KU-158-735

ECONOMICS
OF THE FIRM

PRENTICE-HALL INTERNATIONAL SERIES IN MANAGEMENT

ECONOMICS OF THE FIRM:
Theory and Practice

ARTHUR A. THOMPSON, JR.

Professor of Economics
The University of Alabama

Prentice-Hall, Inc., Englewood Cliffs, New Jersey

Library of Congress Cataloging in Publication Data

THOMPSON, ARTHUR A
    The economics of the firm.

    Includes bibliographies.
    1. Microeconomics.   2. Industrial organization.
    I. Title.
HB171.5.T34   330   72-8183
ISBN   0-13-231381-2

© 1973 by PRENTICE-HALL, INC.
Englewood Cliffs, New Jersey

*All rights reserved. No part of this book may
be reproduced in any form or by any means
without permission in writing from the publisher.*

Printed in the United States of America

10 9 8 7 6 5 4 3 2 1

Prentice-Hall International, Inc., *London*
Prentice-Hall of Australia, Pty. Ltd., *Sydney*
Prentice-Hall of Canada, Ltd., *Toronto*
Prentice-Hall of India Private Limited, *New Delhi*
Prentice-Hall of Japan, Inc., *Tokyo*

In Memory of
My Father

Contents

Preface

This book is about economic behavior in a modern industrial society. It is written expressly for courses in intermediate microeconomic theory at the junior-senior level and for courses in microeconomics for first-year MBA students.

With so many microeconomics books already available, one must necessarily have a very good reason for offering another. My reason is quite simple and straightforward. In its orientation and analytical thrust, this is a different kind of microeconomics book. Much of the conventional text presentations of intermediate microeconomics seems to be at considerable variance with economic reality. Additionally, in a number of cases the gap between theory and practice has become slightly scandalous, especially if one believes the purpose of theory is to explain and to predict real world behavior.

At the heart of the problem is the fact that within the past two decades precious little new material has been added to the typical treatment of intermediate microeconomic theory except to make it more mathematical in line with current fashion. While much progress has been made in dressing up the theory in mathematical clothes, there has been a notable failure to deal with the economics of corporate behavior, the dynamics of technological change, and the long-term performance of product and resource markets. Rather, the theoretical emphasis remains upon the behavior of the single-product entrepreneurial firm operating in a static environment. The reader of conventional treatments of microeconomic theory can scarcely fail to get the largely erroneous impression that profit maximization is the only criterion of business decisions or that any market which is not perfectly competitive results in higher prices, smaller outputs, and a misallocation of resources. The substantial differences between small-firm and large-firm behavior are given scant attention—the actions of IBM are viewed with the same analytical apparatus as the entrepreneurial strategies of a local "monopolist." Current examples of the relevance of theoretical models for explaining real world economic phenomena are few and far between. The impact of major institutional forces are ignored. As a consequence, only the exceptional student is able to bridge the gaps between theory and practice and thereby discern how and why economic theory is useful. Hopefully, this book marks a departure from the current style.

A serious attempt has been made herein to offer a framework for analyzing the workings of a modern industrial economy where the giant corporation is a dominant presence. Accordingly, considerable emphasis has been given to such topics as the evolving structure of business enterprise, the impact of uncertainty upon consumer and business decisions, the unique organizational capabilities and managerial technologies of large corporations, the dichotomies in the behavior of entrepreneurial and managerial firms, the mechanisms of innovation and technological change, the multiplicity of goals of business enterprises, target-return pricing, the competitive strategies of large corporations, and the relative involvement of small firms and large firms in the research and development process. The treatment of oligopoly theory has been made more compatible with readily observable patterns of behavior in a corporate economy. The traditional theory of market structures has been recast to take account of the size and organizational capability of firms as well as the number of firms. Some different views on the dimensions of competition and market power are offered, particularly as concerns corporate behavior and market performance *over time*. Optimum economic performance is discussed in terms of dynamic growth equilibrium for the firm and for the economy rather than solely in terms of static equilibrium. These topics, together with many familiar models, are intended to form a synthesis of the best of all that is old and new in microeconomics. And while a number of them will undoubtedly undergo further thought, extension, and testing, they have been included because it is valuable to consider— if only provisionally—the essence of recent developments in microeconomics and to evaluate quite critically the special coloration which the lenses of American capitalism in its earlier stages may have imparted.

Throughout the entire text, contemporary examples, empirical findings, and applications are accentuated and blended into the theoretical discussion. The correspondence between the predictions of theoretical models and actual events is indicated in the belief that this approach maximizes understanding of microeconomic concepts and minimizes resistance to the use of "theory." In addition, pains have been taken to backstop both the theoretical and practical treatments with enough institutional detail to make them understandable and meaningful to the reader. Special attempts have been made to unravel and to simplify the complexities of graphical analysis. The inclusion of numerous examples and practical applications, coupled with patient explanations of each concept, have necessarily made the book somewhat longer. But the intended effect is a more comprehensible and relevant presentation that will convince the reader of the power of economic analysis and that will help him to hurdle the most difficult theoretical concepts.

As is now customary and proper, the theory is presented in a modestly mathematical vein in the belief that most readers are now equipped to handle nothing more mathematically complex than first derivatives. All mathematical concepts requiring more than college algebra are explained fully and in terms which can be grasped by the mathematically unsophisticated. The more difficult topics in mathematical economics have been placed in self-contained "capsules" at appropriate places in the book and can be omitted without a loss of continuity. Mnemonic symbols have been used throughout the mathematical treatments to facilitate the recognition of economic concepts in mathematical terms.

A set of problems and questions for discussion appears at the end of each chapter. Every problem has been carefully class-tested for its value in developing the skills for using microeconomic concepts. An instructor's manual containing complete solutions to the problems as well as additional problem sets is available to adopters.

On the whole, instructors will find little new in the way of concepts and ideas which have not already appeared elsewhere in the literature of economics. I have borrowed freely from the numerous empirical studies and fertile ideas of other economists, endeavoring of course to acknowledge them in the footnotes. My debts to the works of Professors Schumpeter, Baumol, and Galbraith are especially heavy and will be readily apparent to the reader familiar with their contributions. The material on corporate behavior in oligopolistic markets owes a great deal to Professor F. M. Scherer's very scholarly analysis presented in his *Industrial Market Structure and Economics Performance*.[1] I trust that I have not done great violence to their ideas in my attempts to synthesize them into the body of microeconomic analysis.

In any book of this sort an author owes many acknowledgements.

[1] Skokie, Illinois: Rand McNally and Company, 1970.

My case is very typical. This endeavor has benefited greatly from the comments and criticisms of both students and colleagues. Particularly have I benefited from the comprehensive reviews provided by Professor Keith Lumsden of Stanford University, Professor Robert Clower of UCLA, Professor Howard Dye of Southern Illinois University at Edwardsville, Professor Lloyd Valentine of the University of Cincinnati, and Dr. Richard Hoffman of Arthur Young, Inc. (formerly at the University of Buffalo). Welcome advice and counsel were received from a number of colleagues at The University of Alabama: William D. Gunther, J. F. Vallery and Donald L. Hooks. In one way or another, these persons made each page better than it otherwise would have been. Naturally, however, none of them is responsible for any blunders or inadequacies which remain; for those I bow to tradition and assume full responsibility. I am also indebted to Mrs. Billie Gleisberg and Miss Glenda Wilson for their expert and efficient typing assistance.

Finally, I am grateful for the patience and understanding of my wife and daughters who so graciously accepted my many hours of absence from family activities and who on many occasions gave me the incentive to endure the trials and tribulations of authorship.

A.A.T.

Tuscaloosa, Alabama
October, 1972

Note
to the Student

Courses in intermediate economics typically have the reputation of being among the most challenging in any college or university curriculum. The reputation is well deserved—we might just as well admit this at the outset. But despite the analytical rigor which characterizes economic analysis, the road ahead is exciting and rewarding, and I have tried to clear the way of unnecessary obstacles. For instance, I have endeavored to make this book very readable and to present the material in the most understandable fashion possible. The treatment of each new topic is begun at the lowest level of analysis and proceeds steadily to a fairly sophisticated level; thus, those who have little or no background in economics will find themselves at no serious disadvantage. Pains have been taken to keep the graphs uncluttered and the mathematics simplified. A number of contemporary examples have been included to illustrate the closeness of the links between economic theory and actual economic behavior. Applications of the theory are consistently indicated. When you finish the text, I venture to predict there will be little doubt in your mind that economics is very relevant and that economic theory is a reliable guide for predicting and explaining economic behavior.

The exercises which appear at the end of each chapter are designed to accomplish two things: (1) to reinforce your understanding of the economic concepts discussed in the text and (2) to test your ability to bring the tools of economic analysis to bear upon economic problems. If you cannot work the problems, then you probably do not sufficiently understand the material, and a review of the text material is in order. The exercises serve therefore as a self-test, and you are strongly urged to attempt them conscientiously.

A good textbook is one from which students can learn. This is the only justification for asking you to pay good money to buy one or to spend valuable time in reading it. I trust that when all is said and done you will feel you got your money's worth.

A.A.T.

Introduction: The Methodology of Economic Theory and Model-Building

Economists, like scientists in other disciplines, typically rely upon "theory" and the construction of "models" to broaden and deepen their understanding of real-world events. Therefore, as a prelude to our study of the economics of consumer and business behavior, it will be advantageous to acquire an understanding of the meaning of the terms "theory" and "model" and to become comfortable with the procedures whereby models are built and theories are formulated and judged.

The Methods of Science

Unfortunately, in science there are no set rules of discovery. The methods of scientific investigation vary from discipline to discipline, from one researcher to another within a given discipline, and even from investigation to investigation by a single researcher. Nonetheless, a certain procedural pattern is common to most types of theoretical construction or model-building. This pattern consists of five sequential steps:

1. defining the scope of the problem or the exact phenomena to be investigated,

2. formulating a tentative explanation of relationships pertaining to the problem or phenomena,
3. deducing testable conclusions and/or predictions from the tentative explanation,
4. testing the appropriateness of the conclusions or the accuracy of the predictions by reference to empirical data, and
5. accepting or revising the theory or model on the basis of the tests conducted.

These five elements are worthy of a more detailed discussion—which, for illustrative purposes, will be placed largely in the context of an economic investigation.

DEFINING THE PROBLEM

Defining the problem involves several aspects. The first concerns isolating the exact phenomena of interest to the analyst. Typically, economic behavior contains observable regularities which the analyst seeks to understand. His interest might be stimulated by the need to solve a problem, by the desire to control economic variables in the interest of society, or by his own intellectual curiosity. Once the exact phenomena have been pinpointed and the scope of their study delimited, the investigator must pose the specific questions he seeks to answer with his theoretical model. The most obvious and usual questions pertain to the causes underlying the phenomena, the circumstances in which they occur, and the effects they may produce. The analyst may also be more than incidentally concerned with how his proposed model ties in and interacts with other economic models. The final aspect of defining the problem is to identify the key economic variables that must be studied in the course of the analysis.

FORMULATING THE TENTATIVE EXPLANATION

From an economist's vantage point, economic behavior in the real world is a mass of complex events. Since the economist understandably seeks to generalize, to explain, to predict, and to control economic behavior, he must search for the existence of some degree of order in the real world. That which cannot be described as a manifestation of regularity must be defined as some describable departure from regularity. Such reasoning presumes that economic events can be arrayed according to degrees of regular and predictable behavior. In fact, all systems of knowledge rest upon the assumption of order in the universe, and scientists expend most of their efforts in differentiating among classes of uniformity and relating these to one another. Even when the universe is undergoing rapid change, there exists a degree of order, along with identifiable patterns of change, which can be described and analyzed.

Consequently, the task of the analyst is to seek order out of chaos, to discern what is important and what is not, and to relate events and phenomena to one another. In the course of such an environmental search, many events and factual details are, and should be, ignored because they have no important bearing upon the problem at hand. But even after the relevant facts have been sifted from the irrelevant, it is usually convenient, if not necessary, to simplify the situation still further. Here reliance is placed upon the processes of abstraction and generalization so as to make identification of fundamental relationships between key variables a manageable process. It is not humanly feasible to examine all interrelated events simultaneously. Analytical progress requires some degree of abstraction.

Abstraction involves grouping events or things into a class defined by one or perhaps a few critical attributes (falling prices, low profits, and so on). In addition, it involves concentrating only upon the interrelationships which appear crucial and ignoring those which seem minor. An abstract proposition, consequently, does not (and really cannot) refer to *all* attributes of the elements in the class; it refers only to those which the analyst deems basic. However, the investigator must guard against including empirically false attributes in an abstract proposition. It is fair to conclude that economic theory does not aspire to the task of presenting a complete, exhaustive description of economic phenomena. Rather, the purpose of economic theory is to search for important causes and effects operating in the economy. Selectivity from the mass of detail and events is therefore normal and of the essence; this selectivity is the process of abstraction.

Once abstraction has been used to whittle the situation down to a manageable format, inferences must be made about the nature of the inherent relationships. As an aid to identifying these relationships, the analyst may opt to make some simplifying assumptions which capture the essential features of the economic environment that the model purports to describe. These assumptions need not be *exact representations* of reality; it is enough that they be *reasonable abstractions* of real-world conditions. One of the arts of abstraction is to select basic assumptions that are easy to handle and are capable of producing a theory of substantial scope, but which at the same time are sufficiently realistic that the resulting theoretical model will have an illuminating resemblance to reality. If the assumptions are too detailed and "too realistic," the model becomes unmanageable and unwieldy. On the other hand, if the assumptions of a model are gross oversimplifications of reality, even though very interesting conclusions may be drawn, the model is likely to fail miserably at providing a meaningful explanation of real-world behavior.

What constitutes a reasonable abstraction may be illustrated in terms of the study of consumer behavior. Here we usually introduce the assumption that consumers seek to maximize the satisfaction obtainable from their incomes. In reality this assumption may not be literally true, at least for all consumers in each and every situation. Nevertheless, if over a reasonably interesting range of circumstances many consumers do behave as if they attempted to maximize their satisfaction, then the assumption that "consumers seek to maximize the satisfaction obtainable from their incomes" may be a justifiable and reasonable abstraction of reality. To restate the link between assumptions and reality in another way, even though the assumptions of a model may not be literally exact and complete descriptions of real-world behavior, as long as they are sufficiently realistic to allow for a valid analysis of the phenomena being investigated, no harm is done to reality. More will be said about the realism of assumptions shortly.

Out of the processes of abstracting, making assumptions, and generalizing must result tentative identification of the crucial variables and a tentative explanation as to the nature of the relationships between these variables. This stage of the theoretical process is frequently described as the formulation of hypotheses. *Hypotheses* are tentative explanations or propositions about fundamental relations that are suggested either by previous knowledge or by the theorist's preliminary analysis of the subject matter under investigation. Theoretical standards usually require that the hypothesis be logical and also subject to empirical verification or disproof. Without these qualities there is no way of finding out how good the theoretical model is at advancing our ability to understand real-world behavior, at predicting not-yet-observed phenomena, or at assisting in the control of the environment.

THE DEDUCTION OF PREDICTIONS

Hypotheses do more than establish the pattern of search for cause-and-effect relationships. If properly formulated, they can serve as instruments for deriving predictions about phenomena not yet observed. The deducing of the predictions (forecasts) or conclusions takes place via logical deductive reasoning. To take a concrete example, we might hypothesize that the quantity purchased of any commodity is directly related to the level of advertising expenditures on that commodity, other factors remaining constant. Note that this is a generalized statement applicable to any good or service. We would then logically predict that if RCA increased its promotional expenditures on color TV sets, the sales of RCA color TV's would rise, other factors remaining unchanged. This is a specific testable statement, and one can judge its accuracy by observation. Such is an essential feature of all useful theories and models. They *must* yield predictions or conclusions which are capable of being tested; otherwise there is no appropriate way to evaluate their worth.

TESTING THE ACCURACY OF THE PREDICTIONS

Once tentative relations among the variables are established and predictions are obtained, a multistage process of testing the theoretical model begins.

First, data must be collected for evaluating the accuracy of the predictions derived from the hypothesized relationships. Data collection cannot be initiated prior to this point in the investigation, since some theoretical framework is requisite for deciding just what data are needed.

The sources of such information may be published economic data from either governmental or private institutions, the results of previous research studies, or entirely new data that are generated by the researcher. When the facts are of an empirical character, it may be useful to bring forth the weaponry of *descriptive statistics* and organize the data in the form of charts and tables for economy of presentation and analysis. For example, if the specific economic problem being studied is the nature of the demand function for frozen orange juice concentrate, then one would need to obtain statistics on the quantities of frozen orange juice concentrate purchased, the prices at which these quantities were sold, the prices of other fruit juices, the income of consumers, advertising expenditures, and population. Institutional information about the functioning of the market for frozen orange juice concentrate might also be useful. The items to be included in the actual compilation of information would necessarily depend upon the nature of the problem and the researcher's judgment.

After the necessary data have been compiled, the second stage of testing begins. In the event that quantitative relationships are present in the hypothesis, the constants and parameters must be estimated. A wide variety of powerful quantitative techniques are available for the estimation procedure, but nonquantitative measures may in certain cases be equally useful.

Most of the concepts with which economists deal have a quantitative character. Prices, costs, wage rates, revenues, profits, incomes, production, and so on all involve magnitudes that can in principle be measured. The employment of quantitative techniques is therefore quite natural where relationships among measurable variables are concerned, and it is at this point that econometric techniques enter the picture. *Econometrics* consists of (a) the mathematical formulation of relationships between economic variables, (b) the use of statistical procedures to measure the hypothetical relationships, and (c) the statistical testing of the accuracy of the predictions derived from the hypothesized relationships. Even when mathematical relationships are not absolutely necessary, it is scarcely prudent to discard them if they are able to facilitate the analysis of the problem or render it more concise.

Following the estimation of the constants and parameters in the model comes the formal testing of the accuracy of the model's predictions. New facts and data must be assembled to test these predictions. The data for the formal test should not include any of the observations originally used in estimating the functional form of the model. Often the data for both the parameter estimation stage and the formal testing stage are gathered simultaneously, and the investigator utilizes only part of the data in making the

parameter estimates, reserving the remainder for a test of the model's predictions. Such a practice is followed when the data collection methods are
costly and time-consuming.

EVALUATING THE RESULTS OF THE TEST

If the prediction is confirmed by the facts—that is to say, it corresponds to
what is observed—then the hypothesis is *accepted*. It has *not*, however, been
proved; rather, events have failed to *disprove* it. According to one eminent
authority, generalizations of hypotheses can never be proved, they can only
be tested by seeing whether predictions made from them are in accord with
experimental and observational facts.[1] A favorable finding on the accuracy
of the prediction does not confirm the truth of the hypothesis, because a
prediction deduced from the hypothesis may be true without the hypothesis
being true.

For instance, the truth of the hypothesis that a corporation's profits
arise from the hiring of wise managers is not established by the accuracy
of the prediction that a change in the management of Corporation XYZ will
be followed by a rise in XYZ's profits. Strictly speaking, a hypothesis is
never proved and remains on probation indefinitely, but if it survives all
attempts at disproof, it is accepted in practice, especially if it is compatible
with related theoretical systems.[2] Thus, after a hypothesis successfully survives
a number of tests it becomes part of the knowledge of the discipline, until
evidence appears which shows that it no longer yields an acceptable degree
of accuracy in its predictions.

If the observed facts contradict the predictions, the hypothesis is
disproved or *rejected*; attempts can then be made to revise it in accordance
with the empirical evidence. The cycle of analysis returns to step 2. The
modified hypothesis is then tested and again modified if the test results are
unsatisfactory. The process is continued until the investigator is satisfied that
his *theory* accounts for the observed facts with sufficient accuracy for his
purposes.

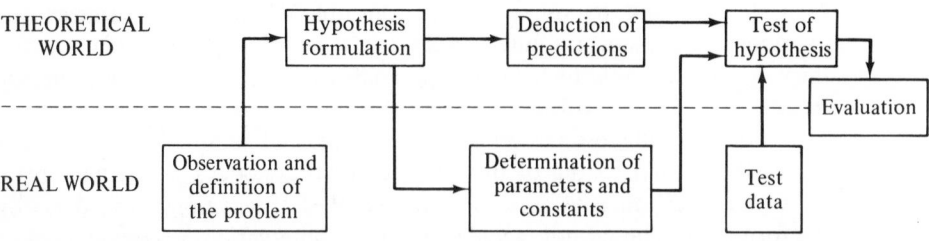

Fig. I-1   The Relationship Between Theory and the Real World

[1] W. I. B. Beveridge, *The Art of Scientific Investigation* (New York: Modern Library, Inc., 1957), p. 118.
[2] *Ibid.*

Figure I-1 summarizes the five steps of the scientific method and its interaction with the real world. Note that the process of scientific investigation begins by observing the real world and finishes by observing the real world. This is as it should be, since the major purpose of theory is to improve our ability to understand and predict real-world phenomena.

What Is a Theory?

In the discussion above, the terms *hypothesis*, *theory*, and *model* appear over and over. Since these terms convey nebulous impressions and often have different connotations to different people, the meaning and function of each can perhaps be clarified at this point. It should be noted, however, that authorities are not in agreement on the "definitions" of these terms, and to some extent, they virtually defy objective specification. What follows represents what is believed to be a general consensus.

A *hypothesis* is a tentative explanation of how phenomena are related. It attempts to pinpoint the key variables in a behavior pattern and describe in preliminary fashion how they interact. A hypothesis may originate as an educated speculation, an informed guess, or a mere conjecture. Supporting evidence is lacking or is scanty and unconvincing. The formulation of a hypothesis necessarily involves abstracting the essential features out of the maze of fact and detail surrounding the phenomena being studied.

A *theory* encompasses both the formulation of the hypothesis and the logical deduction of predictions from it. A theory consists of an accepted explanation of and guide to behavior of phenomena in the real world. It must convey the essence of what happened and why it happened, and it must suggest a cause-effect relationship. In this sense a theory possesses *explanatory power*. Additionally, a theory has the ability to predict how changes in certain variables will affect other variables. In this sense a theory possesses *predictive power*. Because of its explanatory and predictive powers, a theory can be used as the basis for formulating policies designed to modify the environment in whatever ways may be deemed desirable.

A theory assumes its status when the hypothesis it incorporates has been tested a number of times and the accuracy of its predictions accepted. Should the theory be sufficiently profound and universal, it may be termed a *law*. A law implies a very confident degree of empirical regularity; accompanying it is an explanation for its existence and reasons why the law should continue to hold in the future. Thus, in the normal use of the term, a theory is somewhere between a hypothesis and a law. To recapitulate: hypotheses refer to possible relationships with little factual support; theories are better supported, and more confidence can be placed in them; and laws are well-established relationships with a strong empirical foundation.

Often one hears the complaint that theory is "unrealistic" and "impracti-

8

cal."[3] Such complaints can be valid only in the case of "bad" theory. "Good" theory cannot be unrealistic in an important sense, because it *does* explain and predict *real-world behavior*. Nor can good theory be "impractical"; on the contrary, it can serve as a practical man's guide to decision-making, since it has a *demonstrated* ability to explain relationships and to predict phenomena. When a theory truly has appropriate amounts of both explanatory and predictive power, charges of impracticality and lack of realism contain little merit. If a theory is subject to legitimate claims of impracticality and lack of realism, then the time has come to reevaluate it in light of current empirical evidence and to review its predictive and explanatory powers relative to alternative hypotheses and theories.

Some users of theory find the constant review of existing theory unpleasant; they would much prefer the sequence ceased (at the truth). Yet seldom, if ever, in the scientific world has this stopping place been reached, although now and then theories have survived virtually untouched for many years. Unfortunately, the attitude that the truth has already been attained is often a barrier to progress. In economics it is especially necessary to review the existing body of theory on a regular basis. A moment's reflection is enough to convince one that an economic theory of business behavior in the 1920's is likely to be quite impotent when it comes to explaining and predicting business behavior in the 1970's. The emergence of the giant corporation, the international dimensions of competition, and the imperatives of technological change have made the business environment today vastly different from what is was in the 1920's. Not surprisingly, these differences are substantive enough to have generated material changes in the economic theory of business enterprise. Thus, emerging economic developments force economic theorists to keep a close check on the explanatory and predictive powers of the existing body of economic theory.

The term *model* is much harder to describe in unambiguous fashion, simply because it is commonly used in a wide variety of ways. It covers such diverse subjects as the women who display the creations of Paris designers and the scaled-down replicas of an architect's proposed building. Even in scientific investigations there are physical models, abstract models, symbolic models, conceptual models, mathematical models, simulation models, solar models, theoretical models, input-output models, benefit-cost models, and environmental models, to mention only a few. Each of these "scientific" models has its own distinguishing features, yet there is also a common ground; it is the common ground that is of primary interest. The unifying feature of models, as they have been used in many branches of science, is

An "ivory tower" economic theorist is said to have remarked: "And the beauty of this model, which will particularly endear it to the hearts of purists, is that under no conceivable circumstances can it be of any possible practical value." Economic theory is not without its actual examples in this regard. According to John Kenneth Galbraith, "Much economic instruction, and notably so in such fields as advanced theory, foreign trade, and monetary policy, depends not on the relevance of the subject matter but on the existence of an intellectually preoccupying theory." J. K. Galbraith, *The New Industrial State* (Boston: Houghton Mifflin Company, 1967), p. 46.

their attempt to describe the essential features of a system in a way that is simple enough to understand and manipulate, yet close enough to reality to yield successful results. Usually it is neither practical nor possible to represent the system in its original complexity; abstraction must be used, and selecting the appropriate degree of abstraction can greatly enhance the model's value. If the level of abstraction is too low, so that the model resembles the system too closely, the advantages of validity are offset by the unwieldiness of the model and a lack of generalized application. On the other hand, if the model is highly abstract, the advantages gained from its analytic properties may be more than counterbalanced by its dubious connection with the actual system. For example, if one were to assume complete economic rationality, full knowledge of economic information, perfect mobility of economic resources, and an instantaneous economic adjustment process, one might obtain an economic model which is easily manipulated and which yields intellectually appealing conclusions, but there is no compelling reason why it necessarily would replicate an environment bearing significant ties to economic reality. If the model-builder is clever, and extremely lucky, he may develop a model that presents simply and accurately the major dynamics of a complex and poorly understood system—in which case the model could approximate the status of a theory as we have used the two terms.

To state their connection more formally, a theory and a theoretical model are for many intents and purposes synonymous. Both attempt to specify key variables and establish relationships between them. Both provide a logical framework or skeleton in which the complexities of the real world can be understood with greater insight. Both involve predictions or forecasts about phenomena, and both are judged by their accuracy in predicting and explaining the behavior of an actual system. So long as the system that the model is attempting to describe is of sufficient scope and importance, a theory and a model can stand at the same rank. In our examination of consumer and business behavior, we shall use the terms model and theory interchangeably.

The Realism of Assumptions

One problem area remains to be discussed. How valid is a theory which contains what some investigators consider "unrealistic assumptions"? Suppose, for example, a theory of business behavior is based on the assumption that business firms behave as if they seek to maximize profits. Suppose further that this theory is judged to predict rather well, but there is a serious question as to whether the firms involved actually are trying to maximize profits. Is the theory then "invalid" because it is based upon an assumption which appears to be false? How does one determine whether the assumption of profit-maximizing behavior is, in fact, an accurate description of reality? Does it even make any difference whether the assumption of profit maximization is descriptively accurate or not, so long as the predictive power of the theory is judged to be satisfactory for the purpose at hand? Does a theory which predicts behavior also explain behavior? These are very thorny questions, and attempts to answer them have generated a heated debate among some prominent economists.[4]

One of the principals in this debate is Milton Friedman, who in an essay on "The Methodology of Positive Economics," maintained that whether the assumptions made in the course of formulating a hypothesis were "realistic" or "unrealistic" may not really be significant. Friedman argued that the only relevant way to test a hypothesis is to compare its predictions with experience. He stated that there is no meaningful way to test the validity of a hypothesis by comparing its assumptions directly with reality. In support of his position, Friedman said:

> In so far as a theory can be said to have "assumptions" at all, and in so far as their "realism" can be judged independently of the validity of predictions, the relation between the significance of a theory and the "realism" of its "assumptions" is almost the opposite of that suggested by the view under criticism. Truly important and significant hypotheses will be found to have "assumptions" that are wildly inaccurate descriptive representations of reality, and, in general, the more significant the theory, the more unrealistic the assumptions (in this sense). The reason is simple. A hypothesis is important if it "explains" much by little, that is, if it abstracts the common and crucial elements from the mass of complex and detailed circumstances surrounding the phenomena to be explained and permits valid predictions on the basis of them alone. To be important, therefore, a hypothesis must be descriptively false in its assumptions; it takes account of, and accounts for, none of the many other attendant circumstances, since its very success shows them to be irrelevant for the phenomena to be explained.
>
> To put this point less paradoxically, the relevant question to ask about the "assumptions" of a theory is not whether they are descriptively "realistic," for they never are, but whether they are sufficiently good approximations for the purpose in hand. And this question can be answered only by seeing whether ... it yields sufficiently accurate predictions.[5]

Here Friedman is saying that the degree of "realism" in the assumptions is often not apparent in the assumptions themselves, but only becomes apparent after the theory is constructed and its predictive power evaluated. In other words, if a theory predicts accurately, then the assumptions are realistic enough despite appearances to the contrary.

[4] Milton Friedman, "The Methodology of Positive Economics," *Essays in Positive Economics* (Chicago: University of Chicago Press, 1953), pp. 3–43. Friedman's article has provoked a wealth of comment and rebuttal. See, for example, Eugene Rotwein, "On 'The Methodology of Positive Economics,'" *Quarterly Journal of Economics*, Vol. 73, No. 4 (November 1959), pp. 554–575; R. M. Cyert and E. Grunberg, "Assumption, Prediction, and Explanation in Economics," Appendix A in R. M. Cyert and J. G. March, *A Behavioral Theory of the Firm* (Englewood Cliffs, N. J.: Prentice-Hall, Inc., 1963), pp. 298–311; J. W. McGuire, *Theories of Business Behavior* (Englewood Cliffs, N.J.: Prentice-Hall, Inc., 1964), pp. 7–11; and the papers delivered at the session on Problems in Methodology, held at the December 1962 meetings of the American Economic Association and published in the *American Economic Review, Papers and Proceedings*, Vol. 52, No. 2 (May 1963), pp. 204–236.

[5] Friedman, "The Methodology of Positive Economics," pp. 14–15.

Other economists have not found it hard to take issue with Friedman. Naturally, an assumption is "unrealistic" if one is applying the standard that it does not *exhaustively* describe a situation but mentions only some of the traits that are present. Yet it is unlikely that any statement of finite length would suffice to identify the totality of the set of characteristics embodied in a real situation. And it tests the imagination to conceive of uses for such a statement were it constructed. It is in this somewhat trivial sense that Friedman seems at least to be defending the legitimacy of "unrealistic" assumptions.

There are, however, two more worthy instances in which assumptions may be said to be unrealistic. First, an assumption may be unrealistic because it holds only for hypothetical or ideal circumstances. On occasions, models or theories with intentionally unrealistic assumptions are developed, e.g., the frictionless world often posed in physics and the perfectly competitive market model in economics, the latter containing such "ideal" conditions as perfect knowledge on the part of the buyers and sellers, perfect flexibility and mobility in the use of economic resources, and complete freedom of entry and exit of producers into the market. The environmental systems portrayed in these models are admittedly hypothetical and serve as intellectual experiments. Their primary purpose is often to highlight the nature of the interaction between key variables, particularly when they are unaffected by numerous other factors whose influence may never be eliminated in the real world, but whose effects vary in magnitude with differences in attendant circumstances. They may also be used as a standard of comparison against which the functioning of actual environmental systems can be measured. Models of this type are unique in the sense that when observations do not conform to their predictions, this indicates that the conditions upon which the model is predicted are not being met, and *not* that the model is invalid. That society's economic resources are not always deployed in the most efficient manner does not disprove the proposition that perfect competition would achieve this result, but rather suggests the lack of existence of the requirement of perfect competition.

Second, an assumption can be termed "unrealistic" because it appears false or improbable on the basis of available evidence. Here we find the real bone of contention. Ernest Nagel, an eminent authority on methodological matters, has observed that a theory which contains an unrealistic assumption in the sense that it is false is "patently unsatisfactory, for such a theory entails consequences that are incompatible with observed fact, so that on pain of rejecting elementary logical canons the theory must also be rejected."[6] This view supports the consensus that scientific standards require theories and models to possess logical consistency and to provide explanation as well as prediction. One can scarcely be confident in the explanatory power of a theory which contains false or empirically discredited assumptions—regard-

[6] Ernest Nagel, "Assumptions in Economic Theory," *American Economic Review, Papers and Proceedings,* Vol. 52, No. 2 (May 1963), pp. 214–215.

12

less of its ability to predict. Unless the assumptions of a theory or model have been subjected to empirical testing, have not been rejected, and are generally agreed upon as having empirical validity, one has at best *proposed* explanation, not *actual* explanation; moreover, the accuracy of predictions might well be properly ascribed to mere fortuitous circumstances or uncanny chance happenings. Thus, it is imperative that we understand *why* a theory predicts before we give it much credence.

Nor, as Friedman's position implies, does it follow that if a theory containing "unrealistic" assumptions has an impressive degree of predictive power, the theory also possesses satisfactory explanatory power and its assumptions acquire an acceptable degree of "realism." Cohen and Cyert have adequately demonstrated that Friedman's position can lead to prediction without explanation.[7] A theory or model which seems to predict well enough but which explains poorly should arouse suspicion about whether the true variables are correctly represented. In such a case, any predictive power that the model may have could arise from some unknown relationship(s) between variables in the model and/or the influence of unknown variables not included in the model.

It is especially important that a theoretical model possess both predictive power and explanatory power when it is to be used as a guide for control. To employ a theory properly as a basis for formulating control devices, e.g., economic policy, the user must be acutely aware of just how the values of one or more variables must be altered to bring about the desired environmental changes. This clearly requires predictive power, for the user must be able to forecast accurately the consequences of his changing the selected control variables. Were he to rely upon a theoretical model which generated accurate predictions without explanation, it is conceivable that the prescribed changes in the control variables could also trigger changes in some of the unknown variables and/or relationships that had previously led (for reasons unknown) to accurate predictions, thus causing future predictions to be modified in an unpredictable fashion—for the better *or for the worse.*

Summary and Conclusions

The objective of this chapter has been to describe the procedures followed by economists in analyzing economic behavior. Five steps were posed in the development of a theoretical model:

1. defining the scope of the problem,
2. formulating a hypothesis,
3. deducing predictions from the hypothesis,
4. testing the accuracy of the predictions, and
5. accepting or revising the theory on the basis of the tests.

[7] K. J. Cohen and R. M. Cyert, *Theory of the Firm: Resource Allocation in a Market Economy* (Englewood Cliffs, N.J.: Prentice-Hall, Inc., 1965), pp. 22–24.

An examination of these steps reveals that economic theory can provide otherwise unattainable insights into real-world economic behavior. Economic theory consists of a skeletal framework by which the behavior of economic phenomena can be explained and predicted. Theory attempts to account for what happens and why it happens. On not infrequent occasions, a mathematical formulation of economic theory is especially useful because it allows analytical maneuvers to be used that are not feasible with verbal or geometric formulations.

Despite an articulate assertion to the contrary by prominent economist Milton Friedman, the consensus view is that scientific standards require theoretical models to be based upon assumptions that are consistent with observed behavior. Unless the assumptions contained in a theoretical model are reasonable abstractions of reality and have a high degree of empirical validity, the explanatory power of the model is suspect. Moreover, without logical consistency and explanatory power, the usefulness of a theory in assisting to control the environment is suspect; whatever predictive power it may have demonstrated could be due to circumstance or to undetected cause-effect relationships. Thus a theory is judged upon (a) its ability to explain cause-effect relations in logical fashion using reasonable assumptions and (b) its power to predict changes in behavior.

SUGGESTED READINGS

COHEN, K. J., and R. M. CYERT, *Theory of the Firm: Resource Allocation in a Market Economy* (Englewood Cliffs, N.J.: Prentice-Hall, Inc., 1965), Chap. 2.

CYERT, R. M., and E. GRUNBERG, "Assumption, Prediction, and Explanation in Economics," Appendix A in R. M. Cyert and J. G. March *A Behavioral Theory of the Firm* (Englewood Cliffs, N.J.: Prentice-Hall, Inc., 1963), pp. 298–311.

FRIEDMAN, MILTON, "The Methodology of Positive Economics," *Essays in Positive Economics* (Chicago: University of Chicago Press, 1953), pp. 3–43.

LEONTIEF, WASSILY, "Theoretical Assumptions and Nonobserved Facts," *American Economic Review*, Vol. 61, No. 1 (March 1971) pp. 1–7.

MCGUIRE, J. W., *Theories of Business Behavior* (Englewood Cliffs, N.J.: Prentice-Hall, Inc., 1965), Chap. 2.

NAGEL, ERNEST, "Assumptions in Economic Theory," *American Economic Review, Papers and Proceedings*, Vol. 52, No. 2 (May 1963), pp. 211–219.

ROTWEIN, EUGENE, "On 'The Methodology of Positive Economics,'" *Quarterly Journal of Economics*, Vol. 73, No. 4 (November 1959), pp. 554–575.

Questions for Discussion

1. Characterize each of the steps of the "scientific method." Which of these steps encompass what might be termed "theorizing"?

2. Distinguish carefully between the terms hypothesis, theory, and model.

3. Distinguish carefully between "theory" and a "theoretical model."

4. How should a theory be evaluated?

5. What is the role of assumptions in theory construction?

6. Defend Milton Friedman's position regarding the realism of assumptions.

7. On what grounds, if any, is the presence of explanatory power a desirable feature in a theory?

I

THE ENVIRONMENT
OF BUSINESS
ENTERPRISE

1

The Dynamic Structure of Business Enterprise

In all modern nations of the Western world, there exists an implied contract between society and business firms. Society consents to the existence of business firms. In return, business firms agree to serve the needs of society—to the satisfaction of society.

In discharging its obligations to society, the business firm necessarily becomes the principal agent for producing and distributing goods and services. It serves as the focal point of economic activity. As such, it is the economic unit most directly responsible for using the available pool of economic resources in ways that will satisfy human needs and wants to the greatest extent possible. The business firm, for example, is the instrumental factor in providing jobs and expanding career opportunities, in implementing new technologies, in producing new commodities, in raising living standards, and in improving the quality of life in whatever directions society may elect. All major segments of society, including government, are sustained in substantial measure by the economic foundation provided by the business sector. So crucial is its role that the efficiency with which the business sector performs its designated responsibilities is the key determinant of society's overall welfare. For this reason it is appropriate to begin our study of the functioning of a modern industrial economy with a survey of the character of present-day business enterprises.

THE EMERGENCE OF ENTREPRENEURSHIP

In preindustrial America, the typical businessman operated a very small enterprise and had intense daily personal contact with his several employees, often working alongside them. It was in this era that a market-oriented society began to emerge. Men became motivated to pursue their economic self-interest, and a social environment evolved in which the energies of men were directed by raising or lowering the rewards offered for various tasks.[1] Competition appeared, making it hard for any one firm to gain a strategic position for its own advantage. Likewise, buyers were restrained from forcing prices below the costs of production, for other eager buyers would quickly outbid them. The market became a contest wherein buyers sought to pay as little as possible for commodities and sellers sought to extract as high a price as buyers would pay. In the increasingly market-oriented environment of the eighteenth and early nineteenth centuries, consumers catapulted to a new position of prominence. Business firms, prompted by the prospect of profits and a fear of losses, found it advantageous, and even necessary for survival's sake, to synchronize their production decisions with the desires of consumers and the needs of society.

As late as the 1870's, the major business enterprises were engaged in servicing an agrarian economy. Except for a few companies supplying the needs of the rapidly expanding railroad enterprises, the leading firms processed agricultural products and provided farmers with food and clothing. These firms were generally small. They bought their raw materials locally and for the most part sold their finished goods locally. Where they manufactured for a market more than a few miles away, they distributed through commissioned agents or jobbers who handled the business of several other similar firms.

During the next several decades a new form of business enterprise appeared, headed by an entirely new breed of entrepreneur—the industrial capitalist. The industrial capitalist was very much interested in expansion, in growth, and in technological progress and was blessed with a special aptitude for innovation. The factory was his instrument of production. Typically, the industrial capitalist did not immerse himself in day-to-day operational problems inside the factory. These he relegated to salaried production experts—second-echelon plant managers. He himself provided the master touch in overseeing the logistics of the whole operation, seeking new ways to increase production efficiencies, devising financial plans, raising capital, implementing new marketing strategies, and outmaneuvering the competition. Above all, he was an innovator in both production and distribution techniques, a risk-taker, and an opportunist.

A small class of industrial capitalists came to dominate the business

---

[1] For a more complete discussion of this phase of business history see Robert L. Heilbroner, *The Making of Economic Society*, 4th ed. (Englewood Cliffs, N.J.: Prentice-Hall, Inc., 1972), Chap. 4.

environment during the late nineteenth and early twentieth centuries. Among them were many great names from the annals of business history. Edward H. Harriman, William Vanderbilt, and Jay Gould headed an impressive list of railroad entrepreneurs. Until 1900, Andrew Carnegie and Carnegie Steel Company dominated the steel industry. John D. Rockefeller engineered Standard Oil Company to a position of prominence in the oil industry. Most of the meat shipped in interstate commerce came from the packing houses of Philip D. Armour, Gustavus Swift, and Michael Cudahy. The name of McCormick was synonymous with farm machinery. J. P. Morgan became the nation's most outstanding and influential banker, and today Morgan Guaranty Trust Co. is still among the ten largest financial institutions. Persons such as Henry Ford, the DuPonts, Henry Frick, James J. Hill, Andrew Mellon, Jacob Van Astor, James B. Duke, George Westinghouse, and C. P. Huntington were also counted among the most notable of industrial capitalists.

The activities of these men wrought a profound change in the form of business enterprise and the structure of markets. Within the span of thirty years, the economic landscape was transformed and virtually no aspect of social and economic life was left unaffected. Under the regime of the industrial capitalist, the size and complexity of business enterprise was radically enlarged. Large-scale enterprise spread steadily in the areas of manufacturing and transportation, although less so in trade and service. By 1900 the average manufacturing establishment was doing three times as much business as in 1850.[2] Concomitantly, there was a dramatic concentration of production in these large business units.

> By 1900, for example, the number of textile mills, although still large, had dropped by a third from the 1880's; over the same period, the number of manufacturers of agricultural implements had fallen by 60 percent, and the number of leather manufacturers by three-quarters. In the locomotive industry, two companies ruled the roost in 1900, contrasted with nineteen in 1860. The biscuit and cracker industry changed from a scatter of small companies to a market in which one producer had 90 percent of the industry's capacity by the turn of the century. Meanwhile in steel there was the colossal U.S. Steel Corporation, which alone turned out over half the steel production of the nation. In oil, the Standard Oil Company tied up between 80 to 90 percent of the nation's output. In tobacco, the American Tobacco Company controlled 75 percent of cigars. Similar control rested with the American Sugar Company, the American Smelting and Refining Company, the United Shoe Machinery Company, and dozens more.[3]

However, the new world of large business produced by the rise of industrial companies did not *replace* the old world of small business, but rather was

[2] E. A. J. Johnson and Herman E. Krooss, *The American Economy* (Englewood Cliffs, N.J.: Prentice-Hall, Inc., 1960), p. 239.
[3] Heilbroner, *The Making of Economic Society*, p. 114.

simply *superimposed* upon it. Wholesale and retail trade, finance, and service activities remained concentrated in small owner-managed firms; almost one and one-half million enterprises were engaged in these functions in 1900 (and in 1964 over 5.3 million enterprises were so engaged).

The initial impact of the trend to large enterprises, surprisingly enough, greatly enhanced competition. In the largely agricultural, handcraft, small-factory economy of the early nineteenth century, markets were quite small and localized. Each was insulated from its neighbors by slow, high-cost transportation; local producers had neither the means nor the motivation to invade even adjacent markets, much less anything resembling regional or national markets. But the industrial capitalists, wisely employing the strategies of intense penetration of existing markets, expansion into geographically distant markets, vertical integration, and product diversification, precipitated growth rates in their firms which exceeded the rate of the economy as a whole. No longer did they purchase and sell through agents; instead they created their own nationwide buying and marketing organizations. Increasingly markets became interconnected and were unified; local monopolies succumbed to outside competition. The outcome was a steady growth in competitive pressures among large-scale firms, replacing the more restricted local competition of the small-business, small-market environment. Price wars repeatedly broke out as enterprises sought to capture the new markets needed for profitable production levels. Bankruptcy on a multimillion dollar scale for the competing enterprises came to be a disturbing and omnipresent threat.

A reaction set in. Predictably, the firms elected to seek avenues for lessening competitive rigors. Various forms of voluntary cooperation were devised: trade associations, informal pacts to share markets, and gentlemen's agreements to charge mutually satisfactory prices. While these worked modestly well in prosperous times, the temptation to shave prices was powerful when the pressures of depression and shrinking markets periodically appeared. More ingenious and effective devices were needed, and out of this need there developed trusts, holding companies, and mergers.

Yet it would be misleading to presume that the emergence of giant corporations originated solely, or even primarily, from the pyramiding impact of mergers, trusts, and holding companies. The antitrust laws passed in 1890 and 1914 saw in part to that. Equally, perhaps more, important was the process of internal growth. Ford, General Motors, General Electric, DuPont, AT&T, and Carnegie Steel (later U. S. Steel), among others, grew because of rapidly expanding markets for their products and because they were quicker, more able, more efficient, and more aggressive than their rivals. Their gradual ascendency to positions of dominance within their industries is directly attributable to well-executed business strategies and to the significant reduction in unit costs which normally accompanies mass production and distribution techniques.[4] Without the latter, large size could have become a severe liability instead of an asset.

The Structure of Contemporary Business Enterprise

During the first half of the twentieth century, a third stage in the development of business enterprise began to assert itself. An *organizational* revolution began and came to fruition. Whereas key individuals had been instrumental in the initial rise of corporations, now a process of depersonalization set in. Sustained growth in the size of industrial enterprise made it virtually impossible for one individual to continue to play a dominant role in directing operations and in amassing the necessary financial capital. To operate a successful industrial complex (which the corporation had become) required a growing number of managerial skills. The intricacies of finance, accounting, marketing, labor relations and research—all of which the entrepreneur-industrial capitalist formerly performed himself—became major "departmental" tasks within the firm. Major reorganizations in authority and responsibility produced a parceling out of the entrepreneurial functions to *managerial specialists*. Group management replaced the entrepreneur-minded industrial capitalist as the directing force of corporate enterprise, and as it did so, the profession of management took a solid place in the occupational listings.

Simultaneously, the ownership of corporations underwent a definitive change. As the original founders of corporations died, their holdings were fragmented by inheritance, and the heirs frequently preferred to assume a more passive role in the enterprise's operations. In addition, small investors began to acquire stock in corporations; by the 1920's, when it was fashionable for the upper and middle classes to dabble in the stock market, the ownership of most corporations had become widely diluted among hundreds or even thousands of stockholders. No longer was it necessary to own a *majority* of the shares of common stock to exercise effective control over the affairs of a large enterprise. As long as the performance of the firm appeared satisfactory to the average stockholder (in terms of dividends and appreciation in the price of the stock), it was easy enough to get stockholders to sign their voting rights over by proxy to the officers of the corporation. As a result, top management came to be the final arbiter of corporate policy, subject only to perfunctory review by the board of directors. The upshot

---

[4] Several examples can be offered to point up the cost reductions associated with mass production and distribution techniques. In increasing its sales of model-T touring cars frcm 18,664 in 1909–10 to 730,041 in 1916–17, Ford realized such large cost reductions that the price of a typical model fell steadily from $950 in 1909–10 to $360 in 1916–17. Standard Oil Company found, as early as 1884, that by concentrating 75 percent of its production in three giant refineries, its average cost of refining a barrel fell to 0.534 cents as compared to 1.5 cents for the rest of the industry. Gustavus Swift discovered that he could achieve drastic cuts in meat prices by constructing large meat packing houses in the cities on the cattle frontier and then channeling the meat through his own distribution facilities into butcher shops and grocery stores in every major town and city in the East.

was that corporate managements tended to become self-perpetuating groups, nominating their own successors, and directing corporate activities more and less autonomously as sort of "trustees" for the absent owners.[5]

With the last decade a fourth evolutionary stage for major corporations appears in the making—conglomerate diversification. A *conglomerate enterprise* is one that produces and sells a number of economically unrelated products. By operating in many different product markets, the firm detaches its fortunes from a single commodity group, and it can prosper even though one or several of its items lose consumer favor. Product diversification therefore frees the business firm from the life-and-death cycle of either specific products or industries and provides an almost impregnable defense against secular shifts in demand and technology.

The conglomerate type of firm has attained quick maturity and dramatic growth. Its technique involves acquisition of promising, high-growth, small firms coupled with merger with large, well-established enterprises. Diversification by merger or acquisition provides an established management team familiar with the product and the industry; it allows entry under the auspices of an established competitor; and it permits quick entry into profitable, new markets. On occasions an acquisition-minded small conglomerate has merged with or taken over a larger firm and emerged as the parent or surviving firm. The list of conglomerate firms which emerged during the 1960's include Litton Industries, International Telephone and Telegraph, Ling-Temco-Vought, Textron, Walter Kidde, Martin-Marietta, 3M Company, Sperry-Rand, Avco, United Brands, Singer, Gulf & Western, U.S. Industries, Teledyne, Studebaker-Worthington, Loew's Theaters, City Investing, Ogden Corp., Tenneco, Dart Industries, and Olin Mathieson—all of which are among the 500 largest U. S. industrial corporations.

The Two Sectors of Business

As things now stand in the ongoing development of American capitalism, the business sector has evolved into a composite of two essentially distinct sectors. On the one hand there is the sector populated with millions of small firms run by a single individual or family and producing a limited range of products for limited markets. Suppose we designate the firms comprising this segment of the business community as *periphery firms*. On the other hand there is the sector made up of 750 to 800 massively capitalized, technologically dynamic, multimillion dollar corporations with thousands of employees,

---

[5] By 1963, in *none* of the 200 largest nonfinancial corporations in the U.S. was as much as 80 percent or more of the voting stock owned by an individual, family, or group of business associates. In only 9 of the 200 firms was there even majority ownership (where an individual, family, or group owned between 50 and 80 percent) of the voting stock. Minority control (stock ownership of between 10 and 50 percent) or joint minority control (two or more minority interests) characterized but 31 of the 200 firms. The remaining 160 firms were classified as "management controlled" on the basis that no group of stockholders would be able under ordinary circumstances to muster enough votes to challenge management. For more details see Robert J. Larner, "Ownership and Control in the 200 Largest Non-Financial Corporations, 1929 and 1963," *American Economic Review*, Vol. 56, No. 4 (September 1966), pp. 777–787.

a complex organizational structure, and a diversified set of products. Suppose we designate the firms comprising this portion of the business community as *center firms.*[6] We shall use these labels consistently throughout the text to distinguish between "small business" and "big business."

A brief description of both sectors and the interaction between them can sharpen our understanding of the functioning of our economy and of actual business behavior.

THE ECONOMICS OF PERIPHERY FIRMS

The periphery firm coincides very closely with what was described earlier as an owner-entrepreneur type of enterprise. The periphery firm is small in an absolute sense. There is a strong and intimate tie between ownership and control—so intimate in fact that ownership and control are usually bound up in a single individual (or at most a close-knit group) who determines the firm's goals, supplies it with capital, maintains daily personal control over its activities, and enjoys whatever profits it may earn. When the owner-entrepreneur retires or dies, the enterprise is often mortally wounded and may be dissolved or sold. In effect, the periphery firm is the epitome of small business. Taken together, the millions of proprietorships, partnerships, and small- and medium-sized corporations that make up the "small business" sector comprise what we shall refer to henceforth as the *periphery economy.*

Periphery firms, however, are distinguished by a variety of factors other than their size and centralized owner-entrepreneur functions. Their techniques of production, marketing strategies, and overall managerial proficiencies rarely equal those employed in center firms. Generally, but not always, periphery firms are technological followers. On the average, their commitments to research, development, and innovation are relatively small. Access to financial capital can pose a major problem to periphery firms; their cash flow is smaller, their profits and retained earnings lower, their security shakier, their credit rating poorer, their dependency on local credit sources greater, and the interest rates they pay on borrowed funds higher than those of center firms. It is not unusual for shrinking markets to produce severe financial retrenchment or even bankruptcy. Frequently, periphery firm managers are consumed with the short-run problems of daily operations, with little time allocated to long-range business planning.

Periphery firms typically encounter relatively strong competitive forces. The actions of each firm are in large part circumscribed by market forces beyond its control, thereby thrusting it into a defensive and security-conscious posture. Barriers to the entry of new firms are usually low. Expansion potential usually depends on local market growth, yet a rapid growth in the local

---

[6] The terms "center" and "periphery" are taken from Robert T. Averitt, *The Dual Economy* (New York: W. W. Norton & Company, Inc., 1968). What follows draws heavily from his quite fertile work and also contains some embellishments adapted from John Kenneth Galbraith's *The New Industrial State* (Boston: Houghton Mifflin Company, 1967).

market raises a distinct possibility of invasion from center firms searching for a piece of the action. According to Edith Penrose, "There is considerable evidence that small firms, because of their size, are restricted by their environment to certain types of opportunity where the prospects of continued expansion are extremely limited."[7] On occasion, however, periphery firms acquire such a strategic market position (either deliberately or fortuitously) that they are able to grow very rapidly. Some may even become so successful that they are able to cross over into the zone of center firms; Holiday Inns, Xerox, I.T.&T., and Ling-Temco-Vought are good examples.

Three broad types of periphery firms are distinguishable according to the nature of their relationships and interaction with center firms. These may be classified as (1) satellite firms, (2) firms on the competitive fringe, and (3) firms which are independent of and operate independently from the center firms.

Satellite Firms. Periphery firms which function as satellites to center firms can be divided into backward satellites and forward satellites. Backward satellites are small enterprises that supply center firms with raw materials, intermediate goods, or some commodity which the center firm uses as an ingredient in producing its own products. The principal output of the backward satellite is likely to be a minor input for the center firm. The backward satellite may also enjoy a locational advantage from proximity to the center firm. Examples of backward satellites would be local sawmills supplying cordwood to paper mills, upholstery firms selling to automobile manufacturers, apparel firms selling to Sears, Roebuck, and small electronics firms supplying parts to aerospace contractors. Forward satellites operate on the other side of center firms, channeling the center firm's output toward the ultimate consumer. Here the center firm mass-produces the item and then sends it forward to its satellites at the wholesale and retail level for sale to the final buyer. Examples of forward satellites are automobile dealers, gasoline service stations, and most kinds of retail stores. Sometimes center firms use other center firms as satellites. Food packers and appliance manufacturers who use leading retail chains (A&P, Safeway, Kroger, Kresge, Woolworth) as major outlets provide one example.

Some periphery firms are "floating" satellites in the sense that their activities are geared to the requirements of several center firms or industries rather than just one. Other periphery firms function as "attached" satellites and are tied by contract, tradition, personal contact, or some other means to a single center firm (or to a small group of center firms). In certain situations, center firms aid their satellite firms by extending them credit on goods purchased and/or by giving them exclusive franchises to handle their products.

The Competitive Fringe. A second type of periphery firm produces items which compete directly against the products of center firms. Again

---

[7] Edith Penrose, *The Theory of the Growth of the Firm* (New York: John Wiley & Sons, Inc., 1959), p. 215.

two subtypes appear. One subtype is a pioneering, highly innovative small firm operating in an industry dominated by center firms. The pioneering enterprise seeks to be a leader in developing a new product or conceiving of a more efficient production technique, so as to gain a competitive edge on its larger rivals. Center firms are not always major sources of new invention, despite their large expenditures for research and development. A goodly portion of new discovery stems from individuals working alone within the confines of universities or small private laboratories. When center firms are sluggish in their efforts at innovation, the way is opened for pioneer-type periphery firms to compete with them successfully, at least in local or regional markets. By adopting an aggressive approach to the implementation of new production technology and product improvements, the small innovative firm is able to keep one jump ahead of rival center firms and thereby collar a large enough share of the market to remain in business and perhaps even flourish.

The second subtype of competitive fringe firm challenges center firms in their strong markets without relying on pioneering. The U.S. economy is so large that astute periphery firms can capture a niche in the market despite the dominance of center firms. Center firms find it more profitable to launch into new markets and products than to devote time and energy to squeezing the last dollar of sales out of any one market, thereby paving the way for small firms to obtain at least a subsistence market share. Examples of this type of competitive fringe firm include producers of so-called "off-brands," along with the numerous small steel firms, the localized supermarket chains, and small meat packers. A few of the largest periphery firms are able to acquire a nationwide reputation for their products—certain food products and articles of clothing serve as good examples.

Several additional features which typify most, though not all, firms in the competitive fringe include:

1. reliance upon local sources of ingredient inputs for their product;
2. concentration upon one product (or a closely related product group);
3. utilization of technologically inferior production methods and equipment (pioneer-type firms excepted);
4. operating within the framework of a single plant for purposes of production;
5. rare participation in foreign markets;
6. a shorter life span than center firms, owing to a higher rate of failure and to acquisition and merger; and
7. behaving as a price follower in the sense that they tend to charge approximately the same price for their products as do center firms, although when price wars break out, firms in the competitive fringe are usually the initial price cutters.

Independent Periphery Firms.   This category is a residual classification encompassing small firms that are relatively free of center firm influence or affiliation. Such firms operate on the economic fringes of the production-distribution continuum for key commodities, filling in the gaps left by the mainstream of economic activity and specializing in unique articles and services. Manufacturing examples include producers of specialty steel products, jewelry, toys and games, novelty items, small household items (lamps, picture frames, decorative glassware, and kitchenware), men's belts, shoe polish, and leather goods. Independent distributors also are a good example of this type of periphery firm.

THE ECONOMICS OF CENTER FIRMS

Without a doubt, center firms constitute the greatest aggregation of productive potential ever known. Large corporations possess organizational, technological, and production capabilities which overwhelm those of any other type of economic unit. Their sphere of influence is all-pervasive. The prices they charge and the wages they pay strongly influence prices and wages in the remainder of the business community. The rates at which they produce and the aggressiveness with which they expand set the tone of economic activity in general. The degree to which they are able to implement new technologies and to produce new commodities determines the pace of economic progress. Their leadership or their inaction frequently sets the pattern for the extent of business involvement in social problems.

In the United States the 500 largest industrial corporations are the most visible and best known of the center firms. They include such firms as General Motors, Standard Oil, IBM, General Electric, Ford, Texaco, DuPont, RCA, U.S. Steel, Chrysler, Procter & Gamble, Westinghouse, and Gulf. In addition to the 500 largest manufacturing corporations, the category of center firms includes the 250 to 300 largest banks and insurance companies, retail organizations, utilities, transportation companies, and construction firms. Taken together, these 750 to 800 giant corporations comprise the *center economy* of the United States. In 1971 this relatively small group of firms (out of the over 10 million business enterprises in the U.S.) had combined sales of almost $700 billion, combined profits of over $35 billion, combined assets in excess of $1 trillion, and combined employment exceeding 20 million persons.[8] A total of 173 of these enterprises has annual sales or revenues exceeding $1 billion; and four of them (General Motors, Standard Oil of New Jersey, IBM, and American Telephone and Telegraph Co.) have in recent years earned more than $1 billion in profits annually.

Center firms are distinguished by a number of common traits, the most obvious of which is size; they are predominantly large in terms of assets, invested capital, annual dollar sales, profits, and employment. Their operations extend to national and international markets—they seek raw materials from the cheapest source, process them wherever it is most economical, and sell the output in the most advantageous markets irrespective of national

---

8 "The Largest U.S. Corporations," *Fortune*, Vol. 85, No. 5 (May 1972), pp. 188–221.

boundaries. Usually, the markets in which center firms operate consist mainly of a few very large corporate enterprises, each doing its best to outfox its major rivals.

In many respects, the evolution of the large corporation has followed the economic logic of extending the sphere of the firm's activity from raw materials through all phases of manufacturing to the sale of commodities to the ultimate consumer. Thus, center firms characteristically assure themselves of a reliable supply of critical raw material inputs by owning or controlling suppliers, and they frequently operate or control the channels through which their products are distributed. At the same time, many large corporations have diversified into related and sometimes distinctively different products, exercising coordination from a central management point. Only a few center firms have stuck with a single product orientation (bakeries, breweries, cement firms, petroleum firms, and primary metals firms). However, a number of center firms with a multiproduct orientation have concentrated their efforts on a few "bread and butter" products, engaging in the remainder to take up slack in the organization and to round out the product line.

By and large, center firms are technologically progressive; they have discovered that success, and eventually survival, depends upon their staying on the frontiers of innovation. The commitment of center firms to research, development, and innovation is reflected in the fact that firms with over 5,000 employees account for about 90 percent of industrial research and development expenditures. And even though center firms by no means have a monopoly on new ideas and inventions, it is they who nearly always are in the vanguard of applying them and making them practical. They excel especially in rapidly transforming profitable new products into established commodities, even though the ideas for such products may originate elsewhere.[9] Professor Joseph Schumpeter was among the first to recognize the technological exploits of center firms when he observed that inquiry into the origins and evolution of technological progress and the standard of living "leads not to the doors of those firms that work under conditions of comparatively free competition, but precisely to the door of the large concerns . . . and a shocking suspicion dawns upon us that big business may have had more to do with creating (our) standard of life than with keeping it down."[10]

Center firms also have abundant financial resources. Their cash flows are large, especially in prosperous times. Retained earnings generate funds internally which can be used to maintain and to increase technical proficiency. The costs of borrowing tend to fall as center firm profitability rises.

---

[9] According to one study, it is possible to predict with considerable confidence that a large firm will be quicker than a small firm in adopting a new innovation. Given the market structure of an industry and the profitability of an innovation, larger firms can be expected to be early users of new techniques. See Edwin Mansfield, "The Speed of Response of Firms to New Techniques," *Quarterly Journal of Economics*, Vol. 77, No. 2 (May 1963), pp. 290–311.

[10] Joseph Schumpeter, *Capitalism, Socialism and Democracy*, 3rd ed. (New York: Harper & Row, Publishers, 1950), p. 82.

They have ready access to national money markets at highly competitive rates of interest. Only the credit of the federal government is superior to that of center firms. A major consequence of the financial power of the center firm is its ability to marshall whatever resources and technical expertise may be required to break the bottlenecks that most threaten its expansion, its survival, and its profitability.

Along with these rather generalized attributes, center firms exhibit three unique features:

1. the capacity to attract superior managerial and technical talent,
2. the extensive use of managerial technology, and
3. the reliance upon planning and adapting to change.

Each of these is worthy of special discussion.

The Attraction of Superior Managerial and Technical Talent. The quality of managerial and technical talent found in large-scale business enterprises is superior. Because of their adequate financial resources, center firms can offer managerial and scientific employees greater financial and promotional opportunities than periphery firms. It is no accident that center firms typically are salary leaders and pay more than do either governments or educational institutions for people of equivalent training and capability. In addition, the scope of center firms' activities permits them to offer prospective employees a wide variety of career patterns. All in all, not many employers outside the center economy are able to match the calibre of employment opportunities available in center firms. As a consequence, center firms have been able to assemble an impressive array of specialized and highly skilled manpower to meet their needs for managerial and technical capability; this has given them an organizational capability that small enterprises and government agencies are usually unable to match.

The Extensive Use of Managerial Technology. The term *technology* is normally thought of as pertaining to the detailed scientific and engineering aspects of manufacturing intricate products or rendering highly technical services. This, however, is an unduly narrow concept. Broadly construed, technology refers to the systematic application of organized knowledge of any kind to the accomplishment of practical problems and tasks. Thus defined, technology ceases to lie solely within the province of the scientist or the engineer; rather, it extends to the work of specialists of all kinds, including managerial specialists.

Managerial technology is the particular branch of technology concerning the application of organized knowledge to the task of managing business enterprises. The principal function of management is to seek new and better means of overcoming technical inefficiencies, production bottlenecks, and rising costs, and to attack whatever obstacles to growth and profitability may arise. The methodology and the means by which this function is carried out is the essence of managerial technology, and center firms are the masters of its use.

Evidence abounds that an innovative and imaginative application of managerial technology is the critical ingredient of center firm operations which has allowed them to escape the bondage of inefficiency and rising costs customarily thought to inhabit large-scale organizations. In part, center firm managers have circumvented the diseconomies and unwieldiness of large size by optimizing the scale of their several production units. It is simple enough to determine within a narrow range the most economic plant size and then to build as many of these as necessary to satisfy the firm's need for productive capacity. Thus, every center firm has a host of production plants, usually dispersed geographically so as to reduce transportation costs. Secondly, center firms have stemmed rises in raw material costs by expanding their organizational network backward so as to own or control raw material suppliers. Where this has proved uneconomical, center firms have used their large buying power to effect quantity purchase savings. Third, labor costs have been suppressed by heavy investment in capital equipment and automated processes which have released scarce manpower resources for different and more effective uses. Routine, repetitive, mechanistic tasks, performed by either blue- or white-collar workers, have been targeted for reduction or elimination entirely by new machinery or by the imaginative application of computer technology. Fourth, the quality of management science and managerial techniques has been vastly upgraded and streamlined by an increasing use of computers and operations research models, the development of strong financial controls and budget procedures, better methods of market analysis, refinements in forecasting, the design of information systems, and the use of all sorts of quantitative decision tools. The immense speed with which computers can process data and develop new information for decision-making purposes has contributed greatly to this aspect of advances in managerial technology.

Last, but far from least, center firm managers have responded to the technological imperative of mass production and mass marketing by devising innovative styles of management organization. The necessity of this strategy requires a bit of elaboration. An important consequence of a high and rapidly advancing technology is that it forces tasks to be subdivided into fractions small enough that the bits and pieces of new technical knowhow can be applied to greatest advantage. This subdivision must proceed far enough such that the scope of each subtask coincides with the knowledge range of those persons who must perform it. For example, no one person possesses all the knowhow necessary to design and construct a 40-story office building. Hence the design and construction process must be broken down into microfractions, each of which is coterminous with a specific, established segment of knowledge and each of which is within the range of knowledge and capability of an individual specialist. The knowledge of civil engineers and physicists will be required for designing the foundation of such a building and for evaluating the structure's ability to withstand high wind velocity. The expertise of metal-lurgists will be required for deciding upon the particular characteristics which the structural steel should have and whether the plumbing should be copper or galvanized steel. The knowledge of chemists will be especially valuable in assessing the particular molecular structures of the paints to be used, the carpets to be laid, and the upholstery fabrics to be chosen. The services of personnel managers and labor relations experts will be necessary for dealing with the vagaries of union work rules in the building construction industry. And so it goes. A wide variety of detailed and specialized knowledge becomes essential for efficiently producing even simple commodities in a high, rapidly advancing technological environment. It is this phenomenon which accounts for the rise in the demand for specialists of all kinds and for the emphasis upon specialized training programs and professional degrees.

Since center firms typically use very advanced technologies and produce complex commodities, they require many individual skills to bring high-level knowledge to bear upon the microfractions of the production process. A large technical staff may have to be assembled in order to obtain the necessary range and depth of specialized knowledge and expertise. Indeed, modern technology, complex products, and large-scale organization tend to be inseparable. The more intricate the technology or the more complex the product, the larger the organizational network requisite for organizing the production process and for bringing it to a profitable culmination. Thus, to a considerable degree the organizational framework of the large corporate enterprise derives from the *technological imperative* to bring highly specialized knowledge to bear upon each microfraction of each activity in which the firm is engaged, and from the *organizational imperative* to combine and coordinate each of the finished microfractions of the each activity toward efficient and profitable completion of the entire activity. Furthermore, management must see to it that production of each of the firm's products is coordinated to form an integrated, successful operation. Ideally, the various phases of the corporation's activities should mesh together like a well-oiled machine.

It is at this juncture that managerial technology comes into play. Management must devise ways to accommodate large size, yet preserve organizational efficiency. Center firms have responded to this organizational imperative with all sorts of innovative schemes for maintaining their vitality and internal efficiency.[11] Responsibility and managerial functions have been subdivided into manageable proportions and delegated. Likewise, the activities that the managers supervise have been organized according to the most efficient size. In many cases the principal operating parts of the enterprise have been

[11] An excellent analysis of the economic significance of the organizational innovations which corporations have employed to maintain their vitality and internal efficiency is contained in Oliver E. Williamson, *Corporate Control and Business Behavior* (Englewood Cliffs, N.J.: Prentice-Hall, Inc., 1970).

structured as semiautonomous operating divisions, each of which is subsequently organized among both functional and product lines. Decision-making is dispersed throughout the entire organizational structure, yet coordination and control are kept intact by use of computer-based management information systems and tight budget procedures. To some extent, the effective power of decision is lodged not only in the managerial hierarchy but also in the hierarchy of the technical, planning, and specialized staff who possess the information requisite for making decisions and upon whose judgment the managers are obliged to rely. Thus, the processes of decision-making and participation in the various aspects of managerial technology have come to embrace all who bring specialized knowledge, talent, or experience to the organization—extending from the most senior officials of the firm all the way down *to* (but not including) the white- and blue-collar workers whose function it is to conform more or less mechanically to routine instruction.

The principal economic effect of the successful application of managerial technology in center firms is that it has allowed them to escape the prohibitive inefficiencies and rising unit costs which otherwise accompany large-scale operations. Increases in center firm size and output have frequently been accompanied by decreases in unit costs or at least unit costs which are lower than they would otherwise have been. Thus managerial technology has been instrumental in removing the obstacles to center firm growth and expansion and in providing a new source of corporate efficiency. This outcome has been of no small consequence in accounting for the dramatic and successful rise of the large corporation to a position of permanence among the institutions of society.

The Reliance upon Planning. The third distinctive feature of center firms is their increasing propensity to plan. Actually, this is a by-product of the application of managerial technology. Unlike periphery firms, with their preoccupation with short-run problems, center firms combine a long-run perspective with their attention to short-run matters. Not only do center firm managements seek to solve the short-run problems of bringing together and coordinating the resources necessary for production and distribution, but they also display a balanced concern for planning for whatever changes may by required to insulate the firm from unfavorable environmental developments. By and large, the routine decisions involving daily operations are delegated to middle- and lower-echelon management. Top management confines its involvement in regular production operations, with only minor exceptions, to prescribing operational procedures and guidelines. This, in conjunction with tight central office budgetary restraint, is usually sufficient when the start-up kinks are gotten out to ensure operating efficiency, provided plant managers are carefully chosen and trained. Once underway, operations acquire an element of routine and to some degree are propelled by their own momentum. While short-run difficulties are undoubtedly brought to the attention of high-level managers even on a daily basis, the time they allocate to such details is likely to be small relative to the time devoted to intermediate- and long-range planning activities. Responsibility for carrying out the planning function increases as one proceeds *up* the managerial hierarchy, whereas just the reverse is encountered when dealing with short-run managerial tasks.

Sustained success by the center firm hinges upon its correct (or nearly so) anticipation of the form of change and environmental crises. Forecasting the direction of economic changes, anticipating changes in consumer demand, and preparing for new technological developments is particularly crucial, although it is becoming increasingly necessary to undertake planning in regard to every facet of the firm's activities. As concerns new products, for example, proper planning consists of foreseeing the actions required between the initiation of production activity and its completion and preparing for the accomplishment of these actions. Steps must be taken to see that what the firm produces is actually wanted by the consumer in sufficient volume at a profitable price. And the firm must see that the labor, materials, and equipment it needs will be available at costs consistent with the expected selling price. The more technically sophisticated the product, the more time will be required for making the production mechanism operational—hence, the more critical careful planning becomes, since the risks of adverse market change are significantly enhanced. Despite the uncertainty of future events, the scope of the center firm's planning effort includes provisions for adapting to (1) upswings and downswings in the level of business activity, (2) product growth lags and spurts—cycles in the demand for the firm's products, (3) bottlenecks in supplies of required inputs (labor or raw materials), (4) changes in competitive pressures from whatever source, and (5) technological advance. Unless intelligent planning for secular and technological change is undertaken, the center firm cannot long hope to remain a viable organization. Decay will set in, profitability will be impaired, and ultimately the firm's survival will be at stake. Thus, progressive center firms devote a considerable amount of time and energy to planning. In reality, the planning function is simply an added dimension of managerial technology, and in center firms, at least, it is increasingly becoming a normal aspect of managerial methodology and management science.

THE CONCEPT OF THE FIRM RECONSIDERED

From the vantage point of history, the firm has been commonly conceived as consisting of an owner-entrepreneur and a staff of employees. Business leadership has been identified almost exclusively with the owner-entrepreneur —the risk-taking individual who supplies financial capital, who organizes and superivises the economic resources needed for production, and who has a special genius for innovation. "To act with confidence beyond the range of familiar beacons and to overcome that resistance requires aptitudes that are present in only a small fraction of the population and (they) define the entrepreneurial type as well as the entrepreneurial function."[12] The firm typically has been viewed as engaging in whatever activities the owner-entrepreneur deems appropriate. Conformity to the goals of the firm is purchased by payments (wages, salaries, prestige, power, security) made by the owner-entrepreneur to his employees and by a system of internal controls (authority, budgets) which informs the employees of his desires.

This concept of the firm is still appropriate for periphery firms, but it is at considerable variance with reality as concerns center firms. Center firms are large-scale organizations, run by a team of professional managers. Their decisions and their policies cannot correctly be viewed as the product of a single-minded individual entrepreneur. In center firms, the patterns of change in prices, output levels, product lines, product mix, resource allocation, and other standard economic variables are the result of a complex (and little understood) decision-making process.

Moreover, the large corporation has a much more sizable constituency than does the small business enterprise. It comes into touch with a far greater number and range of individuals and its sphere of influence extends to all corners of the economy. As a consequence, it faces different constraints and it behaves in different ways from the periphery firm. These differences are substantive rather than incidental.

For this reason we shall in the following chapters find it necessary to distinguish between entrepreneurial firms and managerial firms. The term periphery firm will be used throughout to symbolize the entrepreneurial firm —the owner-managed firm which epitomizes the concept of small business. The term center firm will be used to symbolize the large corporation run by professional managers. Attention will be called to those instances in which either similarities or differences appear, as between center and periphery firm behavior.

Summary and Conclusions

The American economy's journey from a preindustrial environment through the takeoff into industrialism and thence into economic maturity has left a far-reaching wake of change in the structure of business enterprise. The small proprietorship with a localized market for its products and its stress upon a single line of technically related products which was so characteristic of the nineteenth century still remains the most significant form of enterprise in terms of numbers—but not so in terms of economic importance. The hallmark of organization development in business associated with national economic

---

[12] Schumpeter, *Capitalism, Socialism, and Democracy*, p. 132.

maturity is the phenomenal rise to positions of productive power of large-scale, multiproduct, international corporate enterprises. These enterprises comprise the very heart of a modern industrial system. And it is their dominant presence which gives rise to such popular labels as "the corporate economy" and "the corporate state."

In the chapters which follow we shall analyze this type of economic environment in greater depth. More elaborate embellishments of the center-periphery environment will be added as complete, thoroughgoing theoretical models of business behavior are constructed. By concentrating our attention upon the economics of the firm—its decisions, its behavior, and its impact on society—we can gain a basic understanding and a perspective view of the inner workings of a modern economic system. Our ultimate goal is to explain the complexities of prices, how output rates are determined, why certain patterns of resource usage emerge, the economics of technological change, the foundations of economic progress, and the overall economic welfare of society. Such matters constitute the essence of the branch of economics known as *microeconomics*, and they are the key to understanding the whys and wherefores of economic activity in a technologically dynamic society.

SUGGESTED READINGS

ADELMAN, M. A., "The Two Faces of Economic Concentration," *The Public Interest*, No. 21 (Fall 1970), pp. 117–126.

AVERITT, ROBERT T., *The Dual Economy* (New York: W. W. Norton & Company, Inc., 1967). Chaps. 2, 5, and 6.

BAIN, JOE S., *Industrial Organization* (New York: John Wiley & Sons, Inc., 1959), Chap. 3.

DRUCKER, PETER, "The New Markets and the New Capitatlism," *The Public Interest*, No. 21 (Fall 1970), pp. 44–79.

GALBRAITH, JOHN KENNETH, *The New Industrial State* (Boston: Houghton Mifflin Company, 1967), Chaps. 1–8.

JOHNSON, E. A. J., and HERMAN E. KROOSS, *The American Economy* (Englewood Cliffs, N.J.: Prentice-Hall, Inc., 1960), Chaps. 8 and 9.

KROOSS, HERMAN E., *American Economic Development* (Englewood Cliffs, N.J.: Prentice-Hall, Inc., 1966), Chaps. 6 and 7.

Questions for Discussion

1. What is an entrepreneur? How is an entrepreneur different from a manager? from a corporation president? from a chairman of the board of directors?

2. What characteristics distinguish periphery firms from center firms?

3. To what extent is the concept of an entrepreneur-led enterprise appropriate for center firms? for periphery firms? Explain.

4. What advantages, if any, do center firms possess over periphery firms? Conversely, what advantages if any, do periphery firms possess over center firms?

5. In what types of industry are center firms most likely to be found? In what types of industry are periphery firms most likely to be found? What reasons can you give for this disparity?

6. Can center firms and periphery firms coexist in the same industry? Under what circumstances? Give examples.

7. Explain what is meant by the concept of managerial technology.

2

Decision-Making under Conditions of Certainty, Risk, and Uncertainty

Decision-making lies at the very core of economic activity of any sort. Problems of choice abound in every phase of economics—how much of what commodities to produce, what price should be charged, what to buy, from whom to buy, and so on. It is appropriate therefore to consider that body of knowledge known as *decision theory* for the purpose of learning more about the decision-making process and the conditions under which decisions are made. In this chapter we shall sketch the broad outlines of selected key topics in decision theory which bear directly upon consumer and business behavior. We shall show how and why the framework of decision theory allows for the development of concepts and the explanation of behavior patterns long overlooked in conventional treatments of microeconomics. This chapter is particularly aimed at giving the reader a feeling for the uncertainty confronting the managers of business firms and a respect for the difficulties the manager encounters when trying to improve the quality of his decisions.

Although we focus here upon decision-making in the context of a business enterprise, the fundamental concepts and principles to be presented are equally applicable to the decision processes of consumers, households, nonprofit institutions, government agencies, or any other organization. Decision-making is by no means unique to business enterprise. All human behavior involves, either consciously or unconsciously, the selection of particular actions out of all those available to the individual and over which he exercises influence and authority.

THE NATURE OF DECISION PROBLEMS

A decision problem exists only when the decision-maker can choose among two or more alternative courses of action. When just *one* course of action presents itself, clearly there can be no decision problem. Moreover, for the decision problem to be meaningful, the alternative actions must be separate and distinct, not only in the sense that they represent different choices but also in the sense that they can conceivably result in different outcomes. Otherwise, the choice of alternatives may be of little consequence to the decision-maker.

If the alternatives are to be rationally evaluated, some means must be devised to rank the relative desirability of anticipated outcomes according to the decision-maker's preferences. Often this is the most perplexing aspect of decision problems. Numerous criteria abound, some objective and some subjective. When the choices involve quantifiable variables such as costs, dollar sales, production levels, or profits, the selection of a ranking measure is not so onerous. In this case a *cardinal* ranking pattern, whereby numerical values are assigned to the outcomes, is usually feasible, and the decision rests upon identifying the alternative course of action which possesses the most favorable numerical value. Suppose, for example, the decision-maker must decide which one of three new machines to purchase. Given that the machines have identical purchase prices and life expectancies, it might well be reasonable to base the purchase decision on economy of operating cost. If expected operating costs for machine A are $150 per week, for machine B $175 per week, and for machine C $135 per week, then obviously machine C should be chosen. Furthermore, we could say that we preferred machine C to its closest competitor, machine A, by the definite amount of $15 per week of life expectancy and use. Hence, a cardinal ranking permits an ordering of alternatives based upon numerical values, and the decision-maker can easily ascertain the amount by which one alternative is preferred to another.

In other cases no measures are available for objectively evaluating the outcomes of various courses of action. Then an *ordinal* ranking, using subjective criteria, must be employed. Suppose that the decision problem entails selecting a color combination to be used on boxes of Sparkle detergent. The color combinations available are (a) orange and white, (b) blue and green, and (c) red and yellow. The decision-maker may well arrive at a ranking of these three color combinations utilizing some subjective preference pattern, but he would be hard pressed to describe by how much, in quantitative terms, he preferred one color combination over another. Thus, in an *ordinal* preference pattern it is possible only to array the alternatives in order of preference; no means exists for comparing the *amount* by which one alternative is superior to another.

Whether cardinal or ordinal rankings are used, it is especially critical that the decision-maker's preference pattern satisfy the condition of transitivity. A decision-maker's preferences are transitive if when he prefers A to B in the paired comparison (A, B) and B to C in the paired comparison (B, C), then he also prefers A to C in the paired comparison (A, C). Upon this cornerstone rests the whole of decision theory; unless this condition is met, little can be said about the process of reaching decisions.

The Concepts of Certainty, Risk, and Uncertainty

In many respects the product of modern business decisions is a function of the amount of information managers possess about alternative courses of actions and the possible outcomes which may result from them. A decision-maker's information ranges along a continuum from perfect knowledge to complete ignorance. For analytical convenience, the continuum can be thought of as consisting of three distinct parts: (1) certainty, (2) risk, and (3) uncertainty.

1. *Certainty* is a state of knowledge where the decision-maker has *complete* information about the decision problem confronting him. Each alternative open to him is known, and each alternative is known to result invariably in a specific outcome. Perfect knowledge thus prevails.
2. *Risk* is a state of knowledge where the decision-maker is aware of the alternative courses of action, but is not certain as to their possible outcomes. The distinctive feature of risk is that the probability of each outcome is known or can be reliably estimated. Two kinds of risk are distinguishable.
   (a) *Objective risk* exists when the probability that a particular outcome will result can be computed objectively, either from historical data or on an a priori basis.
   (b) *Subjective risk* exists when the probability that a particular outcome will result is determined or estimated in a subjective fashion, perhaps by a "strong" intuition or hunch based upon experience and familiarity with the sitation—in other words, the decision-maker confidently believes that he has a special insight into the probability of each outcome.
3. *Uncertainty* is a state of knowledge where the decision-maker is aware of fewer than all of the alternative courses of action. Furthermore, he is unable or unwilling to formulate (objectively or subjectively) reliable or believable probabilities of the outcomes from each course of action. Information is too incomplete to allow him to identify every alternative and to make estimates of probable outcomes in which a high degree of confidence may be placed. Historical data may be nonexistent or sketchy, experiences with the situation quite rare, or the structure of the variables insufficiently stable to permit prediction or estimation of the probabilities.

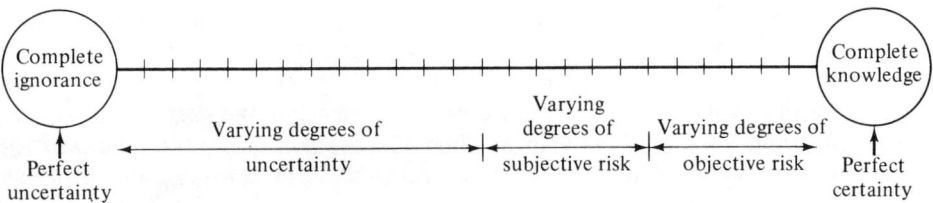

Fig. 2-1   The Continuum of Knowledge

Thus, uncertainty describes a situation where there is no substantial basis for expecting one rather than another of the universe of possible outcomes.

From these descriptions, certainty can be thought of as a special case of risk in which the probabilities of the potential outcomes are either 0 or 1. From another angle, it can be said that risk is "measurable uncertainty."[1] Figure 2-1 provides a useful illustration of the states of knowledge and their relationship to the concepts of certainty, risk, and uncertainty. At the extreme ends of the continuum of knowledge shown in Figure 2-1 are the states of complete knowledge and complete ignorance. The state of complete knowledge coincides precisely with what has been defined as certainty. To the extent that complete knowledge or certainty is not present in a decision problem, some degree of uncertainty must exist. When the degree of uncertainty is small enough so that the probabilities of the possible outcomes are known precisely or can be estimated within a very narrow range, then the state of knowledge is termed objective risk. When the degree of uncertainty is a bit larger so that the probabilities of the outcomes are less precise and entail a high degree of subjectivity, then the state of knowledge is termed subjective risk. Objective risk therefore lies closer to certainty than does subjective risk, as indicated in Figure 2-1. To the left of subjective risk lies a wide band of uncertainty as we have defined it, with the degree of uncertainty increasing as one proceeds leftward toward complete ignorance.

Having introduced the concepts of certainty, risk, and uncertainty, suppose we examine some decision problems which illustrate these three states of knowledge.

DECISION PROBLEMS INVOLVING CERTAINTY

Decision-making under certainty—a phenomenon we would expect to encounter only rarely—encompasses a surprising number of practical problems. In business and economics, situations abound in which the alternatives are

---

[1] Frank H. Knight, *Risk, Uncertainty, and Profit* (Boston: Houghton Mifflin Company, 1921).

known and the problem is to optimize some given index such as profits, dollar sales, and costs—for example, maximizing the output from a given (or known) input-output relationship, determining the profit-maximizing levels of price and output given knowledge of the demand and cost functions, and determining the output rate which minimizes unit costs. Many linear programming problems deal with how best to allocate scarce resources (such as manpower, materials, and equipment) when faced with a set of *known* constraints. Hence, decision-making under certainty describes problems where the decision involves determining the optimum course of action given a known set of circumstances and information.

DECISION PROBLEMS INVOLVING RISK

Risk is a state of knowledge where each alternative has a set of outcomes and where each outcome is known or believed to occur with a well-defined probability. Two approaches can be used in determining the probability of an outcome: (1) logical deduction or *a priori* reasoning and (2) empirical measurement or the *a posteriori* method.

In the a priori method, the probability of an event is deduced from the inherent characteristics of an event. Thus it is not necessary to toss a fair coin a large number of times to discover that the relative frequency of heads (or tails) will approximate $\frac{1}{2}$. Nor is it necessary to draw a card from a deck of 52 cards many times to establish that the probability of drawing the ace of spades (or any other card) is $\frac{1}{52}$.

In the a posteriori method, reliance is placed upon the results of past experience to obtain the probability measure. This procedure assumes that past performances are typical and will continue in the future; it also requires that the number of past experiences be large enough to exhibit stable patterns, the changes in which can be accurately predicted. Insurance companies depend heavily upon empirical measurement of the probabilities of deaths, fire losses, accidents, sickness, and so on, for it is upon these that decisions regarding premium rates are based. Although they cannot predict whether, during a given year, a particular individual will meet his fate or a certain house will be damaged by natural catastrophe, insurance companies can predict with small error how many persons will die, have accidents, or be hospitalized, or how many homes out of a given number will sustain fire damage during that year. *Single* economic units do not experience these events with sufficient frequency to predict such losses for themselves. Thus they plan for objective risk avoidance by shifting the burden of risk to insurance companies, which, in turn, make a careful analysis of the probabilities and use them to determine a reasonable fee for assuming the potential losses. In some cases, a business firm will elect to insure itself against objective risk because the number of occurrences of the event within the firm is sufficient to allow prediction within a narrow margin. For instance, loan companies and banks expect a certain percentage of defaults on the credit they extend, as do most retailers; restaurants expect a certain percentage of spoilage from unsold food; and manufacturing firms have found that they will incur a "normal" loss of production time from breakdowns and employee absenteeism. Typically, the costs of "self-insurance" are planned for by treating the expected losses as a regular cost of doing business.

The preceding discussion pertains primarily to objective risk, since the probabilities can be arrived at by deductive reasoning or empirical measurement. Little subjectivity is involved. Analytically, decision-making under subjective risk is akin to decision-making under uncertainty; hence, the two will be treated jointly in the subsequent sections on uncertainty.

DECISION PROBLEMS INVOLVING UNCERTAINTY

Uncertainty and subjective risk characterize the environment in which most decisions are made. If the future were completely known, business decisions would be relatively trivial; management would need only to plan for the events ahead and to see that the plans were carried out. Objective risk constitutes only a small portion of the decision-making process and can be readily coped with by either self-insurance or the purchase of insurance policies. Hence, the vast majority of decisions are made in a state of incomplete knowledge, where the range of alternatives is imperfectly identified, where the outcomes associated with the perceived alternatives are imperfectly known, and where the probabilities of the outcomes are at best subjectively determined.

Many uncertainty and subjective risk situations arise because business decisions are made in unique circumstances—investment in a new plant, adoption of an imaginative new marketing strategy, selection of a new financing instrument—where information is necessarily incomplete and the future is uncharted. Management cannot predict accurately the outcomes of its decisions because of such unknown factors as (1) changes in technology, (2) shifts in consumer tastes and preferences, (3) entrance of new competition, (4) political uncertainties concerning new legislation, continuation of tariffs and import quotas, and government contracts, (5) impacts of federal fiscal and monetary controls, (6) rates of productivity change, and (7) movements in raw material prices, wage rates, availability of labor, and so on—all of which are beyond the control of the firm.

Decision-makers must attempt to cope with uncertainty, since uncertainty is not insurable and cannot be incorporated into the firm's cost structure as can objective risk. Thus, it is the process of reaching decisions when the knowledge level is below objective risk that is most relevant. How can the decision-maker reach rational decisions in such an environment? What criteria can decision-makers employ to guide their selection of a course of action? A variety of ways exist to deal with imperfect knowledge; to these we now turn.

The Payoff Matrix

Decision theory utilizes a convenient device known as a payoff matrix to tabulate the key information the decision-maker has at his disposal. A *payoff matrix* consists of a set of numbers arrayed into rows and columns. The rows represent courses of action (or "strategies") available for selection by the decision-maker, whereas the columns represent different sets of environmental conditions or "states of nature" over which the decision-maker has no control. Thus the columns in the matrix reflect the fact that the outcome of a specific course of action is partially determined by forces beyond the decision-maker's reach. For each course of action and each state of nature there is a unique outcome or, stated in numerical terms, a "payoff." These payoffs comprise the entries in the cells of the matrix.

The advantage of using a payoff matrix stems from the efficient manner in which it focuses upon the relevant decision variables and reduces the decision problem to manageable proportions. Figure 2-2 depicts a decision problem involving three courses of action and four states of nature. In this matrix the S's are alternative strategies (or courses of action); the N's are states of nature; and the numbers in the matrix are the expected payoffs (objectively or subjectively measured) in dollars. To give concrete meaning to the matrix, the three strategies might represent different amounts of money to spend on promoting a new product, the states of nature might be different levels of consumer acceptance of the new product, and the payoffs might denote profits earned per week from sales of the new product. If the decision-maker chooses strategy S_1 and state of nature N_3 is actually encountered, then the resulting outcome is a payoff of $64 per week. Should the decision-maker select strategy S_3 and encounter state of nature N_1, the outcome is a payoff of $22 per week. The other payoffs are similarly interpreted.

		States of Nature			
		N_1	N_2	N_3	N_4
Alternative Strategies	S_1	$16	$28	$64	$32
	S_2	$70	$42	$12	$ 9
	S_3	$22	$52	$25	$58

Fig. 2-2 An Example of a Payoff Matrix

Notice that the form of the payoff matrix permits recognition and identification of the states of knowledge that prevail—certainty, objective risk, subjective risk, and uncertainty. When the state of knowledge characterizing a decision problem is one of certainty, there is only one state of nature and it is known to occur with a probability of 1. In such cases the payoff matrix will actually have only one column and the decision problem is reduced simply to deciding which strategy will yield the most favorable payoff. When there is more than one possible state of nature and when the probabilities of each state of nature can be *objectively* measured, then the problem is one of decision-making under objective risk. If we can assign a subjectively determined probability to each of the several possible states of nature, then the problem is one of decision-making under conditions of subjective risk. In the event that no meaningful probabilities can be assigned to the states of nature, the problem is one of decision-making under uncertainty.

Some Proposed Decision Rules

Consider the payoff matrix shown in Figure 2-3, where the three strategies represent various pricing policies being considered for adoption by a firm. The three states of nature represent reactions of rival firms, levels of consumer demand, government attitudes and policies, and so on, all combined in different degrees to represent contrasting environmental circumstances which it is believed the firm might well encounter. The dollar payoffs denote the estimated daily profits or losses of the firm. Inspection of the payoff matrix reveals no clear-cut choice as to a strategy; hence a decision problem definitely exists.

		States of Nature		
		N_1	N_2	N_3
Alternative Strategies	S_1	$45	$ 6	$30
	S_2	$66	−$ 21	$90
	S_3	−$12	$120	$24

Fig. 2-3   Selecting the "Best" Alternative

Numerous criteria have been proposed as possible guidelines to the choice of a strategy in a limited-information environment. Among these are (1) the maximin criterion, (2) the maximax criterion, (3) the minimax regret criterion, (4) the maximum-likelihood criterion, and (5) the expected-value criterion.

THE MAXIMIN CRITERION

According to the maximin decision rule, the best strategy is the one which has the largest minimum payoff. In other words, for each strategy the decision-maker determines the minimum (least favorable) payoff and picks the strategy containing the best of the minimum payoffs. Thus, in the matrix in

Figure 2-3, the minimum payoff from S_1 is a profit of $6; the minimum payoff from S_2 is $-$21; the minimum payoff from S_3 is $-$12. The maximum of the minimum (or the largest of the smallest) payoffs is $6, so the maximin criterion in this case would call for selection of strategy S_1.

The maximin criterion can be employed equally well in decision problems which seek to minimize the payoff value rather than maximize it. For instance, to find a strategy that is optimum from a cost standpoint, the maximum cost values associated with each strategy should be identified and the strategy selected which contains the lowest of the maximum values. In this case the maximin criterion is really a minimax criterion, because instead of picking the largest of the minimum values, we base our choice on the strategy containing the smallest of the maximum values.

The maximin criterion is a "pessimistic" decision rule in the sense that the decision-maker attempts to protect himself from the worst state of nature by selecting the alternative with the highest minimum payoff. He hedges against low payoffs by looking only for the best of the worst possible outcomes. Clearly, this is a very conservative decision rule, perhaps overly so, because in making his choice the decision-maker completely disregards the values of the other payoffs. The lack of wisdom in this choice procedure is easily demonstrated by the payoff matrix in Figure 2-4 (which was constructed so as to make the maximin criterion show up badly). Here the maximin criterion calls for selection of strategy S_1 because its smallest payoff of $5 is larger than S_2's smallest payoff of $4. A rational conservative might well prefer S_2, since it offers an attractive hedge against the possibility that neither N_1 or N_3 will occur. If N_1 does occur, the choice of S_2 over S_1 entails an opportunity loss of only $1; if N_3 occurs, the choice of S_2 gives an opportunity loss of only $5; whereas if N_2 prevails, there is an opportunity gain of $80 from selecting S_2 over S_1. Even many conservative decision-makers would be willing to accept the chances for small opportunity losses in return for the prospect of so large an opportunity gain.

			States of Nature		
			N_1	N_2	N_3
Fig. 2-4 Matrix Illustrating Weakness in the Maximin Criterion	Alternative Strategies	S_1	$5	$10	$100
		S_2	$4	$90	$ 95

Fig. 2-4 Matrix Illustrating Weakness in the Maximin Criterion

A second and quite obvious weakness of the maximin rule is its failure to consider the probability of occurrence of the respective states of nature. Knowledge of such probabilities may well be a critical factor. Consider again the payoff matrix in Figure 2-4. If it is thought or known that the probability of occurrence of N_1 is .10 (1 out of 10), the probability of N_2 is .60 (6 out of 10), and that of N_3 is .30 (3 out of 10), then it is scarcely rational to base the *entire* decision upon the fact that the smallest payoff for S_1 ($5) is larger than the smallest payoff for S_2 ($4), when both values are associated with a state of nature (N_1) which is not very likely to occur. Hence, blind use of the maximin rule can sometimes yield what might be considered an irrational choice of alternatives.

Despite its failure to consider all of the payoff values and its lack of provision for incorporating the probabilities of the states of nature, the maximin criterion cannot be roundly dismissed. There is much to be said for careful avoidance of adverse consequences. Where the decision-maker feels or has reason to believe that the worst that *can* happen *will* happen, the maximin rule has great appeal—particularly so, should the financial circumstances of the firm be such that its very survival is endangered in the event of serious losses (or perhaps even negligible profits). Also, as will be seen shortly, the maximin strategy is especially attractive where the decision-maker faces an aggressive opponent (say a rival firm) whose interests are in direct conflict with his own.

THE MAXIMAX CRITERION

Whereas the maximin rule is oriented toward pessimism and conservatism, the maximax criterion is geared toward optimism and venturesomeness. It calls for the decision-maker to elect the strategy which offers the highest possible payoff. In terms of the payoff matrix in Figure 2-3, the decision-maker notes that S_1 has a maximum payoff of $45, S_2 has a maximum payoff of $90, and S_3 has a maximum payoff of $120; since $120 is the maximum of the maximum payoffs, strategy S_3 should be chosen.

Such a decision rule is well suited to the temperament of a perennial optimist or an impulsive gambler desirous of quickly recouping his losses. It is subject to the same shortcomings as the maximin rule: (1) it ignores all values in the payoff matrix other than the highest ones, thereby giving no weight to any dangers that may characterize the strategy with the highest of the highest payoffs; (2) it may suggest to the decision-maker that he forego any attractive advantages inherent in other strategies, for a negligible gain should the most favorable of all outcomes actually appear; and (3) it gives no consideration to the probability of occurrence of the possible states of nature. Again, these weaknesses are quite apparent in the payoff matrix shown in Figure 2-4. In this matrix the maximax strategy is S_1, because its highest payoff of $100 exceeds the highest payoff of $95 offered by S_2. Yet, suppose the prospects for the actual occurrence of state of nature N_3 are slim; then the payoffs for N_1 and N_2 assume greater significance. A comparison of the payoffs for S_1 and S_2 under states of nature N_1 and N_2 strongly indicates a preference for S_2 instead of S_1. Hence the values of the intermediate payoffs offered by S_2, taken in conjunction with the probabilities of the states of nature, may well make it more attractive, to some decision-makers at least, than S_1 (the maximax choice) with its single high payoff of $100.

THE MINIMAX REGRET CRITERION

This decision rule aims at protecting the decision-maker from excessive regret about a wrong or costly decision. Toward this end, the minimax regret criterion maintains that the best strategy is the one that contains the smallest of the maximum regrets. Regret is measured by the difference between the payoff actually received and the payoff that could have been received had the decision-maker known the state of nature in advance. Because all payoffs save the largest for each state of nature will be less than satisfactory, the decision-maker will experience regret should any payoff but the most favorable one materialize. Consequently, there is a unique regret associated with each outcome, and it can be tabulated in what is called a regret matrix.

Suppose we derive a regret matrix from the payoff matrix in Figure 2-3. If strategy S_1 is chosen and state of nature N_1 occurs, the payoff is $45. However, had the decision-maker known in advance that N_1 would occur, he would have selected S_2 and received $66; thus he has a regret of $-$21$ from having chosen S_1, because the payoff he actually received ($45) is $21 *less* than the payoff he could have received ($66) had he known the state of nature would be N_1. The value of $-$21$ is therefore entered in row 1 of column 1 of the regret matrix shown in Figure 2-5. To continue with the calculation of regret, suppose S_2 were selected when N_1 occurred. In this case there is no regret about having made the wrong decision, because the $66 payoff is the largest obtainable given N_1; a zero is entered in row 2 of column 1 in the matrix. Had S_3 been chosen when N_1 occurred, the payoff would be $-$12$, as compared with the most desirable payoff of $66; thus the regret is $-$78$. The remainder of the regret matrix can be derived in like manner, as the reader should verify for himself. Note that the regret matrix contains only negative numbers and zeros. There is a zero in every column; each corresponds to the element of the payoff matrix containing the largest payoff for that state of nature.

| | | States of Nature | | |
		N_1	N_2	N_3
Alterative	S_1	$-$21	$-$114	$-$60
Strategies	S_2	0	$-$141	0
	S_3	$-$78	0	$-$66

Fig. 2-5 Regret Matrix

The decision-maker is now in a position to apply a minimax rule to the information in the regret matrix. The maximum regret value for each strategy is identified and that strategy is chosen which contains the smallest of the maximum values. From Figure 2-5, the maximum regret values are $-\$114$ for S_1, $-\$141$ for S_2, and $-\$78$ for S_3. Strategy S_3 is therefore the recommended course of action under the minimax regret criterion, because it is associated with the best of the worst regrets ($-\$78$).

Like both the maximin and maximax rules, the minimax regret criterion utilizes only a small portion of the payoff information. Just the largest regret value in a strategy is considered; low and intermediate regret values are disregarded. If, for example, strategy one has a *maximum* regret value which is slightly better than the maximum regret value of strategy two, the minimax regret criterion will call for selection of strategy one even though all the other regret payoffs in strategy two are much more favorable than their counterparts in strategy one. Needless to say, this characteristic may be viewed unfavorably by decision-makers. Second, the probabilities of the states of nature, should they be known or reliably estimated, are completely disregarded in the decision process; this is a questionable procedure. Last, it is not clear that the difference between two payoffs is necessarily an accurate measure of the decision-maker's regret when he receives the smaller of the two—especially where the regret is composed of the difference between a profit and a loss as compared to the difference between a large profit and a small profit. The loss might mean bankruptcy and hence a regret more than proportional to the difference in dollars. Even so, the regret measure, while crude and somewhat arbitrary, may not be a totally unreasonable measure of the decision-maker's regret from having chosen the wrong strategy.

Despite its inherent weaknesses, the minimax regret criterion is not without merit. For persons whose reaction is one of dismay, constant worry, and perhaps even mental depression when they discover they have made less-than-optimum decisions, the concept of regret is no doubt valid. Attempting to minimize the maximum regret in such cases may well give these decision-makers greater peace of mind.

THE MAXIMUM-LIKELIHOOD CRITERION

This decision rule seeks to overcome one of the weaknesses noted in the maximin, maximax, and minimax regret criteria—namely, their ignoring the probabilities of the states of nature. The maximum-likelihood criterion requires that probabilities be assigned to the states of nature. These may be arrived at objectively or subjectively. The decision-maker then chooses the best course of action for that state of nature *which is most likely to occur*. Referring again to the payoff matrix in Figure 2-3, suppose that the probabilities of N_1, N_2, and N_3 are, respectively, .10, .60, and .30. Since state of nature N_2 is the most probable, strategy S_3 should be chosen, because $120 is the most favorable payoff associated with N_2.

Although the maximum-likelihood criterion brings the probabilities into consideration, it still involves a decision process which ignores possibly important information in the payoff matrix. The consequences of all states of nature except the one with the highest probability are disregarded. This is a serious indictment in instances when the largest probability is a small value, because the odds may be strongly against actually encountering the most probable state of nature. For example, suppose there are six states of nature; one has a probability of .25 and the others have probabilities of .15 each. Only the payoffs associated with the first state of nature would be considered, even though its chance of occurring is only one out of four. The payoffs associated with the other five states of nature assume great relevance, since the odds are three out of four that one of them will materialize, yet they are ignored under the maximum-likelihood rule. A similar problem would arise were there two states of nature, one having a probability of .51 and one a probability of .49. For practical purposes the two states are equally probable, but under the maximum-likelihood rule we would consider only the state of nature with the probability of .51 and completely ignore the payoffs for the other state. The maximum-likelihood criterion has its greatest appeal when the most probable state of nature has a relatively high probability of occurrence, say .80 or above; then, basing one's decision on a single state of nature makes more sense.

THE EXPECTED-VALUE CRITERION

This decision rule holds that the best strategy is the one whose *expected* payoff is highest. The expected payoff of a strategy is calculated by multiplying the payoff associated with a state of nature by the probability of that state of nature and finding the sum of the resulting products for all the states of nature. The probabilities of the states of nature can be arrived at in either of two ways. If the decision-maker has absolutely no information about the relative frequency with which the states of nature might occur, the expected-value criterion directs him to assign equal probabilities. This is in accordance with a statistical postulate, sometimes designated as Bayes' rule (or the law of equal distribution of ignorance), which says that the different states of nature should be assumed equally probable unless information to the contrary is available. On the other hand, when knowledge permits, subjective (or in rare cases objective) probabilities can be assigned to the possible states of nature. Actually this is the preferable procedure, provided uncertainty is not too great, because it allows the decision-maker to use what information he may have about the states of nature and because it is not very likely that the probabilities of the states of nature are truly equal, as the equal probability postulate implies.

Suppose we determine the optimum strategy according to the expected-value criterion for the payoff matrix in Figure 2-3, under the assumption that no knowledge exists concerning the odds of the states of nature. Following Bayes' rule, the three states of nature are considered as equally probable, producing a probability of 1/3 for each state. The expected value of strategy S_1, symbolized as $E(S_1)$, is calculated as follows:

$$E(S_1) = (1/3)(\$45) + (1/3)(\$6) + (1/3)(\$30) = \$27.$$

In like manner, the expected values or expected payoffs of S_2 and S_3 may be computed:

$$E(S_2) = (1/3)(\$66) + (1/3)(-\$21) + (1/3)(\$90) = \$45,$$

and

$$E(S_3) = (1/3)(-\$12) + (1/3)(\$120) + (1/3)(\$24) = \$44.$$

The expected-value criterion ranks S_2 as the best strategy, because its expected payoff is higher than that for S_1 or S_3. Just what does this mean? The expected payoff may be properly viewed as the *average payoff* which would be realized over an indefinitely large number of trials (or decisions in this case) when the probabilities and payoffs remain unchanged. The expected payoff for S_2 of \$45 is the average outcome over the long run; one-third of the time a \$66 payoff is realized, one-third of the time a \$21 loss is realized, and one-third of the time a \$90 gain is realized—the average of these is \$45 or what is called the expected value. Since the long-run average payoff of strategy S_2 is higher than that of S_1 or S_3, there is a strong rationale and appeal for choosing S_2.

As an example of the expected-value criterion where the probabilities are not equal, consider the matrix in Figure 2-4. Suppose the decision-maker has reason to believe that the probabilities of N_1, N_2, and N_3 are .30, .50, and .20, respectively. The expected payoff of S_1 is \$26.50 and of S_2 is \$65.20 (the student should verify this for himself); S_2, therefore, is the best strategy according to the expected-value criterion.

The expected-value criterion avoids the criticisms leveled at the four previous decision rules. It takes all of the possible payoffs into account and it makes full use of any hard knowledge concerning the relative frequencies with which the states of nature may occur. Nevertheless, the expected-value criterion is not without its faults. First, it is not likely that the conditions under which most decisions are made will repeat themselves over a long period of time. When the strategies, the states of nature, their probabilities, and the payoffs can reasonably be expected to change, the concept of a long-run average payoff derived from "temporary" values is not necessarily a valid basis for decisions.[2] Second, during a short interim, and especially for a period of one or two decisions, the payoff actually received may have an average at considerable variance from the (long-run) expected value or

---

[2] Actually, there is ample room for disagreement here. Some decision theorists would argue that it is best to approach a one-time decision as if it were part of a repetitive series. Still others would admit to instances where the expected-value concept can legitimately be abandoned in the short run in favor of alternative strategies.

expected payoff. Third, the expected-value approach allows no room for the decision-maker to base his selection upon the ability or inability to absorb whatever losses may be associated with the best strategy. And finally, it does not suggest how decision-makers can incorporate their attitudes toward risk and uncertainty into the selective process, Still, the expected-value criterion is well suited to those decision-makers who prefer to "play the odds" and "stack the deck" in their favor. It is a good bet that over the long haul, decisions made according to the expected-value criterion will tend to average out in the decision-maker's favor.

CONCLUSIONS ON DECISION CRITERIA

Although other decision rules have been proposed and still others could be formulated, our survey of five is sufficient to point up several interesting and noteworthy conclusions. Each rule presented presumes that the decision-maker attempts to optimize his choice of alternatives, despite the frustration of uncertainty and imperfect knowledge. Exactly what the optimum choice is, however, is not at all clear. The "optimum" strategy for the payoff matrix in Figure 2-3 varied with the decision rules applied, as noted below:

maximin criterion:	S_1
maximax criterion:	S_3
minimax regret criterion:	S_3
maximum-likelihood criterion:	S_3
expected-value criterion:	S_2

Evidently then, a search for "optimum" decisions in an environment of uncertainty and imperfect knowledge does not produce a unique choice of alternatives. What is optimum hinges upon the makeup and personality of the decision-maker, his objectives, his circumstances, and obviously the decision rule he selects. Moreover, each decision rule can be objected to on legitimate grounds.

Nevertheless, the payoff matrix and the decision rules are quite useful in decision-making. Their use causes the decision-maker to (1) identify the available alternative courses of action, (2) anticipate the various environmental forces that may be encountered, (3) make judgments as to the probable payoffs or outcomes associated with each course of action, (4) set forth the objectives to be reached via the decision, and (5) rationally evaluate the alternatives in light of their payoffs and the desired objectives. There can be little doubt that to follow such procedures in selecting an alternative strategy or course of action should produce higher-quality decisions on the average. Scarcely a neater or more economical way exists to organize the relevant data and information about a decision problem than is offered by the concept of the payoff matrix. The payoff matrix assists in making a decision problem manageable by facilitating rational and logical evaluation of the alternatives.

Decision-Making under Conflict

Another approach to decision-making under conditions of imperfect knowledge concerns situations where the decision-maker is confronted by an aggressive opponent (a rival organization) whose interests are in direct conflict with his own. Here the states of nature facing the decision-maker are really the courses of action of his competitor, and it is reasonable to presume that the actual state of nature which will occur is the one calculated by his competitor to damage him most. Among others, situations of this sort arise in selecting advertising strategies, deciding on capital budgeting, selecting a plant site, deciding which new features to incorporate into the new models of products customarily brought out each year, choosing pricing policies, and engaging in union-management contract bargaining. These types of decision problems may be described as *decision-making under conflict*, and the method of their analysis constitutes the subject matter of *game theory*.

The basic approach in game theory is for one firm first to determine its competitor's "best" counterstrategy in relation to its own "best" strategy and then to formulate appropriate defensive measures to foil the competitor's counterstrategy. Actually, game theory is much like war, where opposing generals marshal their forces and seek to outmaneuver and outguess one another. Each general tries to guess what his enemy's best move is and designs a counterstrategy to subvert it. Since the opposition is following the same train of thought, counters to the counterstrategies must subsequently be devised. And so it goes—a never-ending sequence of devising strategies to counter the actual moves and the anticipated moves of the opposition.

In the remainder of this chapter we shall be concerned with two relatively simple game-theory situations: (1) zero-sum, two-person games and (2) nonconstant-sum, two-person games. The basic ideas of game theory can be grasped from these two cases; besides, the mathematics becomes difficult very quickly in response to even fairly minor extensions of the game environment.

THE ZERO-SUM, TWO-PERSON GAME

The zero-sum, two-person game involves an intensely competitive struggle between two players; each player's gains are at the expense of the other, thereby making the interests of the players diametrically opposed. It is called a zero-sum game because, no matter what is done by either player, the amount that one player wins is equal to what his opponent has lost, so that the total gain for both players is necessarily zero. There is, therefore, no advantage to collusion.

Consider a competitive struggle between two firms, A and B, over the share of the market for a commodity which both produce. Assume that firm A is attempting to decide among three pricing strategies, A_1, A_2, and A_3. Further assume that firm B is considering four alternatives involving various combinations of product promotion and advertising techniques, B_1, B_2, B_3, and B_4.

The payoff matrix in Figure 2-6 describes the market share payoffs for firm A. Observe that there is no need to make a separate payoff matrix for firm B, since it is clear that if firm A captures 40 percent of the market, firm B's share (or payoff) must be 60 percent. We shall assume that both A and B are acquainted with the information in the payoff matrix and that each firm must decide on a strategy without prior knowledge of the strategy actually selected by the other. (Obviously, it is not to the advantage of either firm to reveal the specific strategy it intends to elect until the final moment.)

		Firm B's Strategies			
		B_1	B_2	B_3	B_4
Firm A's	A_1	20	80	15	70
Strategies	A_2	40	35	30	35
	A_3	60	65	25	10

Fig. 2-6 Firm A's Payoff Matrix

Under these circumstances, which of the three strategies should firm A employ so as to capture the largest share of the market? One possibility is for firm A to play it safe and assume that the worst that can happen will happen. Since firm B is "out to get" firm A, it is reasonable for A to seek out a strategy which provides the maximum degree of security against adversity. This calls for adoption of a maximin strategy, for it allows A to guard against receiving less than the minimum share of the market it can possibly get; in other words, a maximin strategy for A would maximize its security level. Firm A's maximin strategy is A_2, since it carries a minimum guarantee of 30 percent of the market, whereas A_1 has a minimum payoff of 15 percent and A_3 a minimum payoff of 10 percent.

For the same reasons, firm B may decide to employ a similar strategy. However, for firm B the worst payoffs in the matrix are the highest values, not the lowest. This is because B's market share is found by subtracting A's market share from 100; thus, the higher firm A's payoff value, the lower will be firm B's and conversely. Looking at Figure 2-6 *from firm B's standpoint*, the worst that can happen should B_1 be chosen is that firm A picks strategy A_3 and obtains 60 percent of the market, leaving only 40 percent for firm B.

Similarly, if firm B elects B_2, the worst payoff level is 80 percent; if it elects B_3, the worst payoff level is 30 percent; and if it elects B_4, the worst is 70 percent. Clearly, the best of the worst outcomes for firm B is 30 percent, since this is the smallest of the largest payoffs for firm A. Firm B's best strategy, therefore, is B_3, because it minimizes the maximum payoff for firm A. Consequently, B_3 is a *minimax* (not a maximin) strategy.

From Figure 2-6 we can see that firm A's *lowest* payoff from choosing A_2 (30 percent of the market) is exactly the same as the *highest* payoff A could receive should B choose B_3 (30 percent of the market). Stated differently, firm A's maximin strategy intersects firm B's minimax strategy at the *same element* in the payoff matrix—A_2B_3. Whenever an element in a payoff matrix is at the same time the best of the worst outcomes for one player and the best of the worst outcomes for the other player, it is indicative of an *equilibrium point* in the matrix. The equilibrium point is also "the value of the game," because it is the outcome which can reasonably be predicted to occur provided the players are rational. In our example, we would expect the outcome of the decisions to result in firm A's obtaining 30 percent of the market and firm B's capturing 70 percent of the market. (Not all payoff matrixes have equilibrium points; we shall deal with these cases in the following section.)

At this point it is worth noting several important attributes of zero-sum situations where one player employs a maximin strategy and one player employs a minimax strategy. First, and perhaps foremost, *if the payoff matrix has an equilibrium point, then a maximin strategy is the most advantageous strategy for one firm when the other firm employs a minimax strategy.* The maximin-minimax combination of strategies gives both firms (players) maximum security or maximum protection from each other's moves and countermoves. Firm A's choice of a maximin strategy effectively prevents firm B from reducing A's market share below 30 percent. No other strategy offers A the security and protection against adversity offered by A_2. In addition, when A selects A_2, any choice of strategies for B other than B_3 (the minimax strategy), will allow A to capture more than 30 percent of the market. Likewise, firm B's choice of a minimax strategy offers B the opportunity of holding A's share of the market down to a level which A can be prevented from increasing any further. When B minimaxes, anything other than a maximin strategy for firm A allows firm B to increase its share of the market. Thus, a minimax strategy for firm B is its best defense against firm A's best strategy.

To illustrate further the degree of security inherent in maximin-minimax combinations, suppose firm A had chosen A_3 over its maximin strategy of A_2, hoping perhaps that B would miscalculate, choose either B_1 or B_2, and thereby allow A the opportunity to get 60 or 65 percent of the market instead of the 30 percent guaranteed by A_2. Firm B's best countermove to selection of A_3 is to adopt strategy B_4, confining A to 10 percent of the market and reaping 90 percent for itself. Hence, firm A leaves its flanks unprotected against a countermove by B whenever A chooses a strategy other than the maximin strategy. Accordingly, it can be concluded that when *one* of the firms deviates from its "optimal" strategy, it is not likely to improve its payoff value and may suffer needlessly.

Second, we may observe that the payoff value corresponding to an equilibrium point is distinguished by being at the same time the smallest value in its row and the largest value in its column. Or, since which player's strategies constitute the rows and which the columns is entirely arbitrary, the players' positions in the payoff matrix could be reversed and the equilibrium payoff value would become the largest value in its row and the smallest value in its column. Fundamentally, then, *the equilibrium payoff is the largest value in one direction (row or column) and the smallest value in the other (column or row)*. In Figure 2-6, the equilibrium value of 30 is the smallest payoff in its row and the largest payoff in its column. Had firm A's strategies been listed in the columns and firm B's in the rows, the equilibrium value of 30 would have been the largest payoff in its row and the smallest payoff in its column.

Last, a maximin strategy may be a poor counterstrategy to a non-minimax strategy. For instance, suppose firm B is not informed about game theory principles, or is poorly directed by dim-witted managers, or is willing and able to take chances, or for various and sundry other reasons is not inclined to pursue a minimax strategy. Take the case where firm B chooses B_4. If firm A persists in a maximin strategy of A_2, it will sacrifice a possible payoff of 70 percent of the market that could be obtained by choosing A_1. Or, take the case where B selects B_2. Here firm A can increase its market share from 35 percent to 80 percent by shifting from A_2 to A_1. We can state as a general principle that *a maximin strategy necessarily produces the best results only when one's opponent cooperates by picking a minimax strategy*. Could it also be said that a minimax strategy is guaranteed to produce satisfactory outcomes only when one's opponent selects a maximin strategy?

MIXED STRATEGIES

Not all payoff matrixes possess equilibrium points. Consider the payoff matrix facing firms A and B shown in Figure 2-7. In this case, firm A's maximin strategy is A_2 and firm B's minimax strategy is B_3. Yet, this does not define an equilibrium point. Why? Because firm A's lowest payoff from choosing A_2 (35 percent) does *not* coincide with the highest payoff which A can receive when firm B chooses B_3 (50 percent). Moreover, if firm A chooses A_2 and firm B picks B_3, firm A does not get just the minimum payoff of 35 percent of the market, but rather captures 50 percent of the market. Even more important, should firm A select A_2, firm B's best choice is definitely *not* its minimax strategy of B_3. Firm B will be much better off to choose B_2 or B_4 and hold A's market share down to 35 percent. If firm B adopts B_4, firm A will prefer A_1, not A_2. But if firm A elects A_1, firm B will like B_1 better than B_4. If firm B chooses B_1, firm A will find it most advantageous to select A_3. But if A selects A_3, firm B will prefer B_4 over B_1. If firm B picks B_4, firm A should choose A_1. And so it goes; the circle is complete. *There is no one best strategy for either firm.* Rather, in this matrix, each firm *always* has a better countermove once its opponent's strategy is known. In addition, as will be proven shortly and as the preceding discussion suggests, firm A can improve its market share by deviating from a maximin strategy no matter what strategy firm B selects. Similarly, it will be shown that firm B will find it advantageous to deviate from a minimax choice no matter what strategy firm A decides to employ.

		Firm B's Strategies			
		B_1	B_2	B_3	B_4
Firm A's	A_1	20	80	25	70
Strategies	A_2	40	35	50	35
	A_3	60	65	25	10

Fig. 2-7   Firm A's Payoff Matrix

The question immediately arises as to what strategy should be chosen by firm A, now that we have indicated that its maximin strategy is not a good choice. Suppose we first attempt to ascertain whether some of the strategies in Figure 2-7 are better than others; in this way we may be able to reduce the number of strategies that need to be considered in making a final choice.

A strategy may be said to be inferior (or dominated) when other alternative strategies are always preferred to it, regardless of the strategy selected by one's opponent. Inspection of the payoff matrix in Figure 2-7 indicates that, from firm B's standpoint, strategy B_3 is inferior; that is, firm B would prefer one of the remaining strategies irrespective of whether firm A chooses A_1 or A_2 or A_3. If firm A chooses A_1, B's best choice is B_1. If firm A chooses A_2, B's best choice is B_2 or B_4, since either yields the same payoff. And if A chooses A_3, B's best choice is B_4. So, no matter which one of A's three strategies is actually selected, firm B will never choose its minimax strategy of B_3, because other choices yield B a higher market share. It is in this sense that we say B_3 is inferior to (or dominated by) the other strategies open to firm B. Further consideration of strategy B_3 and its payoffs is therefore superfluous, since firm B should never rationally select it, and the matrix can be reduced to that shown in Figure 2-8.

		Firm B's Strategies		
		B_1	B_2	B_4
Firm A's	A_1	20	80	70
Strategies	A_2	40	35	35
	A_3	60	65	10

Fig. 2-8   Firm A's Payoff Matrix
(Reduced Form)

Inspection of the payoffs for the remaining strategies, as given by Figure 2-8, shows that A_2 is an inferior choice. If firm B selects B_1, firm A's best choice is A_3; if firm B selects B_2, firm A's best choice is A_1; and if firm B selects B_4, firm A's best choice is again A_1. Strategy A_2 is thus not selected, no matter which strategy B picks. Consequently, we can delete A_2 from further consideration, reducing the relevant strategies and payoffs to those shown in Figure 2-9.

		Firm B's Strategies		
		B_1	B_2	B_4
Firm A's	A_1	20	80	70
Strategies	A_3	60	65	10

Fig. 2-9 Firm A's Payoff Matrix (Reduced Form)

Examination of the payoffs in Figure 2-9 indicates that firm B would not rationally choose strategy B_2. If A chooses A_1, firm B should pick B_1, whereas if A chooses A_3, firm B should pick B_4. Hence, we may conclude that B_2 is inferior to (or dominated by) B_1 and B_4 and that strategy B_2 can now safely be ignored.

This leaves us with the matrix in Figure 2-10. Inspection of A's remaining strategies (A_1 and A_3) and B's remaining strategies (B_1 and B_4) reveals no further inferiority (or dominance). The student should verify for himself at this point that the matrix in Figure 2-10 has no equilibrium point. Thus, *there is no one best strategy* which either firm should select all of the time. Which of the two strategies A selects will depend upon his guess as to whether B will choose B_1 or B_4. If A believes that B will select B_1, it is to A's advantage to choose A_3; but when A expects that B will select B_4, A is better off to choose A_1. Similarly, B's best choice of strategies hinges upon B's judgment as to A's decision. If B believes A will pick A_1, B should select B_1; yet if B believes A will pick A_3, B should respond by choosing B_4.

		Firms B's Strategies	
		B_1	B_4
Firm A's	A_1	20	70
Strategies	A_3	60	10

Fig. 2-10 Firm A's Payoff Matrix (Final Reduced Form)

The decision problem for both firm A and firm B is such that neither should follow a *pure* strategy, but rather both should adopt a policy of *mixed* strategies. Our objective is now to derive some *mixture* of the two remaining strategies for each firm which will improve the position of both parties with respect to the available pure strategies.

Consider first the case of firm A. We have concluded that firm A will find it advantageous to pick A_1 part of the time (when B is believed to choose B_4), and to pick A_3 the rest of the time (when B is believed to choose B_1). Firm A's decision problem, therefore, is *how often* to pick A_1, and *how often* to pick A_3. The guiding principle offered by game theory for these situations says that *each player should alternate among his relevant strategies in such a manner that his expected payoffs from each strategy are equal, no matter what strategy his opponent plays.*

Using this principle, the optimal frequencies with which firm A should choose A_1 and A_3 can be calculated as follows. Let

p = proportion of the time that firm A selects strategy A_1, and
$(1 - p)$ = proportion of the time that firm A selects strategy A_3.

From Table 2-1 we can see that if firm B selects strategy B_1, A's expected market share is

$$20(p) + 60(1 - p).$$

Likewise, if firm B selects strategy B_4, A's expected market share is

$$70(p) + 10(1 - p).$$

Table 2-1   Firm A's Expected Market Share

	If Firm B Selects Strategy B_1	If Firm B Selects Strategy B_4
When Firm A Picks Strategy A_1 p of the Time	Firm A gets 20 percent of the market p of the time.	Firm A gets 70 percent of the market p of the time.
When Firm A Picks Strategy A_3 $(1 - p)$ of the Time	Firm A gets 60 percent of the market $(1 - p)$ of the time.	Firm A gets 10 percent of the market $(1 - p)$ of the time.
Firm A's Expected Market Share	$20p + 60(1 - p)$ when firm B selects strategy B_1.	$70p + 10(1 - p)$ when firm B selects strategy B_4.

Since we have said the guiding principle is that firm A's expected market share (its expected winnings) should be equal, no matter what firm B does, then we may equate A's expected market share when B selects B_1 with A's expected market share when B selects B_4 and solve the resulting equation for the values of p and $(1 - p)$. By so doing, firm A puts itself in a position where it does not care which strategy firm B selects, since A maximizes its market share regardless of firm B's choice of strategies. Accordingly,

$$20(p) + 60(1 - p) = 70(p) + 10(1 - p),$$
$$20(p) + 60 - 60p = 70p + 10 - 10p,$$
$$-40p + 60 = 60p + 10,$$
$$-100p = -50,$$
$$p = \frac{-50}{-100},$$
$$p = .50 \quad \text{or} \quad 50 \text{ percent},$$
$$1 - p = .50 \quad \text{or} \quad 50 \text{ percent}.$$

Hence, firm A should alternate between choosing A_1 and A_3 in such a manner that it picks A_1 50 percent of the time and A_3 50 percent of the time.

Following the same rationale, we can determine how firm B should optimally divide its choices between B_1 and B_4. Let

q = proportion of the time firm selects strategy B_1, and
$(1 - q)$ = proportion of the time firm B selects strategy B_4.

From Table 2-2, we can see that if firm A selects A_1, firm B can expect A's market share to be

$$20(q) + 70(1 - q).$$

Likewise, if firm A selects A_3, firm B can expect A's market share to be

$$60(q) + 10(1 - q).$$

Equating, as before, the two expected market-share payoffs, we get

$$20(q) + 70(1 - q) = 60(q) + 10(1 - q),$$
$$20q + 70 - 70q = 60q + 10 - 10q,$$
$$70 - 50q = 50q + 10,$$
$$-100q = -60,$$
$$q = \frac{-60}{-100},$$
$$q = .60 \quad \text{or} \quad 60 \text{ percent},$$
$$1 - q = .40 \quad \text{or} \quad 40 \text{ percent}.$$

Consequently, firm B can optimize its own share of the market by selecting strategy B_1 60 percent of the time and strategy B_4 40 percent of the time.

Naturally, when we indicate that each player should alternate between his strategies in some proportion, some chance device must be employed

Table 2-2 Firm B's Ability to Influence Firm A's Market Share

	When Firm B Picks Strategy B_1 q of the Time	When Firm B Picks Strategy B_4 $(1 - q)$ of the Time	Firm B's Ability to Hold Down Firm A's Market Share
If Firm A Selects Strategy A_1	Firm A gets 20 percent of the market q of the time.	Firm A gets 70 percent of the market $(1 - q)$ of the time.	$20q + 70(1 - q)$ when firm A selects strategy A_1.
If Firm A Selects Strategy A_3	Firm A gets 60 percent of the market q of the time.	Firm A gets 10 percent of the market $(1 - q)$ of the time.	$60q + 10(1 - q)$ when firm A selects strategy A_3.

which will produce the desired proportions without any discernible pattern. For example, firm B might place 10 cards in a box, 6 of them marked "B_1," and 4 marked "B_4." A card would then be drawn at random to determine firm B's choice of strategies each time a decision needed to be made. This procedure would prevent firm A from correctly anticipating B's decision each time, since B's strategy selection would be completely randomized. Firm A could easily randomize its choice pattern by flipping a coin, choosing A_1 if the coin showed heads and A_3 if it turned up tails. It goes without saying that if one firm displays incompetence and adopts a foolish choice of strategies, then the other firm should quickly discontinue its mixed-strategy pattern as calculated, look for the obvious loopholes in the unwise firm's strategy selection, and act accordingly. Thus, only when both firms employ their mixed strategies in randomized fashion and without a discernible pattern do the strategies we have determined represent the best possible division of time between the relevant alternative courses of action.

Now that we have calculated the mixed-strategy patterns for firms A and B, we can predict the average market share which each firm can reasonably expect to achieve over the long run. Our reduced payoff matrix, including the optimum strategies for each of the firms, is presented below:

		Firm B's Strategies	
		(6/10) B_1	(4/10) B_4
Firm A's	(1/2) A_1	20	70
Strategies	(1/2) A_3	60	10

Looking at the payoffs from firm A's point of view, we can reason as follows:

1. During the 6/10 of the time that firm B selects strategy B_1, firm A's market share is 20 percent 1/2 of the time and 60 percent 1/2 of the time.
2. During the 4/10 of the time that firm B selects strategy B_4, firm A's market share is 70 percent 1/2 of the time and 10 percent 1/2 of the time.

Therefore, firm A's overall expected market share over time is the sum of what happens 6/10 of the time (statement 1 above) and what happens the remaining 4/10 of the time (statement 2 above), or

$$\overbrace{\tfrac{6}{10}[20(\tfrac{1}{2}) + 60(\tfrac{1}{2})]}^{\text{Statement 1}} + \overbrace{\tfrac{4}{10}[70(\tfrac{1}{2}) + 10(\tfrac{1}{2})]}^{\text{Statement 2}}$$
$$= \tfrac{6}{10}[10 + 30] + \tfrac{4}{10}[35 + 5]$$
$$= 40 \text{ percent of the market.}$$

This tells us that firm A, if it selects its strategies optimally, can expect to gain on the average 40 percent of the market for the commodity. Furthermore, we can say that if firm A's expected market share over the long run is 40 percent, then firm B's expected market share over time is 60 percent. This, of course, does not mean every time a decision is made that firm A will obtain 40 percent and firm B will get 60 percent, but rather that A's *average* market share and B's *average* market share will approach 40 percent and 60 percent, respectively, over the course of many decisions made under the same payoff circumstances.

Are these expected payoffs an improvement over the outcome that each firm might reasonably expect were it to choose its maximin (or minimax) strategy? The answer is an unequivocal *yes*. Referring back to Figure 2-10, were firm A to elect to play its maximin strategy, firm B could hold A to a market share of 35 percent by choosing either B_2 or B_4. Obviously, from firm A's standpoint this is *inferior* to the 40 percent share it can achieve over time by adopting the mixed-strategy approach. Similarly, if firm B adopts its minimax strategy of B_3, firm A by choosing A_2 can get 50 percent of the market and leave firm B with only 50 percent. Since firm B can expect to obtain an average market share of 60 percent with mixed strategies, it is not reasonable to expect B to be satisfied with the 50 percent market share realized from its minimax choice.

The "two-by-two" payoff matrix is the simplest illustration of the use of optimal mixed strategies in game theory. Obviously, most decision problems in the real world are characterized by more than two relevant courses of action and involve more than two active participants. However, the concepts of game theory we have introduced can be readily extended to handle problems of larger scope, provided the difficulty of obtaining information to go into the payoff matrix can be overcome. Unfortunately, the information problem increases in geometrical fashion as the payoff matrix is enlarged; the costs of obtaining and processing the information needed for a many-person game rapidly become overwhelming. This feature severely limits the applicability of game theory. Seldom, if at all, do the computations of optimality present a serious problem once the information is developed; computers can be programmed to perform these despite the complexity of the mathematics involved. The important point here is that the principles we have illustrated for the two-by-two payoff matrix are equally applicable in bigger games. Irrespective of the number of players and strategies, each decision-maker seeks to determine whether a pure strategy is optimal, and, if not, to determine the optimum mix of strategies. Basically the same rationale is followed in identifying the best choice(s) of alternatives in large decision problems involving conflict as in small decision problems involving conflict; they differ essentially only in the degree of complexity.

NONCONSTANT-SUM GAMES

The conflict types of decision problems examined thus far have been of the zero- or constant-sum variety and have clear-cut solutions so long as the decision-makers are rational. In practice, however, most real-world conflict situations in economics and business involve decision problems where the payoffs of the participants do not add up to a constant value for all outcomes of the game. Nonconstant-sum games are of two types: (1) noncooperative, where there is no collusion or communication between players prior to the choice of strategies, and (2) cooperative, where opportunity exists for communication and collusion prior to strategy selection.

Noncooperative Decision Problems.   One of the most famous examples of a noncooperative game is "the prisoner's dilemma," where two suspects are taken into custody and interrogated separately. Owing to weaknesses in the evidence against them, each believes they may both go free or at worst receive a light sentence on reduced charges, if neither prisoner talks. However, they are both informed by the district attorney that if one confesses and the other does not, the one who fails to confess will receive a particularly stiff penalty and the confessor will receive lenient treatment for turning state's evidence. Hence the dilemma: should each place confidence in the other's strength of character to not confess; or, should each prisoner, not having any assurance about what the other will do, protect only himself and confess?

Interestingly enough, an analogous dilemma often presents itself in business and other economic situations. Consider the case of two firms, A and B, which produce competing brands of a product and are faced with a decision to initiate or not initiate an intensive TV advertising campaign. Each has two courses of action—advertise or not advertise. Their respective payoffs, expressed in terms of the dollar change in their current profit levels, are shown in Figure 2-11.

Firm A's Payoff Matrix

| | | Firm B's Strategies | |
		Advertise	Not Advertise
Firm A's Strategies	Advertise	−$100,000	$700,000
	Not Advertise	−$500,000	$ 30,000

Firm B's Payoff Matrix

| | | Firm B's Strategies | |
		Advertise	Not Advertise
Firm A's Strategies	Advertise	−$ 80,000	−$600,000
	Not Advertise	$900,000	$ 50,000

Fig. 2-11   Payoff Matrixes for Firms A and B

The payoffs in the pair of matrixes in Figure 2-11 indicate, for example, that if firm A advertises and firm B does not, A will realize a profit gain of $700,000, whereas B will sustain a loss in profits of $600,000. If both firms elect to advertise, firm A's profits drop by $100,000 and firm B's profits drop by $80,000 (perhaps because the heavy costs of a TV advertising campaign are not offset by the profits realized from extra sales).

Inspection of firm B's payoff matrix reveals that B's strategy of advertising dominates B's strategy of not advertising, because the related payoffs are more palatable. If firm A advertises, firm B will also advertise, as it prefers a payoff of − $80,000 to a payoff of − $600,000. If firm A does not advertise, firm B will again prefer to advertise, as it will realize a profit gain of $900,000 compared to a gain of only $50,000 should it not advertise. Thus, initially firm B is rationally motivated to adopt the strategy of advertising. Precisely the same analysis holds for firm A, and it too will select the strategy of advertising for the same reasons as does firm B. Hence the outcome is a $100,000 loss in profits for firm A and an $80,000 loss in profits for firm B. Had A and B not been quite so "rational," they might have perceived the wisdom of *both* not advertising, thus realizing profits gains of $30,000 and $50,000, respectively.

Of course, the reasonableness of both firms' choosing *to advertise* presumes that they cannot communicate their intentions or cooperate. It also applies primarily to a one-time decision process where no learning by the firms can occur. Were the same decision to be made several times, A and B might learn from their unhappy experiences, even without actually communicating, and at a later time each might decide to not advertise. But until each firm can rely upon the other not to "cheat," neither can afford to abandon its strategy of advertising. Analogous business situations include those of producers of detergents, cigarettes, soft drinks, tires, and similar types of consumer goods among which brand competition is intense. In these cases, each producer is compelled to advertise simply to prevent erosion of its market share; all producers of an item cannot be relied upon to not advertise, even if a few voluntarily give it up as a trial signal to the others. The reason is that those who do not cease advertising will reap profits by attracting customers from the nonadvertisers (assuming, of course, that advertising truly influences consumer demand in a positive manner). Consequently, competitive pressures may force firms into advertising activities which they otherwise would reject as unprofitable.

It is not hard to find other real-world examples of the "prisoner's dilemma." Many retail establishments remain open on Sunday, although their proprietors might prefer a holiday, for fear of losing customers to rival stores. Labor-union leaders press hard for wage increases that may be excessive and inflationary in order to enhance their image with the rank and file, even though the resulting gain in labor's real income is actually less than could have been achieved had all union leaders "cooperated" and sought wage increases more in line with productivity gains. Consumers individually often go ahead and pay what they consider to be an outrageous price for an item, lest it not be available later at a lower price; whereas, collectively, were they to wait to buy the item, they might obtain it at sale prices.

Cooperative Games. In cooperative games it is usually postulated that the players will be sufficiently rational to perceive and apply mutually advantageous strategies. In practice this does not always occur, because of the sticky problems encountered in arriving at a mutually acceptable division of the collective payoffs. In fact, most of the analysis of cooperative games focuses on the creating of reasonable or equitable mechanisms for dividing the payoffs among the colluding players.[3]

Suppose we examine briefly a nonconstant-sum cooperative game. Two firms, each with plants located on a small river, are concerned with reducing the level of pollution in the river to which each is contributing. Assume the situation is such that neither firm *by itself* pollutes the river water above acceptable levels, but when their separate waste products are taken together, the pollution factor exceeds socially acceptable limits. Further assume that the authorities have given the two firms a joint ultimatum to reduce the pollution level to tolerable limits or face a $1,000,000 fine each. Each firm has two strategies: to buy pollution control equipment or not to buy; their estimated dollar costs are shown in the payoff matrixes in Figure 2-12.

Firm A's Payoff Matrix

		Firm B's Strategies	
		Buy	Not Buy
Firm A's Strategies	Buy	−$650,000	−$650,000
	Not Buy	0	−$1,000,000

Firm B's Payoff Matrix

		Firm B's Strategies	
		Buy	Not Buy
Firm A's Strategies	Buy	−$650,000	0
	Not Buy	−$650,000	−$1,000,000

Fig. 2-12 Nonconstant-Sum Cooperative Game

[3] See, for example, J. F. Nash, "The Bargaining Problem," *Econometrica*, Vol. 18 (April 1950), pp. 155–162; J. F. Nash, "Two-Person Cooperative Games," *Econometrica*, Vol. 21, No. 1 (January 1953), pp. 128–140; and J. C. Harsanyi, "Approaches to the Bargaining Problem Before and After the Theory of Games: A Critical Discussion of Zeuthen's, Hick's and Nash's Theories," *Econometrica*, Vol. 24 (April 1956), pp. 144–157.

Communication and cooperation between the two enterprises is clearly appropriate (and is not in violation of any antitrust regulations). It does not make sense in this case for both firms to buy pollution control equipment, since the extent of pollution does not warrant it. The rational and least expensive solution is for one firm to install waste treatment procedures. But which one? Herein lies the matter for bargaining and negotiation. Should the firms split the costs equally or according to their relative contributions to the pollution problem? What will be the impact upon the outcome, if anything, of the respective abilities of the negotiators to persuade, to maneuver, to exhort, and so on, thereby perhaps pushing one firm into doing more than its "fair" share? Obviously, the actual outcome is somewhat unpredictable and indeterminate.

Rather than get bogged down in the intricacies of bargaining, suppose we simply present at this point some of the central considerations of cooperative games which shape the final outcome. First, in a many-person cooperative game there exists the possibility that several players will enter into a collusive arrangement against the rest; in the jargon of game theory this sort of combination is called a *coalition*. Many times the formation of coalitions is attractive because it offers members the opportunity to successfully exploit the remaining players. Second, it often occurs that maximizing the welfare of the group entails a sacrifice for one of its members. In order to induce the injured party to cooperate, a *side payment* ("bribe") may have to be paid which will at least compensate him for his sacrifice. Generally speaking, for the coalition to remain viable, each member must receive a payoff equal to or greater than the amount which he can get on his own.

Third, it may be observed that the worst thing that can happen to a coalition, from its point of view, is for all the remaining players to combine against it in one super countercoalition. When this happens and when the total payoff of *all* players is fixed at its maximum possible value, the decision problem is transformed into a zero-sum, two-person (really two-coalition) game which can be solved by methods described above.

Last, the actual outcome from cooperative games of two or more persons hinges largely on the personal, social, institutional, and environmental traits comprising the situation. Until these traits are known and assimilated into the game, prediction of either optimal strategies or final outcomes is largely an exercise in crystal ball gazing.

Summary and Conclusions

In this chapter, decision-making processes have been examined in the context of certainty, risk, and uncertainty. The principal focus of the analysis has been upon the *methods* and *techniques* for making decisions under various states of imperfect knowledge. Issues pertaining to goals and objectives were relegated to a subsidiary role (proper attention will be directed to goals and objectives in forthcoming chapters). Significantly, it is the emphasis of decision theory upon methodology which makes it amenable and flexible to a variety of approaches.

Decision-making under conditions of certainty is much simpler than in instances of objective risk, subjective risk, and uncertainty, because the presence of adequate information allows for easy selection among alternatives. Anytime the decision-maker has less than perfect information upon which to base his choice of alternatives, the principles of decision theory call for him to bring whatever information he does have to bear upon the decision problem. Although fully aware that the information he has may be in error as well as incomplete, the rational decision-maker has no real choice but to attempt to overcome the information gap by using the best available information and knowledge to make the decision.

The hallmark of decision problems under conditions of imperfect knowledge is that the outcomes from alternative strategies are unknown. Although various decision rules are available for assisting the decision-maker in the selection of strategies, it is not at all clear that a unique optimal choice of strategies for any and all circumstances necessarily exists. What is optimum varies with the makeup and personality of the decision-maker, his objectives, his circumstances, and the decision procedure he elects.

In decision-making under conflict, the scope of strategy selection is broadened to include the behavior of two or more decision-makers. In business situations, opposing firms are vitally concerned not only with their own choice of alternatives, but also with those of their competitors. Faced with imperfect knowledge and aggressive opponents, each firm seeks to determine whether a pure strategy is optimal and, if not, to ascertain the optimum mix of strategies.

The theory of games offers a promising framework for examining conflict environments and for developing criteria for rational behavior. The guiding principles posed by game theory in strategy selection provide an illuminating orientation of no small value in the study of business enterprise and business behavior. After all, a chief concern of business management is to watch daily both the moves of competitors and the moods and habits of prospective customers and then to devise appropriate courses of action and adjustment to meet emerging contingencies. Management, especially at the upper levels, spends much of its time planning ways to minimize or eliminate entirely the uncertainties of market influences. And in coping with secular and technological change progressive managers are forced to chart new and ambitious courses of action for future deployment. From one vantage point it can be said that a major function of management is to devise strategies for adjusting and reacting to the environmental elements of risk and uncertainty. Successful direction of an enterprise, large or small, ultimately boils down to attempting to influence the odds and to manage the probabilities to the best advantage of the firm. Yet, as we have seen, this is easier said than done. The path along which optimal decisions are found, given states of imperfect knowledge, is indeed elusive. If you understand why, the mission of this chapter is accomplished.

SUGGESTED READINGS

BAUMOL, W. J. *Economic Theory and Operations Analysis*, 3rd ed. (Englewood Cliffs, N.J.: Prentice-Hall, Inc., 1972), Chaps. 23 and 24.

LUCE, R. DUNCAN, and HOWARD RAIFFA, *Games and Decisions* (New York: John Wiley & Sons, Inc., 1957), Chaps. 2, 4, 5, 6, and 13.

McGUIRE, J. W., *Theories of Business Behavior* (Englewood Cliffs, N. J.: Prentice-Hall, Inc., 1964), Chaps. 6 and 7.

SHUBIK, MARTIN, *Strategy and Market Structure* (New York: John Wiley & Sons, Inc., 1959).

WAGNER, HARVEY M., "Advances in Game Theory," *American Economic Review*, Vol. 48, No. 3 (June 1958), pp. 368–387.

WILLIAMS, J. D., *The Compleat Strategyst* (New York: McGraw-Hill Book Co., Inc., 1954), especially Chaps. 2, 3, and 4.

Applications of decision theory and game theory to actual decision problems are found in the following readings:

BALIGH, H. H., and L. E. RICHARTZ, "Variable-Sum Game Models of Marketing Problems," *Journal of Marketing Research*, Vol. IV (May 1967), pp. 173–183.

BENNION, E. H., "Capital Budgeting and Game Theory," *Harvard Business Review*, Vol. 34, No. 6 (November-December 1956), pp. 115–123.

BROWN, REX V., "Do Managers Find Decision Theory Useful," *Harvard Business Review*, Vol. 48, No. 3 (May-June 1970), pp. 78–89.

FRIEDMAN, LAWRENCE, "Game Theory Models in the Allocation of Advertising Expenditures," *Operations Research*, Vol. 6 (September 1958), pp. 699–709.

HAMMOND, JOHN S., "Better Decisions with Preference Theory," *Harvard Business Review*, Vol. 45, No. 6 (November-December 1967), pp. 123–141.

MOSSIN, J., "Merger Agreements: Some Game-Theoretic Considerations," *Journal of Business*, Vol. 41 (October 1968), pp. 460–471.

Problems and Questions for Discussion

1. Classify each of the following as certainty, objective risk, subjective risk, and uncertainty:
   (a) The weather a week from today.
   (b) The weather tomorrow.
   (c) The weather an hour from now.

(d) The weather a minute from now.
(e) Absenteeism in a plant.
(f) The closing price of Xerox common stock on the New York Stock Exchange on December 29, 1972.
(g) The number of business failures next year.
(h) The average hourly wage for machinists employed by Chrysler in 1972.
(i) Employee turnover in a firm.

2. "Only uncertainty is certain." Comment on the accuracy of this statement.

3. Given the following payoff matrix:

		States of Nature				
		N_1	N_2	N_3	N_4	N_5
Alternative Strategies	S_1	$ 25	$45	−$20	$50	−$ 5
	S_2	$100	−$40	$ 5	$10	$10
	S_3	$ 20	$30	−$50	$20	$30
	S_4	$ 10	$40	$20	−$10	$40

(a) Determine the maximin strategy.
(b) Determine the maximax strategy.
(c) Determine the minimax regret strategy.
(d) Determine the strategy which should be chosen according to the expected-value criterion.
(e) How do you explain the fact that *each* of the above strategies are supposed to be "the best" and yet that they are all different?
(f) Which strategy do you prefer? Why?

4. (a) Might a student on academic scholarship who must maintain a B average to keep his scholarship be attracted to a maximin strategy in studying for his exams? Explain.
   (b) Could the same be said for the strategy to be employed by a football coach (who strongly desires a bowl bid) in playing the final game of the season against the school's fiercest rival?

5. Might a banker or credit officer be inclined to adopt a minimax strategy in allocating loanable funds among potential borrowers? Why or why not?

6. Given the following payoff matrix:

		States of Nature			
		N_1	N_2	N_3	N_4
Alternative Strategies	S_1	4	2	3	1
	S_2	1	8	0	3
	S_3	3	5	1	0
	S_4	2	2	2	2

(a) Which strategy should be chosen if the decision-maker employs the expected-value criterion?

(b) Which strategy should be chosen if the decision-maker employs the maximin criterion?

(c) Which strategy should be chosen if the decision-maker employs the minimax regret criterion?

(d) Which strategy should be chosen if the decision-maker employs the maximax criterion?

(e) Assuming the probabilities of the states of nature are .10, .20, .30, and .40, respectively, which strategy should be chosen if the decision-maker employs the maximum-likelihood criterion?

7. Suppose that two large motels, A and B, are so located on the shore of the ocean and next to a beautiful fishing inlet that, while isolated from other motels, they are in vigorous competition with one another. Aware of the luxury demanded by tourists, each motel owner is considering the desirability of installing color TV in all rooms and/or building a nine-hole golf course in order to take business away from his rival. By chance, both hire the same management consultant, who, after considerable study, furnishes each owner with estimated payoffs from various combinations of actions as follows:

		Motel B's Strategies			
		Color TV	Golf Course	Both	Neither
Motel A's Strategies	Color TV	+$ 80	−$200	−$400	+$ 10
	Golf Course	+$100	+$ 40	−$ 10	+$150
	Both	+$150	+$ 50	+$ 20	+$500
	Neither	−$ 80	−$100	−$450	$ 0

The payoffs in the matrix above are estimated increases and decreases of weekly net payoffs, positive figures being profit gains by Motel A and negative figures profit gains by Motel B. Each motel owner learns that the other has access to the payoff information, and each regards the other as an astute businessman.

(a) What should the owner of Motel A do? Why?

(b) What should the owner of Motel B do? Why?

(c) What can each motel owner expect to gain or lose as the case may be?

8. Suppose that two discount retailers, Dixie Mart and Savadollar, are located at opposite ends of a shopping mall. Each store advertises its specials on a weekly basis, with the ads appearing in the local newspapers on Wednesday afternoon and Thursday morning. Besides the usual "specials," the ads for each store typically feature one to four "loss leaders," selected in such a manner as to attract customers at the expense of the rival stores. Experience over the past year has shown that the most satisfactory loss leaders include (1) recreational equipment, (2) clothing items, (3) toiletries, and (4) automobile accessories. Experience has also shown that the *number* of loss leaders is just as big an influence upon profits as the types of loss leaders. The store manager for Savadollar has kept an accurate record of his store's sales and profits in terms of the various number of loss leaders he selects versus the number the manager at Dixie Mart selects.

In the matrix below, positive payoffs represent estimated weekly profit increases or decreases realized by Savadollar as a result of its loss-leader policies. Analyze this payoff matrix and determine whether Savadollar should employ a pure strategy. If so, explain why. If not, then determine if a mixed strategy is appropriate and calculate the proportion of time Savadollar should pick its strategies.

Savadollar's Payoff Matrix

| | | \multicolumn{4}{c}{Number of Loss Leaders Selected by Dixie Mart} |
		1	2	3	4
Number of	1	10	−30	−100	−200
Loss Leaders	2	70	40	0	−120
Chosen by	3	110	60	60	0
Savadollar	4	100	55	60	−10

9. Assume firm A and firm B produce the only two types of widgets currently on the market. Suppose firm A is endeavoring to choose among four combinations of advertising campaigns and firm B among five. The following payoff matrix shows firm A's estimated payoffs in terms of market share:

Firm A's Payoff Matrix

| | | \multicolumn{5}{c}{Firm B's Strategies} |
		B_1	B_2	B_3	B_4	B_5
Firm A's	A_1	40	60	30	20	50
Strategies	A_2	15	30	20	45	40
	A_3	25	40	50	35	70
	A_4	30	20	40	60	30

(a) Determine firm B's minimax strategy.
(b) Determine firm A's maximin strategy.
(c) If firm A decides to maximize its share of the widget market (believing that this objective will enhance long-run profitability), then what sort of strategy (pure or mixed) should A elect? Why? In the event that you decide a mixed strategy is best, calculate the proportion of time firm A should devote to each of its strategies.
(d) Determine firm B's optimum course(s) of action.
(e) Determine firm A's long-run expected market share. How does this compare with the payoff A can expect if the maximin strategy is chosen?
(f) Determine firm B's long-run expected market share. How does this compare with the payoff B can expect if the minimax strategy is chosen?

10. Barclay and Starr own gasoline stations across the street from one another. No other stations are nearby. There are only two prices they can charge, high and low, and each day they must decide which price they will use for the day. They are not permitted to change prices during the course of the day. If both charge the high price, Barclay's profit is $16 and Starr's is $15. If both charge the low price,

Barclay makes $12 and Starr makes only $8. If one charges the high price and the other one the low price, then the low-priced station owner receives $20 and the high-priced station owner $9.

    (a) Determine the profit matrix for each station owner.

    (b) What should Barclay do? Why?

    (c) What should Starr do? Why?

    (d) How much profit can each station owner expect to make?

11. The Alpha Company and the Beta Company are both producing washing machines domestically and selling them through a foreign subsidiary in the country of Ugandi. The profits per year of the two subsidiaries are: Alpha, $15 million and Beta, $25 million.

The Alpha Company is considering establishing a manufacturing plant in Ugandi. An analyst for Alpha has projected a profit of $35 million after the plant begins operations, assuming the Beta Company continues to market washing machines through its foreign subsidiary.

An analyst for the Beta Company has heard of the plans of the Alpha Company. If the plant is built by Alpha, the analyst projects Beta's profits will fall to $5 million. However, if the Beta Company builds a plant in Ugandi and the Alpha Company does not, the analyst anticipates profits of $30 million for Beta and a decrease in the profits of Alpha to $8 million. If both companies build plants, it is expected that they can each earn $10 million per year.

What are Alpha and Beta's optimum strategies? *Explain your answer.*

II

THE THEORY
AND MEASUREMENT
OF CONSUMER
DEMAND

3

The Theory of Consumer Demand: The Cardinal Utility Approach

Ever since modern man first developed an awareness of material things, human wants have been characterized by two important features: (1) their diversity and (2) their general lack of fulfillment. Consumer wants are diverse in the sense that satisfying the biological, psychological, and cultural desires of millions of people requires an immense variety of commodities. Individual tastes vary, as do individual circumstances regarding age, education, social status, income, life style, and so on—all of which call for a wide and ever-changing mix of goods.

At the same time, we find that no sooner are some human wants partially fulfilled than others are activated. For instance, when one satisfies the need for shelter and acquires a dwelling, there immediately arises a distinct need for furnishings and all of the comforts of home. When the fundamental needs of food, shelter, and clothing are met, there arises a demand for all sorts of goods and services commensurate with higher living standards—washing machines, medical care, vacuum cleaners, convenient transportation facilities, air conditioning, and so forth. When these wants are reasonably well satisfied, there emerges an emphasis on more personal services, recreational goods, travel and tourism, and public accommodations. In addition, new wants are forever being created. Technological advance allows the production of vast numbers of new commodities which consumers find especially useful or satisfying; the strong demands for frozen foods, permanent press fabrics, color television, motorbikes, double-knit suits, instant breakfasts, transistor radios, Polaroid cameras, fluoride toothpaste, automatic ice makers, mobile homes, artificial turf, and small cars serve as examples. Scarcely anyone can claim that he already has all of the material things he would like to have. True, a person may easily obtain all the coffee he wants or all of several other commodities he wants, but this is not to say there are no items on his want list. Were everyone to make a complete list of all the commodities he would like to own or be able to use, there is no doubt but that the sum total would dwarf the ability of producers to fill the orders. And although production might proceed at a furious pace, it is not likely that the list would grow shorter. If past experience is any indication, the persistent emergence of new technological capabilities will generate new wants at a rate sufficient to keep pressure on production activity.

The enormous gap between the human appetite for goods and services and the relatively limited ability to produce them gives rise to a major economic problem. Society is forced to establish some sort of priority system to guide production activity. Plainly enough, since all wants cannot be satisfied, it makes sense to direct production efforts at satisfying as many wants as possible and in order of their urgency. It is at this juncture in a capitalistically oriented society that the business firm comes into play.

Business firms, motivated by the prospect of profits, are induced to choose among the alternative uses of economic resources in such a way that the quantities of those goods which contribute *most* to aggregate want satisfaction are produced *first*. Consumers spend their dollars upon those goods and services which they are most willing and able to buy. These expenditures are in effect "dollar votes" by which consumers register their wants. When the votes for a commodity are great enough to provide a fair profit, resources are steered into its production. The firms producing items for which the dollar votes are insufficient become relatively unprofitable enterprises, and the price mechanism deprives them of the financial wherewithal to obtain resources which are badly needed elsewhere. Changes in consumer tastes and preferences initiate price movements which serve as a signal for producers to alter the composition of their output. Experience has shown that the profit motive, operating through a competitive price system, is an extraordinary device for guiding resources into the production of goods and services most wanted by society. Unless business firms elect to synchronize their production efforts to match the purchasing behavior of consumers (the power of advertising notwithstanding), they face the penalty of unacceptable profits, perhaps even losses and eventual bankruptcy.

Hence, the urgency with which consumers desire various products and their willingness and ability to back up their desires with dollars combine to dictate the course of production activities. Whatever goods and services consumers are willing and able to buy in amounts sufficient to make their production feasible (profitable) *will be forthcoming* in a capitalistically-oriented economy such as that of the United States. This is the genius of capitalism— and proof of its functioning is simple. How many commodities can you think of which it is technologically possible to produce, which consumers truly *want* and for which they are *willing* to pay a price *high enough* to make their production possible, but which are not available to those who have the money to buy them? It is a safe wager that, even if you should come up with one such item, your list will not extend to five. Even the most critical observer of the U.S. economy would have to admit the power of this accomplishment. Consequently, it is fair to state that the avenues of consumer demand for goods and services govern the avenues of production. It would be foolish to produce anything which is not wanted. Economic resources are much too scarce, as witnessed by their prices, to be used in activities no one wants performed.

For these reasons, the analysis of consumer behavior and consumer demand is pivotal in the study of business behavior and the evaluation of economic performance. Production of goods and services to satisfy the human wants is the fundamental *raison d'etre* for business firms. And the efficiency with which business firms satisfy human wants constitutes the basic criterion for judging the performance of our economic system. In this chapter we shall explore the hows and whys of consumer purchases, focusing mainly upon a consumer's optimum disposition of his income and upon how demand functions for particular commodities can be established. We shall examine the *cardinal utility* approach to the analysis of consumer demand and then, in the next chapter, turn to the *ordinal utility* or indifference-curve approach to the theory of consumer demand.

Total and Marginal Utility Functions

The utility approach to the analysis of consumer demand first appeared in economics a century ago, when it was fashionable in psychological circles to assert that much of human behavior could be explained by the desire to achieve pleasure and to avoid pain. Economists borrowed this doctrine and used it to construct a theory of motivated consumer behavior. Specifically, it was held that in the sphere of consumer expenditures, rational consumers manage their purchases of commodities so as to realize as much "pleasure" and as little "pain" as possible. Additionally, it follows that the pleasure derived from commodities varies with the quantity consumed per period of time.

THE CONCEPT OF UTILITY

The pleasure or satisfaction obtained by a consumer from the consumption of goods and services has traditionally been called *utility*. Utility derives from those qualities inherent in a commodity that give it the power to satisfy a want. The utility of a commodity can be formally defined as the amount of satisfaction a consumer receives from consuming various quantities of the commodity per unit of time. By comparing the satisfaction they receive from different consumption rates of different commodities, consumers can establish preferences among commodities.

It is, of course, doubtful that the intensity of satisfaction one gains from a commodity can be measured with *cardinal numbers* such as 14, 84.9, or −115. At least to date no one has devised such a measuring device. One may say "The broiled lobster is excellent" or "I enjoyed the broiled lobster more than anything I have eaten lately"; but if asked "How much did you enjoy the lobster?" one can scarcely reply "About seventeen" and expect to convey any meaningful intelligence. Utility is definitely a subjective concept, insusceptible to precise quantitative measurement. Therefore, in practical applications of the utility concept, *ordinal measures* of utility must usually be employed. In ordinal utility patterns, it is possible to array the subjective degree of utility associated with commodities from highest to lowest, although no means exists for comparing the *amount* by which the subjective utility from one good exceeds the subjective utility from another good. Thus, in ordinal utility analysis, the problem of precisely measuring utility is circumvented, and the consumer has only to be able to distinguish between greater and lesser amounts of utility.

TOTAL UTILITY FUNCTIONS

Although currently we have no way of measuring utility in quantifiable terms, it is still *analytically useful* to *pretend* that we can measure it. By so doing, we can better understand otherwise obscure facets of consumer behavior. For illustrative purposes, assume that we can designate the amount of utility by a unit of measure called a "util." This mythical unit can be viewed as representing some arbitrary amount of satisfaction, and as such it is simply a convenient device whereby utility can be expressed in cardinal numbers.

The *total utility* which a consumer obtains from a specific commodity may be defined as the *entire* amount of satisfaction obtained from the consumption of various quantities of the commodity per period of time. A *total utility function* reflects the relationship between total utility and the rate of consumption of a commodity. The word "function" is nothing more than a shorthand way of referring to how some factors (the independent variables) affect another factor (the dependent variable). In terms of utility functions, this literally means that the total utility obtained from a commodity varies with the amount of it consumed over a period of time. Consequently, the value of total utility *depends* upon (or is a function of) the amount of the commodity consumed during a specific period of time; accordingly,

Table 3-1 The Relationship between Total Utility, Marginal Utility, and the Rates of Consumption of Commodity X (hypothetical data for a hypothetical person)

Units of Commodity X Consumed Per Period of Time	Total Utility (in utils)	Marginal Utility (in utils)
0	0	
1	15	15
2	28	13
3	39	11
4	48	9
5	55	7
6	60	5
7	63	3
8	64	1
9	63	−1
10	60	−3

total utility is the dependent variable and the quantity consumed is the independent variable.

Total utility functions may be represented in any of three ways: tables, graphs, and equations. Consider Table 3-1, which illustrates the total utility that an individual obtains from consuming various quantities of commodity X per period of time. As can be seen from columns 1 and 2, the more of commodity X the individual consumes per period of time, the greater is his total utility or total satisfaction measured in utils, up to a consumption rate of 8 units of X. At 8 units, total utility is at its maximum value of 64 utils of satisfaction. This point is called the *saturation rate*, because the consumer is not capable of deriving any greater satisfaction from consuming more of commodity X per period of time. In fact, were he obliged to consume nine or ten units, his total utility would be decreased, perhaps because such a consumption rate would be overly troublesome (having nine pets to feed and take care of) or physically taxing (eating nine milkshakes a day). From this example it is clear that, although a consumer's wants in general may be unlimited (insatiable), his wants for specific commodities can be totally fulfilled.

A total utility curve corresponding to the information in Table 3-1 is displayed in Figure 3-1(a). Observe that the total utility curve in Figure 3-1(a) rises at a slower and slower rate as the consumption rate approaches 8 units of X; it reaches a peak at 8 units (the saturation rate) and then begins to decline. The implication here is that the more of a specific product a consumer obtains, the less anxious he will be to obtain more units of the same product, because the additional units yield smaller amounts of *extra* satisfaction. Eventually the amounts of extra satisfaction diminish to zero and become negative thereafter.

Each and every total utility function can be expressed mathematically

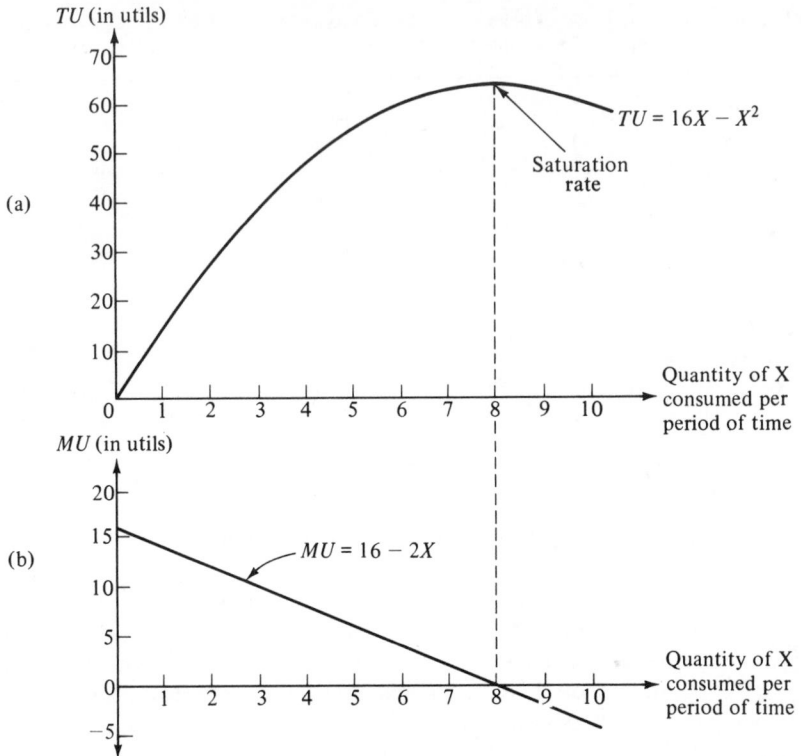

Fig. 3-1 Total and Marginal Utility Functions for a Commodity Whose Total Utility Increases at a Decreasing Rate

by means of an equation which relates total utility to the rate of consumption. It so happens that the total utility function shown in Table 3-1 and in Figure 3-1(a) is equally as well defined by the equation:

$$TU = 16X - X^2,$$

where TU represents the total utility in utils, and X represents the amount of the commodity consumed per unit of time. Hence, if the consumption rate is 5 units of X, then

$$TU = 16(5) - (5)^2$$
$$= 80 - 25$$
$$= 55 \text{ utils.}$$

Observe that the value of 55 utils corresponds exactly to the value for total utility in Table 3-1 when the rate of consumption is 5 units and, likewise, to the value of total utility in Figure 3-1(a) at $X = 5$ units. The use of equations to represent total utility functions allows easy calculation of total utility for any value of X (consumption rate) in which we may be interested.

THE CONCEPT OF MARGINAL UTILITY

Marginal utility may be defined as the change in total utility resulting from a one-unit change in the consumption of a commodity per period of time; it is, in other words, the *extra* satisfaction obtained from an *extra* unit of consumption per period of time. From Table 3-1, we see that when the consumption rate increases from one to two units, total utility rises from 15 utils to 28 utils. Thus, the marginal utility of the second unit of X is 13 utils. In like manner the remaining values for marginal utility may be computed.

During any relatively short period of time, wherein the consumer's tastes can be assumed not to change, it has long been noted that when a consumer continues to increase his consumption rate of a commodity, beyond some point the marginal utility, or extra satisfaction, obtained from successive units becomes smaller and smaller. This phenomenon is known as the *principle of diminishing marginal utility*. The values for marginal utility in Table 3-1 begin to diminish at the outset, so that in the example given, the principle of diminishing marginal utility becomes operative immediately. Each additional unit of X consumed per period of time gives less *extra* utility than the previous unit. For this reason the total utility function increases more slowly as the consumption rate rises. Observe that we can find the total utility corresponding to any consumption rate from the marginal utility values by calculating the cumulative marginal utility values to that point. Thus, from Table 3-1, the total utility for a consumption rate of 3 units of X equals the marginal utility of the first unit (15 utils) plus the marginal utility of the second unit (13 utils) plus the marginal utility of the third (11 utils) for a total utility of 39 utils.

We can illustrate graphically the marginal utility function corresponding to the previously described total utility function by plotting the marginal utility values given in Table 3-1. The graph of the marginal utility curve is presented in Figure 3-1(b). Note that the values for marginal utility are plotted halfway between the two values for total utility from which they were derived. This is as it should be, because the marginal utility values determined in this fashion should be representative of the *range* of consumption from which they were derived, and this is at the midpoint of that range. For the example given, the marginal utility function decreases throughout and reaches a value of zero at precisely the same consumption rate at which the total utility function is at its maximum height.

Actually, there is a very precise relationship between total utility functions and marginal utility functions. The nature of this relationship brings out some critically important factors which are worth deriving and exploring at this point. Among the most useful concepts in the economist's toolkit are the relations between total and marginal quantities. We will have so frequent occasion to use these concepts, not only with reference to utility but also with reference to revenue, production, cost, and other magnitudes, that it is both advantageous and efficient to master them at this point.

Consider again the total utility function described earlier:

$$TU = 16X - X^2.$$

Using this expression, we can easily obtain the value of TU at any consumption rate of commodity X by substituting the units consumed of X into the expression and evaluating the righthand side of the equation.

However, suppose the consumption rate of commodity X rises from some value X to some value $(X + \Delta X)$, where ΔX designates an arbitrary increase of any size. We know that total utility must necessarily *change*. Let us symbolize the change which occurs in total utility by ΔTU. Rewriting the total utility function to incorporate the effect of the increase in X to $(X + \Delta X)$, we have

$$
\begin{aligned}
TU + \Delta TU &= 16(X + \Delta X) - (X + \Delta X)^2 \\
&= 16X + 16\,\Delta X - (X^2 + 2X\,\Delta X + \Delta X^2) \\
&= 16X + 16\,\Delta X - X^2 - 2X\,\Delta X - \Delta X^2.
\end{aligned}
$$

The last expression above is useful for determing the *new* level of total utility corresponding to a consumption rate of $(X + \Delta X)$ units. But our major concern is really with the *change* in total utility (ΔTU) associated with the *change* in the consumption rate of commodity X(ΔX). We can obtain an expression for determining just the *change* in TU by subtracting TU from the lefthand side of the equation and its equivalent of $(16X - X^2)$ from the righthand side. This operation yields

$$
\begin{array}{rl}
TU + \Delta TU = & 16X + 16\,\Delta X - X^2 - 2X\,\Delta X - \Delta X^2 \\
-TU \quad\quad = & -16X \qquad\quad + X^2 \\
\hline
\Delta TU = & \quad + 16\,\Delta X \quad\quad - 2X\,\Delta X - \Delta X^2
\end{array}
$$

We are now in a position to determine the additional utility per additional unit of commodity X by dividing both sides of the expression for ΔTU by ΔX:

$$
\begin{aligned}
\frac{\Delta TU}{\Delta X} &= \frac{16\,\Delta X - 2X\,\Delta X - \Delta X^2}{\Delta X} \\
&= 16 - 2X - \Delta X.
\end{aligned}
$$

The latter equation may be used to evaluate the change in total utility per unit change in the rate of consumption.[1]

Our interest lies yet beyond, however. Up to now all we have done is perform algebraic operations on our original expression of $TU = 16X - X^2$. Something a little more complex is called for at this point. In particular, we need to determine what happens to $\Delta TU/\Delta X$ as the changes in X become smaller and smaller and eventually become very close to zero.[2] Mathematically this interest is expressed as

$$\lim_{\Delta X \to 0} \frac{\Delta TU}{\Delta X},$$

where "lim" is really an abbreviation for limit; however, it is customary to use the symbols dTU/dX to mean the same thing. Since

$$\frac{\Delta TU}{\Delta X} = 16 - 2X - \Delta X,$$

it is clear that as ΔX becomes infinitesimally small,

$$\lim_{\Delta X \to 0} \frac{\Delta TU}{\Delta X} = \frac{dTU}{dX} = 16 - 2X.$$

The symbol dTU/dX may be interpreted to mean the *rate of change in total utility as the consumption rate changes*, and in terms of economics this is a more rigorous and accurate definition of marginal utility. In the language of differential calculus, marginal utility is said to be "the first derivative of the total utility function." Consequently, if total utility is given by the expression

$$TU = 16X - X^2,$$

marginal utility (MU) will be given by the function

$$MU = \frac{dTU}{dX} = 16 - 2X,$$

where $(16 - 2X)$ is the first derivative of the expression $(16X - X^2)$. Thus, for each and every total utility function, there is a corresponding marginal utility function. Fortunately, a shortcut method is available for determining

---

[1] More specifically, this equation defines what is sometimes meant by the term "average marginal utility." Average marginal utility may be described as the average change in total utility per unit change in the rate of consumption. For example, if total utility increases by 50 utils when the consumption rate rises by 10 units, then $\Delta TU/\Delta X = 50/10 = 5$ utils per unit of consumption. In other words, the average change in total utility is 5 utils for each of the 10 additional units consumed. Thus, average marginal utility for this range of consumption is 5 utils. The concept of average marginal utility is very useful, because data do not always permit a unit-by-unit calculation of marginal utility; when this occurs, the concept of average marginal utility may be employed as an estimate of marginal utility.

[2] This is much like asking what happens to the value of y in the expression $y = (x + 1)/x$ as the value of x approaches infinity.

82

the marginal utility function directly from the total utility function without going through the preceding laborious process each time. The purpose of the lengthy derivation is to illustrate, for those readers not familiar with elementary differential calculus, the logic of determining rates of change in variables.

The *general* procedure for finding the marginal function for any variable from the total function for that variable may be illustrated thus: if the total function is given by

$$T = aX^n$$

where *a* and *n* are arbitrary constants and *X* is any variable, then the marginal function is

$$M = \frac{dT}{dX} = naX^{n-1}$$

Example 1 :   If

$$T = 16X^3$$

then

$$M = \frac{dT}{dX} = 3 \cdot 16 \cdot X^{3-1} = 48X^2.$$

Example 2 :   If $T = 160 + 7X + 4X^2 - 2X^3$, then our general rule is applied to *each term* of the expression. Actually the total function may be understood to be

$$T = 160X^0 + 7X^1 + 4X^2 - 2X^3.$$

Hence,

$$M = \frac{dT}{dX} = 0 \cdot 160X^{0-1} + 1 \cdot 7X^{1-1} + 2 \cdot 4X^{2-1} - 3 \cdot 2X^{3-1}$$

$$= \frac{dT}{dX} = 0X^{-1} + 7X^0 + 8X^1 - 6X^2$$

$$= \frac{dT}{dX} = 0 + 7 + 8X - 6X^2.$$

Note that the derivative (or rate of change) of the constant term in the total function turns out to be zero; this is as it should be since the rate of change in a value that is constant is necessarily zero.

Example 3 :   Suppose the total function is expressed in the form of a general algebraic equation:

$$T = a + bX + cX^2,$$

where *a*, *b*, and *c* are constants. Since the total function *T* may be rewritten as

$$T = aX^0 + bX^1 + cX^2,$$

the corresponding marginal function M is

$$M = \frac{dT}{dX} = 0 \cdot aX^{-1} + 1 \cdot bX^0 + 2 \cdot cX^1,$$

which simplifies to

$$M = b + 2cX.$$

For those who feel uncomfortable with the mechanics of derivatives, a number of problems and answers are provided at the end of this chapter to strengthen your ability to use this essential aspect of mathematical economics.

To summarize our brief excursion into the mathematical aspects of economic relationships, we may say that the derivative of a function is the rate of change of the dependent variable as the value of the independent variable changes; in terms of economics, the derivative of a total utility function *defines* the marginal utility function. More specifically, *marginal utility may be rigorously defined as the rate of change in total utility as the rate of consumption of a commodity changes.* The rate of change at a particular consumption rate may be determined precisely by calculating the value of the first derivative of the total utility function at the consumption rate in question.

To return to our original example, we have found that given

$$TU = 16X - X^2,$$

then

$$MU = 16 - 2X.$$

The expression for MU is quite useful because it allows the value of MU to be quickly determined at any value of X. Moreover, these results may be related to both Table 3-1 and Figure 3-1. For instance, the equation of the MU function is the exact equation which describes the graph of the marginal utility function in Figure 3-1(b). Furthermore, we can see from Table 3-1 that the value for MU between one and two units of X is 13 utils (technically, at $X = 1\frac{1}{2}$, $MU = 13$ utils); if we let X assume a value of 1.5 in the equation $MU = 16 - 2X$, we get a value of 13 utils for MU, which corresponds exactly to the value in Table 3-1.

Perhaps the most significant relationship between the TU and MU functions concerns the shape of the total utility function. Marginal utility was defined as the rate of change in total utility as the rate of consumption changes; this is the same thing as saying the value for marginal utility at a particular consumption rate equals the slope of the total utility function at that consumption rate. In other words, viewed geometrically, the derivative of the total utility function gives us the slope of the total utility function at any X-value. When we say that marginal utility is 13 utils at a consumption of 1.5 units of X we really mean that at $X = 1.5$ total utility is increasing at a rate of 13 utils per unit of extra consumption, which is, by definition, the slope of the total utility function at the point where $X = 1.5$ units. When total utility is at its highest point, the slope of the TU curve is zero (because the tangent line drawn to the TU function at its highest point is horizontal). Since marginal utility, by definition, has a value equal to the slope of the total utility function, the value of MU corresponding to the peak of the TU function is also zero.

Using these ideas, the total utility function in Figure 3-1(a) may be said to *increase at a decreasing rate*. Why? Because as the consumption rate increases, the TU function rises more slowly—i.e., its slope gets smaller and smaller. Consequently, the related values for MU must be decreasing, since these values, by definition, are equal to the slope of the TU function. Figure 3-1(b) illustrates just such a pattern of change in the values for marginal utility.

TYPES OF TOTAL AND MARGINAL UTILITY FUNCTIONS

Let us now examine the nature of total and marginal utility functions for various types of commodities. The immense variety of taste and preference patterns among consumers coupled with the diverse character of goods and services gives rise to a whole host of possible utility functions. We shall confine our survey to a few of the more common types.

Consider the case of a wealthy and ardent connoisseur of gourmet food who for reasons of health has been forced to remain on a strict diet for the last six months. His doctor has just given him permission to return to his normal eating habits. To celebrate, he is considering taking an extended world tour so that he may dine at his most favorite restaurants—one each night of the tour. But he is undecided as to the length of the tour and has decided to think about the satisfaction he would have from tours of varying duration. What might be our connoisseur's utility function for eating at these restaurants? Given his long abstention from gourmet food, it is reasonable to expect that for the first several nights his total utility from gourmet dining will *increase* at an *increasing* rate, meaning that each additional meal he eats on the grand tour will increase his level of satisfaction by more than a proportional amount. In this case, the marginal utility derived from eating the second meal will exceed the marginal utility from the first meal. Likewise, the marginal utility of the third meal will be greater than that of the second. However, at some point, the novelty of renewing his acquaintance with good food will begin to wear off, and we can expect the marginal utility of additional meals to level off and decline—say at the end of the first week.

At the point where diminishing marginal utility is reached, total utility begins to *increase* at a *decreasing* rate. Successive meals, although satisfying, will produce smaller and smaller gains in total utility. At the end of a month or so, it is to be anticipated that our connoisseur friend will sate his appetite for eating at fine restaurants; that is, he will reach the saturation rate. To

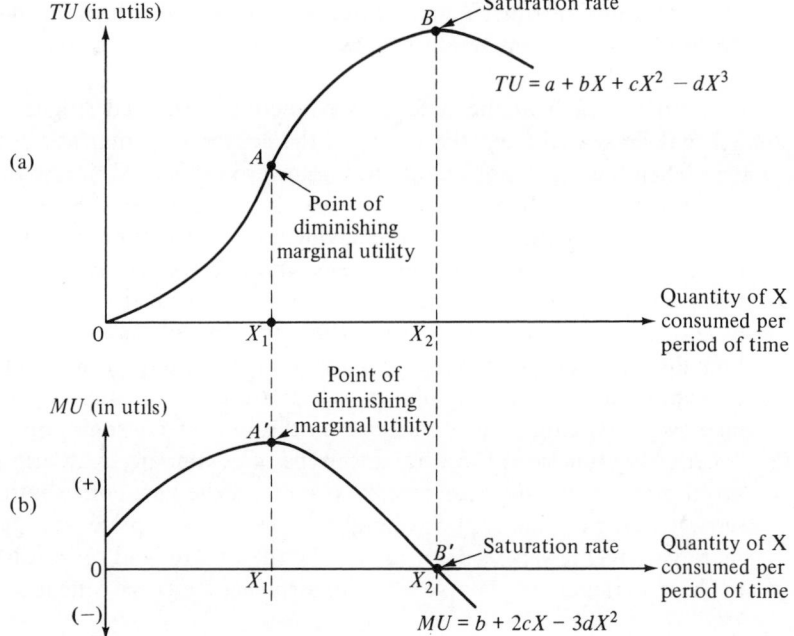

Fig. 3-2   Generalized Total and Marginal Utility Functions for Phases of Increasing and Decreasing Returns as the Rate of Consumption Rises

continue the tour at this point may even result in a decline in total satisfaction, perhaps because he is risking a return to his strict diet after his next trip to the doctor. This type of utility behavior can be described by the curves and equations shown in Figure 3-2. Point A on the TU curve is the point of diminishing marginal utility and corresponds to the same consumption rate as point A' on the MU curve. Point B on the TU curve defines the saturation rate, as does point B' on the MU graph.

Although many forms of equations could represent a total utility function of this shape, one of the simplest is the general equation for a cubic function. Hence, the general equation

$$TU = a + bX + cX^2 - dX^3$$

could be employed to represent our connoisseur's utility function for his tour of world-famous restaurants, where X represents the number of meals eaten, a, b, and c are positive constants, and d is a negative constant. Using the mathematical concepts previously developed, the corresponding general equation for marginal utility is

$$MU = \frac{dTU}{dX} = b + 2cX - 3dX^2$$

Can you think of other commodities or situations in which an individual's *TU* and *MU* functions might behave in the same fashion as those in Figure 3-2?

So far, each of the total utility functions discussed (Figures 3-1 and 3-2) has emanated from the origin of the graph; i.e., total utility has been zero when the consumption rate has been zero. This need not be the case at all; in fact, it is probably not even typical. It is quite possible to incur negative amounts of utility (disutility) from having none of a commodity, as evidenced by the cries of dismay from individuals who find themselves without aspirin when a headache occurs, who run out of gas on a lonely road, or have too little of any item they consider a "necessity." In such cases the total utility function may start below the origin and not reach a zero utility level until the consumption of the commodity is well above the zero rate. Nor is it at all necessary that utility functions rise as the rate of consumption increases. Total utility functions for a nuisance type of commodity may originate at a positive value, and *decrease* rapidly as more of the item comes into the possession of the consumer. For example, people usually prefer less garbage to more garbage, fewer dead leaves to rake than more, and fewer dirty dishes to clean up than more. People who fear airplanes may derive great satisfaction

MATHEMATICAL CAPSULE 1

Determining the Point of Diminishing Marginal Utility and the Saturation Rate: An Application of the Mathematical Concepts of Maxima and Minima

A maximum point on a curve is a point that is higher than its neighboring point to either side, such that the curve is concave downward; a minimum point on a curve is a point that is lower than its neighboring points, such that the curve is concave upward.

All maximum and minimum values of a function $y = f(x)$ occur where $dy/dx = 0$ since the first derivative of a function is indicative of its rate of change or slope. This, characteristic is frequently termed the *first-order* condition.

If, at the value of x at which $dy/dx = 0$, the second derivative is negative, $d^2y/dx^2 < 0$, that value of x defines a maximum value for y, where $y = f(x)$. If at the value of x at which $dy/dx = 0$, the second derivative is positive, $d^2y/dx^2 > 0$, that value of x defines a minimum value for the function $y = f(x)$. This requirement for distinguishing between maximum and minimum values is called the *second-order condition*.

Consider the total utility function

$$TU = 130X - 2.5X^2,$$

which is plotted in the accompanying graph. Suppose we wish to determine the value

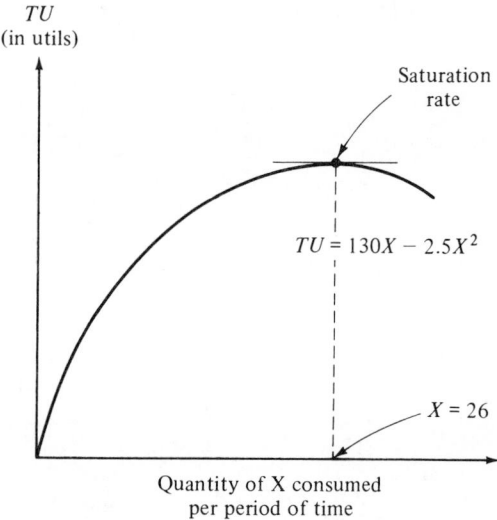

Quantity of X consumed
per period of time

of X at which TU is maximum—the saturation rate. The saturation rate corresponds exactly to that quantity consumed at which the slope of the total utility function is zero. Consequently, we may write

$$TU = 130X - 2.5X^2,$$

$$MU = \frac{dTU}{dX} = 130 - 5X.$$

Setting the marginal utility function equal to zero, we get

$$130 - 5X = 0.$$

Solving for the value of X which satisfies the equation, we find $X = 26$ units. This then is the consumption rate where TU is maximum.

Suppose we wish to find the consumption rate of X at which diminishing MU is encountered for the total utility function presented below:

$$TU = 18X + 7X^2 - \tfrac{1}{3}X^3.$$

Diminishing MU begins at the point where the MU function is at its maximum value. The value of X at which the slope of the MU function is zero $(dMU/dX = d^2TU/dX^2 = 0)$ can be calculated as follows:

$$MU = \frac{dTU}{dX} = 18 + 14X - X^2,$$

$$\frac{dMU}{dX} = \frac{d^2TU}{dX^2} = 14 - 2X = 0,$$

$$-2X = -14,$$

$$X = 7.$$

Hence it is at 7 units of consumption per period of time that diminishing *MU* sets in.

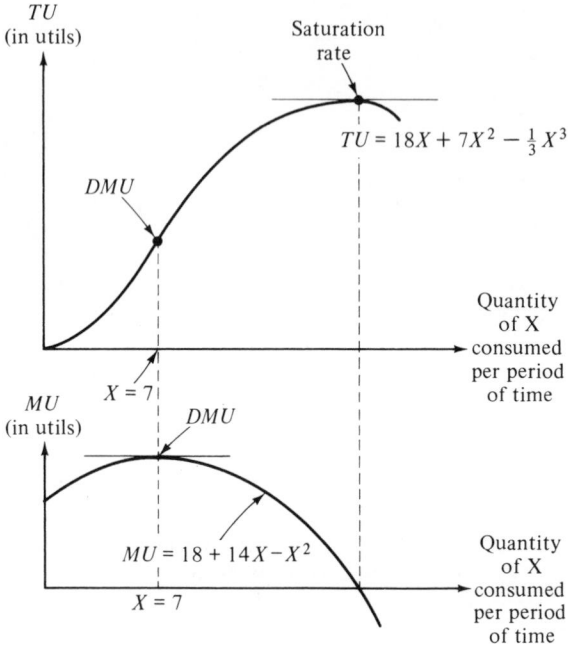

EXERCISES

1. Determine the saturation rate and the point of diminishing marginal utility for each of the following *TU* functions:

   (a) $TU = 36X - X^2$.
   (b) $TU = 10X + 9X^2 - X^3$.

from not traveling by air and may incur increasing disutility the more often they are forced to fly to their destination.

UTILITY FUNCTIONS FOR RELATED COMMODITIES

In many instances it is clear that the utility a person obtains from one commodity is related to his consumption of another commodity. The utility derived from eating biscuits is at least partially dependent upon the availability of butter or margarine; the satisfaction from one's automobile is related to the quantity of gasoline it uses; the satisfaction from eating T-bone steak is related to one's utility for center-cut pork chops; the enjoyment from one's binoculars is related to the frequency with which one goes to football games. Thus, while total utility is a function of the quantities of each commodity consumed per period of time, it need not be simply the sum of the utilities gained separately from each commodity.

Instead of deriving a utility function for each commodity, it is really more appropriate to conceive of a *total utility surface* relating total utility to the joint rates of consumption of all goods simultaneously. This notion is

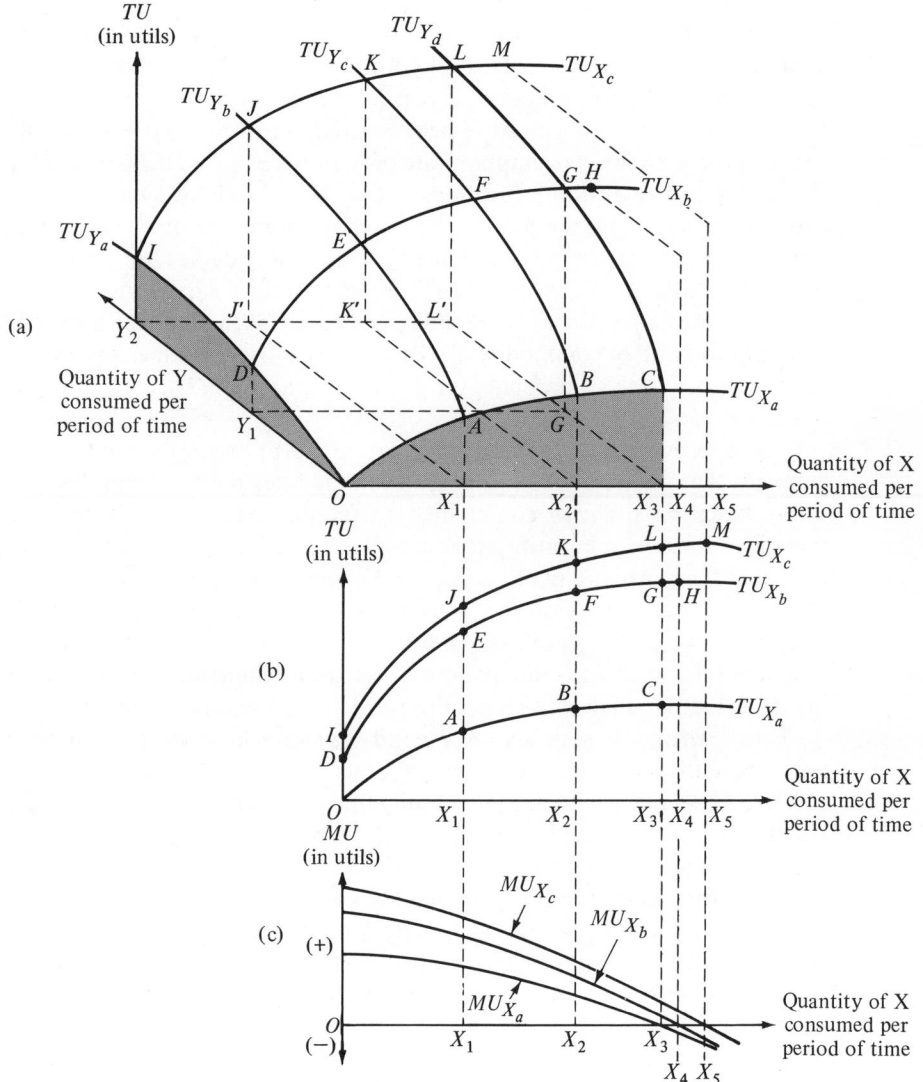

Fig. 3-3   A Total Utility Surface and Corresponding Total and Marginal Utility Functions

illustrated graphically for two commodities X and Y in Figure 3-3(a). The consumption rates for X and Y define a horizontal plane with total utility measured as a vertical distance above it. The total utility surface is $OILC$. If Y_1 units of commodity Y are consumed per unit of time along with X_3 units of commodity X, total utility is GG'; if the respective consumption rates are Y_2 and X_1 per period of time, total utility is JJ'. Points on the total utility surface, such as $A, B, C, D, E, F, G, J, K,$ and L, show total utility for different combinations of X and Y.

The total utility surface pictured in Figure 3-3(a) also indicates how total utility changes as the rate of consumption of one commodity changes, given the rate of consumption of the other. For example, if no units of commodity Y are consumed, then the total utility for commodity X increases along the path $OABC$ as the consumption of X is increased, giving the function TU_{X_a}. If the amount of Y consumed is held constant at Y_1 units, the total utility function for X as the consumption rate of X rises becomes $DEFGH$ or TU_{X_b}. These resulting total utility functions (TU_{X_a}, TU_{X_b}, and TU_{X_c}) are shown in two dimensions in Figure 3-3(b); their corresponding marginal utility functions are shown in Figure 3-3(c). Since the total utility curves for X vary with the consumption of Y, so also do the marginal utility curves for X. In this example, the shape of the total utility surface is such that the higher the consumption rate of commodity Y, the stronger is the consumer's preference for commodity X; this accounts for MU_{X_c} lying above MU_{X_b}, which in turn lies above MU_{X_a}.

The derivation of the curves in Figure 3-3(b) and (c) should make it apparent that interrelationships among commodities produce countless total utility functions for *each* commodity. In the example above, for instance, there is a different total utility function for X associated with each quantity of Y that the consumer might consume. For the same reasons, there is a different total utility function for Y for each different consumption rate of X [see TU_{Y_a}, TU_{Y_b}, TU_{Y_c}, and TU_{Y_d} in Figure 3-3(a)]. Since for each total utility function there is also a unique marginal utility function, there must be innumerable marginal utility functions for both commodities X and Y as well.

Thus, when the satisfaction derived from one commodity hinges in part upon the amounts consumed of other commodities, the effect is to produce a *set* of total and marginal utility functions for each item, rather than a single unique total utility function with its corresponding marginal utility function. In addition, the shape of the total utility surface depends upon the nature of the interrelationship among the commodities. Should total utility by chance increase at an increasing rate for a few units before diminishing marginal utility sets in, the total utility surface would be concave upward for this range of consumption, turning concave downward as diminishing marginal utility is realized. This situation is illustrated in Figure 3-4.

It should be realized that every consumer has his own unique set of total and marginal utility functions, thereby adding still another dimension to

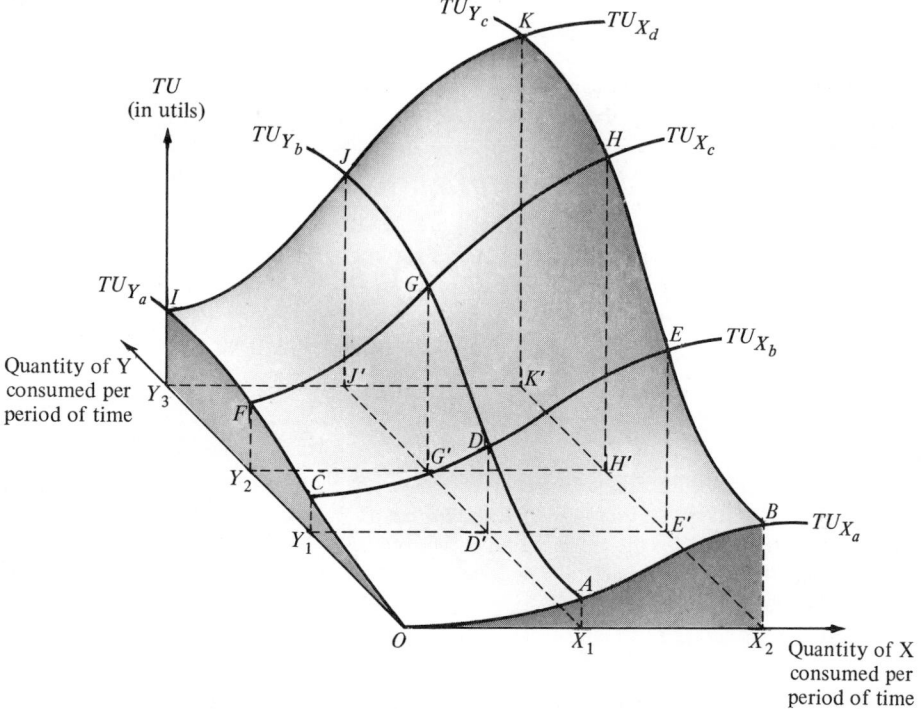

Fig. 3-4 A Total Utility Surface for a Pair of Commodities Characterized by Both Increasing and Decreasing Marginal Utility

the number of existing utility functions. The utility functions for each consumer vary in character according to his own tastes and preferences. Furthermore, these tastes and preferences may be expected to change over time, giving rise to entirely new sets of consumer utility functions and utility surfaces.

MATHEMATICAL CAPSULE 2

Determining Marginal Utility For Multi-Commodity Total Utility Functions

When the satisfaction derived from one commodity is related to the amounts consumed of other commodities, the consumer's total utility function is of the form

$$TU = f(X_a, X_b, \ldots, X_n).$$

where X_a, X_b, ..., X_n represent the array of commodities purchased. Given such multi-commodity TU functions, one is often called to examine the effect of a change in the consumption rate of one commodity upon TU, when the consumption rates of the other commodities do not change. There is a form of the derivative which corresponds to this interest; it is called the *partial derivative*.

Suppose the total utility function for two commodities X and Y is

$$TU = 7X + 4Y - .2X^2 - .3Y^2 - XY.$$

We can find the impact of a change in the rate of consumption of X upon TU when the consumption of Y is kept fixed *by treating Y as a constant* and differentiating the total utility function with respect to X—this gives the partial derivative of TU with respect to X and is denoted by $\partial TU/\partial X$. Accordingly we get

$$\frac{\partial TU}{\partial X} = 7 - .4X - Y,$$

which may be interpreted to represent *the rate of change in TU as the rate of consumption of X changes, the rate of consumption of Y being held constant*. This then is the expression for the marginal utility of commodity X. Similarly, the partial derivative of TU with respect to Y is

$$\frac{\partial TU}{\partial Y} = 4 - .6Y - X,$$

and it represents the expression for the marginal utility of Y.

EXERCISES

1. Determine the relevant marginal utility functions for each of the following total utility functions:
   (a) $TU = 15X^2 Y^2 - X^3 Y^2$.
   (b) $TU = 20X + 40Y - 3X^2 - Y^2$.
   (c) $TU = 30XY + 10XZ - 3XYZ - 10Z$.
   (d) $TU = 5.4X^{1/2} Y^{1/3}$.

2. Determine the values for MU_x and MU_y at $X = 5$ and $Y = 3$ in each of the following total utility functions.
   (a) $TU = 16X - X^2 + 10Y - XY$.
   (b) $TU = 33X + 2X^2 - X^3 + 4Y - XY^2$.
   (c) $TU = 16X^2 + 15XY + 17Y^2 - 4X^2 Y^2$.

Consumer Behavior in the Marketplace

The foregoing utility concepts are useful for explaining the behavior of individual consumers in the marketplace. In approaching the analysis of consumer demand, economists assume that *a rational consumer attempts to arrange his purchases of commodities so as to maximize the total satisfaction he can get from his money income.* In reality, of course, the assumption of maximizing utility may not be literally true, at least for all consumers in each and every situation. Nevertheless, the assumption is a justifiable and reasonable abstraction for a wide range of circumstances. After all, no purpose is served by getting less than one's full satisfaction from consuming commodities. However, imperfect information about alternative purchases and about prices tends to hinder consumer attempts at utility maximization. Consumers, like businessmen, face an uncertain environment in making their decisions, and an exhaustive search for better information may cost more than it is worth. In addition, impulse buying and force of habit work against consumers' actually identifying and purchasing the utility-maximizing combination of goods and services. Nonetheless, the assumption that consumers behave as if they seek to maximize total utility is a viable one, because it allows us to pinpoint some major facets of consumer behavior.

In trying to achieve the maximum degree of satisfaction or utility, the consumer faces two severe limitations: (1) the prices he must pay for the goods he desires to purchase and (2) his available money income. A word about the meaning of money income is in order. Money income is used here to refer to whatever money a consumer has to spend in a given time peiod. Included as money income are (a) dollars currently received, (b) any sums the consumer wishes and is able to borrow, (c) any savings the consumer has accumulated from past income periods, and (d) any other wealth the consumer may wish to allocate to current consumption. Clearly, all consumers, even the most wealthy members of society (including Howard Hughes, J. Paul Getty, and Jacqueline Onassis), have some maximum amount to spend per period of time.

Confronted with a limited number of dollars to spend, the price tags on every commodity, thousands of commodities to choose among, and imperfect knowledge as to all alternatives, the consumer's decision problem is indeed complex. Obviously, he cannot buy everything he wants, because each purchase exhausts a portion of his available income. He is forced to compromise and decide which of the many commodities within his income constraint best suit his needs and tastes.

SOME SIMPLIFYING ASSUMPTIONS

To keep the ensuing analysis of consumer behavior manageable, the following assumptions will be made:

1. Each consumer has full knowledge of all information pertinent to his expenditure decision—a definitive set of tastes and preferences, knowledge of the goods and services available, their capacity to satisfy his wants, his money income, and the prices at which specific commodities can be bought.
2. The consumer's preference pattern for commodities is one of diminishing

marginal utility for each. Actually, this is a more rigorous assumption than need be made. All we need assume is that the marginal utility of one good decreases *relative* to the marginal utilities of other goods as its consumption rate is increased *relative* to the consumption rate of others. Our analysis will be valid in cases where the marginal utility of a good is increasing, so long as it increases less than proportionally to the marginal utilities of other goods.

3. The utility function for each commodity is independent of the rate of consumption of other commodities. Again, this assumption is made for the sake of convenience; it does not change the conditions necessary for utility maximization and it permits an understandable numerical treatment.

None of these assumptions does violence to the principles of consumer behavior we wish to derive, and they offer the distinct advantage of rendering the exposition of them much easier.

MAXIMIZATION OF UTILITY

For the time being, suppose we restrict ourselves to the case of a consumer who is trying to decide what combination of two commodities, X and Y, he should purchase with his weekly income of $40. No matter how many units of X and Y the consumer buys, the price of X remains at $3 per unit and the price of Y at $5 per unit. Table 3-2 summarizes the consumer's preference for the two items, along with his evaluation of the utility he obtains from not spending his money—i.e., the total and marginal utility of saving.[3]

How should the consumer allocate his $40 among buying commodity X, buying commodity Y, and saving in order to obtain maximum satisfaction? To answer this question, let us proceed to ascertain what the consumer should do first. His $40 weekly income allows him to buy some of either X or Y should he decide to do so. If he spends $3 to buy the first unit of X, he receives 54 utils of satisfaction; if he spends $5 to buy the first unit of Y, he receives 75 utils; and if he saves all $40, he is well past the saturation rate for current saving, since his marginal utility for saving a dollar is down to only 1 util when the saving rate reaches $5. Of these alternatives, purchase of X is definitely the better bargain. Why? Because it gives the consumer 18 utils of satisfaction *per dollar spent*, whereas commodity Y yields only 15 untils of satisfaction per dollar spent, and saving yields no more than 9 utils per dollar saved. The proper decision variable in this instance is neither total nor marginal utility, but *marginal utility per dollar of expenditure*. It is the best indicator of value received as it combines the factor of satisfac-

---

[3] The term "saving" is used here to encompass a variety of acts associated with not spending. Consumers may rationally decide not to spend all of their money income during some period because: (a) they place a high value on saving a portion of their income in order to provide for emergencies, accumulate an estate, or any of a hundred other reasons; (b) they are unable to find a commodity precisely suited to their tastes and wish to look further before making a purchase; (c) they wish to postpone spending until some future period so that they may pay cash for the desired items. In any event, the act of not spending or saving may bring the consumer satisfaction or utility just as does the act of consuming goods and services.

Table 3-2 The Utility-Maximizing Combination of Commodities X and Y Obtainable from an Income of $40

Commodity X (Price = $3)				Commodity Y (Price = $5)				Saving		
Quantity	TU (utils)	MU (utils)	MU/Price (utils/$)	Quantity	TU (utils)	MU (utils)	MU/Price (utils/$)	Number of dollars saved	TU (utils)	MU (utils/$1)
0	0			0	0			0	10	
		54	18			75	15			9
1	54			1	75			1	19	
		45	15			60	12			7
2	99			2	135			2	26	
		30	10			40	8			3
3	129			3	175			3	29	
		9	3			25	5			2
4	138			4	200			4	31	
		3	1			15	3			1
5	141			5	215			5	32	
		-3	-1			5	1			0
6	138			6	220			6	32	

tion with the factor of cost; both factors are requisite for valid comparisons between commodities. Since the consumer receives more satisfaction for his money by buying the first unit of X instead of the first unit of Y or instead of saving, his first act should be to exchange $3 for one unit of commodity X. Via the same reasoning, the consumer's second act can be determined. The second unit of commodity X will produce 15 units of satisfaction per dollar spent, as will the first unit of Y; both are superior to saving at this point. Since the consumer has ample funds available for spending ($37 of his original $40), his second and third acts should be to buy the second unit of X and the first unit of Y, leaving him with $29. His fourth act should be the purchase of the second unit of Y. And so it goes. At each step the consumer must decide whether the marginal utility of a dollar's worth of spending is greater than the marginal utility of a dollar's worth of saving. If it is, he should then buy the commodity yielding him the highest marginal utility per dollar of expenditure. If not, he should save his money. In this example, the consumer will maximize total utility by allocating his income so as to purchase 4 units of X and 5 units of Y and to save $3.

No other allocation of the consumer's $40 weekly income will produce as much satisfaction as this one. How do we know? Suppose our consumer were to buy one fewer unit of commodity Y, thereby freeing $5 with which he could buy another unit of X and save an additional $2. This act would reduce his total utility. Giving up the fifth unit of Y entails a loss of 15 utils, whereas increasing the purchase rate of X from 4 to 5 units brings him 3 utils and saving two more dollars yields a combined 3 utils, for a total gain of 6 utils from his alternative expenditure of the $5. He would therefore suffer a net loss of 9 utils of satisfaction by transferring dollars out of the purchase of Y and into X and saving. Alternatively, were our consumer to take his $3 in savings and apply it to the purchase of the fifth unit of X, he would give up 19 utils of satisfaction and acquire only 3 utils of satisfaction, for a net loss in satisfaction of 16 utils. Any act other than buying 4 units of X and 5 units of Y and saving $3 will cause total utility to decline.

Observe carefully the characteristics of the utility-maximizing act. First, the consumer is completely utilizing his purchasing power in the sense that all of his income is allocated either to the purchase of commodities or to saving. There are no idle dollars; the dollars which are saved are constructively deployed every bit as much as are the dollars used for purchasing X and Y—since saving money produces utility. Thus maximization of utility *does not require* that the consumer spend *all* of his money—savings have utility and serve to further the motives of the consumer. Secondly, at the utility-maximizing combination the marginal utilities per dollar spent on the last unit of each item purchased are equal. In other words, the consumer has arranged his purchases such that he is getting an equivalent amount of satisfaction from the last dollar allocated to each of the commodities (including saving) which he actually obtains. He receives 3 utils per dollar spent on the fourth unit of X; he receives 3 utils per dollar spent on the fifth unit of Y; and he receives 3 utils from saving the third dollar.

THE CONDITIONS FOR UTILITY MAXIMIZATION

We are now in a position to state the formal conditions for consumer maximization of utility in a multi-commodity environment. Two equations will suffice:

(1) $P_{Xa} \cdot X_a + P_{Xb} \cdot X_b + P_{Xc} \cdot X_c + \cdots + P_{Xn} \cdot X_n + \text{Saving} = I$

(2) $\dfrac{MU_{Xa}}{P_{Xa}} = \dfrac{MU_{Xb}}{P_{Xb}} = \dfrac{MU_{Xc}}{P_{Xc}} = \cdots = \dfrac{MU_{Xn}}{P_{Xn}} = MU_{\text{saving}}$

Equation (1) says that the sum of the expenditures on each commodity $(X_a, X_b, X_c, \ldots, X_n)$ plus saving must be equal to the money income (I) that the consumer has available per period of time. Total expenditures cannot *exceed* income; any income which is not used to buy goods and services must necessarily be allocated to saving. Thus all of the consumer's money income is accounted for by either spending or saving. Equation (2) says that to maximize total utility the consumer must select and purchase among the different commodities available such that the marginal utilities per dollar of expenditure on the last unit of each item purchased are equal to each other and to the marginal utility of saving an additional dollar.

When the various degrees of satisfaction from marginal outlays are unequal, total satisfaction may be increased by diminishing expenditures for commodities where satisfaction is less and enlarging expenditures for those commodities where satisfaction is greater. To illustrate, consider the following situation:

$$MU_{X_a} = 42 \text{ utils for the last unit purchased,}$$
$$P_{X_a} = \$14 \text{ per unit,}$$
$$MU_{X_b} = 60 \text{ utils for the last unit purchased,}$$
$$P_{X_b} = \$12 \text{ per unit, and}$$
$$MU_{\text{saving}} = 4 \text{ utils for each additional dollar saved.}$$

Then,

$$MU_{X_a}/\$ \text{ spent on } X = \frac{MU_{X_a}}{P_{X_a}} = \frac{42 \text{ utils}}{\$14} = 3 \text{ utils}/\$, \text{ and}$$

$$MU_{X_b}/\$ \text{ spent on } Y = \frac{MU_{X_b}}{P_{X_b}} = \frac{60 \text{ utils}}{\$12} = 5 \text{ utils}/\$.$$

The consumer is realizing more satisfaction per dollar spent on X_b than on X_a. He can increase his total utility by transferring dollars out of the purchase of X_a and into the purchase of X_b until $MU_{X_a}/P_{X_a} = MU_{X_b}/P_{X_b} = MU_{\text{saving}}$. By reducing his expenditure on X_a, the MU of the last unit purchased of X_a would rise (say to 56 utils), thus raising the ratio MU_{X_a}/P_{X_a} (to 4 utils per dollar). By increasing the expenditure for X_b, the MU of last unit purchased would fall (say to 48 utils), thereby lowering the ratio MU_{X_b}/P_{X_b} (to 4 utils per dollar). Since X_a costs \$14 and X_b costs \$12, buying one unit less of X_a and one unit more of X_b would leave \$2 left over either for the purchase of some other commodity whose $MU/\$$ of expenditure exceeded 4 utils per dollar or for saving. Sometimes the indivisibility of units of commodities can preclude the consumer from *exactly* equating the marginal utilities per dollar spent on the last unit for each and every commodity. For example, in the above case the consumer might find that there are no other commodities which he could buy with his \$2 and receive as much as 3.5 utils per dollar; saving the entire two dollars might reduce the MU of the last dollar saved to 3.8 utils. Then equation (2) could not be precisely satisfied because the marginal utilities of the last unit purchased of X_a and X_b would be 4 utils per dollar, whereas the MU of the last dollar saved would be only 3.8 utils. Assuming that fractions of X_a and X_b cannot be bought, the consumer would then have come as close as possible to meeting the condition imposed by equation (2). Practically speaking, equation (2) should be interpreted to mean that the consumer seeking maximum utility from a given money income should spend his dollars so as to approach as nearly as possible the equality of the marginal utilities per dollar spent on the last unit of each commodity purchased and further to approach as nearly as possible the point at which the marginal utility of spending a dollar equals the marginal utility of saving a dollar.

MATHEMATICAL CAPSULE 3

Determination of the Utility-Maximizing Combination of Commodities Subject to an Income Constraint

Let $P_a, P_b, P_c, \ldots, P_n$ be the prices of commodities $X_a, X_b, X_c, \ldots, X_n$, $I = a$ consumer's money income, and $TU = f(X_a, X_b, X_c, \ldots, X_n)$ be the consumer's utility function for n commodities which the consumer wishes to maximize subject to his income constraint

(1) $$I = P_a X_a + P_b X_b + P_c X_c + \cdots + P_n X_n,$$

where saving here is treated as simply one kind of commodity. To find the utility-maximizing combination of commodities, a new function is generated which combines the TU function to be maximized and the constraint equation. In order to keep the solution determinate (as many equations as there are unknowns) an artificial unknown, called a *LaGrange multiplier*, is introduced, giving

(2) $$Z = f(X_a, X_b, X_c, \ldots, X_n) + \lambda(I - P_a X_a - P_b X_b - P_c X_c - \cdots - P_n X_n),$$

where λ is the LaGrange multiplier. The partial derivatives of Z are found for each variable and equated to zero to establish the first-order conditions.

(3) $$\frac{\partial Z}{\partial X_a} = \frac{\partial TU}{\partial X_a} - \lambda P_a = 0$$

(4) $$\frac{\partial Z}{\partial X_b} = \frac{\partial TU}{\partial X_b} - \lambda P_b = 0$$

(5) $$\frac{\partial Z}{\partial X_c} = \frac{\partial TU}{\partial X_c} - \lambda P_c = 0$$

$$\vdots$$

(6) $$\frac{\partial Z}{\partial X_n} = \frac{\partial TU}{\partial X_n} - \lambda P_n = 0$$

(7) $$\frac{\partial Z}{\partial \lambda} = I - P_a X_a - P_b X_b - P_c X_c - \cdots - P_n X_n = 0$$

These equations may be solved simultaneously to determine the utility-maximizing purchase levels for $X_a, X_b, X_c, \ldots, X_n$. From equations (3) through (6), it is seen that

(8) $$\lambda = \frac{\dfrac{\partial TU}{\partial X_a}}{P_a} = \frac{\dfrac{\partial TU}{\partial X_b}}{P_b} = \frac{\dfrac{\partial TU}{\partial X_c}}{P_c} = \cdots = \frac{\dfrac{\partial TU}{\partial X_n}}{P_n}$$

The terms $\partial TU/\partial X_a, \partial TU/\partial X_b, \partial TU/\partial X_c, \ldots, \partial TU/\partial X_n$ really are $MU_{X_a}, MU_{X_b}, MU_{X_c}, \ldots, MU_{X_n}$, and the value of λ necessarily is equal to the marginal utility of the last dollar of expenditure on each item and to the marginal utility of saving. Thus equation (8) translates into

$$(9) \qquad MU_{\text{saving}} = \frac{MU_{X_a}}{P_a} = \frac{MU_{X_b}}{P_b} = \frac{MU_{X_c}}{P_c} = \cdots = \frac{MU_{X_n}}{P_n},$$

which we know to be a necessary condition for consumer maximization of total utility.

As an example of the foregoing, suppose we find the utility-maximizing consumption rate for two commodities X and Y if the total utility function is

$$TU = 10X + 24Y - .5X^2 - .5Y^2$$

and if $P_X = \$2$, $P_Y = \$6$, and $I = \$44$. Then we have

$$Z = 10X + 24Y - .5X^2 - .5Y^2 + \lambda(44 - 2X - 6Y).$$

Finding the partial derivatives and setting them equal to zero gives:

$$\frac{\partial Z}{\partial X} = 10 - X - 2\lambda = 0$$

$$\frac{\partial Z}{\partial Y} = 24 - Y - 6\lambda = 0$$

$$\frac{\partial Z}{\partial \lambda} = 44 - 2X - 6Y = 0$$

Solving $\partial Z/\partial X$, $\partial Z/\partial Y$, and $\partial Z/\partial \lambda$ simultaneously yields $X = 4$, $Y = 6$, and $\lambda = 3$.

EXERCISES

1. Determine the utility-maximizing combination of X and Y when
   (a) $TU = 15X + 22Y - 4XY$ (b) $TU = 17X + 20Y - 2X^2 - Y^2$
       $P_X = \$3$ $P_X = \$3$
       $P_Y = \$6$ $P_Y = \$4$
        $I = \$30$ $I = \$22$

EVALUATION OF THE MAXIMIZING RULES

The foregoing discussion is rather formal and abstract. How realistic is this description of a rational consumer's disposition of his income, especially considering that most consumers have never heard of marginal utility? Does it meet the scientific standards of *explaining* and *predicting* real world consumer behavior?

Basically, the answers to these two questions are "yes." The above conditions, though formal and abstract, simulate quite well the purchase decisions of consumers. Whenever a consumer goes shopping and considers the purchase of a specific item, normally he will mentally ask himself (consciously or unconsciously) whether the price he must pay is "worth it." If his answer is favorable, then he can be expected to buy the item assuming he has the money to pay for it. If he decides the item is not worth the price, then he can be expected not to purchase it and instead to shop around elsewhere. Translated into the language of utility theory, this mental process is equivalent to deciding whether the utility he will get from consuming the item is greater than the utility of keeping his money or buying some other item. If so, he purchases the item; if the utility is less, he elects not to buy the item; and if equality between the two prevails, he is indifferent and may rationally decide to buy or not to buy. In the latter case, he is in a good position to be persuaded by a good salesman to buy the item.

Furthermore, it is quite reasonable to expect any consumer to continue to spend his income as long as he believes the extra satisfaction that he will get from a commodity exceeds the satisfaction of keeping his money. Only when a consumer believes that he obtains more satisfaction from a dollar's worth of saving than he does from a dollar's worth of spending will saving be induced.

Viewed from this perspective, our model of consumer behavior is seen to have widespread validity. Of course, several factors operate to prevent most, if not all, consumers from actually realizing the utmost satisfaction from their money incomes. The most important obstacle is a lack of perfect information about the prices charged by various sellers and about product quality. Consumers often pay more for an item at one store than is charged by another store nearby because they are unaware of the price differential. Sometimes they buy products which turn out to be less satisfactory than originally anticipated. In these ways they exhaust a larger share of their income than they otherwise would have, had perfect knowledge existed. On other occasions they buy impulsively or through force of habit. And on still other occasions they may be unduly influenced by the power of advertising. However, it must be recognized that there are costs to consumers from searching out more accurate information. The time and expense involved in comparing the many types and features of products and in shopping around for the best buy may outweigh the associated benefits. Thus, to be completely rational, the consumer must balance the costs of acquiring better information against the extra satisfaction he gains from having it.

AN ADDED DIMENSION: THE INFLUENCE OF ADVERTISING AND SALES STRATEGY UPON CONSUMER BEHAVIOR[4]

It is customary in economic analysis to presume that the consumer's worst "enemy" in attempting to maximize the satisfaction from his limited money income is his own ignorance or irrationality. By and large, the consumer is

---

[4] The material in this section draws heavily upon ideas expressed by John Kenneth Galbraith. See J. K. Galbraith, *The New Industrial State* (Boston: Houghton Mifflin Company, 1967), Chaps. 18–20.

held to possess the full initiative in buying goods and services. He responds only to wants that he originates or that are given to him by his environment. His purchasing behavior in the marketplace instructs the producers as to what he wants to buy; ultimately, all power is with the consumer—this is what is meant by consumer sovereignty.

Obviously, this overstates the situation somewhat. Much advertising and sales strategy is designed expressly for modifying individual preferences and shaping consumer behavior. To deny that it has any effect would come as a severe shock to those firms who shell out hundreds of thousands and even millions of dollars each year to promote sales of their products. More importantly, such a denial is untenable, and any model of consumer behavior which fails to acknowledge the role of advertising is sorely lacking in its explanation of real-world consumption patterns. The attempt to control or manage consumer demand has, in fact, become a vast and rapidly growing industry in its own right.

Two types of advertising may be distinguished: that which is purely informational and that which is purely persuasive. Most advertising strategy incorporates both features and is therefore not pure in either sense. The persuasive type of advertising is of primary concern here.

The significance of persuasive advertising for the study of consumer behavior is that it permits sellers to try to manipulate consumer tastes and preferences to their own advantage. Consumer behavior is therefore not purely a response of consumers to their utility schedules. If an individual's satisfaction is less from additional expenditures on soft drinks than from on ice cream, this can be just as well corrected by a change in the sales strategy of Coca-Cola as by the consumer's increasing his expenditures on ice cream. In other words, if

$$\frac{MU_{\text{soft drinks}}}{P_{\text{soft drinks}}} < \frac{MU_{\text{ice cream}}}{P_{\text{ice cream}}},$$

either of two acts can restore the equality requisite for consumer equilibrium. The consumer can transfer dollars out of the purchase of soft drinks and into the purchase of ice cream, or the soft-drink manufacturers can attempt to revise upward the consumer's marginal utility for soft drinks by means of a more persuasive advertising and sales strategy.

Consumers, of course, have it well within their powers to reject persuasion. And in due time, enough consumers—by their refusal to continue to purchase items they consider unsatisfactory—can force accommodation by producers. Not even cleverly advertised products can survive if consumers find them seriously deficient. Still, it is clear that persuasive advertising, if effective, can intensify consumer desire for a commodity to the point where its perceived marginal utility per dollar of expenditure becomes high enough to cause its purchase by a sizable number of consumers. Indeed, a major purpose of advertising is to shift the consumer's utility function for the item upward so that he will have a more intense desire for it, thereby becoming willing to buy more of it at a given price or else becoming willing to pay a higher price for the same amount currently being purchased.

INDIVIDUAL CONSUMER DEMAND CURVES

In addition to providing an explanatory and predictive model of how consumers behave in their search for the utility-maximizing combination of commodities, cardinal utility theory can be employed to establish individual consumer *demand curves* for commodities. A consumer's *demand curve* for a commodity shows the amounts of it which the consumer is willing and able to buy at various possible prices during some moment of time wherein all other factors influencing the quantity purchased are held constant.

Suppose we assume, not implausibly, that in the short run a consumer's marginal utility for saving (or not spending) is a constant value—say 21 utils per dollar saved. Suppose the consumer's total utility function for commodity X can be expressed as:

$$TU_X = 225X - 1.5X^2,$$

where X represents the quantity of commodity X consumed per period of time. Maximization of total utility from a given money income requires

$$\frac{MU_X}{P_X} = MU_{saving}.$$

If the total utility function is

$$TU_X = 225X - 1.5X^2,$$

then

$$MU_X = \frac{dTU_X}{dX} = 225 - 3.0X.$$

Since the marginal utility of saving is 21 utils per dollar saved, setting up the condition for maximization and substituting we have

$$\frac{MU_X}{P_X} = MU_{saving}$$

$$\frac{225 - 3.0X}{P_X} = 21$$

$$225 - 3.0X = 21P_X$$

$$-3.0X = 21P_X - 225$$

$$X = -7P_X + 75$$

$$X = 75 - 7P_X.$$

The function $X = 75 - 7P_X$ expresses the relationship between the equilibrium amount of commodity X demanded and the price of X; and it is, accordingly, the equation of the consumer's demand curve for commodity X, given the assumed conditions that (a) the marginal utility of saving additional dollars is constant at 21 utils and (b) the total utility function is $225X - 1.5X^2$.

Utilizing this equation, we can derive a demand schedule for the consumer as follows:

at $P_X = \$5,$ $X = 75 - 7P_X = 75 - 7(5) = 40$ units,

at $P_X = \$6,$ $X = 75 - 7P_X = 75 - 7(6) = 33$ units,

at $P_X = \$7,$ $X = 75 - 7P_X = 75 - 7(7) = 26$ units,

at $P_X = \$8,$ $X = 75 - 7P_X = 75 - 7(8) = 19$ units,

at $P_X = \$9,$ $X = 75 - 7P_X = 75 - 7(9) = 12$ units,

at $P_X = \$10,$ $X = 75 - 7P_X = 75 - 7(10) = 5$ units.

In like manner, the quantity of commodity X demanded by the consumer per period of time can be derived for any other value of P_X. Each of the X values represents an equilibrium level of consumption of commodity X per period of time for that particular value of the price of X. These equilibrium values of X and the associated values of P_X are illustrated graphically in Figure 3-5. It is customary in the graphical analysis of consumer demand curves to let the vertical axis represent price per unit and let the horizontal axis represent the quantity demanded of the good per period of time. The curve in Figure 3-5 is the consumer's demand curve for commodity X.

Observe that the demand curve slopes downward to the right. This indicates that the price of X and the quantity purchased of X per period of

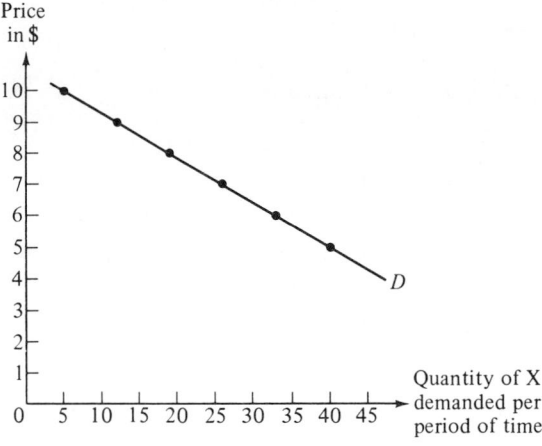

Fig. 3-5   An Illustration of a Consumer's Demand Curve (hypothetical data)

time vary inversely. As P_X rises, the quantity demanded of X falls; or, as P_X falls, the quantity demanded rises. Economists call this relationship the *law of demand*. In truth, this law is pure common sense—*other things remaining equal, a person will be induced to buy more of a commodity per period of time at lower prices than at higher prices*. Additionally, this law is reflected by the negative slope of the demand curve and by the minus sign of the coefficient of P_X in the demand equation. Both of these are indicative of the inverse relationship between product price and the quantity demanded per period of time. On *very* rare occasions, circumstances may combine to cause the quantity demanded to vary *directly* with price, but these exceptions are few indeed.

MARKET DEMAND CURVES

The *market demand curve* for a commodity represents the various amounts of a commodity which consumers as a group are willing and able to purchase at various possible prices at a specific moment of time, wherein other factors influencing consumer behavior are held constant. By summing the quantities of a good that each consumer is willing and able to purchase, we arrive at the market demand curve. Geometrically, the market demand curve can be found by horizontally adding together the individual demand curves for a commodity.

Figure 3-6 illustrates this process for a three-person economy with individual demands as indicated. At a price of P_1 dollars, consumer A is willing and able to buy quantity q_{A_1} per period of time; consumer B is willing and able to buy quantity q_{B_1} per period of time; and consumer C is willing and able to buy quantity q_{C_1} per period of time. Together they are willing and able to buy $q_{A_1} + q_{B_1} + q_{C_1} = Q_1$ units at a price of P_1 dollars as indicated by the market demand curve. Likewise, at price P_2, consumer A is willing and able to purchase q_{A_2}; consumer B is willing and able to purchase q_{B_2}; and con-

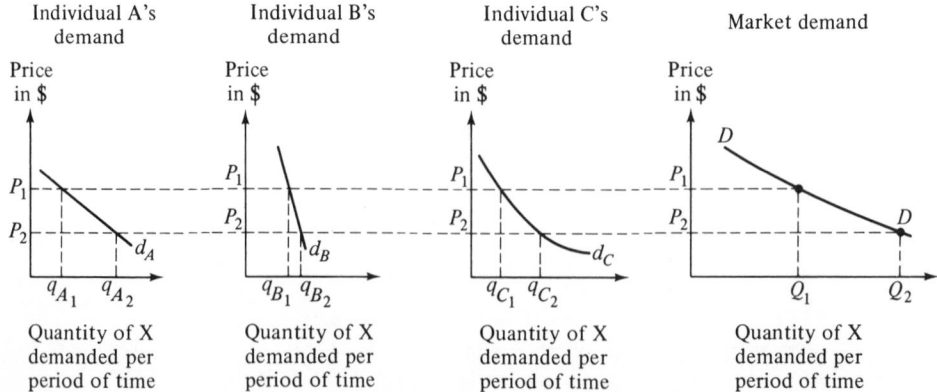

Fig. 3-6 Derivation of the Market Demand Curve for a Commodity for a Three-Person Economy

sumer C is willing and able to purchase q_{C_2}. Taken together, market demand at price P_2 is Q_2 ($= q_{A_2} + q_{B_2} + q_{C_2}$) units. Additional points on the market demand curve can be similarly determined and the market demand curve constructed (line DD in Figure 3-6). Since the individual demand curves are downsloping to the right, the market demand curve must also slope downward to the right. The law of demand holds not only for individual consumer demand but also for market demand.

However, adding together the demand curves of individuals to obtain market demand curves is not entirely satisfactory, since it implies that one consumer's purchases are completely independent of another consumer's. It has, for example, been noted that:

1. People buy goods not so much to satisfy inner wants as to impress other consumers. Thorstein Veblen labled this behavior "conspicuous consumption."
2. The buying habits of some individuals are influenced by the consumption patterns of persons with whom they associate or come into contact. Dusenberry has designated this influence as the "demonstration effect." An example of this effect has been noted in certain neighborhoods regarding the purchase of air conditioners and automobiles.
3. Consumers buy commodities because of the social status they connote. Example of commodities which serve as status symbols include Cadillacs, memberships in exclusive country clubs, diamond necklaces, large homes, fur coats, and original works of fine art.

Consequently, on occasions the amount of a commodity purchased by one consumer has a bearing upon how other consumers behave. The individual demand curves are not therefore independent, and a more complex adding-up process must be used to obtain the market demand curve.

Summary and Conclusions

The utility approach to the analysis of consumer behavior and the formation of individual consumer demand is grounded upon psychological principles. Rational individuals, it is said, will seek to maximize the degree of "pleasure" and minimize the degree of "pain" in choosing among alternative courses of action. In furtherance of this proposition, the concept of utility has evolved into a major tool for analyzing economic behavior. Utility refers to the want-satisfying power of commodities—that is, the amount of satisfaction a consumer receives from consuming various quantities of commodities per period of time.

Although no way currently exists to measure utility precisely, it is analytically useful to pretend it can be measured—this is the foundation upon which the cardinal utility approach to consumer demand is built. Assuming, then, that utility is measurable, a consumer's total and marginal utility functions for a commodity can be represented equally well by tables, graphs, and equations. Marginal utility is defined to be the rate of change in total utility as the rate of consumption of a commodity changes. For each total utility function, there is a corresponding marginal utility function.

Every consumer has his own unique set of total and marginal utility functions; these vary according to his tastes and preferences for different commodities. Moreover, the satisfaction a consumer obtains from one commodity hinges in part upon the amounts consumed of other commodities.

A consumer maximizes the satisfaction he can obtain from his limited money income by meeting two conditions. First, he must fully utilize all of his income, either by spending it on commodities or by saving. Second, he must arrange his purchases so that the marginal utilities per dollar spent on the last unit of each item purchased are equal to each other and to the marginal utility of saving an additional dollar.

It is not likely that many, if any, consumers actually succeed in maximizing satisfaction. Impulsive buying, habit, imperfect knowledge of products and product prices, and the persuasive powers of advertising combine to propel them into purchases with which they may not be fully satisfied.

Extending the conditions of utility maximization permits the derivation of the consumer's demand curve for a commodity. By aggregating the demands of individual consumers, we can obtain the market demand curve for a commodity.

SUGGESTED READINGS

ALCHIAN, A. A., "The Meaning of Utility Measurement," *American Economic Review*, Vol. 43, No. 1 (March 1953), pp. 26–50.

ELLSBURG, D., "Classic and Current Notions of 'Measurable Utility,'" *Economic Journal*, Vol. 64, No. 255 (September 1954), pp. 528–556.

FRIEDMAN, M., and L. J. SAVAGE, "The Utility Analysis of Choices Involving Risk," *Journal of Political Economy* Vol. 56, No. 4 (August 1948), pp. 279–304.

STIGLER, G. J., "The Development of Utility Theory," *Journal of Political Economy*, Vol. 58, Nos. 4 and 5 (August and October, 1950), pp. 307–327 and 373–396.

STROTZ, ROBERT H., "Cardinal Utility," *American Economic Review*, Vol. 43, No. 2 (May 1953), pp. 384–397.

SWALM, RALPH O., "Utility Theory—Insights into Risk-taking,"*Harvard Business Review*, Vol. 44, No. 6 (November-December 1966), pp. 123–136.

VON NEUMANN, JOHN, and OSKAR MORGENSTERN, *The Theory of Games and Economic Behavior*, 3rd ed. (Princeton, N.J.: Princeton University Press, 1953), Chap. 1, Sec. 3, pp. 15–31.

Problems and Questions for Discussion

1. Find the first derivatives of each of the following functions:
   (a) $Y = 124 + 6X$.
   (b) $Y = 15X^2 + 2X^3$.
   (c) $TU_X = 17X - .5X^2$.
   (d) $TU_A = 16A + 5A^2 - .3A^3$.

(e) $TU_B = -185 + 7B + 1.9B^2 - .05B^3$.   (f) $TU_C = .6C^{1/2}$.

(g) $TU_Y = 1.5Y^{.75}$.

[*Ans.*: (a) $\dfrac{dY}{dX} = 6$,   (b) $\dfrac{dY}{dX} = 30X + 6X^2$,   (c) $\dfrac{dTU}{dX} = 17 - X$,

(d) $\dfrac{dTU_A}{dA} = 16 + 10A - .9A^2$,   (e) $\dfrac{dTU_B}{dB} = 7 + 3.8B - .15B^2$,

(f) $\dfrac{dTU_C}{dC} = .3C^{-1/2}$,   (g) $\dfrac{dTU_Y}{dY} = 1.125Y^{-.25}$.]

2. Find the second derivative of each of the following functions (the second derivative is the derivative of the first derivative):

(a) $Y = 124 + 7X^2$.

(b) $TU_X = 9 + 14X - .2X^2$.

(c) $TU_A = 130 + 14A + 15A^2 - .4A^3$.

(d) $TU_B = .6B^{1.5}$.

[*Ans.*: (a) $\dfrac{d^2Y}{dX^2} = 14$,   (b) $\dfrac{d^2TU_X}{dX^2} = -.4$,   (c) $\dfrac{d^2TU_A}{dA^2} = 30 - 2.4A$,

(d) $\dfrac{d^2TU_B}{dB^2} = .45B^{-.5}$.]

3. Explain the nature of the distinguishing features between cardinal and ordinal measures of utility.

4. Adam Smith in *The Wealth of Nations* observed, "Nothing is more useful than water: but it will purchase scarce anything; scarce anything can be had in exchange for it. A diamond, on the contrary, has scarce any value in use; but a very great quantity of other goods may frequently be had in exchange for it."

(a) How do you account for this?

(b) Are the terms "useful" or "usefulness" synonomous with the concept of utility as we have defined it?

5. An individual's total utility function for commodity B is as follows:

$$TU = 18B - .5B^2.$$

(a) Graph the *TU* function and explain the nature of the individual's utility for the product.

(b) Determine the expression for marginal utility and illustrate it graphically.

(c) How much will total utility be at a consumption rate of 10 units? At 15 units?

(d) How much will marginal utility be at a consumption rate of 10 units? At 15 units?

(e) How many units of commodity B can the individual consume and still gain additional satisfaction?

6. An individual's total utility function for commodity Q is as follows:

$$TU = 100Q + 15Q^2 - 2Q^3.$$

(a) Determine the expression for marginal utility.

(b) Graph the total and marginal utility functions and explain the nature of the individual's utility for the product.

(c) How much will total utility be at a consumption rate of 5 units? How much will marginal utility be at 5 units?

(d) At what approximate consumption rate does diminishing *MU* begin?

(e) At what approximate consumption rate does the individual reach saturation for commodity Q?

7. The following table shows the marginal utility, measured in utils of satisfaction, which Mr. Johnson would get by purchasing various amounts of commodities A, B, C, and D, and by saving. The prices of A, B, C, and D are $5, $6, $8, and $20, respectively. Mr. Johnson has a money income of $95 to spend in the current period.

Commodity A		Commodity B		Commodity C		Commodity D		Saving	
Units	*MU*	Units	*MU*	Units	*MU*	Units	*MU*	No. of $ Saved	*MU*
1	31	1	20	1	39	1	50	1	6
2	27	2	19	2	36	2	55	2	5
3	23	3	18	3	33	3	50	3	4
4	19	4	17	4	30	4	45	4	3
5	15	5	16	5	27	5	40	5	2
6	11	6	15	6	24	6	35	6	1
7	7	7	14	7	21	7	30	7	$\frac{1}{2}$

(a) How many units of A, B, C, and D must Mr. Johnson purchase in order to maximize total utility?

(b) How many dollars will Mr. Johnson elect to save?

(c) State algebraically the two conditions for utility maximization and show that your answers to (a) and (b) satisfy these conditions.

8. Given the two conditions requisite for utility maximization, is it likely that a consumer would ever reach his saturation rate for any commodity? Why or why not? Under what circumstances *might* it occur?

9. Dr. Holt has $30 per week available to spend as he wishes on commodities A and B. The prices of A and B, the quantities of A and B he is now buying, and his evaluations of the utility provided by these quantities are as follows:

Commodity	Price	Quantity Bought	Total Utility	*MU* of Last Unit Bought
A	70¢	30 units	500 utils	30 utils
B	50¢	18 units	1000 utils	20 utils

Is Dr. Holt maximizing total utility? If so, *explain why*. If not, what might he do to maximize utility? *Explain* why.

10. Suppose Mr. Pikard has an income of $60 weekly which he is free to spend or save in any way he sees fit. Mr. Pikard believes that *each* dollar he saves gives him 5 utils of satisfaction. This past week, of the thousands of commodities available, Mr. Pikard purchased the following list of items and believes he obtained the indicated degrees of utility from them:

Commodity	Quantity Purchased	Price per Unit	Total Utility	*MU* of Last Unit Bought
A	1 pair	$ 2.50	15 utils	15.0 utils
B	2 jars	.75	16 utils	4.5 utils
C	10 boxes	.50	113 utils	3.0 utils
D	3 pkg.	4.00	248 utils	24.0 utils
E	6 lb.	3.00	618 utils	18.0 utils
F	1 set	15.00	90 utils	90.0 utils

Is it possible, given this information, that Mr. Pikard maximized the total utility he received last week from his $60?

11. Assume that Quentin Roberts' marginal utility for money is 7 utils; that is to say, Mr. Roberts obtains 7 utils of satisfaction for *each* dollar in his possession. Suppose further that his total utility function for commodity A is given by the equation

$$TU = 16.4A - .4A^2.$$

(a) If each unit of A costs $2, how many units should Mr. Roberts purchase in order to maximize total utility?

(b) If the price of commodity A rises to $4, how many units should Mr. Roberts purchase?

4

The Theory of Consumer Demand: The Ordinal Utility Approach

The inability to measure utility in a satisfactory manner was and still is viewed by many economists as a severe limitation of cardinal utility analysis. Out of general dissatisfaction with attempts to instill empirical precision into the concept of utility came the ordinal utility approach to the theory of consumer demand.[1] As will be seen shortly, ordinal utility circumvents the necessity for knowing the quantities of utility; the consumer has only to be able to order or rank the subjective utilities associated with various commodities. Ordinal utility theory is now recognized as both an *alternative* and a *supplement* to the cardinal utility explanation of consumer behavior.[2]

---

[1] Gossen (1854), Jevons (1871), Walras (1874), Edgeworth (1881), Antonelli (1886), Alfred Marshall (1890), and Irving Fisher (1892) were most prominent among the early developers of the concepts of ordinal utility. Vilfredo Pareto, an Italian economist, modified and extended the early versions of ordinal utility theory at the turn of the century. But it was not until the 1930's that John R. Hicks and R. G. D. Allen, two British economists, really popularized ordinal utility analysis and made it a standard component of the economist's toolkit. See, for example, Francis Y. Edgeworth, *Mathematical Psychics* (London: C. K. Paul and Co., 1881); Vilfredo Pareto, *Manuel d'economie politique* (Paris: V. Giard and E. Briere, 1909); and J. R. Hicks and R. G. D. Allen, "A Reconsideration of the Theory of Value," *Economica*, Vol. I (February and May 1934), pp. 52–72, 196–219.

[2] Although the concepts of cardinal and ordinal utility are truly distinct notions, the gap between the two may not be as large as first imagined. Consumers often experience considerable difficulty in deciding which set of commodities they actually prefer. For example, a consumer may have no trouble deciding that he prefers brand X to brand Z and that he prefers brand Y to brand Z, but he may have quite a hard time deciding whether he prefers brand X to brand Y or vice versa. It can then be reliably hypothesized that the cardinal utility difference between the paired comparisons (X, Z) and (Y, Z) is greater than between (X, Y). To put it another way, a consumer may be able to establish an ordinal ranking among three items, X, Y, and Z, ranking X as first, Y as second, and Z as third. Yet it may be quite clear to him that Z is a poor third, while X barely edged out Y for first. Again it can be forcefully argued that the cardinal utility difference between X and Y is much smaller

Neither cardinal nor ordinal utility theory, by itself, is entirely adequate, but taken together they reveal much about patterns of consumer behavior and consumer demand.

THE CONCEPT OF INDIFFERENCE CURVES

The ordinal utility analysis of consumer demand is usually called *indifference-curve* analysis because indifference curves are its primary analytical tool. To understand the origin and meaning of indifference curves, suppose we refocus our attention upon the interrelationships among commodities. As discussed in the preceding chapter, the satisfaction a person derives from consuming one commodity is often related to his rates of consumption of other commodities. In these cases a *total utility surface* describes the relationship between total utility and the rates of consumption of all commodities simultaneously. It is from the total utility surface that the concepts of ordinal utility may be derived.

In Figure 4-1(a) is a typical total utility surface for commodities X and Y, wherein both commodities are deemed desirable by the consumer. Increasing the rates of consumption of X and Y from zero levels produces the total utility surface $OEFG$. Observe that if the consumption of Y is fixed at Y_1 units, then the consumer's total utility from X and Y increases at a decreasing rate along the path $ECAF$ as the consumption of X per unit of time rises from zero to X_1 units. In like manner, whenever the consumption of X is fixed, total utility increases at a decreasing rate as the consumption of Y is increased per period of time.

Suppose we connect all points on the utility surface $OEFG$ which represent a total utility level of CC' (where $CC' = DD'$), thereby obtaining the contour line CD. Thus, all of the points along CD are associated with a specific amount of total utility $CC' = DD'$. Projected vertically downward onto the XY plane, the curve CD traces out the dashed contour line $C'D'$. The contour $C'D'$ defines all of the combinations of commodities X and Y consumed per unit of time that yield the constant amount of total utility $CC' = DD'$. Logically, a consumer would be *indifferent* as to which one of the combinations of X and Y along $C'D'$ he had, since they all yield an equivalent amount of satisfaction.

Following the same procedure, suppose we move up the utility surface to a higher level of total utility, $AA' = BB'$. Connecting all points on the utility surface $OEFG$ with a total utility of $AA' = BB'$ gives the contour line AB. Projecting the image of AB vertically downward onto the XY plane gives the dashed contour line $A'B'$. Any point along AB represents constant total utility of amount $AA' = BB'$, and all combinations of commodities X and Y lying on $A'B'$ yield this amount of total utility. Again, it is reasonable to

---

than between either X and Z or Y and Z. Hence, ordinal utility rankings may permit judgments as to the relative amounts of total utility associated with commodities.

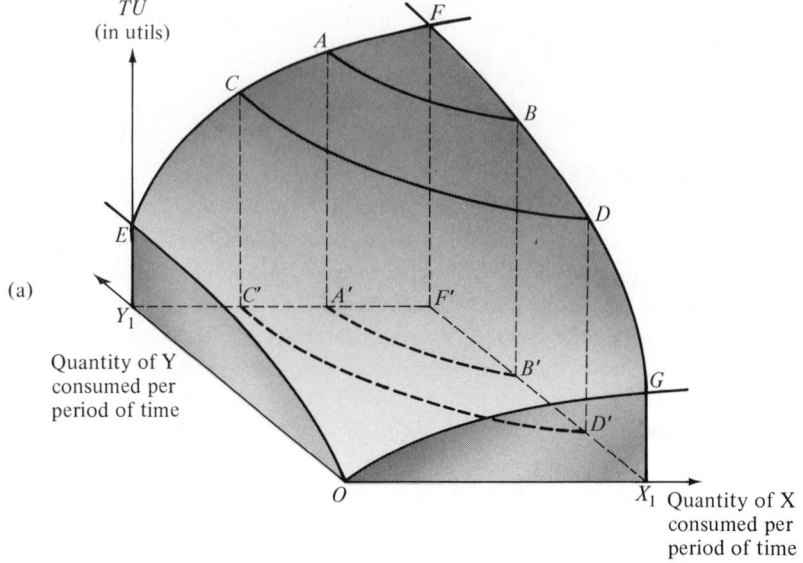

(a)

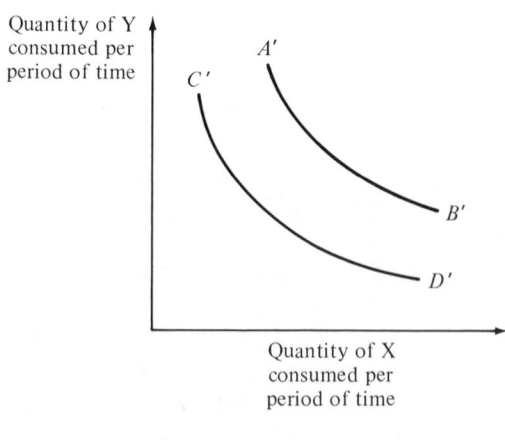

(b)

Fig. 4-1   Derivation of Indifference Curves

conclude that a consumer would be *indifferent* among the combinations of X and Y along $A'B'$ because they all are equally satisfying.

Predictably enough, the contour lines $C'D'$ and $A'B'$ are called *indifference curves*.[3] An indifference curve is the locus of the various combinations of commodities that yield an *equal* amount of satisfaction (total utility) to the consumer, or among which the consumer is indifferent. Figure 4-1(b) illustrates indifference curves $C'D'$ and $A'B'$ in a two-dimensional diagram.

Although a consumer is indifferent as to the various combinations along a particular indifference curve, he is *not* indifferent as to the various combinations between indifference curves. For example, a consumer would prefer *all* combinations of X and Y on $A'B'$ to those combinations on $C'D'$, because the former are associated with a higher total utility ($AA' > CC'$). Greater degrees of total utility are shown by contour lines higher up on the utility surface, lower degrees by lower contour lines. Consequently, in a two-dimensional diagram like Figure 4-1(b), indifference curves lying farther from the origin represent higher levels of satisfaction than do those closer in. Therefore, an indifference curve may additionally be thought of as a boundary between combinations of commodities which a consumer views as less satisfying and those combinations which he views as more satisfying.

There is an indifference curve associated with each distinct degree of total utility on the total utility surface. Thus, indifference curves are "everywhere dense;" that is to say, an indifference curve passes through each point in the XY plane. The family of indifference curves which may be derived from the total utility surface comprises an *indifference map*. The indifference map provides a complete description of a consumer's preferences for various combinations of commodities.

It is important to note that the information provided by an indifference curve says nothing whatsoever about the *amount* of satisfaction produced by the commodity combinations comprising it. In Figure 4-1(b), the total utility attached to $C'D'$ and $A'B'$ could be 10 utils and 20 utils, respectively, or 112 utils and 547 utils, or any other pair of numbers where the size of the second number exceeds the size of the first. The fact that knowledge of the total utility associated with an indifference curve is in no way crucial is the distinctive feature of the indifference curve concept. All that is essential in indifference analysis is for the consumer to know his preferences; he must be able to distinguish whether he prefers one combination of goods to another or whether he views them as equally satisfying.[4] The *amount* by

---

[3] The utility surface in Figure 4-1(a) may be represented mathematically by $TU = f(X, Y)$. The equation for one indifference curve is $TU_1 = f(X, Y)$, where TU_1 is a constant. Other indifference curves may be generated by assigning different values to TU. The family of indifference curves produced by letting TU assume every possible value defines the consumer's indifference map. The values for TU need only reflect the order of consumer preferences; it is not at all imperative that the TU values be cardinal utility (numerical) values.

[4] The consumer must be able to avoid being thrust into a position similar to that of Buridan's ass. The ass, it will be recalled, stood midway between two equally sized bundles of hay, and finally died of hunger because it could not decide which bundle to eat.

which he prefers the combinations on a higher indifference curve to those on a lower indifference curve is of no particular concern. Accordingly, the height of the total utility surface from which indifference curves are derived is inconsequential. In this sense ordinal utility or indifference-curve analysis is free of the need to measure utility.

THE SHAPES OF INDIFFERENCE CURVES

Although the height of the total utility surface is immaterial, its *shape* is not. In fact, the *shape* of the utility surface determines the shape of the indifference curves, thereby describing a consumer's taste and preference pattern. Any set of consumer tastes can be portrayed by indifference curves and utility surfaces. Several examples may be given in support of this statement.

First, consider the taste and preference pattern of an individual who enjoys commodity X immensely but considers commodity Y completely useless. Commodity X might be filet mignon and commodity Y might be tickets to last night's concert performance. Panel (a) of Figure 4-2 displays a utility surface and corresponding indifference map for this situation. Having more of Y neither raises nor lowers total satisfaction (its marginal utility is zero); only commodity X has the power to change the level of total utility. Thus, each indifference curve in the bottom half of Figure 4-2(a) is a vertical line. As the consumption rate of X is increased per unit of time, utility increases; hence on the indifference map higher levels of satisfaction are shown by rightward movement along the *X*-axis.

Panel (b) of Figure 4-2 illustrates a total utility surface and corresponding indifference map for a pair of commodities that are *perfect substitutes*. Commodities are said to be perfect substitutes when their qualities are so similar that a consumer would just as soon have more of one as more of the other. Examples could be nickels and dimes (at a constant ratio of two to one), competing brands of gasoline, or competing brands of many food products—milk, eggs, sugar, and black pepper, for example. The indifference curve is a straight line because the consumer considers perfect substitutes as being absolutely equivalent and is willing, therefore, to substitute one for the other at some *constant* ratio, no matter how much he has of either.

Figure 4-3 is the indifference map for a pair of commodities, X and Y, that have a rigid one-to-one complementary relationship in the mind of the consumer (right and left gloves, a pair of socks, nuts and bolts). Here, each indifference curve is a right angle, because the consumer is no better off having more of just one commodity—more units of one commodity have a marginal utility of zero unless combined with more units of the other commodity. Therefore, total satisfaction can be increased only by having more of both commodities. The nature of the utility surface from which these curves are derived is left as an exercise at the end of this chapter.

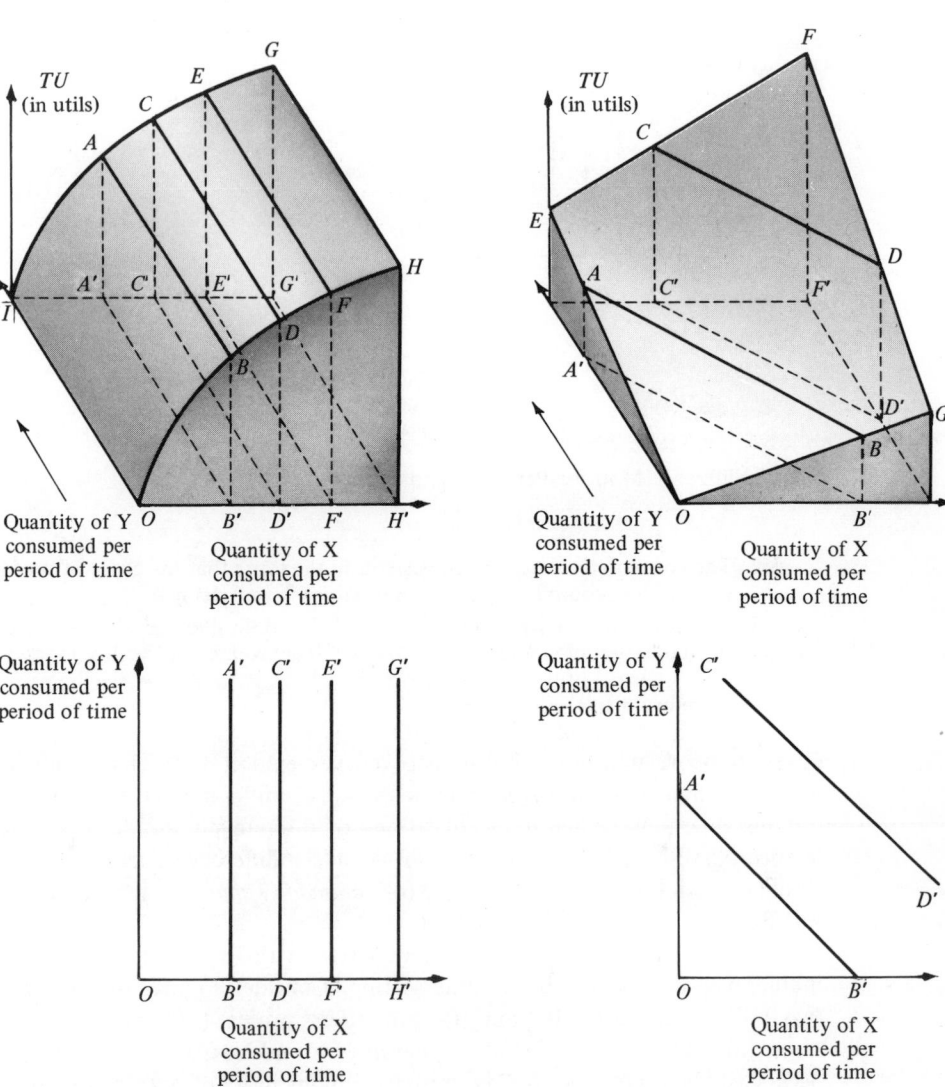

(a)   (b)

Fig. 4-2 Total Utility Surfaces and Indifference Maps for Special Commodities

THE CHARACTERISTICS OF TYPICAL INDIFFERENCE CURVES

In order to simplify the exposition of indifference-curve analysis, it is customary to make three assumptions:

   1. The commodities are continuously divisible into subunits, so that a con-
      sumer is not constrained by the size of the units in which the item is sold.

116

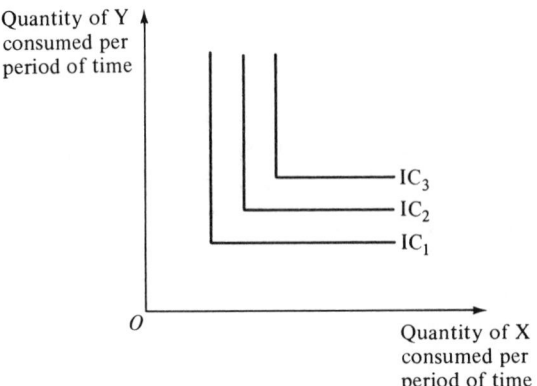

Quantity of Y consumed per period of time

IC_3

IC_2

IC_1

O

Quantity of X consumed per period of time

Fig. 4-3   An Indifference Map for Perfect Complements

2. The consumer's tastes are consistent, in the sense that his order of preference among combinations of commodities is well-defined.

3. The consumer views commodities as being desirable; he always prefers having more of something to having less, which means his marginal utility for additional units is positive. Useless and nuisance items are therefore disregarded.[5]

Given these assumptions, indifference curves exhibit four characteristics. From the first assumption it follows that (a) indifference curves are continuous functions rather than collections of discrete points and (b) indifference curves are "everywhere dense"—some indifference curves will pass through every point in the XY plane (or *commodity space*, as it is sometimes called).

The second assumption, in conjunction with the third, ensures that indifference curves will be nonintersecting. Consider Figure 4-4, in which two indifference curves, IC_1 and IC_2, are shown; points A, B, and C represent three different combinations of commodities X and Y. Combination B must necessarily be preferable to C because it contains more of both commodities (assumption 3). A and C are equally satisfying because they both lie on IC_1; by the same token, A and B are equivalent because they lie on IC_2. If A and C are equivalent and A and B are also equivalent, logical consistency dictates that B and C be equivalent; yet they are not, because combination B contains more of both X and Y than does C. Moreover, it is quite illogical for combination A to produce simultaneously two levels of satisfaction—

[5] It is easy enough to redefine a nuisance commodity to make it a desirable commodity: instead of garbage, the commodity can be called garbage removal; instead of polluted water, the commodity can be defined as clean water.

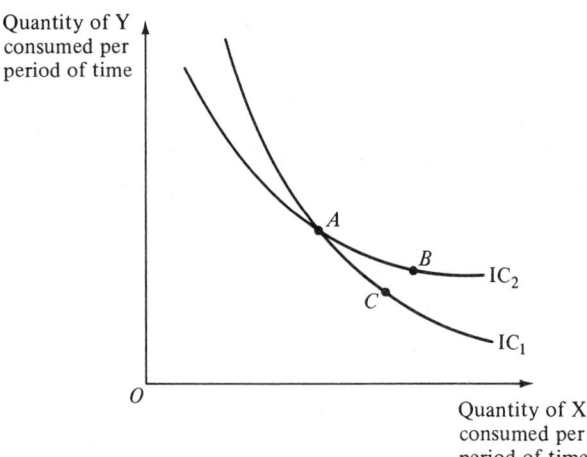

Fig. 4-4 Indifference Curves Do Not Intersect

as would be the case were it to lie on two different indifference curves. Hence, intersecting indifference curves deny the condition of consistency (or transitivity).[6] This is *not* to say, however, that indifference curves must be equidistant from one another. Two indifference curves may or may not be the same distance apart throughout. In many, even most, cases they may be closer together at some points than at others; the only requirement is that they do not intersect.

The third assumption produces the fourth characteristic of indifference curves: they have a negative slope, which is to say they slope downward to the right. Negatively-sloped indifference curves reflect the condition that when a consumer gives up units of one commodity, the loss must be compensated for by his having more of another commodity or else the consumer's satisfaction cannot be maintained constant. Stated differently, a negative slope implies that by having more of one commodity (say X) and by giving up an appropriate amount of another commodity (say Y), the consumer can be made to feel just as well off as originally (when he had less of X and more of Y). By *substituting* one commodity for another in such a way that the gain in satisfaction from consuming more of one is exactly offset by the loss of satisfaction from consuming less of another, we can hold the consumer's overall satisfaction level constant.

[6] In Chapter 2, transitivity was defined as a scale of preference such that if A is preferred to B, and B is preferred to C, then A must be preferred to C. Clearly, transitivity cannot be present if (a) A and B are viewed as equivalent, (b) A and C are viewed as equivalent, and (c) B is preferred to C—as is precisely the situation in Figure 4-4.

THE MARGINAL RATE OF SUBSTITUTION

Except in the case of perfect substitutes and perfect complements, indifference curves for desirable commodities not only slope downward to the right, but they are also *convex* to the origin of the indifference map. We can see the reasons for this convexity in better perspective by introducing the concept of the marginal rate of substitution of one good for another.

The *marginal rate of substitution* (*MRS*) is defined as the rate at which a consumer is willing to exchange some of one commodity for more of another commodity while at the same time maintaining a constant level of satisfaction. Consider the indifference curve shown in Figure 4-5. The consumer is indifferent among combinations $X_1 Y_1$, $X_2 Y_2$, $X_3 Y_3$, $X_4 Y_4$, and $X_5 Y_5$. The horizontal axis is measured so that distances $OX_1 = X_1 X_2 = X_2 X_3 = X_3 X_4 = X_4 X_5 = 1$ unit of X. Starting at combination $X_1 Y_1$ and proceeding down the indifference curve, observe that initially the consumer is willing to give up a considerable amount of Y ($Y_1 Y_2$ units) to get an additional unit of X and yet have just as much satisfaction as before. But as he acquires more and more of X and has less and less of Y left, the amount of Y he is willing to give up to get another unit of X becomes progressively smaller. Hence, economists say that the marginal rate of substitution of X for Y (MRS_{XY}) diminishes as we move *down* an indifference curve. This

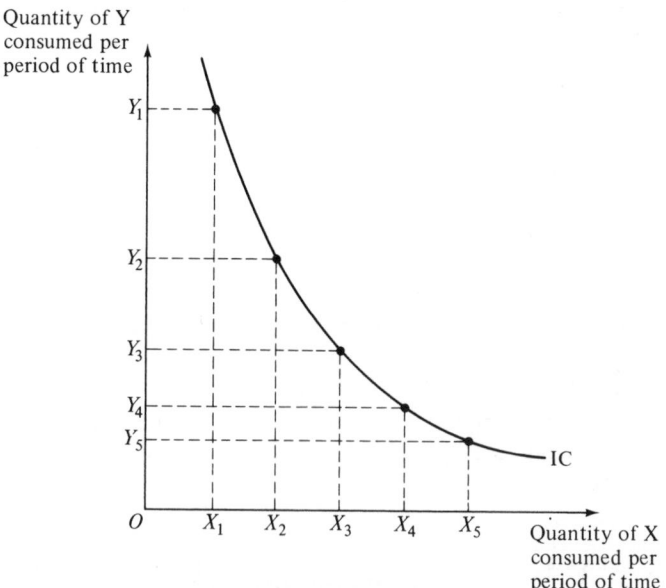

Fig. 4-5   The Marginal Rate of Substitution Along an Indifference Curve

description indicates that the marginal rate of substitution represents the ratio at which a consumer is willing to exchange one commodity for another. Algebraically, this translates into

$$MRS_{XY} = \frac{\Delta Y}{\Delta X},$$

where ΔY represents the number of units of Y the consumer is willing to give up and ΔX represents the number of units of X it will take to compensate the consumer for his loss of Y. The expression $\Delta Y/\Delta X$, therefore, defines the exchange ratio (or the rate of substitution) between Y and X that will precisely maintain the consumer's level of satisfaction. Clearly, this ratio changes as we move along an indifference curve: the ratio becomes smaller as we move down the curve or larger as we move up the curve.

It is also apparent from Figure 4-5 that the consumer is indifferent between combinations $X_1 Y_1$ and $X_2 Y_2$, since both combinations are on the same indifference curve. Accordingly, the consumer would be willing to trade $Y_1 Y_2$ units of Y for $X_1 X_2$ units of X. The marginal rate of substitution of X and Y between these two points is

$$MRS_{XY} = \frac{Y_2 - Y_1}{X_2 - X_1} = \frac{Y_1 Y_2}{X_1 X_2} = \frac{\Delta Y}{\Delta X}.$$

Furthermore, we know that in moving from one point to the other, there is no change in utility. Hence, we can say that the amount of utility "lost" from consuming fewer units of Y is exactly compensated for by the "gain" in utility from consuming more units of X. In more formal terms

$$\underbrace{-\Delta Y \cdot MU_Y}_{} \qquad = \qquad \underbrace{\Delta X \cdot MU_X}_{}$$

"loss" in utility from consuming $Y_1 Y_2$ (or ΔY) fewer units of commodity Y

"gain" in utility from consuming $X_1 X_2$ (or ΔX) units more of commodity X

Dividing both terms of this equality by $\Delta X \cdot MU_y$ gives

$$\frac{-\Delta Y \cdot MU_Y}{\Delta X \cdot MU_Y} = \frac{\Delta X \cdot MU_X}{\Delta X \cdot MU_Y},$$

which reduces to

$$-\frac{\Delta Y}{\Delta X} = \frac{MU_X}{MU_Y} \quad \text{or} \quad \frac{\Delta Y}{\Delta X} = -\frac{MU_X}{MU_Y}.$$

But since $MRS_{XY} = \Delta Y/\Delta X$, then we have

$$MRS_{XY} = \frac{\Delta Y}{\Delta X} = -\frac{MU_X}{MU_Y},$$

which says that the marginal rate of substitution of X and Y is equal to the ratio of MU_X to MU_Y. This expression for MRS_{XY} holds true for any two points on an indifference curve. The negative sign in the expression reflects the fact that having more of one commodity (X) entails having less of the other commodity (Y). Furthermore, it follows that if any two points on a given indifference curve become so close together that they are really one point, then the marginal rate of substitution of X for Y equals the slope of the indifference curve at that point.

To summarize, the marginal rate of substitution of X for Y is a measure of the rate at which a consumer is willing to give up some of commodity Y in order to get more of commodity X, all the while maintaining a constant level of satisfaction. The marginal rate of substitution is defined by the expression

$$MRS_{XY} = \frac{\Delta Y}{\Delta X} = (-) \frac{MU_X}{MU_Y},$$

and is numerically equal to the slope of the indifference curve. Its value decreases as one proceeds down along an indifference curve. The marginal rate of substitution is meaningful only for movements along an indifference curve, never for movements among curves.

One final point deserves examination: why is it that marginal rate of substitution diminishes as X is substituted for Y in such a way as to leave the consumer on the same indifference curve? One explanation for diminishing MRS_{XY} is that as we move down an indifference curve, the remaining units of Y become dearer and the additional units of X yield smaller amounts of extra satisfaction; i.e., the marginal utility of the remaining units of Y rises, whereas the marginal utility of additional units of X decreases. This argument, although quite plausible—since a state of diminishing marginal utility for X and Y is fairly normal—is not always sufficient. When the utility derived from commodity Y is partially dependent on the amount consumed of X, increasing the consumption of X may decrease the marginal utility from Y and spoil the argument. Fortunately, more powerful evidence for convexity exists. It has, for example, been proven that if the consumer buys some of each of two commodities, his indifference curves must be convex to the origin; otherwise only one of the commodities would be bought.

THE LINE OF ATTAINABLE COMBINATIONS

A consumer's indifference map indicates his subjective attitudes toward various combinations of commodities. It shows what combinations are preferred to others and the rates at which he is willing to substitute one commodity for another. However, the extent to which the consumer is *able* to satisfy these tastes and preferences hinges upon his money income and the respective prices of the commodities he is desirous of consuming.

For the sake of simplicity and convenience, suppose we continue to restrict ourselves to a situation where there are just two commodities, X and Y, with prices of P_x and P_y. As we saw in the previous chapter, the consumer's money income is fixed in the short run; he has only so much to spend per period of time. Let this amount of income be designated as I.

The consumer's total expenditure on commodity X is equal to the selling price (P_x) times the amount purchased (X) or $P_x X$; similarly, the consumer's total expenditure on commodity Y is $P_Y Y$. The sum of the consumer's expenditures for X and Y must be equal to or less than his income I. Thus we may write

$$P_X X + P_Y Y \leq I.$$

If the consumer elects to spend all of his income on X and Y and save nothing, then

$$P_X X + P_Y Y = I.$$

Otherwise, saving accounts for the margin of difference between the consumer's total expenditures on X and Y and his money income I.

Suppose the consumer's money income is \$50, $P_x = \$5$, and $P_Y = \$2$. Should the consumer decide to spend the entire \$50 on commodity X, he could buy a maximum of 10 units (I/P_x); or should he decide to spend the entire \$50 on Y, he could buy as much as 25 units (I/P_Y). These combinations are illustrated in Figure 4-6. A straight line joining these two points on the graph shows *all* of the other combinations of X and Y that the consumer's

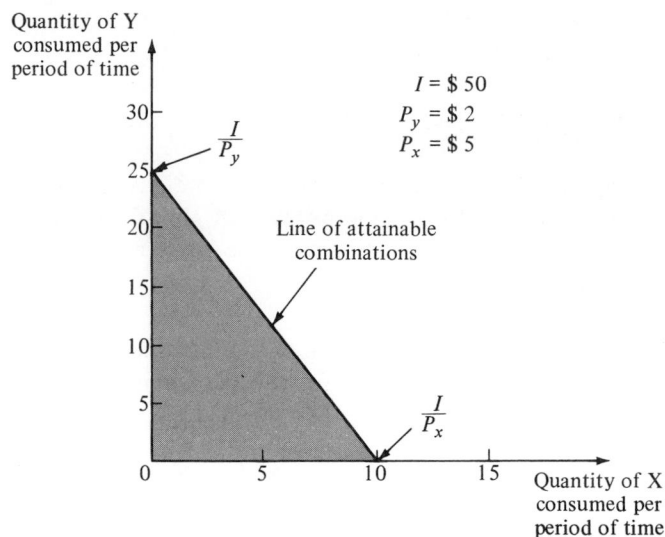

Fig. 4-6   The Line of Attainable Combinations

income will allow him to purchase at these prices. This line is called the *line of attainable combinations* because it represents the locus of combinations of X and Y which can be purchased when the consumer spends his entire money income.[7] The consumer can also buy any of the combinations of X and Y inside the line (the shaded area); however, if he does so, he will not be spending all of his income and will have money left over for saving (or for spending on other commodities). The equation of the line of attainable combinations in Figure 4-6 is

$$\$5X + \$2Y = \$50,$$

where $\$5$ = the price of commodity X,
$\$2$ = the price of commodity Y, and
$\$50$ = the consumer's money income.

The set of values for X and Y which satisfy this equation are given by the points comprising the line of attainable combinations. In drawing the line as a continuous function we continue our assumption of the preceding sections that commodities X and Y are perfectly divisible into subunits and can be purchased in any quantity.

The general equation for the line of attainable combinations in a two-commodity economy is

$$P_X X + P_Y Y = I.$$

For *n* number of commodities and where saving is indicated as a separate activity, the general equation of the line of attainable combinations may be written as

$$P_{X_a} X_a + P_{X_b} X_b + P_{X_c} X_c + \cdots + P_{X_n} X_n + \text{Saving} = I,$$

where I = money income and $P_{X_a}, P_{X_b}, P_{X_c}, \ldots, P_{X_n}$ are the prices of commodities $X_a, X_b, X_c, \ldots, X_n$.

The slope of the line of attainable combinations is negative and is numerically equal to the ratio of the prices of X and Y. This is easily verified by considering the slope of the line in Figure 4-6 between the two extreme points I/P_X and I/P_Y:

$$\frac{\text{slope of the line}}{\text{of attainable combinations}} = \frac{\text{change in the quantity of Y}}{\text{change in the quantity of X}} = \frac{-\dfrac{I}{P_Y}}{\dfrac{I}{P_X}}$$

$$= -\frac{I}{P_Y} \cdot \frac{P_X}{I} = -\frac{P_X}{P_Y}.$$

[7] In the literature of indifference-curve analysis the line of attainable combinations is known variously as the budget line, the price line, the budget restraint, the expenditure line, the price-income line, and the consumption possibility line.

To use the values of I, P_X and P_Y in our numerical example, the slope of the line of attainable combinations in Figure 4-6 is

$$\text{slope} = \frac{\dfrac{I}{P_Y}}{\dfrac{I}{P_X}} = \frac{-\dfrac{50}{2}}{\dfrac{50}{5}} = -\frac{50}{2} \cdot \frac{5}{50} = -\frac{5}{2} = -2.5.$$

Essentially, the value of -2.5 means that with $P_X = \$5$ and $P_Y = \$2$, the consumer must give up $2\frac{1}{2}$ units of Y in order to acquire the $5 needed to purchase an additional unit of X. This ratio remains constant at -2.5 no matter how much of X and Y are purchased, so long as the prices of X and Y remain fixed at $5 and $2, respectively. Thus, the line of attainable combinations is defined as a linear, negatively-sloped function with the general equation of $P_X X + P_Y Y = I$, given constant commodity prices.[8]

SHIFTS IN THE LINE OF ATTAINABLE COMBINATIONS

In forthcoming sections we will be concerned with the impact that changes in money income and in commodity prices have upon consumer purchases. Changes in money income and prices are graphically portrayed by shifts in the position of the line of attainable combinations.

Consider first the effect of an increase in money income from I_1 to I_2 when the prices of X and Y remain constant at P_{X_1} and P_{Y_1}. The larger money income permits the consumer to purchase more of X, more of Y, or more of both. The maximum amount of X which can be purchased increases from I_1/P_{X_1} to I_2/P_{X_1}, as shown in Figure 4-7(a). The maximum purchase level of Y rises from I_1/P_{Y_1} to I_2/P_{Y_2}. Since the prices of X and Y are fixed, the slope of the new line of attainable combinations must be identical to the slope at an income of I_1, and it must pass through points I_2/P_{X_1} and I_2/P_{Y_1}. Thus an increase in money income from I_1 to I_2, commodity prices remaining constant, is shown graphically by a parallel shift in the line of attainable combinations upward and to the right. Likewise, another increase in income (to I_3) will shift the line parallelwise even further outward. Conversely, it follows that decreases in money income can be represented by parallel shifts in the line downward and to the left.

Figure 4-7(b) displays the change in the line of attainable combinations when the price of X decreases, the price of Y (P_{Y_1}) and money income (I_1) remaining unchanged. Since I_1 and P_{Y_1} do not change, the maximum quantity

---

[8] Normally the amount an individual consumer buys of a commodity is so small relative to the total amount bought that the price of it can reasonably be anticipated to remain constant irrespective of the amount purchased. Thus, a linear line of attainable combinations may be considered typical. However, if by chance the prices of X and Y depend on the amounts the consumer buys, then the line of attainable combinations becomes curvilinear. When commodity prices fall as the consumer buys more of them, the line of attainable combinations is bowed in or convex towards the origin. When commodity prices rise with increasing purchase levels, then the line is bowed out or concave towards the origin.

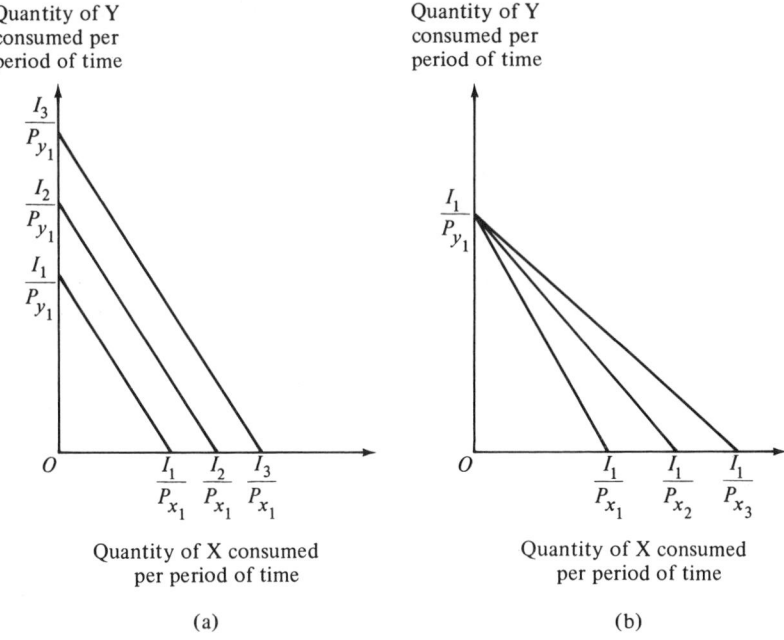

Fig. 4-7   Shifts in the Line of Attainable Combinations

of Y which may be purchased (I_1/P_{Y_1}) is unaffected by any change in P_X. As the price of X declines from P_{X_1} to P_{X_2}, the maximum quantity of X which can be purchased with I_1 is raised from its original value of I_1/P_{X_1} to I_1/P_{X_2}. Accordingly, the line of attainable combinations becomes flatter and rotates to the right about the point I_1/P_{Y_1}. Should the price of X decline to P_{X_3}, the line of attainable combinations rotates rightward even more. In contrast, to represent increases in the price of X the line of attainable combinations is rotated to the left around the point I_1/P_{Y_1}, causing the new line to be more steeply sloped. These changes in the slope of the line follow directly from our finding that the slope of the line of attainable combinations is $-P_X/P_Y$. Clearly, if P_Y is fixed and P_X falls, the slope of the line becomes smaller (or flatter); and when P_X rises, the slope of the line becomes larger (or steeper).

MAXIMIZATION OF SATISFACTION

Granting the validity of the postulate that a rational consumer seeks to obtain the maximum degree of satisfaction from his money income, the consumer's decision problem is to select from among all of the various possible commodities that particular combination which he perceives to be the

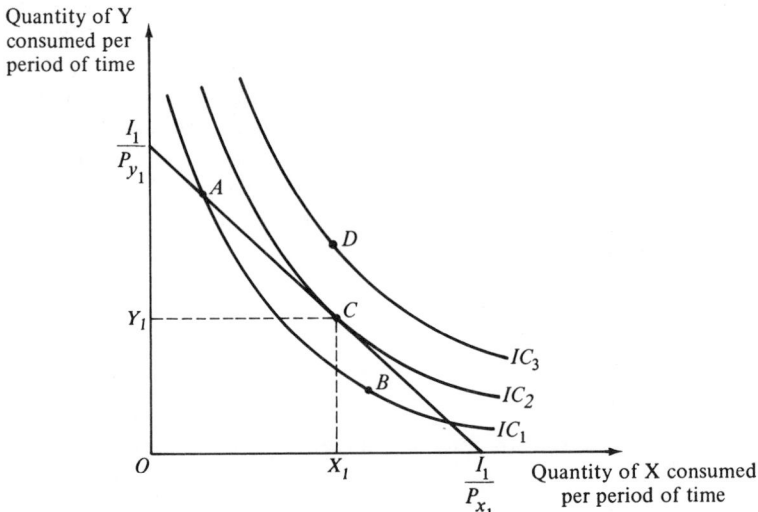

Fig. 4-8   Maximization of Satisfaction

most satisfying. The consumer's indifference map provides a diagrammatic representation of his tastes and preferences—that is to say, his subjective evaluation of the intensity of his desire for different commodity combinations. The consumer's ability to satisfy his material impulses is reflected by the line of attainable combinations. Putting these two concepts together gives the insight into the consumer's decision problem requisite for pinpointing that allocation of the consumer's income which will maximize his satisfaction.

In Figure 4-8, the most satisfying combination among all those which can be purchased is at point C, where the consumer buys X_1 units of X and Y_1 units of Y. Combinations A and B, while attainable, are on a lower indifference curve from C and hence entail lower degrees of satisfaction. Combination D is superior to C, but it costs more than the consumer can afford and therefore must be eliminated from consideration. Indifference curve IC_2 is the highest possible indifference curve which can be reached given the consumer's income constraint, and combination C is the only obtainable combination on that curve. Consequently, C represents the *most preferred* combination of X and Y and may be said to represent *consumer equilibrium. Satisfaction is maximized at the point of tangency between the line of attainable combinations and an indifference curve, provided the commodities in question are desirable.*

It is relevant to ask at this point: what are the conditions for maximizing satisfaction via indifference-curve analysis? First, we may note that the equilibrium combination of X and Y lies *on* the line of attainable combinations, rather than to the inside. This means that the consumer must *fully utilize* his available income to maximize satisfaction. Such a requirement does not preclude saving, since saving may appropriately be considered as a commodity available for "purchase" by the consumer.

Second, at the equilibrium point the slope of the indifference curve is precisely equal to the slope of the line of attainable combinations. This necessarily results from their being tangent at this point. As shown earlier, the respective slopes can be expressed as

$$\text{slope of an indifference curve} = MRS_{XY}$$

$$= (-)\frac{MU_X}{MU_Y},$$

$$\text{slope of the line of attainable combinations} = (-)\frac{P_X}{P_Y}.$$

Consequently, the second condition for maximizing satisfaction requires the consumer to so allocate his available money income that the marginal rate of substitution of X for Y be equal to the ratio of the price of X to the price of Y. The interpretation of this condition is straight forward. The MRS_{XY} defines the *rate* at which the consumer is *willing to exchange* X and Y. The price ratio (P_X/P_Y) shows the *rate* at which the consumer *can exchange* X and Y. Unless the two rates are equivalent, it is possible for the consumer to alter his purchases of X and Y and achieve a greater degree of satisfaction. For example, suppose the $MRS_{XY} = (-)4$, meaning that the consumer is willing to give up 4 units of Y in order to get 1 more unit of X. If $P_X = \$6$ and $P_Y = \$2$, then the consumer need only give up 3 units of Y at \$2 each to obtain the \$6 he needs to buy another unit of X. Clearly, the consumer can benefit by exchanging Y for X, since his preference for X and Y at this level is such that he is willing to trade off 4 units of Y for 1 unit of X, but he only has to give up 3 units of Y to get 1 more unit of X. In general terms, therefore, consumer maximization of satisfaction requires equality between the marginal rate of substitution for any pair of commodities and the ratio of their prices; otherwise, some exchange can be made which will increase the consumer's overall level of satisfaction.

However, the income allocation that will maximize consumer satisfaction can be approached from a more familiar angle. Not only is the slope of the indifference curve equal to the MRS_{XY} at any point, but it is also equal to the ratio of the marginal utilities (ordinally interpreted) of the two commodities:

$$MRS_{XY} = (-)\frac{MU_X}{MU_Y}.$$

Thus we may write the second condition for maximizing satisfaction as

$$(-)\frac{MU_X}{MU_Y} = (-)\frac{P_X}{P_Y}.$$

This equation states that the consumer's income should be allocated so as to equate the ratio of the marginal utilities with the ratio of the commodity prices. Rewriting this last expression, we get

$$MU_X \cdot P_Y = MU_Y \cdot P_X.$$

Dividing each term by $P_X \cdot P_Y$ yields

$$\frac{MU_X \cdot P_Y}{P_X \cdot P_Y} = \frac{MU_Y \cdot P_X}{P_X \cdot P_Y},$$

which reduces to

$$\frac{MU_X}{P_X} = \frac{MU_Y}{P_Y}.$$

In an n-commodity economy, this latter expression expands to

$$\frac{MU_{X_a}}{P_{X_a}} = \frac{MU_{X_b}}{P_{X_b}} = \frac{MU_{X_c}}{P_{X_c}} = \cdots = \frac{MU_{X_n}}{P_{X_n}} = MU_{\text{saving}},$$

which, combined with the requirement for full utilization of the consumer's income, yields exactly the same conditions imposed upon the maximization of consumer satisfaction via the cardinal utility approach. There is one important distinction: we reached these same conditions *without* the necessity for quantifying utility or satisfaction.

THE IMPACT OF INCOME CHANGES UPON CONSUMER EQUILIBRIUM

Consumers typically respond to changes in their money incomes by altering the amounts of commodities they purchase. Suppose we trace the impact of a change in an individual consumer's money income upon his commodity purchases, assuming that commodity prices and the consumer's preference pattern remain unchanged.

Given the price of X at P_{X_1}, and the price of Y at P_{Y_1}, the consumer's equilibrium purchase level at an income of I_1 is shown in Figure 4-9 as point A on indifference curve IC_1, where he buys X_1 units of X and Y_1 units of Y. If the consumer's money income rises to I_2, the prices of X and Y remaining unchanged, the line of attainable combinations shifts in parallel fashion upward and to the right. The higher income level allows the consumer to

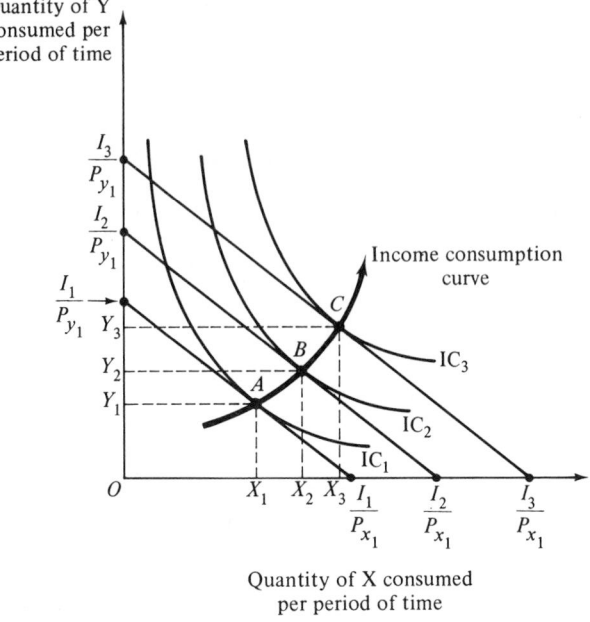

Fig. 4-9   The Impact of Income Changes Upon Consumer Equilibrium

buy more of X, or more of Y, or more of both. According to the preference pattern reflected by the shapes of his indifference curves, an increase in his money income to I_2 will result in equilibrium purchases of X_2 units of X and Y_2 units of Y at point B on indifference curve IC_2. This is a more satisfying combination of X and Y than was permitted by an income of I_1, because it lies on a higher indifference curve. The consumer would realize a further gain in satisfaction should his money income rise to I_3, thereby allowing him to reach point C on indifference curve IC_3 and to purchase X_3 units of X and Y_3 units of Y. The line joining the points of consumer equilibrium as income changes is called the *income consumption curve*. The income consumption curve is the locus of utility-maximizing combinations of commodities associated with various levels of money income and constant commodity prices.

When the resulting income consumption curve is positively-sloped, then the commodities are *normal goods*, meaning that more of both goods are purchased at higher levels of income than at lower levels. Such is not always the case. Some commodities, designated as *inferior goods*, are purchased in smaller amounts when income rises, in which case the income consumption curve is negatively-sloped, as in Figure 4-10. From Figure 4-10 it can be seen that as income rises from I_1 to I_2 to I_3, the equilibrium purchases of Y fall from Y_1 to Y_2 to Y_3. Hence, commodity Y is an inferior good; commodity

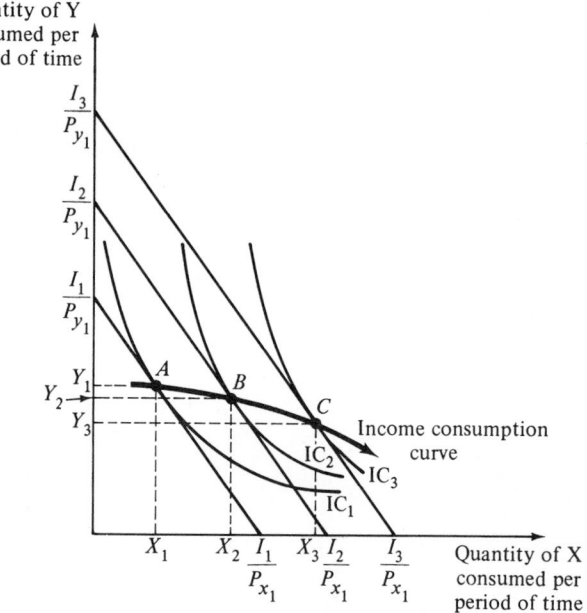

Fig. 4-10   An Income Consumption Curve for an Inferior Good

X, however, is a normal good, because its purchase level rises from X_1 to X_2 to X_3 as income rises from I_1 to I_2 to I_3. Examples of goods which many consumers view as inferior include bologna, dried beans, chewing tobacco, used clothing, recapped automobile tires, black and white camera film, economy or budget-priced durable goods, reconditioned shock-absorbers, and used textbooks.

ENGEL CURVES

The information provided by the income consumption curve may be used to derive *Engel curves* for each commodity.[9] Engel curves show the equilibrium (utility-maximizing) quantities of a commodity which a consumer will purchase at various levels of income, other things remaining equal.

An Engel curve for commodity X is constructed in Figure 4-11. From Figure 4-11(a), we can see that at an income level of I_1 the consumer's equilibrium purchase level is X_1 units of commodity X. The values of I_1 and X_1 are plotted as point A in Figure 4-11(b). Again from Figure 4-11(a), we see that when money income is I_2, the consumer will purchase quantity X_2; these values form point B. In like manner, point C corresponds to a money

[9] Engel curves are named for Christian Lorenz Ernest Engel, a nineteenth-century German statistician who was a pioneer in the study of consumer budgets.

income of I_3 and the resulting equilibrium purchase of X_3 units of X; and point D is formed from an income of I_4 and the related purchase of X_4 units of X. Connecting points A, B, C, and D gives the Engel curve relating purchases of X to changes in money income.

Three frequently encountered shapes of Engel curves are shown in Figure 4-12. An Engel curve of the shape in Figure 4-12(a) indicates that as the consumer's money income increases from very low levels, his consumption of the commodity rises rapidly at first. However, as his income continues to increase, his purchases begin to rise ever more gradually, becoming

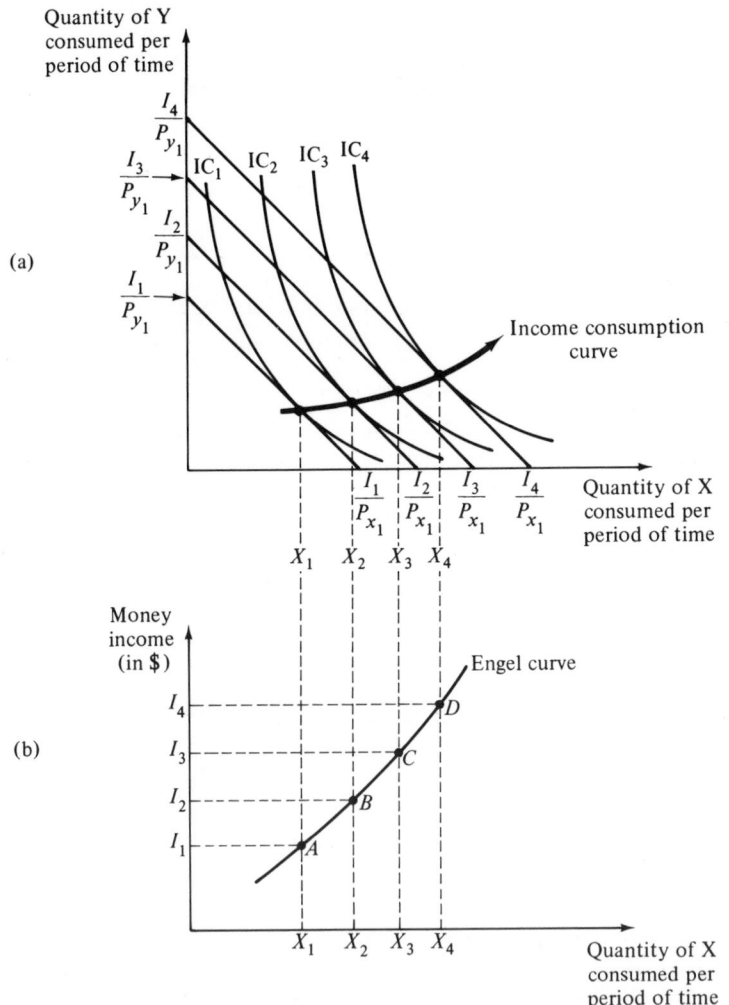

Fig. 4-11   Derivation of an Engel Curve From an Income Consumption Curve

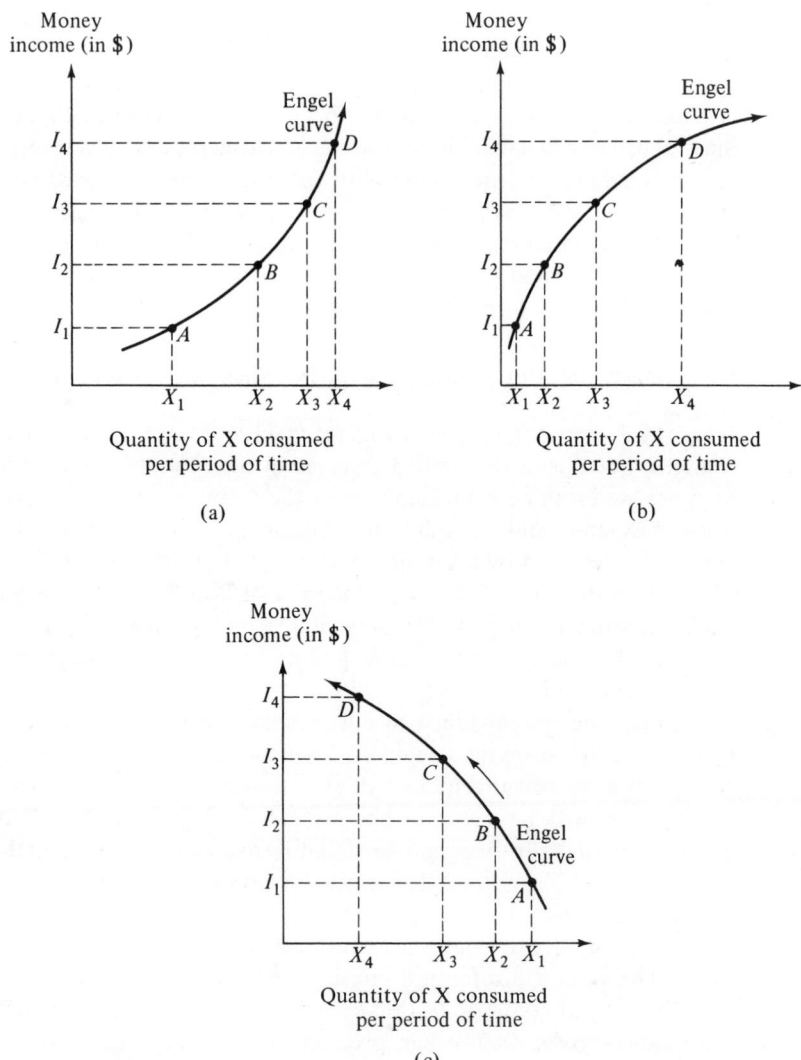

Fig. 4-12   Types of Engel Curves

less than proportional to the gains in money income. Although more of the commodity continues to be bought as income rises, additional purchases become increasingly less sensitive to further gains in income. This sort of consumption pattern causes the Engel curve to become more steeply sloped at higher and higher levels of income. Real-world examples of such commodities abound: newspapers, grain products, fuel, expenditures on food, and many types of basic "necessities."

For other items, the consumer's expenditures expand more rapidly than does income. Figure 4-12(b) illustrates this type of situation. Observe that here the Engel curve increases at a decreasing rate [in contrast to increasing at an increasing rate, as does the Engel curve in Figure 4-12(a)]. Such consumer behavior is indicative of an increasing degree of sensitivity in the purchases of the commodity to income changes; examples include restaurant meals, steak, recreation activities, travel, educational activities, medical care, "luxuries," and saving. Figure 4-12(c) shows an Engel curve for an inferior good; purchases of X decline from X_1 to X_2 to X_3 to X_4 units per period of time as income rises from I_1 to I_2 to I_3 to I_4 dollars.

THE IMPACT OF PRICE CHANGES UPON CONSUMER EQUILIBRIUM

Not only do consumers typically adapt their consumption patterns to income changes, but they also react to changes in the price of goods and services. Suppose we examine what happens to the quantity of X when we vary the price of X and hold constant the consumer's income, his tastes and preferences (as reflected by his indifference map), and the price of Y.

Given the price of X at P_{X_1}, the price of Y at P_{Y_1}, and money income at I_1, the consumer will maximize satisfaction by purchasing X_1 units of X and Y_1 units of Y, as shown in Figure 4-13(a). Now suppose the price of X falls to P_{X_2}; the line of attainable combinations will pivot to the right about point I_1/P_{Y_1} allowing the consumer to purchase as much as I_1/P_{X_2} units of X were he to spend his entire income on X. The new line of attainable combinations will necessarily be tangent to a higher indifference curve than previously. Equilibrium will be reestablished by purchasing quantity X_2 of X and quantity Y_2 of Y. In like manner it can be ascertained that a further decline in the price of X to P_{X_3} will permit the consumer to reach an even higher indifference curve, maximizing satisfaction at X_3 and Y_3. The line joining the various points of consumer equilibrium is called the *price consumption curve*. The price consumption curve is the locus of the utility-maximizing combinations of commodities that result from variations in the price of one commodity, given that other product prices, the consumer's tastes and preferences, and his money income are held constant.

The *demand curve* of the individual consumer for commodity X can be derived directly from the information contained in the price consumption curve. A consumer's demand curve for a commodity graphically illustrates the different amounts which he is willing and able to buy at various possible prices during some moment of time wherein all other factors influencing the quantity purchased are held constant. From Figure 4-13(a) it can be seen that when the price of X is P_{X_1}, the consumer's equilibrium purchase is quantity X_1 of X. This establishes one point on his demand curve for commodity X, shown as point A in Figure 4-13(b). At the lower price of P_{X_2}

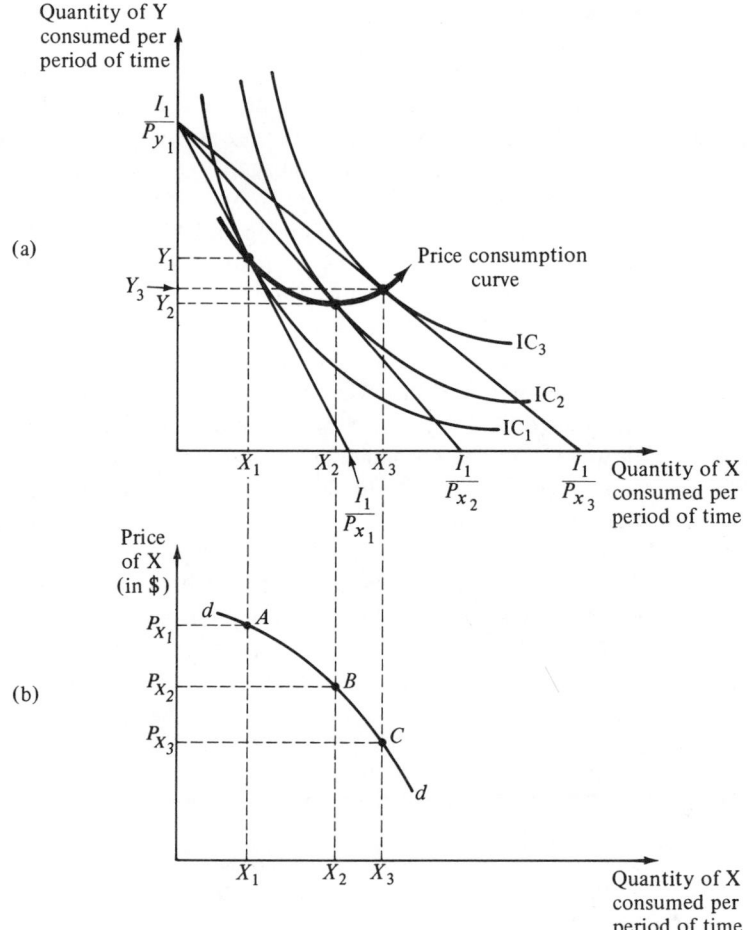

Fig. 4-13   The Price Consumption Curve and the Consumer's Demand Curve

the consumer's purchases rise to X_2 units; this becomes a second point on the demand curve for commodity X [point B in Figure 4-13(b)]. At the still lower price of P_{x_3} the consumer buys X_3 units of X, which gives a third point on his demand curve [point C in Figure 4-13(b)]. Other points on the demand curve can be derived in analogous fashion, thereby producing the demand curve—line dd in Figure 4-13(b). Again, we find that the consumer's demand curve for a commodity slopes downward to the right; there exists an inverse relationship between the price of a commodity and the corresponding quantity purchased—the *law of demand* is upheld by the ordinal utility approach to consumer demand as well as by the cardinal utility approach.

THE INCOME AND SUBSTITUTION EFFECTS

When the price of a commodity changes, other factors remaining constant, two forces are activated to cause the consumer to alter his purchase level of the commodity. One, a decrease in price increases the consumer's real income (purchasing power), thus enhancing his ability to buy more of all commodities to some extent. Two, a decrease in the price of a commodity induces some consumers to substitute it for other now relatively higher-priced items. Indifference-curve analysis enables us to readily measure the potence of both the income effect and the substitution effect.

Consider Figure 4-14. The consumer's money income is I_1, and the price of Y is P_{Y_1}. If the price of X initially is P_{X_1}, then the original equilibrium is at point A on indifference curve IC_1, where the consumer buys X_1 units of X. When the price of X decreases to P_{X_2}, the line of attainable combinations rotates rightward, and the consumer moves to a new equilibrium position at B on indifference curve IC_2. Here he purchases quantity X_2 of X. Suppose we designate the overall change in the quantity demanded of X from the first equilibrium point at A to the second equilibrium point at B as the *total effect* of the price change. It is the associated change in X from X_1 to X_2 that we seek to decompose into the substitution effect and the income effect.

Let us first isolate the substitution effect and determine its magnitude. The decline in the price of X precipitates an increase in the consumer's real

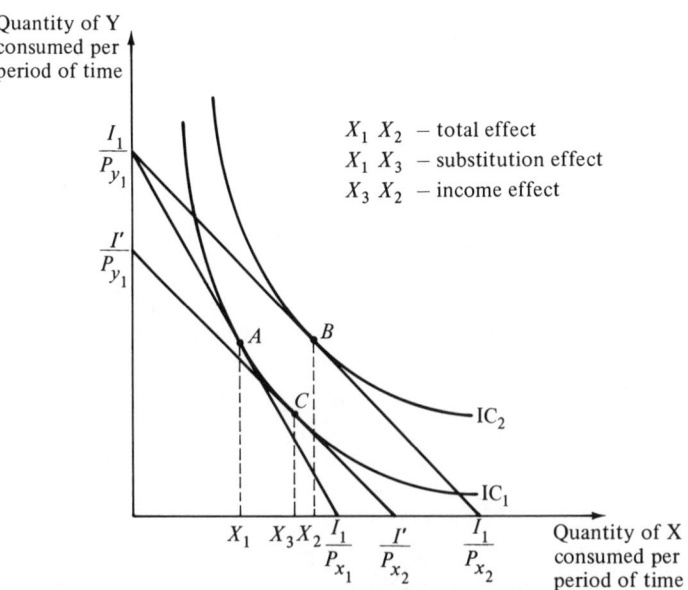

Fig. 4-14 The Income and Substitution Effects for a Normal Good in the Case of a Price Decline

income, as evidenced by the movement to a higher indifference curve even though money income remains fixed. Now imagine that we decrease the consumer's income by an amount just sufficient to return him to the same level of satisfaction he enjoyed before the price decline. Graphically this is accomplished by drawing a fictitious line of attainable combinations with a slope corresponding to the *new* ratio of the commodity prices (P_{X_2}/P_{Y_1}) so that it is just tangent to the original indifference curve (IC_1). This produces the line in Figure 4-14 with extreme points I'/P_{Y_1} and I'/P_{X_2} which is tangent to IC_1 at point C.

Combination C is equally as satisfying as combination A because they both lie on the same indifference curve. Yet, given the decline in the price of X from P_{X_1} to P_{X_2}, the consumer would prefer combination C to combination A, as it is cheaper. The sole reason for the consumer's preference for C over A is the lowering of the price of X; this induces the consumer to increase his consumption of X and cut his consumption of Y—i.e., to substitute X for Y. Hence the increase in the consumption of X from X_1 to X_3 is the substitution effect, and it is represented by a movement along the original indifference curve IC_1 from point A to the imaginary intermediate equilibrium at point C. Accordingly, the *substitution effect may be defined as the change in the quantity demanded of a commodity resulting from a change in its price when the consumer's real income is held constant, thereby restricting the consumer's reaction to the price change to a movement along the original indifference curve.*

The income effect is determined by observing the change in the quantity demanded of a commodity that is associated solely with the change in the consumer's *real* income. In Figure 4-14, letting the consumer's real income rise from its imaginary level (defined by the line of attainable combinations tangent to point C) back to its true level (defined by the line of attainable combinations tangent to point B) gives the income effect. Thus the income effect is indicated by the movement from the imaginary equilibrium at point C to the actual new equilibrium at point B; the increase in the quantity of X purchased from X_3 to X_2 is the income effect. Formally, the *income effect may be defined as the change in the quantity demanded of a commodity exclusively associated with a change in real income, commodity prices and money income being held constant.*

Comparatively speaking, the magnitude of the substitution effect is usually greater than that of the income effect. Ordinarily the change in the consumer's real income resulting from changes in the price of one commodity is indeed slight and provides little room for the consumer to alter the quantities of commodities he purchases.[10] However, when commodities are easily

---

[10] For instance, if a consumer with an annual income of $10,000 finds that the price of a good he buys once a month has declined in price from 73 cents to 69 cents, then the consumer's real income has increased—but ever so slightly. The 48 cents which he saves on the purchase of the good over the period of a year does technically increase the consumer's real income, but it scarcely is sufficient to cause even a minor realignment in his purchases.

substituted for one another, a change in the price of one does provide the consumer with a strong motivation for substitution, and a relatively large substitution effect may result.

Usually the income and substitution effects reinforce one another; that is, they operate in the same direction. A *lower* price for a commodity results in an *increase* in its quantity demanded due to the substitution effect and an *increase* in its quantity demanded due to the income effect. As Figure 4-15 illustrates, when the price of a commodity *rises*, the substitution effect will bring about a *decrease* in quantity demanded and the income effect likewise will bring about a *decrease* in quantity demanded. Note that in the event of either a price decrease or a price increase (Figures 4-14 and 4-15, respectively), the quantity demanded of a commodity varies inversely with its price—the law of demand is operative. Second, note that in either event, the change in quantity demanded stemming from the income effect moves in the *same* direction as the change in real income—if real income rises, the quantity demanded rises; if real income falls, the quantity demanded falls. This latter relationship between income and quantity purchased characterizes the class of goods we earlier delineated as *normal goods*.

In the case of an *inferior good*, however, the income and substitution

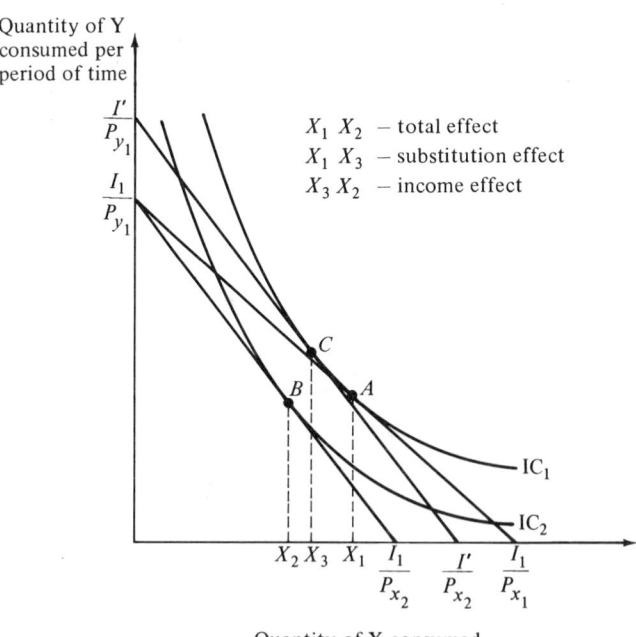

Fig. 4-15 The Income and Substitution Effects for a Normal Good in the Case of a Price Increase

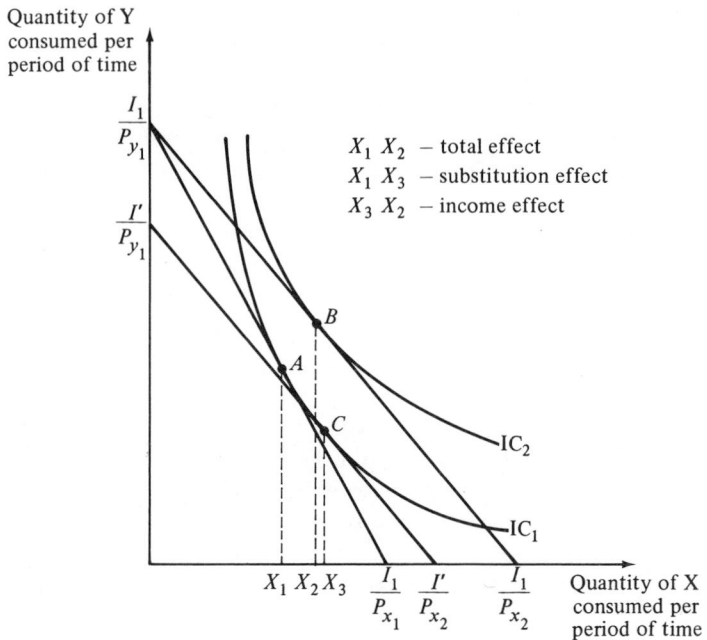

$X_1 X_2$ – total effect
$X_1 X_3$ – substitution effect
$X_3 X_2$ – income effect

Fig. 4-16   The Income and Substitution Effects for an Inferior Good in the Case of a Price Decline

effects work in the *opposite* direction. For an inferior good, a *decrease* in the price of X causes the consumer to buy *more* of it (the substitution effect), but at the same time the higher real income of the consumer tends to cause him to *reduce* his consumption of X (the income effect). The income and substitution effects for this situation are diagrammed in Figure 4-16. Observe that the substitution effect still is the more powerful of the two; even though the income effect works counter to the substitution effect, it does not override it. Furthermore, it follows for an inferior good that in the case of a price *increase*, the substitution effect causes *less* of the commodity to be purchased, whereas the related decline in real income activates a tendency for the consumer to purchase *more* of the commodity. (The diagrammatics of this situation are left as an exercise for the student.)

On the very rarest of occasions, a good may be so strongly inferior that the income effect actually overrides the substitution effect. Such an occurence means that a decline in the price of a commodity will lead to a *decline* in the quantity demanded and a rise in price will induce an *increase* in the quantity demanded—in other words, price and quantity move in the *same* direction. The name given to such a unique situation is Giffen's paradox; it constitutes the only exception to the law of demand. Figure 4-17 illustrates the income and substitution effects for an inferior good subject to Giffen's paradox.

It should be emphasized at this point that the phenomenon of Giffen's paradox is so infrequently observed in the modern world that no current examples can be offered. It does appear that one example occurred in the nineteenth century. According to Alfred Marshall, Sir R. Giffen noted cases where a rise in the price of bread "makes so large a drain on the resources of the poorer labouring families and raises so much the marginal utility of money to them, that they are forced to curtail their consumption of meat and the more expensive farinaceous foods; and, bread being still the cheapest food which they can get and will take, they consume more, and not less of it. But such cases are rare; when they are met with, each must be treated on its own merits."[11] Even in the case of this outdated example one may surmise that had the price of bread continued to rise, there quickly would have come a point when the purchases of bread began to decline. Thus Giffen's paradox is likely to hold only for a fairly narrow range of prices. In our type of society Giffen's paradox is likely to be observed in at most a small minority of consuming units (individuals and households) and then only for precious few types of inferior goods. It is a safe bet that when individual demand

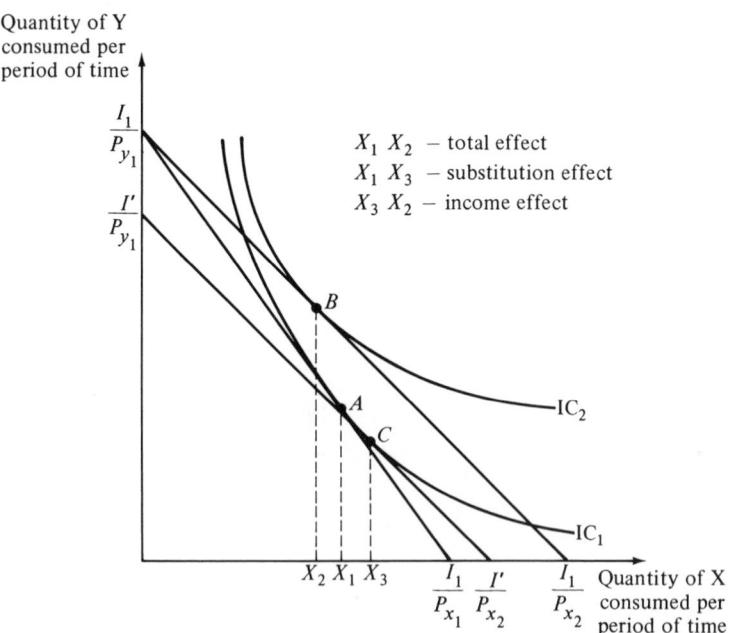

Fig. 4-17 Income and Substitution Effects for an Inferior Good Subject to Giffen's Paradox

[11] Alfred Marshall, *Principles of Economics*, 8th ed. (London: The Macmillan Company, 1920), p. 132.

curves are aggregated to obtain the market demand curves, the quantity demanded in the total market will vary inversely with market price for every commodity—*other things being equal.*

Summary and Conclusions

The ordinal utility approach to consumer demand offers both a supplementary and an alternative approach to the cardinal utility approach for describing individual consumer behavior and for establishing the foundations of market demand. Indifference analysis is preferred by some economists, in part because it does not require the precise quantification of utility and in part because it does not depend so heavily upon the requirement of diminishing marginal utility.

A consumer's taste and preference pattern can be represented by a family of indifference curves. The shapes of the indifference curves are the critical features for displaying a consumer's set of tastes for a pair of commodities. Depending upon the consumer's evaluation of the satisfying power of particular commodities, indifference curves can assume a variety of shapes and can be drawn so as to represent any set of tastes and preferences.

A consumer's ability to satisfy his tastes and preferences is represented by the line of attainable combinations. This line incorporates into the consumer's choice pattern the restraints imposed by his money income and by the prices of the commodities he may be desirous of purchasing. The point of tangency between the line of attainable combinations and an indifference curve defines the highest possible level of satisfaction which the consumer can attain. It was concluded that the conditions requisite for maximizing satisfaction via the ordinal utility or indifference-curve approach are exactly identical to the conditions imposed by the cardinal utility approach.

By allowing income to vary, while holding commodity prices and the consumer's tastes fixed, we can establish the consumer's income consumption curve. The income consumption curve illustrates the various commodity combinations which will maximize the consumer's satisfaction at different levels of income. From the data provided by the income consumption curve, an Engel curve showing the relationship between money income and purchases of a commodity can be derived. Positively-sloped Engel curves are indicative of normal goods, whereas negative slopes are indicative of inferior goods.

We can find the consumer's price consumption curve by observing the equilibrium path traced out when we change the price of a commodity and hold constant money income and tastes and preferences. Data for plotting the consumer's demand curve is obtained from the price consumption curve.

When the price of a commodity changes, other factors remaining unchanged, two forces are activated to cause a change in the equilibrium purchase levels for commodities. The most powerful force, typically, is the substitution effect; it represents the extent to which the consumer is induced to alter his purchase levels *solely* because of the change introduced in the relative prices of commodities. The second, and usually less powerful, force is the income effect; it represents the extent to which the consumer is motivated to buy more or less of a commodity because of the change in real income brought about by the price change.

Usually the income and substitution effects operate in the same direction and reinforce one another. Such is the case for normal goods. For inferior goods, however, the substitution and income effects work in opposite directions. For most inferior goods, the substitution effect overrides the income effect and causes the quantity demanded of a commodity to vary in the opposite direction from the change in its price, thereby validating the law of demand. On the very rarest of occasions, a good may be so strongly inferior that the income effect overpowers the substitution effect and causes the quantity demanded to vary in the *same* direction as the change in price. Such a situation, termed Giffen's paradox, constitutes the only exception to the law of demand.

SUGGESTED READINGS

BAILEY, MARTIN J., "The Marshallian Demand Curve," *Journal of Political Economy*, Vol. 62 (June 1954), pp. 255–261.

FRIEDMAN, MILTON, "The Marshallian Demand Curve," *Journal of Political Economy*, Vol. 57 (December 1949), pp. 463–495.

————, "The 'Welfare' Effects of an Income Tax and an Excise Tax," *Journal of Political Economy*, Vol. 60 (February 1952), pp. 25–33.

HENDERSON, JAMES M., and RICHARD E. QUANDT, *Microeconomic Theory*, 2nd ed., (New York: McGraw-Hill, Inc., 1971), Chap. 2.

HICKS, JOHN R., *Value and Capital*, 2nd ed. (Oxford: Clarendon Press, 1946), Chaps. 1 and 2.

MARSHALL, ALFRED, *Principles of Economics*, 8th ed. (London: The Macmillan Company, 1920), Books 3 and 5.

MISHAN, EDWARD J., "Theories of Consumer's Behaviour: A Cynical View," *Economica*, N.S., Vol. 28 (February 1961), pp. 1–11.

SAMUELSON, PAUL A. "Consumption Theory in Terms of Revealed Preference," *Econonica*, N.S., Vol. 15 (November 1948), pp. 243–253.

VICKREY, WILLIAM S., *Microstatics* (New York: Harcourt Brace Jovanovich, Inc., 1964), Chap. 2.

Problems and Questions for Discussion

1. Illustrate by means of indifference curves the taste and preference pattern suggested by the following statements:

(a) "There is not enough money to make me eat a raw oyster."
(b) "What good is a cigarette if you don't have a light?"
(c) "I would just as soon eat broiled lobster as filet mignon."
(d) "What good is money if you don't spend it? After all, you can't take it with you!"

2. Graphically illustrate in three dimensions the nature of the total utility surface for two commodities which are perfect complements.

3. Suppose a particular consumer has an especial dislike for eating turnips but immensely enjoys eating barbecued spareribs. Draw an indifference map for these two commodities. Indicate the direction of higher degrees of satisfaction.

4. Explain the logical inconsistency involved were two indifference curves to intersect.

5. Suppose that the equation of an indifference curve for a consumer is as follows:

$$XY = 48$$

where X = units of commodity X,
        Y = units of commodity Y,
        48 = amount of utility or satisfaction expressed in utils.

(a) Graphically determine the shape and location of this indifference curve. (Use graph paper.)
(b) Determine the consumer's MRS_{XY} at $X = 4$ and $Y = 12$.
(c) Suppose the price of X is $10 per unit and the price of Y is $4 per unit. Determine the equation for the line of attainable combinations if the consumer's income level is $20. What is the slope of the line of attainable combinations at this income? Determine the equation and slope of the line of attainable combinations at an income of $30. Does the change in income from $20 to $30 influence the slope of the line of attainable combinations? Why or why not?
(d) Illustrate graphically the point of tangency between the indifference curve $XY = 48$ and a line of attainable combinations where $P_X = 10 and $P_Y = 4. How much income will it take for the consumer to attain 48 utils of satisfaction, given these prices?

6. Is a consumer's satisfaction level increased, decreased, or unaffected when the price of a commodity he is purchasing goes down? Illustrate graphically.

7. If indifference curves for perfect substitutes are negatively-sloped and linear and if indifference curves for perfect complements are right angles, is it then true that the degree of convexity of an indifference curve reflects the degree of substitutability and complementarity among commodities? Explain.

8. Graphically illustrate the combination of goods X and Y that will maximize satisfaction when goods X and Y are perfect substitutes, $MRS_{XY} = (-)1$, $P_X = 2, $P_Y = 2.25, and $I = 18.

9. Diagrammatically illustrate the income and substitution effects for an inferior good in the case of a price increase.

10. Diagrammatically illustrate the income and substitution effects for an inferior good subject to Giffen's paradox in the case of a price increase.

11. Suppose two commodities X and Y are judged by consumers to be perfect substitutes for each other. Suppose further that the price of X is higher than the price of Y.

(a) If consumers behave rationally, what would you predict to happen to sales of the two commodities?

(b) Where consumers view products which compete against one another as being nearly perfect substitutes, is it surprising to find that their prices are identical or at least nearly so? Explain your answer.

5

Consumer Demand, Revenue Functions, and Elasticity

Our surveys of cardinal and ordinal utility analysis firmly established that an individual's demand for a commodity tends to vary inversely with the price of the commodity, other things remaining equal. In other words, the amount of a commodity which an individual is willing and able to purchase at a particular moment of time tends to rise as the commodity's price falls and to fall as its price rises. The sole exception to the law of demand is Giffen's paradox —an extremely limited and undoubtedly insignificant occurrence.

This chapter will extend the analysis of consumer demand, first by exploring the full complement of determinants of individual demand, second by relating the concept of demand to the firm and examining the demand curve for the product of a particular firm, and third by deriving the revenue functions corresponding to these demand curves. With regard to the latter, attention will be focused upon the total and marginal revenue functions associated with various types of product demand functions and upon the sensitivity of the demand for a firm's product to changes in price and consumer income.

THE MAJOR DETERMINANTS OF INDIVIDUAL DEMAND

It is evident from previous discussions that *the price of the commodity* itself is a primary factor influencing the quantity demanded by an individual consumer. Other factors also are relevant; these include:

—a consumer's taste and preference pattern as reflected by his utility functions or indifference maps,
—a consumer's money income (or purchasing power),
—the prices of related products, both substitutes and complementary goods,
—a consumer's expectations with respect to future commodity prices, income levels, and product availability,
—the range of goods and services available for selection by the consumer.

A word or two about each of these is in order.

Consumer Tastes and Preferences.   The relevance of consumer tastes for determining demand is easily apparent. When a person's taste for a commodity lessens, so does his demand for the commodity. By the same token, an increase in the intensity of a consumer's desire for a commodity tends to increase his willingness to pay a higher price for the commodity or to buy more of it or both. Needless to say, an individual's taste and preference pattern undergoes continuous review and is subject to change, sometimes gradual and sometimes rapid, over time. In the modern world the constant flow of innovation is a powerful instigator of changes in consumer tastes and preferences; new substitutes for old products appear quite regularly. Estimates have it that between 6,000 and 10,000 new products are introduced each year through grocery and drug channels alone. Advertising, also, exerts a pervasive and dynamic influence upon consumer tastes. Even more fundamentally, individual values and priorities are modified by changing economic circumstances, rising living standards, and affluence.

Consumer Income.   The impact of income upon demand is plain enough and warrants little discussion. Clearly, the consumer's ability to purchase commodities, as given by his money income, is what permits him to satisfy his material desires. Willingness to buy is in itself insufficient; the consumer must be *able* to pay for the commodities he wants. Typically, the greater a consumer's purchasing power the greater will be his demand for goods in general and for goods in particular. Only in the case of inferior goods is an increase in income accompanied by a weakening of demand.

Prices of Related Commodities.   The prices of related commodities are an important determinant of the demand for a commodity because of interrelationships among goods. In the case of goods which are substitutes for each other, *relative* prices are perhaps the critical factor in the consumer's selection process. If Schlitz is cheaper than Budweiser, this fact is sure to influence, at least partially, the consumer's choice of which to buy. In the case of goods which have a complementary relationship and are demanded jointly (golf clubs and golf balls, automobiles and gasoline, Scotch and soda), it is equally clear that relative prices are pertinent. Should the price of men's suits rise by 20 percent, the demand for new ties is certain to be affected; should the prices of stereo sets fall, the demand for phonograph records is likely to increase.

Consumer Expectations. A consumer's expectations with respect to future price levels can influence his current purchase behavior. If he believes that the prices of goods he expects to buy shortly are going to rise in price, he will be motivated to buy them now and escape paying the higher prices. Similarly, if a consumer for some reason expects a good to be unavailable or in short supply in the near future (because of a strike, delays in shipping, production bottlenecks, or whatever), he will be induced to make his purchases now, so as to have the commodity on hand when he needs it. Other consumers may purchase goods currently with a view toward paying for them later out of expected increases in income. Some college seniors, for example, in the months just prior to graduation purchase automobiles in the expectation of paying for them out of future income from their new jobs.

Range of Available Commodities. The range of goods and services available for a consumer's selection is a demand determinant in the sense that it indicates the number of alternatives open to him in spending his income. Generally speaking, the greater the number of commodities from which the consumer can choose, the fewer units of a commodity the consumer will buy. Diminishing marginal utility for additional units of a particular good is likely to motivate a consumer to spread his income out over a wider range of commodities should the opportunity present itself.

To the foregoing list of the major demand determinants of *individual* consumer demand we may add one more and obtain the list for overall *market* demand—the number of consumers. Since the market demand for a commodity is the summation of individual consumer demands for the commodity, then by adding the factor of the number of consumers to the list of determinants of individual consumer demand, we necessarily end up with the determinants of market demand.

SOME ADDED DIMENSIONS TO THE NATURE
AND NUMBER OF DEMAND DETERMINANTS

The preceding discussion of demand factors is more suggestive than exhaustive. While the seven factors above are generally acknowledged as the major demand determinants, other factors commonly exert minor influence on demand.

1. It makes a great difference in the level of demand whether a product

is a "luxury" or a "necessity." Although classifying a commodity as a luxury or a necessity is largely a matter of taste and living standards, it is often useful to consider whether, under present conditions, certain classes of consumers view a good as a necessity. This then introduces into the analysis various sociological influences on demand and permits a more definitive delineation of who buys what and with what degree of urgency.

2. The demand for some goods is derived from the demand for other goods and thus is known as a *derived demand*. The demand for steel is derived from the demand for commodities containing steel or requiring steel somewhere in the course of their production. The demand for newsprint is derived from the demand for newspapers. The demand for typewriters is derived from the demand for secretarial services. The point here is that, in investigating the demands for intermediate goods and capital goods, we may gain considerable insight by examining the markets for the final goods to which they are related.

3. The extent to which the market for a product is *saturated* can be a critical factor in the level of demand for new products and for durable goods. To cite a familiar case, the current market for black and white TV sets is largely restricted to a replacement demand, with some sales going to newly formed households. Why? Because over 95 percent of today's households have a TV set. In contrast, the market potential for color TV sets is far greater. Less than 35 percent of American households have color TV, thus offering color TV producers a much larger sales potential than if the household saturation level were higher. The limited demand for commodities having high saturation levels has prompted many producers of durable goods to adopt a policy of "planned obsolescence," whereby their products are restyled periodically, new features are added, and consumers are in turn induced to increase the frequency with which they replace their "worn-out" and "out-of-date" durable goods.[1]

4. For consumer goods which are typically purchased with the aid of credit (automobiles, appliances, furniture, houses), the level of consumer debt and prevailing interest rates may be valuable additions to the dimensions of the consumer's buying power and may, in fact, be more closely related to the demand for such commodities than is current money income. We can logically predict that the higher the ratio of consumer debt to consumer income and the higher the rates of interest on borrowed funds, the less able and less eager will consumers be to make additional commitments toward the purchase of durable goods. Rather, they will prefer to postpone the purchase of such items until more favorable buying conditions present themselves.

5. For those commodities whose purchase is truly discretionary, a superior measure of consumer purchasing power may be derived by considering

---

[1] For a good discussion of the economics of planned obsolescence, see Ronald J. Dornoff and Esmond T. Adams, "Planned Obsolescence: Stimulus or Crutch," *Mississippi Valley Journal of Business and Economics*, Vol. 6, No. 2 (Winter 1970–71), pp. 10–19.

the consumer's *discretionary income.* This is the residual amount of income remaining after subtracting necessary living expenses and fixed payment charges from disposable personable income. A consumer's discretionary income is likely to be closely related to his purchases of consumer durables and his recreation and travel activities, and, therefore, it may be a more valid demand determinant for some goods than other income measures. The National Industrial Conference Board publishes a discretionary income series. Somewhat more refined measures add such items as cash balances, near liquid assets, and the availability of new consumer credit, thereby providing a more comprehensive indicator of consumer purchasing power for items which are not in the category of "necessities."

Additional reflection would, no doubt, suggest still other factors which bear upon the amounts purchased of certain commodities. Obviously enough, each commodity has its own peculiar set of demand determinants, which in turn act to influence demand in their own peculiar ways.

THE CONCEPT OF THE DEMAND FUNCTION

The discussion of the circumstances prompting consumers to buy or not to buy a commodity suggests that the market demand for a commodity is the result of the complex interaction of a wide variety of forces. In mathematical terms, the demand function for a commodity can be symbolized as

$$Q_d = f(P, T, I, P_r, E, R, N, O),$$

where Q_d = quantity demanded of a commodity,
      P = the market price of the commodity,
      T = consumer tastes and preferences,
      I = the level of consumer incomes,
     P_r = prices of related commodities,
      E = consumer expectations regarding future prices, incomes, and product availability,
      R = range of goods and services available to consumers,
     N = number of potential consumers, and
     O = all other factors which may influence Q_d.

The major demand determinants are likely to be influential in the case of nearly every commodity, though their individual impacts certainly will vary in degree and intensity from commodity to commodity. The term "all other factors" will be composed of factors related directly to the commodity's own specific characteristics.

Using the functional notation to symbolize the relationship between the quantity demanded of a particular product and the specific factors which influence it is, unquestionably, a more explicit and conceptually accurate way of representing the demand for a commodity than is the graphic portrayal of price-quantity relationships in the form of demand curves.

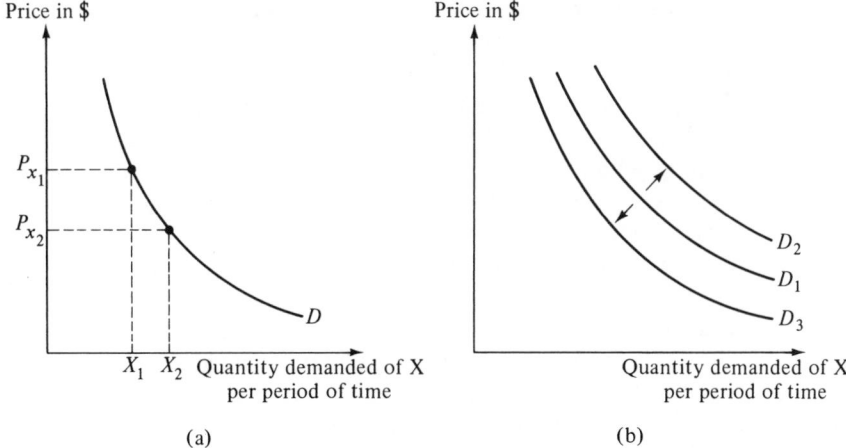

Fig. 5-1 The Nature of Shifts in Consumer Purchases and Demand Intensity

Nevertheless, it is usually convenient to segregate demand determinants into two groups: (1) the price of the commodity and (2) all other demand determinants. Using this dichotomization, variations in the purchases of a commodity associated solely with changes in product price are customarily termed "changes in the quantity demanded" and are represented graphically by movements *along* a given demand curve. In Figure 5-1(a), a decrease in the price of X from P_{X_1} to P_{X_2} increases the quantity demanded from X_1 to X_2. Hence, a change in the quantity demanded is the result of a change in the price of the good itself when *all* other factors influencing the purchase level remain unchanged. On the other hand, variations in the purchases of a commodity which are associated with changes in one or more of the demand determinants other than the commodity's price are referred to as "changes in demand" and are represented graphically by shifts in the demand curve [Figure 5-1(b)].[2] For example, such circumstances as increases in consumer incomes, a larger advertising budget, a more intensive desire for a good, or an increase in the price of substitutes would tend to shift the position of a given demand curve to the right, say from line D_1 to D_2. Such circumstances as a decline in the number of consumers, an increase in the range of

---

[2] The terms "change in the quantity demanded" and "change in demand" can be explained readily in the language of mathematics. Suppose the equation of the demand curve is given by

$$P = a - bQ,$$

where P represents the selling price of a commodity and Q represents the quantity bought. As long as all of the demand determinants other than P remain constant, the parameters a and b also remain constant and the equation $P = a - bQ$ defines a unique demand curve. A change in P will result in a movement along this demand curve to the corresponding value of Q—this is what has been termed a "change in the quantity demanded." However, shifts in demand determinants other than P are reflected by changes in the values of a and b. A change in the value of a shifts the level of the curve and a change in the value of b alters the slope of the curve—either or both of which represent a "change in demand" and define the equation of a new demand curve.

goods (especially substitutes) available to consumers, or the expectation of a forthcoming price decrease tend to shift the demand curve to the left, as illustrated by shifting D_1 to position D_3.

The distinction between the terms "change in quantity demanded" and "change in demand" should make it perfectly clear that graphically representing the price-quantity relationship in the form of a demand curve does *not* mean that the price of a commodity is the sole, or even the principal, determinant of the amount purchased of a commodity during a moment of time. All the demand curve purports to show is the impact that different prices will have upon the amounts purchased of a commodity *when the remaining factors comprising the demand function are fixed in value.*

Average, Total, and Marginal Revenue

Consider, for the time being, a demand curve as representing the intensity of consumer demand for the product of a particular business firm. This opens the way to introducing several new dimensions to the concept of demand and demand curves.

The demand curve for the product of a particular business firm is shown in Figure 5-2. This curve portrays the *maximum quantities* per unit of time that consumers are willing to buy from this firm at alternative prices. Equally accurate is the concept that a firm's demand curve shows the *maximum prices* that buyers are willing to pay the seller to obtain given quantities of the commodity. Naturally, consumers would gladly pay less for the item were the opportunity to present itself, but they cannot now be induced to pay the firm more than the price shown by the demand curve. Hence, should a firm

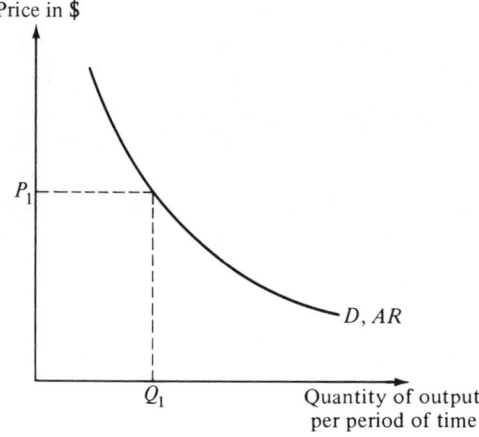

Fig. 5-2   A Firm's Demand or Average Revenue Curve

elect to offer quantity Q_1 for sale, the maximum price for which it can be sold is P_1. Moreover, price P_1 represents the *average* amount of revenue the firm will receive *per unit sold*, and from the point of view of the firm this is properly called *average revenue* (*AR*). Accordingly, a *firm's* demand curve can with equal propriety be labeled an average revenue curve.

The average revenue function may be expressed as a function of the quantity sold and written as

$$AR = f(Q).$$

When a firm sells all of its output at the same price, its selling price and its average revenue are the same value. In this case, it is correct to say

$$AR = P = f(Q).$$

However, if the firm has a multiple price policy, whereby it sells its product at different prices to different customers, average revenue is equal to a weighted average of the selling prices with the weights being the proportions sold at each price. In this case we can still write

$$AR = P = f(Q),$$

but P must be interpreted as representing the *average* selling price.

Now let us consider the properties of a firm's revenue functions for selected demand conditions.

AVERAGE, TOTAL, AND MARGINAL REVENUE
WHEN THE DEMAND CURVE IS HORIZONTAL

Consider first the simple, but rather unusual, case where the firm perceives the demand curve for its product to be horizontal as in Figure 5-3(a). A horizontal demand curve means that a firm can sell all the units it wishes at the price given by the intersection of the demand curve with the price axis; in Figure 5-3(a) this is shown as a price of $10.[3] If the firm raises its price above $10, no units can be sold. Obviously, if the firm can sell all it wishes at a price of $10, it can also sell all it wishes below $10. However, we would logically expect the firm to offer its product for sale at the maximum price of $10, as no advantage can be gained from any lower price. The equation of the firm's average revenue and demand functions in this situation is

$$AR = P = \$10.$$

[3] Just because a *firm's* demand curve is horizontal, it does not follow that the law of demand is suspended. Although a firm may be able to sell all it wishes within the limits of its production capacity at a particular price, it still is true that a single consumer will prefer to buy more at lower prices than at higher prices. Likewise, it is still true that consumers as a group will prefer to buy more at lower prices than at higher prices. What may make the demand curve horizontal for a *firm* is the fact that *many* other sellers are offering consumers an *identical* product; thus all firms may be driven by the market forces of demand and supply to sell at the same price. Because each firm is so small relative to the total market, they are able to sell all they wish at the prevailing price and their individual demand curves are, therefore, horizontal.

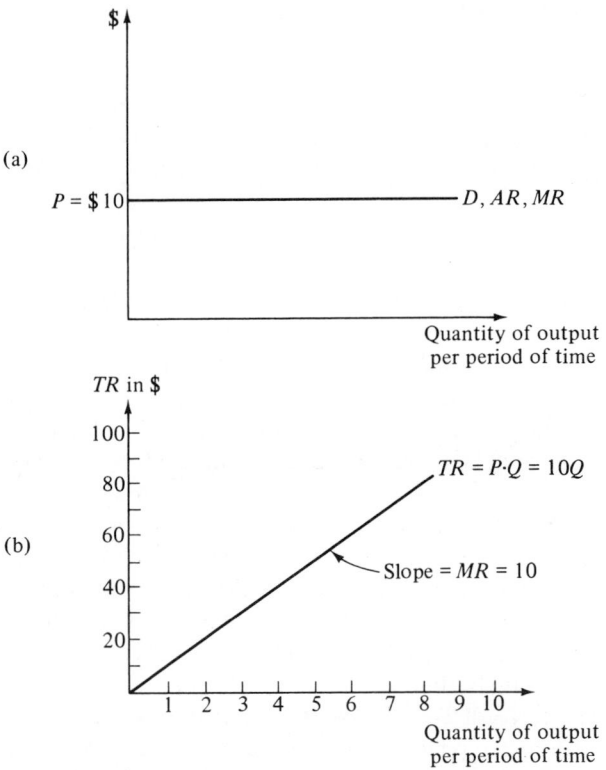

Fig. 5-3 The Average, Total, and Marginal Revenue Functions for a Firm Whose Demand
Curve is Horizontal

The *total revenue* function is found by multiplying average revenue by the
number of units sold, and may be written as

$$TR = AR \cdot Q = P \cdot Q.$$

When the demand curve is horizontal, the corresponding total revenue curve
is a positively-sloped linear function starting from the origin and having a
slope equal to the product price [see Figure 5-3(b)]. In this example, the slope
of the total revenue function is equal to 10, because every time one more
unit is sold, the firm's total revenue rises by $10; the related equation for
TR is

$$TR = P \cdot Q = 10Q.$$

Marginal revenue is rigorously defined as the rate of change in total
revenue as the rate of output changes. The *marginal revenue function*, then,

is the first derivative of the total revenue function. Since, in our example,

$$TR = 10Q,$$

then

$$MR = \frac{dTR}{dQ} = 10.$$

A marginal revenue value of 10 means that a one-unit increase in sales will cause total revenue to rise by $10. Geometrically, it also means that marginal revenue equals the slope of the total revenue function. Because the slope of a linear TR function is constant, the value of MR is likewise a constant. Since the firm can sell all it wishes at a price of $10, marginal revenue is fixed at $10 and is exactly equal to the firm's selling price and average revenue. In this case the marginal revenue function is graphically identical, therefore, to the firm's demand and average revenue functions and is so shown in Figure 5-3(a).

On occasion, it is useful to conceive of marginal revenue as the change in total revenue resulting from a *one unit* increase in sales. This definition is appropriate when one wishes to calculate the change in total revenue associated with a *discrete* change in output. We shall refer to this concept of MR as *discrete marginal revenue*. When output can be varied continuously—that is, changes in Q can be infinitesimally small—MR is most appropriately conceived as the derivative of TR. We shall refer to this latter concept of MR as *continuous marginal revenue*. It will be necessary to rely upon both concepts of MR in future analyses.

In the example above, the nature of the demand function is such that the values for discrete MR and continuous MR are both $10. This is typical for horizontal demand functions but is not true of other types of demand functions, as the next case illustrates.

AVERAGE, TOTAL, AND MARGINAL REVENUE
WHEN THE DEMAND CURVE IS LINEAR AND DOWNSLOPING

Somewhat more plausible is the circumstance where the demand curve for a firm's product is linear and downsloping. The general equation for linear, downsloping demand and average revenue functions can be expressed as

$$AR = P = a - bQ.$$

The value of a in the equation is the price at which the demand curve intersects the price axis and, in economic terms, is the price just high enough so that no consumers will be willing to purchase the firm's product. The value of b in the equation is the slope of the demand curve. The minus sign $(-)$ means that the demand curve is negatively-sloped and that there exists an

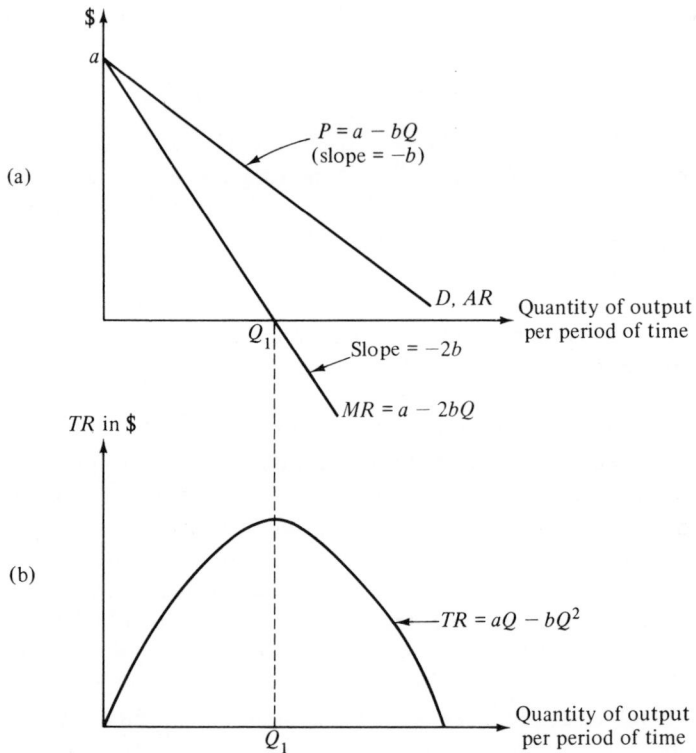

Fig. 5-4 The Average, Total, and Marginal Revenue Functions for a Firm Faced with a Linear Downsloping Demand Curve

inverse relationship between P and Q—all of which is, of course, the usual case. The graph of a linear, downsloping demand curve is shown in Figure 5-4(a).

Since a firm's total revenue from the sale of a commodity equals average revenue times the quantity sold (or price times the quantity sold), the expression for TR can be obtained by multiplying the average revenue (demand) function by Q:

$$TR = AR \cdot Q = P \cdot Q.$$
$$= (a - bQ)Q$$
$$= aQ - bQ^2.$$

A total revenue function of this type is graphically portrayed by a parabola of the shape in Figure 5-4(b).

As before, the corresponding marginal revenue function is the derivative of the total revenue function. Since $TR = aQ - bQ^2$, then

$$MR = \frac{dTR}{dQ} = a - 2bQ.$$

Plotting the MR function on the same diagram as the demand and AR functions [Figure 5-4(a)] reveals that the MR curve lies below the demand curve. Both curves originate at the same value a, but the slope of the MR function is twice as great as the slope of the demand curve ($-2b$ as compared to $-b$).[4] In geometric terms, the MR curve is located by drawing it so as to bisect the horizontal distance between the demand curve and the vertical axis. However, this procedure is accurate only in the case of a linear demand curve.

Marginal revenue is less than price (average revenue) because with a downsloping demand function the firm must lower its selling price to boost the quantity sold. The lower price applies not only to the additional units sold but also to the units of output which otherwise could have been sold at a higher price. For instance, suppose a firm can sell 50 units at a price of $1 and realize total revenue of $50, but that to increase sales to 51 units the firm must lower its price, say to $0.99 on all units sold. The increase in total revenue is *not* the $0.99 gained from the sale of the 51st unit, because the firm must give up revenue of $0.01 on each of the previous 50 units formerly selling at $1.00. Thus the net gain in total revenue is $0.99 − $0.50 or $0.49, as can easily be verified by multiplying 51 units times $0.99, which gives a total revenue of $50.49. Hence, the marginal revenue of the 51st unit is $0.49, which is less than its selling price of $0.99.

One further very important relationship remains to be pointed out. This concerns the MR and TR functions. Observe in Figure 5-4 that the TR function increases at a decreasing rate up to a sales volume of Q_1 units; over this same range, MR is *positive* but decreasing in value. Earlier it was stated that MR at any sales volume Q equals the slope of the TR function at that value of Q. Since the TR function has a positive slope up to an output of Q_1, MR of necessity must be positive; likewise, just as the slope of the TR function diminishes as the sales level approaches Q_1 units, so also does the value of MR diminish. Marginal revenue is zero at exactly the same output level (Q_1) at which total revenue is maximum. Past a sales volume of Q_1, TR falls and MR is negative. Consequently, when the slope of the TR function is positive, MR is positive; when the slope of the TR function is zero, MR is zero; and when the slope of the TR function is negative, MR is negative.

A numerical example at this point may serve to clarify and illuminate these relationships between AR, TR, and MR. Suppose a firm's demand and

---

[4] Technically, the demand and MR functions originate at the common sales level of one unit. Yet, if we assume the distance measuring one unit of output on the horizontal axis is infinitesimally small, both curves can be viewed as originating from a common point on the vertical axis.

average revenue functions can be represented by the following equation:

$$AR = P = 12 - Q.$$

The total revenue and marginal revenue functions can be calculated as follows:

$$TR = AR \cdot Q = P \cdot Q$$
$$= (12 - Q)Q$$
$$= 12Q - Q^2,$$
$$MR = \frac{dTR}{dQ} = 12 - 2Q.$$

Table 5-1 contains representative values for P, Q, AR, TR, continuous MR, and discrete MR as derived from the preceding equations. Several attributes of the values in Table 5-1 are worth noting. First, when price is \$12 or higher, no consumer is willing to purchase any of the firm's product. Second, selling price and AR are identical; as stated earlier, this is a necessary result of a single-price policy. Third, TR increases rapidly at first, then more slowly, reaches a maximum at six units of output, and declines thereafter as sales continue to increase. Fourth, the values for continuous MR are positive but steadily declining for the first five units of output; MR is zero where TR is at its maximum value of \$36; and MR is ever more negative as the sales volume extends beyond six units. Fifth, the discrete MR values (which are computed by subtracting successive values of TR in order to obtain the change in TR associated with a one-unit change in Q) do not correspond exactly to the values for continuous MR. This is not because the two concepts are inconsistent, but rather because they are really associated with different output or

Table 5-1   Demand and Revenue Data for a Linear Demand Function

Quantity of Output Demanded	Price $(P = 12 - Q)$	Average Revenue $(AR = 12 - Q)$	Total Revenue $(TR = 12Q - Q^2)$	Continuous Marginal Revenue $(MR = 12 - 2Q)$	Discrete Marginal Revenue $(MR = TR_Q - TR_{Q-1})$
0	\$12	\$12	\$ 0	\$12	
					\$11
1	11	11	11	10	
					9
2	10	10	20	8	
					7
3	9	9	27	6	
					5
4	8	8	32	4	
					3
5	7	7	35	2	
					1
6	6	6	36	0	
					−1
7	5	5	35	−2	
					−3
8	4	4	32	−4	
					−5
9	3	3	27	−6	
					−7
10	2	2	20	−8	

sales levels. For instance, when TR rises from \$11 to \$20 as a consequence of a rise in sales from one to two units, it is fair to say that the \$9 gain in revenue is not MR when TR is \$20 and sales are two units, but is instead MR *between* one and two units of output. The values for discrete MR in Table 5-1 are more correctly associated with output levels of $\frac{1}{2}$, $1\frac{1}{2}$, $2\frac{1}{2}$, and so on. This can easily be confirmed by plugging these values of Q into the equation for continuous MR; the resulting values for MR correspond exactly to the values for discrete MR presented in the table. Thus the discrete and continuous measures of MR are perfectly compatible and define the same MR function and curve. If the TR function is known, it is usually more convenient to use the continuous measure of MR. If MR must be determined from a table of TR values, the discrete measure of MR is the simplest to calculate.

Plotting the values in Table 5-1 will yield curves which possess the relationships alluded to in Figure 5-4. The reader should verify this for himself.

AVERAGE, TOTAL, AND MARGINAL REVENUE FUNCTIONS
WHEN THE DEMAND CURVE IS CURVILINEAR

The demand curve for a commodity can assume a wide variety of curvilinear forms. No attempt here is made to catalog the diverse types. We shall be content with examining two basic curvilinear demand curves with relatively simple equations.

Suppose for an output range of 0 to 40 units the demand function for a firm's product is given by the expression

$$P = 400 - 20Q + .25Q^2.$$

The firm's average revenue function will likewise be

$$AR = 400 - 20Q + .25Q^2.$$

Again, the total revenue function is found by multiplying the average revenue function (or demand function) by the quantity sold:

$$\begin{aligned} TR = AR \cdot Q &= P \cdot Q \\ &= (400 - 20Q + .25Q^2)Q \\ &= 400Q - 20Q^2 + .25Q^3. \end{aligned}$$

The marginal revenue function is the first derivative of the total revenue function, giving

$$MR = \frac{dTR}{dQ} = 400 - 40Q + .75Q^2.$$

These functions are pictured in Figure 5-5. The solid portions of the curves

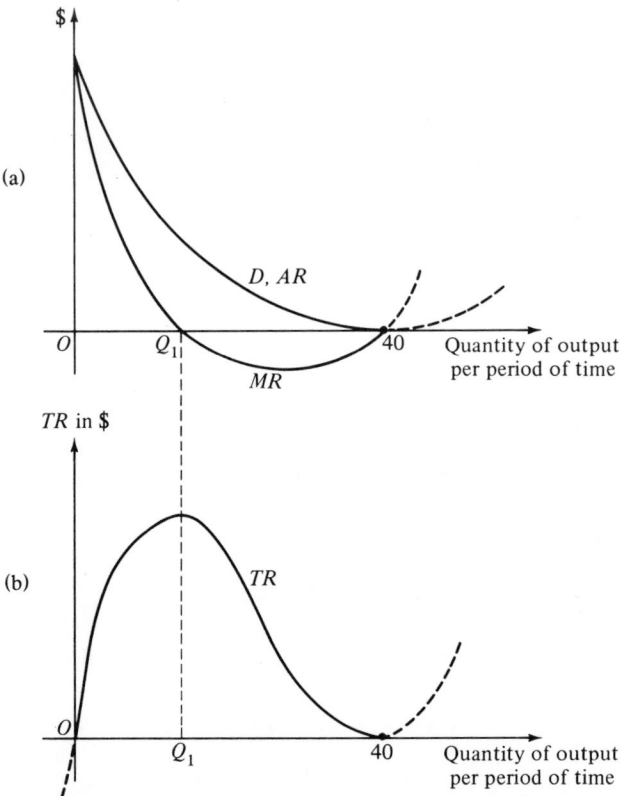

Fig. 5-5   The Average, Total, and Marginal Revenue Functions for a Firm Whose Demand
Equation is of the General Form $P = a - bQ + cQ^2$

are the only relevant parts of the functions for our analysis, because the
demand function ($P = 400 - 20Q + .25Q^2$) describes the price-quantity
relationship only for values of Q from 0 to 40. Negative values of Q have no
economic meaning. Values of Q above 40 are not meaningful for the *given*
function, as they result in a positively-sloped curve, which we earlier stated
does not characterize demand functions except in the rarest of circumstances.
In other words, we are saying that the equation $P = 400 - 20Q + .25Q^2$
describes the firm's demand curve only for the output range 0 to 40. The
dashed portions of the curves in Figure 5-5 indicate the parts which are defined mathematically but which have no economic significance; these portions
are shown only for the sake of completeness.

Observe that the MR function lies everywhere below the demand function except at their common beginning value of 400. The values for MR
are declining but greater than zero for the output range where TR is rising;

MR is zero where TR is maximum. When the demand curve is convex to the origin, as in this example, the MR curve lies to the left of a line bisecting the horizontal distance between the vertical axis and the demand curve.

The generalized equations for the demand, AR, TR, and MR functions of this type and shape are as follows:

$$P = a - bQ + cQ^2,$$
$$AR = a - bQ + cQ^2,$$
$$TR = aQ - bQ^2 + cQ^3,$$
$$MR = a - 2bQ + 3cQ^2,$$

where a, b, and c are constants.

Another fairly common type of demand function is that associated with the general equation

$$P = a + bQ - cQ^2.$$

In this case, the AR function is also given by the equation

$$AR = a + bQ - cQ^2.$$

The TR function is again derived by multiplying the AR (or demand) function by Q:

$$TR = AR \cdot Q = P \cdot Q$$
$$= (a + bQ - cQ^2)Q$$
$$= aQ + bQ^2 - cQ^3.$$

Taking the derivative of the TR function, we get the MR function:

$$MR = \frac{dTR}{dQ} = a + 2bQ - 3cQ^2.$$

The graphs of these functions are plotted in Figure 5-6. The same basic relations between demand, AR, TR, and MR hold in this instance as well. The significant difference between this case and the previous example is the location of the MR function. Although MR still lies below the demand function, this time it is located to the right of a line bisecting the horizontal distance between the vertical axis and the demand curve.

Elasticity of Demand

The concept of *elasticity of demand* is one of the most important analytical devices in microeconomics. In general terms, elasticity of demand is a mea-

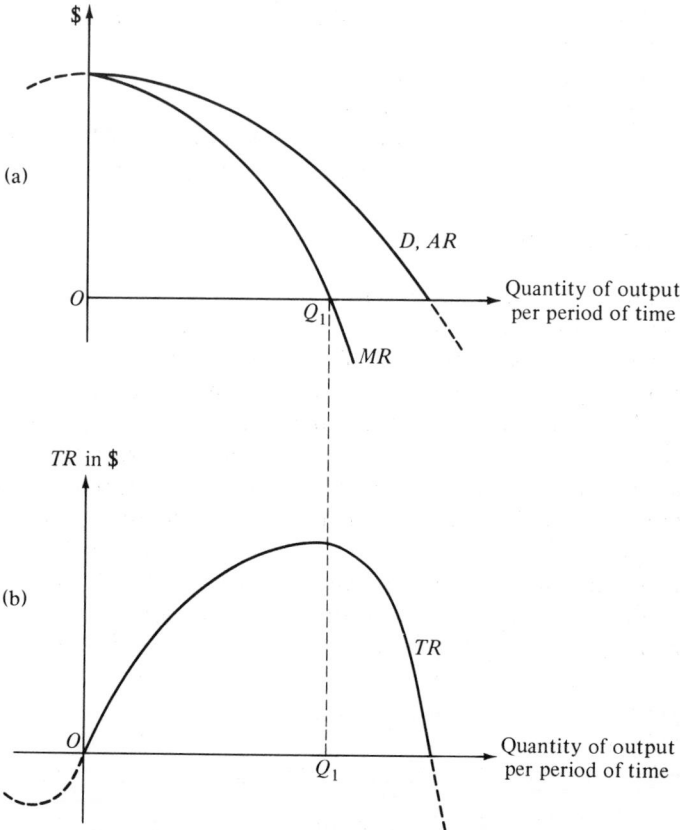

Fig. 5-6   The Average, Total, and Marginal Revenue Functions for a Firm Whose Demand Equation is of the General Form $P = a + bQ - cQ^2$

sure of the *responsiveness* or *sensitivity* of the quantity demanded of a commodity to a change in some demand determinant. There are as many kinds of demand elasticity as there are numbers of demand determinants for a commodity.

Mathematically, the elasticity of demand, ϵ (epsilon), can be conceived as

$$\epsilon = \frac{\text{percent change in quantity demanded}}{\text{percent change in any demand determinant}}.$$

Elasticity is *always* measured in relative or percentage terms rather than in absolute or unit terms. This permits comparisons of demand sensitivity for different products, irrespective of the units in which products or product prices are quoted. (A 5 percent change has the same meaning whether it is measured in tons, dozens, crates, cans, cents, or dollars.) However, because elasticity is calculated by dividing a percentage change by a percentage change, the result is a pure number and must be so interpreted.

The general concept of elasticity of demand can be given more concrete meaning in terms of specific measures of elasticity of demand. We shall begin with the measure most familiar and widely used—price elasticity of demand.

PRICE ELASTICITY OF DEMAND

The relation of product price to sales volume is of major interest to business concerns as a basis for pricing policy, sales strategy, and achievement of the profit objective. Consider the case of products X and Y with demand curves as shown in Figure 5-7. The negative slopes of both curves indicate that as the prices of X and Y fall, the quantities demanded of X and Y rise. From the diagram, when the prices of X and Y are P_{X_1} and P_{Y_1}, such that $P_{X_1} = P_{Y_1}$, the quantities purchased are X_1 units and Y_1 units, respectively. However, if the prices of X and Y decline by an identical amount to P_{X_2} and P_{Y_2} (where $P_{X_2} = P_{Y_2}$), the percent change in the quantity demanded of X (X_1 to X_2) is greater than the change in the quantity demanded of Y (Y_1 to Y_2). In other words, the demand for X is more sensitive or responsive to a change in the price of X than the demand for Y is to a change in the price of Y at the indicated prices. Or, in the language of economics, we can say that the price elasticity of demand for X is greater than the price elasticity of demand for Y over the indicated price range.

Price elasticity of demand can be defined more precisely as:

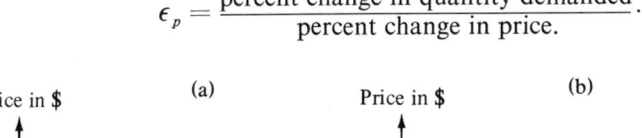

$$\epsilon_p = \frac{\text{percent change in quantity demanded}}{\text{percent change in price}}.$$

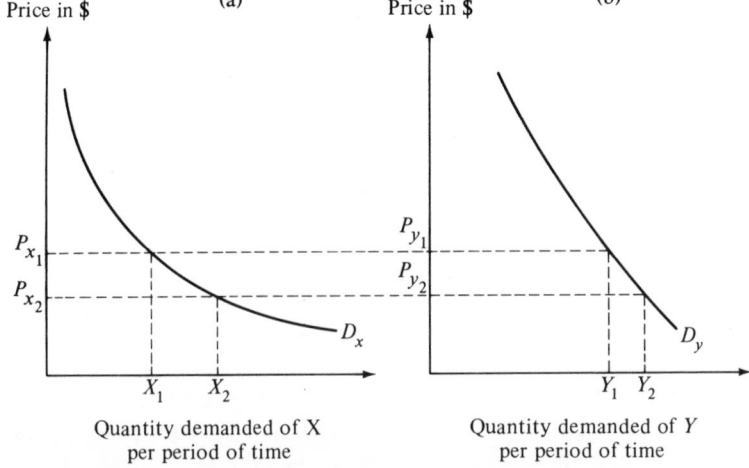

Fig. 5-7 The Sensitivity of Product Demand to Price Changes

The number or coefficient denoting price elasticity is necessarily a pure number independent of any units of measurement, because it is obtained by dividing a percentage value by a percentage value. The coefficient for price elasticity of demand is negative, since price and quantity are inversely related; when price falls we expect the quantity demanded to rise and when price rises we expect the quantity demanded to fall. Thus one of the percentage changes will be negative and the other will be positive, thereby producing a negative coefficient.

Two distinct measures of price elasticity exist: arc elasticity and point elasticity. *Arc elasticity* is a measure of the responsiveness of the quantity demanded between two separate points on a demand curve. *Point elasticity* is a measure of the sensitivity of the quantity demanded at a single point on the curve for an infinitesimal change in price. Both measures are useful and each shall be discussed in turn.

Arc Elasticity.   To illustrate the arc technique for computing price elasticity, consider a demand curve having two points *A* and *B* with price-quantity combinations as follows:

	Price	Quantity Demanded
point *A*	$12	30 units
point *B*	$10	50 units

Now suppose we determine the degree of responsiveness of quantity demanded to a *decrease* in price from $12 to $10—this is equivalent to moving down along the demand curve from point *A* to point *B*. It will be recalled that the usual way of computing percentage change is to find the change in a value relative to its original value and multiply by 100 to convert the ratio to a percentage figure. Algebraically, then, our definition of price elasticity is equivalent to

$$\epsilon_p = \frac{\text{percent change in quantity demanded}}{\text{percent change in price}} = \frac{\dfrac{Q_2 - Q_1}{Q_1} \times 100}{\dfrac{P_2 - P_1}{P_1} \times 100}$$

where the pairs (Q_1, P_1) and (Q_2, P_2) represent, respectively, the quantity and price values *before* and *after* their change. In this instance, the multiplication by 100 of both the numerator and the denominator is superfluous and can be omitted, as it will be canceled out in dividing. Substituting the appropriate values into the formula gives

$$\epsilon_p = \frac{\dfrac{Q_2 - Q_1}{Q_1}}{\dfrac{P_2 - P_1}{P_1}} = \frac{\dfrac{50 - 30}{30}}{\dfrac{10 - 12}{12}} = \frac{\dfrac{20}{30}}{\dfrac{-2}{12}} = \frac{2}{3} \cdot -\frac{6}{1} = -4.0.$$

Yet, if we compute the sensitivity of the quantity demanded to an *increase* in price from \$10 to \$12, which is to move up the demand curve from point *B* to point *A*, the coefficient of price elasticity is

$$\epsilon_p = \frac{\dfrac{Q_2 - Q_1}{Q_1}}{\dfrac{P_2 - P_1}{P_1}} = \frac{\dfrac{30 - 50}{50}}{\dfrac{12 - 10}{10}} = \frac{\dfrac{-20}{50}}{\dfrac{2}{10}} = \frac{-2}{5} \cdot \frac{5}{1} = -2.0.$$

Clearly, the percentage changes in price and quantity demanded in moving from point *A* to point *B* differ substantially from those in going from *B* to *A*. This is because the *sizes* of the original price and quantity influence the percentage value every bit as much as do the *changes* in the price and quantity.

This example serves to demonstrate that arc elasticity calculations are no more than approximations.[5] The farther apart are the two points between which arc elasticity is computed, the greater will be the discrepancy between the coefficients of price elasticity obtained from the above formula. For the arc elasticity coefficient to be reliable and to have any real meaning, it must be computed between points on the demand curve which are reasonably close together.

Nevertheless, the bias introduced by computing the percentage changes using the original values of price and quantity as the reference point can be partially overcome by averaging Q_1 and Q_2 and P_1 and P_2 and using the formula

$$\epsilon_p = \frac{\dfrac{Q_2 - Q_1}{\left(\dfrac{Q_1 + Q_2}{2}\right)}}{\dfrac{P_2 - P_1}{\left(\dfrac{P_1 + P_2}{2}\right)}}.$$

This modification allows for a superior estimate of arc elasticity and will be used henceforth. In terms of our previous numerical example, the coefficient of price elasticity for a decline in price from \$12 to \$10 now becomes

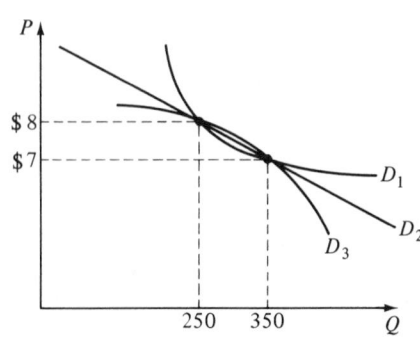

[5] This is especially true when the shape of the demand curve is not known and data for only a few prices and quantities are given. For example, it may be observed that when price is \$8, 250 units of a commodity are purchased, and when price is \$7, 350 units are purchased. However, as the accompanying figure suggests, an infinite number of demand curves can pass through these two points, and these curves reflect quite different price-quantity relationships over this price range.

$$\epsilon_p = \frac{\dfrac{Q_2 - Q_1}{\left(\dfrac{Q_1 + Q_2}{2}\right)}}{\dfrac{P_2 - P_1}{\left(\dfrac{P_1 + P_2}{2}\right)}} = \frac{\dfrac{50 - 30}{\left(\dfrac{30 + 50}{2}\right)}}{\dfrac{10 - 12}{\left(\dfrac{12 + 10}{2}\right)}} = \frac{\dfrac{20}{40}}{\dfrac{-2}{11}} = \frac{1}{2} \cdot -\frac{11}{2} = -\frac{11}{4} = -2.75.$$

The −2.75 can be interpreted to mean that over the indicated range of prices and quantities a 1 percent change in price will be followed by approximately a 2.75 percent change in quantity demanded in the *opposite* direction.

Since the sign of the coefficient is negative in accordance with the law of demand, it is the *size* of the coefficient itself which is relevant. It has become customary, therefore, to ignore the minus sign in speaking of the magnitude of elasticity. By convention, economists say that when the coefficient is a number greater than 1, demand is *elastic*, and when the coefficient is less than 1, demand is *inelastic*. Should, by chance, the coefficient turn out to be exactly 1, demand is said to be *unitary* or of *unitary elasticity*. The rationale for this classification is not hard to understand. When the coefficient is greater than 1, the percentage change in quantity demanded must necessarily be *larger* than the percentage change in price. It follows, then, that *in relative terms* the quantity demanded is responsive or sensitive to price changes—or, in the language of economics, that demand is elastic. On the other hand, when the coefficient is less than 1, the percentage change in quantity demanded is *smaller* than the percentage change in price, clearly implying that the quantity demanded is *relatively unresponsive or insensitive* or inelastic with regard to price changes.

The student should verify for himself at this point that when the modified arc elasticity formula is used, exactly the same coefficient is obtained for an increase in price from $10 to $12 as was obtained from a decrease in price from $12 to $10. Hence, the modification of averaging the prices and quantities eliminates any difference in the size of the coefficient arising from an arbitrary designation of one of the two points on the demand curve as the "starting point;" it also produces an "average" of the two results gotten with the simple version of the formula. More precisely, the modified arc elasticity formula yields an estimate of the responsiveness or sensitivity of the quantity demanded at the middle of the range defined by the two points.

Point Elasticity.   Measuring elasticity at a point eliminates the imprecision of the arc elasticity concept. Point elasticity, as the name implies, refers to the responsiveness of quantity demanded to very small price changes from a given point. Algebraically, this translates into the following:

$$\epsilon_p = \frac{\dfrac{\Delta Q}{Q}}{\dfrac{\Delta P}{P}} = \frac{\Delta Q}{Q} \cdot \frac{P}{\Delta P} = \frac{\Delta Q}{\Delta P} \cdot \frac{P}{Q}.$$

The last expression says that price elasticity at a point equals the ratio of the change in quantity demanded to the change in price multiplied by the ratio of price to quantity demanded at that point. As the changes in price get smaller and smaller and actually approach zero, the ratio of $\Delta Q/\Delta P$ becomes equivalent to the derivative of the demand function with respect to price, or

$$\lim_{\Delta P \to 0} \frac{\Delta Q}{\Delta P} = \frac{dQ}{dP}.$$

Hence, the formula for point elasticity becomes

$$\epsilon_p = \frac{dQ}{dP} \cdot \frac{P}{Q}.$$

As illustrations of the point elasticity concept, consider the following two examples.

Example 1: Suppose the demand function for a commodity is defined by the equation

$$Q = 245 - 3.5P.$$

We might ask, what is the price elasticity of demand at a price of $10? To determine ϵ_p we need to know P, Q, and dQ/dP. At a price of $10,

$$Q = 245 - 3.5(10) = 245 - 35 = 210.$$

The rate of change in Q as P changes, dQ/dP, is found by calculating the first derivative of the demand function:

$$\frac{dQ}{dP} = -3.5.$$

Hence, we can now substitute directly into the point elasticity formula, obtaining

$$\epsilon_p = \frac{dQ}{dP} \cdot \frac{P}{Q} = -3.5 \cdot \frac{10}{210} = -\frac{1}{6} = -.167.$$

This may properly be interpreted to mean that if the price of the commodity changes by a small amount (say 1 percent) from its value of $10, then the quantity demanded will change by approximately .167 percent in the opposite direction. Demand would appear to be quite inelastic at a price of $10.

Example 2: On occasion, the demand function may be expressed in terms of quantity rather than price. Consider the demand function

$$P = 940 - 48Q + Q^2.$$

What is the price elasticity of demand at an output of 10 units?
At $Q = 10$,

$$P = 940 - 48(10) + (10)^2$$
$$= 940 - 480 + 100 = \$560.$$

Now, it remains to find the value of dQ/dP. However, since the equation is expressed in terms of quantity rather than price, we must find dQ/dP by a slightly more circuitous route. We can determine dP/dQ quite easily as follows:

$$\frac{dP}{dQ} = -48 + 2Q.$$

It so happens (the mathematicians have formally proved it) that

$$\frac{dQ}{dP} = \frac{1}{\frac{dP}{dQ}},$$

thereby giving

$$\frac{dQ}{dP} = \frac{1}{-48 + 2Q}.$$

At $Q = 10$, this becomes

$$\frac{dQ}{dP} = \frac{1}{-48 + 2(10)} = -\frac{1}{28}.$$

Subsituting into the point elasticity formula, we have

$$\epsilon_p = \frac{dQ}{dP} \cdot \frac{P}{Q} = -\frac{1}{28} \cdot \frac{560}{10} = -2.$$

Again, the proper interpretation for the elasticity coefficient in this case is that for a 1 percent price change from the current price of \$560, the quantity demanded will change by about 2 percent in the opposite direction. And we would conclude that at a price of \$560 demand is elastic.

ELASTICITY AND THE SLOPE OF THE DEMAND CURVE

The concepts of slope and elasticity are frequently confused. It is sometimes fallaciously assumed that the flatter the demand curve, the greater its elasticity, and the steeper the demand curve, the smaller its elasticity. This assumption is categorically false and is so indicated in the definitions of the terms themselves. The slope of a demand curve depends entirely upon the size of an absolute change in price as compared to the size of the associated absolute change in the quantity demanded. At any given point on a demand curve the slope equals dP/dQ. Yet, as we have just seen, elasticity is defined mathematically as

$$\epsilon_p = \frac{dQ}{dP} \cdot \frac{P}{Q}.$$

Elasticity is, therefore, equal to the reciprocal of the slope of the demand curve multiplied by the ratio of P to Q and is a measure of the relative or *percentage* changes in P and Q. Clearly, then, since the slope (flatness or steepness) of a demand curve is based upon *absolute* changes in P and Q, whereas price elasticity has to do with *percentage* changes in P and Q, the value of the slope of the demand curve can equal the value of the coefficient of price elasticity only by the rarest of coincidences. Moreover, in the case of a linear, downward-sloping demand curve, the slope is constant, whereas the price elasticity varies from point to point along the curve according to the ratio of P to Q. Thus, any notion that elasticity and slope have any valid relationship to one another must be dispelled.

ELASTICITY AND TOTAL REVENUE

We are now ready to examine some of the practical applications of the price elasticity concept. Of prime interest to business firms is the effect that a price change will have upon sales volume and total revenue. Also, from the viewpoint of consumers it is pertinent to determine the effect of a price change upon the total amount of money consumers are willing and able to spend on a given commodity. Price elasticity can provide insight into these matters.

Consider the demand schedule in Table 5-2 and the corresponding demand curve for a firm shown as line dd' in Figure 5-8(a). At a price of $120 ($P_1$), the firm can sell 100 units (Q_1). If price is lowered to $110 ($P_2$), sales increase to 200 units (Q_2). The *percentage* change in price obviously is small in comparison with the *percentage* change in quantity demanded—the price decline is but a fraction of its original value of P_1, whereas the increase in quantity demanded from Q_1 to Q_2 is double the original volume of 100 units. From the arc elasticity formula, it can be verified that the coefficient of price elasticity over this range is -7.67. Thus, demand is *elastic* between points A and B. What happens to the firm's total revenue as it lowers price from $120 to $110? It increases. This can be seen geometrically from Figure 5-8(b), as well as from Table 5-2. Since total revenue is price times quantity sold, the size of the area shown by rectangle OP_1AQ_1 in Figure 5-8(a) is the firm's TR at P_1 and corresponds to the value for TR (distance $A'Q_1$) at Q_1

Table 5-2   Elasticity and Total Revenue

Price	Quantity Demanded	Total Revenue	Coefficient of Price Elasticity	Elasticity
$120	100	$12,000		
			-7.67	elastic
110	200	22,000		elastic
			-3.13	
100	270	27,000		elastic
			-1.90	
90	330	29,700		elastic
			-1.03	
85	350	29,750		
			-0.91	inelastic
80	370	29,600		inelastic
			-0.58	
70	400	28,000		inelastic
			-0.39	
60	425	25,500		

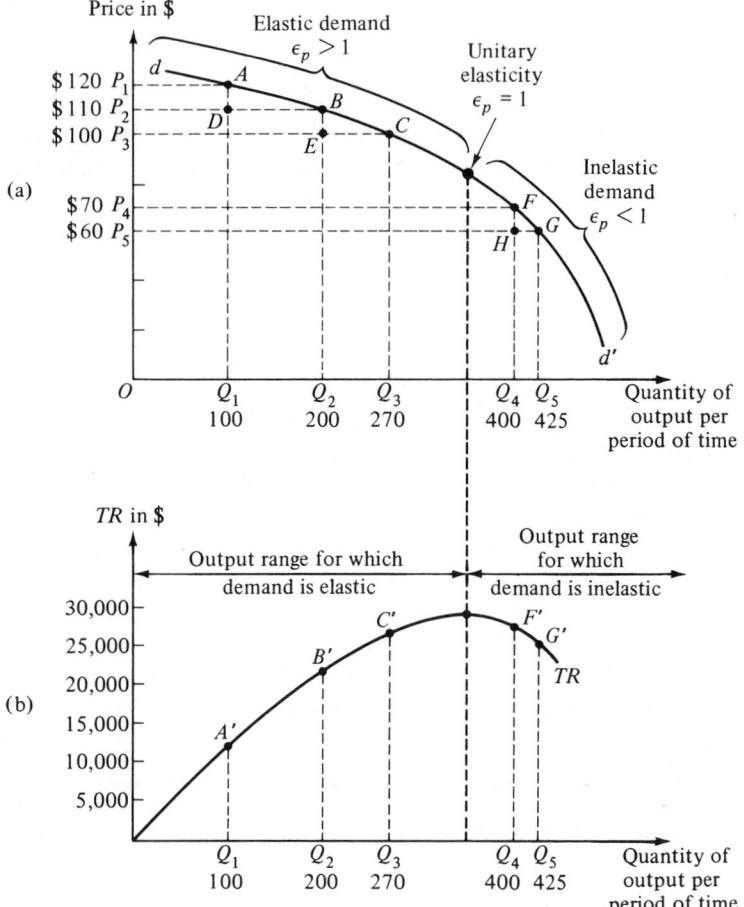

Fig. 5-8   The Relationships Between Demand Curves, Total Revenue, and Price Elasticity

in Figure 5-8(b). At price P_2, the firm's TR is given by the area of rectangle OP_2BQ_2 in Figure 5-8(a) and by distance $B'Q_2$ in Figure 5-8(b). By inspection, the area of rectangle OP_2BQ_2 exceeds that of rectangle OP_1AQ_1, and as indicated in Table 5-2 and Figure 5-8(b), TR at P_2 ($22,000) is larger than TR at P_1 ($12,000). It is larger because the *loss* of revenue due to the lower price per unit (area P_2P_1AD) is *less* than the *gain* in revenue resulting from increased sales (area Q_1DBQ_2). In other words, even though the firm sells its product at a lower price, the increase in sales at the lower price *more* than makes up for the smaller amount of revenue received per unit sold.

Should the firm lower its price further to P_3 ($100), sales will rise to Q_3 (270 units). Again, inspection of the graph shows that the decline in price

(P_2 to P_3) measured in percentage terms is *smaller* than the increase in quantity sold (Q_2 to Q_3) measured in percentage terms. And, again, we may correctly conclude that demand is *elastic* between points B and C. According to the arc formula, the coefficient of price elasticity over this range is -3.13. Also, from Figure 5-8(a) we see that the firm's total revenue at P_3 (area OP_3CQ_3 or \$27,000) is larger than the firm's total revenue at P_2 (area OP_2BQ_2 or \$22,000), because the *loss* in revenue associated with lowering price from P_2 to P_3 (area P_3P_2BE) is *less* than the *gain* in revenue due to greater sales (area Q_2ECQ_3).

This behavior of total revenue over elastic portions of the demand curve is not merely coincidental. In fact, we may state, as a general principle, that *whenever demand is elastic, a decline in price will result in an increase in total revenue*. The reasoning is reversible: *when demand is elastic, an increase in price will result in a decline in total revenue*. This is because should price rise, for example, from P_3 to P_2, the gain in total revenue associated with selling the commodity at a higher price (area P_3P_2BE) is smaller than the loss in revenue stemming from selling fewer units (area Q_2ECQ_3).

When demand is inelastic with regard to price, a lower price will cause a decline in total revenue. This situation exists for a decrease in price from P_4 (\$70) to P_5 (\$60) as shown in Figure 5-8(a). Over this price range, the coefficient of price elasticity is -0.39 (Table 5-2). At a price of \$70 and sales of 400 units, TR is \$28,000, whereas at a price of \$60 and sales of 425 units, TR is \$25,500. Graphically, at a price of P_4 (\$70), TR is equal to the area OP_4FQ_4, which is larger than TR at P_5 (\$60) shown as area OP_5GQ_5. Total revenue is lower because the modest increase in sales precipitated by the price decline is inadequate to offset the adverse impact of the fall in average revenue; consequently, the *loss* in revenue due to the lower price (area P_5P_4FH) *exceeds* the *gain* in revenue associated with selling more units (area Q_4HGQ_5). As before, the relationship is reversible: when demand is price inelastic, a rise in price (say from P_5 to P_4) will increase total revenue.

To recapitulate, whenever the demand for a commodity is elastic with respect to price changes, a decline in its price will cause total revenue to increase. In contrast, whenever the demand for a commodity is price inelastic, a price decline will be accompanied by a fall in total revenue. In the case of price increases, TR will rise when demand is price inelastic and will fall when demand is price elastic. Table 5-3 summarizes these principles.

It follows, then, that the positively-sloped portion of the TR function

Table 5-3 Price Changes, Price Elasticity, and Total Revenue

	$\epsilon_p > 1$	$\epsilon_p < 1$
$P \downarrow$	$TR \uparrow$	$TR \downarrow$
$P \uparrow$	$TR \downarrow$	$TR \uparrow$

corresponds to the elastic portion of the demand curve and vice versa (as is illustrated in Figure 5-8). By the same token, the negatively-sloped segment of the TR function is associated with inelastic demand. Starting from the top of the demand curve and moving down along it, the coefficient of price elasticity is a decreasing value but remains, nevertheless, larger than 1.0; simultaneously TR is increasing. Where TR is maximum, the elasticity of demand is unitary ($\epsilon_p = 1$). As we move further down the demand curve past the point of unitary elasticity, the coefficient of price elasticity is less than one and decreasing, and TR is declining. These relationships are typical of down-sloping demand functions.

There is a tendency, therefore, for most demand curves to be elastic at "high" prices and inelastic at "low" prices. As price falls from high levels, consumers respond vigorously and strong sales gains are posted, as well as healthy increases in TR. The point where $\epsilon_p = 1$ is the price at which consumers are willing to spend the greatest number of dollars on the commodity (TR is maximum). Further price cuts will not induce consumers to buy enough more units to compensate for the price decline. In other words, they are approaching their saturation level for the commodity and their marginal utility for additional units is rapidly diminishing; thus, price cuts have less impact upon consumer purchases.

Furthermore, it may be noted that the more elastic demand is, the further TR will rise when price falls. The more inelastic demand is, the further TR will fall when price is lowered. This feature may be verified from Table 5-2. For a price change from \$120 to \$110, over which range the coefficient of price elasticity approximates -7.67, TR rises from \$12,000 to \$22,000. However, for a price decline from \$110 to \$100, where $\epsilon_p = -3.13$, TR rises but from \$22,000 to \$27,000. And as price falls from \$100 to \$90, with ϵ_p approximating -1.90, TR rises by even less (from \$27,000 to \$29,700). On the inelastic portion of the demand curve, where demand is only slightly inelastic, as between prices of \$85 and \$80 ($\epsilon_p = -0.91$), a price decrease causes only a slight decline in TR (\$29,750 to \$29,600). As demand becomes more inelastic, as for a price decrease from \$70 to \$60 where $\epsilon_p = -0.39$, the decline in TR becomes more sizable (\$28,000 to \$25,500).

Elasticity, Total Revenue, and Profitability. The relationship between price elasticity and total revenue has a subtle, but highly important, implication for the pricing of commodities. Should a business firm discover, or have good reason to believe, that at its current price the coefficient of price elasticity is less than one (demand is inelastic), then the firm can increase its profits by raising its price. This principle derives from the fact that when demand is inelastic at the prevailing price an increase in price will cause total revenue to rise and total costs to fall, thereby widening the gap between the firm's revenues and costs. As was shown above, a price increase precipitates an increase in total revenue whenever the coefficient of price elasticity is less

170

than one. Total costs fall as a result of a higher price, since the higher price will reduce purchases of the commodity and cause the firm to produce fewer units, buy smaller amounts of economic resources, and, consequently, spend fewer dollars in the course of its activities. With *TR* rising and total costs falling, the overall profitability of the enterprise will, of necessity, be improved. Pursuing the same line of reasoning, a firm contemplating a lowering of its price should beware of an inelastic demand situation. A price decrease in face of an inelastic demand will lead not only to a decline in total revenue, but also to an increase in total costs due to a rising sales volume. The firm's profits will be lowered, and under such circumstances a lower selling price would seem ill-advised.

It is fair to state, therefore, that the most profitable level of output lies somewhere on the *elastic* portion of a firm's demand curve—just where, is a matter which will be explored fully in Chapters 10 and 11.

ELASTICITY AND LINEAR DEMAND CURVES

Although the law of demand requires only that a demand curve slope downward to the right, it is often convenient to represent the demand curve in its simplest form—as a straight line. This is legitimate, especially for an abstract discussion of "the" demand for "a" product. Also, empirical demand studies have revealed approximate linearity for some commodities, so such a portrayal is neither unrealistic nor unwarranted. Because of its simplicity, we shall employ the linear demand curve frequently. Familiarity with its character will, therefore, be quite useful.

Figure 5-9 illustrates a typical linear demand function along with its corresponding total revenue and marginal revenue function. It will be recalled that the general equatons for these functions are

$$P = a - bQ,$$
$$TR = P \cdot Q = aQ - bQ^2,$$
$$MR = \frac{dTR}{dQ} = a - 2bQ.$$

Additionally, the slope of the *MR* function is twice the slope of the demand curve; and *MR* equals zero where *TR* is maximum. The geometry of the relationships among the three functions is such that the price and quantity at which $MR = 0$ and *TR* is maximum is the midpoint of the demand curve; that is to say, the length of the segment of the demand curve above this point is equal to the length of the segment below it.

From the discussion in the preceding section it should be evident that demand is elastic on the *upper half* of the linear demand curve and is inelastic

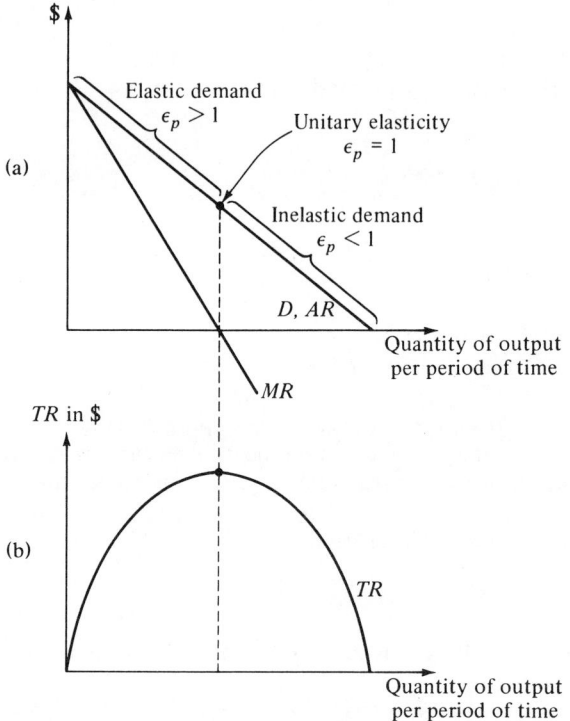

Fig. 5-9   Linear Demand Curves, Total Revenue, and Price Elasticity

along the *lower half* of the curve (see Figure 5-9). The coefficient of price elasticity is one at the *midpoint* of the curve. Moreover, starting at the top of the demand curve and proceeding down along it, the coefficient of price elasticity declines from very large values to a value of one at the midpoint, becomes less than one upon passing the midpoint, and approaches zero as price declines toward zero. The explanation for this behavior is not complicated. Near the top of the demand curve the percentage declines in price are quite small compared to the percentage increases in quantity demanded which they cause. The coefficient of price elasticity is, accordingly, large, since it is equal to the percentage change in the quantity demanded divided by the percentage change in price. Yet, moving down along the demand curve, as price continues to fall and quantity demanded continues to rise, the percentage changes in price get larger, while the percentage changes in quantity demanded get smaller. As a consequence, the coefficient of price elasticity necessarily declines in value.

It is not accurate, therefore, to describe linear demand curves as being

172

either elastic or inelastic; rather, the upper half of the demand curve is elastic and the lower half is inelastic. It is proper to speak of the price elasticity of demand at a given point or between two given points, but it is inappropriate to speak of the price elasticity of the demand curve as a whole.

MATHEMATICAL CAPSULE 4

The Elasticity of Demand at the Midpoint of a Linear Demand Function

It is relatively simple to show for a linear downsloping demand function that the price elasticity of demand at the midpoint of the demand curve is -1. All we need do is compute the coefficient of price elasticity at the midpoint utilizing the point elasticity formula.

The general equation for a linear demand curve is

$$P = a - bQ.$$

The general equations for the associated TR and MR functions are

$$TR = P \cdot Q = aQ - bQ^2,$$

$$MR = \frac{dTR}{dQ} = a - 2bQ.$$

To compute point elasticity, we must obtain values for dQ/dP, Q, and P at the midpoint of our generalized demand curve. We can find dQ/dP from the demand equation itself as follows:

$$P = a - bQ,$$

$$\frac{dP}{dQ} = -b.$$

Since

$$\frac{dQ}{dP} = \frac{1}{\frac{dP}{dQ}},$$

we have

$$\frac{dQ}{dP} = \frac{1}{-b} = -\frac{1}{b}.$$

The value of Q at the midpoint of the demand curve can be derived from the fact that at the midpoint of a linear demand curve $MR = 0$ and TR is maximum. The quantity at which $MR = 0$ can be found by setting the equation for MR equal to zero and solving for the value of Q which will satisfy this condition:

$$MR = a - 2bQ = 0,$$
$$-2bQ = -a,$$
$$Q = \frac{-a}{-2b} = \frac{a}{2b}.$$

When $Q = a/2b$, the corresponding value for P is

$$P = a - bQ$$
$$= a - b\left(\frac{a}{2b}\right)$$
$$= a - \frac{a}{2}$$
$$= \frac{a}{2}.$$

Substituting the values for dQ/dP, P, and Q into the point elasticity formula, we have

$$\epsilon_p = \frac{dQ}{dP} \cdot \frac{P}{Q}$$
$$= -\frac{1}{b} \cdot \frac{\frac{a}{2}}{\frac{a}{2b}}$$
$$= -\frac{1}{b} \cdot \frac{a}{2} \cdot \frac{2b}{a}$$
$$= -1.$$

Therefore, the coefficient of price elasticity equals -1 at the midpoint of all linear downsloping demand functions, irrespective of the values that a and b may assume.

SOME SPECIAL CASES IN PRICE ELASTICTIY

Certain kinds of demand curves have unique price elasticity properties. Three special cases will be noted.

Sometimes the demand situation confronting a firm is such that its demand curve is horizontal at a given price, meaning that at the given price the firm can sell all it wishes within the limits of its production capacity. A de-

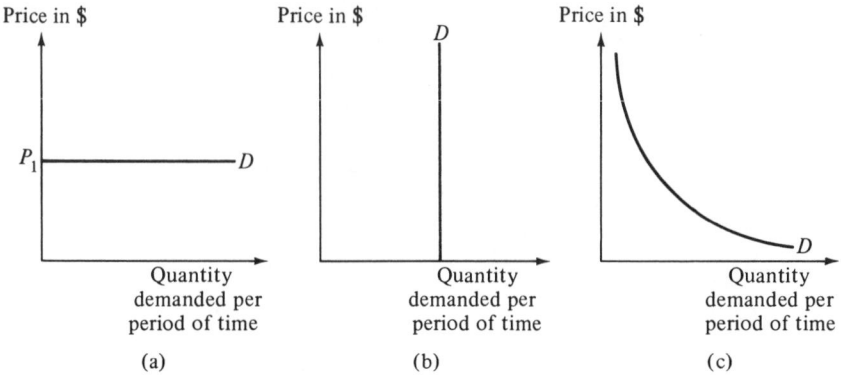

Fig. 5-10   Special Cases in Price Elasticity

mand curve of this type is illustrated in Figure 5-10(a). The firm may sell all it wishes at price P_1, but should it raise its price above P_1, buyers will shift *all* of their purchases to other firms. Since in this case the response of buyers to a price increase is total and complete, demand is said to be *perfectly elastic*, and the coefficient of price elasticity is infinity ($\epsilon_p = -\infty$).

In the very unusual event that the demand curve is vertical [Figure 5-10(b)], then there is no response in the quantity demanded to a price change. The coefficient of price elasticity is zero ($\epsilon_p = 0$) and demand is said to be *perfectly inelastic*.

The third special case arises when consumers spend a fixed amount of dollars upon a commodity irrespective of the price charged and the quantity bought. Every price-quantity combination results in the same amount of expenditure upon the product. Total revenue is constant no matter what the values of P and Q; the equation of the demand curve becomes

$$P \cdot Q = TR = k,$$

where k is a constant. The graph of a curve of this type is known as a rectangular hyperbola and is shown in Figure 5-10(c). The price elasticity of demand for such a demand curve is unitary ($\epsilon_p = -1$) for every point along the demand curve.

FACTORS INFLUENCING PRICE ELASTICITY

It is relevant to ask at this point just what causes a commodity to be responsive or unresponsive to price changes. By and large, a commodity tends to be more sensitive to price changes (1) the greater the number of good substitutes available at competitive prices, (2) the larger the price of the item relative to the income of buyers, and (3) the more the product is regarded as a luxury item. A couple of illustrations may highlight the reasoning for these propositions.

The demand for toothpaste is highly inelastic on all three counts. Good substitutes for toothpaste are scarce; indeed, consumers have no place to turn if its price rises from 89 cents to $1.05 for the family-size tube. Furthermore, a family's expenditures for toothpaste are so small a fraction of monthly income that the impact of a 16-cent price increase is negligible. And, finally, toothpaste is a virtual necessity.

On the other hand, the demand for brand X sailboats is likely to be highly elastic. Good substitutes are available in the form of competing brands, not to mention other forms of boats and recreational activities. Since the price of the item is large in relation to income, the consumer is likely to be quite price-conscious and substitute-conscious; a given percentage change in price can be expected to have a significant sales impact, as well as an impact upon the consumer's budget. And to most families a sailboat is a luxury and an expendable item in their budget.

Other factors also influence price elasticity. There is a tendency for the demand for a commodity to be more elastic the wider the range of its uses. With a larger number of uses, more opportunity exists for variation in the quantity sold when price changes. Increases in price reduce the number of economical uses to which a commodity may be put, whereas price declines expand the range of economically feasible uses. This aspect of demand elasticity is especially pertinent for steel, aluminum, other primary metals, plastics, wool, and various paper products. Also, it may be noted that the demand for a product tends to be more elastic in the long run than in the short run. Primarily, this is due to lags in consumer response to price changes and in the associated alterations in their patterns of expenditure. Lastly, the durability of some products influences the degree of elasticity. Postponing the purchase of new durable goods by repairing them may be an effective, albeit temporary, substitute for replacement, thus making for a more elastic demand than would otherwise be the case.

Before passing, it should be recalled that the elasticity of demand is affected by the position on the demand curve. Demand is more likely to be elastic at prices on the upper end of the demand curve than on the lower end. As discussed previously, this is a purely mathematical aspect of price elasticity, and its validity hinges upon the shape of the demand curve.

INCOME ELASTICITY OF DEMAND

Although our analysis has focused upon price elasticity of demand, other measures of demand elasticity exist. We noted in Chapter 4 that the purchase levels of many commodities are quite sensitive to variations in consumer incomes. The responsiveness of the quantity demanded to a change in consumer income (other demand determinants being held fixed) is called *income elasticity of demand.*

Just as price elasticity was found by determining the ratio of the percentage change in the quantity demanded to some percentage change in price, so income elasticity is calculated by finding the ratio of the percentage change in quantity demanded to a percentage change in income. Hence, we may write

$$\epsilon_I = \frac{\text{percent change in quantity demanded}}{\text{percent change in income}}.$$

As with price elasticity, there are also two measures of income elasticity: arc elasticity and point elasticity. The arc formula for computing income elasticity is

$$\epsilon_I = \frac{\dfrac{Q_2 - Q_1}{\left(\dfrac{Q_1 + Q_2}{2}\right)}}{\dfrac{I_2 - I_1}{\left(\dfrac{I_1 + I_2}{2}\right)}},$$

where ϵ_I represents the coefficient of income elasticity and I is income. The point formula for income elasticity is

$$\epsilon_I = \frac{dQ}{dI} \cdot \frac{I}{Q},$$

where dQ/dI symbolizes the rate of change in the quantity demanded as income changes.

For all commodities except inferior goods the sign of the coefficient of income elasticity is positive, because for normal goods income and quantity purchased vary in the same direction. If the value of the income elasticity coefficient is greater than $+1$, the demand for the commodity is said to be income elastic; if it is less than $+1$, then demand is said to be income inelastic. The coefficient of income elasticity is negative for inferior goods. The greater the size of the coefficient, the greater the degree of responsiveness of the quantity demanded to a change in income.

Income elasticity varies widely from commodity to commodity. Light bulbs, dairy products, haircuts, aspirin, and cigarettes are examples of commodities whose income elasticities are typically low. In contrast, jewelry, T-bone steak, Cadillacs, objects of art, education, foreign travel, and scotch have high income elasticities. Generally, commodities which consumers regard as necessities have low income elasticities, while luxuries tend to have high income elasticities. Indeed, perhaps the most accurate way of designating commodities as either luxuries or necessities is by the size of their income elasticities.

CROSS ELASTICITY OF DEMAND

Insofar as demand is concerned, commodities can be related in any one of three ways:

1. They may be *competing* products or *substitutes*, in which case an increase in the purchase of one is at the expense of another. So it is with various *brands* of margarine, soap, razor blades, and gasoline; likewise, hamburgers may be a substitute for hot dogs, a trip to Florida may be a substitute for a trip to the Great Smoky Mountains, and a Pinto may be substitute for a Vega.
2. They may be *complementary* products, in which case an increase in the purchase of one causes a rise in the purchase of another. Complementarity implies that goods are consumed *together*. Examples include electric appliances and electric power, shoes and socks, notebook paper and ball-point pens, and carpets and vacuum cleaners.
3. They may be *independent*, so that the purchase of one has no direct bearing upon the demand for another. Independence implies that goods are consumed neither together nor in place of each other. Pairs of commodities whose purchases are independent include shrimp and pillows, football tickets and spools of thread, and shotgun shells and lingerie.

Cross elasticity of demand is a measure for interpreting the relationship between commodities. As between two products X and Y, cross elasticity measures the percentage change in the quantity demanded of product Y in response to a percentage change in the price of product X. In mathematical terms,

$$\epsilon_{YX} = \frac{\text{percent change in quantity of Y}}{\text{percent change in price of X}},$$

where ϵ_{yx} symbolizes the coefficient of cross elasticity between X and Y. Again, there are two ways of actually computing cross elasticity. The arc formula for calculating the coefficient of cross elasticity is

$$\epsilon_{YX} = \frac{\dfrac{Q_{Y_2} - Q_{Y_1}}{\left(\dfrac{Q_{Y_1} + Q_{Y_2}}{2}\right)}}{\dfrac{P_{X_2} - P_{X_1}}{\left(\dfrac{P_{X_1} + P_{X_2}}{2}\right)}}.$$

The point formula for cross elasticity is

$$\epsilon_{YX} = \frac{dQ_Y}{dP_X} \cdot \frac{P_X}{Q_Y}.$$

The cross elasticity coefficient may be either positive or negative. When ϵ_{yx} is positive, products X and Y are substitutes for each other. This is illustrated by a simple example. Other factors remaining constant, if the price of shipping goods by rail increases, the freight traffic via motor carrier should rise. Conversely, if the price of shipping goods by rail declines, the freight traffic via motor carrier should decrease. In either case, the percentage changes in rail rates and the volume of motor freight are in the same direction. Thus, whether the price changes are up or down, the cross elasticity coefficient is positive.

Complementary goods have negative cross elasticity coefficients. Automobiles and automobile insurance serve as a case in point. Other things being equal, an increase in the price of automobiles reduces purchases of automobiles and cuts back on the sales of automobile insurance. In contrast, lower automobile prices stimulate car sales, thereby boosting sales of auto insurance. Hence, a change in the price of automobiles is followed by a change in sales of auto insurance in the opposite direction. As a consequence, the coefficient of cross elasticity is negative.

The strength of the relationship between substitute and complementary products is reflected by the absolute size of the cross elasticity coefficient. The larger the coefficient, the stronger the relationship. Furthermore, it follows that the closer the coefficient is to zero (approached from either the positive or negative side), the weaker is any substitute or complementary relationship between two commodities and the more independent the two products are. This is so because as ϵ_{yx} approaches zero, variations in the price of one commodity induce no appreciable change in the quantity demanded of the other; hence, purchases of the products would seem unrelated or independent.

Measures of the cross elasticity of demand may indicate the boundaries of an industry. High cross elasticities indicate close relationships and suggest that the goods are part of the same industry, whereas low cross elasticities imply weak relationships and that the goods may be in different industries. If a commodity has a low cross elasticity with respect to all other commodities, then it may be considered to constitute an industry by itself. Similarly, should a group of products have high cross elasticities among themselves but low cross elasticities with respect to other commodities, then the product group may define an industry. For instance, various brands of TV sets have high cross elasticities among each other but low cross elasticities with other household appliances and fixtures.

MATHEMATICAL CAPSULE 5

Partial Elasticities of Demand: A More Rigorous Concept of Demand Elasticity

In its most general form, the demand function for a commodity can be expressed as

$$Q_1 = f(P_1, P_2, \ldots, P_n, I, E, R, N, T, Q),$$

where Q_1 = the quantity demanded of commodity "1,"
P_1 = the market price of the commodity,
$P_2, \ldots, P_n$ = prices of other commodities,
I = the level of consumer incomes,
E = consumer expectations regarding future prices, incomes, and product availability,
R = range of commodities available to buyers,
N = number of potential buyers, and
Q = all other factors relevant in influencing Q_1.

The elasticity of demand with respect to any demand determinant refers to the degree of responsiveness of the quantity demanded relative to some percentage change in that demand determinant *when the values of all other demand determinants are held fixed.*

In mathematical terms, this definition translates into the following expressions for point elasticity:

(1) $$\epsilon_p = \frac{\partial Q_1}{\partial P_1} \cdot \frac{P_1}{Q_1}.$$

which is the partial elasticity of good 1 with respect to its price, P_1, or price elasticity of demand;

(2) $$\epsilon_{12} = \frac{\partial Q_1}{\partial P_2} \cdot \frac{P_2}{Q_1},$$

which is the partial elasticity of good 1 with respect to the price of good 2, or cross elasticity of demand between good 1 and good 2;

(3) $$\epsilon_{1n} = \frac{\partial Q_1}{\partial P_n} \cdot \frac{P_n}{Q_1},$$

which is the partial elasticity of good 1 with respect to the price of good n, or cross elasticity of demand between good 1 and good n;

(4) $$\epsilon_I = \frac{\partial Q_1}{\partial I} \cdot \frac{I}{Q_1}.$$

which is the partial elasticity of good 1 with respect to income, or income elasticity of demand; and so on for the other demand determinants. Hence, when given the demand function for a commodity containing more than one variable, the procedure for determining point elasticity requires using the *partial derivative* of the demand function with respect to that demand determinant rather than the first derivative.

EXERCISES

1. Suppose the demand function for commodity X is specified by the equation

$$Q_X = 34 - .8P_x{}^2 + .3P_y + .04I.$$

   (a) Determine the price elasticity of demand for X when $P_x = \$10$, $P_y = \$20$, and $I = \$5,000$.
   (b) Determine the cross elasticity of demand for X with respect to commodity Y when $P_x = \$10$, $P_y = \$20$, and $I = \$5,000$. Are X and Y substitutes or complements?
   (c) Determine the income elasticity of demand for X when $P_x = \$10$, $P_y = \$20$, and $I = \$5,000$. Is X a normal or an inferior good?

2. Suppose the demand function for commodity Y is specified by the equation

$$Q_y = 1,665 - .5P^3{}_y - .1P^2{}_x - .05I.$$

   (a) Determine the price elasticity of demand when $P_y = \$10$, $P_x = \$20$, and $I = \$2,500$.
   (b) Determine the cross elasticity of demand for Y with respect to commodity X when $P_y = \$10$, $P_x = \$20$, and $I = \$2,500$. Are X and Y substitutes or complements?
   (c) Determine the income elasticity of demand for Y when $P_y = \$10$, $P_x = \$20$, and $I = \$2,500$. Is Y a normal or an inferior good?

Summary and Conclusions

The analysis of the demand for a commodity can be approached from the standpoint of an individual consumer (individual consumer demand), from the standpoint of all consumers taken as a group (market demand), or from the standpoint of a particular business firm (product demand or firm demand). Individual consumer demand for a commodity is determined in the main by (1) the selling price of the commodity, (2) consumer tastes and preferences, (3) the money income of consumers, (4) the prices of related products, (5) consumer expectations with regard to future prices, income levels, and product availability, and (6) the range of goods and services available for selection. By adding to this listing the number of consumers, we get the seven major determinants of the market demand for a commodity. Other peripheral considerations include whether the good in question is a luxury or a necessity, whether its demand is derived from the demand for other goods, the size of its market saturation level, the price and availability of consumer credit, and the discretionary purchasing power of consumers. The separate impacts of the major and minor demand determinants vary in degree and intensity from commodity to commodity; each commodity has its own unique set of demand determinants.

A firm's demand curve provides the basis for deriving its revenue curves. A firm's average revenue (*AR*) curve summarizes the relationship between average revenue (i.e., price) and quantity sold; it is identical to the firm's demand curve. A firm's total revenue (*TR*) curve represents the total receipts it obtains from the sale of its output. A firm's marginal revenue (*MR*) curve shows the change in total revenue that results from a very small increase or decrease in output sold. Marginal revenue may be thought of as either *continuous* or *discrete*. Continuous marginal revenue is appropriate when output changes by infinitesimally small amounts. Discrete marginal revenue is used in situations where output changes in amounts of 1 unit (or more). A firm's average revenue can be found by dividing total revenue by the number of units sold. The shapes of the various *TR*, *MR*, and *AR* functions depend upon the shape of the demand curve.

Elasticity of demand measures the responsiveness or sensitivity of the quantity demanded to changes in a demand determinant. Price elasticity of demand is defined specifically as a ratio of the percentage change in quantity demanded resulting from a percentage change in price. Arc elasticity is an approximate measure of demand sensitivity between two points, while point elasticity measures elasticity at a single point on the demand function. When the coefficient of price elasticity is greater than one, demand is elastic and a price decrease will cause *TR* to rise. When the coefficient of price elasticity is less than one, demand is inelastic and a price decrease will cause *TR* to fall. Total revenue is maximized at the output level where the price elasticity coefficient is one. The degree of price elasticity for a commodity varies according to (1) the region of the demand curve within which price changes, (2) the number and availability of substitutes, (3) the price of the item relative to consumer income, (4) whether the item is a luxury or a necessity, (5) the number of uses for the good, (6) the length of the time period being considered, and (7) the durability of the item.

Two other elasticity concepts of particular importance are income elasticity and cross elasticity. High, positive income elasticities characterize luxury items; low, positive income elasticities are typical for necessities; and negative income elasticities denote inferior goods. Cross elasticity is a measure of the sensitivity of the demand for one commodity relative to price changes in another commodity. When the cross elasticity coefficient is positive, the two commodities are substitutes; when the coefficient is negative, a complementary relationship is indicated. The closer the coefficient is to zero, the more independent are the two commodities.

SUGGESTED READINGS

For some empirical measures of the elasticity of demand, see:

DEAN, JOEL, *Managerial Economics* (Englewood Cliffs, N.J.: Prentice-Hall, Inc., 1951), pp. 177–210.

WOLD, H., *Demand Analysis* (New York: John Wiley & Sons, Inc., 1953).

SCHULTZ, HENRY, *Theory and Measurement of Demand* (Chicago: University of Chicago Press, 1938).

SUITS, DANIEL B., "The Demand for New Automobiles in the U.S., 1929–1956," *Review of Economics and Statistics*, Vol. 40 (August 1958), pp. 273–280.

Problems and Questions for Discussion

1. The following table presents hypothetical data for the market demand for a commodity. Complete the table.

Price	Quantity Demanded	AR	TR	Discrete MR	Coefficient of Price Elasticity
$50	1	_____	_____	_____	_____
$40	2	_____	_____	_____	_____
$30	3	_____	_____	_____	_____
$20	4	_____	_____	_____	_____
$13	5	_____	_____	_____	_____
$ 8	6	_____	_____	_____	_____

2. Given the following demand function:

$$P = 81 - 9Q.$$

(a) What is the equation for TR? for MR?

(b) At what output is $MR = 0$?

(c) At what output is TR maximum?

(d) Determine the price elasticity of demand at the output where TR is maximum.

3. Given the following demand function:

$$Q = 20 - 3P,$$

what is the price elasticity of demand at a price of $1? At a price of $4?

4. Given the following demand function:

$$Q = 16 + 9P - 2P^2,$$

what is the price elasticity of demand at a price of $4? A price of $3?

5. Given the following demand function:

$$P = 1000 + 3Q - 4Q^2,$$

(a) determine the equations for TR and for MR.
(b) graphically illustrate the demand, TR, and MR functions.
(c) determine price elasticity of demand at an output of 10 units.

6. Given the following hypothetical data for a consumer, compute *all* meaningful elasticity coefficients (price elasticity, income elasticity, and cross elasticity). Remember that prices must be constant when income elasticity is computed and that income and the prices of other products must be constant when price elasticity is computed, and so on. In other words, the computation of elasticities of any kind is valid *only* when *all other* variables are held constant.

Period	Price of X	Quantity of X Purchased	Price of Y	Income
1	$1.00	200	$.50	6000
2	1.05	190	.50	6000
3	1.05	200	.52	6500
4	1.05	220	.54	6500
5	1.03	210	.53	6500
6	1.03	215	.55	6500
7	1.03	205	.55	6300
8	1.07	190	.55	6300

7. Given the following market demand equation for widgets:

$$Q = 840 - .50P,$$

where Q = quantity demanded per period of time, and P = price of widgets in dollars.

(a) If the price of widgets were lowered from $40 to $38, would you expect consumer expenditures for widgets to rise, fall, or remain unchanged?
(b) If the economy's sole producer of widgets lowered its price from $40 to $38, what predictions, if any, can you make about the effect the price reduction would have upon the firm's *profits*?

8. Given the following relationship between product A and product B:

$$Q_A = 80P_B - .5P_B^2,$$

where Q_A = units of product A demanded by consumers each day, and P_B = selling price of product B.

(a) Determine the cross elasticity coefficient for the two products when the price of product B = $10.
(b) Are products A and B complements, substitutes, or independent, and how "strong" is the relationship?

9. Given the price levels now prevailing for steel products, would you expect that the price elasticity of demand for the output of U.S. Steel Corporation is higher or lower than the price elasticity of demand for the output of the steel industry as a whole? Why?

PRODUCTION
AND
COST ANALYSIS

6

Production Processes
and Technological Change

Having obtained an understanding of the formation of consumer demand and the composition of demand functions, we are ready to proceed with the economics of decision problems concerning how best to produce the output which consumers are willing and able to purchase. This chapter will examine some of the properties of a firm's production process and pinpoint the factors governing a firm's choice of production technologies. Specifically, we shall consider (1) the concept of production, (2) the properties of the production functions of firms, (3) the role of technology and technological advance in altering the capabilities of a firm to produce commodities, and (4) the pressures upon firms for adopting new technologies.

THE CONCEPT OF PRODUCTION

It is common to conceive of "production" as simply the manufacture of a commodity. It is more accurate, however, to give the term production a much broader connotation. As used in economics, it includes such diverse activities as:

    —collecting taxes,
    —delivering newspapers,
    —operating a grocery store,

—hiring and training new employees,

—cutting a person's hair,

—repairing equipment,

—conducting a marketing research study of changes in consumer taste and in product demand,

—storing commodities or transporting them from one place to another,

—conceiving of an imaginative advertising campaign and quarreling with the Federal Trade Commission over its use,

—dictating a letter,

—managing a United Fund drive,

—offering professional advice on new applications of computer technology, and

—teaching a course in intermediate microeconomic theory.

Thus, production does not refer simply to the process of manufacturing commodities, but also involves any activity concerned with storing, transporting, or selling these commodities, as well as the rendering of personal and business services of all kinds. In general, *activities which create value represent production*. Thus production covers virtually all phases of economic activity except consumption. Nevertheless, manufacturing activity is, in many respects, typical of what production means to economists as well as others, and we shall discuss production theory and production decisions largely in the context of manufacturing processes. Still, the principles of production are equally applicable to the whole range of an organization's activities.

PRODUCTION PROCESSES

Were a production engineer asked how to make some simple product, he might well reply in terms of the kinds of raw materials needed, the proportions and order in which these ingredients should be combined, and the processing times and temperatures needed to produce the desired characteristics. Such an answer would serve as a beginning, though it would, of course, be incomplete. Other inputs are needed. Raw material ingredients do not get combined and processed of their own volition; these operations require human intervention or *labor* input. In addition, various tools, machinery, equipment, and physical facilities will likely be required to assist in converting the raw material ingredients into the final product—these types of inputs constitute a general category of resources called *capital*. Furthermore, production activity must occur in some location and so occupies space or *land* (this is particularly apparent in the case of agricultural production), and the activity takes *time*, even if only the time involved in transporting and mixing ingredients. Finally, production activity requires supervision, planning, control, coordination, and leadership—in other words, an input of *managerial talent and capability*.

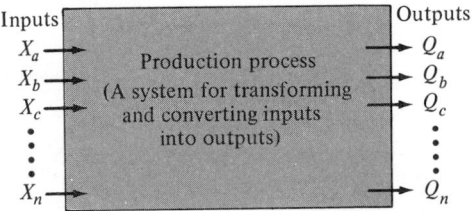

Fig. 6-1   The Production Process

By *production process* is meant, therefore, an integrated system of activities by which inputs (raw materials, labor, capital, land utilization, and managerial talents) are transformed over some period of time into outputs of goods or services. The time period requisite for the transformation is variable among products and from recipe to recipe for a given product. It should be noted that a production process may result in more than one output. In meat packing, for example, the slaughter of beef cattle produces numerous kinds of meat products, hides for leather goods, and lard for cooking purposes. Outputs produced from the same production process are designated as *joint products*.

Figure 6-1 summarizes in simple terms the basic nature of a production process. The boundaries of the box tend to change over time as a consequence of modifications in technical requirements, the qualities of inputs, and the composition of output. It is important to recognize that a production process is composed of a series of intricately integrated phases. To introduce a change in one of the phases nearly always requires changes elsewhere. Introducing a piece of labor-saving equipment, for example, typically has the effect of adjusting materials specifications and of modifying the skill levels of the labor input needed to operate the new equipment. These, in turn, may necessitate changes in procurement patterns and in hiring and training programs. The high productivity of the new equipment may cause bottlenecks at either or both ends of the phase, causing even further adjustments.

THE PRODUCTION FUNCTION

The term *production function* refers to the physical relationship between a firm's input of productive resources (raw materials, labor, capital, land, managerial talents) and its output of goods or services per unit of time. A firm's production function thus relates the size of a flow of output to the size of the corresponding flow of input required to generate it. It can be expressed symbolically as

$$Q = f(X_a, X_b, X_c, \ldots, X_n),$$

where $X_a, X_b, X_c, \ldots, X_n$ represent quantities of various types of inputs and the variable Q represents the quantity of output obtainable per period of time from specific combinations of the array of inputs. Such an expression furnishes a convenient analytical device for relating output flows to input flows and for clearly indicating that the quantity of a commodity produced per period of time is a function of the quantities of resource inputs used by the firm per period of time.

The specific character of the production function depends partly upon the quantities of resources employed and partly upon the way in which they are combined (the production techniques adopted by the firm). For illustration, consider the following circumstance, in which a firm has two technically feasible ways of combining inputs X_a, X_b, X_c, and X_d:

Production Technique	Resource Inputs	Output
Technique A	50 units each of X_a, X_b, X_c, and X_d	5,000 units
	100 units each of X_a, X_b, X_c, and X_d	10,000 units
	150 units each of X_a, X_b, X_c, and X_d	15,000 units
Technique B	50 units each of X_a, X_b, X_c, and X_d	6,000 units
	100 units each of X_a, X_b, X_c, and X_d	12,000 units
	150 units each of X_a, X_b, X_c, and X_d	18,000 units

By employing Technique A the firm can produce 5,000 units of output with 50 units each of inputs X_a, X_b, X_c, and X_d. One hundred units of each input yield 10,000 units of output, and 150 units of each input yield 15,000 units. However, the input-output relationship is quite different for technique B. Technique B generates more output for the same volume of input than does technique A; consequently, it is more efficient than A. It follows that a production function exists for *each* production technique or recipe for producing a commodity. A firm can alter its quantity of output by varying the amounts of input it combines according to its given production technique, by switching from one production technique to another, or by doing both. The efficiency of a production technique determines the output yield from each combination of inputs, while the state of technological know-how determines the number of available techniques.

In order to distinguish between the many production techniques available to a firm and the one it actually employs, economists customarily assume that the profit motive induces a firm to utilize the production technique that is most efficient. Moreover, a firm is presumed to employ this technique in such a way as always to obtain the maximum output from each alternative combination of inputs it uses. In symbolic language, for a production function of the form

$$Q = f(X_a, X_b, X_c, \ldots, X_n),$$

each numerical value of Q corresponding to specified numerical values of $X_a, X_b, X_c, \ldots, X_n$ is interpreted as being the largest possible value of Q obtainable, given the production technology employed by the firm. For instance, in studying the production function for a firm producing red fireplugs, interest centers only upon the *maximum* number of red fireplugs per period of time that can be produced from specific combinations of machine time, hours of skilled labor, floor space, electricity, hours of managerial input, metal casting, red paint, and so on. The rationale for this presumption is that no firm would knowingly seek to get anything less than the largest possible amount of output for a specified set of inputs, although, of course, in reality various frictions and imperfections in the production process may prevent a firm from always realizing the maximum output.

Actually, it is equally accurate to conceive of a firm's production function as specifying the minimum input requirements for a designated level of output, given its production technology. To use the fireplug example again, the input-output relationship for a firm producing red fireplugs can be estimated by studying the *minimum* amounts of machine time, hours of skilled labor, floor space, electricity, hours of managerial input, metal casting, red paint, and so on requisite for producing specified quantities of red fireplugs per period of time.

As either of the foregoing approaches suggests, the production function for a firm defines the limits of the firm's technical production possibilities. At any point in time, should a firm producing at these limits wish to increase its rate of output, it must use more inputs; similarly, the firm cannot use fewer inputs without decreasing its rate of output. Clearly, then, given that a firm is using the most efficient production technique permitted by the state of technology, its output rate is dependent upon the quantities of resource inputs employed in the production process and upon how efficiently it is using these quantities of resource inputs.

Knowledge of the production function is of crucial importance to a firm because it permits answers to the following questions:

1. To what extent will the total output of a production process be changed if the quantity of some input employed in this process is held constant, while the quantity of some other input is increased?
2. To what extent will the total output of a production process be changed if the quantity of one input employed in this process is decreased, while the quantity of some other input is simultaneously increased?
3. To what extent will the total output of a production process be changed if the firm increases *in equal proportions* all of the inputs employed in its process?

A firm can also ascertain from its production function whether its operating level is technically efficient. Because the production function gives the maximum output obtainable from a given input combination, should the actual output flow be less than the potential maximum flow, then the firm can produce its present output with a smaller volume of one or more inputs (and thereby reduce costs), or else it can use its present inputs to produce a larger volume of output than it is currently getting. To put it another way, unless a firm is operating at some input-output combination defined by its production function, its output rate is technically inefficient.

THE IMPACT OF TECHNOLOGICAL ADVANCE
UPON PRODUCTION FUNCTIONS

It is a matter of historical fact that technical knowledge and capability has broadened and deepened over time, and presumably will continue to do so. This kind of technological change is pertinent for production analysis, because an advance in the state of technology increases the number of recipes available for producing commodities, and in time it will alter the production functions of enterprises as they incorporate new technologies into their production processes. While technological advance brings to light *more efficient* recipes for producing commodities, the nature of the efficiency improvement may assume several forms, of which the following four are the most relevant and pervasive:

1. A new production process may permit the same amounts of resource inputs to be combined differently so as to yield a greater output than before.
2. A new production process may utilize the same types of inputs to produce the same type of output as previously known processes, but require a *smaller* quantity of one or even several inputs and *no more* of the remaining inputs to produce the same quantity of output as before.
3. A new production process may employ the same types of inputs to produce the same type of output as previously known processes, using *less* of some inputs and *more* of others, yet with a smaller total cost and rate of input usage, to produce the same quantity of output as before.
4. A new production process may require inputs, or yield outputs, that are of a kind not heretofore used or available at all.

Technological change which results in the discovery of production processes that are less efficient than those already known can safely be ignored, since an enterprise has no motive to employ more than the minimum amount of input.

It should be noted that the state of technological knowledge is not necessarily uniform among those firms engaging in the production of a commodity. Different firms are very likely to have built their production facilities at points in time when the state of technological know-how was different. Steel mills built in the 1920's are of far different efficiency from those being built today. Also, the managers, engineers, and technical staff of some firms may simply have failed to keep up with current developments and may not know the processes that other firms are keeping secret. For these reasons, the production functions for firms producing the same commodity can be—and usually are—heterogeneous.

THE CONSEQUENCES OF TECHNOLOGICAL CHANGE FOR PRODUCTION PROCESSES

As explained in Chapter 1, technology refers to the systematic application of scientific, engineering, administrative, or other organized bodies of knowledge to the accomplishment of practical tasks and problem-solving. It includes ways to teach economics, plant corn, count votes, supervise people, or manufacture trucks. The application of modern technology requires production activity to be subdivided to such an extent that specialists can bring their full expertise to bear upon various phases of each production process. Hence, whenever the scope of production activity exceeds the range of capability of an individual, it must necessarily be broken down into parts coterminous with a specific segment of knowledge and within the range of accomplishment by an individual. Furthermore, the broader and deeper is society's technical capability, the greater is the technological inperative to subdivide production activity so that the full contribution of each specialized bit of knowledge can be gained.

Plainly, an expanding state of knowledge permits the production of commodities which heretofore could not be produced or were not even discovered. Often these new commodities are quite complex (electronic computers, diagnostic equipment for detection of illness, electron microscopes, supersonic transport planes) and/or require highly specialized manpower during the course of their production (technical instruments, spacecraft, and prescription drugs). As a consequence, technological advance induces fundamental and persistent changes in both production processes and production functions. This is particularly true of technological progress in the twentieth century. Several of these changes deserve brief mention.[1]

First, as elaborate production processes are developed to produce commodities more efficiently, an increasing span of time separates the beginning from the completion of the production process. An analogy may be made to the root system of a tree. A production process is subdivided into phases and stretches back into time just as the root system of a tree penetrates and spreads through the ground. The bigger the tree, the larger and more complex its root system. Similarly, the more complex the commodity to be produced or the production process required to produce it

---

[1] The following discussion is based largely upon ideas expressed by John Kenneth Galbraith in Chapter 2 of *The New Industrial State* (Boston: Houghton Mifflin Company, 1967).

efficiently, the longer the time span required for its accomplishment and the greater the number of phases into which the production process must be divided. Specialized knowledge and technical expertise can then be brought to bear upon the performance of each phase of the whole task. As the first-level phases are completed, their results must be combined with the results of related phases so as to effect completion of the second level of the process; these second-level results must be combined again, and so on, until the phases have been put together to complete the whole process. The more complex the process, the more individuals with specialized, technical skills are required.

Second, advances in technology are typically accompanied by increases in the capital goods which must be committed to the production process as a whole. The application of more knowledge to some phase of a process often involves the development of tools, machinery, or equipment to perform or assist in performing the function. Hence, the incorporation of greater degrees of technological sophistication tends to mean that even more time, money, and human effort than previously will be integrated into the production process.

Third, the added commitment of more time, money, and effort associated with the introduction of specialized capital equipment tends to render production processes somewhat less adaptable to short-run changes in the composition of the final product or in the means of producing it. The new equipment may be *useful* only for performing certain well-defined and delimited aspects of the overall task. To further alter the means of performing specific segments of the process may well make some pieces of capital equipment obsolete or useless and cause still greater investments of knowledge and equipment to be brought to bear in revising the phase in question. The expense of accommodating such a change may be prohibitive until a larger portion of the projected life of the specialized equipment is used up and its replacement falls within the range of economic feasibility. When this occurs, changes in the production process may be effected more easily. Meanwhile, in the short run, change in the production recipe is inhibited.

Fourth, technological advance alters the types of manpower needed to staff the human element of production processes. For example, the introduction of computers into business operations has greatly reduced the needs for payroll clerks, billing clerks, bookkeepers, and similar kinds of office staff while at the same time creating entirely new demands for keypunch operators, programmers, statistical consultants, systems analysts, computer engineers, and so on. Also, one may note that over the last several decades, the character of technological change has dictated that more highly specialized manpower be used in conjunction with the introduction of new production techniques and new equipment. The requirement of specialized manpower, however, does not necessarily reflect a need for a higher order of human talent so much as it calls for the specialist to have a deeper knowledge of a smaller range of subjects.

Fifth, with a higher order of technology and more intensive specialization must come organization and proficient administration. Organization is what brings the work of the specialists in their performance of the various phases of the production process to a coherent result. When a product is complex or the production process is lengthy and complicated, the job of coordinating the work of the many specialists will itself be a major task—so major, in fact, that business enterprises will have a need for managerial and administrative specialists. A higher order of *managerial technology* will be required if the enterprise is to function with proficiency.

Sixth and last, there arises from the persistent introduction of more advanced technology the necessity of building into business organizations a mechanism for the orderly handling of change and for coping with unscheduled developments and contingencies. Tasks must be performed so that they are right not only for the present, but also for that time in the future when, companion and related functions having also been finished, the whole production process is brought to a conclusion. Conditions at the time the production process is completed and any stumbling blocks along the way must be anticipated. The unreliability of market forces must be overcome or subverted, and the tastes and needs of consumers must be forecast months and sometimes years in advance. The labor, materials, and equipment to be used must be acquired at costs consistent with the expected sales price. A mechanism for taking steps to prevent, offset, or otherwise neutralize the effect of adverse developments and to insure that what was foreseen actually comes to pass rapidly becomes a necessary feature in structuring complex and time-consuming production processes.

With a primitive technology where the production process takes only a matter of days, it can rightly be assumed that the conditions under which the output is marketed, being near at hand, will be virtually identical to the present. Should the product not meet customer approval, it can be readily modified with scarcely any lasting harm to the producer's reputation. Similar shortcomings in a technologically sophisticated production process approach the intolerable—the correction time is longer, the expense costlier, and the scars on a firm's reputation long in healing. By the same token, a complicated technology makes it equally imperative that planning for the procurement of resource inputs be undertaken. If clerical staffs of electric utilities use hand calculators to determine payrolls and to process customer sales, a staff of people can be put together on short notice to do the job—labor of this skill level being readily available with little more than the promise of higher wages. Likewise, hand calculators, being useful in a variety of business enterprises, are stocked in easily obtainable quantities. But when the specifications for data processing are raised to electronic computer standards, planning is of the essence. Computer technicians, programmers, data processing engineers, and others who participate in the operation of data processing systems may not be readily available, even with offers of sizable pay increases. Nor can a computer, high-speed printers, keypunch machines, and so on be acquired with the same facility as hand calculators. In more technical terms, we can say that the supply prices of highly specialized labor, equipment and components are inelastic in the short run; offers of large wage increases or a willingness to pay higher prices brings little or no added supply immediately. Anticipatory steps (planning) must be taken to insure that the required resource inputs are available when needed at acceptable prices. In addition, the more sophisticated the product, the more time will be required for making the production process operational and for processing the final output through the various stages. In such cases, careful planning and provisions for meeting unscheduled contingencies become critical to the success of the enterprise, since the risks of adverse market developments are significantly enhanced.

The technological imperative to subdivide production processes into manageable tasks, the organizational imperative to coordinate these tasks to effect a coherent result, and the market imperative to do so efficiently and profitably—all combine to explain, at least partially, why large firms usually produce complex, technically sophisticated commodities and why small enterprises are often relegated to producing simpler commodities. Many observers, unfortunately, are lulled by the once accurate, but now somewhat obsolete, notion that the advance of large corporate enterprise at the expense of small enterprise is motivated by the urge for monopoly power and ultimately monopoly profits.[2] A more revealing explanation for size is, however, the long-run impact which technological advance has had upon the production functions for the many commodities now being produced by large corporate enterprises.

CHARACTERISTICS OF TECHNOLOGICAL PROGRESS IN BUSINESS ENTERPRISES

New technological knowledge and, subsequently, technological progress in business enterprises stem from the internal research efforts of a firm and from knowledge transfer between firms, industries, governments, and educational institutions. A portion of new knowledge originates with basic research—investigations conducted without special concern for the usefulness of the results. Nonetheless, chances are that most new knowledge

---

[2] Such a simplistic explanation for size may well have characterized the era of trusts, holding companies and mergers that prevailed in the 1880's and 1890's and to some extent on into the first two decades of this century. But circumstances were different then. A few individuals dominated the business scene and technology was certainly more primitive. The same circumstances cannot be said to exist now. As future discussions will suggest, the motives for large-scale enterprise have many dimensions. To attribute the existence of giant corporations to the desire for monopoly power is at variance with the dictates of technology, production efficiency, marketing strategy, market pressures, and consumer demand.

is derived from purposive investigations where the intent is to obtain results for specific uses. Implicit in a firm's search for improved production techniques is the hope that successful research and development activities will increase the productive efficiency of its operations, which in turn will give the firm a cost advantage and ultimately allow for a higher degree of profitability. Business firms obtain access to new (and existing) knowledge via the education, training, and experience possessed by their employees. Increases in usable technological knowledge are most frequently the possession of some individual, and only in the case of innovations which can be patented does knowledge become an owned asset of the firm.

The application of new production techniques is not, however, the sole means of technological progress. Progress in the form of higher degrees of productive efficiency commonly derives from learning to apply existing techniques more effectively. Obviously enough, as more units of a commodity are produced with a given process, opportunities are identified for using the technique more effectively. Particularly during the early stages of using a new technique are gains in productive efficiencies realized, partially by an evolving historical process. This facet of technological progress, called *learning by doing*, is often neglected as a feature of progress and as a factor causing gradual, yet persistent, shifts in a firm's production function. Experience in industry has shown that the "bugs" in a new technology survive for sustained periods—even as much as three to ten years. Bits and pieces of complex processes do not always fit as neatly together as was originally envisioned. Parts of the process may have to be torn down and rebuilt; start-up and break-in costs may exceed expected forecasts. Meanwhile, output is nonexistent or not up to acceptable standards, expected revenues from the sale of output are not forthcoming, working capital is used up and not regenerated from the sale of output, with the result that the firm is sometimes caught in a classic, but temporary, profit squeeze. Even with a known technology, new plants may take up to three years to get on stream at the level of efficiency originally foreseen.

Plainly, the impact of technological change is uneven among both firms and industries. Some firms are more financially able to engage in invention and innovation. Still others are firmly convinced that improvement of their competitive position is more permanently achieved from technological innovation than from the adaption of unique marketing strategies that can be duplicated more easily; hence, they place strong emphasis on research and development activities and tend to be technologically progressive. In some cases advancing technology seems to allow firms to purchase greater amounts of production capacity per dollar of investment. In other instances it appears that it takes more investment in production facilities per unit of output. By and large, modern production technology is designed to substitute machines for manpower. In addition, new technologies are designed more and more for large production units and large markets.

Firms and industries have displayed a wide disparity in the rates with which they have adopted new technologies.[3] Taking into account a period of fifteen years after the discovery of a new technology, it has been observed that some innovations languish in oblivion for as much as ten years and then are rapidly adopted, that other innovations never mount a serious challenge to displace predecessor processes and facilities, and that still other innovations come quickly into general use and soon are being used to produce 80 or more percent of the total output of the industry. The differences in the diffusion rates of new production techniques have several root explanations. In the first place, some innovations are slow to be employed because while they are technologically possible they nevertheless are not economically feasible. An innovation may require resource inputs which are not readily available or which have prohibitive costs, thereby undercutting the incentive to incorporate it into the production process.[4] Second, there usually is ample room for the managers of firms to possess different perceptions of the actual degree of technological superiority of an innovation, thus partially accounting for why one firm adopts an innovation and another does not. Unless an innovation has substantial technological and economic superiority over existing processes, firms are likely to switch to the new technology only in the normal course of replacing worn-out equipment. Third, an innovation may require capital commitments beyond reach of small firms; this may explain why larger firms are, on occasion, technologically superior to smaller firms.

One economist has demonstrated that larger enterprises tend to be early users of new production technologies.[5] This is to be expected. Because much technological development and innovation is costly, it is more easily conducted and implemented by firms having considerable financial resources and having a sufficiently large share of the market as to be able to employ the innovation profitably. Without the latter there is less compelling incentive among business enterprises to undertake the expensive process of developing new technologies and initiating innovation. That large enterprises, especially center firms, are more strongly oriented toward technical development and innovation than small periphery firms is readily verified. The American farmer, an entrepreneur in the classic sense, does almost no research and

[3] F. Lynn, "An Investigation of the Rate of Development and Diffusion of Technology in Our Modern Industrial Society," in *Studies prepared for the National Commission on Technology, Automation,, and Economic Progress*, Appendix Vol. II, Technology and the American Economy (Washington, D.C., 1966); E. Mansfield, "The Speed of Response of Firms to New Techniques," *Quarterly Journal of Economics* Vol. 77, No. 2 (May 1963), pp. 290–311; and E. Mansfield, "Size of Firm, Market Structure and Innovation," *Journal of Political Economy*, Vol. 71, No. 4 (December 1963), pp. 556–576.

[4] A good example is provided by the fact that only recently have nuclear-powered generators of electricity become economically feasible alternatives to hydroelectric or coal-fired steam generators, yet the technical know-how to build nuclear reactors for this purpose has existed for some ten to fifteen years. Prior to the late 1960's the cost of constructing and operating nuclear power plants exceeded the costs of conventional means of generating electricity; now the differential has shifted slightly in favor of nuclear facilities, which accounts for the growing propensity of electric utilities to install them as they add to their generating capacity.

[5] Mansfield, "The Speed of Response of Firms to New Techniques," pp. 290–311. Mansfield concluded that if one firm is four times as large as another, and given equal profitability of the innovation to each firm, there is an 80 percent probability that the larger firm will introduce an innovation more rapidly than the smaller firm.

development on his own behalf. It is taken for granted that technological advance in agriculture is the product of the agricultural experiment stations of state universities, the U.S. Department of Agriculture, and the center firms which devise and sell products to the farmer. Obviously, a farm enterprise, even a corporate farm enterprise, is quite unable to support a staff for conducting agricultural research and experimentation. Other small enterprises find themselves in the same position. Less than 10 percent of the firms with fewer than 1,000 employees have formal research and development programs.[6] All told, firms with fewer than 1,000 employees spend only 5 percent of the total amount spent by the U.S. firms on research and development endeavors. In addition, they employ fewer than 10 percent of the scientists and engineers engaged in research and development activities.

A comparison of the oil and bituminous coal industries usefully illustrates the differential commitment of center and periphery firms to supporting technical advance and the ultimate effect this has upon society's economic welfare.[7] The oil industry is unquestionably dominated by center firms; seven are among the twenty largest industrial enterprises in the United States. Over the years they have been charged with violations of the antitrust laws; they have been, and still are, widely suspected of charging prices above the level that would prevail were price competition more vigorous; and they have earned quite acceptable profits. In contrast, the bituminous coal industry is populated with several thousand enterprises, none of which is large enough to visibly affect price much less dominate the coal market; their profits are relatively small and many of their number include "marginal" firms barely able to survive. Competition among the bituminous coal firms approaches what many economists view as the ideal amount. Yet few would be inclined to trade the results of competition in the oil industry for the results of competition in the bituminous coal industry. The oil industry is plainly progressive. The consumer of gasoline and fuel oil has fared quite well from the enterprise of center firms in petroleum exploration and recovery, in improving production efficiency, and in developing new and better petroleum products. The consumer of coal has had to put up with rising prices and no product improvement. The technology used to crack petroleum and to refine crude oil is of an advanced form, whereas the process of coal extraction is by comparison quite primitive and only recently has undergone any real progress at all.

Had the same technical expertise employed by the oil industry been brought to bear on coal mining, it is doubtful that coal miners would still toil like moles in mineshafts, even the best of which are unsafe, inefficient, unpleasant, uninspiring, and a hazard to health. As further evidence of the

---

[6] National Science Foundation, *Research and Development in Industry, 1966* (Washington, D.C.: U.S. Government Printing Office, 1968), pp. 6, 54.
[7] This example is adapted from John Kenneth Galbraith, *American Capitalism* (Boston: Houghton Mifflin Company, 1952), Chap. 7.

very limited ability of small enterprises to innovate when confronted with strong competitive forces, efforts to spur advances in coal mining technology have required government-sponsored coal research programs and cooperative ventures among the small firms. Experience in the bituminous coal industry clearly indicates that industries composed of thousands of small firms pose exceedingly difficult problems for the development of modern industrial research programs. The outcome tends to be a meager rate of technological progress and below-average increases in output per unit of input, unless government takes up the slack.

Significantly, the marvels of technology and the showcases of American industrial achievement are to be found largely in the very same corporate enterprises that the attorneys for the Antitrust Division of the Department of Justice visit in their ongoing crusade against the real and imagined "evils" of big business. This is mainly because R&D efforts are heavily concentrated in the largest corporations, or the center economy. The close relationship between large firm size and R&D effort is not mere circumstance; rather, it is to be expected. The reasons, however, require an understanding of center firm behavior. Hence, we shall postpone consideration of this economic facet until Chapters 12 and 13.

THE MOTIVATION AND PRESSURES
FOR INNOVATION WITHIN BUSINESS FIRMS

Business firms, even when well sheltered from the cold winds of competition, are beset with a multitude of motivations and pressures for seeking out better production techniques and adopting proven innovations.[8] Naturally, the overriding motivation for the adoption of new technologies is to improve the profitability of the firm and, ultimately, to safeguard its market position and chances for survival. Yet such an explanation is too simplistic, for it reveals little about the many subtle profit-enhancing facets of technological change and innovation.

Not only is new product innovation a major avenue for increasing profits, but it becomes a virtual necessity in the face of competition. Firms consistently attempt to drive their rivals out of a particular market by coming out with a product that outperforms the others. To successfully combat such product market pressures a firm must aggressively seek new products that can satisfy consumer demand, provide a stronger defense against substitute products, and fulfill recognized market potentials. In addition, pressures for quality improvements, for product standardization in terms of sizes or performance, and for greater quantities of output dictate a pro-

---

[8] Even firms with a stranglehold on the production of an item cannot long afford to be complacent about technological developments. In a world where the threat of potential substitutes grows more ominous every day and where innovation is proceeding elsewhere at accelerating rates, it is not likely that many firms, even monopolies, will choose to risk the fates of stagnation and obsolescence. The inherent desires of firms for long run survival and profitability are indeed powerful forces and virtually preclude the election of a course of technological restraint.

gressive technology. Technical innovation and virtuosity is a weapon of rivalry which pervades nearly every industry.

Adverse developments in the market for resource inputs provide added pressures for innovation and technological change. A portion of the trend to automate production processes originates from the desire of firms to escape rising labor costs. In the same vein, pressures to eliminate human labor due to physical limitations, hazard to life, the frequency of human error, and the like are a very real motivation for technological change in some industries. In addition, the deterioration of sources of supply for raw materials and fuels tends to precipitate a search for technological remedies in the form of new raw materials and fuels or the ability to use lower-quality inputs (such as lower grades of ore). For example, rising costs of mining and transporting coal have been a major factor in inducing electric utilities to switch from coal-fired stem generators to nuclear-powered generators. On occasion, price competition among suppliers of new capital equipment can so reduce the cost of an innovation as to make it feasible on a broader scale. From an internal standpoint, the operating benefits from relieving bottlenecks in the production process can serve to motivate firms to seek technological solutions to their problems.

During the 1970's a new factor has emerged as a propelling force for technological advance—widespread social concern for the pollution of air and water resources. The solution to environmental pollution is clearly technological in character. Where the means does not currently exist to reduce pollution to tolerable limits, we can be sure that the powerful social pressures now being brought to bear upon business enterprises (as well as upon municipalities in the matter of their waste treatment practices) will greatly intensify the rate of increase in technological capabilities for dealing with pollution abatement.

Rare is the firm which can insulate itself from the pervasive compulsion to remain technologically up-to-date in the long run. To do otherwise spells almost certain extinction for a firm, subject only to the propensity of government to rescue it by the granting of subsidies, protective tariffs, or regulation. Indeed, casual empiricism suggests that government-protected and government-regulated industries are among the least progressive in terms of the rate of technological advance; whether a cause-effect relationship exists here must remain a matter of conjecture until more evidence is available.[9]

Aside from the product market pressures, the resource input pressures, and the operating efficiency requirements that combine to motivate firms to adopt new technologies, several other considerations make firms intent upon advancing their levels of technological capability.[10] The managers of some firms apparently feel that because the future will undoubtedly differ markedly

---

[9] For a survey of the technological progressivity of regulated enterprises, see William M. Capron, ed., *Technological Change in Regulated Industries*, (Washington, D.C.: The Brookings Institution, 1971).

[10] Bela Gold, "Values and Research," in *Values and the Future*, ed. Kurt Baier and Nicholas Rescher (New York: The Free Press, 1969), pp. 389–430.

from the present, survival and protection of their competitive position require participation in the stream of innovation, even if one is not sure of where it leads and even if attractive estimates of the rates of return from technologically progressive undertakings cannot be contrived. A similar view holds that "technically sound" innovations can be made to pay off eventually, even though investment does not seem warranted at the outset. Another bootstrap view holds that innovation is requisite for maintaining the quality and morale of technical and engineering staffs; the reasoning has even been extended to affect the progressive image of the firm and its capacity to attract high-calibre personnel. The point here is that personalities and organizational considerations prevailing inside the firm combine with economic forces from the outside to virtually compel an enterprise to participate in or even initiate major innovation programs.

Summary and Conclusions

Production as commonly used in economics involves manufacturing, storing, transporting, or selling commodities, as well as the rendering of personal and business services of all kinds. Production includes virtually all phases of economic activity except consumption. By *production process* is meant an integrated system of activities whereby resource inputs are transformed into outputs of final goods and services ready for consumption. A *production function* indicates in quantitative terms the physical relationship between the input of resources and the output of goods or services per unit of time.

During the twentieth century technological advance has induced fundamental and persistent changes in both production processes and production functions. These include (a) increasing the span of time separating the beginning from the completion of the production process, (b) increasing the use of capital goods in the production process, (c) rendering production processes somewhat less adaptable to short-run changes in the composition of the final product and in the means of producing it, (d) altering the types of manpower needed to staff the human element of production processes, (e) requiring a higher order of administrative organization and managerial technology, and (f) requiring the creation of a mechanism within the enterprise for the orderly managing of change and for coping with unforeseen difficulties. The technological imperative to subdivide production processes into manageable tasks, the organizational imperative to coordinate these tasks to effect a coherent result, and the market imperative to do so efficiently and profitably combine to explain, at least partially, why large firms frequently produce sophisticated commodities and small firms produce simpler commodities.

Rarely can firms insulate themselves from the necessity to remain technologically up-to-date. Product innovation and progressive production methods are weapons of rivalry which pervade nearly every industry. In addition, pressures to innovate arise from production bottlenecks, from the desire to escape rising labor or raw material costs, from social pressures to eliminate environmental pollution, from pressure to eliminate hazard to life or human error—all of which ultimately bear upon the profitability, market position, and chances for the survival of an enterprise.

SUGGESTED READINGS

ARROW, KENNETH J., "The Economic Implications of Learning by Doing," *Review of Economic Studies*, Vol. 29 (June 1962), pp. 155–173.

AVERITT, ROBERT T., *The Dual Economy* (New York: W. W. Norton & Company, Inc., 1968), Chap. 3.

GALBRAITH, JOHN KENNETH, *American Capitalism* (Boston: Houghton Mifflin Company, 1952), Chap. 7.

GOLD, BELA, "Economic Effects of Technological Innovations," *Management Science*, Vol. II, No. 1 (September 1964), pp. 105–134.

JOHNSTON, ROBERT E., "Technical Progress and Innovation," *Oxford Economic Papers* (July 1966), pp. 158–176.

HAMBURG, DANIEL, *R & D: Essays on the Economics of Research and Development*, (New York: Random House, Inc., 1966).

MANSFIELD, EDWIN, *The Economics of Technological Change* (New York: W. W. Norton & Company, Inc., 1968), Chaps. 2, 3, and 4.

_____, *Industrial Research and Technological Innovation* (New York: W. W. Norton & Company, Inc., 1968), Chaps. 1 and 10.

_____, "Size of Firm, Market Structure, and Innovation," *Journal of Political Economy*, Vol. 71, No. 6 (December 1963), pp. 556–576.

_____, "The Speed of Response of Firms to New Techniques," *Quarterly Journal of Economics*, Vol. 77, No. 2 (May 1963), pp. 290–311.

NELSON, RICHARD, MERTON PECK, and EDWARD KALOCHEK, *Technology, Economic Growth and Public Policy* (Washington, D.C.: The Brookings Institution, 1967), Chaps. 1–5.

SCHERER, FREDERIC, *Industrial Market Structure and Economic Performance* (Skokie, Ill.: Rand McNally & Company, 1970), Chap. 15.

Questions for Discussion

1. Explain carefully what is meant by the terms "production process" and "production function."

2. What are the several effects which technological change can have upon a firm's production function?

3. Does the pace of technological change seem to be accelerating? Can you cite examples in support of your position?

4. How have technological advances changed the basic nature of production processes during the course of the twentieth century?

5. Why is it important for business firms to keep their production techniques close to the frontier of technological know-how?

6. Do you think that business enterprises on the whole are technologically progressive? Give examples to support your position.

7

The Principles
of Production Technology

Having indicated the influence of technology and technological change upon production processes, we are now in a position to examine the principles underlying input-output relationships. Attention will be focused especially upon the conditions for achieving peak production efficiency and for optimizing the mix of resource inputs in both the short run and the long run. Analyzing the principles of production is of fundamental import, because it provides the foundation for estimating production costs and for selecting the most economical production techniques.

FIXED AND VARIABLE INPUTS

To facilitate the exposition of production analysis we shall divide inputs into two somewhat artificial, yet quite convenient, categories—fixed inputs and variable inputs. A *fixed input* is one whose quantity cannot *readily* be changed in response to a desire to alter *immediately* the rate of output. Admittedly, inputs seldom are fixed in an absolute sense, even for very short periods. Practically, though, the costs of quickly varying the amount of some kinds of inputs may be prohibitive. Even where they are not, changing an input's usage rate may be severely impeded by the unavailability of additional supplies and/or by the length of time it takes to effect acceptable changes in their usage. Examples of fixed inputs include major pieces of equipment and machinery, the space available for productive activity, and key managerial personnel.

On the other hand, a *variable input* is one whose usage rate may be altered quite easily in response to a desire to raise or lower the quantity of output. Resource inputs that can be varied in quantity within a very short time include electric power, raw materials, transportation services, and most types of blue- and white-collar labor services.

Parenthetically, it should be pointed out that in a number of production processes the quantities of raw material inputs may be readily changed but only in some fixed proportion to one another and to output. Aspirin provides a good example. The various chemicals comprising aspirin must be blended in fixed proportions or else the quality and character of the product will change. And a fixed amount of these ingredients must be used in each adult aspirin produced. It is the same with such commodities as specialty steel products, food and beverage products, drugs, cigarettes, paint, and fertilizers.

THE SHORT RUN AND THE LONG RUN

To accompany the fiction of fixed and variable inputs, economists distinguish between the short run and the long run. The *short run* refers to a period of time so short that the firm does not have time to vary the quantity of its fixed inputs (major pieces of equipment, key managerial personnel, and space for production activities). Yet, the short run is long enough a time period to allow for variation in the firm's variable inputs. Hence, in the short run output changes are effected exclusively by initiating changes in the usage of variable inputs.

The *long run* is defined as a period of time sufficiently long to allow *all* inputs to be varied. All resources are variable in the long run; no inputs are considered as fixed. Thus, in the long run output changes can be accomplished by altering the usage of any resource input in whatever way may be most advantageous to the firm. Whereas in the short run a firm may be forced to expand production by operating its facilities several more hours per day, and incurring overtime wage rates for labor, in the long run the firm may find it more economical to construct larger facilities and return to a normal work shift.

The length of the short run varies from industry to industry. In some industries, where the quantities of fixed inputs are small or where the character of production permits fixed inputs to be changed in a short span of time, the short run can easily be a period of several months or less. The apparel, mobile-home, and food-processing industries are cases in point. For other industries the short run may be a year or more. It takes time to add to a firm's capacity to produce copying machines, sports cars, sheet aluminum, or aircraft. In the case of electric utilities, orders for new steam generators must be placed five or more years in advance of actual installation and operation.

By differentiating between fixed and variable inputs and between the short and long runs, we can make some statements about the environment in which production takes place. The quantities of a firm's fixed inputs determine the size of the firm's plant or its *scale of operations*. This scale sets an upper limit to the amount of output per period that the firm is capable of producing in the short run. Output can, in the short run, be varied up to that limit by increasing or decreasing the usage of variable inputs in conjunction with the amount of fixed input. The limits of output can, in the long run, be raised or lowered by changing the scale of production, the entire character of the production process, and the utilization rate of any and all inputs.

SHORT-RUN PRODUCTION FUNCTIONS

The short-run production function for a firm indicates the output obtainable from combining various amounts of variable inputs with a given amount of fixed input. As stated earlier, the production function may be expressed symbolically as

$$Q = f(X_a, X_b, X_c, \dots, X_n),$$

where Q refers to the quantity of output per unit of time and is a function of specific quantities of inputs $X_a, X_b, X_c, \dots, X_n$. In the short run, since the quantity of output (Q) will be the result of combining variable input factors (say labor and raw materials) with the fixed inputs (size of plant, major pieces of equipment, managerial capacity), the functional relationship may be more appropriately written as

$$Q = f(X_a, X_b \,|\, X_c, \dots, X_n).$$

The vertical bar indicates that the input factors to the right are regarded as fixed in the production process, whereas the inputs to the left are variable. The fundamental problem in the study of short-run production functions is to estimate the quantity of output which can be produced by combining alternative amounts of variable inputs with the available amount of fixed inputs.

As an example, consider a firm producing a commodity with a fixed amount of equipment, space, and managerial capability—the so-called fixed inputs.[1] In the ensuing discussion it will be convenient to refer to the amount of these fixed inputs, so suppose we arbitrarily designate them as constituting

---

[1] Actually the fixed inputs are not really as fixed as it might first appear. While a firm may possess a given amount of fixed input, say ten machines, the operating pattern for the fixed inputs involves a choice among several dimensions of operation. The effective amount of available fixed input can be "changed" by altering (a) the speed at which the machines are operated, (b) the number of hours per day the machines are used, and (c) the number of days of operation per year. However, firms rarely have full flexibility in choosing among these dimensions, owing to the constraints imposed by maintenance requirements, union work rules, and wage differentials among work shifts.

two "units." A unit of fixed input may be defined in whatever way we please
or find most convenient. Let the variable inputs be man-hours of labor time
along with the necessary raw materials. Now suppose we conduct an experiment in which successively larger doses of variable input are combined with
the given amount of fixed input and that the resultant output levels are
observed and recorded.[2]

Tabular Illustration. The results of the hypothetical experiment are
listed in Table 7-1. The equation corresponding to these values of variable
input and output, given the amount of fixed input, is

$$Q = 21X + 9X^2 - X^3,$$

where Q is the quantity of output of the commodity and X represents the
units of variable input. The values in column three can be obtained by
substituting values for variable input $(1, 2, 3, \ldots, 9)$ into the equation and
finding the corresponding value of Q. From the table we see that when
progressively larger doses of variable input are combined with the available
fixed inputs, the quantity of output rises more rapidly at first, then more
slowly, reaches a maximum and begins to decline. The exact change in output
associated with the use of one more unit of variable input per period is known
in economics as the *marginal product of the variable input*.[3] The change in the
quantity of output per unit of time resulting from a *one-unit change* in the
quantity of that input used per unit of time is defined as *discrete marginal
product*. In our example the values for discrete marginal product are shown
in column 4 of Table 7-1; the reader should verify their derivation. However, a superior concept of the marginal product for an input is given by the
first derivative of the equation expressing the mathematical relation between
the flow of output and the flow of that input.[4] Hence, if the relationship
between the quantity of output and the units of variable input is

$$Q = 21X + 9X^2 - X^3,$$

[2] Strictly speaking, the different amounts of variable input are best conceived as being applied to different plants of equal size and type, rather than to a progressively larger application of additional units of variable input to a single plant. Practically, however, real-world implementation of this concept of measuring a firm's production function is usually not possible—many identical plants may simply not exist. The sensible alternative, therefore, is to observe the relation between input and output for a single plant operation at various points in time where the rates of variable input usage are different.

[3] It cannot be inferred from the definition of marginal product that the change in output is due just to the efforts and contribution of variable input. An increase in variable input by itself is not *the cause* of changes in output; output changes as a consequence of having more units of variable input employed in conjuction with the fixed input. An example may serve to clarify this point. Suppose a firm has five pieces of machinery, each requiring one skilled operator. As the firm increases its labor inputs from one to five skilled operators to run the five machines, it is clear that the resulting output gains are not due solely to the productive powers of labor but rather are the joint products of using more labor with the five available machines. Economists, how-ever, customarily refer to the gains in output from using more labor as being the marginal product of labor, despite the fact that gains in output from employing more units of labor reflect the *joint* contributions of labor and the other inputs with which it is combined.

[4] Should more than one variable input be present in the expression defining the short-run production function, the relevant concept of the marginal product of an input is the partial derivative of the production function. See Mathematical Capsule 6.

Table 7-1 Data for a Hypothetical Short-Run Production Function

(1) Units of Fixed Input	(2) Units of Variable Input	(3) Quantity of Output $Q = 21X + 9X^2 - X^3$	(4) Discrete Marginal Product of Variable Input	(5) Continuous Marginal Product of Variable Input $MP = 21 + 18X - 3X^2$	(6) Average Product of Variable Input $AP_{vi} = 21 + 9X - X^2$	(7) Average Product of Fixed Input $AP_{fi} = \dfrac{21X + 9X^2 - X^3}{2}$
2	0	0		—	—	0
2	1	29	29	36	29	14.5
2	2	70	41	45	35	35
2	3	117	47	48	39	58.5
2	4	164	47	45	41	82
2	5	205	41	36	41	102.5
2	6	234	29	21	39	117
2	7	245	11	0	35	122.5
2	8	232	-13	-27	29	116
2	9	189	-43	-60	21	94.5

then the marginal product of the variable input is

$$MP = \frac{dQ}{dX} = 21 + 18X - 3X^2.$$

This concept of marginal product is called *continuous marginal product* to distinguish it from discrete marginal product.[5] Continuous marginal product represents the rate of change in total output as the rate of variable input changes per period of time and can be calculated in the manner shown in column 5 of Table 7–1. In the case of a short-run production function, marginal product is meaningful only for inputs whose rate of usage can be changed; logically, then, there can be no marginal product for the fixed inputs, since the fixed inputs by definition do not change in the short run.

MATHEMATICAL CAPSULE 6

Determining Marginal Product When the Production Function is Composed of Several Variable Inputs

In most production processes the quantity of output in the short-run is a function of several variable inputs such that

$$Q = f(X_a, X_b, X_c, \ldots, X_n).$$

The marginal product of a specific variable input, say X_a, is found by observing the impact upon Q of a change in the usage of X_a, when the quantities of the remaining variable inputs $(X_b, X_c, \ldots, X_n)$ are held constant. Mathematically, this procedure involves determining the *partial derivative* of the production function with respect to X_a.

Suppose the production function for a commodity is

$$Q = 7X_a^2 + 8X_b^2 - 5X_aX_b.$$

We can find the effect of a change in the rate of usage of resource input X_a, when the usage of X_b is held constant by treating X_b as a constant and differentiating the production function with respect to X_a—this gives the partial derivative of Q with respect to X_a and is symbolized as $\partial Q/\partial X_a$. Thus we obtain

$$\frac{\partial Q}{\partial X_a} = 14X_a - 5X_b,$$

---

[5] The definitions and concepts of discrete and continuous marginal product are analogous to our earlier definitions of marginal utility and marginal revenue. In drawing marginal product as a continuous function, we assume that both variable input and output can be varied by extremely small amounts.

which is the expression for the marginal product of input X_a. In economic terms it may be interpreted precisely to mean the rate of change in output as the usage of input X_a changes, the usage of input X_b remaining constant. In less formal terms, the expression for the marginal product of X_a tells us how changes in the use of X_a will affect the quantity of output provided X_b does not change.

Similarly, the marginal product for input X_b is the partial derivative of the production function with respect to X_b, or

$$\frac{\partial Q}{\partial X_b} = 16X_b - 5X_a.$$

It shows the impact of changes in X_b upon Q when X_a is held constant.

EXERCISES

1. Determine the marginal product functions for labor (L) and capital (C) for each of the following production functions:
   (a) $Q = 18L^2 + 14C^3 - L^2C$
   (b) $Q = 10L^{.5}C^{.5}$
   (c) $Q = 17L + 9C + .6L^{.4}C^{.5}$
2. Determine the values for MP_L and MP_C at $L = 10$ and $C = 20$ for each of the following production functions.
   (a) $Q = 36L - L^2 + 20C - LC$
   (b) $Q = 5L^2 + 4LC + 6C^2 - 8\frac{L}{C}$

The average product of the variable input is shown in column six of Table 7-1. It is found by dividing the quantity of output by the required number of units of variable input. Algebraically,

$$AP_{vi} = \frac{\text{units of output}}{\text{units of variable input}}.$$

Thus, if $Q = 21X + 9X^2 - X^3$, where X represents the units of variable input, the expression for AP_{vi} becomes

$$AP_{vi} = \frac{Q}{X} = \frac{21X + 9X^2 - X^3}{X} = 21 + 9X - X^2.$$

Likewise, the average product of the fixed input (shown in column seven of Table 7-1) is defined as the quantity of output divided by the available units of fixed input. Algebraically,

$$AP_{fi} = \frac{\text{units of output}}{\text{units of fixed input}}.$$

Given that $Q = 21X + 9X^2 - X^3$ and that two units of fixed input are present, AP_{fi} can be calculated as follows:

$$AP_{fi} = \frac{Q}{FI} = \frac{21X + 9X^2 - X^3}{2}.$$

Alternatively, AP_{fi} can be computed by dividing the output values in column three by the number of units of fixed input given in column one, yielding the values in column seven of Table 7-1.

In our example observe that marginal product increases for the first three units of variable input to its maximum value of 48 (column five). As additional units of variable input are added past three, marginal product diminishes; it reaches zero at an input of seven units per period and becomes increasingly negative beyond an input of eight units. The reasons for this behavior on the part of output and marginal product are found in the *principle of diminishing marginal returns*.

The principle of diminishing marginal returns describes the direction and the rate of change of the firm's output when increasingly larger amounts of a variable input per period of time are combined with a constant amount of fixed input. Specifically, the principle states that *as the amount of a variable input is increased by equal increments and combined with a specified amount of fixed inputs, a point will be reached* (*sometimes more quickly and sometimes less quickly*) *where the resulting increases in the quantity of output will get smaller and smaller;* or, in other words, eventually the marginal product of variable input will begin to diminish. Furthermore, it can be added that should the amounts of variable input applied to a given fixed input get large enough, the quantity of output will reach a maximum and may then *decrease* as still additional amounts of variable input are used in conjunction with the fixed inputs.

Before the inevitable point of diminishing marginal returns is reached, the gains in output from larger applications of variable input may either increase at an increasing rate such that marginal product of variable input increases, or output may increase at a constant rate such that marginal product is constant. For example, in Table 7-1 the first three units of variable input cause the quantity of output to increase at an increasing rate. Such may occur because small amounts of variable input combined with the fixed inputs tend to be relatively inefficient.[6] When the variable input is being used in too sparse a proportion to the fixed input, additional units of variable input can help diminish the associated inefficiencies and thereby cause output to increase at an increasing rate.

---

[6] Examples of this condition are commonplace in manufacturing. Suppose a plant of a given size has been designed to operate with 400 employees. If an attempt is made to operate with 50 employees, the multiplicity of functions to be performed by each employee with the attendant inefficiencies in execution, coupled with the time lost in changing from job to job, will no doubt cause output to be more than proportionately *less* than might be gotten, say, from 100 employees. Thus, up to some point, equal increments in the amount of labor used may well produce successively larger gains in the quantity of output.

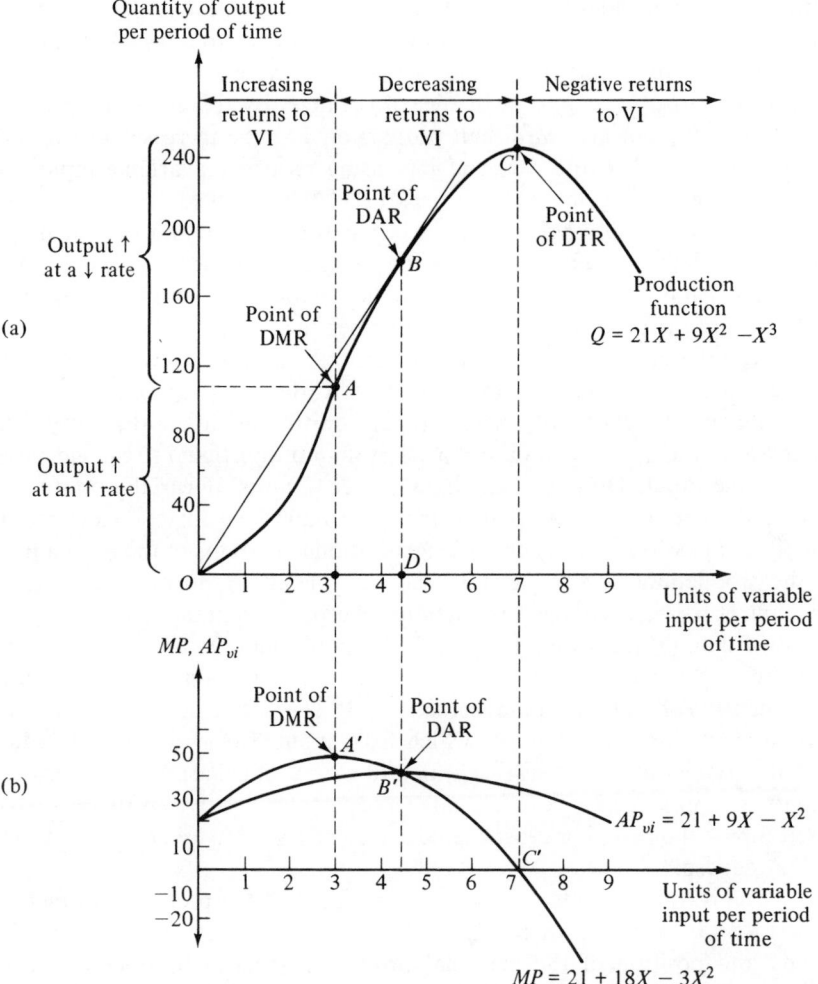

Fig. 7-1   A Short-Run Production Function and Its Corresponding Marginal and Average Product Functions

Graphic Illustration.   The hypothetical data in Table 7-1 are graphed in Figure 7-1. Since output is a function of variable input, output is the dependent variable and variable input is the independent variable. Accordingly, output per period of time is plotted on the vertical axis, and the units of variable input are plotted on the horizontal axis. Joining the points by a smooth curve yields a graphical illustration of the firm's production function for the commodity [Figure 7-1(a)].

The production function of Figure 7-1(a) conveys the same input-output relation as does the production schedule in Table 7-1.[7] Note that the production function increases at an increasing rate up to a level of usage of variable input of 3 units per period; accordingly, we may say that *increasing returns to the variable input* exist over this range. By this is meant that the increases in output are *more* than proportional to the increases in variable input. At the end of the range of increasing returns to variable input the point of diminishing marginal returns (*DMR*) is reached. Here the principle of diminishing marginal returns becomes operative, and heavier usage of variable inputs results in a declining marginal product; i.e., extra units of variable input yield successively smaller amounts of extra output. The curvature of the production function becomes such that it rises more slowly; that is to say output increases at a decreasing rate. In turn, we can say that between a level of usage of 3 and 7 units of variable input per period there exist *decreasing returns to variable input;* or, to put it another way, the increases in the quantity of output are *less* than proportional to the increases in variable input. Output is maximum when 7 units of variable input per period of time are combined with the fixed input. No further increases in output are possible without employing additional amounts of the fixed inputs in the production process and this is not feasible in the short run. For reference purposes we may label the maximum output level in the short run as the point of diminishing *total* returns (*DTR*). Should more than 7 units of variable input per period of time be used in conjunction with the fixed inputs, the quantity of output would actually fall. The rationale for this derives from the existence of a limit to which fixed inputs can accommodate additional variable input and still yield additional output. Past 7 units, variable inputs are present in excessively large proportions relative to the available fixed input; the resulting gross inefficiencies in resource usage cause output to be reduced.

The marginal product curve corresponding to the production function described above is shown in Figure 7-1(b). The data for ascertaining the shape and position of the marginal product curve can be obtained from columns 4 and 5 in Table 7-1.

Since by the marginal product of the variable input we mean the rate of change in the quantity of output as the usage rate of variable input changes, the slope of the production function at any level of variable input is the value of marginal product at that quantity of variable input. When the quantity of output is increasing at an increasing rate (as it does up to a level

---

[7] In this example the production function is shown as beginning from the origin of the diagram. This is the case only when the variable input under consideration is absolutely essential to the production of the commodity and when output may be obtained immediately upon applying variable input. Needless to say, these characteristics do not typify all production processes or all kinds of variable inputs. For variable inputs not essential to the production of the commodity, the production function may begin above the origin (installing carpets in an office building to reduce noise and to enhance the esthetic quality of the working conditions, thereby boosting employee productivity, is a case in point). In other situations no output may be forthcoming until several units of variable input are used with the complex of fixed inputs. For example, five men in a huge pulp and paper mill can produce nothing. Ten men can do no better. Where a minimum complement of variable input is requisite for any production to take place, the production function or total product curve begins to the right of the origin and at that point on the horizontal axis corresponding to the minimum input requirement.

of 3 units of variable input), marginal product is increasing. Marginal product attains its maximum value at the point of diminishing marginal returns, which in this example is at 3 units of variable input where $MP = 48$ [point A in Figure 7-1(a)]. Between 3 and 7 units of variable input, where the quantity of output increases at a decreasing rate, the values of marginal product are positive but diminishing. At 7 units of variable input, the rate of output is maximum and marginal product is zero. Beyond 7 units, additional units of variable input cause output to decline, meaning that in this range the marginal product of variable input is negative. The negative values for marginal product in the range beyond 7 units reflect the fact that the production function is declining and, therefore, has a negative slope.

The average product curve for the variable input originates from the same point as does the marginal product curve (in this instance, both assume a value of 21 when $X = 0$). From this point the average product curve rises until it reaches its maximum value at 4.5 units of variable input. It subsequently declines, conceivably becoming zero should variable input ever be added to such an extent that output falls back to zero. The average product curve has a definite relationship to the marginal product curve. So long as the value for MP is greater than the value for AP_{vi}, the average product curve will rise. The value for MP equals the value of AP_{vi} when AP_{vi} is at its maximum value. When the value for MP is less than the value for AP_{vi}, the average product curve falls. The explanation for this relationship is rooted in simple arithmetic; an example may suffice to illustrate it.

Consider a student who after two years of college has managed to earn a 2.5 overall grade average in his coursework. If *this term* he earns a 2.8 average in his courses, then his new *overall* grade average will *rise* above the 2.5 level. However, if he earns a 2.0 average *this term*, his new overall grade average will *fall* below 2.5. The overall grade average of our hypothetical student is analogous to average product, while the grade average this term is analogous to marginal product. Thus, for average product to be increasing, marginal product must exceed the average. And for average product to be decreasing, marginal product must be less than average product.

MATHEMATICAL CAPSULE 7

The Relationship Between an Input's Marginal and Average Product

That an input's marginal and average products are necessarily equal at the maximum value of average product is easily proven mathematically. Let the production function be of the general form $Q = f(X)$. Then,

$$AP_{vi} = \frac{Q}{X} = \frac{f(X)}{X}$$

$$MP = \frac{dQ}{dX} = f'(X).$$

From Mathematical Capsule 1 in Chapter 3 we know that the condition which must be satisfied for AP_{vi} to be maximum is that the slope of AP_{vi} be zero. This in turn means that the derivative of the AP_{vi} equation must be zero:

$$\frac{dAP_{vi}}{dX} = 0.$$

Using the rule of calculus for finding the derivative of a quotient, and calculating dAP_{vi}/dX, where $AP_{vi} = f(X)/X$, gives

$$\frac{dAP_{vi}}{dX} = \frac{X \cdot f'(X) - f(X)}{X^2}.$$

For dAP_{vi}/dX to equal zero requires that the numerator of the above expression be equal to zero, or that

$$X \cdot f'(X) - f(X) = 0.$$

Rewriting the above condition yields

$$f'(X) = \frac{f(X)}{X}.$$

Since $f'(X) = MP$ and $f(X)/X = AP_{vi}$, then the input rate that makes AP_{vi} maximum is also the value of X at which $MP = AP_{vi}$.

Furthermore, if the expression for dAP_{vi}/dX is rewritten as follows:

$$\frac{dAP_{vi}}{dX} = \frac{f'(X) - \dfrac{f(X)}{X}}{X^2},$$

then it becomes apparent that the slope of the average product function will be positive if $f'(X)$, marginal product, is greater than $f(X)/X$, average product. This reflects the fact that so long as the value for marginal product exceeds the value for average product, the average product curve is rising. Conversely, it is clear that if marginal product is less than average product, then the slope of the average product curve is negative and the value of average product is declining.

The rate of variable input usage at which the average product curve of the variable input reaches its maximum value can be ascertained directly from the graph of the production function. Suppose a ray is drawn from the origin to point B on the production function in Figure 7-1(a). Since average product equals the quantity of output divided by the units of variable input employed, AP_{vi} at point B equals distance BD (the quantity of output) divided by distance OD (the number of units of variable input), or, more simply, BD/OD, which in turn is equivalent to the slope of the ray OB. As the number of units of variable input increases from zero to 4.5 units (point D), the slopes of rays drawn from the origin to the corresponding points on the production function become progressively greater. Since the average product of the variable input is mathematically equivalent to the slope of a ray from the origin to the corresponding point on the production function, AP_{vi} is maximum at that value of variable input where the slope of such a ray is steepest. This occurs when the ray from the origin is just *tangent* to the production function (point B) or at 4.5 units of variable input. We shall designate the peak of the average product curve for variable input as the point of diminishing *average* returns to variable input (DAR).

SOME ALTERNATIVE TYPES OF SHORT-RUN PRODUCTION FUNCTIONS

It is not at all necessary that a firm's production function exhibit the shape illustrated in Figure 7-1. Under certain circumstances other shapes may be quite appropriate. We shall look at three alternative shapes of production functions and their distinctive properties.

Constant Returns to Variable Input. As we shall verify later in this chapter, some production processes have qualities such that the firm's short-run production function is linear over the *normal* ranges of output. A production function of this type, along with the corresponding marginal and average product curves, is shown in Figure 7-2. The general equation describing such production behavior is

$$Q = a + bX,$$

where Q is the quantity of output, X represents the units of variable input per period of time, and a and b are constants. In the case of the production function shown in Figure 7-2(a) it is assumed that variable input is essential for production to occur and that some output can be obtained as soon as variable input is combined with the available units of fixed input. The effect of this rather reasonable assumption (and we shall continue to use it in the succeeding illustrations) is that the production function begins at the origin and the value of a in the equation for the production function is zero, thereby reducing the equation of the production function to

$$Q = bX.$$

From the preceding definitions of average and marginal product, we can

218

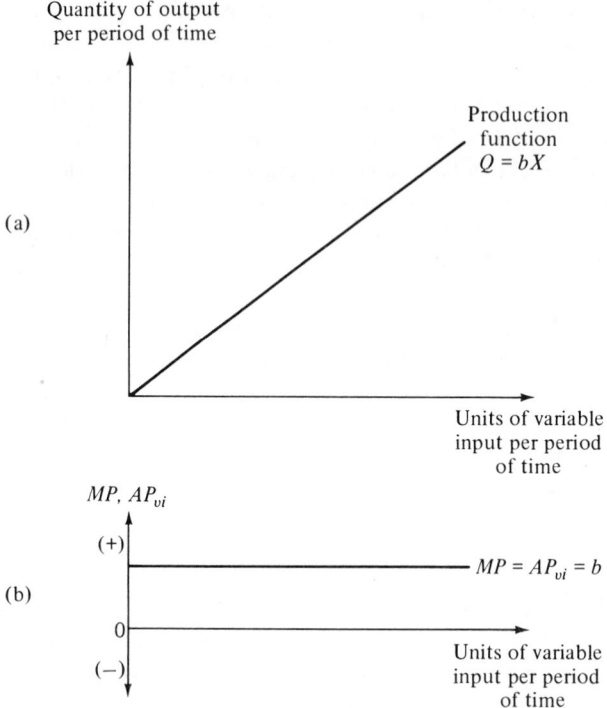

Fig. 7-2   A Production Function Characterized by a Phase of Constant Returns to Variable
Input

write

$$AP_{vi} = \frac{Q}{X} = \frac{bX}{X} = b$$

and

$$MP = \frac{dQ}{dX} = b.$$

Thus the equations for both marginal and average product in the case of a
linear production function are constants and $MP = AP_{vi}$. These relationships are illustrated in Figure 7-2(b).

The shapes and behavior of the production function in Figure 7-2(a)
and its corresponding MP and AP_{vi} curves may be explained as follows.
A linear production function means that as additional units of variable input
are combined with the given units of fixed input, the quantity of output
increases at a *constant rate*—there exist *constant returns to variable input*.
Each unit of variable input contributes just as much to total output as did

the previous unit and as will the next unit. Since successive units of variable input are *equally* productive, their marginal products are necessarily equal. This factor makes the production function linear, because marginal product is the rate of change in the quantity of output as variable input changes. When this rate is constant, the production function is linear. Moreover, with additional units of variable input being equally productive, the average product of the units of variable input is itself a constant value equal in size to the value of the marginal product of the variable input.

It does not follow, however, that a linear production function contradicts the principle of diminishing marginal returns. Rather, linearity implies that the point of diminishing marginal returns is yet to be reached. There can be *no doubt* that if *enough* units of variable input are combined with the given amount of fixed input, diminishing returns will set in. But in production processes where a standard man-machine ratio is employed, this point might not be encountered until the limit of the plant's capacity is approached, say around 90 to 95 percent of practical capacity. Thus, up to this limit, experiencing constant returns to the variable input is neither inconceivable nor unrealistic.

Decreasing Returns to Variable Input. Another type of production function displays *decreasing returns to variable input* as soon as the *first* dose of variable input is combined with the fixed input. Although several equations can be used to describe this behavior, the simplest is the quadratic equation:

$$Q = a + bX - cX^2$$

or, more simply,

$$Q = bX - cX^2$$

if the variable input is essential for production. Here b is a positive constant and c, as indicated, is negative. The corresponding average and marginal product functions are:

$$AP_{vi} = \frac{Q}{X} = \frac{bX - cX^2}{X} = b - cX,$$

$$MP = \frac{dQ}{dX} = b - 2cX.$$

These three curves are illustrated in Figure 7-3. Observe that the MP curve lies below the AP_{vi} curve; in fact, it declines at twice the rate of AP_{vi}, as can be verified from the equations of the two functions (the slope of AP_{vi} is $-c$ and the slope of MP is $-2c$).

Here the nature of the production process is such that each additional unit of variable input adds *less* to total output than the preceding unit. Therefore, the quantity of output increases at a decreasing rate up to the maximum output. Diminishing marginal returns to variable input are

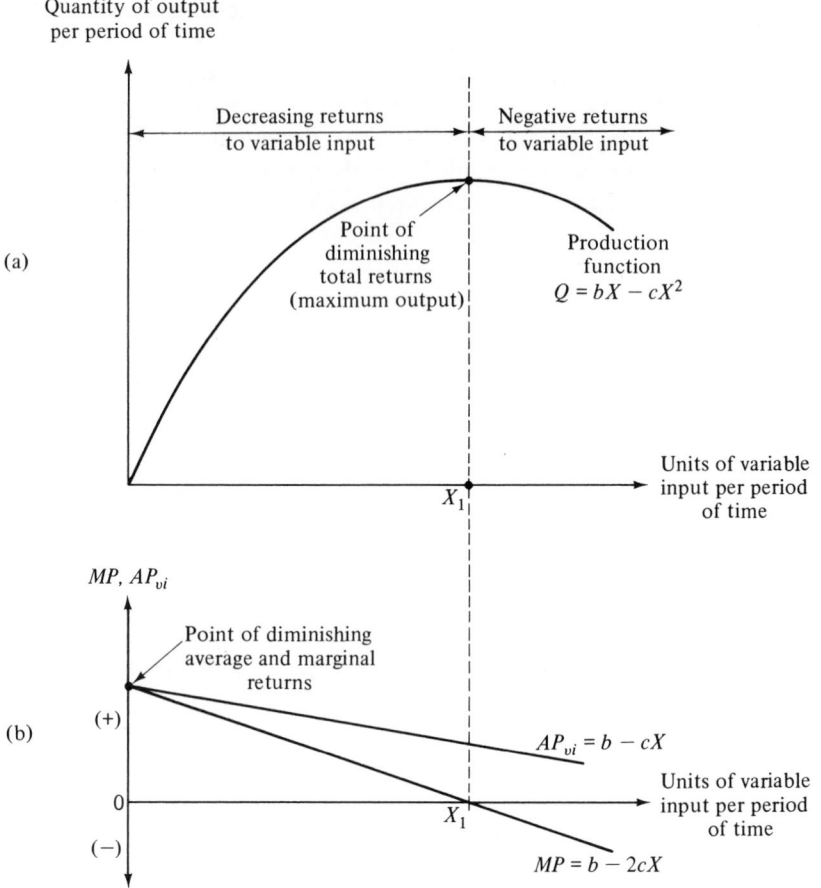

Fig. 7-3 A Production Function Characterized by a Phase of Decreasing Returns to Variable Input

encountered with the first increment of variable input. Increases in the intensity of use of the fixed input brought about by larger doses of variable input yield progressively less and less in additional output. The marginal product of variable input then is a declining, but positive, value up to X_1 units of variable input, at which point the peak of the production function is reached. Since additional usage of variable input lowers marginal product, the average product of variable input is always falling, being pulled downward by the declining values of *MP*.

When X_1 units of variable input have been combined with the fixed input, the units of fixed input are being utilized to their fullest extent so that no greater output can be gotten until the fixed inputs are increased. Larger applications of variable input beyond the level of X_1 will cause the quantity of output to fall and the marginal product of variable input to become negative, since the fixed input is being *overutilized* to such an extent that all inputs become less efficient and less productive.

Increasing Returns to Variable Input.   The last and least likely type of production function has the quantity of output increasing at an increasing rate as large amounts of variable input are used with the fixed input. The simplest form of this function is given by the equation:

$$Q = a + bX + cX^2.$$

Again, if $a = 0$ and if b and c are positive constants as indicated, the equation for this production function reduces to

$$Q = bX + cX^2.$$

The general equations for the corresponding average and marginal product curves can be derived as follows:

$$AP_{vi} = \frac{Q}{X} = \frac{bX + cX^2}{X} = b + cX$$

and

$$MP = \frac{dQ}{dX} = b + 2cX.$$

The graph of these three functions is shown as Figure 7-4.

For production functions of this type, output increases at an increasing rate. Adding extra units of variable input results in larger and larger gains in output as reflected by the rising marginal product of variable input. *Increasing returns to variable input* are said to prevail, because the gains in the quantity of output are *more* than proportional to the increased usage of variable input. The average product of variable input rises persistently, being pulled up by the increases in marginal product.

It is important to note that a production function of this form is likely to describe the behavior of output *only* for relatively small values of variable input, where the fixed input is being utilized far less than it could be. In other words, increasing returns to variable input are likely to prevail only for low levels of output for the plant—and then only in those instances where combining more variable input with the fixed input causes a dramatic increase in the productivity of the inputs such that output can be increased at an increasing rate. Situations of this nature can be anticipated only when the fixed inputs are being so grossly underutilized that additional variable input will permit great reductions in inefficiencies, thereby making for disproportionately greater gains in output.

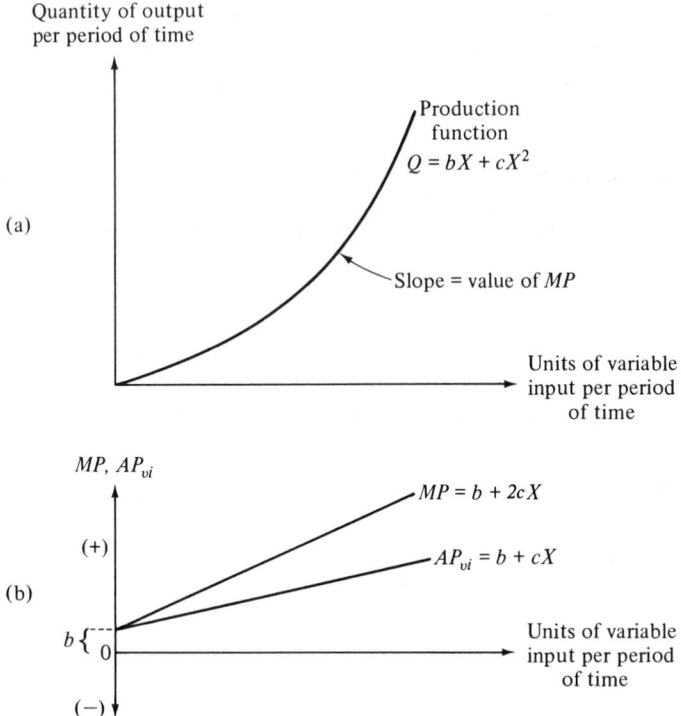

Fig. 7-4   A Production Function Characterized by a Phase of Increasing Returns to Variable Input

A More General Type of Production Function.   When one considers the *entire* range of output of which a firm is capable, the most probable type of input-output relation is that where first is encountered a (short) range of increasing returns to variable input, then a (perhaps long) range of approximately constant returns to variable input, and finally a range of decreasing returns to variable input as production capacity is approached. A simple form of a production function which captures these basic elements is like that described earlier and shown in Figure 7-1. The general equation for a production function of this shape and character is

$$Q = a + bX + cX^2 - dX^3;$$

or, given our assumption that $a = 0$, we have

$$Q = bX + cX^2 - dX^3,$$

where b and c are positive constants and the coefficient of the X^3 term (d)

is negative as indicated. The general equations for the corresponding average and marginal product curves are

$$AP_{vi} = \frac{Q}{X} = \frac{bX + cX^2 - dX^3}{X} = b + cX - dX^2$$

and

$$MP = \frac{dQ}{dX} = b + 2cX - 3dX^2.$$

The general applicability of this type of production function is wide. No doubt many production processes contain a stage of increasing returns to variable input at very low output levels, and almost every production process is certain to reflect decreasing returns to variable input as the upper limit to production capacity is approached. Moreover, for many production processes constant returns (or nearly so) to variable input can characterize the range in between. This can be seen from Figure 7-1(a), where the production function assumes an almost linear shape along the range from point A to just beyond point B.

Because the cubic type of production function does incorporate the key characteristics of other production functions, we will in future discussions use it to describe input-output relations over the entire range of a firm's output capacity. However, when there is some special reason to expect increasing, decreasing, or constant returns to the variable input to dominate the input-output relationship over the relevant range of output, we will depart from use of the cubic form of production function and employ instead the indicated form.

THE STAGES OF PRODUCTION

Production functions of the form

$$Q = a + bX + cX^2 - dX^3$$

and the associated average and marginal product curves can be divided into three stages, as illustrated in Figure 7-5. Stage I extends from zero usage of the variable input to the level where the *average* product of variable input is maximum. Stage II extends from maximum AP_{vi} to where the quantity of output is maximum (or to where the marginal product of variable input is zero). Stage III coincides with the range of variable input where output is falling and the marginal product of variable input is negative. These stages are of special significance for analyzing the efficiency with which resource inputs are used.

Stage I.   In stage I we find the entire range of increasing returns to

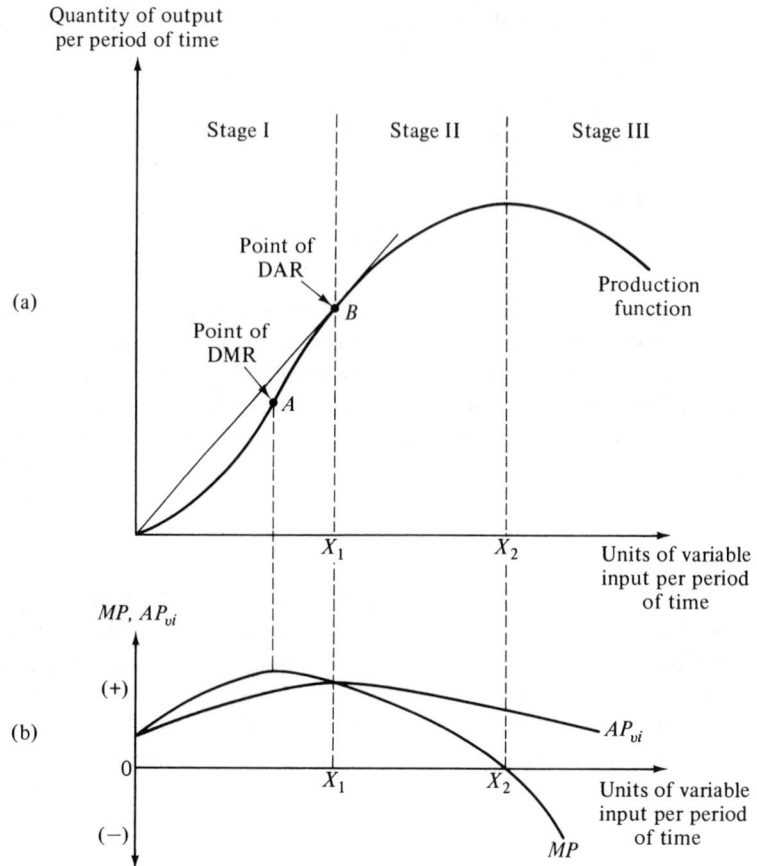

Fig. 7-5   The Stages of Production

variable input and the point of diminishing marginal returns is reached (point *A*) and passed. Up to the point of diminishing marginal returns, output is increasing at an increasing rate; past this point it increases at a decreasing rate. The marginal product of variable input rises to its peak and begins to fall, yet it remains a greater value than average product throughout the stage. Stage I ends when the point of diminishing *average* returns is reached (point *B*).

What about the efficiency with which the fixed and variable inputs are being used in stage I? The *efficiency* of an input is best measured by its *average* product, because it indicates the average amount of output obtained *per unit* of input. An input's marginal product is a measure of the efficiency of a *single* unit of variable input, but it is not relevant for purposes of determining the efficiency of *all* the units of an input taken as a group. Since the average product of variable input is rising throughout stage I, it is evident that variable input is being employed with *increasing* efficiency as the end of stage I is approached. Indeed, maximum efficiency of the variable input is attained at the border between stages I and II, where the average product of variable input is maximum. So much for variable input; now what about the efficiency of the fixed inputs in stage I? Although we have no curve representing the average product of fixed input (AP_{fi}), a definite statement regarding its behavior can nevertheless be made. The quantity of output rises throughout stage I, and the level of fixed input remains unchanged. Thus, because

$$AP_{fi} = \frac{\text{units of output}}{\text{units of fixed input}},$$

the average product of fixed input must also be rising throughout stage I. We can conclude, therefore, that increasing the quantity of variable input applied to a given quantity of fixed inputs in stage I increases the efficiency with which *both* fixed and variable inputs are utilized.

It is pertinent to understand *why* the efficiency of both fixed and variable inputs rises in stage I. The reason rests with an imbalance between the fixed and variable inputs. Throughout stage I the amount of fixed input is excessive compared to the amount of variable input employed. The unduly large proportions of fixed input to variable input in stage I cause the fixed inputs to be underutilized and the variable inputs to be overutilized. Hence, as more variable input is used, the imbalance is relieved and the efficiencies of both inputs rise.

The rising efficiencies of fixed and variable inputs have important implications for the costs of production. As will be demonstrated in the next chapter, when both the average products of fixed and variable inputs are increasing, the *unit* costs of producing more output are declining. Thus, *from the standpoint of cost and efficiency, a firm would always prefer to move through stage I to at least the border of stage II before ceasing to use more variable input.*

Stage II   In stage II the quantity of output rises at a decreasing rate; accordingly, the marginal product of variable input is declining, although it remains greater than zero. More significantly, the average product of variable input is falling throughout stage II. The average product of fixed input, however, continues to rise in stage II, since the quantity of output rises while the amount of fixed input is held constant. In stage II, then, additional units of variable input add to the efficiency of fixed input but diminish the efficiency of variable input.

Stage III.   At the boundary between stages II and III, short-run output is maximum and the fixed input is being utilized to its fullest extent—the efficiency of the fixed input has reached its peak level. With further doses of variable input, the amount of variable input relative to fixed input becomes so large that the quantity of output falls. There simply is too little fixed input relative to the amounts of variable input being used. Thus, the use of larger quantities of variable input per period of time reduces its average product still more, and the marginal product of variable input becomes negative. Since output falls, the average product of fixed input also decreases. *The efficiency of variable input and the efficiency of fixed input both diminish as soon as stage III is entered.*

The Optimum Stage. The foregoing description of the three stages should make it apparent that operating in stage II is best from the standpoint of cost and efficiency. In stage I, variable input is used too sparingly with the available fixed input; increases in variable input will so increase the efficiency of all inputs that the *unit costs* of producing more output will decline. Thus, efficiency and cost considerations will induce the firm to employ at least an amount of variable input sufficient to reach stage II.

Stage III is obviously irrational. It makes no sense whatsoever for the firm to incur the added expense of purchasing and using more units of variable input per period of time when the payoff is a decline in the quantity of output.

Therefore, stage II is the optimum stage in which to produce if criteria of efficiency and cost are applied. Just where in stage II the best rate of variable input usage lies depends upon the prices of fixed and variable input; we shall examine this matter more thoroughly shortly. *Stage II is not, however, the stage in which profit will necessarily be maximized.* Demand for a firm's product may in the short run be so low that it is actually more profitable to operate in stage I. We shall indicate this more clearly in a later chapter. It should be apparent at this point, however, that stage III can never be more profitable than stage I or stage II, because the decline in output is associated with rising total costs and potentially lower revenues.

FIXED INPUTS AND THE SHORT-RUN PRODUCTION FUNCTION

Generally speaking, the greater the quantity of fixed input employed in the short run, the larger will be the values of output, MP, and AP_{vi} for any given amount of variable input. In other words, the amount of fixed input influences the heights of the production function and its associated complement of curves. This relationship has serveral pertinent implications.

We have seen in the preceding section that economical production occurs only in stage II; yet what can a firm do if its level of product demand does not warrant an output sufficiently high to reach stage II? Suppose, for instance, that a firm's production function is as shown in Figure 7-6(a), where stage II is reached at an output of Q_2 units, and that the quantity

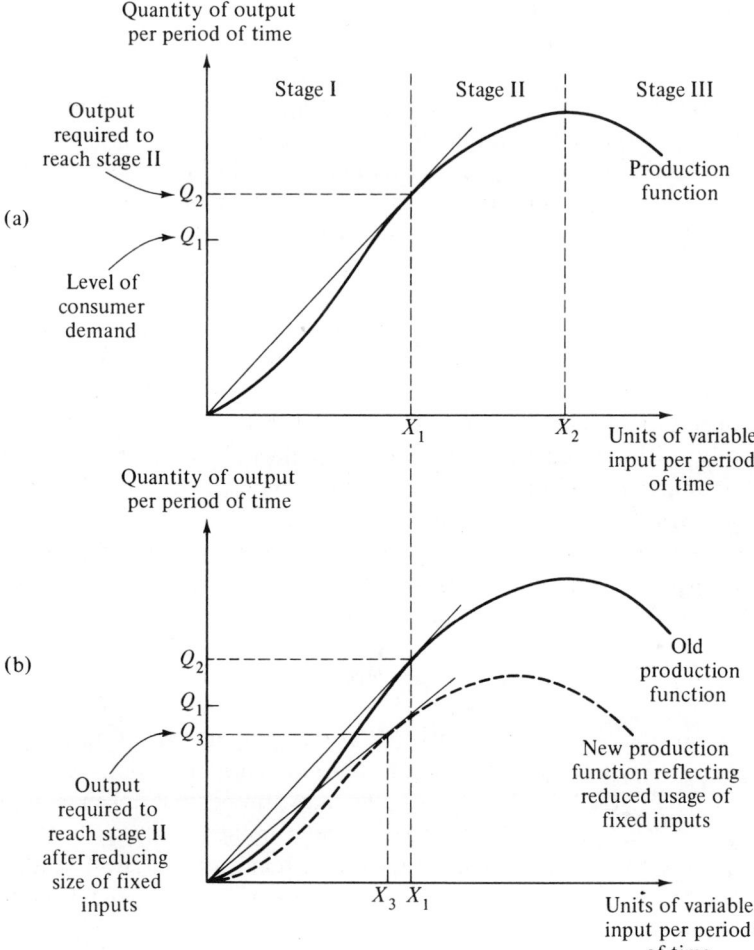

Fig. 7-6   The Impact of Reductions in the Use of Fixed Inputs Upon the Production Function

demanded is only Q_1 units at the current selling price. Several alternatives are open to the firm. In the short run it can (1) tolerate the production inefficiency—which may, incidentally, allow ample room for profit to be earned, (2) seek to increase product demand by lowering its selling price and/or increasing promotional and selling efforts, or (3) add new products to its product line to take up the slack in production capacity. If these prove unsatisfactory for a variety of reasons, in the long run the firm can reduce its scale of production operations by cutting back on the size of fixed inputs. Reducing the size of fixed inputs has the impact of shifting the production function down and to the left, as shown in Figure 7-6(b).[8] Then the firm can reach stage II at a lower output (Q_3 as compared to Q_2) and with a smaller amount of variable input (X_3 as compared to X_1). Demand for the firm's product can be satisfied by using fewer inputs, thereby cutting production costs and widening the firm's profit margin at the current price.

Likewise, when a firm encounters a level of product demand exceeding its ability to produce (as indicated by the peak of its production function), several options are again present. If the strong demand for the commodity is perceived to be temporary, a price increase to ration the available supply among potential buyers is in order, and no increase in production capacity is called for. But when demand seems likely to remain above production capacity on a relatively permanent and profitable basis, a price increase in the short run should be combined with an expansion of the firm's scale of operations in the long run. To accomplish this, the size of the fixed inputs must be increased; such action has the effect of shifting the production function upward and raising the maximum obtainable level of output.

In summary, whenever output must be produced in quantities not covered by producing in stage II, long-run productive efficiency requires a change in the usage of fixed inputs and in the firm's scale of operations.

Determining Optimal Input Proportions

So far, the firm has been pictured as changing its rate of output in the short run by employing more or less units of variable input. In the long run, changes in the usage of fixed inputs may also be undertaken to adjust output capabilities. Although the fixed-variable input approach to output adjustment is adequate for indicating the fundamental physical relationships of production, it does not permit determination of the optimal proportions of different resource inputs. To gain a better understanding of the most economical combination of resource inputs, we must shift our attention away from the relationships between input-output flows and concentrate upon the relationships between resource inputs.

THE PRODUCTION SURFACE

To simplify the analysis of relationships between resource inputs, let us begin by assuming that capital and labor are the only two types of resource inputs available for use in the production of a commodity. No disservice to reality is done by this assumption, since the relevant principles apply for two inputs

---

[8] In the event that fixed inputs are "lumpy" and can be reduced only by a relatively large proportion, the production function conceivably could shift downward and *to the right*, meaning that the firm can reach stage II at a lower output provided its usage of variable input is increased. Whether the firm would prefer to use less fixed input and more variable input in producing its product would depend upon the relative prices of fixed and variable inputs.

as well as for a whole host of alternative types of input. Capital is symbolic of those kinds of resource inputs which are fixed in the short run, and labor symbolizes those kinds of inputs which are variable in the short run. By letting capital serve as the proxy for fixed inputs in the short run and labor as the proxy for variable inputs, we can learn more about the optimal combination of fixed and variable inputs in the long run.

In the three-dimensional diagram of Figure 7-7(a), the coordinates in the horizontal plane show the alternative combinations of capital and labor. The quantity of output associated with each combination of the two types of resource inputs is measured vertically above the plane. Varying the quantities of capital and labor generates the inverted bowl-shaped production surface $OCPL$.[9] If OC units of capital are used, varying the quantity of labor generates

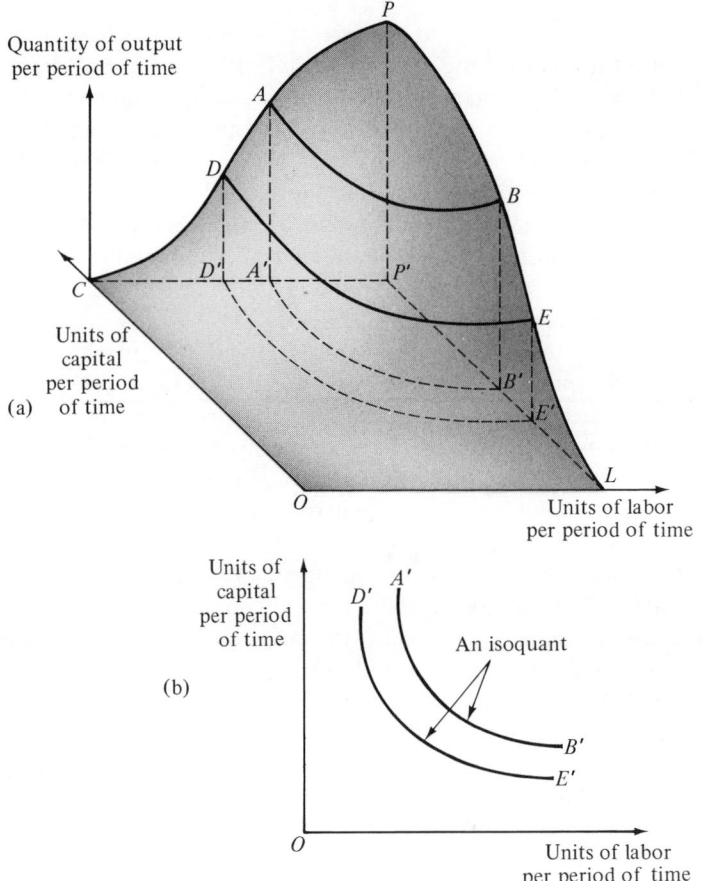

Fig. 7-7   Derivation of Isoquants from a Production Surface

---

[9] Observe that the concept of the production surface is analogous to the utility surface discussed in Chapters 3 and 4.

the production function *CDAP*. Similarly, given *OL* units of labor, varying the quantity of capital input gives the production function *LEBP*. Notice that the shapes of the production functions generated by holding the input of one resource constant and letting the other change correspond to the cubic type of production function, which often typifies the entire output range for a plant.

Suppose we connect all points on the production surface *OCPL* associated with an output of *AA′* units (where *AA′ = BB′*), obtaining the contour line *AB*. All of the points along *AB* are associated with the *same* amount of output (*AA′ = BB′*). Projecting line *AB* vertically downward onto the horizontal plane gives the dashed contour line *A′B′*. The line *A′B′* defines all of the combinations of capital and labor employed per unit of time that will yield an output flow of *AA′ = BB′*; such a line is called an *isoquant*.[10] For movements along an isoquant the rate of output remains constant, but the input ratio (in this case the ratio of capital to labor) changes continuously.

Following the same procedure, suppose we move down the production surface to a lower level of output, say *DD′*, and connect all points on the production surface *OCPL* representing an output of *DD′* (where *DD′ = EE′*). This gives the contour line *DE* which projected vertically downward onto the horizontal plane traces out the dashed contour *D′E′*. Any point along *DE* represents constant total output, and all combinations of capital and labor lying on *D′E′* are capable of producing this amount of output. Contour line *D′E′* is also an isoquant.

Figure 7-7(b) illustrates isoquants *A′B′* and *D′E′* in a two-dimensional diagram. All input combinations lying on *A′B′* yield more output than the input combinations on *D′E′*. Hence, higher rates of output are represented by isoquants lying farther from the origin, as can easily be seen from the positions on the production surface of the contour lines from which isoquants are derived. A complete set of isoquants for a production surface is called an *isoquant map*.[11]

Isoquants may be viewed as analogous to the contour lines on a geographical map; each isoquant connects all points of the same altitude or output rate. From this standpoint, the entire production surface (of which only a section is shown in Figure 7-7) can be considered as a "production mountain" with isoquants as the contour lines encircling it.

Although, the previous discussions have portrayed a firm's production function and production surface as being continuous with the isoquants derived therefrom also being continuous it is more realistic to acknowledge that the "lumpiness" of resource inputs produces a discrete production function and a discrete production surface with correspondingly discrete

[10] The term isoquant is derived from the prefix *iso-*, meaning equal, and the word *quantity;* hence, it literally means equal quantity (of output). In the literature of economics isoquants are sometimes referred to as product indifference curves, equal product curves, or isoproduct curves.

[11] Suppose a firm's production function is $Q = f(L, C)$; then a particular isoquant is defined by assigning a value to Q and observing all of the different technically feasible values of L and C which will yield that value of Q. The firm's isoquant map is derived by repeating this procedure for many values of Q.

isoquants. Seldom does any resource (especially capital) lend itself to being used in any quantity; which is to say that most resources are not continuously divisible in subunits. After all, anything less than a whole machine is less than satisfactory. More importantly, technology is not of such a character that an infinite number of combinations of resources can be used to produce equivalent amounts of output. A firm is necessarily constrained in its selection of resource inputs to the finite number of recipes known to exist for producing a commodity. In these cases, isoquants are represented by a series of points, where each point represents a technically feasible combination of resource inputs that yields the specified level of output. Such isoquants are discontinuous or discrete and emphasize the limited potentials of substituting one resource input for another. However, as long as the "lumpiness" of resource inputs is recognized, it does little harm to simplify our discussion by drawing isoquants as smooth curves. Certainly, our exposition of the pertinent relationships is made easier by considering smooth curves instead of a series of points.

THE CHARACTERISTICS OF ISOQUANTS

At the outset, it is evident that the properties of isoquants are remarkably similar to those of indifference curves. First, isoquants are nonintersecting. Second, all *rational* combinations of resource inputs lie on that portion of an isoquant which slopes downward to the right. Third, the rational segments of isoquants tend to be convex to the origin. Each of these properties warrants some discussion.

The intersection of isoquants defies logic, for it means that two different amounts of output can be produced with the same combination of resource inputs. This can occur only when a firm uses its inputs inefficiently and thereby reduces their productivity. To knowingly combine resources so as to obtain less output than is possible makes no sense and is irrational. Hence, an isoquant is conceived as showing only the maximum output which can be gotten from resource inputs.

As indicated above, an isoquant map consists of a series of concentric rings around the production surface. A single such isoquant is reproduced in Figure 7-8. All of the points along the isoquant in Figure 7-8 represent input combinations capable of producing the same level of output. Suppose a firm wishes to produce the output represented by this isoquant. Although all of the combinations of capital and labor lying on this isoquant represent possible recipes for producing this output, some of the combinations are more rational than others. For example, combination B would never be chosen over combination A. Why? Combination A requires the same amount of capital input as B (C_2 units) but requires considerably less labor input (L_1 units as compared to L_3 units); hence, combination A is *cheaper* than B. Similarly, combination D is always preferable to combination C, since it requires much

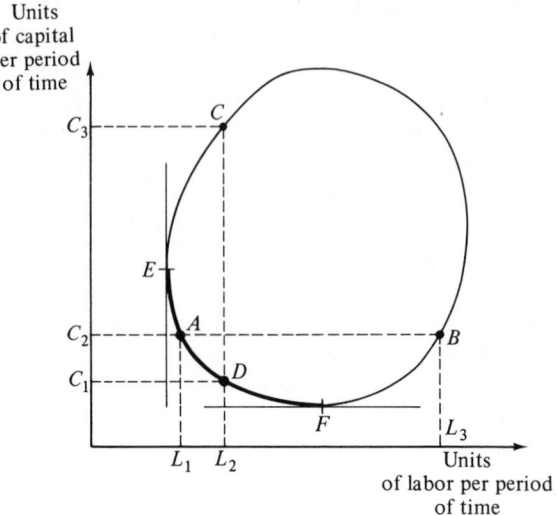

Fig. 7-8   The Economic Region of a Isoquant

less capital input (C_1 as compared to C_3 units) while using the same amount of labor input (L_2 units). It follows that the economically practical resource combinations fall within the lower left quadrant of the isoquant—the boldly inscribed portion in Figure 7-8 lying between the vertical and horizontal tangents to the isoquant at points E and F. The remaining points on the isoquant constitute economically foolish resource combinations, even though they represent technically feasible recipes. Thus, for reasons of economy in resource use and cost, the rational segment of an isoquant is the portion sloping downward to the right and bowed in toward the origin.

The downward slope of the economic region of an isoquant derives from the possibility of substituting one resource input for another in the production process and still maintaining the same production level. Consider the *rate* at which one input must be substituted for another to keep output constant. From Figure 7-9, we see that a change from input combination C_1L_1 to input combination C_2L_2 involves a substitution of labor for capital. The rate at which labor is substituted for capital over this range is

$$\frac{C_2 - C_1}{L_2 - L_1} = \frac{-\Delta C}{\Delta L}$$

and is called the *marginal rate of technical substitution* of labor for capital. The marginal rate of technical substitution ($MRTS$) measures the reduction in one input (ΔC) per unit increase in the other (ΔL) that is just sufficient to maintain a constant level of output.

In moving from C_1L_1 to C_2L_2 in Figure 7-9, the output rate remains unchanged; consequently, the "loss" in output from using fewer units of

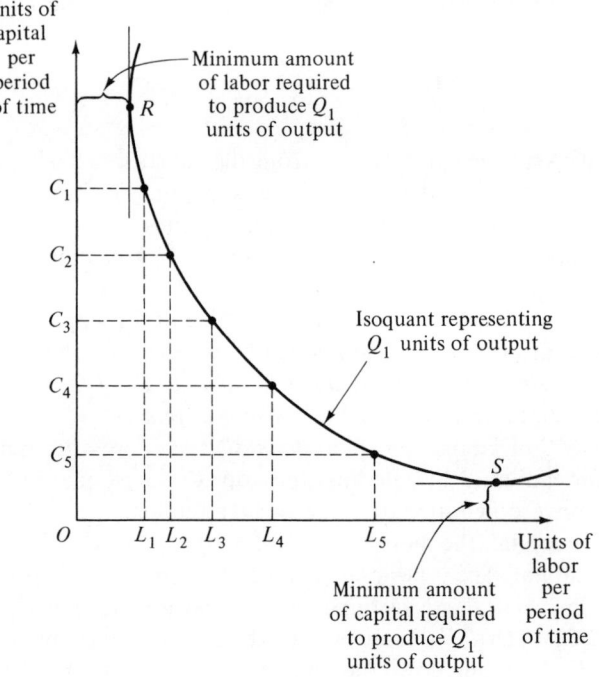

Fig. 7-9   The Marginal Rate of Technical Substitution

capital input is exactly compensated for by the "gain" in the output from using more units of labor input. The "loss" in output from using less capital equals the reduction in capital usage multiplied by the marginal product of these units, or

$$-\Delta C \cdot MP_C.$$

By the same token, the "gain" in output from using a larger dose of labor equals

$$\Delta L \cdot MP_L.$$

Since the "loss" and the "gain" are equivalent in size, we can say

$$-\Delta C \cdot MP_C = \Delta L \cdot MP_L.$$

Dividing both sides of this equation by $\Delta L \cdot MP_C$ gives

$$-\frac{\Delta C \cdot MP_C}{\Delta L \cdot MP_C} = \frac{\Delta L \cdot MP_L}{\Delta L \cdot MP_C},$$

which reduces to

$$-\frac{\Delta C}{\Delta L} = \frac{MP_L}{MP_C}.$$

234

Therefore, it is apparent that between combinations C_1L_1 and C_2L_2

$$MRTS_{LC} = (-)\frac{\Delta C}{\Delta L} = (-)\frac{MP_L}{MP_C}.$$

That both ratios are negative derives from the substitution of one resource for the other and the negative slope of the isoquant; however, for our purposes it is the *size* of the ratio that is important, not its sign.

Now suppose combination C_1L_1 in Figure 7-9 is moved closer and closer towards C_2L_2 so as to merge eventually with it to form a single point. The ratio $(-)\Delta C/\Delta L$ will then approach the value of the slope of the tangent to the isoquant at point C_2L_2. Consequently, we may say that *the marginal rate of technical substitution of one input for another input at any point along an isoquant is equal to the slope of the isoquant at that point.*[12]

The *MRTS* of labor for capital *diminishes* as more and more labor is substituted for capital. Why? Because the slope of the isoquant becomes less steep as we move down along it. The greater the extent to which labor is substituted for capital, the more labor it takes to compensate for a reduction in the use of capital. The other points along the isoquant in Figure 7-9 make this clearer. The vertical axis in Figure 7-9 is measured so that $C_1C_2 = C_2C_3 = C_3C_4 = C_4C_5 = OC_5 = 1$ unit of capital. Starting at resource combination C_1L_1 and proceeding down the isoquant, we find that it takes a relatively small increase in the use of labor (L_1L_2 units) to compensate for using one less unit of capital and still produce the same quantity of output. But, as we move further down the isoquant and continue to substitute labor for capital, reductions in capital must be offset by progressively larger increases in labor input ($L_1L_2 < L_2L_3 < L_3L_4 < L_4L_5$). Plainly, then, the *MRTS* of labor for capital diminishes as the degree of substitution is increased. Where the isoquant becomes horizontal, the substitution of labor for capital has reached its maximum limit, and the $MRTS_{LC} = 0$. Further reductions in capital will cause output to *fall*; no longer is it possible to reduce the use of capital and maintain the output level by using more labor. The amount of capital corresponding to point S in Figure 7-9 is the minimum amount of capital which can be used to produce an output of Q_1. By the same rationale, as we move

[12] Mathematically, the *MRTS* can be found by taking the first derivative of the equation defining an isoquant. For example, if the expression

$$LC = 100$$

defines an isoquant, then the $MRTS_{LC}$ can be found as follows:

$$C = \frac{100}{L} = 100L^{-1},$$

$$\frac{dC}{dL} = -100L^{-2} = -\frac{100}{L^2}.$$

Since $MRTS_{LC} = dC/dL$, then we have

$$MRTS_{LC} = -\frac{100}{L^2}$$

for any value of L in which interest may focus.

back up the isoquant toward point R, capital is being substituted for labor, and the $MRTS$ of capital for labor is rising. At point R capital has been substituted for labor to the maximum possible extent; the $MRTS$ of capital for labor is infinity and the slope of the isoquant is vertical. The amount of labor corresponding to point R is the minimum amount of labor which can be used to produce output Q_1.

It is the changing marginal rate of technical substitution that makes the isoquant convex to the origin. Should two inputs be perfect substitutes for each other, the isoquant is linear and downsloping. Such a relationship between inputs is rare, especially regarding inputs as diverse as labor and capital. That most isoquants are convex is easily demonstrated. Consider labor and capital in making fenders for automobiles. A metal-stamping machine with a single operator can transform a piece of sheet steel into the shape of an automobile fender in a matter of seconds. Within limits, less expensive stamping machines requiring more labor time can be used to make same fender. But the more labor and the less capital used to shape sheet steel into fenders, the more difficult it becomes to carry the degree of substitution further without jeopardizing the quantity and quality of output. To hammer out the fender, for example, would require an inordinate amount of labor time and cost, as well as entailing a major reduction in fender quality. The same reasoning applies equally well to other resource inputs; consequently, a diminishing marginal rate of technical substitution of one resource input for another is a generally encountered phenomenon in production processes.

THE ISOCOST CURVE

Up to now, we have examined production theory from the standpoint of the possible ways that firms can combine resource inputs—no restrictions, save those of a technical nature, have been imposed. In reality, though, firms are limited in their choice of production techniques by the prices of resource inputs and by the amount of funds available for purchasing these inputs.

An *isocost curve* portrays the various alternative combinations of resource inputs which a firm can purchase, given the prices of resource inputs and the stipulated amount of expenditure on resources.[13] Continuing our assumption of only two inputs, capital and labor, let the price of labor be P_L, the price of capital be P_C, and the stipulated amount of expenditure on resources be TC (total cost). The firm's expenditure for labor is equal to the purchase price per unit (P_L) times the amount purchased (L) or $P_L \cdot L$; similarly, the firm's expenditure for capital is $P_L \cdot C$. With only two resource inputs to choose from, the sum of the firm's expenditures for labor and capital must be equal to or less than the maximum allowable expenditure (TC).

---

[13] The concept of isocost curves is analogous to the concept of lines of attainable combinations (Chapter 4). The only difference is that isocost curves deal with the resource combinations which a firm can purchase, whereas lines of attainable combinations relate to a consumer's ability to purchase goods and services.

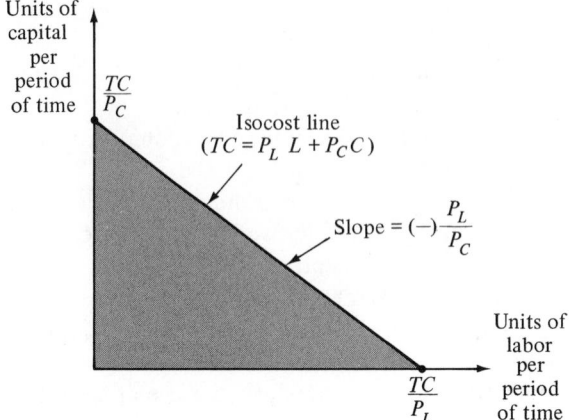

Fig. 7-10   The Isocost Curve

Thus, the expression defining the isocost curve may be written as

$$P_L L + P_c C = TC.$$

Provided P_L and P_c are unaffected by the quantity of labor and capital the firm decides to purchase, then if the firm elects to use only labor a maximum of TC/P_L units can be employed; if the firm elects to use only capital a maximum of TC/P_c can be bought. A straight line joining TC/P_c and TC/P_L shows all of the combinations of capital and labor obtainable from an expenditure of TC dollars. Figure 7-10 illustrates such an isocost curve.[14] The slope of the isocost curve may be found by considering points TC/P_c and TC/P_L. Between these two points:

$$\text{Slope of isocost curve} = \frac{(-)\dfrac{TC}{P_c}}{\dfrac{TC}{P_L}}$$

$$= -\frac{TC}{P_c} \cdot \frac{P_L}{TC}$$

$$= (-)\frac{P_L}{P_c}.$$

THE OPTIMUM MIX OF RESOURCE INPUTS

A basic objective of firms is to realize the greatest amount of output from a stipulated total cost outlay. In terms of isoquant-isocost analysis this means

[14] Resource prices need not remain constant irrespective of the amounts purchased of labor and capital. A large employer in a tight labor market may have to raise wage rates to attract and hire more labor. A large purchaser of capital goods may be able to squeeze price concessions from suppliers of capital goods as the firm's usage of capital increases. Likewise, quantity discounts may be received on raw material purchases. When the prices of resource inputs fall as the amounts purchased go up, the isocost curve is bowed in toward the origin. In the event that resource prices rise as their levels of usage are increased, the isocost curve is bowed out from the origin.

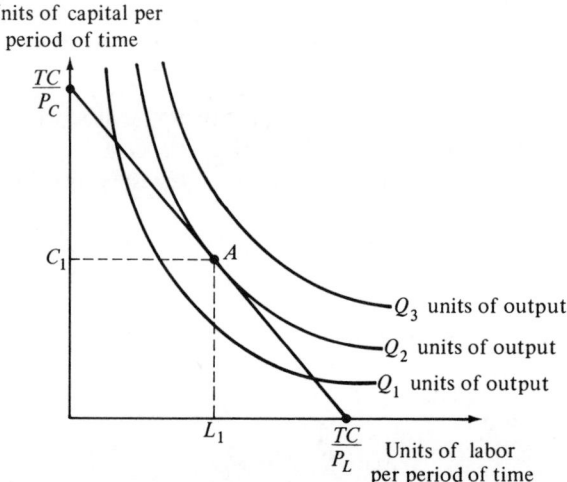

Fig. 7-11   Determining the Optimum Resource Combination

getting to the highest isoquant permitted by the firm's isocost curve. In Figure 7-11, the output rate corresponding to isoquant Q_2 is the highest output which can be attained given an outlay of TC dollars and prices P_L and P_C. Accordingly, the optimum combination of resource inputs for producing output Q_2 is C_1 units of capital and L_1 units of labor. From a slightly different viewpoint, this resource combination may also be designated as the *least-cost resource combination*, since it represents the minimum cost of producing Q_2 units of output when the prices of capital and labor are P_C and P_L, respectively. In other words, the point of tangency between the isocost and isoquant curves defines the optimum resource combination, whether interest centers upon (a) finding the maximum output for a given total cost outlay and at given resource prices, or (b) finding the minimum cost for producing a given output at given resource prices.

If we conceive of capital as symbolic of fixed input and of labor as symbolic of variable input, then the mix of capital and labor at the least-cost resource combination in Figure 7-11 defines the optimal proportions of fixed and variable input for a firm in producing output Q_2. This proportion is optimum because, given the prices of the two inputs, no other combination of fixed (capital) and variable (labor) input can produce Q_2 units of output as cheaply—hence the term *least-cost* resource combination.

The Conditions for Optimizing the Resource Mix.   At this point we are ready to explore the conditions for optimizing the combination of labor and capital inputs. First, we may note that the optimum resource combination of capital and labor lies *on* the isocost line rather than inside it. This means the firm must fully utilize its available dollars in purchasing inputs if it is to maximize output. Translated into the language of mathematics, we can say that optimization requires

$$P_L L + P_C C = TC.$$

Second, at the point of tangency between the isocost line and the maximum attainable isoquant, the slope of the isocost line is equal to the slope of the isoquant. From prior discussions, the respective slopes are

$$\text{slope of the isoquant} = MRTS_{LC} = (-)\frac{MP_L}{MP_C},$$

and

$$\text{slope of the isocost} = (-)\frac{P_L}{P_C}.$$

Since the slopes are equal, we may write

$$MRTS = (-)\frac{P_L}{P_C},$$

which states that to optimize the resource mix the firm must allocate its expenditures so that the marginal rate of technical substitution of labor for capital equals the ratio of the price of labor to the price of capital. The interpretation of this result is straightforward. The $MRTS_{LC}$ defines the *rate* at which the firm is *technically able* to substitute labor for capital. The price ratio P_L/P_C shows the *rate* at which the firm is *economically able* to substitute labor for capital. Unless the two rates are equivalent, the firm can alter its resource mix and obtain a larger output or else reduce its costs for a given output. For example, suppose the $MRTS_{LC} = -\frac{1}{2}$, meaning that the firm is technically able to substitute two units of labor input for one unit of capital input without changing output. If $P_L = \$10$ and $P_C = \$30$, then the firm is economically able to give up one unit of capital in return for 3 units of labor. Giving up one unit of capital releases $30, of which only $20 is needed for purchasing labor, since two units of labor at $10 each will compensate for a one unit reduction in capital input. The remaining $10 can be applied to the purchase of additional resources for increasing output or else to reducing the total costs of the current output level. In either event the firm will be better off. In general terms, therefore, optimizing the input combination requires equality between the marginal rate of technical substitution for any pair of resource inputs and the ratio of their prices; in the absence of equality some substitution of one resource for another can be initiated to increase output, or else expenditures on resource inputs can be reduced.

However, we can approach this second condition for optimizing the resource mix from yet another and more familiar angle. Not only is the slope of the isoquant equal to the $MRTS$ at any point, but it is also equal to the ratio of the marginal products of the resource inputs:

$$MRTS_{LC} = (-)\frac{MP_L}{MP_C}.$$

Thus we may rewrite the second condition for optimizing the resource combination as

$$(-)\frac{MP_L}{MP_C} = (-)\frac{P_L}{P_C}.$$

This equation states that the firm's total cost outlay should be allocated among labor and capital so as to equate the ratio of their marginal products with the ratio of their prices. Transforming the latter equation still further by cross multiplying, we get

$$P_L \cdot MP_C = P_C \cdot MP_L.$$

Dividing both sides by $P_L \cdot P_C$, we get

$$\frac{P_L \cdot MP_C}{P_L \cdot P_C} = \frac{P_C \cdot MP_L}{P_L \cdot P_C},$$

which reduces to

$$\frac{MP_C}{P_C} = \frac{MP_L}{P_L}.$$

The latter expression says that the firm should arrange its input purchases so as to obtain an equivalent amount of additional output from the last dollar spent on each input. When the extra outputs per dollar spent on the last unit of each resource are unequal, the quantity of output can be increased (or total costs reduced) by diminishing expenditures where the marginal product per dollar spent is less and by enlarging expenditures where the marginal product per dollar spent is greater. For example, if

MP_L = 42 units output for the last unit of labor purchased,
P_L = $7 per unit,
MP_C = 80 units of output for the last unit of capital purchased,
P_C = $10,

then

$$\frac{MP_L}{P_L} = \frac{42 \text{ units}}{\$7} = 6 \text{ units of output/\$ spent on labor,}$$

and

$$\frac{MP_C}{P_C} = \frac{80 \text{ units}}{\$10} = 8 \text{ units of output/\$ spent on capital.}$$

The firm is realizing more extra output per dollar spent on capital than on labor. The situation calls for (1) reallocating dollars away from the purchase of labor, thereby raising the MP_L and increasing the output per dollar spent on labor and (2) spending more dollars on the purchase of capital, thereby decreasing MP_C and decreasing the output per dollar spent on capital. Substituting capital for labor will tend to equalize the ratios MP_L/P_L and MP_C/P_C.

When There Are More Than Two Resource Inputs. The preceding conclusions are easily expanded for cases where more than two distinct kinds of resource inputs are used in a production process. In the event that a production process requires multiple types of resource inputs $(X_a, X_b, X_c, \ldots, X_n)$ obtainable at prices $(P_{X_a}, P_{X_b}, P_{X_c}, \ldots, P_{X_n})$, the optimal mix of resource inputs is attained by meeting the following two conditions:

(1) $$P_{X_a}X_a + P_{X_b}X_b + P_{X_c}X_c + \cdots + P_{X_n}X_n = TC,$$

(2) $$\frac{MP_{X_a}}{P_{X_a}} = \frac{MP_{X_b}}{P_{X_b}} = \frac{MP_{X_c}}{P_{X_c}} = \cdots = \frac{MP_{X_n}}{P_{X_n}}.$$

MATHEMATICAL CAPSULE 8

Determination of the Optimum Resource Combination

Let P_L and P_C be the prices of units of labor (L) and capital (C); let TC symbolize the budget a firm has available for purchasing the three resource inputs; and let $Q = f(L, C)$ represent the firm's production function for a commodity. The issue is how to best allocate the available dollars (TC) among purchases of labor and capital input so as to maximize the quantity of output (Q) subject to the constraint that the total expenditures on inputs just exhaust TC. More formally, what values of L and C will cause $Q = f(L, C)$ to be maximum, yet just meet the constraint that

$$TC - P_L L - P_C C = 0?$$

The mathematical solution requires using the Lagrangian multiplier method of finding the maximum value of a function. A new function is generated which combines the production function to be maximized with the constraint to be met. In order to keep the solution determinate (as many equations as there are unknowns) an artificial unknown, called a Lagrange multiplier and symbolized by λ, is introduced into the new function, giving

$$Z = f(L, C) + \lambda(TC - P_L L - P_C C).$$

Note that the constraint has been expressed in such a way that it is satisfied when $TC - P_L L - PC_C = 0$. Next, the partial derivatives of Z are found for each variable and equated to zero to establish the first-order conditions:

$$\frac{\partial Z}{\partial L} = \frac{\partial Q}{\partial C} - \lambda P_L = 0,$$

$$\frac{\partial Z}{\partial C} = \frac{\partial Q}{\partial C} - \lambda P_C = 0,$$

$$\frac{\partial Z}{\partial \lambda} = TC - P_L L - P_C C = 0.$$

These three equations are then solved simultaneously to determine the combination of L and C which will maximize the quantity of output subject to the cost constraint.

As an example of the foregoing, suppose the production function is

$$Q = 20L + 65C - .5L^2 - .5C^2$$

and that $TC = \$2200$, $P_L = \$20$ per unit, and $P_C = \$50$ per unit. To find the maximum output obtainable from an expenditure of $2200, we generate the function

$$Z = 20L + 65C - .5L^2 - .5C^2 + \lambda(2200 - 20L - 50C).$$

Finding the partial derivatives of Z and setting them equal to zero, we have

$$\frac{\partial Z}{\partial L} = 20 - L - 20\lambda = 0,$$

$$\frac{\partial Z}{\partial C} = 65 - C - 50\lambda = 0,$$

$$\frac{\partial Z}{\partial \lambda} = 2200 - 20L - 50C = 0.$$

Solving these three equations simultaneously gives $L = 10$, $C = 40$, and a maximum Q of 1950 units.

EXERCISES

1. Determine the optimum resource combination of labor and capital when

(a) $Q = 140L + 160C - 5L^2 - 2C^2$,   (b) $Q = 60L + 88C - 4LC$,
$P_L = \$12$, $P_L = \$5$,
$P_C = \$24$, $P_C = \$10$,
$TC = \$732$. $TC = \$180$.

THE EXPANSION PATH

It is not likely that a firm will maintain its output at the same rate for long. Market conditions, particularly demand, change frequently and cause the firm to adjust its output rate accordingly. For this reason, the firm has an interest in knowing the least-cost resource combinations for several rates of output. Especially pertinent is the issue of how much more of each input to use should market conditions warrant a long-term expansion of output.

Consider Figure 7-12, where inputs of C_1 units of capital and L_1 units of labor are being used to produce an output of Q_1 units at a total cost of TC_1 dollars. Now suppose the firm wishes to expand output to Q_2 units per period of time. Clearly, a greater total cost outlay is required. Assuming the prices

242

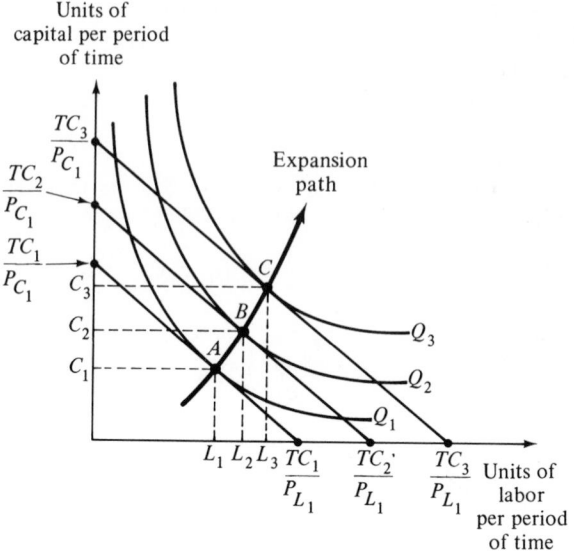

Units of
capital per period
of time

Expansion
path

Units of
labor
per period
of time

Fig. 7-12 Maintaining the Optimum Resource Combination for Various Quantities of Output

of capital and labor remain constant at P_{L_1} and P_{C_1}, an increase in the expenditure level for resource inputs will shift the isocost curve outward *parallel* to itself. Thus, an outlay of TC_2 dollars using C_2 units of capital and L_2 units of labor represents the least possible cost of producing output Q_2. Similarly, an outlay of TC_3 dollars with inputs of C_3 units of capital and L_3 units of labor is the least possible cost of producing Q_3 units of output. The line joining these and all other least-cost resource combinations is called the *expansion path* of the firm. *The expansion path shows the locus of optimum input combinations for each possible rate of output when the prices of the resource inputs remain constant.*

The shape of the expansion path for labor and capital has a certain amount of economic significance. It is probable that increasing the output of most commodities over the long run entails a technological and economic bias towards using relatively more capital than labor, meaning the expansion path is as shown in Figure 7-13(a). This stems from the readily observable tendency of large firms to use a more capital-intensive production recipe than do smaller firms producing the same item. The explanation for this bias is twofold. In the first place, for mass-produced items capital-intensive technology is more efficient than labor-intensive production techniques. Second, in the United States at least, labor is scarcer than capital; consequently, to attempt to expand output with even proportional increases in labor would create labor shortages and touch off significant increases in

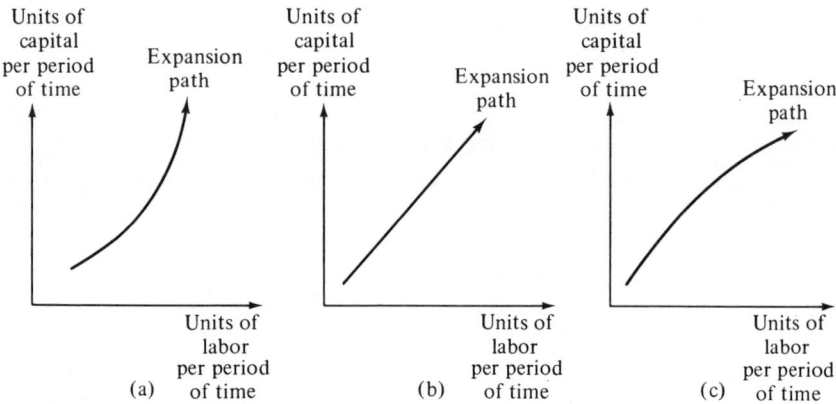

Fig. 7-13   Alternative Shapes for the Expansion Path

wage rates, thereby effectively frustrating output expansion. Occasionally, the expansion path may be linear or very nearly so [Figure 7-13(b)]. A linear expansion path for a commodity implies that the costs of additional output are minimized by using more of both inputs *in the same proportion* as before, perhaps because technological requirements call for a constant ratio between inputs. It is conceivable that the expansion path could assume the shape of that in Figure 7-13(c), where expanding output requires using relatively more labor than capital.

If we look upon capital as symbolizing the fixed inputs, the expansion path shows the amounts of resource inputs which the firm should use as it expands its *long-run* rate of output; in the short run, the firm has no alternative but to expand output by using more variable input with the given amount of fixed input. However, in order to minimize costs in the short run it is imperative that the firm adjust its usage of the several variable resources so as to keep the ratios of the marginal products per dollar spent on these variable resources equivalent. In other words, if *in the short run* a firm uses four *variable* inputs (X_a, X_b, X_c, and X_d), even though the fixed inputs cannot be changed, minimization of cost requires the quantities of variable inputs be adjusted such that

$$\frac{MP_{X_a}}{P_{X_a}} = \frac{MP_{X_b}}{P_{X_b}} = \frac{MP_{X_c}}{P_{X_c}} = \frac{MP_{X_d}}{P_{X_d}}.$$

THE IMPACT OF CHANGES IN RESOURCE PRICES

The prices of resource inputs, as with the prices of goods and services, are subject to change. Business firms typically respond to changes in input prices by adjusting the purchase levels of the resources they use. Suppose

244

we examine the frequently encountered circumstance of an increase in the price of labor and observe its impact upon the optimum mix of capital and labor.

Given the price of labor P_{L_1}, the price of capital P_{C_1}, and the firm's total cost outlay TC_1, the firm will optimize its inputs at an output of Q_1 by combining L_1 units of labor with C_1 units of capital as shown by point A in Figure 7-14. Now suppose the price of labor rises to P_{L_2}; the isocost curve will pivot to the left about point TC_1/P_{C_1}, restricting the maximum usage of labor to TC_1/P_{L_2} units were the entire total cost outlay used to buy labor. The new isocost curve will necessarily be tangent to a lower isoquant than previously and it will not be possible to product Q_1 units of output with an expenditure of TC_1 dollars. The optimum input mix becomes L_2 units of labor and C_2 units of capital (point B in Figure 7-14) at an output of Q_0 units. The firm must choose between being content with a lower output (Q_0) or else increasing TC to permit maintenance of output at Q_1. If the latter alternative is chosen and assuming the input of capital is fixed *in the short run* at C_1 units (as is truly the case in the real world), then the firm will find it most advantageous *in the short run* to continue to produce Q_1 units of output by using C_1 units of capital and L_1 units of labor (point A). Why? Because when the firm's capital input is fixed at C_1 units, the *smallest* amount of labor which can be used to produce an output of Q_1 units is L_1 units of labor.

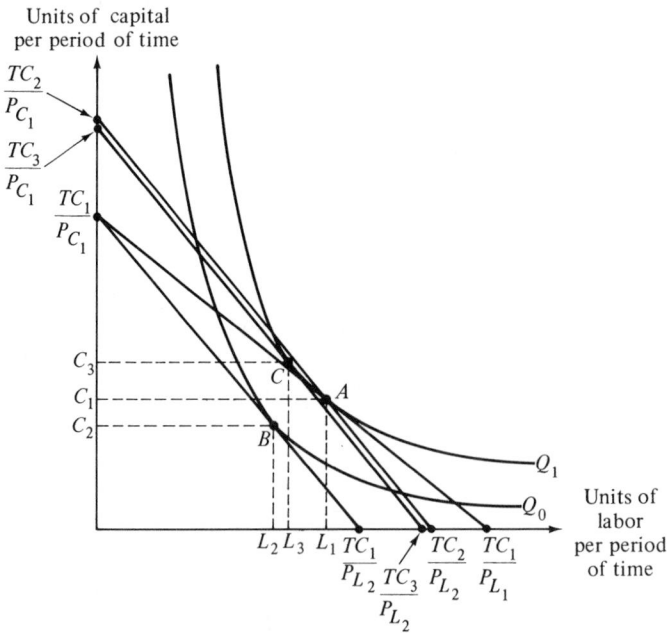

Fig. 7-14   Adjusting to Changes in Resource Prices

An examination of Figure 7-14 verifies this statement. Consequently, *in the short run* point A represents the least cost of producing Q_1 units when no more than C_1 units of capital are available, despite the fact that the price of labor has risen from P_{L_1} to P_{L_2}. But, since the price of labor has gone up, it is clear that the cost of producing Q_1 units of output must be greater than TC_1. The higher cost can be illustrated graphically by drawing a new isocost line with a slope of P_{L_2}/P_{C_1} (so as to reflect the new ratio of resource prices) through point A. The extreme points of this isocost line are TC_2/P_{C_1} and TC_2/P_{L_2}, where $P_{L_2} > P_{L_1}$ and $TC_2 > TC_1$. *In the short run*, therefore, the fixed aspect of capital input may cause the firm to leave its input combination unchanged in response to an increase in the price of labor, provided it elects to continue to produce Q_1 units and provided it can afford to increase its expenditures on resource inputs from TC_1 to TC_2.

However, *in the long run* the firm will wish to change its usage of capital and labor in response to the higher price of labor. As soon as time and money permit, the firm will be induced to produce Q_1 units of output by shifting from point A to point C in Figure 7-14. Point C is determined by finding the point of tangency between isoquant Q_1 and an isocost line with a slope of P_{L_2}/P_{C_1}; this isocost line is parallel to the isocost line defined by extreme points TC_2/P_{C_1} and TC_2/P_{L_2}, because both lines reflect the resource inputs obtainable when the price of labor is P_{L_2} and the price of capital is P_{C_1}. The shift in the optimum resource mix from point A to point C will reduce the costs of producing Q_1 units of output from TC_2 to TC_3, an amount which is indicated graphically by the distance between the isocost line defined by extreme points TC_3/P_{C_1} and TC_3/P_{L_2} and the isocost line defined by extreme points TC_2/P_{C_1} and TC_2/P_{L_2}.

Thus, in the long run an increase in the price of labor relative to the price of capital will induce the firm to substitute capital for labor. The logic of such action is compelling. Whenever a resource becomes more expensive, it makes sense to use less of it and more of the now less expensive input. This is precisely what business firms have proceeded to do. In manufacturing, for example, as unions and other wage increasing forces have combined to drive up the relative price of labor, firms have put forth a concerted effort to substitute capital for labor. Rising labor costs are, in fact, a major motive for introducing automated production processes. Substitution of capital for labor is most evident in the steel, coal mining, chemical, petroleum, automobile, aluminum, and pulp and paper industries, as well as in the use of computers to perform tasks formerly handled by white-collar employees.

However, the degree to which firms have substituted capital for labor has been obscured somewhat by growing output rates. Suppose a firm simultaneously experiences a rise in the price it must pay for labor inputs and an increase in the demand for its product. As just explained, the increase in the price of labor, given the price of capital, will eventually precipitate a substitution of capital for labor. This result is shown in Figure 7-15 as the move-

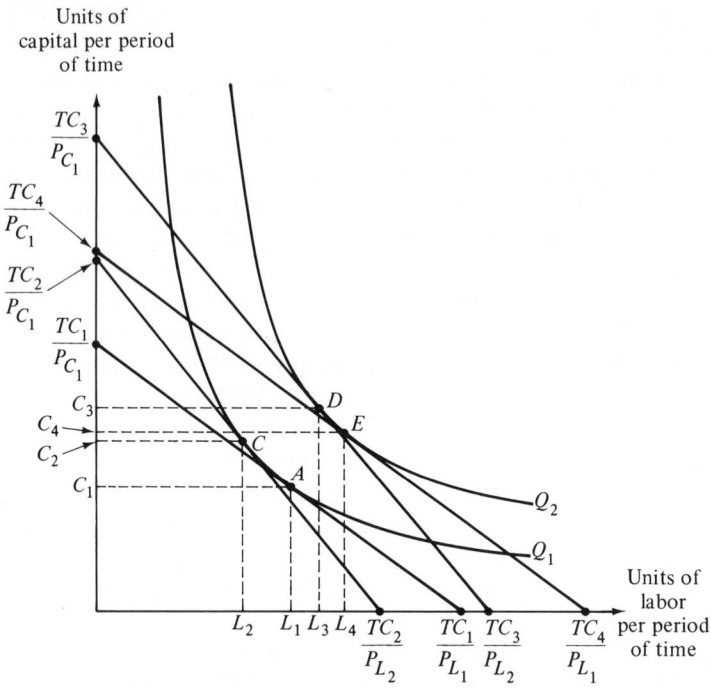

Fig. 7-15 The Effect of Simultaneous Changes in Resource and Output Rates Upon the Optimum Resource Combination

ment from point A to point C. But should the increase in demand for the firm's product dictate a change in output from Q_1 to Q_2 units, then the firm will find it advantageous to shift from the input mix at point C to the input mix at point D. The movement from point C to point D ultimately calls for using both more capital and more labor than originally. In this case, the labor-increasing effect of raising the firm's output rate more than offsets the labor-decreasing effect of the rise in the price of labor input. But had the price of labor input not risen, the firm would have preferred to use L_4 units of labor instead of L_3 units to produce Q_2 units of output. Thus, the increase in the price of labor input served to restrict the use of labor and caused the firm to select a more capital-intensive production technology (point D) than it otherwise would have selected (point E).

By and large, it is strong and sustained increases in consumer demand which have prevented unemployment rates from rising to socially unacceptable levels as business enterprises have gradually shifted to more capital-intensive production technologies. Therefore, the net effect of increases in labor input prices, insofar as the entire economy is concerned, has been to restrict the growth of employment opportunities to less than what would have been realized had the increases in the price of labor not induced firms to substitute capital for labor. And fortunately, the demand for output has grown fast enough to override the labor-decreasing effect of automation.

RETURNS TO SCALE

Up to now, the firm and its technology have been examined primarily from a short-run point of view, where a portion of the firm's resource inputs are fixed. The concept of *returns to scale* deals with production relationships over a time span sufficiently long to allow changes in any and all inputs, especially those inputs such as plant space, major pieces of capital equipment, and managerial capability, which are typically fixed in the short run. Specifically, the phrase "returns to scale" refers to the character of changes in output when *all* resource inputs are changed in *equal* proportions.

Consider a firm using L units of labor in combination with C units of capital to obtain an output of Q units. Then

$$L + C \rightarrow Q.$$

Now suppose the amounts of both labor and capital are increased by some arbitrary proportion a. Plainly, output will rise; the question is by what proportion. Suppose we designate the proportion by which output increases as b. Then

$$aL + aC \rightarrow bQ.$$

1. If the change in output is more than proportional to the change in input ($b > a$), *increasing returns to scale* are said to prevail. For example, if the inputs of capital and labor are increased by 20 percent per period of time, and output rises by 30 percent, the firm enjoys increasing returns to scale.
2. If the change in output is equal to the proportional change in input ($b = a$), *constant returns to scale* are present. In this case a doubling of the inputs of both capital and labor per period of time leads to a doubling of the number of units produced.
3. If the change in output is less than proportional to the change in input ($b < a$), the firm experiences *decreasing returns to scale*. An illustration of decreasing returns to scale would be where inputs are increased by 40 percent but output rises by only 30 percent.

Given the state of technology, it is generally believed that in expanding its scale of operation a firm will pass successively through

(a) a short range of increasing returns to scale,
(b) a lengthy range of constant returns to scale, and
(c) a range of decreasing returns to scale.

Conceivably, a firm can increase its usage of resource inputs to the point where output becomes maximum; subsequent increases in input then would produce a stage of negative returns to scale where output actually falls.

However, if the concept of returns to scale is broadened to permit changes in a firm's technical capabilities as its size increases, firms may well be (and, indeed, are) able by skillful application of new technologies to expand their scale of operations without ever encountering decreasing returns to scale.[15] Constant returns to scale over a wide range of output appear to characterize many manufacturing industries. The reasons for increasing, constant, and decreasing returns to scale are worth exploring further.

Factors Contributing to Increasing Returns to Scale. Five factors combine to produce increasing returns to scale for a firm. The most pervasive of these five factors originates with opportunities for specializing in the use of resource inputs as a firm's scale of operations is increased. The gains in efficiency from specialized use of production-type labor are well chronicled.[16] In the case of labor, small-scale production facilities employing few workers require that the typical employee perform several different operations in the course of producing the commodity. It is difficult for employees to be proficient at each of these tasks; mediocre performance in some of them, with an attendant loss of efficiency, is almost unavoidable. In addition, time is lost in changing from task to task and in moving about the plant. Larger-scale operations, in contrast, allow employees to be assigned only to those tasks for which they are particularly adept. In concentrating upon a single, well-defined task, workers tend to develop speed and accuracy; also, they are better able to devise short cuts and identify ways for improving the production flow—all of which combine to enhance efficiency. Time lost in switching from task to task and moving about the plant is eliminated. Also, the

---

[15] Several recent empirical studies confirm this finding. See, for example, J. Haldi and D. Whitcomb, "Economies of Scale in Industrial Plants," *Journal of Political Economy*, Vol. 75, No. 4 (August 1967), pp. 373–385; and John R. Moroney, "Cobb-Douglas Production Functions and Returns to Scale in U.S. Manufacturing Industry," *Western Economic Journal*, Vol. 6, No. 1 (December 1967), pp. 39–51.

[16] The productive powers of specialized use of labor are amply illustrated in a famous passage from Adam Smith's, *The Wealth of Nations*, written over two hundred years ago: "To take an example . . . from a very trifling manufacture; but one in which the division of labor has been very often taken notice of, the trade of the pinmaker; a workman not educated to this business (which the division of labour has rendered a distinct trade), nor acquainted with the use of the machinery employed in it (to the invention of which the same division of labour has probably given occasion), could scarce, perhaps, with utmost industry, make one pin in a day, and certainly could not make twenty. But in the way in which this business is now carried on, not only the whole work is a peculiar trade, but it is divided into a number of branches, of which the greater part are likewise peculiar trades. One man draws out the wire, another straights it, a third cuts it, a fourth points it, a fifth grinds it at the top for receiving the head; to make the head requires two or three distinct operations; to put it on, is a peculiar business, to whiten the pins is another; it is even a trade by itself to put them into the paper; and the important business of making a pin is, in this manner, divided into about eighteen distinct operations, which, in some manufactories, are all performed by distinct hands, though in others the same man will sometimes perform two or three of them. I have seen a small manufactory of this kind where ten men only were employed, and where some of them consequently performed two or three distinct operations. But though they were very poor, and therefore but indifferently accommodated with the necessary machinery, they could, when they exerted themselves, make among them about twelve pounds of pins in a day. There are in a pound upwards of four thousand pins of a middling size. Those ten persons, therefore, could make among them upwards of forty-eight thousand pins in a day. Each person, therefore, making a tenth part of forty-eight thousand pins, might be considered as making four thousand eight hundred pins in a day. But if they had all wrought separately and independently, and without any of them having been educated to this peculiar business, they certainly could not each of them have made twenty, perhaps not one pin in a day; that is, certainly, not the two hundred and fortieth, perhaps not the four thousand eight hundredth part of what they are at present capable of performing, in consequence of a proper division and combination of their different operations."

costs of training individual workers is reduced by increased specialization. However, specialization in the use of labor can be carried so far that the monotony of performing the assigned task fatigues the employee and neutralizes gains in the efficiency of his performance. Hence, firms must be wary of dividing up production line operations into too many small tasks.[17]

Second, the larger the scale of production the greater the feasibility of utilizing the most advanced productive equipment and technology and obtaining the benefits of using specialized capital equipment.[18] Frequently, the most efficient recipe from a technological point of view involves making a commodity via mass production methods. Small enterprises cannot justify the use of such large-volume production technology, let alone raise the money to install it. Thus small-scale operations often must rely upon multipurpose machinery and equipment, which seldom can attain the speed and precision of the single-purpose pieces of capital equipment used in larger-sized production units. Not only can larger-scale enterprises afford to employ mass production methods and to embrace new technologies, but they also have the organizational ability to market larger volumes of output, to diversify, to integrate vertically and horizontally (when antitrust will allow), and to decentralize. Hence, they tend to realize more-than-proportional increases in output from their production, selling, and administrative inputs.

Purely dimensional factors are a third reason for increasing returns to scale. Doubling the diameter of a natural-gas pipeline can more than double the flow through it. A 100-watt light bulb does not require $2\frac{1}{2}$ times as much labor and materials as a 40-watt light bulb. Doubling the labor and materials in a motor can easily more than double the horsepower of the motor. To build and operate a pulp and paper plant capable of producing 5,000 tons of paper products per week does not require 5 times as much labor, managerial talent, equipment, and building space as a pulp and paper plant capable of producing only 1,000 tons per week. In a somewhat related fashion, tripling the rate of output of an assembly line may require only one additional inspector instead of two; a diesel locomotive may have sufficient power to pull fifty freight cars as adequately as twenty; and a book salesman may be able to sell books in both economics and business administration subjects as well as just those in economics with less than a proportional increase in time, effort, and cost. Thus, larger-scale enterprises frequently require proportionately less input per unit of output, which also translates into proportionately more units of output per unit of input.

Fourth, since technologically complex production processes require several major pieces of equipment, the scale of production may have to be

---

[17] The September 4, 1971, issue of *Business Week* reported an interest on the part of several firms, Motorola in particular, for enriching the content of assembly-line jobs and thereby improving worker motivation and job satisfactions. See p. 32.

[18] M. A. Adelman found that employment among the 200 largest firms was about 60 percent more capital intensive than in the economy as a whole. See M. A. Adelman, "The Measurement of Industrial Concentration," *Review of Economics and Statistics*, Vol. 33, No. 4 (November 1951), p. 278.

large to overcome potential bottlenecks in the process. Suppose two machines A and B are required for packaging a commodity, machine A being used to fill the package with the proper amount of the product and machine B being used to wrap the package in cellophane. If machine A can fill 15,000 packages per day and machine B can wrap 20,000 packages per day, then at an output of 60,000 units per day, where four type A machines and three type B machines are used, both types of machines can be efficiently utilized. At less than 60,000 units of output full utilization of both machine types is not possible, and some amount of idle capacity will be present.

Finally, larger firms can put together highly specialized managerial staffs which have the ability to perform the functions of planning, control, coordination, and administration more efficiently than can smaller firms whose managers, being fewer, must necessarily be equipped to solve a wider range of managerial problems. Many owner-managers simply do not have the skill or taste for the kind of management style needed to guide an enterprise to maturity. More important, however, the large corporation has repeatedly demonstrated a remarkable vitality for devising organizational schemes which enhance, or at worst only renew and preserve, internal operating efficiency. Decentralization, the multidivisional organizational form, and, most recently, the matrix form of organization have all been employed in their several varieties to effect substantial operating efficiencies.[19] At the same time, the larger the enterprise the greater is its ability to attract a superior calibre of managerial talent and thereby obtain access to a higher order of managerial technology. Larger enterprises are better suited for utilizing the capacities of high-speed computers; they are better able to implement proven managerial techniques emerging from operations research, simulation processes, and the other tools of management science; and they have more opportunities for experimenting in the use of new manageral methodologies. Thus, on the whole, the organizational and managerial capabilities of the large firm exceed those of the small enterprise by more than a proportionate margin. This aspect of size is a principal reason for the vitality and success of large corporate enterprises and it derives in part from their superior access to and use of *managerial technology*.

Factors Contributing to Constant Returns to Scale. It is clear that the phase of increasing returns cannot continue indefinitely; the factors responsible for increasing output at rates more than proportional to the volumes of resource inputs will become exhausted sooner or later—and usually sooner. Particularly is this true for the production unit of a firm—the plant. It is no secret in business that certain size plants are more efficient than others. Moreover, experts in technology and engineering can peg quite closely the

[19] Alfred D. Chandler, Jr., *Strategy and Structure* (New York: Doubleday, Anchor Books edition, 1966), pp. 126–127, 156–157, 195–196, 230, 256, 321–323, 369, 382–383; Oliver E. Williamson, *Corporate Control and Business Behavior* (Englewood Cliffs, N.J.: Prentice-Hall, Inc., 1970), Chapters 7 and 8; Jay R. Galbraith, "Matrix Organizational Designs," *Business Horizons*, Vol. 14, No. 1 (February 1971), pp. 29–40.

most efficient plant size for producing a given commodity. It is then a simple matter for large-scale enterprises to build as many of these optimum-sized facilities as may be necessary to satisfy the firm's need for productive capacity for that product. For example, if the most efficient plant size is one capable of producing 100,000 units per year, a large firm selling 1,000,000 units per year can realize constant returns to scale in producing this commodity by building 10 plants, each capable of producing 100,000 units. Where a firm produces several products, it can use the multidivisional form of corporate organization, each division being scaled to the most efficient size. Large firms are able, therefore, to realize constant returns to scale in their production activities for an almost indefinitely large volume of output by organizing their several production units according to the most efficient size. And by centralizing purchasing, selling, and administrative activities under one management, it may even be possible to realize increasing returns from these latter inputs, making the firm's overall operations slightly more efficient than that achievable by a smaller enterprise. Since the ability to build as many optimum-sized plants as demand will permit is restricted only by a firm's capacity for obtaining financial resources to construct these plants, the range of output for which a firm can experience constant returns to scale in its production activities is virtually unlimited. To the extent that larger firms have superior managerial talent and managerial technology, they have the inherent ability to be more efficient—or at least no less efficient—than smaller firms. Herein lies a major reason why large enterprises dominate many industries and account for almost 70 percent of the U.S. economy's manufacturing output.

Factors Contributing to Decreasing Returns to Scale. The principal factor causing a firm to experience decreasing returns to scale is the limit to which the managerial function can be efficiently performed. As the firm becomes larger, the problems of integrating the many facets of the firm's activities multiply. Decision-making is more complex, and the burdens of administration become disproportionately greater. Conventional wisdom insists that "diminishing returns" to management will be encountered as top management loses touch with the daily routine of operation and finds it increasingly necessary to delegate authority to lower-echelon managers whose level of competence may not be as great. Red tape and paper work expand with size; bureaucratic procedures creep in, causing the managerial hierachy of larger firms to be sluggish and unwieldy in responding to the operational requirements of the organization.

This view of the limits to managerial efficiency is not without merit; yet, it is not altogether valid and convincing. Many of the very large corporate enterprises (General Motors, General Electric, IBM, Proctor and Gamble, Xerox, Atlantic Richfield, Sears, International Telephone and Telegraph) are well noted for their managerial expertise. Indeed, the corporate mechanism is extremely adept at circumventing and subverting managerial bottle-necks and inefficiencies. Advances in managerial technology in the form of innovative organizational schemes, systems analysis, new information systems, managerial techniques, and operations research models, coupled with the immense speed with which computers can process information for decision-making purposes have so streamlined the managerial function that billion dollar corporations can be managed quite efficiently.[20] Hence while it is undoubtedly true that limits exist regarding efficient performance of the managerial function, enterprises are as attentive to managerial bottlenecks and inefficiencies as they are to inefficiencies from other sources. Thus, in actual situations the limits to efficient performance of the managerial function will rarely hinder the growth of enterprises any more than will ineffi-cient perfomance of other phases of business activity.

AN APPLICATION OF THE RETURNS TO SCALE CONCEPT

Suppose a large, diversified enterprise carefully examines the input-output relationships for each of its three major products (X, Y, and Z) and concludes that the production functions for these products are

$$Q_X = 1.6L^{.4}C^{.4}M^{.1}$$
$$Q_Y = \sqrt{.4L^2CM}$$
$$Q_Z = 10L + 7C + M$$

where Q represents output per period of time, L is units of labor input, C is units of capital input, and M is units of managerial input. The question immediately arises as to what returns to scale are encountered in manufac-turing the three products. The answer can be determined by observing what happens to output when the inputs of labor, capital, and management are increased *in equal proportions*. The production function is "tested" by multiplying each input by a constant factor (say a) and ascertaining whether output changes (1) by an amount greater than a in which case increasing returns to scale are signified, (2) by an amount equal to a in which case constant returns to scale are signified, or (3) by an amount less than a in which case decreasing returns to scale are indicated.

The returns to scale indicated by the production function for product X is found in the following manner. Multiplying each of the three inputs by a, where $a > 1$ so as to indicate an increase in the inputs, we obtain

[20] One cannot fail to be impressed by the rapid development we are witnessing of analytical and manage-rial techniques that stimulate and assist firms to find more efficient ways of accomplishing their current activ-ities. Operations research and mathematical programming are among the more fancy of this new form of managerial technology. Other improvements include new accounting and budgeting procedures, better methods of market analysis, refinements in forecasting, and all sorts of quantitative decision tools. The unifying charac-ter of these new developments in managerial technology is that they bring the principles of rational problem-solving to bear even more heavily upon raising the quality of organizational planning and decision-making.

$$1.6(aL)^{.4}(aC)^{.4}(aM^{.1})$$

which becomes

$$1.6a^{.4}L^{.4}a^{.4}C^{.4}a^{.1}M^{.1}.$$

Factoring a out of the function gives

$$a^{.4+.4+.1}(1.6L^{.4}C^{.4}M^{.1})$$

or

$$a^{.9}(1.6L^{.4}C^{.4}M^{.1}).$$

The expression in parentheses defines the level of output prior to the change in input, and $a^{.9}$ represents the proportional change in the output of product X when each input is increased by a. Because the exponent for a is less than 1, increasing the inputs by a results in a *less than proportional* increase in the output of X and the production function for X may be said to exhibit decreasing returns to scale.

In the case of product Y, increasing each input by an arbitrary proportion a, where $a > 1$, yields

$$\sqrt{.4(aL)^2(aC)(aM)}.$$

Simplifying this expression, we get

$$\sqrt{.4a^2L^2aCaM} = \sqrt{.4a^4L^2CM} = a^2\sqrt{.4L^2CM}.$$

Hence, increasing each input by a causes output to expand by a^2—obviously, increasing returns to scale are present, since output expands at a rate more than proportional to the input increase. This result is easily confirmed by means of a numerical example. Suppose, originally $L = 5$, $C = 5$, and $M = 2$; then

$$Q_Y = \sqrt{.4L^2CM}$$
$$= \sqrt{.4(5)^2(5)(2)}$$
$$= \sqrt{100}$$
$$= 10.$$

If all of the inputs are doubled ($a = 2$), we have $L = 10$, $C = 10$, $M = 4$, and

$$Q_Y = \sqrt{.4(10)^2(10)(4)}$$
$$= \sqrt{1600}$$
$$= 40.$$

Consequently, doubling the inputs of labor, capital, and management causes the output of product Y to quadruple (since $a^2 = 4$ when $a = 2$), and increasing returns to scale may be said to characterize the production function for product Y.

Increasing the inputs by a for the production function for product Z gives

$$10(aL) + 7(aC) + aM$$

or, more simply

$$a(10L + 7C + M).$$

Here output changes by the same proportion as input, so constant returns to scale are present.[21] Again, a simple example verifies existence of constant returns to scale for product Z. If $L = 15$, $C = 10$, and $M = 5$, then

$$Q_Z = 10L + 7C + M$$
$$= 10(15) + 7(10) + 5$$
$$= 225.$$

Doubling the inputs ($a = 2$) so that $L = 30$, $C = 20$, and $M = 10$, we get

$$Q_Z = 10(30) + 7(20) + 10$$
$$= 450.$$

Therefore, doubling each input causes the output of product Z to double—a constant returns to scale situation.

The character of the production functions for the three products X, Y, and Z provides a guide to management for choosing the products upon which to concentrate its limited resources. *Other things being equal*, cost and efficiency considerations call for steering resources (financial and otherwise) to those products with the most favorable returns to scale. The most favorable, of course, is increasing returns to scale, followed in order by constant returns and decreasing returns. Hence, products Y, Z, and X in that order yield the enterprise the greatest amounts of output for a given amount of input.

---

[21] The mathematics of production functions is not always as neat and clear-cut as the above three cases might indicate. Consider the production function

$$Q = 16L + .5LCM + 1.4L^{.5}C^{.3}M^{.1}.$$

Changing the inputs by a yields

$$16(aL) + .5(aL)(aC)(aM) + 1.4(aL)^{.5}(aC)^{.3}(aM)^{.1},$$

which simplifies to

$$16aL + .5a^3LCM + 1.4a^{.9}L^{.5}C^{.3}M^{.1}.$$

Inspecting the above expression term by term, we find that the first term ($16aL$) has the characteristic of constant returns to scale, the second term ($.5a^3LCM$) has the characteristic of increasing returns to scale, and the third term ($1.4a^{.9}L^{.5}C^{.3}M^{.1}$) displays decreasing returns to scale. Whether the entire production function exhibits increasing, constant, or decreasing returns to scale on balance depends upon the relative strengths of the three terms. In this instance the strong increasing-returns influence found in the second term will overpower the mildly decreasing returns shown in the third term, with the result that the entire production function shows increasing returns to scale.

However, a word or two of qualification must be offered. Returns to scale in no way reflect the demand side of the picture. The mere fact that the output of a commodity is characterized by decreasing returns to scale does not mean that it is unprofitable. The price which can be obtained for product X may be so favorable that it is relatively more profitable than either product Y or Z. In fact, the competitive forces prevailing in the markets for Y and Z could make those commodities unprofitable, even though they can be produced under very favorable conditions. Returns to scale indicate only the direction of change in productive efficiency and unit costs which can be anticipated if the size of the firm's production operations is increased or decreased. Also, the nature of the production function for a commodity can change over a period of time because of scientific and engineering developments, innovation, and advances in managerial technology. Thus, in the long run the production process for a commodity can be transformed from decreasing to constant or increasing returns to scale.

Summary and Conclusions

In analyzing production processes, resources are generally divided into two categories: fixed and variable. Corresponding to the notion of fixed and variable inputs is the notion of the short run and the long run. In the short run, output can be changed only be altering the amount of variable input used in conjunction with the given fixed input. In the long run, output can be changed by altering the scale of production, the technology of the production process, and the rate of usage of any and all inputs.

The principle of diminishing marginal returns states that as the amount of a variable input is increased by equal increments and combined with a specified amount of fixed input, eventually a point will be reached where the resulting increases in the quantity of output will get smaller and smaller. Should the usage rate of variable input get sufficiently large, the quantity of output will reach a maximum and may then decrease as still larger amounts of variable input are employed.

The relationships between the production function, average product, and marginal product can be used to define three stages of production. Stage I covers the range of variable input where AP_{vi} is rising; stage II includes the range where AP_{vi} is falling *and* where *MP* is declining yet positive; and stage III encompasses the range where *MP* is negative and total output is falling.

The optimum resource combination is in stage II at the input rate where (a) the firm is fully utilizing its dollars in purchasing inputs and (b) an equivalent amount of output is being obtained from the last dollar spent on each input. Graphically, this condition is achieved at the point of tangency between the isocost curve and an isoquant.

If the firm increases all of its inputs by the same proportion and output increases by *more* than this proportion, increasing returns to scale prevail. If the firm increases all of its inputs by a given proportion and output rises by this *same* proportion, constant returns to scale characterized the production process. If the firm increases all of its inputs by the same proportion and output rises by *less* than this proportion, decreasing returns to scale are present. Increasing returns to scale occur because of increased specialization in use of resources, technological considerations, dimensional factors, and indivisibility of inputs. Constant returns to scale arise when the production process embodies standard man-machine ratios and when it is feasible to assimilate a number of optimum-sized production units under a single management. Decreasing returns to scale occur primarily because of limitations to efficient performance of the managerial function.

SUGGESTED READINGS

HALDI, J., and D. WHITCOMB, "Economies of Scale in Industrial Plants," *Journal of Political Economy*, Vol. 75, No. 4 (August 1967), pp. 373–385.

MAXWELL, W. DAVID, "Short-Run Returns to Scale and the Production of Services," *Southern Economic Journal*, Vol. 32, No. 1 (July 1965), pp. 1–19.

MOORE, F. T., "Economics of Scale: Some Statistical Evidence," *Quarterly Journal of Economics*, Vol. 73, No. 2 (May 1959), pp. 232–245.

MORONEY, JOHN R., "Cobb-Douglas Production Functions and Returns to Scale In U.S. Manufacturing Industry," *Western Economic Journal*, Vol. 6, No. 1 (December 1967), pp. 39–51.

STIGLER, GEORGE, "The Economies of Scale," *Journal of Law and Economics*, Vol. 1 (October 1958), pp. 54–71.

Problems and Questions for Discussion

1. Fill in the values for discrete MP, AP_{vi}, and AP_{fi} based upon the information given in the table below:

Units of Fixed Input	Units of Variable Input	Quantity of Output	Discrete MP	AP_{vi}	AP_{fi}
3	0	0			
3	1	120	———	———	———
3	2	270	———	———	———
3	3	390	———	———	———
3	4	480	———	———	———
3	5	540	———	———	———
3	6	560	———	———	———
3	7	540	———	———	———

2. Given the following production function:

$$Q = 12X,$$

where Q = units of output per period of time and X = units of variable input.

    (a) Determine the equations for MP and AP_{vi}.

    (b) Assuming 5 units of fixed input are presently being employed in the production process represented by the above production function, determine AP_{fi} when 10 units of variable input are combined with the 5 units of fixed input.

    (c) Graphically illustrate the production function and the corresponding MP and AP_{vi} functions.

    (d) How would you describe the important properties of this production function?

3. Production mangers for the Cosmic Paper Corporation estimate that their production process is currently characterized by the following short-run production function:

$$Q = 72X + 15X^2 - X^3,$$

where Q = tons of paper products per production period, and X = units of variable input employed per production period.

    (a) Determine the equations for MP and AP_{vi}.

    (b) What is MP when 7 units of variable input are employed?

    (c) By how much does output rise when the usage of variable input is increased from 7 to 8 units per production period?

    (d) At what rate of usage of variable input is the point of diminishing marginal returns encountered?

    (e) What is the maximum output capability per production period? What rate of usage of variable input is required to reach the maximum output level?

    (f) Graphically illustrate this production function and the corresponding MP and AP_{vi} functions. Indicate on your graph the output ranges where output is increasing at an increasing rate and where output is increasing at a decreasing rate. Also indicate the output where the point of diminishing average returns to variable input is encountered.

4. Graphically illustrate the stages of production for each of the general types of production functions given below:

    (a) $Q = bX$

    (b) $Q = bX - cX^2$

    (c) $Q = bX + cX^2 - dX^3$

5. The production department of the National Cabinet Corporation is employing 20 unskilled laborers, 45 semi-skilled workmen, and 60 skilled craftsmen. A careful assessment of the productivity of the three types of labor indicates that the marginal product of an unskilled laborer is currently 10 units of output per man-day, the marginal product of a semi-skilled workman is 20 units per man-day, and the marginal product of a skilled craftsman is 50 units per man-day. The wage rates for the three types of labor result in labor costs of $20 per man-day for unskilled labor, $30 per man-day for semi-skilled workmen, and $50 per man-day for skilled craftsmen. Output is currently at the desired level. Would you suggest a change in the labor mix used by the production department? Why or why not?

6. The Paper Dress Fashion Corporation is considering the construction of

a new plant. Engineers have submitted the following possible plant designs—all of which are equally capable from a physical standpoint of producing the desired output of 1000 dresses per day.

	Units of Capital	Units of Labor
Plant Design No. 1	50	500
Plant Design No. 2	75	400
Plant Design No. 3	150	200
Plant Design No. 4	250	100
Plant Design No. 5	350	50

(a) Illustrate the technically feasible production alternatives by means of an isoquant.

(b) Suppose the price of capital is $100 per unit and the price of labor is $50 per unit, which plant design should be selected? Justify your answer with an isocost-isoquant graph.

(c) What will be the required total cost outlay for capital and labor for the selected plant design?

7. Suppose that Apex Manufacturing Corporation has its choice of three production processes for producing its product. With process A, Apex can produce 100 units of output per hour using 5 units of labor and 20 units of capital; by process B, 100 units per hour with 10 units each of labor and capital; by process C, 100 units per hour with 20 units of labor and 5 units of capital. All three processes are characterized by constant return to scale.

(a) Graphically illustrate isoquants for outputs of 100, 200, and 300 units per hour.

(b) If the price of labor is $5 per unit and capital costs $10 per unit, which process should be selected to produce 200 units? *Illustrate* your answer by means of isoquant and isocost curves.

(c) If the price of labor is $8 per unit and the price of capital is $8 per unit, which process should be selected to produce 100 units per hour? Verify your answer with an isoquant-isocost graph.

(d) If the price of labor is $14 per unit and capital is $7 per unit, which process should be selected to produce 300 units per hour? What will be the necessary total cost outlay?

8. Jupiter Products, Inc., has derived the following production function for its operation:

$$Q = .65L^{.42}C^{.38}M^{.20}Z^{.08},$$

where Q = units of output per period of time,
L = man-hours of labor,
C = hours of machine services,
M = man-hours of managerial input,
Z = miscellaneous resource services.

(a) Assuming that Jupiter's operations are sufficiently flexible to vary the usage of L, C, M, and Z, what kind of returns are indicated by this production function? Why?

(b) What inference, if any, can you make about the firm's unit costs for producing additional units of output?

9. A rapidly developing conglomerate has employed a team of operations researchers to advise it on acquiring prospective enterprises. Four small firms, each producing the same commodity but employing radically different production technologies, are currently being carefully scrutinized for possible acquisition by the conglomerate. The operations research team has initiated investigations of the production, marketing, and financial aspects of the four firms for the purpose of singling out one of them as the best candidate for acquisition. As part of their investigation they have sought to estimate the production functions for each of the four firms; their estimates are as follows:

Firm A: $Q_A = .8L^{.6}C^{.2}M^{.1}$
Firm B: $Q_B = \frac{7}{3}L + \frac{3}{2}C + M$
Firm C: $Q_C = \sqrt{.09L^{.5}C^{1.0}M^{.5}}$
Firm D: $Q_D = 6L^2 + 7C^2 - LC + .1M^2$

On the basis of these preliminary estimates, which of the four firms appears to offer the expansive-minded conglomerate the best prospects? Why?

10. What is the difference between "returns to variable input" and "returns to scale"?

8

Analyzing
the Costs of Production

The costs of goods and services derive from the character of the process by which they are produced. The analysis of cost behavior is founded, therefore, upon the principles of production. This chapter translates the relationships among production technology, inputs, and outputs into cost functions. After exploring the nature of "cost," we shall derive the short-run and long-run cost curves of a business enterprise for a variety of possible production functions and production technologies.

The Concept of Cost

Mention of the word "cost" immediately conjures up the thought of "money outlays." In the context of business operations, costs are commonly viewed as a firm's actual or historical expenditures for resource input. However, for most business purposes this notion of cost is overly narrow and confining, if not inappropriate. In the first place, the costs that really matter for business decisions are future costs; in this regard, historical costs are useful primarily as benchmarks for anticipating future production costs and for estimating the costs of alternative courses of action. And even here past costs are of limited significance, since rarely does the past represent the best guess con-

cerning the future. Second, anyone familiar with the vagaries of cost accounting is aware that two manufacturers of physically identical commodities who
use different, but acceptable, cost accounting methods could differ in their
reported costs of making the commodity by 20 percent or more.[1] Historical
cost statistics convey little information unless one knows a great deal about
the particular cost accounting system from which they are derived. And,
finally, to view costs in exclusively monetary terms is to leave out a large
portion of what may rightfully be considered as cost. The social costs of
noise, congestion, and environmental pollution are not easily reduced to
dollars and cents. Nor are psychic costs readily expressed in monetary terms;
these involve the mental anguish and mental dissatisfaction associated with
such business activities as dismissing employees, moving one's family to
accept a transfer in an undesirable location, working on holidays, pressures
from one's boss for outstanding performance, and the monotony of repeti-
tious tasks.[2] Plainly, social costs and psychic costs abound in many business
situations, yet they never appear in an enterprise's financial accounts.

A thread common to all of the many dimensions of cost can be summed
up in the word "sacrifice." All costs entail a *sacrifice* of some type; the form
of the sacrifice may be tangible or intangible, objective or subjective, monetary or nonmonetary. For this reason, it is not possible in many cases to
quantify costs in terms of dollars, nor is it possible to have a single universally
acceptable measure of cost.

THE MANY ASPECTS OF COST

As a means of illustrating the multidimensional aspects of cost, consider the
apparently innocuous statement: "General Electric's cost of producing an
electric toaster in 1972 was $6.13." The most obvious interpretation of this
statement is that General Electric's money outlays for the resource inputs
needed to produce an electric toaster amounted to an average of $6.13 in
1972. No doubt the basis for such a figure would be the historical expenses
for resources bought outright or hired by GE and which were routinely
recorded in its accounts according to GE's scheme of accounting practice.
These explicitly incurred expenses might consist of production labor costs,

---

[1] Cost differentials can "artificially" be produced by judiciously selecting among the following options for measuring a firm's costs:
    (a) using an accelerated depreciation schedule instead of the straight-line method,
    (b) using the first-in, first-out (FIFO) method of inventory valuation instead of the last-in, first-out (LIFO) method,
    (c) employing a direct costing system rather than a full-cost accounting system,
    (d) selecting any one of several acceptable rules for determining the time period to which certain kinds of expenses will be charged, and
    (e) using artificial transfer prices for intermediate goods passing from one operating division to another instead of realistic transfer prices.

[2] Psychic costs are not unique to business enterprise, nor can they be lightly dismissed as inconsequential. For example, few students would question that they incur significant psychic costs in preparing for and taking final exams; nor would professors deny the existence of psychic costs in preparing and grading exams and in assigning final grades. The examination process is very painful indeed, and to ignore the psychic costs which it entails would probably mean omitting the greatest of the costs of administering examinations.

payments for component parts purchased from suppliers, managerial salaries, interest costs, payments for electric power, transportation costs, telephone services, depreciation charges, administrative expenses, property taxes, and other miscellaneous payments. Such outlays are known as *explicit costs*.

Despite the apparent accuracy and completeness of explicit cost figures, the stated costs of $6.13 per toaster will not in all probability prove to be all-inclusive.[3] Most likely to be overlooked is the cost of capital supplied by the firm's owners.[4] In the case of corporate enterprises such as General Electric, no provision is made for including as an expense the cost of capital furnished by stockholders (equity capital). When firms borrow money from banks or other financial institutions, the interest costs are shown as an expense on the profit and loss statement; yet, if the same funds are raised by selling new issues of common stock, no interest cost is entered on the firm's ledger.[5] Nevertheless, a cost is incurred by the firm's use of equity capital. Unless GE stockholders receive a return on their funds equivalent to what could be earned were they to invest their funds in the best alternative investment of equal risk, they cannot be expected to supply the enterprise with capital in the future. Thus, if General Electric wishes to use equity capital as a source of financing for its activities (including making toasters), then it must plan not only on covering its explicit costs but also on having enough revenue left over to reward stockholders with a return on their investment at least equivalent to the return GE's owners are sacrificing by not having put their money in the best alternative venture. GE must cover this cost in order to induce continued stockholder participation and confidence. This minimum acceptable return to stockholders is just as legitimate a cost as are explicit costs, and this is the chief reason that the stated costs of $6.13 per toaster underestimate the total costs of producing a GE toaster. There may be other owner-related cost omissions, however. All those costs of resources supplied by owners which are not explicitly recorded as expenses according to conventional accounting practices are called *implicit costs*. These include an allowance for rent on company-owned facilities and a cost

[3] From a broader social viewpoint the cost of producing a toaster can be measured by the utility consumers forego from giving up the commodities that could have been produced had not some of society's existing pool of economic resources been used to manufacture electric toasters. Resources used to produce toasters cannot be used to produce other commodities—commodities from which certain segments of society may derive great satisfaction. Thus, the cost to society of a GE toaster is not $6.13 but is the sacrifice of utility associated with not having more of some other commodity which GE or some other firm could have produced instead.
[4] In the case of entrepreneurial or owner-managed firms the cost of other owner-supplied resources may be overlooked. For example, the proprietor may elect not to pay himself a salary but instead rely upon "profits" as payment for his services. Such a practice clearly understates the operating costs of the enterprise, since the value of the managerial skills furnished by the proprietor is not included. Likewise, if no allowance is made for the costs of land and working capital supplied by the proprietor, total costs will be underestimated.
[5] The concepts governing measurement of total costs in an accounting period are less than logical. For example, if GE were to lease a plant to produce toasters from a second party, the lease payment would generally include a margin for the cost of both debt and equity capital, and such lease payments are allowable expenses in their entirety. If GE were to build its own plant with funds borrowed from the Chase Manhattan Bank, the interest expense for the cost of this debt capital would be allowed. Yet, if GE financed the same plant with the proceeds of a common stock issue, no expense for the cost of equity capital would be permitted.
The Internal Revenue Service is insistent that explicit costs be the standard upon which profits and, subsequently, corporate profits taxes are computed. The inclusion of implicit costs is strictly illegitimate.

allowance for fully depreciated property and equipment still in use, as well as the costs of equity capital.

A second category of costs not appearing as an operating expense in historical accounting records may be referred to as opportunity costs. *Opportunity costs* represent the benefits (monetary or otherwise) which could have been received had an alternate course of action been chosen. They are, in other words, the sacrifices incurred by not having done something else. Several examples may be offered to make the relevance of opportunity costs more apparent. The cost to General Electric of making its own heating elements for use in GE electric toasters is really the price at which GE could sell these heating elements to other firms were they not to use them in their own toasters. In periods of strong demand for GE products, the cost to GE of using available resources for toaster production is the profit GE gives up by not devoting these resources to the production of other GE appliances and products. The costs to GE of using scarce executive and managerial talents in toaster production is not so much the related salaries as it is the contribution to profits that these executives and managers could make by devoting their time to other GE activities. The cost of building a new $2 million plant to manufacture GE toasters is not just the interest that GE might have to pay on the borrowed money but rather the profits or cost savings that could be achieved by investing the $2 million in making color TV's, vacuum cleaners, numeric-controlled process equipment, longer-lasting light bulbs, or in producing any of GE's other many products. Opportunity costs are, therefore, nothing more than the sacrifice incurred from a decision not to take advantage of an alternative opportunity; the measurement of opportunity costs involves a comparison between the chosen course of action and the best alternative course of action.

Although precise calculation of either implicit or opportunity costs is rarely possible, considering these two aspects of cost in conjunction with historical costs leads to a more comprehensive approach to the analysis and determination of costs. Certainly, adjusting historical costs for implicit and opportunity cost considerations improves the accuracy with which the profitability of an enterprise can be judged. For unless GE's revenues from the sale of toasters exceed both the explicit and implicit costs of toaster production, GE cannot be said to be truly earning a profit on toasters. Moreover, unless GE's return on its dollar investment in toaster production is at least equivalent to what it could earn by putting this investment in another activity, GE should discontinue toaster production and shift its resources into the better alternative. Thus, while the size of a firm's opportunity costs is difficult to determine, some estimate of their size is crucial to key decisions. In this regard it is better to have a rough estimate of the right concept of cost than an accurate estimate of the wrong concept.

But even after adjusting historical costs for implicit and opportunity costs we are left with a cost concept of limited usefulness for business decisions. Given again the stated cost of $6.13 for producing a GE toaster, consider the following questions:

1. How much of the $6.13 represents costs directly related to the production of toasters (direct costs) and how much represents costs not directly traceable to toasters—e.g., the chief executive's salary and other costs common to the production of several of GE's products (common costs)?
2. How much of the $6.13 represents fixed charges associated with the plant, equipment, and management needed for toaster production (fixed costs) and how much is accounted for by direct production labor and raw materials (variable costs)?
3. To what extent would the $6.13 cost be altered by a 10 percent increase in GE's production of toasters (incremental costs)?
4. What portion of the $6.13 represents controllable costs (property taxes as compared to managerial salaries) and what portion represents cuttable costs (the use of skilled union labor as compared to advertising)?
5. How would a labor strike affect the costs of producing a toaster (shutdown costs and start-up costs)?
6. To what extent can the $6.13 cost be expected to change in the long run (long-run vs. short-run costs)?
7. How is the $6.13 cost of a toaster divided between manufacturing costs and such selling costs as salesmen's salaries and commissions, promotional expenses, maintenance of channels for distribution, and operation of repair centers and warehouses?
8. How would the introduction of a completely automated assembly line alter the $6.13 cost?
9. What portion of the $6.13 could be postponed in the event of a decision to trim the costs of toaster production (postponable costs)?
10. How much of the $6.13 could be avoided if it became necessary to reduce toaster production by 20 percent (escapable vs. unavoidable costs)?

These questions suffice to indicate that no one measure of the costs of production is adequate for decision-making purposes. Different decision problems call for different kinds of cost information. Depending upon the purpose at hand, one may wish to determine total costs, average costs, marginal costs, fixed costs, variable costs, direct costs, common costs, explicit costs, implicit costs, opportunity costs, controllable costs, shutdown costs, postponable costs, long-run costs, short-run costs, escapable costs, replacement costs, incremental costs, production costs, selling costs, administrative costs, labor costs, and so on *ad infinitum*.[6]

Cost-Output Relationships

The fundamental starting point in cost analysis is that a functional relationship exists between the costs of production and the rate of output per period

[6] More complete discussions of the many aspects of cost are found in J. M. Clark, *The Economics of Overhead Costs* (Chicago: University of Chicago Press, 1923), Chaps. 4–6; Joel Dean, *Managerial Economics* (Englewood Cliffs, N.J.: Prentice-Hall, Inc., 1951), Chap. 5; and Milton H. Spencer, *Managerial Economics*, 3rd ed. (Homewood, Ill.: Richard D. Irwin, Inc., 1968), Chap. 7.

of time. A cost function shows the various costs which will be incurred at alternative output rates; in other words,

$$\text{cost} = f(\text{output}).$$

But, as indicated in Chapter 7, the rate of output is, in turn, a function of the rate of usage of the resource inputs:

$$\text{output} = f(\text{inputs}).$$

Since the production function establishes the relationships between input and output flows, once the prices of the inputs are known the costs of a specific quantity of output can be calculated. As a consequence, the level and behavior of costs as a firm's rate of output changes is largely dependent upon two factors: (1) the character of the underlying production function, and (2) the prices the firm must pay for its resource inputs. The former determines the shape of the firm's cost functions while the latter determine the level of costs. To simplify our examination of cost-output relationships, we shall assume that the prices a firm pays for its resource inputs are not affected by changes in its output rate.

THE SHORT RUN AND THE LONG RUN

In discussing the relationships between cost and output it is useful to differentiate between cost behavior in the short run and cost behavior in the long run. From Chapter 7 it will be recalled that the short run refers to a period of time so short that the firm cannot readily vary such inputs as the amount of space available for production activity, major pieces of equipment, and key managerial personnel (the so-called fixed inputs); output is alterable only by increasing or decreasing the usage of variable inputs (production labor, raw materials, and so on). In the long run, however, sufficient time exists for modifying the usage of any and all inputs so as to maintain an optimum combination—all inputs are therefore variable in the long run.

The classification of resource inputs as being fixed or variable in the short run and as being all variable in the long run provides a convenient approach to investigating cost behavior. We shall first examine short-run then long-run cost functions.

Cost-Output Relationships in the Short Run

THE FAMILY OF TOTAL COST CONCEPTS

Three concepts of total cost are important for analysis of a firm's cost structure in the short run: total fixed cost, total variable cost, and total cost.

Corresponding to the category of fixed inputs is short-run fixed cost. The fixed inputs of a firm give rise to costs the amount of which depends upon the quantity of each of the various fixed inputs and the respective prices paid for them. Hence, a firm's explicit fixed cost is simply the sum of the quantities of the fixed inputs multiplied by their associated prices. In the short run, implicit costs are also constant; thus they are part of a firm's fixed costs. Accordingly, *total fixed cost* may be defined as the sum total of the explicit costs of all the fixed inputs plus the implicit costs associated with the firm's operations.[7] Fixed costs do not vary as the rate of output is changed, and they continue even if production facilities are idle. Salaries of top-management officials, property taxes, interest on borrowed money, depreciation charges, rents on office space, the implicit costs of equity capital, and insurance premiums are examples of fixed costs.

Similarly, those inputs that are variable in the short run give rise to short-run variable costs. Since in the short run a firm modifies its output rate by buying more or less units of variable input, variable costs depend upon and vary with the quantity of output. *Total variable cost* is the sum of the amounts a firm spends for each of the variable inputs employed in the production process.[8] Examples of variable costs include payroll expenses, raw material outlays, power and fuel charges, and transportation costs.[9] Total variable cost (TVC) is zero when output is zero, because no variable inputs need be employed to produce nothing. However, as output increases, so does the usage of variable inputs and the level of total variable cost.

The *total cost* of a given level of output in the short run is the sum of total fixed cost and total variable cost:

$$TC = TFC + TVC.$$

At zero output, total variable cost is zero and total cost is equal to total fixed cost. As soon as output rises above zero in the short run, some variable inputs must be used, variable costs are incurred, and total cost is the sum of the fixed and variable expenses.

[7] In terms of more formal mathematics, total fixed costs may be defined as:

$$TFC = \sum_{i=1}^{n} p_i x_i,$$

where p_i = price of a specified fixed input,
       x_i = quantity of the specified fixed input, and
       n = number of various kinds of fixed inputs (explicit as well as implicit).

[8] Total variable costs may be defined in mathematical terms as

$$TVC = \sum_{j=1}^{m} p_j x_j,$$

where p_j = price of a specified variable input,
       x_j = quantity of the specified variable input, and
       m = number of various kinds of variable inputs.

[9] A variety of expenses incurred by firms have both fixed and variable aspects. These include telephone service, advertising outlays, research and development costs, office supplies, expense account allowances, payroll taxes, and fringe benefit costs.

THE FAMILY OF UNIT COST CONCEPTS

There are four major unit cost concepts: average fixed cost, average variable cost, average total cost, and marginal cost. All of these may be derived from the total cost concepts discussed above.

Average fixed cost is defined as total fixed cost divided by the units of output, or

$$AFC = \frac{TFC}{Q}.$$

Since total fixed cost is a constant amount, average fixed cost declines continuously as the rate of production increases. For example, if $TFC = \$1000$, at an output of 10 units $AFC = \$1000/10 = \$100$; at an output of 20 units $AFC = \$1,000/20 = \$50$; at an output of 50 units $AFC = \$1,000/50 = \$20$; and so forth. The reduction of AFC by producing more units of output is what businessmen commonly call "spreading the overhead." The calculation of average fixed cost can also be approached from a slightly different direction. If we conceive a firm's fixed inputs as consisting of a number of identical units, then total fixed cost equals the number of units of fixed input (FI) multiplied by the unit price of the fixed input (P_{FI}), or $TFC = (P_{FI})(FI)$. Substituting into the expression for AFC gives

$$AFC = \frac{TFC}{Q} = \frac{(P_{FI})(FI)}{Q} = P_{FI}\left(\frac{FI}{Q}\right).$$

Consider the term FI/Q, the number of units of fixed input divided by the quantity of output. In Chapter 7 we defined average product of the fixed input as total output (Q) divided by the number of units of fixed input (FI). Thus, the term $FI/Q = 1/AP_{fi}$ and

$$AFC = P_{FI}\left(\frac{1}{AP_{fi}}\right).$$

Average variable cost is total variable cost divided by the corresponding number of units of output, or

$$AVC = \frac{TVC}{Q}.$$

As with AFC, the concept of AVC may be related to the underlying production function. Total variable cost equals the units of variable input employed (VI) multiplied by the price per unit of variable input (P_{VI}). Assuming a single type of variable input is used, $TVC = (P_{VI})(VI)$. Hence we have

$$AVC = \frac{TVC}{Q} = \frac{(P_{VI})(VI)}{Q} = P_{VI}\left(\frac{VI}{Q}\right).$$

Since the average product of variable input equals Q/VI by definition, it follows that

$$AVC = P_{VI}\left(\frac{1}{AP_{VI}}\right).$$

Average total cost is defined as total cost divided by the corresponding units of output, or

$$ATC = \frac{TC}{Q}.$$

However, since $TC = TFC + TVC$,

$$ATC = \frac{TC}{Q} = \frac{TFC + TVC}{Q} = \frac{TFC}{Q} + \frac{TVC}{Q}$$
$$= AFC + AVC.$$

Last, *marginal cost* is the change in total cost associated with a change in the quantity of output per period of time. As with previous marginal concepts, we can make a distinction between discrete marginal cost and continuous marginal cost. *Discrete marginal cost* is the change in total cost attributable to a one-unit change in the quantity of output. For example, the marginal cost of the 500th unit of output can be calculated by finding the difference between total cost at 499 units of output and total cost of 500 units of output. Hence the increase in cost from producing one additional unit of output equals the marginal cost of that unit. *Continuous marginal cost* may be thought of as the *rate* of change in total cost as the quantity of output changes, and it can be calculated from the first derivative of the total cost function. Thus,

$$MC = \frac{dTC}{dQ}.$$

However, because all changes in total cost associated with changes in the output rate are attributable *solely* to changes in total variable cost (*TFC* is constant), it is equally accurate to measure discrete marginal cost by observing changes in total variable cost. Consequently, the marginal cost of the 500th unit of output can be calculated by finding the difference between *TVC* at 499 units of output and *TVC* at 500 units of output; continuous marginal cost is also equivalent to the first derivative of the TVC function:

$$MC = \frac{dTVC}{dQ}.$$

As with the other unit cost concepts, marginal cost is related to the underlying production function. Marginal costs stem from the changes in variable costs associated with altering the quantity of output. Since in the short run output is altered by increasing or decreasing the usage of variable inputs, changes in total variable cost (ΔTVC) may be calculated by multiplying the price of variable input (P_{VI}) by the associated change in variable input (ΔVI), giving

$$\Delta TVC = P_{VI}(\Delta VI).$$

As indicated above, $MC = \Delta TVC$ for a one-unit change in output; or, if output changes by several units, then

$$MC = \frac{\Delta TVC}{\Delta Q}.$$

But since $\Delta TVC = P_{VI}(\Delta VI)$, we have

$$MC = \frac{P_{VI}(\Delta VI)}{\Delta Q} = P_{VI}\left(\frac{\Delta VI}{\Delta Q}\right).$$

In Chapter 7, marginal product (MP) was defined as the change in output attributable to a change in variable input, or $MP = \Delta Q / \Delta VI$. It follows, therefore, that

$$MC = P_{VI}\left(\frac{1}{MP}\right).$$

Marginal cost is of central interest because it reflects those costs over which the firm has the most direct control in the short run. More particularly, MC indicates the amount of cost which can be "saved" by reducing output by one unit or, alternatively, the amount of additional cost which will be incurred by increasing production by one unit. Average cost data do not reveal this valuable bit of cost knowledge.

Now let us use these definitions to investigate the behavior of a firm's costs for a variety of production functions. Specifically, we shall examine the total, average, and marginal cost functions for each of the following types of short-run production functions:

(a) $Q = a + bX + cX^2$ (increasing returns to variable input),
(b) $Q = a + bX$ (constant returns to variable input),
(c) $Q = a + bX - cX^2$ (decreasing returns to variable input),
(d) $Q = a + bX + cX^2 - dX^3$ (increasing and decreasing returns to variable input),

where Q = quantity of output and X = units of variable input.

COST BEHAVIOR WITH INCREASING RETURNS TO VARIABLE INPUT

When a firm's production function exhibits increasing returns to variable input, each additional unit of variable input adds more to total output than does the previous unit. Graphically, then, the production function increases at an increasing rate and has, in the simplest case, the general equation $Q = a + bX + cX^2$, where $a = 0$, provided that variable input (X) is essential for any output (Q) to be produced. Figure 8-1(a) illustrates this type of production function. The corresponding marginal and average product functions are shown in Figure 8-1(b).

As indicated earlier, a firm's fixed inputs, not being easily susceptible

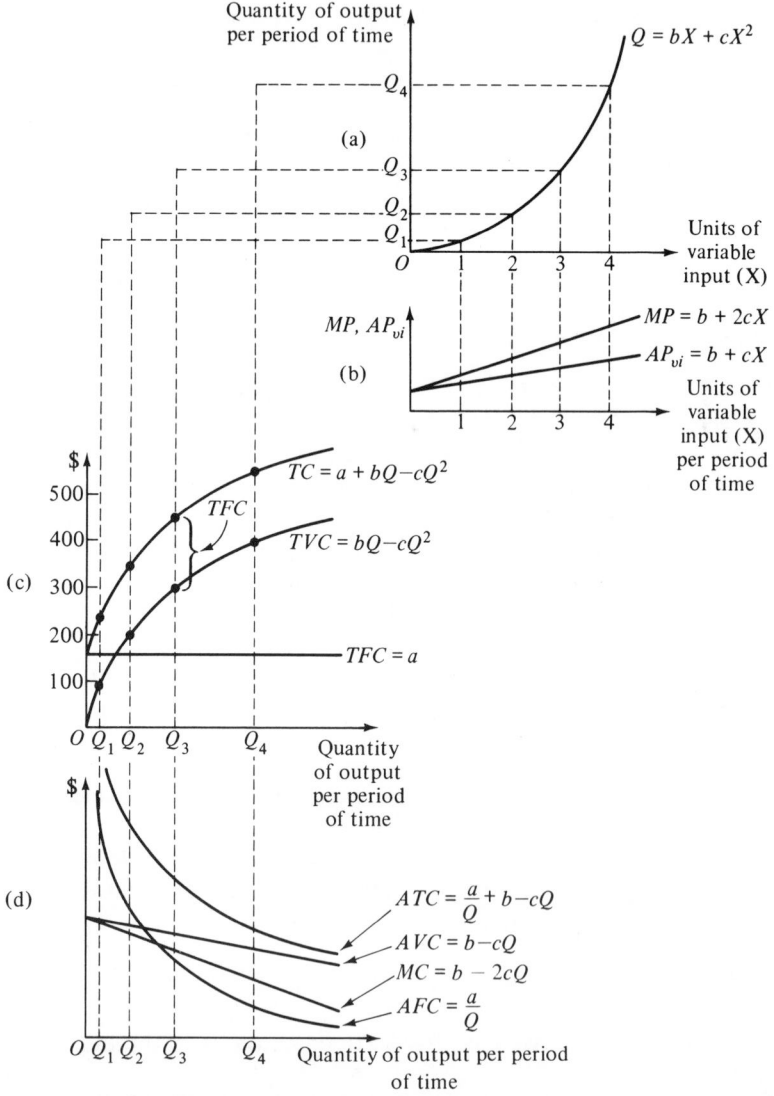

Fig. 8-1   Production and Cost Behavior for an Increasing Returns to Variable Input Situation

to change in the short run, give rise to a constant amount of cost, barring any change in the prices of the fixed inputs. This amount of cost (*TFC*) represents the sum total of the explicit costs of all the fixed inputs plus an allowance for implicit costs. Graphically, the *TFC* function is a horizontal line, reflecting the fact that *TFC* does not vary with the quantity of output. [Figure 8-1(c)]. Costs in dollars are plotted on the vertical axis, and the quantity of output is on the horizontal axis. Algebraically, the amount of *TFC* can be represented by a constant, say *a*, making the general equation for the total fixed cost function:

$$TFC = a.$$

The total variable cost (*TVC*) function gets its shape directly from the production function. To illustrate the tie between the production function and *TVC*, consider the behavior of *TVC* as successive units of variable input per period of time are added to the given amount of fixed inputs. Suppose the price of variable input is $100 per unit. From Figure 8-1(a) it can be seen that employing one unit of variable input with the given fixed input will yield an output of Q_1 units; this translates into *TVC* of $100 for Q_1 units of output [Figure 8-1(c)]. Similarly, employing two units of variable input yields Q_2 units of output and results in *TVC* of $200. Note that in panel (a) the marginal product of the second unit of variable input is larger than the marginal product of the first unit (distance $Q_1Q_2 >$ distance OQ_1) in accordance with increasing returns to the usage of variable input. Adding the third unit of variable input causes the quantity of output to increase even faster to Q_3 units (distance $Q_2Q_3 >$ distance Q_1Q_2), and *TVC* at Q_3 is $300. When the fourth unit of variable input per period of time is employed, output rises by yet a greater increment to Q_4 units (distance $Q_3Q_4 >$ distance Q_2Q_3), and *TVC* becomes $400. From Figures 8-1(a) and (c) it is apparent that when the quantity of output increases at an increasing rate, *TVC* must necessarily increase at a decreasing rate. With each additional unit of variable input, *TVC* rises by a constant amount equal to the price per unit of variable input, yet the associated increases in output get larger and larger owing to the rising productivity of additional variable input. To put it another way, when increasing returns to variable input characterize the production function, the quantity of output rises faster than does total variable cost. The simplest equation for representing *TVC* which captures the properties of such cost behavior is the equation

$$TVC = bQ - cQ^2.$$

(It must be emphasized that while the equation for the production function [$Q = bX + cX^2$] and the *TVC* function [$TVC = bQ - cQ^2$] are very similar in form, the values of the constants *b* and *c* in the production function *are not equal* to the values of *b* and *c* in the *TVC* equation—except in the rarest of coincidences.) Notice that *TVC* equals zero at an output of zero units and that the *TVC* function begins at the origin. Also, the greater is the usage of variable input, the greater is both the quantity of output and the level of total variable costs.

Given that $TC = TFC + TVC$, the total cost curve is found by vertically summing the *TFC* and *TVC* functions. The equation for the total cost function in this case is

$$TC = a + bQ - cQ^2,$$

where a represents the *TFC* component of *TC* and $(bQ - cQ^2)$ represents the *TVC* component. From Figure 8-1(c), it can be seen that the shapes of the *TVC* and *TC* curves are identical. At every rate of output their slopes are equal and the two curves are separated by a constant vertical distance equal to the amount of *TFC*. At zero output, $TVC = 0$ and $TC = TFC$.

The *AFC* curve decreases continually as the quantity of output increases —as indicated in Figure 8-1(d). Its equation is

$$AFC = \frac{TFC}{Q} = \frac{a}{Q}.$$

As explained earlier, the decline in *AFC* derives from the spreading of *TFC* over a greater number of units of output. Geometrically speaking, the *AFC* curve is a rectangular hyperbola, meaning that the curve approaches the vertical and horizontal axes asymptotically. In addition, were we to pick any point on the *AFC* curve, draw lines perpendicular to the two axes, and calculate the area of the resulting rectangle, this area will be the same irrespective of the point chosen. Why? Because this area measures $AFC \times Q$ and because $AFC \times Q = TFC =$ a constant value.

The nature and behavior of average variable cost can be deduced from the total variable cost function. When the production function exhibits increasing returns to variable input, *TVC* may be represented by the equation $TVC = bQ - cQ^2$. It follows that

$$AVC = \frac{TVC}{Q} = \frac{bQ - cQ^2}{Q} = b - cQ.$$

The *AVC* curve corresponding to this type of production function is shown in Figure 8-1(d). The significant point here is that unit variable costs *fall* as output increases under conditions of increasing returns to variable input. That this is so can be verified by means of the relationship between *AVC* and the production function:

$$AVC = P_{vi}\left(\frac{1}{AP_{vi}}\right).$$

Given increasing returns to variable input, the average productivity of variable input rises as more units of variable input are added [see Figure

8-1(b)]. As AP_{vi} goes up (and provided the price of variable input does not change), then AVC must necessarily fall.

The average total cost function can be derived by dividing the equation for total cost by the units of output, obtaining

$$ATC = \frac{TC}{Q} = \frac{a + bQ - cQ^2}{Q} = \frac{a}{Q} + b - cQ.$$

The equation for ATC could just as well have been found by adding together the equation for AFC and the equation for AVC. Since

$$ATC = AFC + AVC,$$

$$AFC = \frac{a}{Q},$$

$$AVC = b - cQ,$$

then

$$ATC = \frac{a}{Q} + b - cQ.$$

The shape of the average total cost curve is obtained by vertically summing the AFC and AVC curves at every rate of output. This gives the ATC curve shown in Figure 8-1(d). Average total cost declines throughout because both its components—AFC and AVC—are decreasing. Observe that the ATC curve is asymptotic to the AVC curve. Why? The difference between ATC and AVC is the amount of AFC. At low levels of output AFC is relatively large and the values of ATC are well in excess of the AVC values; however, as output increases, the values of AFC decline and the values of ATC more closely approach the values of AVC. Thus, while ATC always exceeds AVC, the greater the quantity of output the smaller the value of AFC and the smaller the distance between the AVC and ATC curves. This asymptotic relationship between AVC and ATC is not unique to cost behavior in the instance of increasing returns to variable input, but rather is a general and necessary trait for all types of production and cost situations.

The marginal cost function is obtained by differentiating either the TC or the TVC function—the result is the same in either event. Given that $TC = a + bQ - cQ^2$ and $TVC = bQ - cQ^2$, we have

$$MC = \frac{dTC}{dQ} = \frac{dTVC}{dQ} = b - 2cQ.$$

The MC function is, therefore, both linear and downsloping, as shown in Figure 8-1(d). The downward-sloping feature of the marginal cost curve stems from the fact that the marginal product of successive units of variable input is rising. Recalling that

$$MC = P_{vi}\left(\frac{1}{MP}\right),$$

it follows that if MP is increasing and if the price of the variable input is constant, then MC must necessarily be falling. Moreover, it should be noted that the slope of the MC curve $(-2c)$ is twice as large as the slope of the AVC curve $(-c)$; both curves originate at a common point (b). And, finally, the value of MC at a given output is equal to the slope of the TVC curve and the TC curve at the given output rate.

The salient feature of increasing returns to variable input is that the efficiency with which resource inputs are used rises as the quantity of output increases, with the concomitant result of declining unit costs. In other words, the larger the quantity produced, the lower the costs of each unit—clearly, a most favorable set of circumstances. Unfortunately for the firm, increasing returns to variable input are not likely to be encountered except at output rates well below the normal operating range.

Table 8-1 presents hypothetical production and cost data for a production function exhibiting increasing returns to variable input. Before proceeding, the reader would do well to examine the cost figures in this table to be sure that he fully understands how each one is computed.

Table 8-1   Hypothetical Production and Cost Data for Increasing Returns to Variable Input

Units of Fixed Input	Units of Variable Input	Quantity of Output	TFC^a	TVC^b	TC	AFC	AVC	ATC	"Average" MC
2	0	0	$100	$ 0	$100	—	$ 0	—	$4.00
2	1	10	100	40	140	$10.00	4.00	$14.00	2.67
2	2	25	100	80	180	4.00	3.20	7.20	2.00
2	3	45	100	120	220	2.22	2.67	4.89	1.60
2	4	70	100	160	260	1.43	2.29	3.72	1.33
2	5	100	100	200	300	1.00	2.00	3.00	

[a] The price of fixed input is assumed to be $50 per unit.
[b] The price of variable input is assumed to be $40 per unit.

COST BEHAVIOR WITH CONSTANT RETURNS TO VARIABLE INPUT

When a firm's production process is characterized by constant returns to variable input, each additional unit of variable input used per period of time adds the same amount to total output as the preceding unit. The quantity of output increases at a constant rate, and the production function is linear. The related MP and AP_{vi} functions are horizontal lines, indicating that the values of MP and AP_{vi} are the same for every unit of variable input. The general equation for the production function is

$$Q = a + bX,$$

where $a = 0$. The related equations for marginal and average products are

$$MP = b, \qquad AP_{vi} = b,$$

where b is a constant equal to the slope of the production function. Panels (a) and (b) in Figure 8-2 illustrate the family of product curves corresponding to a constant returns to variable input situation.

The *TFC* curve for a production process displaying constant returns to variable input is also a horizontal line. The character of *TFC* is not affected by the relationship between variable input and output—the level of *TFC* does not vary with the short-run quantity of output. The equation for total

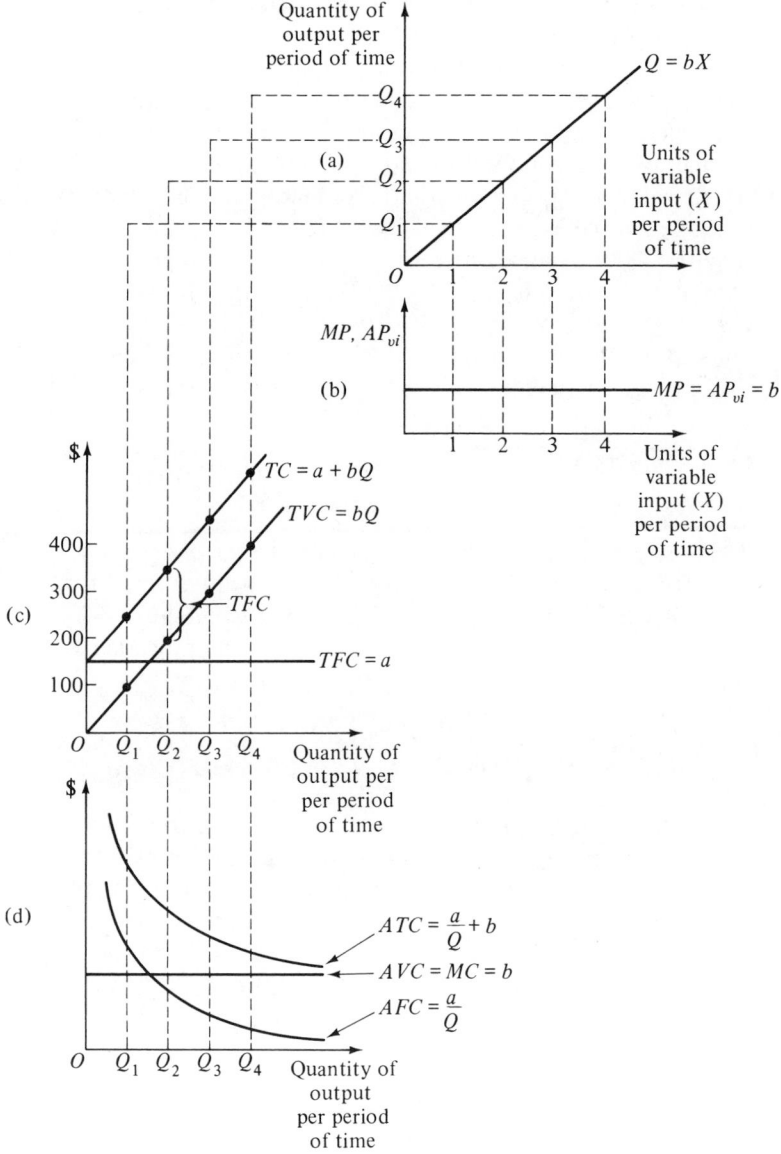

Fig. 8-2   Production and Cost Behavior for a Constant Returns to Variable Input Situation

fixed cost remains

$$TFC = a,$$

where a is a given amount of dollars and is determined by the amount and prices of fixed inputs present. The *TFC* function is graphed in Figure 8-2(c).

The shape of the total variable cost function is tied directly to the nature of the production function. Consider the impact upon *TVC* when additional units of variable input costing $100 each are combined with the fixed input. From Figure 8-2(a) it can be seen that combining one unit of variable input per period of time with the given amount of fixed inputs will yield an output of Q_1 units; accordingly, the total variable cost of Q_1 units is $100, as shown in Figure 8-2(c). Combining two units of variable input with the available fixed input yields an output of Q_2 units [Figure 8-2(a)]; the marginal product of the second unit of variable input equals the marginal product of the first unit $(OQ_1 = Q_1Q_2)$ in accordance with the condition of constant returns to variable input [Figure 8-2(b)]. *TVC* at Q_2 units of output is $200 [Figure 8-2(c)]. Adding the third unit of variable input causes the quantity of output to rise to Q_3 $(OQ_1 = Q_1Q_2 = Q_2Q_3)$, and the total variable cost of Q_3 units is $300. And so it goes. Each additional unit of variable input produces an equivalent rise in output (*MP* is constant), and *TVC* rises by a given amount ($100 in this case) with each unit increase in variable input. Plainly then, the *TVC* curve is *linear*, begins from the origin, and has the general equation

$$TVC = bQ.$$

The *TVC* function is illustrated in Figure 8-2(c).

Since $TC = TFC + TVC$, the shape of the total cost curve is derived by vertically adding the *TFC* and *TVC* curves [see Figure 8-2(c)]. It follows that the equation for *TC* may be found by adding together the expressions for *TFC* and *TVC*:

$$TFC = a, \qquad TVC = bQ,$$
$$TC = TFC + TVC = a + bQ.$$

Since all changes in total cost are solely attributable to changes in variable cost items, the shape of the *TC* curve is identical to the shape of the *TVC* curve. Given constant returns to variable input, the *TC* curve is therefore a linear function with a slope equivalent to the slope of *TVC*; the two curves are separated by a constant vertical distance equal to the amount of *TFC*. At zero output, $TVC = 0$ and $TC = TFC$.

As before, the *AFC* curve decreases continually as the quantity of output increases and it assumes the shape of a rectangular hyperbola. Its equation is

$$AFC = \frac{TFC}{Q} = \frac{a}{Q}.$$

The reasoning is the same as previously. As a constant value (TFC) is divided by an increasing value (Q), the resulting values (AFC) get smaller and smaller. Figure 8-2(d) illustrates the AFC curve for a situation of constant returns to variable input.

Average variable cost can be derived from the expression for total variable cost:

$$AVC = \frac{TVC}{Q} = \frac{bQ}{Q} = b.$$

This means that AVC is a constant value. That this is so can be confirmed from the relationship

$$AVC = P_{vi}\left(\frac{1}{AP_{vi}}\right).$$

With constant returns to variable input, AP_{vi} is also a constant and, assuming a given price for variable input, AVC must necessarily be a constant. For instance, suppose each unit of variable input costs \$100 and that the average product of variable input is fixed at 50 units of output. Then,

$$AVC = P_{vi}\left(\frac{1}{AP_{vi}}\right) = \$100\left(\frac{1}{50}\right) = \$2.$$

Graphically, the AVC curve is a horizontal line with a height of b dollars above the horizontal axis, as shown in Figure 8-2(d).

Since, by definition, average total cost equals total cost divided by the units of output, the equation for ATC under conditions of constant returns to variable input becomes

$$ATC = \frac{TC}{Q} = \frac{a + bQ}{Q} = \frac{a}{Q} + b.$$

Observe that the term a/Q is AFC and the term b is AVC. Plainly, the equation for ATC can be found by adding the equation for AFC to the equation for AVC. Since in this instance AVC is a constant value, the ATC curve assumes a shape precisely identical to that of the AFC curve and lies above it by the amount of AVC [see Figure 8-2(d)]. The ATC curve is, therefore, asymptotic to the horizontal AVC curve and decreases throughout.

With marginal cost being equal to the first derivative of the TC function (or the TVC function) and the equation for TC being $TC = a + bQ$, the equation for MC becomes

$$MC = \frac{dTC}{dQ} = \frac{dTVC}{dQ} = b,$$

where b is a constant. That MC is a constant value follows from its relationship with marginal product:

$$MC = P_{vi}\left(\frac{1}{MP}\right).$$

MP is itself a fixed value when constant returns to variable input are present. Letting the price of variable input remain fixed, MC becomes the product of a constant times a constant. For example, if $P_{vi} = \$100$ and if the marginal product of every additional unit of variable input equals 50 units of output, then

$$MC = P_{vi}\left(\frac{1}{MC}\right) = \$100\left(\frac{1}{50}\right) = \$2.$$

Thus, with constant returns to variable input, $MC = AVC = b$, and the MC curve is a horizontal line. Also, the value of MC is equal to the slope of the TVC and TC curves.

Figure 8-2(d) illustrates the shapes and relationships of the unit cost curves. Table 8-2 presents hypothetical production and cost data for a production function exhibiting constant returns to variable input. Observe that the greater the output rate, the lower the average total cost of producing a unit of output. Unit cost falls solely because total fixed costs are being spread over a larger volume of output. As best as can be determined, constant MC and AVC and slowly declining ATC typify many production processes over the "normal" range of output (more about this presently).

Table 8-2 Hypothetical Production and Cost Data for Constant Returns to Variable Input

Units of Fixed Input	Units of Variable Input	Quantity of Output	TFC[a]	TVC[b]	TC	AFC	AVC	ATC	"Average" MC
2	0	0	$100	$ 0	$100	—	0	—	$4.00
2	1	10	100	40	140	$10.00	$4.00	$14.00	4.00
2	2	20	100	80	180	5.00	4.00	9.00	4.00
2	3	30	100	120	220	3.33	4.00	7.33	4.00
2	4	40	100	160	260	2.50	4.00	6.50	4.00
2	5	50	100	200	300	2.00	4.00	6.00	

[a] The price of fixed input is assumed to be $50 per unit.
[b] The price of variable input is assumed to be $40 per unit.

COST BEHAVIOR WITH DECREASING RETURNS TO VARIABLE INPUT

Having a production process characterized by decreasing returns to variable input means that the marginal product of variable input declines throughout the output range. Each additional unit of variable input used per period of time with the available fixed input adds less to total output than the previous unit and the quantity of output increases at a decreasing rate. Both the marginal and average product functions are downsloping. The product curves are illustrated in panels (a) and (b) of Figure 8-3.

As is the case each time, the *TFC* curve is a horizontal line having the equation

$$TFC = a,$$

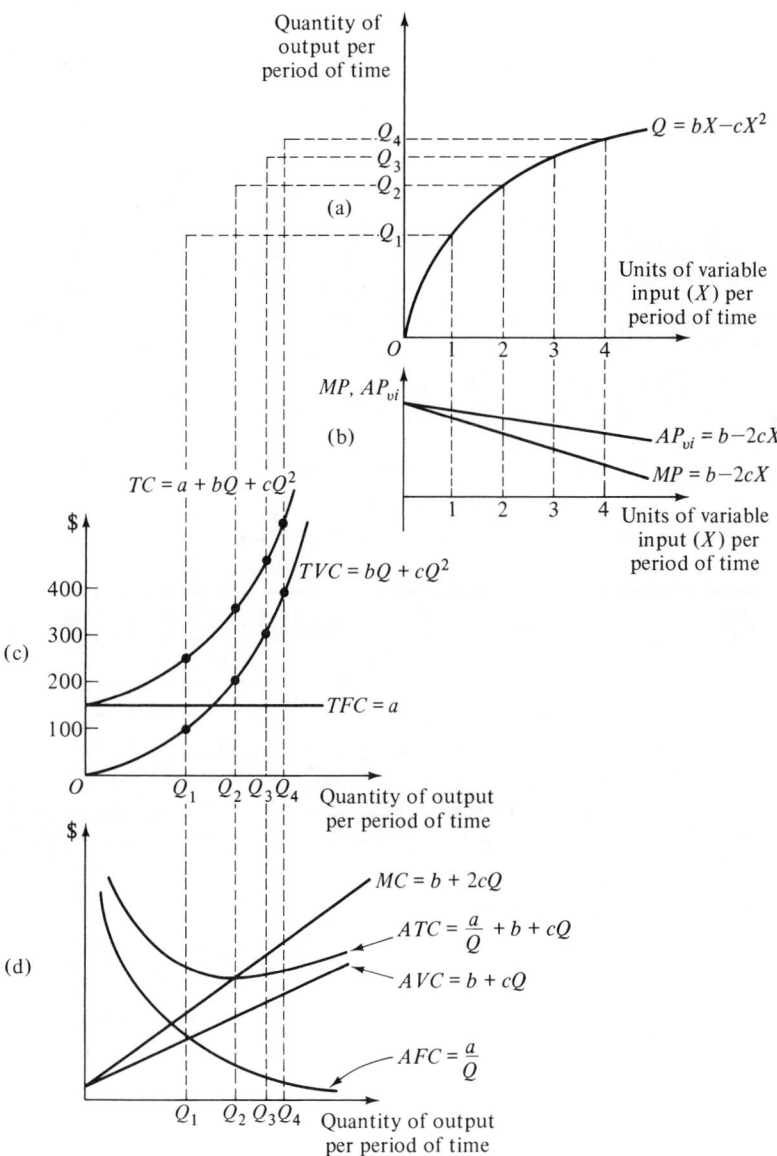

Fig. 8-3   Production and Cost Behavior for a Decreasing Returns to Variable Input Situation

where a is a constant. In the short run, neither the amount nor the cost of the available fixed inputs is affected by the character of the production function; for this reason TFC does not vary with the quantity of output. The TFC curve is illustrated in Figure 8-3(c).

To determine the shape of the TVC curve we must again look to the corresponding production function. Letting $P_{vi} = \$100$ per unit, each additional unit of variable input employed will cause TVC to rise by \$100. From Figure 8-3(a) it is evident that combining one unit of variable input per period of time with the given fixed input yields an output of Q_1 units. This translates into a TVC of \$100 at an output of Q_1 units, as shown in Figure 8-3(c). Combining two units of variable input with the fixed input produces a less-than-proportional increase in output to Q_2 units ($OQ_1 > Q_1Q_2$), and TVC becomes \$200 at an output of Q_2. Adding the third unit of variable input yields yet a smaller increment in the quantity of output ($Q_1Q_2 > Q_2Q_3$); TVC rises to \$300. Successive additions of variable input produce similar results. The declining marginal product of variable input causes output to rise ever more slowly, while costs increase by a given amount (\$100 in this example) with each unit increase in variable input. Such behavior produces a TVC curve which increases at an increasing rate, as indicated in Figure 8-3(c). The simplest equation to represent this type of function is

$$TVC = bQ + cQ^2.$$

Since $TC = TFC + TVC$, the equation for TC under conditions of decreasing returns to variable input becomes

$$TC = a + bQ + cQ^2.$$

The graph of this function, shown in Figure 8-3(c), starts from the point where the TFC curve intersects the vertical axis and thereafter increases at an increasing rate. The shape of the TC curve is identical to the shape of the TVC and lies above it by a constant amount equal to TFC.

As is the case irrespective of the character of the production function, the AFC curve is a decreasing function that is asymptotic to the horizontal axis [see Figure 8-3(d)]. Its equation is

$$AFC = \frac{TFC}{Q} = \frac{a}{Q}.$$

The nature and behavior of AVC are easily established. Since the equation for TVC is

$$TVC = bQ + cQ^2,$$

the equation for AVC becomes

$$AVC = \frac{TVC}{Q} = \frac{bQ + cQ^2}{Q} = b + cQ.$$

The graph of the AVC function is linear with a positive slope equal to the value of c. Thus, when the production function exhibits decreasing returns to variable input, AVC rises as output is increased. That AVC rises throughout can be confirmed by examining the expression

$$AVC = P_{vi}\left(\frac{1}{AP_{vi}}\right).$$

With decreasing returns to variable input, AP_{vi} decreases over the entire output range [see Figure 8-3(b)]. Assuming a constant price for variable input, as output is increased the smaller and smaller values of AP_{vi} result in larger and larger values of AVC. Aside from the mathematics of the situation, the logic for rising AVC is compelling. When the production function displays decreasing returns to variable input, both the marginal and average productivity of variable inputs decline as output is increased. Hence, the efficiency of variable input falls as more variable input is added and as output rises. Lower efficiency in the usage of variable input clearly implies higher variable costs per unit of output.

Since $ATC = TC/Q$, the equation for average total cost is

$$ATC = \frac{TC}{Q} = \frac{a + bQ + cQ^2}{Q} = \frac{a}{Q} + b + cQ.$$

However, the graph of ATC is somewhat less obvious. Whereas the AFC component of ATC (a/Q) decreases as the quantity of output rises, the AVC component of ATC $(b + cQ)$ rises continuously as output rises. Hence, whether ATC rises or falls hinges upon the decreases in AFC relative to the increases in AVC. At low output rates the declines in AFC are larger than the increases in AVC, so the ATC curve declines up to an output of Q_2 units. At Q_2 the decline in AFC is exactly offset by the increase in AVC, and ATC is a minimum. Beyond Q_2, the increases in AVC override the decreases in AFC, with the result that the ATC curve turns upward. But despite the U-shaped behavior of ATC, the ATC curve is still asymptotic to the AVC curve for the reason previously given.

A production function displaying decreasing returns to variable input is associated with a rising marginal cost function. Given that $TC = a + bQ + cQ^2$,

$$MC = \frac{dTC}{dQ} = b + 2cQ.$$

Alternatively, the MC function can be found from the TVC equation. Since $TVC = bQ + cQ^2$, then

$$MC = \frac{dTVC}{dQ} = b + 2cQ.$$

The graph of such an equation is a linear function with a positive slope equal to $2c$ [see Figure 8-3(d)]. The increasing aspect of MC stems from its relationship to marginal product:

$$MC = P_{vi}\left(\frac{1}{MP}\right).$$

By definition, decreasing returns to variable input means that the marginal product of additional units of variable input is a declining, yet positive, value. With MP falling as output rises, MC must necessarily rise. Note that in this instance the slope of the MC curve ($2c$) is twice as great as the slope of the AVC curve (c). Also, the MC curve passes through the minimum point of the ATC curve. The latter property is an inherent feature of the mathematical relationship between average and marginal values. MC is the additional cost for one unit of output; ATC is the average for all the units produced up to that point. So long as MC is below ATC, ATC is pulled down by the lower cost of the additional output. When the cost of an additional unit is greater than the average cost of previous units, ATC is pulled up by the higher cost of the incremental output. At the point of intersection of MC and ATC, ATC has ceased declining but has not begun to rise; this, then, is the minimum point on the ATC curve.

The production and cost functions in Figure 8-3 are not likely to typify the entire output range for many production processes. But they are quite typical of production and cost behavior at near-capacity levels of output. The closer capacity is approached, the harder it becomes to increase production without encountering the point of diminishing marginal returns. If for no other reason, the plant will eventually become so crowded that labor, equipment, and materials get in each other's way, with an attendant loss of time and efficiency—when this happens MC, AVC, and ATC will rise sharply.

Table 8-3 illustrates production and cost behavior for a situation characterized by decreasing returns to variable input throughout the output range. Note that the patterns of change in the total and unit cost values parallel exactly the shapes of the cost curves in panels (c) and (d) of Figure 8-3.

Table 8-3 Hypothetical Production and Cost Data for Decreasing Returns to Variable Input

Units of Fixed Input	Units of Variable Input	Quantity of Output	TFC[a]	TVC[b]	TC	AFC	AVC	ATC	"Average" MC
2	0	0	$100	$ 0	$100	—	0	—	
									$2.00
2	1	20	100	40	140	$5.00	$2.00	$7.00	
									2.50
2	2	36	100	80	180	2.78	2.22	5.00	
									3.33
2	3	48	100	120	220	2.08	2.50	4.58	
									5.00
2	4	56	100	160	260	1.79	2.86	4.65	
									10.00
2	5	60	100	200	300	1.67	3.33	5.00	

[a] The price of fixed input is assumed to be $50 per unit.
[b] The price of variable input is assumed to be $40 per unit.

COST BEHAVIOR WITH INCREASING
AND DECREASING RETURNS TO VARIABLE INPUT

A more pervasive type of production function which incorporates many of the essential features of the three preceding types of production functions is illustrated in Figure 8-4(a). The general equation representing this type of production function is

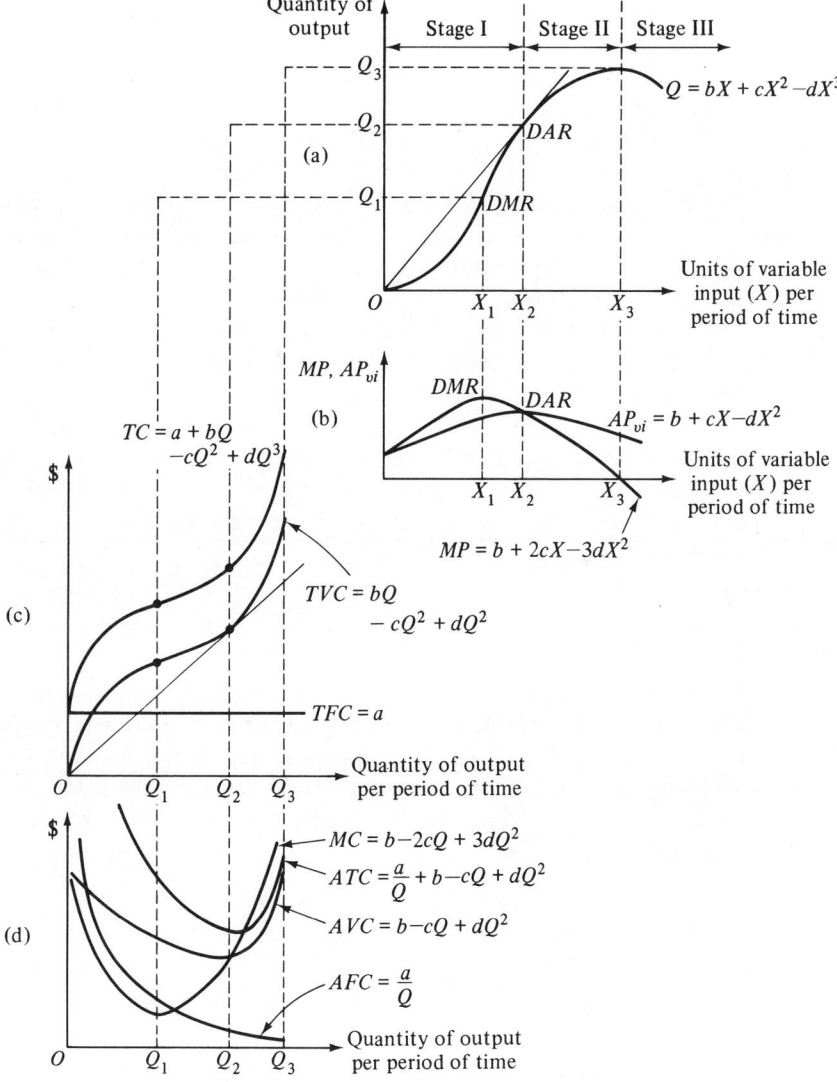

Fig. 8-4   Production and Cost Behavior Where Both Increasing and Decreasing Returns to Variable Input Are Present

$$Q = a + bX + cX^2 - dX^3,$$

where X represents the units of variable input. Up to X_1 units of variable input, the quantity of output increases at an increasing rate. From X_1 to X_3 units of variable input, output increases at a decreasing rate. The corresponding MP and AP_{vi} functions are shown in Figure 8-4(b).

As before, the TFC curve is a horizontal line with an equation $TFC = a$ [see Figure 8-4(c)]. The TVC curve for this type of production function combines the shapes of the TVC curves for both increasing and decreasing returns to variable input. From panels (a) and (c) of Figure 8-4 it can be seen that over the range of output where increasing returns to variable input prevail (0 to Q_1), the TVC curve increases at a decreasing rate, whereas over the range of output where decreasing returns to variable input are encountered (Q_1 to Q_3), the TVC curve increases at an increasing rate. At the short-run capacity level of output (Q_3) the slope of the TVC curve becomes vertical. The explanation for the shape of TVC rests with the principle of diminishing marginal returns. Where the quantity of output increases at an increasing rate, marginal product is also increasing, and smaller and smaller increases in variable inputs are required to produce successive units of output. This means that TVC will increase by progressively smaller amounts as output rises. But when the point of diminishing marginal returns is encountered and marginal product begins to decline, it becomes necessary to use larger and larger amounts of variable input to obtain more units of output. Total variable costs therefore increase at an increasing rate over this output range. The simplest form of general equation for a TVC curve with these traits is

$$TVC = bQ - cQ^2 + dQ^3.$$

Total cost is again the sum of TFC and TVC at each rate of output. At zero units of output, $TC = TFC$, and for each successive unit produced TC varies in precisely the same fashion and at precisely the same rate as does TVC. As indicated in Figure 8-4(c), the TC curve is the same shape as the TVC curve, but lies above it by the amount of TFC. The equation for a total cost curve of this nature is

$$TC = a + bQ - cQ^2 + dQ^3,$$

where a equals the amount of TFC and the expression ($bQ - cQ^2 + dQ^3$) equals the amount of TVC at each value of Q.

The graph and equation of the AFC curve are identical to the preceding cases and are shown in Figure 8-4(d). The behavior of AVC can be determined from TVC. Since $TVC = bQ - cQ^2 + dQ^3$, the average variable cost equation is

$$AVC = \frac{TVC}{Q} = \frac{bQ - cQ^2 + dQ^3}{Q} = b - cQ + dQ^2.$$

When plotted on a graph, an equation of this type produces a curve which declines initially, reaches a minimum, and then increases. The AVC curve is therefore U-shaped, as shown in Figure 8-4(d). The rationale for this behavior of AVC can be seen from its relationship with AP_{vi}:

$$AVC = P_{vi}\left(\frac{1}{AP_{vi}}\right).$$

Given a fixed price for units of variable input, when AP_{vi} is rising [Figure 8-4(b)], AVC must be falling; when AP_{vi} is declining, AVC must be rising. Minimum AVC (an output of Q_2) corresponds to the output rate where AP_{vi} is maximum (X_2 units of variable input). It is at this quantity of output that the point of diminishing average returns is encountered and the stage II phase of production begins. Thus, stage I rates of output correspond to the output range where AVC is declining, whereas stage II quantities correspond to the range of output where AVC is rising.

As previously indicated, ATC is calculated by dividing total cost by the quantity of output—or, more simply, by adding AFC and AVC at each rate of output. Here the equation for ATC is

$$ATC = \frac{TC}{Q} = \frac{a + bQ - cQ^2 + dQ^3}{Q} = \frac{a}{Q} + b - cQ + dQ^2,$$

where a/Q is the AFC component of ATC and ($b - cQ + dQ^2$) is the AVC component of ATC. As usual, the vertical distance between ATC and AVC reflects the value of AFC at any output. Because AFC decreases as output expands, the distance between ATC and AVC gets progressively smaller. Thus, the ATC curve is again asymptotic to the AVC curve and is also U-shaped [see Figure 8-4(d)]. Note that the minimum point on the ATC curve corresponds to a quantity of output in stage II. This result is in accord with the rationale for operating in stage II presented in Chapter 7. Also, the minimum point of the ATC curve is at a larger volume of output than is the minimum point of the AVC curve. Why? ATC continues to fall beyond the output where AVC is minimum because the continuing declines in AFC more than offset the slight increases in AVC. As output expands further, however, the growing increases in AVC begin to override the decreases in AFC, and ATC turns upward. The minimum point on the ATC curve defines the most efficient and economical rate of operation in the short run.

Marginal cost can be determined by calculating the first derivative of the equation for either *TC* or *TVC*:

$$MC = \frac{dTC}{dQ} = \frac{dTVC}{dQ} = b - 2cQ + 3dQ^2.$$

The *MC* function in this instance is a quadratic equation which, when graphed, assumes the U-shape shown in Figure 8-4(d). The curvature of the *MC* function reflects its relationship with marginal product. Since

$$MC = P_{vi}\left(\frac{1}{MP}\right),$$

then so long as *MP* is rising, *MC* must be declining. But when diminishing marginal returns set in and *MP* is falling, then the marginal cost of the extra unit of output is rising. Hence, assuming a constant price for variable input, increasing returns to variable input result in declining marginal costs, and decreasing returns are associated with rising marginal costs. Marginal cost is minimum at the point of diminishing marginal returns where *MP* is maximum (note that this quantity of output is in stage I). Furthermore, the *MC* curve intersects the *AVC* and *ATC* curves at their minimum points— a relationship of mathematical necessity [see Figure 8-4(d)].[10] When the cost of producing an additional unit is less than the average total cost of the previously produced units, the newly computed *ATC* will fall, being pulled down by the lower *MC*. Similarly, when the cost of producing an additional unit is greater than the average total cost of the preceding units, the new value of *ATC* rises, being pulled up by the higher value of *MC*. It follows that *ATC* is minimum at the point of intersection of *MC* and *ATC*. By analogous reasoning the *MC* curve must pass through the minimum point of the *AVC* function.

Table 8-4 illustrates the patterns of change in the total and unit cost values for a production function having phases of both increasing and decreasing returns to variable input.

---

[10] The mathematical proof of this point is relatively simple and follows the procedure presented earlier in Mathematical Capsule 7. Let *TC* be some function of the quantity of output:

$$TC = f(Q).$$

Then, by definition,

$$MC = \frac{dTC}{dQ} = f'(Q).$$

For *ATC* to be a minimum value, it is necessary that the slope of the *ATC* curve be zero, which, in turn, requires that the derivative of the *ATC* equation be equal to zero:

$$\frac{dATC}{dQ} = \frac{Q \cdot f'(Q) - f(Q)}{Q^2} = 0.$$

For $dATC/dQ$ to equal zero, the numerator of the above expression must be zero, or

$$Q \cdot f'(Q) - f(Q) = 0.$$

This can be rewritten as

$$f'(Q) = \frac{f(Q)}{Q}.$$

Since $f'(Q) = MC$ and $f(Q)/Q = ATC$, then the output rate that makes *ATC* minimum is also the value of *Q* at which $MC = ATC$.

By analogous logic, it can be shown that $MC = AVC$ at the minimum point of the *AVC* curve when the equation for total variable cost is of the form $TVC = f(Q)$.

Table 8-4   Hypothetical Production and Cost Data for Increasing and Decreasing Returns to Variable Input

Units of Fixed Input	Units of Variable Input	Quantity of Output	TFC^a	TVC^b	TC	AFC	AVC	ATC	"Average" MC
2	0	0	$100	$ 0	$100	—	0	—	$4.00
2	1	10	100	40	140	$10.00	$4.00	$14.00	2.00
2	2	30	100	80	180	3.33	2.67	6.00	1.14
2	3	65	100	120	220	1.54	1.85	3.39	1.33
2	4	95	100	160	260	1.05	1.69	2.74	1.60
2	5	120	100	200	300	.83	1.67	2.50	2.00
2	6	140	100	240	340	.71	1.71	2.42	2.67
2	7	155	100	280	380	.64	1.81	2.45	4.00
2	8	165	100	320	420	.61	1.94	2.55	8.00
2	9	170	100	360	460	.59	2.12	2.71	

^{b} The price of fixed input is assumed to be $50 per unit.
^{a} The price of variable input is assumed to be $40 per unit.

SHORT-RUN COST FUNCTIONS IN THE REAL WORLD: THE EMPIRICAL EVIDENCE

Economists have conducted a great many studies of the short-run cost functions of particular firms and industries. A wide variety of accounting, engineering, and econometric methods have been used to analyze historical cost and output data. Although both the methods employed and the data used suffer from a number of deficiencies, the results of these studies point quite consistently to one conclusion: *constant marginal cost in the short run is the pattern that best seems to describe actual cost behavior.* For the firms and industries examined, the relationship between total cost and output more often than not appears as linear, implying constant returns to variable input over the "normal" operating range of output. U-shaped marginal and average cost curves have been found to exist, but seem to be less general than commonly thought. Table 8-5 summarizes the findings of a number of these studies.

Despite a lack of empirical confirmation, we can be relatively confident that the closer the firm approaches its short-run maximum rate of production the greater becomes the pressure for rising marginal and average costs. As the firm attempts to squeeze more and more output from its production facilities, a wage premium must be paid for overtime. If second and third shifts are used, the productivity of labor tends to be noticeably lower than on the day shift. Constant use of equipment induces more breakdowns, improper maintenance, and production bottlenecks. Marginal, and perhaps obsolete, pieces of equipment may have to be brought on stream to achieve rated capacity. Hiring standards may have to be lowered to obtain the needed labor. As the firm literally "scrapes the ceiling" of production

Table 8-5   Results of Empirical Studies of Short-Run Cost Functions

Name	Type of Industry	Finding
Lester (1946)	Manufacturing	*AVC* decreases up to capacity levels of output.
Hall and Hitch (1939)	Manufacturing	Majority have decreasing *MC*.
Johnston (1960)	Electricity, multiple-product food processing	"Direct" cost is a linear function of output and *MC* is constant.
Dean (1936)	Furniture	Constant *MC* which failed to rise.
Dean (1941)	Leather belts	No significant increases in *MC*.
Dean (1941)	Hosiery	Constant *MC* which failed to rise.
Dean (1942)	Department store	Declining or constant *MC*, depending upon the department within the store.
Ezekiel and Wylie (1941)	Steel	Declining *MC* but large variation.
Yntema (1940)	Steel	Constant *MC*.
Johnston (1960)	Electricity	*ATC* falls, then flattens, tending toward constant *MC* up to capacity.
Mansfield and Wein (1958)	Railways	Constant *MC*.

SOURCE: A.A. Walters, "Production and Cost Functions," *Econometrica*, Vol. 31, No. 1 (January 1963), pp. 1–66.

capacity, it may become imperative to utilize less productive capital and labor inputs.[11] A loss of efficiency accompanied by rises in *MC* and *ATC* can therefore be expected at near maximum production rates.

Evidence that this is so is furnished by McGraw-Hill Publishing Company's annual survey of manufacturing firms. Among other things, Mc-Graw-Hill inquires of manufacturing firms (a) what percentage of their production capacity they are currently using and (b) at what percentage they would prefer to operate. The preferred rates of operation usually range in the neighborhood of 90 percent, which strongly implies belief that the minimum points of their *ATC* curves are reached at about 90 percent of the maximum rate of production. Apparently, producing within the 90 to 100 percent range would entail, as expected, rising marginal and average costs. Then, too, the reason for the failure of empirical studies to detect rising unit costs could well be that the firms and industries examined were for the most part operating short of the output range where their unit cost curves turned upward.

On the basis of available indications, the cost functions shown in Figure 8-5 are fair representations of total and unit cost behavior for a large

[11] According to a 1970 McGraw-Hill survey *How Modern Is American Industry*, 17 per cent of U.S. manufacturing capacity is more than 20 years old, 35 percent is less than 5 years old. Shipbuilders, makers of railroad and other transportation equipment, and iron and steel producers tend to have the highest proportion of obsolete equipment, while instrument, mining, electrical machinery, petroleum firms, and the airlines have the smallest proportions of facilities more than 20 years old. Naturally, older facilities and equipment are less efficient and more costly to operate; thus, as firms approach production capacity and find it necessary to bring such facilities on stream unit costs are bound to rise.

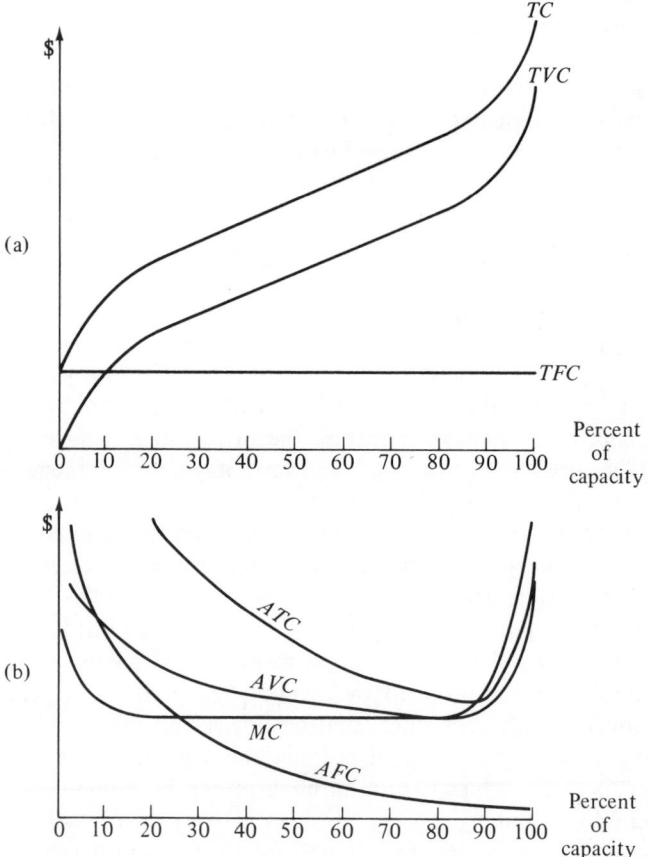

Fig. 8-5   Total, Average, and Marginal Cost Behavior Frequently Found in Business Enterprises

number of diverse production processes. The properties of these functions suggest increasing returns to variable input at exceptionally low production rates, constant returns to variable input thereafter up to about 90 or 95 percent of capacity, and decreasing returns to variable input beyond the 90 to 95 percent level. Thus, while the marginal cost curve is U-shaped, the bottom of the U has a wide, flat range that encompasses the "normal" and "preferred" rates of output. *AVC* continues to fall over this entire range because *MC* is below *AVC*. This follows from the fact that the slope of *TVC* in the linear portion is a smaller value than the slope of a ray drawn from the origin of the diagram in Figure 8-5(a) to the *TVC* curve; the former slope value equals *MC* while the latter equals *AVC*.

Cost-Output Relationships in the Long Run

In the long run all resource inputs are variable; a firm can alter its usage of major capital equipment, change top management personnel, build new plant capacity, close down obsolete facilities, update its use of technology, or in any other way modify its production process and use of resources per period of time. There are no total or average fixed cost curves in the long run, since no inputs are fixed, and as a consequence, the discussion of unit costs can be limited to just average costs.

Along with its concern for short-run operations, a firm must be cognizant of the future and develop strategies for the long run. Decisions concerning the long run will determine the character of the short-run positions the firm will occupy in the future. For instance, before a firm makes a decision to expand its productive potential, the firm is in a long-run position; it has several options among the types and sizes of equipment, the technology, and the labor mix for producing the extra output. But once the investment is made and the new production capacity is installed, the firm is confronted with a short-run situation where the types and amounts of certain inputs are frozen for the time being.

In the long run the firm will seek to adjust its scale of production so as to be able to produce the desired output at the lowest possible cost. Sometimes economies can be attained by dividing the production process into smaller production units. On other occasions lower unit costs can be achieved by enlarging the size of its scale of production. A plant can be "too small" as well as "too big." Likewise, an entire firm can be "too small" as well as "too big." In examining the relationships between cost behavior and the scale of production it is therefore important to distinguish between *plants* and *firms*, because the advantages and disadvantages of each are different. We begin with the former, then turn to the latter.

COST BEHAVIOR AND PLANT SIZE

Suppose technological constraints allow a firm the choice of constructing any one of three plant sizes: small, medium, and large. The short-run average cost curve for each of these plant sizes is represented by $SRAC_S$, $SRAC_M$, and $SRAC_L$ in Figure 8-6. Whatever size plant the firm has currently, in the long run it can convert to or construct any one of these three plant scales. Obviously, the firm's choice of plant size is conditioned by its perceived need for future production capacity. For example, if the anticipated output rate is OQ_1, the firm should elect to build the small-sized plant, since it can produce OQ_1 units of output per period of time at a cost of AC_1 which is well below either the unit cost of the medium-sized plant (AC_2) or the unit cost of the large-sized plant (AC_3). If the expected output rate is OQ_2, the

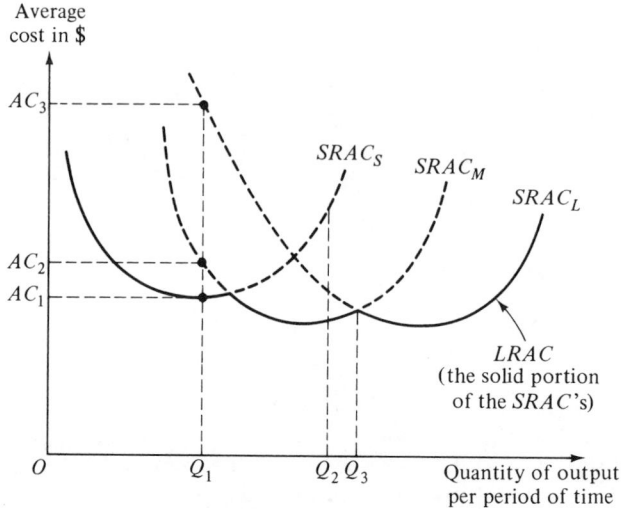

Fig. 8-6   The Long-Run Average Cost Curve When Only Three Plant Sizes are Available

medium-sized plant plainly offers the lowest unit cost. On the other hand, at an output of OQ_3 the medium- and large-sized plants are equally efficient from a unit cost standpoint. Here the final choice of plants might depend on the forecasted growth in consumer demand, with an expectation of strong growth tipping the scales in favor of the large plant. Otherwise, the medium-sized plant is likely to be the more attractive because of its smaller capital investment requirements.

The portions of the three short-run average cost curves which are pertinent for selecting the optimum plant size are indicated by the solid, scalloped line in Figure 8-6. This line is called the *long-run average cost* curve (*LRAC*) and shows the minimum cost per unit of producing at each output rate when all resource inputs are variable and any desired scale of plant can be built. The broken line segments of the *SRAC* curves are all associated with higher average costs for each output rate.

Actually a firm's choice of plant sizes will usually number well in excess of three alternatives. When a host of alternative plant sizes confront the firm, the long-run average cost curve is an "envelope" of the short-run curves and is tangent to each of the short-run average cost curves. This type of *LRAC* curve is pictured in Figure 8-7 and again represents the least unit cost attainable for a given output rate when the firm has time to change the rate of usage of any and all inputs. Suppose the firm estimates that an output of OQ_1 is most desirable; then the plant represented by $SRAC_1$ is the most efficient because it can produce OQ_1 units at a lower cost per unit than can any other sized plant. If consumer demand should expand sufficiently to

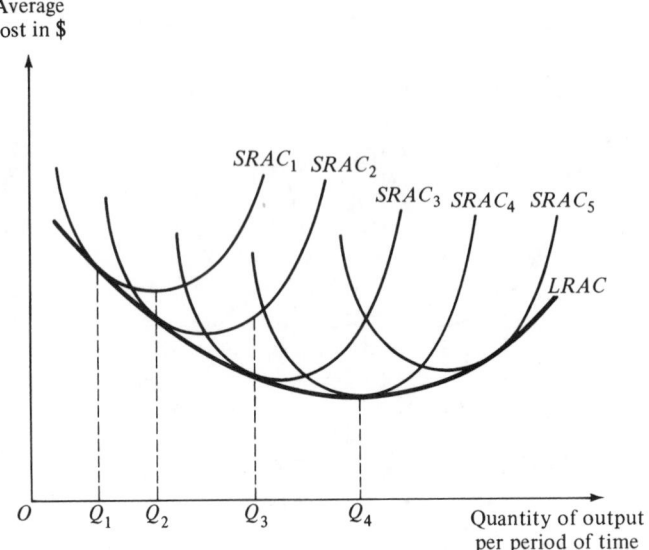

Fig. 8-7 The Long-Run Average Cost Curve for Alternative Plant Sizes

warrant an output of OQ_2 units, the output of the plant represented by $SRAC_1$ could be increased to meet this demand in the short run. Nevertheless, in the long run the firm would prefer to construct the plant represented by $SRAC_2$ because this slightly larger plant is capable of producing OQ_2 units at a lower cost. Should the level of demand expand even further to OQ_3, although the plant represented by $SRAC_2$ is capable of producing OQ_3 units, the plant represented by $SRAC_3$ is preferable because of its ability to produce OQ_3 units at a lower average cost.

Of all the possible plant sizes, the one which is most efficient of all is the one whose *SRAC* curve is tangent to the *LRAC* curve at the *minimum point* of the *LRAC* curve.[12] The plant capable of producing the commodity at the lowest unit cost of all the other plants is termed the *optimum plant size*. In Figure 8-7 the optimum plant size is the one corresponding to $SRAC_4$— no other plant is capable of producing the commodity at as low an average cost as is the plant associated with $SRAC_4$. It is in this sense that $SRAC_4$ represents the optimum plant size.

Observe that the *LRAC* curve is *not* tangent to the *SRAC* curves at their minimum points except in the one case of the optimum plant size. When the *LRAC* curve is decreasing (up to an output of OQ_4 in Figure 8-7), the *LRAC* curve is tangent to the *SRAC* curves to the left of their minimum-cost points. Therefore, for outputs smaller than OQ_4, it is more economical to produce the desired output by "underusing" a slightly

---

[12] In the event that the *LRAC* curve has a horizontal segment, several plant sizes will qualify as the most efficient.

larger plant operating at *less* than its minimum-cost output than it is to construct a plant that will produce the desired output at the minimum point of its *SRAC* curve. However, when the *LRAC* curve is rising (past an output of OQ_4 in Figure 8-7), the *LRAC* curve is tangent to the *SRAC* curves to the right of their minimum cost points. Hence, at outputs greater than OQ_4 it is more economical to produce the desired output by "overusing" a slightly smaller plant than it is to build a larger plant to produce the desired output at the minimum point of its *SRAC* curve.

The U-shape of the *LRAC* curve clearly implies that, up to a certain output, constructing a larger-sized plant results in greater efficiency and lower unit costs, but beyond this output larger plants become progressively less efficient and entail higher unit costs. The *LRAC* curve is U-shaped because for a time successively larger plants entail greater efficiency and lower costs due to *economies of large-scale production*—thus the decline in *LRAC*. Eventually, the economies associated with larger size are exhausted and the *LRAC* reaches its minimum level. Thereafter, increases in plant size may be accompanied by *diseconomies of scale* such that there is an attendant loss in productive efficiency and a rise in the unit costs of production. The reasons for economies and diseconomies in plant scale are worth exploring.

Reasons For Economies of Scale At The Plant Level. At the plant level, lower unit costs basically derive from production economies. A larger plant can achieve greater subdivision of the production process and greater specialization in the use of resource inputs (labor, capital equipment, and supervision). In small plants each production worker typically performs several component tasks (or in extreme cases performs the whole task), whereas in a large plant the production operation is finely subdivided into a large number of small tasks. Although it may be monotonous for a worker to go through the same few motions for hours at a time, he learns to do his task much faster and with greater accuracy, no time is lost in switching from task to task, and machines and tools can be designed to assist him in doing his particular job. In fact, to mechanize production processes it is essential to subdivide them into segments which can be machine-executed. The result of specialization in the use of labor and machinery is almost invariably a dramatic rise in productivity.

In some production processes, the capital investment for using the most advanced and efficient technology runs into the millions of dollars. For example, in automobile plants the huge presses which stamp out automobile bodies in a matter of seconds, the automatic equipment which drills holes in the cylinder block in one operation, the large ovens which spray and bake paint on the car, the miles of assembly lines, and the mechanized equipment used to transport materials and finished parts from station to station on the production floor are simply too expensive and impractical to be used for producing a small number of cars. Only when thousands of cars are produced daily can the costs of capital-intensive technology be sufficiently spread out to reduce the cost per car to acceptable levels. Another example of the economies of large-scale plants is found in industries characterized by continuous-process production technologies. Steel firms have found it advantageous to have pig iron, raw steel, and semifinished steel products produced in one continuous operation in order to economize on reheating materials between phases of the production process.

Also, the larger a plant, the greater the opportunities for taking advantage of and utilizing by-products. Large steel mills usually maintain their own coking operations. Naptha is a by-product of producing coke from coal and can be commercially marketed by steel plants with a large enough coking facility to make the capture of naptha worthwhile. Similarly, in segments of the petroleum refining, meat packing, chemicals, and paper products industries, plants are constructed on a scale that allows advantage to be taken of various by-products. In capturing by-products firms realize salable output not otherwise obtainable and can use the revenues from their sale to defray production costs associated with the primary product.

A larger plant necessarily uses more raw materials. Once a plant reaches the size where it can buy raw materials in large volume, it can take advantage of quantity discounts on its purchases. Similarly, larger plants can ship their products in carload lots and/or realize transportation economies by instituting their own shipping system.

Finally, the costs of purchasing and installing larger machines and equipment are usually *not* proportionately greater that the costs of smaller machines with less capacity.[13] This gives large-sized plants an inherent ability to achieve lower average fixed costs, since they produce more units of output over which to spread proportionately smaller overhead costs.

Eventually, of course, plants can be enlarged to the point where all economies of scale are taken full advantage of; larger plants then bring no additional savings in unit costs. It is here that the minimum level of the *LRAC* curve for plants is reached. Whether the *LRAC* curve begins to rise immediately with further increase in plant size or whether it has a flat portion before turning upward depends upon technological, spatial, and managerial considerations, along with the specific nature of the production process itself. It is quite conceivable, even likely in many situations, that the *LRAC* curve remains horizontal for somewhat larger plants before it begins to rise, meaning that there may be a number of optimum-sized plants, each capable of producing at the lowest achievable unit cost. But there can be little doubt that continued increases in plant size will sooner or later result in diseconomies of scale.

Reasons for Diseconomies of Scale at the Plant Level. The more acres over which a plant is spread, the greater the bottlenecks and costs of getting labor, materials, and semifinished and finished goods from one place in the

---

[13] This point was made at greater length in the section on returns to scale in the preceding chapter.

plant to another. Moreover, the larger the plant the greater its raw materials requirements and the more likely that raw materials will have to be shipped to the plant from more distant suppliers, thereby driving up the cost of incoming shipments of raw material inputs. Similarly, the larger the plant, the greater its output and the further outputs must be shipped to reach potential buyers, thereby raising the costs of transporting the product from the point of manufacture to the final consumer. To these must be added the growing difficulties of maintaining efficient supervision and coordination. As an extreme example, imagine the incredible problems that would beset General Motors were it to try to produce all of its Buicks, Cadillacs, Chevrolets, Oldsmobiles, and Pontiacs at a single plant site—the logistics of managing 350,000 employees and millions of tons of material inputs would entail a colossal logjam and gross inefficiency.

The optimum plant size varies tremendously from industry to industry, mainly according to whether the industry's production technology requires large and indivisible units of capital input for low-cost production. Railroads, electric power facilities, automobile firms, steel mills, oil refineries, glassware firms, aluminum plants, and inorganic chemical firms all involve multi-million-dollar capital investments in a single plant before operations begin. On the other hand, the manufacture of garments, mobile homes, shoes, furniture, sporting goods, and precision instruments, as well as printing and publishing, coal mining, and farming, can be efficiently conducted in relatively small production units.

COST BEHAVIOR AND FIRM SIZE

Even after plants have been expanded to their most efficient size and all economies of *plant* size taken advantage of, there may arise additional cost savings in putting a number of plants under common management. These plants may perform the same kind of operation—a chain of motels or a number of garment plants—in which case the resulting firm is said to be *horizontally integrated*. Or the plants may be *vertically integrated* such that they perform successive phases of the same overall production process. All the major steel firms in the United States are vertically integrated in that they mine and ship iron ore, make pig iron, transform pig iron into steel, and produce a wide variety of finished steel products. Or further, the plants may involve the production of a number of unrelated commodities—such multiplant enterprises are called *conglomerates*. Some firms may exhibit these three characteristics simultaneously, such as General Electric, Standard Oil of New Jersey, General Motors, DuPont, Chrysler, RCA, Georgia-Pacific, and Ford—all of which are horizontally and vertically integrated and produce a variety of different commodities.

Reasons for Economies of Scale at the Firm Level. A number of factors combine to allow larger firms to achieve lower production costs than smaller firms. In the first place, putting several plants under common management economizes on top management costs. Every firm must have a board of directors, a president, vice-president, comptroller, sales manager, personnel director, legal counsel, and so on. Spreading the salaries of key executives and administrative staff over 5 million units of output a year instead of 1 million units lowers average cost. Second, larger firms are able to realize certain advantages in marketing their output. A nationwide distribution organization can be established to funnel goods from factory to retail outlets in the most efficient way. National advertising campaigns offer the opportunity for more effective canvassing of consumers per advertising dollar spent.[14] For example, General Motors in selling 5 million cars annually can well afford to spend $90 million advertising its cars (a paltry advertising cost of only $18 per car), but for American Motors to spend $90 million on advertising to sell 300,000 cars ($300 cost per car) would place them at a distinct price disadvantage. Third, a large enterprise can afford expert specialists for research, development, design, and production engineering, thereby maneuvering it into a better position to introduce new and improved products and to embrace new technologies. Fourth, the cost of capital tends to fall for larger firms as their credit rating rises, their securities assume blue-chip status, and internally generated funds accumulate. Large firms often are able to borrow at interest rates 1 to 3 percentage points below small- and medium-sized firms. Fifth, larger firms with their more ample financial strength can afford to acquire an able, creative management with all the attendant gains in managerial efficiency; this, in turn, gives larger firms organizational capabilities that tend to exceed those of smaller firms. Large corporations tend to have a greater capacity for generating new managerial technologies and this, in turn tends to result in superior strategies for competing in the marketplace. When exploited to its fullest potential, their higher order of managerial technology gives larger firms an organizational economy of scale that can produce sizable reductions in unit costs, thereby giving them an inherent and material cost advantage.[15]

Last, but far from least, large size achieved via vertical integration can be a distinct asset in superseding the market uncertainties associated with unreliable sources of supply and channels of distribution. Efficient production and low costs require minimal interruption of the routine of day-to-day operation. Where a firm is especially dependent on an important material or service, the danger exists that the requisite supplies will be disrupted and occasionally subject to unfavorable price increases. To own or at least control the supply of essential ingredient inputs is an elementary and sometimes quite beneficial way of subjecting these highly strategic cost factors

[14] This contention is documented in a study by William S. Comanor and Thomas A. Wilson, "Advertising and the Advantages of Size," *American Economic Review, Papers and Proceedings*, Vol. 59, No. 2 (May 1969), pp. 87–98.

[15] This point is developed in more detail in Oliver E. Williamson, *Corporate Control and Business Behavior* (Englewood Cliffs, N.J.: Prentice-Hall, Inc., 1970), especially Chaps. 8 and 9.

to internal decision. Similarly, unreliable outlets for a firm's products may prompt the establishment of a distribution network to permit the firm to realize the cost savings obtainable from steady and continuous operation of production facilities. Thus, it is not without design that heavy users of coal buy and operate coal mines, that major steel firms have their own sources of iron ore, that major oil refiners maintain aggressive divisions to search out deposits of crude oil on the one hand and to sell their products on the other hand, that Sears has a controlling interest in an appliance manufacturer, that General Motors has its own divisions to supply it with batteries, shock absorbers, air conditioning units, and various other automobile parts, that A&P has a division to supply it with bakery products and canned goods, and that Goodyear, Firestone, and B.F. Goodrich all give special attention to maintaining an effective chain of retail stores, including a number of company-owned and operated outlets.

Reasons for Diseconomies of Scale at the Firm Level.   It is argued that there are at least temporary limits to the economies derived from increasing size. The reason for supposing that a firm's long-run average cost curve eventually turns upward lies in the increasing difficulties and costs of managing ever larger enterprises. Conventional wisdom instructs that bureaucracy is not restricted to governmental units; it inhabits large corporations as well and with the same costly results.

However, in an age of computers, operations research, and rapidly advancing managerial technology, the case for an upward rising long-run average cost curve is less convincing. Certainly, decentralized management and improved managerial techniques combine to minimize, if not prevent, rising administrative costs per unit as size increases. To large enterprises, diminishing returns to managerial inputs present only temporary limits to firm size and growth; given sufficient time and imagination, ways can be found to surmount management-related obstacles to growth. This is the essence of advances in managerial technology, which is just as effective as the use of technology and innovation to solve other types of operating bottlenecks.

That firms can attain almost gigantic sizes without encountering any significant diseconomies is amply testified to by General Motors, General Electric, Sears, AT&T, IBM, and other multimillion-dollar enterprises. General Motors is reputed to produce at lower unit costs than its smaller competitors, and its profit *margins* are widest in those years when its sales volume is greatest. On the other hand, it is true that in some industries the long-run average cost curve turns upward rather quickly—most notably in farming and in services.

Actually, the limits to firm size may be less related to economics than to legal and political considerations. Having a disproportionately large share of the market for a commodity means flirting with the antitrust laws and inviting investigation from Justice Department officials crusading against the "evils of monopoly power." Likewise, it is questionable strategy to use aggressive tactics to drive one's rivals out of business. The Justice Department is just as suspicious of too much competition as it is of too little, especially when the former appears deliberately predatory or cutthroat.

Finally, it should be noted that large firms usually are at a price disadvantage in obtaining the services of blue-collar labor. Unions have had their greatest success in dealing with large enterprises; large firms often pay higher hourly wage rates than do small- and medium-sized firms. Thus, to the extent that larger size is accompanied by an increase in the ability of unions to secure higher wage rates, the large enterprise may find itself confronted with diseconomies of scale, unless it takes steps to offset them by means of automation or some other productivity-increasing strategy.

The Long-Run Average Cost Curve for Firms. As the foregoing discussion suggests, it is difficult to pinpoint the output when diseconomies of scale set in or when they become strong enough to override economies of scale. In some industries economies of scale are negligible, and diseconomies assume paramount importance at relatively low output rates. Panel (a) of Figure 8-8 shows a long-run average cost curve for firms in such situations. The points on the curve show the lowest feasible unit cost of production for various *firm* sizes when the *firm* has sufficient time to adjust its input combinations to optimum levels. Examples of firms with an *LRAC* curve of the shape in Figure 8-8(a) include those involved in farming, many of the retail trades, printing, and certain types of light manufacturing such as baking, electronics, instruments, concrete products, and soft drink bottling. Fairly small firms tend to be more efficient than large-scale producers in such industries.

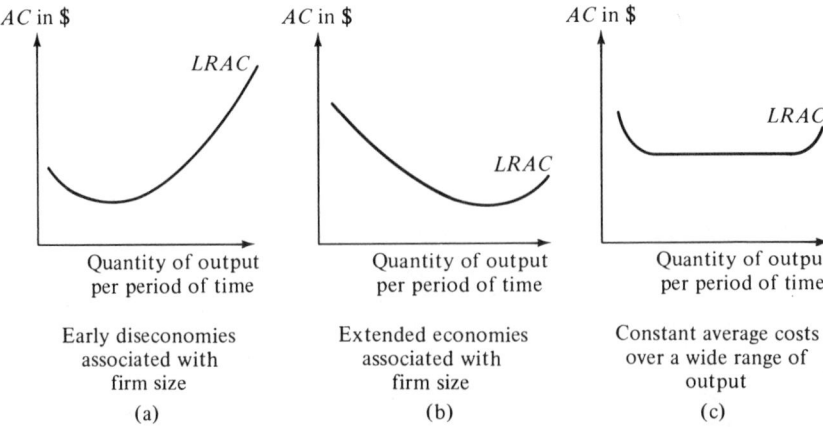

Fig. 8-8 Alternative Shapes for the Long-Run Average Cost Curve

In other industries economies of scale are extremely important, and the firm's *LRAC* curve declines significantly over a long range of output as in panel (b) of Figure 8-8. Here the limitations of consumer demand dictate that efficient production be achieved primarily with a small number of large firms. The automobile, aluminum, steel, railroad, aircraft, and farm implement industries are cases in point.

In still other industries the *LRAC* curve of firms is virtually horizontal over a wide range of output [see Figure 8-8(c)]. Economies of scale are quickly exhausted, yet diseconomies are not forthcoming until very large outputs are produced. Or, alternatively, economies and diseconomies cancel each other out over an extended range of output. The result is that small, medium, and large firms can operate with roughly an equivalent degree of efficiency. The meat-packing, apparel, furniture, oil, household appliance, coal mining, textile, food products, rubber, and chemical industries are representative of this type of long-run cost behavior.

Statistical analyses of long-run cost behavior in a preponderance of cases reveal an L-shaped pattern for the *LRAC* curve. Table 8-6 summarizes the results of several major studies of long-run cost functions. None of these studies presents conclusive evidence that large firms actually encounter significant diseconomies of scale in the range of observed data. Rather, the long-run average cost curve has generally been found to decrease and then level off as output rises. However, the failure to find much evidence of diseconomies of large size does not mean that the *LRAC* does not turn up-

Table 8-6   Results of Empirical Studies of Long-Run Cost Functions

Name	Type of Industry	Finding
Bain (1956)	Manufacturing	Small economies of scale for multi-plant firms.
Holton (1956)	Retailing	*LRAC* is L-shaped.
Alpert (1959)	Metal	Economies of scale up to an output of 80,000 lb. per month; constant returns to scale and horizontal *LRAC* thereafter.
Moore (1959)	Manufacturing	Economies of scale prevail quite generally.
Lomax (1951) and Gribbin (1953)	Gas (Great Britain)	*LRAC* of production declines as output rises.
Lomax (1952) and Johnston (1960)	Electricity (Great Britain)	*LRAC* of production declines as output rises.
Johnston (1960)	Life assurance	*LRAC* declines
Johnston (1960)	Road passenger transport (Great Britain)	*LRAC* either falling or constant.
Nerlove (1961)	Electricity (U.S.)	*LRAC* (excluding transmission costs) declines, then shows signs of increasing.

SOURCE: A. A. Walters, "Production and Cost Functions," *Econometrica*, Vol. 31, No. 1 (January 1963), pp. 1–66.

ward at some point. Instead, the evidence suggests that most firms have been wise enough to avoid becoming so large as to incur rising unit costs. The lack of large firms in several industries is adequate testimony to the existence of diseconomies, though it does appear that diseconomies may not be as pervasive as once imagined.

Summary and Conclusions

A constructive approach to measuring the cost of an activity is to consider the amount of sacrifice associated with conducting the activity. Completeness requires that the nature of the sacrifices considered be both tangible and intangible, objective and subjective, monetary and nonmonetary.

No one measure of cost is adequate for analytical and decision-making purposes. Depending on the type of problem, one may wish to determine explicit costs, implicit costs, opportunity costs, total costs, average costs, marginal costs, fixed costs, variable costs, direct costs, common costs, long-run costs, short-run costs, labor costs, controllable costs, shutdown costs, escapable costs, replacement costs, incremental costs, production costs, selling costs, administrative costs, and so on.

The cost-output relationships for a firm in the short run are governed by the character of the underlying production function. Given that the production function exhibits increasing returns to variable input, as output rises TFC remains constant, TVC and TC increase at a decreasing rate, and unit costs (AFC, AVC, ATC, and MC) decline.

When the underlying production function displays constant returns to variable input, rising output is associated with the following cost behavior: TFC is a fixed value, TVC and TC rise at a constant rate, MC and AVC are equal and constant, and AFC and ATC decline.

When the underlying production function is characterized by decreasing returns to variable input, increases in the output rate of the firm cause the TFC and TC functions to increase at an increasing rate, TFC remains fixed, AVC and MC rise, AFC decreases, and ATC is U-shaped.

When the production function has a range first of increasing returns and then of decreasing returns to variable input, the firm's TFC function is again a constant, but the TVC and TC functions both increase at a decreasing rate over the range of output where increasing returns to variable input prevail, then increase at an increasing rate over the output range where decreasing returns prevail. As usual, AFC decreases with increases in output irrespective of the nature of the returns to variable input. And the AVC, ATC, and MC are U-shaped functions, with the MC curve intersecting the AVC and ATC curves at their minimum points.

According to the best available empirical evidence, the behavior of total, average, and marginal costs in many firms combines elements of the four preceding basic types of production-cost-output relationships. At output rates well below "normal," increasing returns to variable input are encountered and unit costs fall as output rises. Beyond these abnormally low output rates constant returns to variable input prevail up to approximately 85 or 90 percent of capacity; over this output range total costs rise linearly, MC is a constant, and ATC declines. Past 90 percent of capacity, decreasing returns to variable input are encountered; TVC and TC begin to rise disproportionately to the additional increases in output, and AVC, MC, and ATC rise sharply.

In the long run, when the firm has time to alter its usage of any and all inputs, the firm will seek to adjust its scale of production so as to be able to produce the desired output at the lowest possible cost. In examining the relationships between long-run cost behavior and the scale of production it is important to distinguish between the optimum plant size and the optimum firm size. The $LRAC$ for a *plant* shows the minimum average cost of producing a commodity for various *plant* sizes when all resource inputs are variable and any desired scale of *plant* can be built. The $LRAC$ for a *firm* shows the minimum average cost of producing a commodity for various *firm* sizes when the firm has adequate time to adjust any and all of its inputs to optimal levels. By and large, the $LRAC$ curves for both plants and firms are U-shaped.

The behavior of long-run costs is a key force in determining the number and size of firms in a particular industry. Generally speaking, where significant economies are associated with mass production technologies, the structure of the industry will consist of a small number of large-scale producers. When there are few cost advantages to producing in large quantities and many cost disadvantages, production units will be large in number and small in size. In those cases where cost is virtually unaffected by the output rate, small, medium, and large firms may be able to compete on fairly equal terms.

SUGGESTED READINGS

ALCHIAN, ARMEN A., "Costs and Outputs," *The Allocation of Economic Resources*, edited by Moses Abramovitz *et al.* (Palo Alto, Calif.: Stanford University Press, 1959), pp. 23–40 .

APEL, HANS, "Marginal Cost Constancy and Its Implications," *American Economic Review*, Vol. 38, No. 5 (December 1948), pp. 870–885.

CLARK, J. M., *The Economics of Overhead Cost* (Chicago: University of Chicago Press, 1923), Chaps. 4–6.

DEAN, JOEL, *Managerial Economics* (Englewood Cliffs, N.J.: Prentice-Hall, Inc., 1951), Chap. 5.

EITEMAN, W. J., "Factors Determining the Location of the Least Cost Point," *American Economic Review*, Vol. 37, No. 5 (December 1947), pp. 910–918.

JOHNSTON, J., *Statistical Cost Analysis* (New York: McGraw-Hill, Inc., 1960), Chaps. 4 and 5.

KOOT, RONALD S., and DAVID A. WALKER, "Short Run Cost Functions of a Multiproduct Firm," *Journal of Industrial Economics*, Vol. 18, No. 2 (April 1970), pp. 118–128.

SPENCER, MILTON, *Managerial Economics*, 3rd ed. (Homewood, Ill.: Richard D. Irwin, Inc., 1968), Chap. 7.

TANGRI, OM P., "Omissions in the Treatment of the Law of Variable Proportions," *American Economic Review*, Vol. 56, No. 3 (June 1966), pp. 484–493.

VINER, JACOB, "Cost Curves and Supply Curves," reprinted in *Readings in Price Theory* (Homewood, Ill.: Richard D. Irwin, Inc., 1952), pp. 198–232.

WALTERS, A. A., "Production and Cost Functions," *Econometrica*, Vol. 31, No. 1 (January 1963), pp. 1–66.

WILLIAMSON, OLIVER E., "Hierarchical Control and Optimum Firm Size," *Journal of Political Economy*, Vol. 75, No. 2 (April 1967), pp. 123–138.

Problems and Questions for Discussion

1. Complete the following table:

Units of Output	TFC	TVC	TC	AFC	AVC	ATC	"Average" MC
0	——	——	$ 500	——	——	——	
100	——	——	750	——	——	——	——
200	——	——	1100	——	——	——	——
300	——	——	1500	——	——	——	——
400	——	——	2000	——	——	——	——
500	——	——	2600	——	——	——	——

2. Complete the following table. Assume that units of fixed input cost $10 each and units of variable input cost $20 each.

Units of Fixed Input	Units of Variable Input	Units of Output	"Average" Marginal Product of Variable Input	Average Product of Variable Input	TFC	TVC	TC	AFC	ATC	"Average" MC
100	0	0	——	——	——	——	——	——	——	——
100	20	600	——	——	——	——	——	——	——	——
100	40	1500	——	——	——	——	——	——	——	——
100	60	2000	——	——	——	——	——	——	——	——
100	80	2200	——	——	——	——	——	——	——	——
100	100	2300	——	——	——	——	——	——	——	——

3. Given the following total cost function:

$$TC = 10,000 + 9Q,$$

where Q = units of output.

(a) Determine the equations for *TFC* and *TVC* and illustrate graphically the relationships between *TFC*, *TVC* and *TC*.

(b) Determine the equations for *AFC*, *AVC*, *ATC*, and *MC*. Graphically illustrate their relationships to one another.

(c) What, if anything, can you infer about the nature of the underlying production function?

(d) How much is the marginal cost of the 100th unit of output? How much is *AVC* at an output of 100 units? Explain why $MC = AVC$ at each rate of output.

4. Given the following total cost function:

$$TC = 20,000 + 4Q + .5Q^2,$$

where Q = units of output

(a) Determine the equations for *TFC* and *TVC*. Graph the *TFC*, *TVC*, and *TC* functions and show their relationships to one another. How would you describe the behavior of *TVC* as output increases?

(b) Determine the equations for *AFC*, *AVC*, *ATC*, and *MC*. Graph each of these functions and show their relationships to one another.

(c) What is the nature of the underlying production function? What will its shape be?

5. Given the following information:

(a) $Q = 6X$, where X = units of variable input and Q = units of output.

(b) There are 10 units of fixed input,

(c) Price of the fixed inputs = \$10/unit,

(d) Price of the variable inputs = \$5/unit.

Determine the corresponding equations for *TFC*, *TVC*, *TC*, *AFC*, *AVC*, *ATC*, and *MC*.

6. The total cost function of a shirt manufacturer is

$$TC = 10 + 26Q - 5Q^2 + .5Q^3,$$

where *TC* is in hundreds of dollars per month and Q is output in hundreds of shirts per month.

(a) What is the equation for *TVC*?

(b) What is the equation for *AVC*?

(c) What is the equation for *ATC*?

(d) What is the equation for *MC*?

(e) Plot (or sketch) the relationship between *TFC*, *TVC*, and *TC*.

(f) Plot (or sketch) the relationships between *AFC*, *AVC*, *ATC*, and *MC*.

(g) What, if anything, can you infer about the nature of the underlying production function?

7. Given: $TC = 2000 + 15Q - 6Q^2 + Q^3$, where Q = units of output.

(a) How much is *TFC* at an output of 2000 units? at 5000 units?

(b) How much is *AFC* at an output of 2000 units? at 5000 units?

(c) How much is *AVC* at an output of 20 units?

(d) How much is *MC* at an output of 20 units?

(e) How much is *ATC* at an output of 20 units?

(f) At approximately what output rate is the point of diminishing marginal returns to variable input encountered?

(g) At approximately what output rate does diminishing average returns begin?

(h) At approximately what rate of output does stage II begin?

8. Given the following production function:

$$Q = 15X,$$

where X = units of variable input and Q = units of output. Units of variable input cost \$30 each and units of fixed input cost \$100 each. Ten units of fixed input are available.

    (a) Determine AFC at an output of 400 units.

    (b) Determine AVC when 10 units of variable input are combined with the 10 available units of fixed input.

    (c) How much is MC at an output of 300 units?

9. Prove that $MC = AVC$ at the minimum point of the AVC curve when the equation for TVC is of the general form $TVC = bQ - cQ^2 + dQ^3$. [*Hint:* See footnote 10.]

10. What is the relationship, if any, between marginal costs and fixed costs?

11. Given the following cost information:

    (a) AFC for 5 units of output is \$2000.

    (b) AVC for 4 units of output is \$850.

    (c) TC rises by \$1240 when the 6th unit of output is produced.

    (d) The ATC of 5 units of output is \$2880.

    (e) It costs \$1000 more to produce 1 unit of output than to produce nothing.

    (f) TC for 8 units of output is \$19,040.

    (g) TVC increases by \$1535 when the 7th unit of output is produced.

    (h) AFC plus AVC for 3 units of output is \$4185.

    (i) ATC falls by \$5100 when output rises from 1 to 2 units.

Using this information, fill in the table below:

Output	TFC	TVC	TC	AFC	AVC	ATC	MC
0	——	——	——	——	——	——	
1	——	——	——	——	——	——	——
2	——	——	——	——	——	——	——
3	——	——	——	——	——	——	——
4	——	——	——	——	——	——	——
5	——	——	——	——	——	——	——
6	——	——	——	——	——	——	——
7	——	——	——	——	——	——	——
8	——	——	——	——	——	——	——

IV

BUSINESS BEHAVIOR AND MARKET PERFORMANCE

9

The Goals
of Business Enterprises

A major task of microeconomic theory is to explain and to predict changes in prices and outputs as a consequence of changes in particular economic forces and public policies. This is not a simple matter in a trillion-dollar economy, where the forms of business enterprise range from the free-wheeling independent proprietorship to the multiproduct, billion-dollar modern corporation and where competition rarely assumes the same proportions from one industry to the next. However, all enterprises have a common trait which helps unify the approach to microeconomic analysis. Each firm's market strategies—its product mix, its prices, its advertising expenditures, its research and development activities and so on—are the result of decisions made by those in control of the enterprise. From the numerous alternatives available, and subject to the constraints imposed by each firm's economic environment, a firm's decision-makers can be relied upon to select the market strategies which they perceive best contribute to achieving the firm's goals. The goals of the firm are therefore fundamentally important in influencing its character, and they serve as a convenient starting place for analyzing business behavior in a market environment.

In this chapter we shall examine the goals of business enterprises, concentrating mainly on the profit motive. Particular consideration will be given to the character, source, and use of profit, the role and functions of profit in a modern economy, and whether firms seek to maximize profit. The last section of the chapter will present some major alternatives to profit maximization.

The Ambiguous Meaning of Profit

Profit is generally viewed as the difference between total revenue and total cost. In terms of symbols, $\pi = TR - TC$, where π represents profit. This concept of profit, although widely accepted and seemingly straightforward, is nevertheless quite ambiguous in its application. To the accountant "profit" usually means total revenue minus explicit costs; thus *accounting profit* is an *ex post* concept based upon past transactions and historical fact. To the economist "profit" means total revenue minus *all* costs—not just the money expenses incurred by the firm, but implicit and opportunity costs as well. This less than unanimous agreement over what constitutes a cost and how cost should be measured is a source of much of the controversy about how profits are or should be calculated.[1] In particular, various interpretations of cost give rise to the concepts of accounting profit, normal profit, and economic profit.

In the literature of economics much attention has been paid to discrepancies in profit measurement that may arise from failure to account for all of the costs (or sacrifices) incurred by the producer. It is easy to see, for instance, that valuing resources in terms of foregone alternative uses (the economist's opportunity-cost doctrine) is likely to be at variance with the accountant's practice of costing resources at their original purchase price less depreciation. Since accounting conventions for determining profit do not allow for a comprehensive inclusion of implicit and opportunity costs, the accountant's measure of profit typically exceeds the economist's. The most significant element of discrepancy relates to the treatment of the stockholders' capital investment in an enterprise. Suppose we explore this point briefly.

It is clear that in a capitalistic economy the stockholders of an enterprise must over the long run receive a profit of sufficient magnitude to induce their continued participation in the firm. Whenever their actual return on investment falls (for a period of significant duration) below what can generally be earned elsewhere on investments of equivalent risk, then stockholders can be expected to seek greener pastures for their investment funds.[2] Because

---

[1] Several illustrations of the alternative ways of calculating profits may be easily indicated. To begin with, differences in the amount of profit arise in determining the "correct" revenues and costs attributable to a given period as distinct from past and future periods. For example, fixed costs such as research, advertising, public relations, and managerial activities normally are allocated to the period in which such costs are incurred rather than to the future periods in which they are expected to influence sales, production costs, or the profits of the firm. Obviously, this accounting procedure is dictated by practical necessity, since only an oracle could accurately decide just how present costs should be distributed over future accounting periods. Still, the fact remains that the profit reported in any current period can be increased or decreased substantially by the amount and costs of future-oriented activities that are undertaken. Opportunities for wide differences in profit measurement also stem from the number of discretionary techniques with which depreciation may be calculated, inventories valued, maintenance undertaken, and the costs of fixed assets adjusted for price-level changes.

[2] The actual or realized return to stockholders takes two forms: dividends and increases in the value of their stock in terms of price per share.

additional resources and capital will tend to be withheld from an enterprise if and when the realized profits fall below "minimum acceptable levels," it is appropriate to conceive of this minimum return as a genuine cost. It is a cost in the sense that unless revenues from the firm's operations are adequate to provide an acceptable profit to the stockholders, the enterprise will lack the external financial support required for sustaining its activities and for undertaking expansion.

How large is this minimum acceptable return? Five percent? Ten percent? Actually a precise answer to this question is not feasible, since competitive rates of return vary with the circumstances—the risk involved, the time period, the amount of required investment, the health of the economy, the type of industry, the potential of the enterprise, and so forth. Nevertheless, it is evident that an enterprise must earn some minimum amount of profit if it is long to remain a viable entity. Accordingly, it has become customary in economics to think of the minimum profit that is necessary to keep a firm in business in the long run as being a cost of production. We shall refer to this minimum return to ownership as *normal profit*. Profit in the economic sense can therefore be thought of as the difference between the actual returns and the minimum acceptable returns to enterprise; or, to put it another way, *economic profit* is a return over and above a normal profit. Economic profit may be either positive or negative—positive if total revenue exceeds *all* costs, negative if total revenue is below total costs. Consider the following examples, which serve to illustrate the relationships between accounting profit, normal profit, and economic profit.

Example 1: Company A owns production facilities valued at $100 million. Its net earnings after taxes in 1970 were $12 million—as determined by accounting techniques. Assuming that the "normal" rate of return for firms of comparable position is 8 percent, then the company's normal profit should approximate $8 million (8 percent of $100 million). Company A's *economic profit* is $12 million − $8 million = $4 million. The $4 million represents that portion of the overall return to owners (stockholders) *over and above* what could be earned in comparable alternative ventures.

Example 2: Company X has made an investment of $50 million in facilities to produce high-speed copying equipment. According to conventional accounting measures, its earnings after taxes in 1970 were $5 million or 10 percent on investment. However, an evaluation of the alternatives open to Company X indicate that had the firm directed its energies to producing electronic desk calculators, net earnings after taxes could have been $6 million. Hence, even though Company X realized 10 percent return on its investment, it forewent the opportunity of earning 12 percent, thereby resulting in an *opportunity loss* of 2 percent.

Significantly, it is economic profit which serves as the prime motivator of business behavior.

Henceforth we shall endeavor to use the term profit to mean economic profit; a normal return or normal profit will be treated as part of total cost.

Still, even with this distinction well delineated, the concept of profit is replete with other ramifications that makes its definition elusive. For example, should profit be viewed with or without regard to profit taxes? Should profit be measured in dollars or as a rate of return—and if as the latter, as a rate of return on stockholders' equity or on total investment? And over what time period should profit be calculated?

One final point needs to be made. Insofar as both decision-making and the analysis of firm behavior are concerned, interest centers more on *expected* profit than upon realized profits.[3] Realized profits are relevant as a guide to action and to behavior only to the extent that they influence future profit expectations. Realized profits can also serve as the yardstick for measuring performance. Nonetheless, expected profit considerations must in the final analysis serve as the basis for making decisions and for predicting business behavior.

Theories of Profit

Ever since the emergence of the profit-oriented capitalistic type of economic system, the matter of profit has been the central point of attention and controversy. Economic literature abounds with discussion of the many aspects of profit—from whence it derives, the economic functions it performs, its ethical and moral qualities, whether profit is socially justified, and so forth. It will be instructive therefore to present a brief summary of various profit theories. For convenience our discussion of profit theories will be grouped into three broad categories:

1. Compensatory and functional theories of profit.
2. Friction and monopoly theories of profit.
3. Technology and innovation theories of profit.

This grouping is indicative of historical patterns of thinking on profit issues and for our purposes offers a logical approach to examining the manner in which profit arises.

COMPENSATORY AND FUNCTIONAL THEORIES OF PROFIT

As applied to small business, the compensatory and functional theories of profit hold that profit arises primarily from successful performance of the

---

[3] More precisely, managers are primarily interested in the size of the time-discounted profit flow—or, to put it another way, the *present value* of the expected stream of profits. The present value of the stream of profits flowing in from an investment is the amount of money that must be invested *now*, at some rate of return, to produce a cash flow equivalent to the expected profit flow. For a more complete explanation of present-value concepts, see Milton H. Spencer, *Managerial Economics*, 3rd ed. (Homewood, Ill.: Richard D. Irwin, Inc., 1968), Chap. 11.

entrepreneurial function. Specifically, it is said that profit is a payment to the entrepreneur in return for the services he performs in coordinating and supervising the many facets of the firm's activities and in bearing the risks of enterprise. The entrepreneur is the key force in initiating, integrating, and guiding the course of production to a successful conclusion; it is, in fact, the active exercise of business leadership toward productive ends that constitutes the essence of the entrepreneurial function. Profit is therefore the entrepreneur's reward for fulfilling his function successfully. Losses are the penalty for unsuccessful entrepreneurship.

In this view, the entrepreneur appears as a laborer of a very high type and talent. Profit becomes the special creation of the gifted entrepreneur, who by his comprehension of the marketplace, his capacity for organization, his administrative ability, and his energy, wisdom, and economy is able to generate an excess of total revenue over total cost. Profit, then, is more than something that just happens to be left over after all costs are covered; rather, its existence signals astute entrepreneurship, a vitality of enterprise, and economic progress.

While this explanation provides a valid rationale for the profits earned by individual proprietorships, partnerships, and small enterpreneurial corporations, it is at considerable variance with the realities of large corporate enterprise. There, salaried managers perform much of the entrepreneurial function, but the profits accrue to "absentee" stockholders. Consequently, other bases must be found for justifying the earning of normal and economic profit.

One such basis pertains to the entrepreneurial functions which stockholders perform even though they are absentee owners. In corporate enterprises the stockholder assumes a central role, since the firm depends heavily on capital supplied by risk-taking investors. In furnishing the corporation with money capital, the investor receives no assurance of a return on his investment in the form of dividends and/or capital gains. He may even lose money if the corporation's activities prove to be unprofitable. Unpredictable changes in the general economic environment, along with sudden changes in consumer tastes, resource supplies, government policy, and technology, combine to produce an abundance of uncertainty that tends to enrich some firms and impoverish others. Persons willing to accept the uncertainties of enterprise are entitled to a reward for the use of their capital —a reward which includes a premium for the degree of uncertainty borne by the investor.

The stockholder's profits, then, can be considered as a reward for bearing uncertainty and supplying venture capital. Naturally, a 20 percent *expected* return will not be valued as highly as a 20 percent *guaranteed* return. Depending upon the confidence investors place in the estimated profitability of a venture and upon their immediate inclinations toward either taking risks or avoiding them, they may evaluate a 20 percent expected return as equivalent to 10 percent on a sure thing, or just 8 percent, or even just 5 percent. Hence, while the stockholder is indeed an absentee owner, he still performs the essential entrepreneurial functions of bearing the uncertainties of enterprise and of supplying capital—both of which are crucial to the survival and success of the corporation. And the element of uncertainty explains why business firms must sometimes earn "high" profits if they are to keep investors willing to supply risk capital.

Another basis for the earning of profit is the service which the firm renders to the buyer. In this instance the profit earned by an enterprise reflects, at least in part, the value buyers place on the service the firm provides its customers. To the extent that the price a customer pays more than covers the cost of labor, materials, capital, taxes, and other expenses involved in manufacturing the commodity, the excess can be considered as *compensation* to the supplier for having solved the customer's problem—that of how to obtain a certain product or service at an acceptable price and at a convenient time and place. The proponents of this viewpoint observe that when firms are rewarded with profit for successfully combating market uncertainties and for fulfilling society's material wants, they tend to be more efficient, and living standards tend to rise faster. Why? Primarily because enterprises are more willing to innovate, more venturesome, and therefore more progressive when the prospects of above-average profits present themselves. It is to be expected that when the stakes are attractive, business firms will be more daring and their entrepreneurial spirit more vibrant. Moreover, the earning of economic profit enhances the financial ability of firms to invest in new activities and to absorb the periodic losses of those high-risk endeavors that turn sour.

FRICTION AND MONOPOLY THEORIES OF PROFIT

The theme underlying this grouping of profit theories is that various market frictions and the lack of vigorous competition combine to allow firms to earn "monopoly" profits. Profit is considered as resulting from positions of advantage. Ideally, the free play of market forces results in competitive forces that are powerful and responsive enough to prevent any "exploitation" of consumers. No firm is able to maneuver itself into the position of being able to fix prices or otherwise "rig the market" to its own advantage.

In the real world, of course, these ideal conditions are seldom, if ever, strictly met. Institutional and market rigidities exist in such abundance that many firms, both large and small, are able to achieve some degree of monopolistic advantage; accordingly, the ability to earn "monopoly profits" is not uncommon. Several illustrations of market imperfections can be readily cited. The granting of patents, trademarks, and copyrights enables the holder to legally exclude competitors from the field. Unusually favorable locations for businesses (motels, service stations, restaurants, and similar establishments) give them distinct advantages over less fortunately situated rivals. International trade barriers may give domestic producers a more strategic position in domestic markets. Military and other government installations bring profit bonanzas to adjacent localities. Where one or even a few producers dominate the market for a commodity, prices may be higher than would prevail if competition were more rigorous; examples include the local hotel in a small community, the convenience foodmart which stays open 24 hours a day, and the drug manufacturer with a new antibiotic cure. Windfall profits may be obtained for short periods of time as the result of circumstances (labor strikes, extreme weather conditions, natural disasters) that cause demand temporarily to exceed supply.

It would, however, be erroneous to conclude that monopoly power is a truly *important* contributor to the profits of very many firms in the sense that it accounts for or explains their abilities to earn more than a normal return. The capacity of firms to extort monopoly profits from consumers is easily and often exaggerated. Nor is it valid to conclude that monopoly profits are always socially undesirable relative to the alternatives. For example, society undoubtedly benefits from the practice of granting patents (a legal monopoly); to do otherwise would surely discourage inventive and innovative activities. And to expect powerful competitive conditions to pervade every nook and cranny of an economy is unreasonable—imagine the duplication of effort and inefficiency that would prevail were *every* local, regional, national, and international market for *every* commodity served by a large enough number of suppliers to guarantee that no one supplier have any advantage over its rivals. Scarcely anything could be more foolish or economically undesirable. We shall have more to say about the source and character of so-called monopoly profits, as well as their impact on society, in the chapters to come.

TECHNOLOGY AND INNOVATION THEORIES OF PROFIT

The unifying feature of the third group of profit theories is the potential of technology and innovation for providing the impetus for above-average profitability.[4] New methods of production and distribution can be introduced to lower costs or else neutralize cost-increasing factors. New and improved products can be introduced to generate favorable changes in revenues and/or

---

[4] The "innovation theory of profit" is chiefly associated with the late Joseph A. Schumpeter. He made a distinction between invention and innovation; the former he termed as the creation of something new, whereas the latter he viewed as the actual application of an invention in the production process. As originally expounded, Professor Schumpeter used innovation theory to explain business cycles rather than to identify the causes and character of profits. See especially his *Theory of Economic Development* (Cambridge, Mass.: Harvard University Press, 1934), Chap. 6.

prices. New managerial, financial, marketing, or accounting practices can be devised to allow more effective and efficient operation. Taken together, these practices constitute perhaps the most powerful and pervasive weapon business firms have for earning sustained economic profits.

Indeed, there can be no doubt that technologically superior production techniques and product innovations in large measure account for the ability of enterprises to realize large and growing profits. (Witness the billions of dollars earned by IBM, Xerox, Polaroid, DuPont, General Electric, and Eastman Kodak from precisely such strategies.) And especially can innovation bring economic profit to the first few adopters. However, after the few have shown the way, the many will follow. Unless there are legal or artificial barriers to wider use of an innovation, rival firms, attracted by the prospect of higher profits, will be induced to incorporate the innovation into their operations. As the innovation is widely adopted, competitive pressures stiffen, product prices are shaved in response to rising supply capabilities, and profits drift back down to "normal" levels as firms gradually lose their initial advantage. Thus the profits associated with a particular innovation tend to vanish, although it may take a long time before they completely melt away. But despite the temporary aspect of innovation profits, in a technologically dynamic environment innovation-generated profits are an ongoing feature; new successful innovations are constantly being introduced to replace older innovations whose associated profitability has already been undermined— such is the "perennial gale of creative destruction."[5]

A PERSPECTIVE VIEW OF PROFIT THEORIES

The foregoing presentation of profit theories makes it apparent that profit is a mixture resulting from a variety of influences, any number of which may be present at a given time. No single theory can adequately explain profit. Furthermore, the theories are not mutually exclusive; for example, the profit earned by an innovating firm derives in part from the monopoly which the superiority of its innovation provides. Also, careful studies and exhaustive analyses notwithstanding, firms do not know in advance whether an innovation will produce the results the blueprints predict; in this sense, the profits associated with innovation may be viewed as compensation for successful risk-taking.

While the above discussion of profit theories is intended to be suggestive rather than comprehensive, it should be helpful in delineating the role played by profit in business behavior. Profit must be a return to a firm resulting from

[5] The chemical and pharmaceutical industries offer classic examples of the process of creative destruction. In both these industries the pace of technological progress is rapid and competition is keen. Large profits are earned for short periods of time as new products are introduced, but the forces of competition soon cut severely into earnings as other firms develop similar products or as patents expire. Hence, the maintenance of high earnings is almost entirely dependent upon a firm's ability to sustain a steady flow of new products.

some element either within the firm or in its environment which differentiates it from other firms—in other words, *profit arises from the differential advantages among firms*. Since the advantages which can accrue to a firm are diverse, the sources of profit are heterogeneous.

THE SOCIAL BENEFITS OF PROFIT

Our discussion of profit theories has emphasized the sources of business profit and the role of profit as a reward for business acumen. Yet is important to recognize that the owners of enterprise are not the sole beneficiaries of profit—major benefits accrue to society as well. In line with traditional capitalist theory, the social justification for profit may be encapsuled as follows.

Profit-seeking enterprises find the rewards greatest for doing what society most wants done. It is virtually impossible for a firm to earn a profit by producing a commodity for which consumer demand is lacking. The size of the profit flow acts as a feedback mechanism, informing managers clearly and quickly in which direction to alter the composition of output. When an enterprise's profits exceed normal or expected levels, the clear indication is for managers to consider increasing the quantity of output and thereby to exploit the profit opportunities offered by strong consumer demand. Rising profits serve as society's signal for an industry to expand. At the same time, rising profits provide firms with the funds to assist in adding to their productive capacity. When profits are less than satisfactory, a reevaluation of the firm's product offering is warranted; if the low profitability is viewed as permanent, then a reallocation of the firm's resources to other more profitable ventures is in order. Consequently, the relative profitability of firms is ultimately a major determinant of both the level of utilization of society's resource pool and the allocation of resources among alternative uses.

With a profit-minded business sector there is an almost ironclad guarantee that production will be in harmony with demand. One might even say that business firms behave responsibly by seeking to earn the largest practicable amount of profit, for by so doing they will be producing what society is most desirous of having performed.[6] To put it a little differently, socially responsible business behavior requires that firms vigorously pursue the earning of profit, for it is through the profit mechanism that society signals business firms just which goods and services are most preferred by consumers. Indeed, one of the basic functions of the profit-loss discipline is to induce economic resources to be used in accordance with the tastes and preferences of consumers.

[6] For a more thorough discussion of this issue see Milton Friedman, *Capitalism and Freedom* (Chicago: The University of Chicago Press, 1962), pp. 133–136.

Society is also a prime beneficiary of the profit stemming from innovation. Innovation is a fundamental contributor to the process of economic growth and to advances in the standard of living, and it is, of course, the prospect of profit which stimulates innovative activity. Innovation acts as a spur to heavier capital investment, to expanded production capacity, to higher levels of output, and to growth in employment. These socially beneficial spinoffs from innovative activities are critical to the realization of economic progress and cannot be lightly dismissed.

But the strongest argument of all in behalf of profit relates to the role profit plays in allowing the firm to discharge its obligation to society as society's principal agent for producing and distributing goods and services. An unprofitable firm is not a healthy firm, nor is a firm which earns very low profits. Firms which are losing money or which earn substandard profits are in no position to grow and prosper; the job prospects they offer are dim; they are unlikely to be able to pay higher wages and salaries; they find it difficult to obtain credit; they are financially unable to commit substantial resources to innovation and technological advance; and they are thrust sooner or later into a weak competitive position. As a consequence, they contribute little, if anything, towards providing new jobs and expanding career opportunities, implementing new technologies, marketing important new commodities, raising living standards, and meeting the new and constantly emerging needs of society—all of which are crucial to enhancing society's overall economic welfare. The earning of what is generally considered to be at least adequate profits is, therefore, an essential prerequisite for business to be able to respond to society's needs in a positive and efficient fashion.

THE PROFIT RECORD OF BUSINESS ENTERPRISES

On the whole, profit-seeking enterprises are not totally deserving of the moral disapproval and greedy image which they have inherited. For instance, manufacturing profits before taxes as a percentage of sales have ranged in the neighborhood of 7 to 12 percent since 1949 (see Table 9-1); after-tax profits have approximated only 4 to 6 percent of sales. The rate of return before taxes on stockholders' ownership has fluctuated from 16 to 22 percent, depending upon overall economic conditions; the rate of return after taxes has usually been in the 8 to 12 percent range. Assuming a normal profit of 6 percent, then economic profits have amounted to an average of 2 to 6 percent annually—an amount which would not seem excessively large in terms of the associated degrees of uncertainty. The cynical view of the businessman as a cigar-smoking plutocrat who exploits helpless consumers to raise his already high rate of return is thus at variance with the evidence. And even to the extent that the profits of some firms are truly excessive, tax rates are easily adjusted to separate them from their large profits.

Table 9-1 Profits as a Percentage of Sales and as a Percentage of Stockholders' Equity, All
Manufacturing Corporations, 1949–1971.

	Profits as a Percentage of Sales		Profits as a Percentage of Stockholders' Equity	
Year	Before Federal Income Taxes	After Federal Income Taxes	Before Federal Income Taxes	After Federal Income Taxes
1949	9.3	5.8	18.6	11.6
1950	12.8	7.1	27.9	15.4
1951	11.2	4.8	27.9	12.1
1952	9.2	4.3	22.1	10.3
1953	9.2	4.3	22.6	10.5
1954	8.4	4.5	18.5	9.9
1955	10.3	5.4	23.8	12.6
1956	9.7	5.3	22.6	12.3
1957	8.8	4.8	20.0	10.9
1958	7.4	4.2	15.4	8.6
1959	8.8	4.8	18.9	10.4
1960	8.0	4.4	16.6	9.2
1961	7.7	4.3	15.9	8.9
1962	8.2	4.5	17.6	9.8
1963	8.5	4.7	18.4	10.3
1964	8.9	5.2	19.8	11.6
1965	9.4	5.6	22.0	13.0
1966	9.3	5.6	22.5	13.4
1967	8.3	5.0	19.3	11.7
1968	8.8	5.1	20.8	12.1
1969	8.4	4.8	20.1	11.5
1970	6.8	4.0	15.7	9.3
1971[a]	7.1	4.2	16.4	9.7

a For the first nine months only.

SOURCE: *The Economic Report of the President*, February 1972, pp. 281–282.

Do Business Firms Seek to Maximize Profits?

As a consequence of the role and function of profits in a capitalistically-oriented economy, most economists in the course of analyzing business behavior have assumed that firms behave as if they seek to maximize profits. Traditional theory of the firm does not merely postulate that profit is a goal of business enterprise. It states that *the* goal is maximum profit, and that businessmen will pursue this goal in a rational, deliberate manner. Although it would be stretching matters somewhat to conceive of profit maximization as meaning that a firm will point its *every* action and decision in a direction coldly calculated to obtain the largest excess of revenue over cost, it does imply that a decision-maker faced with two or more alternatives resulting in different outcomes can usually be counted upon to select the alternative that will move the firm towards (or to) the greatest profit.

A wealth of literature has sprung up regarding the validity of relying upon the assumption of profit maximization in constructing theoretical models to explain and predict business responses to market forces.[7] Both sides have argued from positions of strength, though each appears vulnerable on certain points. Table 9-2 summarizes the main arguments in support of profit maximization. Table 9-3 presents the chief criticisms of the assumption that firms behave as if they seek to maximize profits. The reader is urged to study the content of these tables carefully, since the issues involved are especially pertinent for analyzing business behavior and for developing a satisfactory theory of modern American capitalism.

A SENSE OF PROPORTION

A close examination of Tables 9-2 and 9-3 suggests that both the critics and the defenders of the profit-maximization assumption have persuasive arguments in their favor. Fortunately, it is not necessary to choose between full acceptance or all-out condemnation of the profit-maximizing assumption. An intermediate position is especially attractive, for it allows use of the meritorious arguments on both sides. As it turns out, assuming that firms seek to maximize profits is for many analytical purposes a fruitful postulate, capable of yielding good explanatory and predictive results. It gives us a conception of the broad purpose, the stance, and the unifying intent of business firms as a group. Yet, on other occasions, use of this assumption is not so satisfactory. The important thing is to be able to discriminate between the circumstances where the profit maximization assumption will suffice and the circumstances where other goals should be recognized and incorporated into the analysis.

Insofar as the analysis of firm behavior is concerned, profit is sure to be a goal of nearly every enterprise—probably the predominant goal. Profit is a universal measure of business performance; invariably, financial statements of firms focus upon the amount of profit. Few managers consistently and knowingly will go so far as to pursue policies calculated to yield long-run profits far below what their firms could otherwise earn. Nonetheless, some

---

[7] The interested reader may wish to consult the discussions by Lester, Machlup, Oliver, Blum, and Gordon beginning in the *American Economic Review* in 1946. Pertinent literature of more recent vintage includes Joseph W. McGuire, *Theories of Business Behavior* (Englewood Cliffs, N.J.: Prentice-Hall, Inc., 1964); H. A. Simon, "Theories of Decision Making in Economics and Behavioral Science," *American Economic Review*, Vol. 49, No. 3 (June 1959), pp. 253–283; William Baumol, *Business Behavior, Value and Growth*, 1st ed. rev. (New York: Harcourt Brace Jovanovich, Inc., 1967); Edith Penrose, *The Theory of the Growth of the Firm* (New York: John Wiley & Sons, Inc., 1959); Robin Marris, "A Model of the 'Managerial' Enterprise," *Quarterly Journal of Economics*, Vol. 77, No. 4 (May 1963), pp. 185–209; R. M. Cyert and J. G. March, *A Behavioral Theory of the Firm* (Englewood Cliffs, N.J.: Prentice-Hall, Inc., 1963); O. E. Williamson, *The Economics of Discretionary Behavior: Managerial Objectives in a Theory of the Firm* (Englewood Cliffs, N.J.: Prentice-Hall, Inc., 1964); R. F. Lanzilotti, "Pricing Objectives in Large Companies," *American Economic Review*, Vol. 48, No. 5 (December 1958), pp. 921–940; William L. Baldwin, "The Motives of Managers, Environmental Restraints and the Theory of Managerial Enterprise," *Quarterly Journal of Economics*, Vol. 78, No. 3 (February 1964), pp. 238–256; and Gerald L. Nordquist, "The Breakup of the Maximization Principle," *Quarterly Journal of Economics and Business*, Vol. 5, No. 3 (Fall 1965), pp. 33–46.

Table 9-2   Summary of Arguments Why Firms Behave As If They Seek To Maximize Profits

Arguments for Profit Maximization	Supporting Rationale
The profit motive is the strongest, the most universal, and the most persistent of the forces governing business behavior.	Although firms may pursue goals other than profit, the impact of such goals upon behavior is quite small. Hence, imputing "more realistic" goals to the firm yields no *significant* improvement in explanation or prediction while greatly increasing the complexity of the analysis.
Competition forces firms to adopt a goal of maximum profits.	Where competition is keen, firms must display a behavior pattern very closely akin to profit maximization in order to stand a chance of earning any profit at all. Knowledge that only the fittest will survive is a powerful incentive for all firms to direct their energies in profit-maximizing directions, learning whatever skills are required and emulating firms which are visibly successful in the battle for survival.
Assuming that business firms behave as if they seek to maximize profits is an appropriate theoretical approach so long as such an assumption allows accurate predictions to be made about behavior.	The only valid test of a theory is its predictive power. Whether an assumption is realistic enough can be settled only by examining the predictive ability of the theory. Since economists have had considerable success in using the profit-maximizing assumption as a basis for predicting the price and output behavior of business firms, the merit of using this assumption in theoretical models is well established.
The profit-maximizing assumption is a useful aid in obtaining a general understanding and explanation of the behavior of groups of firms.	Microeconomic theory is not designed to explain and predict the behavior of *particular* firms; instead it is designed to explain and predict changes in observed prices and outputs as consequences of particular market forces (such as changes in wage rates, resource prices, or taxes). In accomplishing this purpose, the firm serves only as a theoretical link for identifying how one gets from the causes of business behavior to the effects of business behavior. This is altogether different from conceiving of the firm as an object of study in itself and of trying to predict and explain the behavior of Texaco or Holiday Inns.

REFERENCES: 1. Milton Friedman, "The Methodology of Positive Economics," *Essays in Positive Economics* (Chicago: The University of Chicago Press, 1953), pp. 22–23.
2. Fritz Machlup, "Theories of the Firm: Marginalist, Behavioral, Managerial," *American Economic Review*, Vol. 57, No. 1 (March 1967), p. 9.
3. Melvin W. Reder, "A Reconsideration of the Marginal Productivity Theory," *Journal of Political Economy*, Vol. 55, No. 5 (October 1947), pp. 453–454.
4. George J. Stigler, *The Theory of Price* (New York: The Macmillan Company, 1952), pp. 148–149.

Table 9-3 Summary of Arguments Why Firms Do Not or Cannot Maximize Profits

Arguments Against Profit Maximization	Supporting Rationale
Uncertainty prevents firms from maximizing profits, even if they wish to do so.	Business decisions are made in a fog of uncertainty; managers are not aware of all the alternative courses of action much less the possible outcomes associated with each known alternative. Consequently, the path along which profit can be maximized is not easily identified because of imperfect information about demand, costs, competitive responses of firms, and general economic conditions.
Because of imperfect information and uncertainty, it is usually not possible to say unequivocally which of several courses of action appears to be the profit-maximizing alternative. Hence, profit maximization becomes a meaningless goal and prescription for decision-making.	Although a variety of "rules" and approaches have been devised to aid in decision-making under conditions of uncertainty (Chapter 2), the "best" rule for a firm in one decision situation may not be "best" in another decision situation. Nor is the "best" rule for one firm necessarily identical to the "best" rule for another firm. If, because of uncertainty, each firm concludes that profit maximization can be attained by a different route, then the profit-maximizing assumption has little utility in predicting business behavior.
In the large corporation the separation of control from ownership gives managers the discretion to pursue goals other than maximum profit.	Why should managers assume the onerous task of maximizing the monetary gains of stockholders? What motive is there for them to do so? Managers rarely encounter interference from stockholders so long as earnings remain "acceptable" and show a persistent tendency to increase. Furthermore, competitive pressures are often neither powerful nor quick enough to keep firms on the tightrope of economic survival; this gives corporate managers the discretion to pursue goals other than profit.
Many readily observable business practices are inconsistent with profit maximization.	Separation payments to discharged employees, beautification projects around plant facilities, donations to charity, the failure of executives to spend their whole day hard at work, and the failure of cost-accounting practices to generate the data required for maximizing profits are all examples of deviations from profit-maximizing behavior. Also, managers may be anxious to maintain such harmonious relations with employees that they tolerate lax work habits and agree to restrictive work practices and cost-increasing union work rules.
Firms find it advantageous to avoid making as large a profit as possible.	Some of the most important reasons for not maximizing profits include (a) a fear of attracting competition from firms which have the potential to enter the industry, (b) a fear of provoking antitrust action, and (c) a belief that holding profits down to "satisfactory" levels will restrain union wage demands and will promote stronger public relations.

Table 9-3 (cont.)

Arguments Against Profit Maximization	Supporting Rationale
Maximizing profit is too difficult, unrealistic, and immoral.	Strictly speaking, profit maximization requires businessmen to use every trick in the trade to keep wages and fringe benefits down, to charge as high a price as the consumer can and will pay, to sell as low a quality of merchandise as they can legally hoodwink the consumer into buying, to disclaim any community responsibility, to finagle the lowest prices from suppliers, and so on. Firms seldom pursue these tactics as zealously as is suggested by profit-maximizing behavior.

REFERENCES: 1. R. N. Anthony, "The Trouble with Profit Maximization," *Harvard Business Review*, Vol. 38, No. 6 (November-December 1960), pp. 126-134.
2. Neil W. Chamberlain, *Enterprise and Environment* (New York: McGraw-Hill, Inc., 1968), Chap 4.
3. John Kenneth Galbraith, *The New Industrial State* (Boston: Houghton-Mifflin Company, 1967), p. 117.
4. Melvin W. Reder, "A Reconsideration of the Marginal Productivity Theory," *Journal of Political Economy*, Vol. 55, No. 5 (October 1947), pp. 452.

firms are almost certain to evidence more profit-conscious and profit-oriented behavior than are others. The most intensely profit-seeking firms may approximate profit-maximizing behavior so closely that we may safely assume profit is the only goal of the firm that really matters for decision-making. At the other extreme, however, is a group of firms with goals other than profit—firms with a primary objective of earning at least a minimum acceptable profit, but desirous of satisfying some secondary set of objectives as well.[8] Their decisions will be only partially conditioned by profit considerations, and if their behavior is to be explained and accurately predicted, analysts cannot be content to rely upon the profit-maximizing assumption.

By and large, proprietorship, partnerships, and enterpreneurial corporations—the so-called periphery firms—are most likely to exemplify profit-maximizing behavior. On the other hand, objectives other than profit are likely to assume their greatest prominence in large, multiproduct corporations (center firms). The reasons are fairly simple.

In small firms, the owner has close personal contact with the daily operation of the enterprise. The goals of the firm conform closely to the goals of the owner. An intimate relationship exists between profit and the reward for successful ownership; in faet, the owner's economic welfare is a direct function of the profit performance of the firm. Frequently, the firm's profits constitute the owner's primary source of income. Moreover, as was suggested in Chapter 1 and as will be examined in more detail in Chapter 10, owner-managed firms typically operate in highly competitive markets where profit margins are thin, security is shaky, and the ability of firms to absorb losses is weak—there exists a fierce struggle in which only the fittest will survive. Market forces allow little room for discretionary action. Under such conditions, profit becomes an overriding concern, and profit considerations virtually dominate all policy decisions. The elected courses of action are extremely likely to be those *perceived* to have the greatest expected profit. Thus, it is reasonable to anticipate that the behavior of these firms will parallel that of profit maximization. In methodological terms, the profit-maximizing assumption, although not always an exact representation of reality, is nevertheless a sufficiently good approximation to the real-world behavior of most small enterprises in most situations. Certainly it is the best *single* assumption which can be made about the goals of these firms.

On the other hand, the large corporation, operating in markets where short-run competitive pressures are less intense, exemplifies the type of enterprise most likely to deviate from a profit-maximizing pattern of behavior. The assumption underlying this line of reasoning is that corporate managers, emancipated from the stockholders' control and from the rigors of short-run

---

[8] Conceivably, there may be some firms in which the profit goal is consistently subordinate to the achievement of other goals. But the list of firms which can afford the luxury of relegating profit to positions of lesser importance in the goal hierarchy is very short, and their role in the private sector of the economy is minimal.

competition, have some discretion to formulate and pursue goals of their own choosing so long as profits remain at or above levels sufficient to satisfy the stockholders. It would, however, be a gross exaggeration to presume that managers' goals alone motivate the market behavior of these large corporations. Both market and nonmarket factors restrain managers in selecting and pursuing goals other than profit. Not the least of these is the imperative to keep profits at a satisfactory level. No firm can long remain viable if it fails to earn a profit. Consequently, there can really be no doubt that profit is far and away the chief concern of the managers of large corporations *unless and until profits reach an acceptable minimum.*[9] But once managers see to it that minimum acceptable profit levels are assured, secondary goals can begin to assume attention in the councils of decision-making, although managers seldom lose sight of the impact that satisfaction of other goals will have on profits.[10] However, the success that large corporations have in pursuing goals other than profit depends upon the presence of a favorable economic environment. If actual or potential competition is sufficiently strong, consumer demand is weak, or the state of the economy depressed, then the firm may be effectively thwarted in its pursuit of secondary objectives.

Therefore, in constructing models for analyzing microeconomic problems, the assumption of profit-maximizing behavior is especially suitable in those situations where (1) *large* groups of firms are involved and nothing has to be predicted about the behavior of individual firms, (2) competitive forces are relatively intense, (3) the *effects* of a specified change in conditions upon prices, outputs, and resource inputs are to be explained and predicted rather then the values of these magnitudes before or after the change, and (4) only the directions of change are sought rather than precise numerical results.[11] Problems concerning large corporations, situations where the number of firms is small and the behavior of any one firm affects the behavior of others, and questions calling for numerical answers require a rather explicit identification of firm goals before a meaningful analysis can be conducted. Generally speaking, an assumption of profit maximization usually suffices for analyzing the behavior of periphery firms, whereas the profit goal must frequently be considered in conjunction with other goals if corporate behavior is to be understood.

Suppose we now turn to a consideration of some of the more prominent alternatives to the singular goal of maximum profits.

---

[9] Witness, for instance, the wave of cost-cutting campaigns, firm reorganizations, and overall belt-tightening that hits the business community when business turns sour and profits fall (as during late 1969 and 1970). It is when profits turn into losses that management discovers how much inefficiency it has been tolerating. Also, the plight of the Penn Central Railroad, and the recurrent losses realized by American Motors, Chrysler, Ling-Temco-Vought, Admiral, and other "name" firms serve as additional cases in point.

[10] Oliver Williamson contends that the multidivisional form of corporate organization makes considerable use of profit criteria within its units and also relies heavily upon profit criteria in its overall resource allocation decisions within the enterprise. See Oliver E. Williamson, *Corporate Control and Business Behavior* (Englewood Cliffs, N.J.: Prentice-Hall, Inc., 1970).

[11] Machlup, "Theories of the Firm," p. 31.

The Alternatives to Profit Maximization

Observers of contemporary corporate capitalism have advanced a host of alternative goals which conceivably can assist in explaining and predicting the market behavior of business firms, especially large corporations. Some of these alternatives, if achieved, will cause profits to be less than they might be otherwise, while others actually support the earning of profit in the long run.

SATISFICING BEHAVIOR

It has been suggested by a number of observers that business firms aim at a "satisfactory" rate of profit rather than maximum profit.[12] That is, firms *satisfice* rather than maximize with respect to their pursuit of the profit goal. This contention is founded upon the theory that managers in guiding corporate activities basically pursue satisficing strategies and not maximizing strategies. According to Herbert Simon, "Administrative theory is peculiarly the theory of intended and bounded rationality—of the behavior of human beings who *satisfice* because they have not the wits to *maximize*."[13]

From a practical standpoint, seeking the optimum course of action at each and every decision fork (a necessary act if one is to maximize) is an especially difficult and burdensome chore. More particularly, it simply is not man's nature to maximize; it is far easier to seek *satisfactory* solutions to problems than it is to seek *optimum* solutions.[14]

Briefly, the picture of the modern corporation as seen through the eyes of the satisficing theorists is as follows. The corporation operates in an uncertain environment with imperfect information and aspires to earn future profits at least as great as, and probably greater than, current earnings. When confronted with the necessity of making a decision, corporate managers draw upon past and present experiences and upon decision-making conventions, finally choosing an alternative from among the number known to exist that they expect will produce a satisfactory stream of profit. Thus, despite uncertainty, managers are able to use the information at their disposal to steer the firm in specific directions. But they abandon the attempt to maximize profits because the search process for finding the maximizing alternatives is too complicated and the available data are too poor. The preference instead is for attaining certain satisfactory standards of performance.

Besides uncertainty considerations, there is another rationale for

---

12 For example, see Herbert A. Simon, *Models of Man* (New York: John Wiley & Sons, Inc., 1957); Simon, "Theories of Decision Making in Economics and Behavioral Science"; Cyert and March, *A Behavioral Theory of the Firm*, and other works by the same authors. Also, see Julius Margolis, "The Analysis of the Firm: Rationalism, Conventionalism, and Behaviorism," *Journal of Business*, Vol. 31, No. 3 (July 1958), pp. 187–199.

13 Herbert Simon, *Administrative Behavior*, 2nd ed. (New York: The Macmillan Company, 1957), p. xxiv.

14 Satisficing has been tested in experimental goal-seeking and problem-solving situations and appears to be a verifiable trait of human behavior. See J. G. March and H. A. Simon, *Organizations* (New York: John Wiley & Sons, Inc., 1958), pp. 140–141, and R. M. Cyert and J. G. March, "Organization Factors in the Theory of Oligopoly," *Quarterly Journal of Economics*, Vol. 70, No. 1 (February 1956), pp. 44–64.

satisficing behavior on the part of corporate managers. Contemporary corporate theory views management as being trustees of the organization with responsibilities not only to stockholders but to employees, customers, creditors, suppliers, communities, government, and society as well. Modern professional managers face the sticky problem of reconciling the claims of stockholders for dividends and higher stock prices with the demands of employees for higher wages and better fringe benefits, consumers for lower prices and higher-quality products, retailers for wider profit margins, government for more tax revenues, suppliers for more stable purchasing arrangements, communities for a cleaner environment—all within a framework that will be constructive and acceptable to society. According to this philosophy of corporate management, the manager's function as trustee for all these participants and constituencies is to seek a statesmanlike balance among the diverse interests, resolving conflicts and competing claims and, to whatever extent is feasible, advancing the welfare of *all* groups who have a stake in the organization.

Moreover, within the management group itself, there are large numbers of people in middle management as well as in top management who occupy key decision-making and policy-formulating positions. Many of these people share the same interests—production, sales, personnel relations, finance, research and development, public relations, and so on—and form coalitions to further their common interests. For example, those managers involved with production (along with the affected employees) are likely to evidence considerable concern about keeping production from varying more than a tolerable amount from one time period to another and about future production equaling or exceeding current production. Those persons most intimately associated with the production phase of the firm's operations therefore have production goals which reflect organization pressures for stable employment, ease of production scheduling, developing acceptable cost performance, and output expansion. Still another portion of the managerial hierarchy can be counted upon to focus upon the importance of sales effectiveness—including the level of sales and the firm's market share. Sales goals reflect the demands of the sales department and secondarily the demands of those who view effective sales performance as critical to the success and stability of the organization. And, of course, along with production and sales goals, other coalitions of interest in the corporation will press for goals relating to wages and salaries, profits, inventory levels, security, leisure, status, financial liquidity, public relations, research and development activities, technological superiority, and so on.

Thus, the large corporation is confronted with many centers of power of varying potency. Top management has the function of presiding over the complex of diverse interests involved. According to the satisficing theorists, decisions on the goals of the corporation are reduced to a matter of politics, tradeoffs, and compromises. In such an environment, maximizing the monetary well-being of stockholders is not acceptable, nor is maximizing the achievement level of any of the goals of the other participants and constituencies in the enterprise. Instead, managers are forced to conduct the affairs of the enterprise in ways that will maintain some sort of equitable working balance among the claims of the various directly-interested groups (stockholders, employees, customers, managerial factions, government, various interest groups, and the public at large). The result is a balancing of conflicts and not the simple maximization of profit at the expense of all other considerations. The pursuit of any one goal is constrained by the requirement to *satisfy* at least minimally the demands of competing interests; no one center of power, especially the stockholders—who have the least detailed knowledge about the organization of all the competing groups involved—has the organizational support needed to impose its goal on all the others and thereby maximize its attainment. As a consequence, satisficing behavior and the seeking of satisfactory standards of performance become the rule rather than the exception in the formulation of corporate policy and corporate strategy. Corporate managers are induced to adopt strategies for earning a "satisfactory profit," charging "fair prices," obtaining a "satisfactory share of the market," and growing at an "acceptable rate." And they are forced to adopt policies that make the corporations responsive to all of its constituencies and to the whole of society.

SALES REVENUE MAXIMIZATION

One of the most widely discussed alternatives to profit maximization has been proposed by Professor William Baumol.[15] He contends that large corporations rank dollar sales ahead of profits as the main object of their concern. Baumol sets forth a number of reasons why corporations tend to be primarily concerned about the magnitude of sales revenues. Declining (or even constant) sales entail potentially serious consequences. Consumers shun products they believe are losing popularity; more critically, distributors may decide to switch over to competing brands where sales prospects are more attractive, thereby dealing a grave marketing setback to firms with lagging sales. Investors and lenders become both hesitant and stringent in committing funds to support enterprises whose absolute or relative sales revenues are declining. In static or declining firms, personnel relations become more difficult, owing to the unpleasantness associated with departmental budget cuts, layoffs, and dismissals. Any position of advantage a firm has in its markets is undermined and its ability to respond effectively to competitive pressures is weakened when sales fall off. Such firms are particularly vulnerable to a deterioration in general business conditions. And, finally, managerial self-interest dictates an expansive sales strategy, since executive salaries appear to be more closely correlated with the scale of a firm's operations than with its

---

[15] Baumol's thesis is fully developed in Chapter 6 of his *Business Behavior, Value and Growth* previously cited. This section draws heavily from his discussion therein.

profitability. The gist of these concerns about the magnitude of sales revenues is that gains in sales revenue serve as one of the most important yardsticks by which successful performance is measured.

Although Baumol maintains that profit considerations are subordinated to sales, he indicates they are by no means disregarded altogether. It is imperative that profits be kept high enough to satisfy stockholders and to help finance an expansion of sales and output. These funds can be gotten internally from retained earnings, or they can be obtained externally from new stock issues and borrowing. However, the willingness of bankers and investors to supply the firm with money capital depends directly on profits— the larger are profits (current and expected), the more funds a firm can attract from the capital market. Large corporations therefore find it advantageous to keep profits high enough to attract capital, though not so high that they severely impair selling additional outputs and pushing sales revenues to new peaks. But according to Baumol, once profits reach the level required to sustain the firm's need for capital, greater sales revenues rather than greater profits become the overriding objective of corporate strategy.

MARKET-SHARE CONSIDERATIONS

A number of large corporations profess to have a market-share goal.[16] Needless to say, a firm's competitive position is jeopardized unless it gains acceptance for its products; for this reason alone, a corporation can be expected to have some goal relating to sales effectiveness. It is obvious that good market position is a valuable asset—so valuable, in fact, that its achievement will govern short-term marketing decisions. The value of a firm's market share is not merely defensive; it also indicates the firm's ability to respond positively to unanticipated developments. In this sense, achievement of a strong market position supports attainment of profit and sales goals under conditions of uncertainty.

Market share, however, is not likely to be the principal goal of the firm. Too diligent a pursuit of market share may endanger profitability (as indicated by the deleterious effect on Armour of its efforts to overtake Swift in the meat packing industry).[17] Too successful a pursuit of an ever-larger market share may produce a market dominance that invites antitrust action.[18] A goal which a firm can attain only by risking survival, or which a firm is capable of exceeding but must be careful not to, ceases to be by itself an adequate goal or a standard of performance.

[16] Robert F. Lanzilotti, "Pricing Objectives in Large Companies," *American Economic Review*, Vol. 48, No. 5 (December 1958), pp. 921–40; A. D. H. Kaplan, J. B. Dirlam, and R. F. Lanzilotti, *Pricing in Big Business: A Case Approach* (Washington: The Brookings Institution, 1958), pp. 181–200; and Burnard H. Sord and Glenn A. Welsh, *Business Budgeting* (New York: Controllership Foundation, 1958), p. 149.

[17] The Armour-Swift story is told in "Beat Swift and Go Broke," *Fortune*, October 1959, p. 123.

[18] General Motors is said to exercise care that its share of the automobile market does not go much beyond the 55 percent level. General Electric officials have stated they do not wish to exceed 50 percent of any given market; moreover, "the company would rather be pushing to expand a 25 percent share than defending a 50 percent share." See Lanzillotti, *Pricing in Big Business*, p. 933.

328

LONG-RUN SURVIVAL

Some economists express the opinion that business behavior is motivated most strongly by the urge to survive.[19] The firm as a social and economic organization, like living organisms, has a compelling instinct to survive that is even more fundamental than the profit motive. In the view of these economists, expanding sales, market shares, and profits are relevant because they contribute to the long-run survival and viability of the firm. However, they point out that a firm might maximize profit and still not survive. Inadequate liquidity, shrinking markets, takeovers by acquisition-minded firms, and so on may spell the end even for profitable firms.

The relevance of long-run survival is apparent. Yet survival seldom is an explicit primary goal of a firm; usually, long-run survival considerations serve to provide a pervasive set of limitations upon the pursuit of all other goals including profit. But once survival over the near future seems assured, other goals are sure to motivate managerial decisions. The primary significance of the survival goal lies in permitting the firm to pursue its principal purpose(s), just as survival is a necessary condition for individuals to accomplish their objectives. It is doubtful whether the goals of survival distinctly characterize the motives of either business firms or individuals; as an explanation of behavior it is relevant only to a limited segment of the population (people or firms) that is in such severe stress that nothing else matters.

PERSONAL OBJECTIVES OF MANAGERS

The separation of ownership and control in corporations has led many economists to emphasize how the motives of managers may differ from those of the profit-maximizing owner-manager. Motives such as personal vanity, the desire to control the largest possible business empire, the quest for professional recognition in executive circles, an affinity for lavish office accommodations, and larger managerial incomes are held to divert managerial decisions down avenues other than profit maximization. The desires of managers for a quiet, easy life and for more leisure time have also been said to blunt the drive for maximization, since managers with "normal" preferences will attempt to maximize their satisfactions from both money income and leisure.[20]

Professor Fellner has observed the tendency toward asymmetry in the rewards to managers.[21] When risky investments turn out badly, stockholders

[19] Kenneth E. Boulding, *A Reconstruction of Economics* (New York: John Wiley & Sons, Inc., 1950), pp. 26–27; J. K. Galbraith, *The New Industrial State*, p. 167.
[20] Tibor Scitovsky, "A Note on Profit Maximization and Its Implications," *The Review of Economic Studies*, Vol. II, No. 4 (Winter 1943), pp. 57–60, and John R. Hicks, "Annual Survey of Economic Theory: The Theory of Monopoly," *Econometrica*, Vol. 3, No. 1 (February 1935), p. 8. Such a characterization may do considerable justice to some European businessmen of past generations, but whether it describes the psychology of present-day corporate executives in either the United States or Europe is dubious indeed.
[21] William Fellner, *Competition among the Few* (New York: Alfred A. Knopf, 1949), pp. 172–173.

lose their assets and managers their jobs. But when they turn out well, while managers may receive salary increases or bonuses, their rewards seldom are in proportion to stockholders' gains. Faced with this reward structure, managers are likely to decide to forego the higher profits associated with higher-risk ventures for more secure (though still acceptable) profits associated with low-risk endeavors. A related manifestation is the preference of managers for stable (steadily rising) profits over widely fluctuating profits, even though the latter may average higher than the former. This is because sharp declines in earnings may arouse stockholder demands for a management change, while an outstanding rise in earnings may produce investor expectations of repeat performances and embarrassing questions when the gains are not duplicated.

On another level, a pride of workmanship, the urge to create, a pervasive interest in technological feats, and an ambition to demonstrate professional excellence may lead to managerial actions in conflict with the greatest possible profits. Technological virtuosity serves the personal needs of all those members of the firm (engineers, technical specialists, research scientists, managers with technical and scientific backgrounds, and so on) concerned with keeping the firm on the frontiers of technical know-how and capability. Progressive technology means opportunities for the technologists to pursue their favorite interests as well as opportunities for personal advancement in the form of better jobs, higher salaries, and promotions.

THE IMPERATIVES OF SOCIALLY RESPONSIBLE BEHAVIOR

Within the past few years professional managers—quite correctly—have come to view the corporation as a social as well as an economic organization, functioning in the whole of society as well as in the markets for its products.[22] This has led to the adoption of corporate policies aimed at integrating the various interests of the major constituencies of the corporation into its governance structure and its decision-making process. The goal here is to relate the entire enterprise to the needs of society. Much more attention is being given to how the corporation looks from the outside and how its behavior impacts on society. Considerable emphasis is also being given to adapting the corporation to the changing requirements of society, especially as concerns the growing public insistence that corporations help solve the social ills of society while continuing to improve upon the performance of its basic economic function.

The philosophy underlying the trend to "social responsibility" on the part of corporate enterprise is that it is in the enlighted self-interest of corporations to promote the public welfare in a positive way. The success of the corporation is inexorably tied to the well-being of society, and unless the

---

[22] This section reflects one of the most recent trends in corporate management. For more complete details see *Social Responsibilities of Business Corporations*, issued by the Research and Policy Committee of the Committee for Economic Development, June 1971.

corporation accepts a fair measure of responsibility for social improvement, the long-term interests of the corporation are certain to be jeopardized. Insensitivity to the changing demands of society will sooner or later result in government intervention and regulation to require firms to do what they were reluctant to do voluntarily. Hence, the corporation's self-interest is best served by responding positively to social demands and by demonstrating a willingness to take needed action ahead of confrontation. The exercise of social responsibility thus has both "carrot" and "stick" aspects. There is the positive appeal for the corporation to pursue policies that will enhance its opportunities to grow and profit in a healthy and well-functioning society. And there is the negative threat of harassment and onerous regulation if it does not do its part in creating a better society.

The consequence of the emerging corporate emphasis on social responsibility, insofar as the goals of the firm are concerned, is that it almost certainly forces the firm to abandon short-run profit *maximization* in favor of policies more consistent with making a substantive contribution toward whatever social and economic goals society has placed high priority upon achieving. The responsibility of management to the stockholders must be balanced against the larger interest of society as a whole. Undoubtedly, some sort of satisficing approach to profits and to social priorities will have to be devised. By no means can the firm's short-term profitability be ignored, because the earning of profit is a prerequisite for giving the firm the organizational ability and the financial wherewithal to respond to social objectives, but it certainly does not follow that it is necessary to maximize profits in the strictest sense of the term.

It may well be, however, that socially responsible behavior on the part of the corporation is quite consistent with a goal of long-run profit maximization. Inasmuch as corporate enterprise clearly has a vital stake in a prosperous economy and a progressive society, logic dictates that stockholder interest in the long run is best served by corporate policies which contribute to development of the kind of society in which business can grow profitably. In fact, the pursuit of profit and the pursuit of social objectives can usually be made complementary. From the standpoint of business firms, profit can be earned by serving public needs for social improvements as well as for goods consumed individually. From the standpoint of society, social objectives can be achieved more rapidly and more efficiently by enlisting the productive power of business firms through the opportunity for profit and by imposing harsh penalties for business activities which are deemed socially harmful.

In any event, it is evident that corporations are becoming seriously concerned about social responsibility and are taking steps to modify their policies and their behavior. These actions have as yet undetermined implications for the goals of the firm, but they probably will have the ultimate effect of curtailing short-run profit-maximizing activities in favor of long-run profit maximization or else of making a satisficing approach to goal formation an even more viable and more attractive managerial practice.

SECURITY, AUTONOMY, AND GROWTH

Galbraith imputes a specific hierarchy of goals to the large corporate enterprise. In his view, the directing force of the large corporation consists not only of those persons plainly identified with management (the chairman of the board, the president, vice-presidents and their staffs, division and department heads) but also of all those technicians, engineers, scientists, and specialists who bring specific knowledge, talent, and experience to the organization.[23] He argues that the guiding intelligence or brain of the large corporation embraces those individuals from the most senior officials all the way down to those white- and blue-collar workers whose function is to conform more or less perfunctorily to instruction or routine. This is because the corporate decision-making process involves all those individuals who furnish the specialized scientific and technical knowledge, the accumulated information, the experienced judgment, and the abilities to systematize and interpret sophisticated analyses. Thus, decisions in the large corporation are the product not of individuals but of a complex of groups, teams, and committees which operate formally and informally and are subject to constant change in composition. Each contains the individuals possessed of the expert information that bears on the particular decision, together with those who are skilled in testing the reliability and relevance of this information and in obtaining a conclusion. Galbraith calls this decision-making hierarchy the "technostructure."

The goals of the technostructure and therefore the goals of the corporation, argues Galbraith, are its own security, autonomy, and self-interest.[24] The first concern of the corporate technostructure is to preserve the autonomy on which its decision-making power depends; this means the firm must have a secure minimum of earnings. The power of the technostructure is secure only so long as earnings are great enough to generate ample rewards to the stockholder (dividends and capital gains) and to provide a supply of funds for reinvestment in the firm's operations. Unless stockholders receive what they consider to be an acceptable return, they may become aroused and precipitate a struggle for control. And if retained earnings are insufficient, appeals must be made to bankers and other monied interests who may ask questions, impose conditions on the capital they supply, and thereby compromise the autonomy of the technostructure. However, the effects of low and high earnings on the technostructure are not symmetrical. With low earnings or losses the technostructure becomes vulnerable to outside influence,

[23] John Kenneth Galbraith, *The New Industrial State*, Chap. 6.
[24] *Ibid.*, Chap. 15.

and its autonomy dissipates. But once profits reach a certain level and show a persistent tendency to increase, higher profits add little or nothing to the technostructure's security, and its autonomy becomes nearly absolute.

At this point the technostructure's chief concern becomes the achievement of the greatest possible rate of corporate growth as measured by sales. This goal commends itself strongly to the self-interest of the technostructure, since expansion of sales and output means expansion of the technostructure in the form of more jobs with more responsibility, more promotions, and higher salaries. Growth as a goal is wholly consistent with the personal and pecuniary interest of those who participate in decisions and direct the enterprise. Growth serves another important purpose as well. It is the best tactic to protect against contraction of the firm's activities. Any contraction of output is painful and damaging to the technostructure, for it entails such distasteful consequences as dismissal, curtailment of pet projects, and possible loss of autonomy.

Associated with growth, as a goal of the technostructure, is technological virtuosity. Progressive technology means more and better jobs and promotions for the technologists. It is also the pathway to growth, since it is by innovation that the firm holds and recruits customers for its existing products and opens up entirely new markets for its products. However, the pursuit of technological virtuosity cannot be so aggressive that it prejudices the minimum level of profits.

Next in the technostructure's goal hierarchy comes a progressive rise in the dividend rate. This goal is clearly secondary but is sought as an added means of enhancing the technostructure's autonomy from stockholder interference.

Thus, in Galbraith's scheme of things, large corporations have a distinct array of goals determined largely by the devices and desires of the technostructure. A secure level of earnings and a maximum rate of growth consistent with providing adequate retained earnings to finance expansion are the prime goals. Technological virtuosity and a rising dividend rate are secondary in the sense that they are not pursued to the detriment of the prime goals. After these ends are achieved to some adequate extent, there is further opportunity to seek satisfaction in lesser goals. But since lesser goals sometimes impinge upon earnings and/or growth, their role tends to be closely circumscribed. On occasions, though, lesser goals serve the primary and secondary goals—they contribute to a "sound corporate image," employee morale, or a better public attitude toward the firm's products.

THE DOMINATING INFLUENCE OF GROWTH AND EXPANSION

We have seen that large corporations may be variously interested in such goals as maximum profits, satisfactory profits, secure profits, sales maximization, a target market share, long-run survival, managerial autonomy, technological virtuosity, a rising dividend rate, "socially responsible" behavior, and achievement of the personal goals of top management. A range of "corporate personalities" may be said to exist, with each corporation reflecting or responding to a characteristic set of goals. Some firms are especially profit-conscious, others appear less so. Some firms tend to be risk-taking and innovative, others more cautious and imitative. Some firms limit their interests to a single industry or product group, and have managers who pride themselves upon being "steel" men or "railroad" men or "oil" men; other firms (the conglomerates) emphasize diversification and the penetration of a wider range of markets. Some firms integrate horizontally, others find comfort in vertical integration. Some firms seek growth by internal expansion, others by merger and acquisition. Some firms seek positions of market advantage through technology and innovation; other firms emphasize quality, service, and marketing superiority; and still others display a propensity towards monopolistic behavior. And so it goes.

However, the diversity of goals and strategies among large corporations is not without its common elements. The profit objective is one; another is the tactic of growth and expansion.[25] In the domain of the large corporation, growth is a pervading influence and goal. The reason is easy to comprehend. Growth is far and away the most powerful and effective tactic the large corporation has for attaining both its primary and secondary goals. Rising profits, increased sales, target market shares, security and survival, managerial autonomy, technological virtuosity, and rising dividends, as well as the fulfillment of the personal objectives of managers, tend to be by-products of growth and expansion.

Corporate managers are fully aware of the importance of avoiding the throes of stagnation and remaining aggressive at seizing new opportunities. The routine activities on which a firm relies for its existence will in time lose their sustaining power, through changes in consumer tastes, technological change, the appearance of superior commodities, increased competition from domestic rivals and importers, and growth in the market power of suppliers and customers. Although a corporation may elect to maintain the status quo and gradually divert its inputs from declining activities into expanding activities, profits can be expected to show little movement, and progress in achieving the firm's other goals is likely to be slim. Not many firms will willingly choose this strategy—the only thing more damning in the business world than the status quo is decline. In contrast, no other test of business success has such nearly unanimous acceptance as growth. Indeed, rising sales and rising profits are absolutely essential for even satisfactory long-term performance.

---

[25] As previously indicated, Galbraith has emphasized the pervasiveness of growth. Others include Penrose, *The Theory of the Growth of the Firm;* Chamberlain, *Enterprise and Environment*, Chap. 6; Baumol, *Business Behavior, Value and Growth*, Chap. 10; and Robert T. Averitt, *The Dual Economy* (New York: W. W. Norton & Company, Inc., 1968), pp. 12–17.

Inducements to Growth and Expansion. The specific appeals of growth as a strategy for long-term goal achievement are worth further exploration. One ostensible reason for an expansive policy is the desire of firms to establish some degree of control over the markets in which they operate. The smaller a firm's market share, the less it has to say about major industry decisions, especially price. Growth by greater penetration of its markets thus offers the firm more influence and market power. To the extent that a firm can gain on or overtake its rivals, it has greater freedom for maneuver. There are fewer firms it must worry about matching or besting or with whom it must come to terms. It also achieves a stronger, more secure market position vis-à-vis competitors, suppliers, and customers, particularly when economies of scale are a factor.

But the drive to expand is by no means *entirely* motivated by a wish to attain a more influential position in a given market. This fails to touch those firms which have sought growth by moving into new markets. Besides, a firm which absorbs an increasingly larger market share, especially by acquisition or merger, moves closer to the boundary of scrutiny by antitrust officials.

A second inducement for growth is security. Growth is the best defense against adversity. Where security is a consideration to a firm, it is likely to seek growth not just through greater dominance in its principal markets but through diversification as well. Diversification allows firms to free themselves from too much dependence on one or a few products. Sometimes the aim for growth by diversification is better balance in a seasonally-oriented product line or in a cyclically-oriented product line. It is also a hedge against an inevitable slowdown in some of its principal products.

Size itself can promote corporate security. If one phase of the firm's operations declines, the firm can survive and even grow on the strength of its other activities. If its research and development ventures along one course of action prove fruitless, as can recurringly be expected, other ventures may reveal new vistas of opportunity. In other words, growth and larger size permit the spreading of risks over a greater number of activities. Security, therefore, is related directly to the scale of a firm's operations.

Third, the managers of corporate enterprises pursue a growth strategy because of the personal rewards it brings. To have had a part in building a successful, dynamic organization is a direct source of personal gratification.[26] There is pride in size and growth. It also wins the attention and respect of other managers and executives, institutional investors, stockholders, and business journals. A growth strategy expands the range of opportunities for achieving dramatic technological feats, for bold and imaginative new designs and styles of products, and for putting together an organizational network and team which is a model for industry. And, as previously indicated, there is

---

[26] The psychological satisfaction attending growth is by no means limited to corporate managers. It is found in abundance among university presidents, city officials, labor union leaders, heads of churches, and chiefs of state.

a financial incentive. Managerial remuneration may be linked to levels of responsibility in the corporate hierarchy. The larger the enterprise, the greater the number of managerial positions and the greater the opportunities for personal advancement.

Undoubtedly, there are other good reasons for a policy of growth and expansion, but the list above is sufficient to indicate that a good many corporations will look upon expansion as desirable if not essential. That large corporations are acutely growth-conscious is rather easily confirmed, albeit in a casual and somewhat unscientific way. Growth and expansion is a recurrent theme in annual reports, and it receives constant emphasis in the financial pages and journals devoted to busines affairs. The worth of an enterprise is measured not so much by current performance as it is by growth potential. This is obvious from the price-earnings multiples of the so-called growth stocks relative to those of the slow-growth firms. Also, far more attention is paid to *growth* in sales and *growth* in profit than to the levels of sales and profits. To most managers, the concept of a stationary optimum is abhorrent; they are well aware of the consequences of stagnation and decline. Hence, their main concern is not at what size their enterprises should finally settle down but, rather, how rapidly to grow and in what directions.[27] Current profitability, once regarded as the exclusive objective, is increasingly being viewed as a vital means and powerful motivating force for achieving long-term ends, rather than as an end in itself. Thus, modern managers are much more prone to trade off short-run profits to achieve a stronger position from which to puruse long-run profitable growth.

Summary and Conclusions

Few economic terms or concepts are used with a more bewildering variety of well-established meanings than profit. Not only is there accounting profit, normal profit, and economic profit, but each of these may be measured in several ways, depending upon the specific accounting conventions employed and upon whether the desired profit measure is a dollar amount or a rate of return. Accounting profit is based on a firm's income statement and is conceived as the excess of revenue over historical costs after corporate taxes have been deducted. Normal profit is the minimum amount of profit (or rate of return) sufficient to keep the firm in business in the long run; normal profit is considered by the economist as part of total cost. Economic profit is a return over and above a normal profit. It is economic profit which business firms really seek and which motivates much of their behavior.

Profit is a mixture resulting from a variety of influences including business acumen, successful performance of the entrepreneurial function,

27 Baumol, *Business Behavior, Value and Growth*, p. 87.

services rendered to the consumer, a fortuitous coping with uncertainty, the presence of market frictions which inhibit a quick response of competitive forces, monopoly power and positions of advantage, technological superiority, and new product innovation.

Wide disagreement exists among economists over whether business firms, especially large corporations, behave as if they seek to *maximize* profits. But, by and large, it is generally agreed that periphery firms (proprietorships, partnerships, small owner-managed corporations, and entrepreneurial firms) are among the most profit-conscious and intensely profit-seeking of all business enterprises. A consensus exists that the profit-maximizing assumption does no great violence to reality when applied to owner-managed firms.

However, the feud rages ever more vigorously regarding the validity of assuming that large corporations (center firms) seek to maximize profits. Diffused ownership, conditions of uncertainty, and insulation from heavy competitive pressures of the classical variety are held to allow corporate managers the discretion to pursue goals other than profit maximization. Among the most prominent alternatives are satisficing, sales revenue maximization, and growth. Lesser and/or corollary goals include a target market share, long-run survival, satisfactory and secure profits, a rising dividend rate, financial liquidity, technological virtuosity, autonomy of the "technostructure," attainment of a "good" image, behaving in a "socially responsible" manner, maintaining a strong competitive image, and achievement of personal goals of top management (power, prestige, sense of accomplishment, professional recognition, and high incomes). An aggressive growth strategy offers quite an effective means of simultaneously pursuing and achieving many of these goals.

If anything is to be learned from this chapter, it should be that no *single* goal can capture the *whole* truth about the motivations of business behavior in each and every situation. There simply are too many subtle shadings of behavior, and the decision constraints are far too complex. Furthermore, diverse goals and variations in motivations are a natural outgrowth of a dynamic trillion-dollar economy populated by a variety of business firms ranging from the small proprietorship to the giant multiproduct corporation. Given the sizable differences among firms in matters pertaining to ownership and control, size, competition, uncertainty, technological capabilities, personalities of owners and managers, and so on, rational behavior does not require that all firms pursue the *same* set of goals with the *same* degree of intensity.

Nevertheless, the profit motive is deeply ingrained in the folklore of modern business behavior, and rightly so. All firms have a profit goal, and few knowingly follow strategies calculated to cut long-run profits substantially below levels they could otherwise achieve. Moreover, there can be little doubt that profit maximization is the most satisfactory single assumption which can be made about the goals of business enterprises. Just how satisfactory an assumption it is depends upon the purpose of the analysis and upon how well the underlying implicit qualifications are understood. If business firms really do act as if they seek to maximize profits, then an assumption of profit maximization should yield a good first approximation to predicting and explaining business behavior. But if business behavior is not compatible with profit-maximizing actions, then profit-maximizing models are suspect and the assumption may need to be modified. In the following chapters we shall find it helpful to use models which incorporate goals other than pure profit maximization in order to predict and to explain the full range of business behavior.

SUGGESTED READINGS

FARMER, RICHARD N., "Two Kinds of Profit," *California Management Review*, Vol. 8, No. 2 (Winter 1965), pp. 21–28.

GALBRAITH, JOHN KENNETH, *The New Industrial State* (Boston: Houghton Mifflin Company, 1967), Chaps. 6, 7, 8, and 10–15.

LANZILOTTI, ROBERT F., "Pricing Objectives in Large Companies," *American Economic Review*, Vol. 48, No. 5 (December 1958), pp. 921–940.

MACHLUP, FRITZ, "Theories of the Firm: Marginalist, Behavioral, Managerial," *American Economic Review*, Vol. 57, No. 1 (March 1967), pp. 1–33.

NORDQUIST, GERALD L., "The Breakup of the Maximization Principle," *Quarterly Journal of Economics and Business*, Vol. 5, No. 3 (Fall 1965), pp. 33–46.

SIMON, H. A., "Theories of Decision Making in Economics and Behavioral Science," *American Economic Review*, Vol. 49, No. 3 (June 1959), pp. 253–283.

Social Responsibilities of Business Corporations: A Statement on National Policy by the Research and Policy Committee of the Committee for Economic Development (New York: Committee for Economic Development, 1971).

WHITE, C. MICHAEL, "Multiple Goals in the Theory of the Firm," in K. E. Boulding and W. A. Spivey, *Linear Programming and the Theory of the Firm* (New York: The Macmillan Company, 1960), pp. 181–201.

WILLIAMSON, OLIVER E., *Corporate Control and Business Behavior* (Englewood Cliffs, N.J.: Prentice-Hall, Inc., 1970).

Problems and Questions for Discussion

1. (a) The Vista Corporation has invested $10 million in producing greeting cards. In 1972 its after-tax profits according to conventional accounting measures amounted to $800,000. During 1972 an average return of 6 percent could have been obtained by purchasing government securities. Do you think Vista Corporation earned an economic profit in 1972? Why or why not? Explain.

   (b) Suppose the financial vice-president of Vista Corporation conducts a thorough study and finds that the prospects are excellent (90 percent chance of success) that an annual profit of $900,000 could be earned by shifting Vista's $10 million investment into the production of business forms. What implications, if any, does this estimate have for evaluating the profitability of Vista's greeting card operations? for future resource allocation within the firm?

2. How should an enterprise go about estimating normal profit?

3. In which of the following circumstances would an assumption of profit maximization be appropriate and in which would the analysis probably be improved by a consideration of goals other than profit? Justify your answer in each case.

(a) The effect of steel import quotas on steel prices.

(b) The effect of the UAW's winning a lucrative wage increase from General Motors upon the prices of GM cars.

(c) The effect of increased liquor taxes upon the price of liquor.

(d) The effect of the ban on cigarette advertising upon the sales strategy of the three largest cigarette producers.

(e) The effect upon coal prices of the major oil firms' acquiring producers of coal and thereby gaining control over a large segment of the nation's coal deposits.

(f) The effect of strong antipollution laws upon the prices of paper products, chemicals, steel, and other products produced by processes with a heavy pollution by-product.

4. "No single goal of business enterprise is pure in its purpose. Goals tend to be overlapping and interdependent." Discuss the validity of this viewpoint and give examples in support of your answer.

5. Is it possible to determine whether or not a particular firm is maximizing profits? Or, to put it another way, is it possible to ascertain at some moment of time what the maximum potential profit performance of a firm is, thus allowing a comparison with the firm's actual profit performance to see if the firm is maximizing profits? Justify your answer.

6. The Hall-Prentiss Corporation is weighing two alternative projects costing $50 million, one offering a best-guess profit expectation of $10 million with a 10 percent chance of losing $5 million, the other offering an expected profit of $20 million with a 30 percent chance of losing $5 million. Which is the profit-maximizing alternative? How does this decision situation illustrate the problem of trying to maximize profits under conditions of uncertainty?

10

The Price
and Output Decisions
of Periphery Firms

Now that the goals of business enterprises have been investigated, we are ready to examine price and output behavior in a variety of market circumstances. Our study of market behavior will be from the vantagepoint of firms, on the assumption that the policies they set actually reflect not only their own decisions but also the preferences and constraints imposed by competitive forces and by buyers. We begin with a brief survey of some key factors that condition the operation of markets.

THE CHARACTERISTICS OF MARKETS

Of critical importance in the market for any commodity is the *number of firms*—whether there are *many* or *few* sellers of the commodity. The terms "many" and "few" are delineated not so much by specific numbers as by the behavior of firms. There are "many" sellers of a commodity when no one firm is important enough for the remaining firms to watch its actions closely. Each firm is virtually an anonymous entity, free to make decisions independent of what rival firms decide to do. Firms are so numerous that they have no occasion to pay any attention to one another; competition is *impersonal*. In contrast, we say there are "few" sellers of a commodity whenever the actions of any one firm will be noticed and reacted to by rival sellers. "Few" means few enough so that firms find it imperative to follow each other's moves closely. Fewness of sellers also means that each firm is large *relative to the size of the market* in which it operates; often, when firms are few, each firm is large in absolute size as well.[1]

A second characteristic of markets relates to whether the products of sellers are identical or differentiated. Identical products typically have a small number of measurable qualities which can be graded and which tell the buyer all he needs to know about the product. Examples include cotton, meats, sulfuric acid, natural gas, iron ore, copper wire, and coffee beans. In such cases, the products of the firms tend to be perfect substitutes, because consumers have no particular reason to prefer one firm's product over that of another firm.

On the other hand, where the products of firms are distinctive or unique they are not perfect substitutes for one another. Different brands of furniture, shoes, wines, cereal, cigarettes, tires, cosmetics, and soft drinks provide examples. The ultimate test of differentiation is in the mind of the buyer; the differences he perceives in the products of the various firms may be either real or imaginary. "Real" differences involving performance, materials, design, workmanship, and service are obviously important aspects of product differentiation. But "imaginary" differences brought about by brand names, trademarks, packaging, and advertising can also be significant. It matters not whether different brands of aspirin are of differential effectiveness so long as buyers are convinced they are different. A major function of advertising is to initiate and strengthen such convictions. In addition, it should be recognized that a firm's product extends beyond the physical and functional characteristics of the item itself. Although a large number of stores in an area may sell Crest toothpaste, they may not be viewed as equally attractive to buyers of Crest. The sales clerks in one store may be more courteous, or its location more convenient, or its check-out system faster, or its delivery service more dependable, or its credit terms more accommodating. Such factors can cause buyers to prefer one seller over another, even though the item purchased is the same.

Three other aspects of markets are worth noting here. Often the number of buyers in the market can be important. In retail markets the buyers are nearly always numerous, but in other markets they are few: the milk producer who buys from dairy farmers, the computer manufacturer who buys parts from the many electronics suppliers, the nationwide discount chain which handles the products of hundreds of manufacturers, and the Department of Defense which buys from the several producers of military wares. The buying and selling sides of the market need not be symmetrical in terms of numbers; there may be many sellers and few buyers or few sellers and

---

[1] Fewness does not always mean bigness. A small community has only a few banks, dry cleaners, movies, florists, doctors, lawyers, and hairdressers—none of which is big in an absolute sense. Such cases, while relatively numerous, are not very important as compared to the center economy of large corporations where giants compete among giants and where the outcome has implications for the entire economy.

many buyers, just as well as many sellers and many buyers or few sellers and few buyers. The number of buyers and sellers is significant because of its implications for competition and market performance.

Entry into and exit from a market is an important characteristic of market behavior. Not unexpectedly, prices and outputs under conditions of restricted entry and exit differ from what they would be if firms were completely free to enter or leave the production of a commodity.

Lastly, the degree to which firms reach decisions independently, or whether they cooperate in various ways, has an effect upon market behavior. The antitrust laws usually suffice to preclude formal collusive arrangements from being effective. Occasionally, however, firms find clever ways of administering prices to their own advantage, dividing up the market according to some prearranged scheme, and in general creating a very relaxed competitive environment. Nearly always, such forms of collusion are found in industries where the firms are few, owing to the difficulty of establishing a stable, enforceable agreement among a larger number of firms.

Viewed from the seller's side of the market, four main forms of market structure stand out:

1. *Perfect competition*—many sellers of a standardized product.
2. *Monopolistic competition*—many sellers of a differentiated product.
3. *Oligopoly*—few sellers of either a standardized or a differentiated product.
4. *Monopoly*—a single seller of a product for which there is no close substitute.

There is no preordained sequence for studying market structures, so we shall take them up in the order listed. This chapter presents the standard theoretical models of perfect competition and monopolistic competition. In its final section we shall use these two models to explain price and output behavior in the periphery firm sector of the economy—the domain of markets comprised of *large* numbers of *small* firms. The next two chapters concern monopoly and oligopoly models as they apply to center firm behavior and the markets in which center firms operate.

The Classic Model of Perfect Competition

A perfectly competitive market environment is distinguished by four main features. First, the products of the firms are identical—or at least are so much alike that buyers do not care whether they buy the product of one firm or another. Since the products of the firms are indistinguishable and therefore homogeneous, no buyer is willing to pay one firm a higher price than that charged by rival firms. Buyers are totally indifferent as to the firm from which they purchase, so long as price is the same. In fact, differences in price constitute the only reason a buyer might prefer one seller to any other.

Second, perfect competition requires every buyer and seller to be unable to affect the price of the product. The purchases of each buyer must be a sufficiently small portion of the total bought by all buyers that he cannot wrangle a lower price from sellers than can any other buyer. Likewise, the sales made by a particular firm must be a sufficiently small portion of the total sold by all firms that the price of the product is not materially affected by any one firm's decision to increase or decrease its output rate. In other words, market conditions must be such that all buyers and sellers are without power to influence the going price of the product. Of course, should buyers or sellers act in concert, they could influence price and output levels. But it is presumed that any buyer or seller acting alone cannot do so.

Third, in a perfectly competitive environment resource inputs of all kinds are completely mobile. In the long run, there are no important restrictions upon the freedom of firms to enter or leave the industry. Resources can be switched from one use to another very readily. Workers are willing and able to move from region to region in response to new job opportunities and changing wage rates. The supplies of raw materials are in no way monopolized, but are made freely available to the highest bidders.

Fourth, perfect competition is characterized by a state of perfect knowledge. Decisions are made under conditions of *certainty*. Firms know exactly what their revenue and cost functions are. They also know the prices of all resource inputs and the various alternative technologies which can be used to produce their products. Consumers are aware of the prices charged by all firms. Resource owners are aware of the prices firms are paying for resource inputs and all relevant opportunity costs.

Obviously, these four conditions are so stringent that no market in the real world ever has or ever can meet them. A few markets satisfy the first three requirements fairly well (numerous agricultural products, bituminous coal, and some stocks and bonds), but naturally none satisfies the fourth requirement of perfect knowledge. Nonetheless, the study of perfectly competitive markets is not without value. Recall from the introductory chapter that a model may yield valid conclusions even though its assumptions are "unrealistic." As we shall see in the last section of this chapter, the perfectly competitive model characterizes fairly well the behavior of owner-managed, periphery firms in certain market circumstances. In addition, it illuminates several basic principles underlying the economics of business behavior. For these reasons perfect competition is worthy of study, even though the assumptions upon which it rests are not always "reasonable" abstractions of real-world phenomena. We shall, however, be careful not to claim too much for the model of perfect competition, and we shall be especially judicious in applying its conclusions to the behavior of firms in actual situations. With these points fixed firmly in mind, suppose we examine how a firm would behave in a perfectly competitive market environment.

SHORT-RUN EQUILIBRIUM OF A FIRM IN
A PERFECTLY COMPETITIVE MARKET

In perfect competition the prevailing market price of a commodity is established in classic fashion by the interaction of the market forces of demand and supply. Given the market demand and supply curves in Figure 10-1(a), a short-run market equilibrium is attained at a price of P_1 dollars and at a total industry output of Q_T units.[2] If price were higher than P_1, then excess supply conditions would drive it downward. By the same token, if price were lower than P_1, excess demand conditions would force it upward. The establishment of market price at the intersection of the supply and demand curves determines the shape and position of each firm's demand and average revenue (demand-AR) curve.

Under conditions of perfect competition, each firm has a *horizontal* demand-AR curve which intersects the vertical axis at the price established by market supply and market demand conditions. This is illustrated in Figure 10-1(b). No firm can sell its output at a price even slightly higher than P_1 dollars, because buyers will immediately shift their purchases to other firms selling the same item at a lower price. And since each firm is so small relative to the total market, it can sell its entire output at the market price of P_1; hence, there is no inducement whatsoever to sell at a price lower than P_1. The result is that firms all sell their products at the same price. At any one time a *single* price prevails throughout the market, determined via the familiar process of equating demand and supply.

When the firm's demand-AR curve is horizontal, it can sell additional units of output without reducing price. Thus, marginal revenue equals price at every output rate, since each additional unit sold will cause total revenue to rise by an amount equal to the price of the product. For example, if price is fixed at $10, then the sale of each additional unit causes total revenue to rise by $10; MR is therefore constant and equal to $10. The firm's MR function corresponds precisely to its demand-AR curve, as shown in Figure 10-1(b). Both marginal and average revenue are equal to the market price of the product at all possible outputs of the firm.

Since the firm can sell whatever amount it wishes at a given price, its total revenue (TR) function will be a linear upward-sloping curve starting from the origin, as depicted in Figure 10-1(c). If the firm sells zero output, total revenue is also zero. If sales are one unit of output per period of time, the firm's revenue will equal the price of the product. Each additional unit sold will increase TR by an amount equal to the selling price. Marginal revenue (MR) is constant, so the TR curve rises at a constant rate (equal to MR and price) and is therefore linear and upward-sloping. The general

---

[2] The total industry output, Q_T, is the sum of the outputs of all the firms in the industry. It is important to remember that no one firm's output constitutes a significant portion of Q_T.

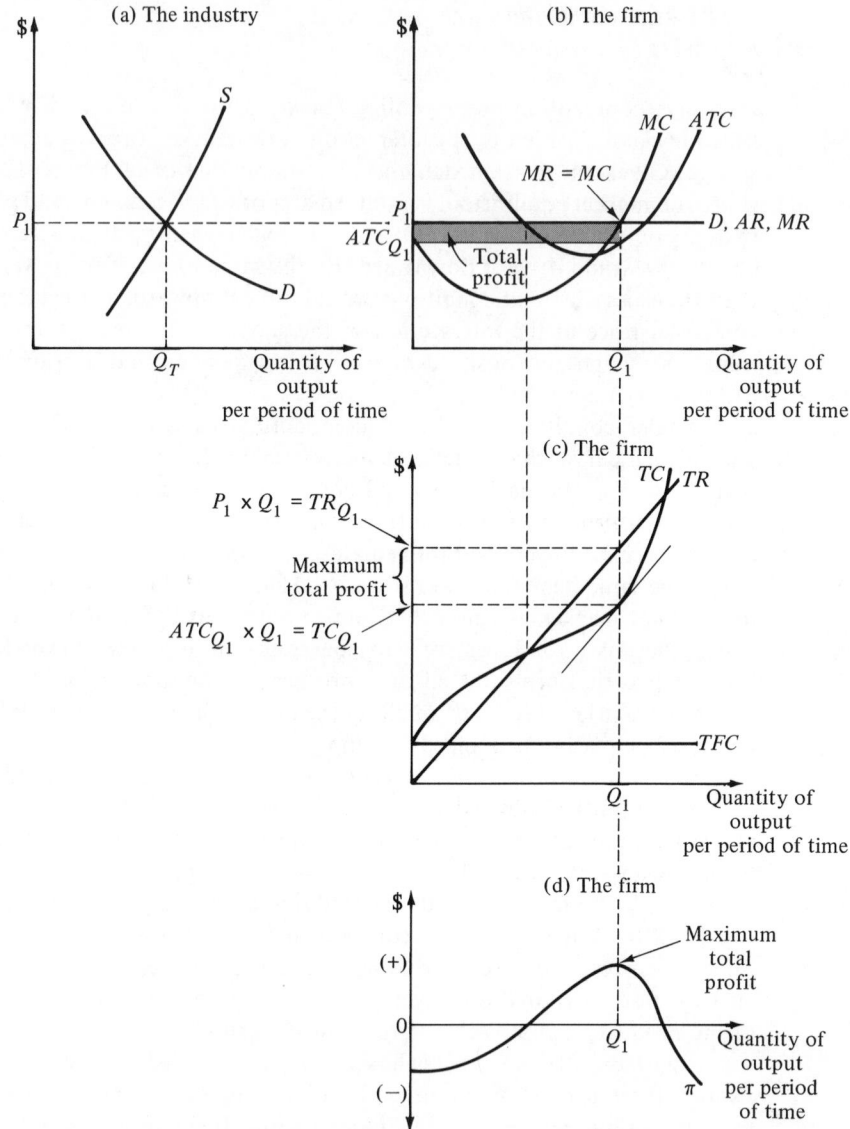

Fig. 10-1 The Profit-Maximizing Price and Output for a Firm Operating in a Perfectly Competitive Market Environment

equation for the TR function can be written as

$$TR = P \cdot Q.$$

Now suppose the firm has a cost structure represented by the average total cost (*ATC*) and marginal cost (*MC*) curves in Figure 10-1(b) and by the associated total cost (*TC*) curve in Figure 10-1(c).[3] Questions immediately arise as to what price the firm will charge for its product and what amount of output it will decide to offer for sale. To answer these questions properly, we must first consider the goal or goals of business enterprises in an environment of perfect competition. As indicated in Chapter 9, small entrepreneur-dominated enterprises, such as those which typically comprise the population of firms in perfect competition, are among the most intensely profit-seeking and profit-conscious of all firms. Therefore, suppose we assume that the prime objective of perfectly competitive firms is to maximize profits (or to minimize losses if they cannot make profits). The validity of this assumption will be confirmed shortly.

Since price is established by the market, a perfectly competitive firm has no pricing decision to make. It is a *price-taker*. The determination of price in a perfectly competitive environment is well beyond the control of any one firm; rather, each firm must live with whatever price that market demand and supply conditions establish. However, alternatives do exist regarding the firm's short-run output. The firm *is* able to exert some measure of control over its destiny by adjusting its output to any rate it is capable of producing. Assuming, then, a goal of profit maximization, consider the optimum output decision of a perfectly competitive firm.

Profit Maximization: The Total Cost - Total Revenue Approach. In order to maximize profits, the firm must determine the output at which it obtains the greatest excess of revenue over all costs of production. The point where *TR* exceeds *TC* by the greatest amount must be the operating rate at which profits will be highest. In Figure 10-1(c) the profits of the firm are maximum at an output of Q_1 units, where the *vertical distance* between *TR* and *TC* is greatest. Geometrically, it so happens that the maximum vertical distance between *TR* and *TC* occurs at the output rate where a tangent to the *TC* curve has the same slope as and is parallel to the *TR* curve, as indicated on the diagram.

The firm's profit function [Figure 10-1(d)] is derived by subtracting *TC* from *TR* at each rate of output. It indicates how the firm's short-run profits vary with its output rate. The peak of the total profit (π) curve defines the output rate corresponding to maximum short-run profits.

---

[3] It should be recognized that the cost curves portrayed in Figures 10-1(b) and 10-1(c) represent just one of the several types of short-run cost functions which firms may possess. As discussed in Chapter 8, the cubic type of *TC* function is viewed by many economists as representative of the most typical type of cost behavior. However, firms may well possess other types of cost functions, depending upon the character of the technology employed in the production process. The chapter-end exercises incorporate other types of cost functions to illustrate the perfectly competitive firm's output decision under a variety of cost circumstances.

Profit Maximization: The Unit Cost - Unit Revenue Approach. On a unit cost and unit revenue basis, *maximum profits are obtained at the output rate where marginal cost equals marginal revenue.* The validity of this proposition may be established as a matter of common sense. If the production and sale of one more unit of output will add more to a firm's total revenue than to its total costs, the sale of the unit must necessarily add something to the firm's total profits. If, however, the extra cost of producing and selling one more unit is greater than the extra revenues the firm gains, the firm's total profits will be reduced by selling that unit. Marginal revenue (MR) is defined as the *addition* to total revenue attributable to the sale of one more unit of output, while marginal cost (MC) is defined as the addition to total cost resulting from the production and sale of one more unit of output. Hence, to maximize profits the firm must be cognizant of the marginal revenue and the marginal cost of each successive unit of output.

Thus in Figure 10-1(b) the most profitable output level is at Q_1 units, where the MC curve intersects the MR curve. If the firm stops short of selling Q_1 units, then the revenue from selling an additional unit will exceed the cost of selling another unit. Plainly, the firm can increase profits by increasing its rate of output to Q_1. Should the firm produce beyond an output rate of Q_1 units, the marginal costs of all the units in excess of Q_1 will exceed the additional revenue which the firm can obtain from selling them. The firm will lose money on all the units sold past an output of Q_1 units, thereby causing total profits to be smaller than that obtainable at lesser outputs.

The profit-maximizing output rate in Figure 10-1(b) corresponds exactly to the output rate in Figure 10-1(c) where TR exceeds TC by the greatest amount. How do we know? Because at an output of Q_1 units in Figure 10-1(c), the slope of the TR curve equals the slope of the TC curve. MR, by definition, equals the slope of TR; and MC, by definition, equals the slope of the TC function. Hence, since the values of the slopes are equal, MC must necessarily equal MR at the same output where total revenue exceeds total cost by the largest amount. Logical consistency requires further that the profit-maximizing output rate in Figure 10-1(b) coincide with the output rate in Figure 10-1(d) where the total profit function reaches its maximum height.

The profit-maximizing rule may be stated in yet another way: *total profit is maximum at the output rate where marginal profit equals zero.* Marginal profit is the change in total profit resulting from a one-unit change in output; this is equivalent to saying that

$$M\pi = MR - MC,$$

where $M\pi$ is marginal profit. More technically, marginal profit equals the rate of change in total profit as the rate of output changes, or

$$M\pi = \frac{d\pi}{dQ}.$$

Marginal profit is, therefore, geometrically equal to the slope of the total profit function. At the peak of the total profit function, its slope equals zero, hence the rationale for saying that total profit is maximized where $M\pi = 0$. So long as marginal profit is positive, the total profit function is rising and it pays to increase output. When the profit earned on the next unit of output has shrunk to zero ($M\pi = 0$), the peak of the total profit function has been reached. If the firm produces beyond the output rate associated with zero marginal profit, marginal profit becomes negative, and the loss incurred on each of these extra units causes the total profit function to turn downward. This is evident from inspection of the total profit function in Figure 10-1(d).

Calculation of the Profit-Maximizing Output.   It is useful to examine the mathematics of determining the perfectly competitive firm's optimum output decision. Suppose the going market price for the commodity is $20 and the firm's total cost function is $TC = 75 + 4Q - 11Q^2 + Q^3$. From the preceding discussion we know that profit is maximized at the output where $MR = MC$. Both the MR and MC functions can be obtained from the information given. At a constant price of $20, MR is also $20 at every output rate. The MC function is the first derivative of the TC function, giving

$$MC = \frac{dTC}{dQ} = 4 - 22Q + 3Q^2.$$

Equating MR with MC, we have

$$20 = 4 - 22Q + 3Q^2.$$

Solving for Q yields the two roots $Q = -\frac{2}{3}$ and $Q = 8$. Since output can never be negative, the profit-maximizing rate of output is 8 units. Actually, it can be proved that the larger of the two roots is always the profit-maximizing (or loss-minimizing) output rate. It is a simple matter, however, to resolve the issue by calculating total profit at each of the values of Q for which $MR = MC$ and observing firsthand which Q yields the greatest total profit.

The profit-maximizing output can also be determined using the rule that total profit is maximum where marginal profit is zero. Again, let $P = MR = \$20$ and $TC = 75 + 4Q - 11Q^2 + Q^3$. Total profit is defined as

$$\pi = TR - TC.$$

Total revenue, being equal at every output to $P \cdot Q$, can in this case be represented by the expression $20Q$. Substituting into the expression for total profit, we have

$$\pi = 20Q - (75 + 4Q - 11Q^2 + Q^3).$$

Since marginal profit is precisely defined as the rate of change in total profit as the rate of output changes, the expression for marginal profit becomes

$$M\pi = \frac{d\pi}{dQ} = 20 - (4 - 22Q + 3Q^2).$$

Given that total profit is maximum where $M\pi = 0$, the expression above is set equal to zero, yielding

$$20 - (4 - 22Q + 3Q^2) = 0,$$
$$20 - 4 + 22Q - 3Q^2 = 0,$$
$$16 + 22Q - 3Q^2 = 0.$$

Solving for Q gives the roots $Q = -\frac{2}{3}$ and $Q = 8$, the same results given by the $MR = MC$ approach.

Total Profit or Loss. Whether the firm realizes a profit or a loss depends upon the relationship between price and average total cost at the intersection of MR and MC. If price exceeds ATC, the firm will enjoy short-run profits, whereas if price is less than ATC, losses will be incurred.

In Figure 10-1(b), selling price is P_1 dollars and ATC at the profit-maximizing output of Q_1 units is ATC_{Q_1} dollars. Profit per unit is therefore $(P_1 - ATC_{Q_1})$ dollars at an output of Q_1 units. Total profit is profit per unit multiplied by the number of units sold, or

$$\pi = (P_1 - ATC_{Q_1})Q_1,$$

which is numerically equivalent to the size of the shaded area in Figure 10-1(b). This shaded area has a numerical dollar value equal to the vertical distance between TR and TC at an output of Q_1 units in Figure 10-1(c) and equal to the height of the total profit function in Figure 10-1(d). It should also be clear from Figures 10-1(b) and (c) that multiplying P_1 by Q_1 gives TR_{Q_1} and that ATC_{Q_1} times Q_1 equals TC_{Q_1}.

Observe that at output Q_1, profit *per unit* is *not* maximized; in other words, total profit is not maximum at the same output at which profit per unit is maximum. Profit per unit is maximized at the output rate where price exceeds ATC by the greatest vertical distance, whereas total profit is maximized where $MR = MC$. These two output rates do not coincide, as an examination of Figure 10-1(b) will confirm.

It does not, of course, always work out that perfectly competitive firms can earn positive economic profits in the short run. The equilibrium market price in the short run may fall below the firm's *ATC* curve at every level of output, thereby making it impossible for the firm to cover all of its costs in the short run. What then is the firm's optimum output decision? Should it shut down operations and wait for price to return to a more profitable level, or should it produce at a loss? If it continues to operate, at what output will the firm's losses be minimized?

The firm's decision rests on whether or not the market price is high enough to cover the firm's average variable costs (or whether enough total revenue can be obtained to cover total variable costs) at some output rate. Suppose we define *unit contribution profit* as the difference between price and average variable cost:

$$\text{unit contribution profit} = P - AVC.$$

The relevance of unit contribution profit is easily demonstrated. If a product sells for $10 per unit and average variable cost is $6, the firm is able to cover all of the expenses associated with the variable inputs needed to produce the product and has $4 left over to help pay total fixed costs and to contribute to the earning of profit. Hence, even though price may not be sufficient to cover *ATC*, so long as the prevailing price is high enough to permit the firm to obtain a margin over and above *AVC*, it pays the firm to produce in the short run. Covering part of *AFC* is better than covering none of *AFC*.

A related concept is that of *total contribution profit*. Total contribution profit is the difference between total revenue and total variable costs:

$$\text{total contribution profit} = TR - TVC.$$

It should be apparent that even if *TR* is not sufficient to cover *TC*, so long as *TR* more than covers *TVC*, the firm earns some amount of total contribution profit which can be used to pay at least a portion of the firm's total fixed costs. This is a superior outcome to the situation of shutting down. When the firm ceases selling in the short run, *TR* falls to zero, and the firm's loss will be equal to its total fixed costs. Furthermore, it stands to reason that the larger the amount of total contribution profit a firm can obtain, the better will be its short-run profit and loss position. The greater the amount by which *TR* exceeds *TVC*, the more dollars the firm will have to pay fixed costs. And when total fixed costs have all been paid, then any remaining total contribution profit represents economic profit.

We are now ready to use the concepts of contribution profit in determining a firm's optimum output decision when price temporarily falls below average total cost. Consider Figure 10-2. Suppose supply and demand conditions establish an industrywide price of P_1 dollars. Given the firm's *MC*,

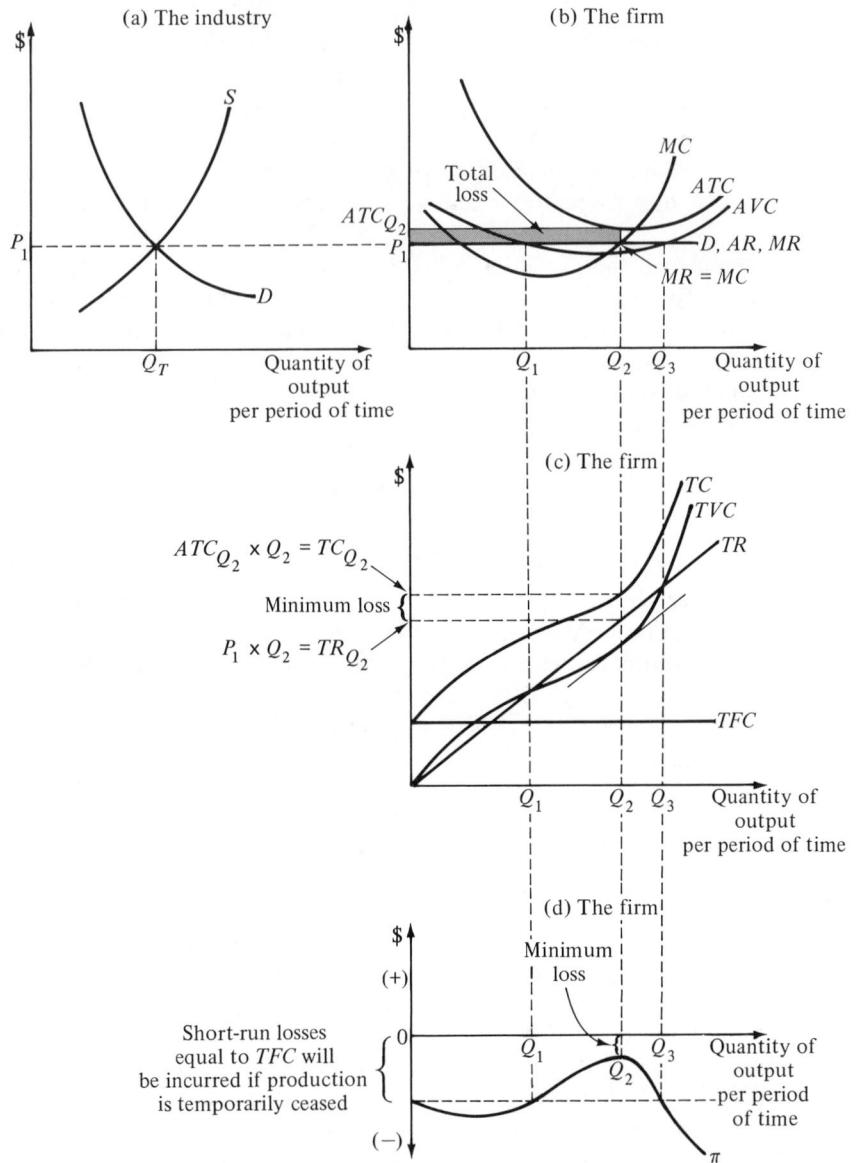

Fig. 10-2 The Short-Run Loss-Minimizing Price and Output for a Perfectly Competitive Firm

AVC, and ATC curves, what is the optimum output rate? Clearly, the firm cannot make a profit because the ATC curve lies above price P_1 at every output rate; the firm's decision then turns on how to minimize its losses. Observe that between outputs Q_1 and Q_3 in Figure 10-2(b) price exceeds AVC;

similarly, between the same outputs in Figure 10-2(c), TR exceeds TVC. Thus, there are a number of output rates at which both unit and total contribution profits are positive. The significance of this finding is that the firm will minimize its losses by producing somewhere between Q_1 and Q_3, since in this output range TR will exceed TVC, and the resulting total contribution profit can be applied to the payment of total fixed costs. Common sense tells us that the firm will want to obtain as much total contribution profit as possible, so as to have the maximum number of dollars available for covering total fixed costs and thereby keeping losses to a minimum. Note in Figure 10-2(c) that the output at which TR exceeds TVC by the greatest vertical distance occurs at output Q_2, where a tangent to the TVC curve is parallel to the TR curve; this is the output rate associated with maximum total contribution profit. It is also apparent from Figure 10-2(c) that the vertical distance by which TC exceeds TR is less at Q_2 than at any other output rate, meaning that here the firm's short-run losses are minimized. Thus, from the standpoint of TC-TR analysis, *short-run losses are minimized at the output where TC exceeds TR by the smallest vertical distance.* In Figure 10-2(d) the total profit function reaches its highest level at an output of Q_2 units; short-run losses are measured by the vertical distance from the peak of the profit function to the horizontal axis. Insofar as the firm's unit costs and revenues are concerned [Figure 10-2(b)], an output of Q_2 units per period of time corresponds exactly to the output where $MR = MC$ and $M\pi = 0$. Thus, we find that the $MR = MC$ rule, and its corollary, $M\pi = 0$, not only identify the short-run profit-maximizing output but also identify the short-run loss-minimizing output.

Now consider Figure 10-3, where the forces of supply and demand combine to establish a short-run equilibrium price of P_1 dollars, such that the firm's demand-AR-MR curve is just tangent to the minimum point of its AVC curve. Again, there exists no opportunity for earning a normal profit, much less an economic profit, and the firm's output decision must be aimed at minimizing short-run losses. If the firm elects to produce where $MR = MC$ and where $M\pi = 0$, then it will produce Q_1 units [Figure 10-3(b)] and will obtain total revenues of TR_1 dollars [Figure 10-3(c)]. Price will be just equal to AVC [Figure 10-3(b)] and total variable costs will be equal to total revenue [Figure 10-3(c)]. Unit contribution profit will be zero and total contribution profit will be zero. The firm's revenues will just cover variable expenses and the firm's losses will be equal to total fixed cost. Insofar as minimizing losses is concerned, the firm will be indifferent as to producing and selling Q_1 units or closing down its operations in the short run. In either case, short-run losses will equal total fixed costs, and this is the best the firm can do. At any other output rate revenues will not even be sufficient to cover TVC, contribution profit will be negative, and losses will exceed TFC by the amount of TVC not covered by TR. However, given that short-run losses will

352

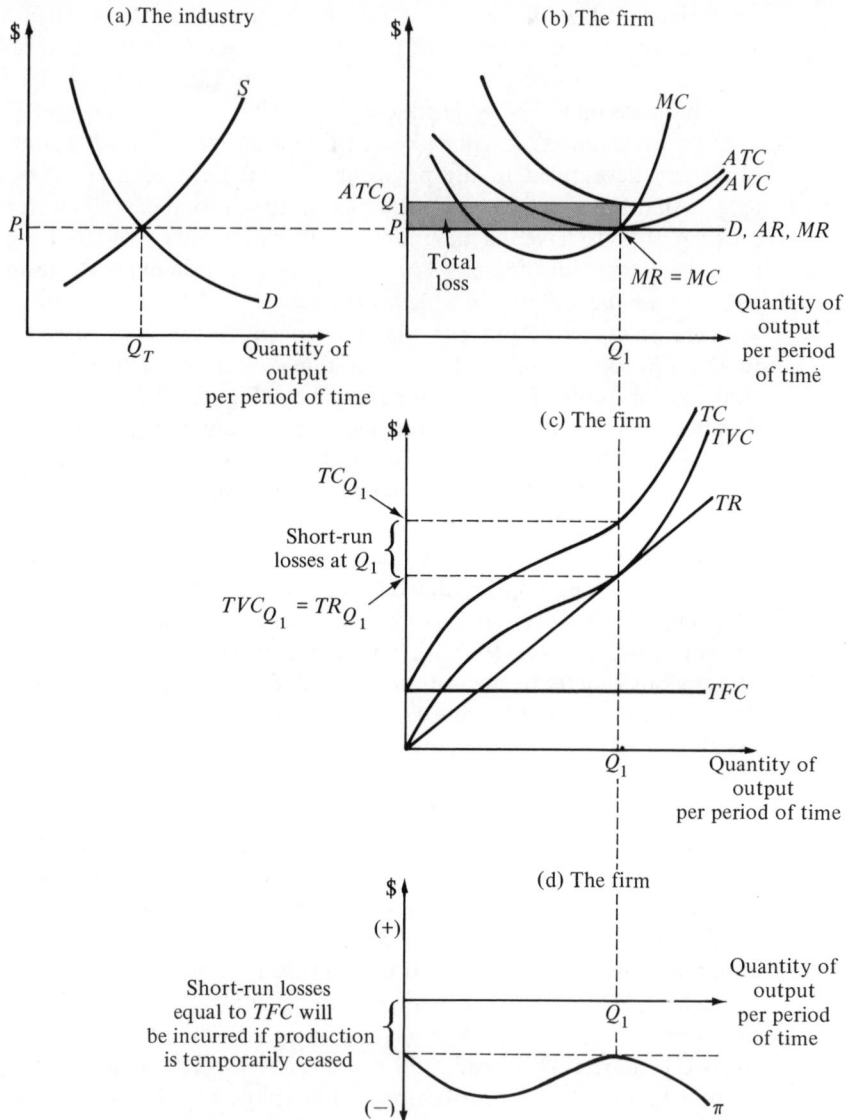

Fig. 10-3 The Short-Run Loss-Minimizing Price and Output for a Perfectly Competitive Firm When the Demand Curve Is Just Tangent to the *AVC* Curve

be no more by operating at Q_1 than by closing down, the firm will in all probability elect to produce and sell Q_1 units. By so doing, the firm continues to serve its customers and to offer employment to its workers, with no adverse effects on its profit and loss statement.

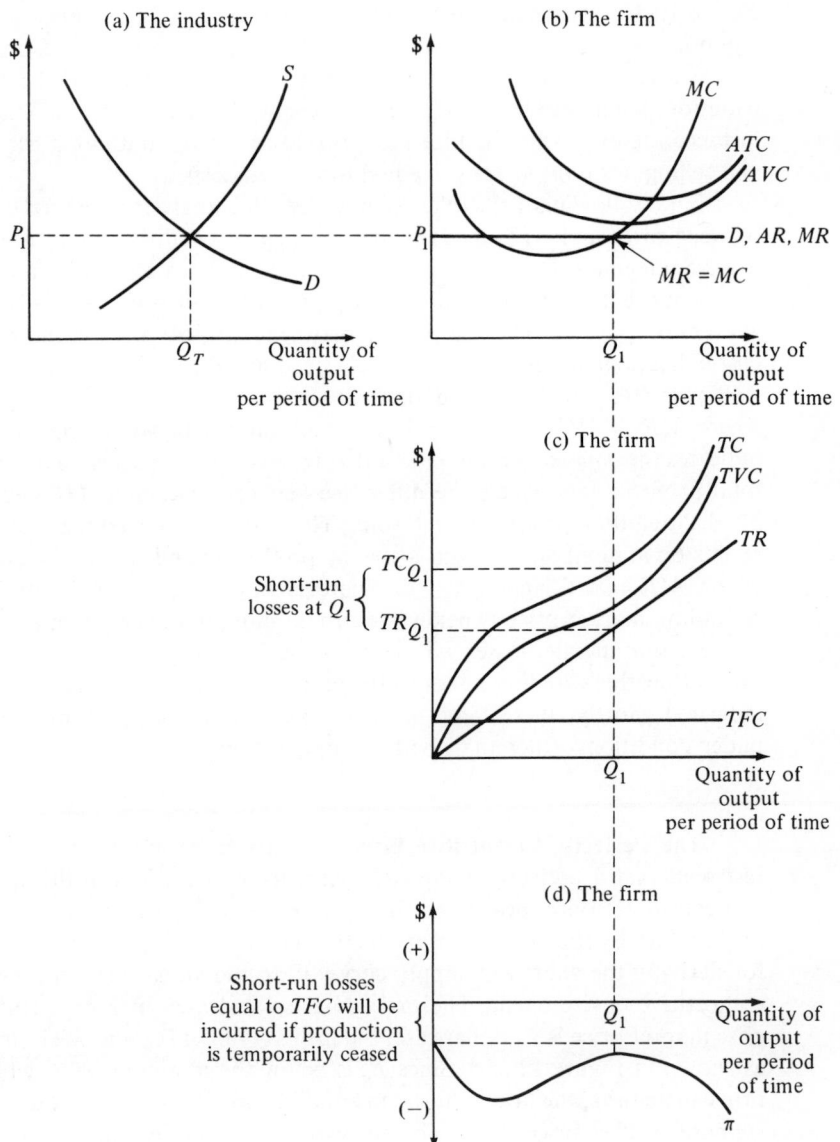

Fig. 10-4   The Short-Run Close-Down Position for a Perfectly Competitive Firm

However, Figure 10-4 shows a situation where the short-run èquilib-
rium market price falls below even minimum *AVC*. Should the firm again
follow the rule of producing at the point where $MR = MC$ [Figure 10-4(b)],
then total losses will be equal to the vertical distance between *TR* and *TC* in

Figure 10-4(c). Observe that *TR* will not even cover *TVC* at this output—or any other output for that matter. The vertical spread between *TR* and *TC* is always greater at outputs above zero than at zero. Both unit and total contribution profits are negative at every output above zero. Therefore, in this instance the firm will minimize short-run losses by discontinuing production and selling nothing; losses will equal total fixed costs.

The following principles summarize the analysis: The relationship between price and *AVC* tells the firm *whether* to produce; the firm will find it advantageous to continue production if price equals or exceeds *AVC* at one or more output rates and to cease production if price falls below *AVC* at every output rate. The relationship between marginal revenue and marginal cost indicates *how much* the firm should produce when price equals or exceeds *AVC*; profits are maximized or losses are minimized at the output rate where $MR = MC$ and $M\pi = 0$. The relationship between price and *ATC* indicates the *amount of profit or loss* that results from the decision to produce; total profit or loss equals the difference between price and *ATC* multiplied by the quantity produced and sold. Thus, the firm maximizes short-run profits or minimizes short-run losses by producing and selling the output at which $MR = MC$ and $M\pi = 0$. There is only one exception. When the prevailing market price is below the firm's minimum average variable costs at every output rate, losses will be minimized by stopping short-run operations altogether, holding losses to the amount of total fixed costs. As will be indicated shortly, these same principles also hold true for firms operating under conditions other than perfect competition.

The Perfectly Competitive Firm's Short-Run Supply Curve. We have just seen that a perfectly competitive firm incurring a loss in the short run will continue to produce in the short run provided it loses no more by producing than by shutting down production entirely. This proposition is useful for deriving the short-run supply curve of an individual firm in a perfectly competitive environment. The procedure is illustrated in Figure 10-5. Suppose market price is P_0 dollars and the firm's *AVC*, *ATC*, and *MC* curves are as shown in Figure 10-5(a). Since P_0 is below the minimum *AVC* which the firm can achieve, the firm's short-run equilibrium rate of output is zero. Next, suppose market price is P_1. The corresponding equilibrium rate of output for the firm is Q_1 units, as this is the output at which $MR = MC$ and at which losses are minimum. Thus, the firm is ready, willing, and able to supply Q_1 units at a price of P_1 dollars; the values (P_1, Q_1) define a point (S_1) on the firm's supply curve in panel (b). Now suppose market price is P_2, generating D_2, AR_2, and MR_2. In this case, the firm's optimum output decision is to produce Q_2 units and thereby minimize its short-run losses. The values (P_2, Q_2) are associated with point S_2 in Figure 10-5(b). Similarly,

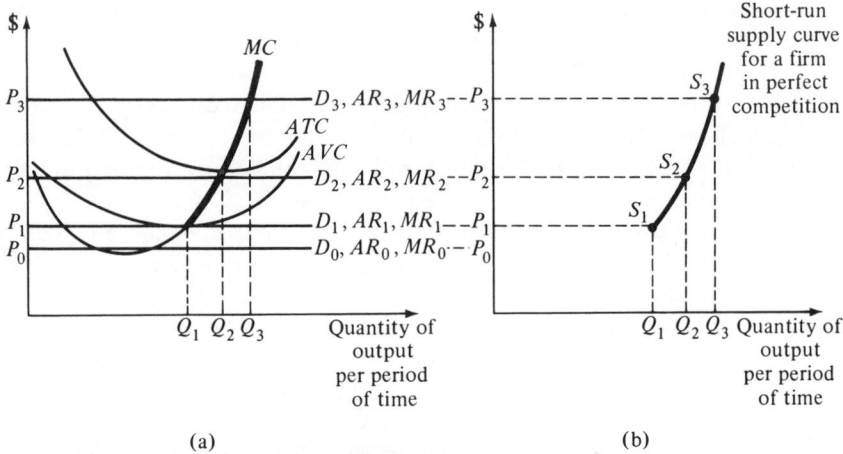

Fig. 10-5   Derivation of the Short-Run Supply Curve for a Perfectly Competitive Firm

a price of P_3 leads to a profit-maximizing output of Q_3 units and point S_3. Other supply points can be derived in like fashion.

Connecting the price-output combinations in Figure 10-5(b) gives the short-run supply curve of the perfectly competitive firm. The supply curve indicates the quantity of output per period of time which a profit-maximizing firm would supply at various alternative prices under conditions of perfect competition. It should by now be apparent that the firm's supply curve is identical in shape and position to that portion of the firm's MC curve lying above its AVC curve. This is illustrated in Figure 10-5(a) as the boldly inscribed portion of the firm's MC curve. In other words, *the short-run supply curve for a perfectly competitive firm coincides with its marginal cost curve for all rates of output equal to or greater than the output at which AVC is minimum.* The firm's supply of output drops to zero at any price below AVC. Herein lies the link between production costs and output rates in the short run for a perfectly competitive enterprise.

The Perfectly Competitive Industry's Short-Run Supply Curve. In Chapter 3 the market demand curve was derived by horizontally adding together the demand curves of individual consumers. However, factors are present which may preclude a similar determination of the short-run industry supply curve for the commodity in question. The perfectly competitive firm's marginal cost curve is derived from the underlying production function (Chapter 8) on the assumption that the price of variable input is constant, no matter how many or how few units the firm purchases. This is a reasonable assumption in the case of perfectly competitive firms, because any one firm uses such a small amount of the total supply of the variable input that changes in its rate of input usage have no perceptible effect on the market price of the variable input. In other words, a single firm can expand or reduce its output rate, and consequently its variable input usage, without affecting the price it pays for variable input.

Yet, should *all* firms in a perfectly competitive industry simultaneously decide to expand or to reduce output, there may be a marked effect upon the supply price of the variable input. For example, suppose one chicken producer decides to raise more chickens and therefore buys more chicken feed. The prevailing price of chicken feed is quite unlikely to be affected. But if all chicken producers decide to raise more chickens, upward pressure on the price of chicken feed becomes a distinct possibility, particularly in the short run when the supplies of chicken feed are limited by the available production capacity.

As a consequence, the short-run supply curve for the product of a perfectly competitive industry cannot necessarily be obtained by horizontally summing the relevant portion of the marginal cost curves of each firm. It all depends upon what happens to the price of variable input when *all* firms in the industry alter their usage of variable input. In the event that the supplies of variable input to a perfectly competitive industry are perfectly elastic (the input supply curves are horizontal), then it is valid to conceive of the short-run industry supply curve for the product as being the horizontal summation of the relevant portions of the *MC* curves of the individual firms. If the use of more variable input by all firms in the industry precipitates an increase in the price of variable input, then the marginal cost curve of each individual firm will shift upward by the increase in input price, and the short-run industry supply curve will be *more steeply sloped* than had input prices remained constant. If the use of more variable input by all firms in the industry causes the price of variable input to decline (perhaps because it can be supplied more economically in larger quantities), then the marginal cost curve of each individual firm will shift downward by the decrease in input price and the short-run industry supply curve will be *less steeply sloped* than had input prices remained constant.

But whatever happens to the price of variable input when all firms use more or less of it, we can be confident that the short-run industry supply curve is upward sloping. How steeply sloped it is depends upon the factors determining the shape of the marginal cost curve of each firm and upon the effect of changes in industrywide output on variable input prices. Suffice it to say at this point that to induce greater supplies of output in the short-run from a perfectly competitive industry, higher prices will have to be offered. This characteristic gives rise to a short-run industry supply curve that slopes upward to the right—such then is the basis for the industry supply curves drawn in Figures 10-1 through 10-4.

LONG-RUN EQUILIBRIUM OF A FIRM IN
A PERFECTLY COMPETITIVE MARKET

Although a perfectly competitive firm finds its short-run output decision constrained by the limitations of the fixed inputs, in the long-run the options are more numerous. An established firm can alter its plant size, implement new technologies, or modify the character of its products in line with changing consumer tastes. More importantly, the firm can abandon production entirely and leave the industry if below-normal profits are being earned and the prospects are dim for any improvement. On the other hand, new firms may enter the industry if the profits of established firms are sufficiently attractive. Consider now the transition of a firm from short-run to long-run equilibrium in a perfectly competitive market.

Two assumptions will greatly simplify the analysis without invalidating the important conclusions:

1. We shall suppose that all firms in the industry have comparable cost structures. By so doing we can talk in terms of a typical firm with the knowledge that all other firms in the industry will be similarly affected. (This assumption is not implausible, given that all the firms are producing identical products.)

2. We shall assume for the moment that the prices of resource inputs are unaffected (a) by changes in the long-run output rates of existing firms, (b) by the entry of firms into industry, or (c) by the exodus of firms from the industry. In other words, the firms in the industry can, singly or as a group, alter their input requirements without affecting the prices they pay for them.

Let the short-run forces of market demand (D_1) and supply (S_1) result in a market price of P_1 dollars [Figure 10-6(a)]. Further suppose that the typical firm has a short-run cost structure represented by $SRAC_1$ and $SRMC_1$ at the indicated position on the $LRAC$ curve [Figure 10-6(b)]. With these revenue and cost functions, short-run equilibrium output for the firm is Q_1 units. At this output rate the firm realizes an economic profit because price exceeds $SRAC$ at Q_1 units. Recall from Chapter 9 that an economic profit means the firm is receiving a rate of return on its investment greater than it could earn by diverting its resources into the production of other commodities. Under these circumstances the earning of an economic profit will have two significant effects. First, it will encourage the firm to expand its production capability and take advantage of any available economies of scale indicated by the firm's $LRAC$ curve. Expanding its long-run output potential offers the firm the prospect of even greater economic profits. Second, the existence of above-normal profits in this industry will induce new firms to initiate production of the commodity. The process of new entry may be very slow or very rapid, depending upon the amount of economic profits being

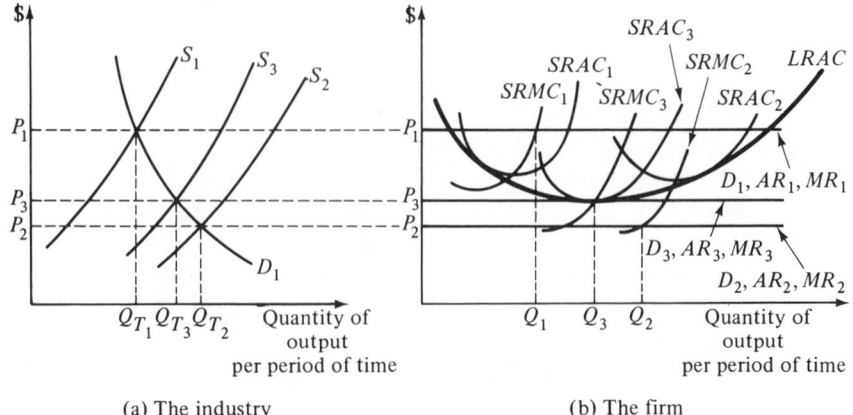

(a) The industry   (b) The firm

Fig. 10-6   The Transition to Long-Run Equilibrium for a Firm Operating in a Perfectly Competitive Market Environment

earned by established firms and upon the length of time it takes new entrants to begin their production operations.

As time elapses and these two effects take hold, the industry supply curve will shift to the right, say from S_1 to S_2, thereby driving the market price from P_1 down to P_2 and increasing the equilibrium industry output from Q_{T_1} to Q_{T_2}. The larger volume of industry output is a result of both the entry of new firms and the expansion of firms already in the industry.

Suppose that the profit attraction is strong enough to induce the typical firm to expand its production capacity to the output range where it has a cost structure represented by $SRAC_2$ and $SRMC_2$. Then, when price falls to P_2, the profit-maximizing (loss-minimizing) output of the typical firm becomes Q_2 units per period of time, where $SRMC_2$ equals MR_2. It is apparent from Figure 10-6(b) that in this particular case entry and expansion have driven market price down to the point where the typical firm will sustain losses in the short run, since P_2 is below $SRAC_2$ at every output rate. Obviously, in this example the typical firm and the industry have both overexpanded; no longer is it possible for firms to earn normal profits. The result will be another readjustment in the industry's production rates. Given that firms can earn higher rates of return in other industries, some firms—perhaps the least efficient firms incurring the greatest losses—will elect to cease production of the commodity in question and shift their energies into the production of products where the profit outlook is brighter. The firms that choose to remain in the industry will find it advantageous over the long term to reduce unit costs by adjusting their production capabilities to the optimum size— where the $SRAC$ curve is tangent to the minimum point of the $LRAC$ curve. In terms of Figure 10-6(b), the typical firm will be induced to construct production facilities having a cost structure represented by $SRAC_3$ and $SRMC_3$.

Gradually, the outmigration of firms, coupled with the retrenchment of the production capacity of those that remain, will shift the industry supply curve to the left, say to S_3. Given the market demand curve (D_1), market price will rise to P_3 and total industry output will contract to Q_{T_3}. The optimum output rate for the typical firm will be Q_3 units, where MR_3 intersects $SRMC_3$. Observe that at this output price is just equal to short-run average total cost and to long-run average cost. The typical firm earns no economic profit but is able to squeeze out a normal profit. Taken together, these conditions define long-run equilibrium for a perfectly competitive market.

Given our initial assumptions of (a) perfect mobility of resources into and out of the industry and (b) a goal of profit maximization, the position of long-run equilibrium is ordained to occur at the point where price equals the minimum value of long-run average cost and where the typical firm earns no more and no less than a normal profit. This is, indeed, the only conceivable point of long-run equilibrium. The reasoning is straightforward. So long as market price is above the long-run average costs of the typical firm, economic profits can be realized. Established firms will be induced to expand, provided it is profitable to do so, and new firms will be attracted into the industry. Over time the market supply curve will be shifted to the right, thereby driving market price down and lowering the horizontal demand, AR, and MR curves confronting each firm. Economic profits will tend to vanish. On the other hand, whenever price is below the long-run average costs of the typical firm, losses will be incurred. As their plants and equipment depreciate, some firms will leave the industry, being attracted by the higher profit prospects elsewhere; the remaining firms will attempt to lower their costs by constructing facilities of more economical size. The industry supply curve shifts leftward and market price is raised along with the horizontal demand, AR, and MR curves for the individual firms. Losses will gradually be eliminated. The number of firms in the industry and the production capacity of each firm will stabilize only when the opportunities for earning an economic profit are exhausted and when economic losses can be avoided. Therefore, since the position of long-run equilibrium must be consistent with *zero* economic profit and *zero* economic loss, it is necessary that the long-run equilibrium price be exactly equal to minimum short-run average cost and to minimum long-run average cost. Unless $P = MR = SRAC = SRMC = LRAC$, a change in firm size or in the number of firms will lead to the appearance of either economic profits or economic losses, in which case the forces of adjustment will spring into motion.[4]

It should now be apparent that we are entirely justified in our earlier

[4] In practice, however, the profit thermostat regulating the number of firms and the outputs they produce works much better for expansion than contraction. Economic profits and free entry are reliable stimulants for increasing industry output, given sufficient time for firms to construct new facilities and bring new production capacity on stream. But to squeeze firms out of an overexpanded industry where profits are below normal or negative can be a slow and painful process. It takes time for entrepreneurs to accept the harsh fact that profit prospects are bleak, time for production facilities to wear out, and time to shift into the production of other commodities or else go out of business entirely. The long death of the small farmer is a case in point.

assumption that perfectly competitive firms will seek to maximize profits. Actually, perfectly competitive firms have no choice—they are placed in a position of *forced profit maximization*. Under conditions of long-run equilibrium a firm which operates at any output rate other than the equilibrium rate will not earn even a normal profit; it will, in other words, sustain economic losses. Few firms are likely to pursue alternative goals when their earnings record is so dismal. They simply cannot afford it. For this reason, it seems justifiable to assume that perfectly competitive firms will behave as if they seek to maximize profits. Firms that behave otherwise in this type of competitive environment are not likely to survive for long.

It is also fair to conclude at this point that perfect competition is a very "competitive" business environment. The impersonal market forces of supply and demand are so powerful that in the long run firms are unable to make a profit any larger than that just sufficient to induce them to remain in business. The only discretionary action a firm has relates to its output decision. And in the long run even here the firm's option is taken away; it is forced to produce where $P = MR = SRAC = SRMC = LRAC$ if it wants to earn at least a normal profit. Thus, the firm is truly a servant of the market. All of this, according to conventional wisdom, works to the advantage of consumers and society as a whole. Under long-run equilibrium conditions the consumer pays a price no higher than is required to cover all costs of production, thereby obtaining the commodity at as low a price as is economically feasible. Moreover, all firms produce at the minimum points of their cost curves, thus utilizing in the most efficient manner the pool of resources which society makes available to the industry.

A CONSTANT-COST INDUSTRY

In the preceding section it was assumed that the expansion or contraction of industry output had no effect on *input* prices. An industry having this characteristic is referred to as a *constant-cost* industry. The existence of such an industry has several implications which merit further exploration.

Figure 10-7 depicts long-run equilibrium under conditions of constant costs. Let D_1 and S_1 be the original short-run market demand and supply curves, with an equilibrium price at P_1 dollars. Assume that each firm in the industry is in long-run equilibrium at Q_1, where the firm's horizontal demand, AR, and MR curve is just tangent to the minimum points of the firm's $SRAC$ and $LRAC$ curves, as shown in Figure 10-7(b). Now consider the impact of a shift in the short-run market demand curve to D_2. The market price will rise to P_2 dollars and the profit-maximizing output for the firm becomes Q_2 units per period of time. However, at a price of P_2 dollars and an output of Q_2 units each firm will earn an economic profit, thereby triggering the entry of new firms into the industry and shifting the industry supply curve rightward, eventually to S_2. In the case of a constant-cost

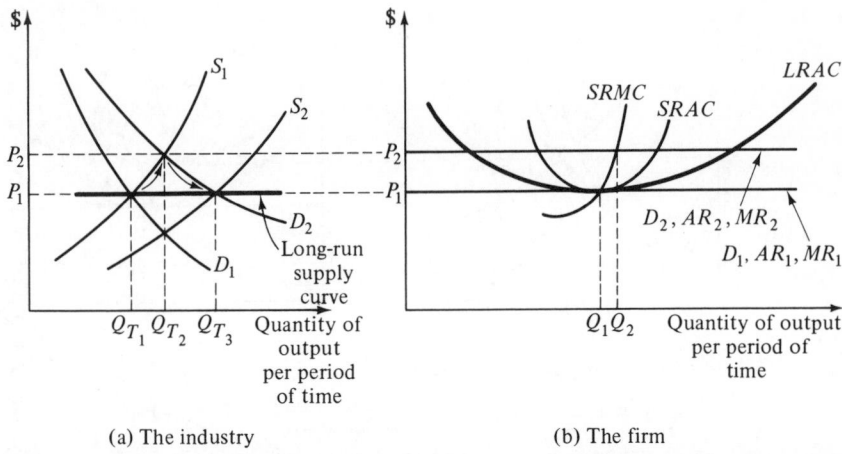

(a) The industry   (b) The firm

Fig. 10-7   The Long-Run Supply Curve for a Constant-Cost Industry

industry the entry of new firms and the expansion of industry output will not affect the costs of the existing firms. The reason is that the resource inputs employed by this industry are available in such sufficiently large quantities that the appearance of new firms does not bid up the prices of the inputs and raise the costs of the existing firms. As a consequence, the $LRAC$ curve of established firms remains fixed and the new firms can operate with an identical $LRAC$ curve.

Long-run equilibrium adjustment to the shift in demand is accomplished when the entry of new firms has caused the market price to fall back to P_1 where $P_1 = MR_1 = SRAC = SRMC = LRAC$, and each firm is producing Q_1 units and earning only a normal profit. The important point here is that the industry has a *constant long-run supply price*, which means industry output can be expanded or contracted in accordance with market demand conditions without altering the *long-run* equilibrium price charged by the firms. To put it another way, *a constant-cost industry operating under conditions of perfect competition has a horizontal long-run supply curve.* Such a curve is illustrated in Figure 10-7(a).

AN INCREASING-COST INDUSTRY

Obviously, a situation can easily arise where changes in the output rate of an industry can cause the prices of resource inputs to change. In this section we examine the case where the expansion of industry output has the effect of *raising* input prices, thereby giving rise to an *increasing-cost industry.*

As illustrated in Figure 10-8, suppose the industry is in long-run equilibrium. D_1 and S_1 portray the initial market demand and supply conditions, market price is P_1 dollars, and each firm is operating at the output

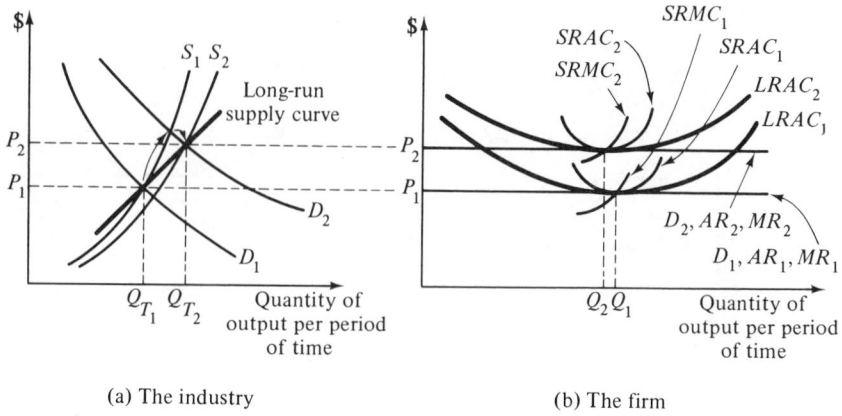

(a) The industry   (b) The firm

Fig. 10-8   The Long-Run Supply Curve for an Increasing-Cost Industry

rate where price equals minimum $SRAC$ and minimum $LRAC$. Now suppose market demand increases to D_2, temporarily causing an increase in market price to the level where D_2 intersects S_1. The higher price allows established firms to earn an economic profit, which in turn attracts the entry of new firms. As output expands more resources are needed; at this point resource input prices are bid up by firms competing for the available resource supplies. The effect of rising input prices is to increase the operating costs of both established firms and new entrants. As industry output expands and input prices rise, the marginal and average cost curves for the typical firm all gradually shift upward from $SRMC_1$, $SRAC_1$, and $LRAC_1$, say to a position represented by $SRMC_2$, $SRAC_2$, and $LRAC_2$. Moreover, the short-run industry supply curve is shifted to the right by the expansion of industry output. The process of adjustment continues until all economic profits have been eliminated. In Figure 10-8, this is depicted by the intersection of D_2 and S_2 and its associated price of P_2 dollars. Each firm selects the rate of output where $P_2 = MR_2 = SRMC_2 = SRAC_2 = LRAC_2$. The long-run industry supply curve is found by joining the points of long-run equilibrium; in Figure 10-8 these points are represented by the intersection of D_1 and S_1 and the intersection of D_2 and S_2.

    The salient feature of an increasing-cost industry is the presence of a positively sloped long-run supply curve. Whereas in a constant-cost industry the expansion of industry output has no effect on the long-run price of the industry's product, in an increasing-cost industry the effect of greater industry output is a higher product price. The long-run supply curve of an increasing-cost industry slopes upward, because greater rates of output entail rising input prices and hence rising costs. Under these circumstances, higher market prices will be required to give firms the incentive to expand output.

A DECREASING-COST INDUSTRY

Price and output behavior in a *decreasing-cost industry* is depicted in Figure 10-9. The initial long-run equilibrium is given by the market demand curve D_1, the short-run industry supply curve S_1, a market price of P_1 dollars, and each firm producing at the minimum points of $SRAC_1$ and $LRAC_1$. As before, suppose market demand increases to D_2. Market price rises to the point where D_2 intersects S_1, and established firms find themselves in the position of being able to earn an economic profit. New firms are induced to enter the industry, and the short-run industry supply curve shifts rightward, say to S_2. In a decreasing-cost industry the expansion of output results in *lower* input prices and hence lower costs for the firms in the industry. Thus, as the entry of new firms causes input prices to fall, the short-run and long-run cost curves of the firm shift downward. The adjustment process will continue until a new long-run equilibrium is established. In Figure 10-9

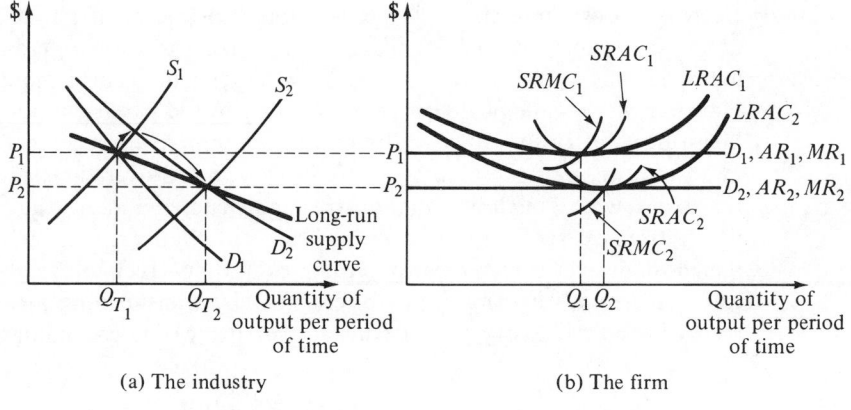

(a) The industry   (b) The firm

Fig. 10-9 The Long-Run Supply Curve for a Decreasing-Cost Industry

this occurs at the intersection of D_2 and S_2, where the resulting price of P_2 dollars is just equal to the minimum points of $SRAC_2$ and $LRAC_2$. Connecting the two points of long-run equilibrium gives the long-run industry supply curve.

Clearly, a decreasing-cost industry has a negatively-sloped long-run supply curve, meaning that the equilibrium price of the industry tends to fall as industry output increases. Although it is rare for input prices to fall when industry output expands, it does occur. One example is the case of a young industry which springs up in a relatively underdeveloped area, where resource markets are poorly organized, marketing facilities are primitive, and transportation is inadequate. An increase in the number of firms and in the output of the industry may stimulate the development of marketing and transportation facilities that reduce the costs of individual firms; in addition, supplies of labor and other support services may become more dependable and more efficient. Another example arises in the case of capital goods purchases. The more firms there are in an industry and the larger its output, the more economically suppliers of capital goods may be able to provide these firms with specialized machinery, continuous-process equipment, and higher-quality tools because of their own economies of scale in producing them. By and large, the individual firm has little control over these sorts of decreasing costs; consequently, cost reductions of this type are often referred to as external economies of increasing production, or simply as *external economies*. They result solely from growth of the industry and from forces outside the control of the individual firm. External economies should not be confused with the internal economies of scale which are under control of the firm and which can be secured by enlarging the scale of the firm's operations.

In the absence of technological change, most economists regard increasing-cost industries as being the most prevalent of the three types. Decreasing-cost industries are perhaps the most unusual situation. Both decreasing- and constant-cost industries are likely to evolve gradually into industries of increasing cost as they grow larger and become more mature. However, if technological change is admitted to the picture, a downsloping long-run industry supply curve becomes more probable. Technical progress in an industry can cause costs of production to fall over time, thus giving rise to a downsloping long-run industry supply curve.[5] Indeed, the industries which are most successful in lowering costs and relative prices tend to show the most dramatic increases in output over time. Technological progress can also neutralize rising input prices, thereby transforming an otherwise increasing-cost industry into a constant- or decreasing-cost industry.

SUMMARY OF THE PERFECTLY COMPETITIVE MODEL

The chief feature of a perfectly competitive market structure is the presence of powerful forces which drive market price to the level where each firm earns no more and no less than a normal rate of return. The position of long-run equilibrium is characterized by a "no profit-no loss" situation—firms earn only an accounting profit equal to the rate of return generally obtainable elsewhere. Whenever demand and supply conditions allow firms in the industry to earn more than a normal profit, new firms are induced to enter and, where economies of scale permit, existing firms are induced to expand. Subsequently, price is driven to the point of minimum $SRAC$ and minimum $LRAC$, thereby foreclosing the opportunity to earn more than a normal return. Should demand and supply conditions result in a price that inflicts losses upon the firms in the industry, then some firms are induced to shift into the production of other commodities where the profit prospects

---

[5] The manufacture of transistors and solid state components is an excellent example of an industry which has experienced declining costs as a result of new technologies.

are more favorable; the remaining firms seek to adjust their scale of operations in the direction of minimum long-run average cost. As a consequence, price and output will tend to move toward levels consistent with the earning of a normal profit.

It should be emphasized that in perfectly competitive markets the market forces of supply and demand *compel* firms to produce the quantity of output with the lowest possible long-run average cost. Market price is wholly determined by the interaction of market demand and market supply; therefore, perfectly competitive firms are *price takers* and *quantity adjusters*. Ultimately, firms which wish to avoid losses have *no choice* but to adjust their output rates in the long run to the point where $P = MR = SRMC = SRAC = LRAC$. Perfect competition thus represents a powerful competitive struggle in which the firm must respond passively to forces well beyond its control. The perfectly competitive firm in long-run equilibrium has absolutely zero market power; it is able to exercise no control whatsoever over price, and if it wishes to earn a normal profit it has no choice but to adjust its output rate to correspond to the lowest point on the $LRAC$ curve. Consequently, consumers are well protected from exploitation by business firms. The market result is the outcome of freely made decisions of consumers to buy and freely made decisions of producers to sell. Neither is able to control the other or rig the market to his own advantage. Hence, the model of perfect competition is the very epitome of a *free market*.

The major conclusions to be derived from the model of perfect competition concern the benefits derived by the consumers of the industry's product and the efficiency with which resources are allocated. Under conditions of long-run equilibrium, consumers are able to buy the product at the lowest price consistent with covering all costs of production. Since price is barely sufficient to give the firm a normal profit and keep it in business in the long run, the consumer obtains the product at as low a price as is economically feasible. In addition, every firm is forced to produce at the most efficient output rate. All scale economies are realized, and all diseconomies of size are avoided. Thus perfectly competitive firms utilize resources in the most efficient manner possible—full production efficiency is attained. Society obtains the greatest output from the resources used in producing the commodity and at the lowest feasible price. Herein lies the social justification for a free-market (or capitalistic) economy. The perfectly competitive model is indeed the way pure capitalism theoretically works; in other words, the model describes the operation of a market economy and provides the theoretical underpinning for *laissez faire* capitalism.

In practice, of course, it is not really expected that a perfectly competitive industry would reach and maintain a state of long-run equilibrium. Consumer tastes and preferences undergo constant adjustment and modification as do other demand determinants; the result is frequent shifts in the market demand curve. Technological progress, changing resource prices, and changes in other supply-determining factors likewise cause firm and industry supply curves to shift. As a consequence, few markets are ever in equilibrium, and if they were they would not remain there long. The typical market is in a state of constant flux, always responding to changes in demand and supply and chasing the newly created equilibrium point. The main practical use of the perfectly competitive model is, therefore, to explain change and to predict its direction rather than to determine the conditions for stability.

The Model of Monopolistic Competition

In actual markets the products of firms are seldom homogeneous. Ordinarily, the product of each firm is in some way *differentiated* from the product of every other firm. In fact, most enterprises devote considerable time and effort to engineering special features into their products and to making their products unique through advertising, packaging, brand names, terms of credit, service, and so on. The particular concern of the model of monopolistic competition is with price and output behavior in a market environment comprised of *many* firms selling products that are very close, but not perfect, substitutes for each other. The two distinctive features of monopolistic competition are large numbers of firms and differentiated products.

In practice, some difficulty may arise in determining the boundaries of a monopolistically competitive industry, since each firm produces a somewhat different product. Nonetheless, it is usually feasible to group similar products together and refer to them as a *product group*; firms which participate in the product group can then be said to constitute the industry. For example, we can speak of a product group called women's dresses or furniture, knowing full well that the products they include, while exceedingly diverse in detail, are still similar enough to be classified together.

Introducing the element of product differentiation causes some consumers to prefer the products of particular firms over those of other firms. Each firm in producing its own unique version of the product obtains a kind of limited monopoly. There is only one producer of Schlitz beer, only one manufacturer of Hart, Schaffner, and Marx suits, and only maker of Ritz crackers even so, each of these firms faces stiff competition from rival firms—hence the label "monopolistic competition." Ultimately, product differentiation has the effect of giving a monopolistically competitive firm limited influence over the price it charges for its output—the firm in a very restricted sense is a "price maker." It derives this power from consumer preferences for some product over others; some consumers are willing, within limits, to pay a higher price to satisfy their preferences for the products of specific firms. The price differential which a firm is able to charge is a function of the firm's success in differentiating its product in the minds of consumers, thereby creating "brand loyalties" and "store loyalties." However, the price differential obtainable by any one firm is likely to be slight, since close similarity among the products of rival firms makes it quite difficult to create strong brand attachment when price differences are sizable. In more formal terms, we can say that the cross elasticity of demand between products of monopolistically competitive firms is quite high; so also is the price elasticity of demand for any one firm's product over the relevant range of prices.

Like perfect competition, monopolistic competition is characterized by a sufficiently large enough number of firms that no one firm has the production capacity to supply a significant share of the industry's output. Monopolistically competitive firms are typically small, both absolutely and relatively. Entry into monopolistically competitive industries is usually easy, though a bit more difficult than in perfect competition. This is so because of product differentiation. A new firm must not only possess the capacity for producing the product, but it must also be able to win customers away from established firms. Securing a niche in the market is likely to entail research and development costs by the new firm to discover features which will distinguish its product from products already on the market. Moreover, unlike perfect competition, advertising and sales promotion may be necessary to inform consumers of the availability of a new brand and to persuade enough customers to switch to the new brand. Therefore, a newcomer into a monopolistically competitive industry faces somewhat greater financial and marketing obstacles than a comparably situated firm in perfect competition.

The final feature of monopolistic competition is the presence of vigorous *nonprice competition* among the firms. Economic rivalry is based partially on price and partially on product quality, service and other conditions of sale, and sales promotion. A firm under monopolistic competition can simultaneously undertake three strategies for influencing its sales volume. First, the firm can change the price it charges. Second, the firm can modify the nature of its product. Third, the firm can revise its sales promotion tactics. The first strategy represents an attempt to move along the demand curve confronting the firm, whereas the latter two strategies involve an attempt to shift the firm's demand curve. Significantly, from a theoretical standpoint all three strategies can be pursued without explicit regard for the behavior of rival firms and without much concern for retaliation by rival firms. The reason? With a large number of firms in the industry, the impact of the strategy of a single firm spreads itself over so many of its rivals that the effect felt by any one rival is greatly diluted and does not usually lead to the formulation of a counterstrategy or a readjustment. Accordingly, each firm may expect its actions to go unnoticed by its competitors and to be unimpeded by countermeasures on the part of any one firm.[6]

Suppose we examine each of these three strategies in turn.

---

[6] Some economists challenge the view that a firm can rationally assume its actions will go undetected by rival firms. From a behavioral standpoint a firm can be expected to learn, sooner or later, that its strategies will in fact invoke retaliation from competitors—especially if its strategies prove successful. One must search long and hard to find a businessman who does not believe his actions will be noticed by his competitors and who, in turn, does not keep close tabs on what rival firms are doing—irrespective of how many rivals he may have. Thus, the ability to act independently is relative, not absolute. But despite this legitimate objection, it still seems fair to conclude that the larger the number of firms in an industry, the more able a firm will be to implement new strategies without provoking direct retaliation from rival firms. The fact that a firm with many rivals can act more independently than a firm with few rivals does indeed lead to differences in firm and market behavior.

PRICE AND OUTPUT DECISIONS OF MONOPOLISTICALLY COMPETITIVE FIRMS

Under conditions of monopolistic competition, each firm is confronted with a downsloping demand and average revenue curve. Herein lies the fundamental difference between the model of perfect competition and the model of monopolistic competition, and it stems from the presence of differentiated products. Because the particular product of each firm has certain distinguishing features which set it apart from those of other firms, a monopolistically competitive firm has a small measure of discretion in establishing the price of its product. By shaving its price to levels somewhat below the prices of rival firms, a firm can usually induce proportionately more customers to buy its product because it is a good substitute for the products of its competitors. On the other hand, a firm which raises its price can expect a significant decline in sales as many of its customers switch to lower-priced brands. Accordingly, the firm must have a downsloping demand curve, for it can sell more of its product at lower prices than at higher prices. The firm cannot raise price without losing sales and it cannot gain sales without charging a lower price (assuming, of course, the demand curve does not shift). Moreover, the presence of large numbers of good substitutes makes the demand curve of a particular firm highly elastic over the relevant range of possible prices.[7] Graphically, this means that the firm's demand curve tends to be *gently* downsloping, as depicted in Figure 10-10(a); the demand curve is drawn as a straight line merely for simplicity and convenience. Generally speaking, the exact degree of price elasticity reflected in a monopolistically competitive firm's demand curve is a function of the number of rival firms and the degree of product differentiation. The larger the number of competitors and the weaker the product differentiation, the greater the price elasticity of demand for a firm's product and the flatter is its demand-AR curve over the relevant price range.

When the firm's demand curve is downsloping, the firm's marginal revenue function does not coincide with the demand-average revenue function; rather, it lies below the demand-AR curve.[8] If the firm's demand-AR curve is linear and downsloping, the firm's MR curve is also linear and downsloping and has a slope twice that of the demand-AR curve. Recall from Chapter 5 that if the demand function is given by the general linear equation

$$P = a - bQ,$$

---

[7] The results of one study showed a coefficient of price elasticity of -5.7 for different brands of frozen orange juice, -5.5 for instant coffee, -4.4 for regular coffee, and -3.0 for margarine. Indirect evidence of high elasticity also stems from the fact that rival firms in monopolistic competition act as though they believed that their demand curves were highly price elastic. They usually sell their products at very nearly the same price and display a distinct hesitancy to test consumer loyalty by pricing their products much above the prices charged by rival firms. For some empirical evidence as to the degree of consumer loyalty see the two articles by Lester G. Telser: "The Demand for Branded Goods as Estimated from Consumer Panel Data," *Review of Economics and Statistics*, Vol. 44, No. 3 (August 1962), pp. 300-324; and "Advertising and Cigarettes," *Journal of Political Economy*, Vol. 70, No. 5 (October 1962), pp. 471–499.

[8] The reader is urged to refresh his memory on this point by reviewing the section on "Average, Total, and Marginal Revenue" in Chapter 5 (p. 149).

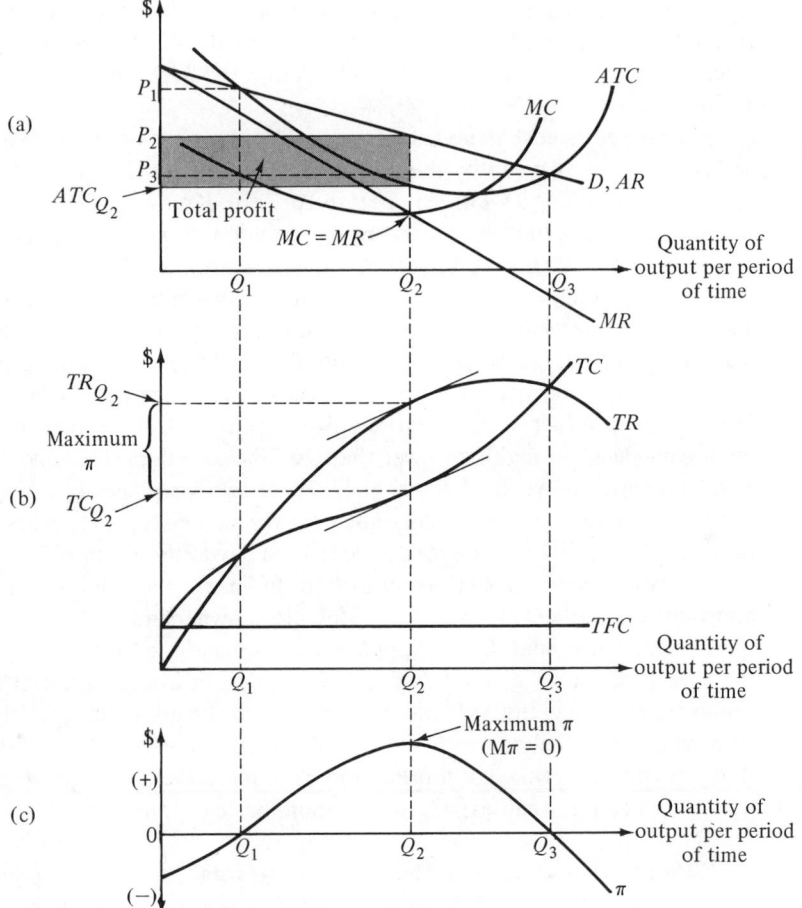

Fig. 10-10   Short-Run Profit Maximization for a Firm in Monopolistic Competition

then the equation for TR becomes

$$TR = P \cdot Q = (a - bQ)Q = aQ - bQ^2.$$

Since the expression for marginal revenue is found by taking the first derivative of the TR equation, the general equation for MR is

$$MR = \frac{dTR}{dQ} = a - 2bQ.$$

Both the demand-AR curve and the MR curve originate at the same value a; but the slope of the MR function is twice as great as that of the demand-AR curve ($-2b$ as compared to $-b$). In geometric terms, the MR curve is located by drawing it so as to bisect the horizontal distance between the demand-AR curve and the vertical axis [Figure 10-10(a)]. The total revenue function corresponding to the demand-AR and the MR functions is depicted in Figure 10-10(b).

Suppose the cost structure of a typical firm in a monopolistically competitive industry is given by the ATC and MC curves in Figure 10-10(a) and by the corresponding TC curve in Figure 10-10(b). Knowing, then, its cost and revenue functions, the firm must now decide upon its price and output levels. Since monopolistically competitive industries are composed of numerous firms that, by and large, are both small and owner-managed, it is appropriate again to assume that the firm's decisions are motivated by the desire to maximize profits. However, we cannot be completely confident about assuming firms will behave as if they seek to maximize profits, because the element of product differentiation gives each firm somewhat more discretionary decision-making power than was the case in perfectly competitive environments. As we shall see shortly, there are more variables to be considered, a greater degree of uncertainty is present, and market forces operate in ways which allow firms a modest leeway in deviating from profit-maximizing behavior. Nevertheless, a goal of profit maximization is a reasonable approximation of reality because of the close ownership and control which typifies relatively small firms. Suppose, also, we assume for the moment that the firm produces a given product and engages in a fixed amount of sales promotion activity; this will allow us to pinpoint the principles underlying the price and output behavior of a monopolistically competitive firm. Following this, we will relax this assumption and examine the effect of product variation and promotional expenditures upon price-output behavior.

Profit Maximization: The Total Cost-Total Revenue Approach. A firm in monopolistic competition, like the perfectly competitive firm, will maximize short-run profits at the output where total revenue exceeds total cost by the greatest amount. Given the TR and TC functions in Figure 10-10(b), the firm will be able to earn an economic profit at any output rate between Q_1 and Q_3 units; but short-run profits will be maximum at an output of Q_2 units, where the vertical distance between TR and TC is the greatest. Geometrically, TR exceeds TC by the greatest amount at the output rate where a tangent to the TC curve has the same slope and is parallel to a tangent to the TR function. The total profit function in Figure 10-10(c) is again derived by subtracting TC from TR at each output rate. Logic dictates that the peak of the total profit function correspond to an output rate of Q_2, where TR exceeds TC by the largest amount.

Profit Maximization: The Unit Cost-Unit Revenue Approach. On a unit cost and unit revenue basis, short-run profits are maximized at the output where $MC = MR$ and $M\pi = 0$. The reasoning is precisely the same as in the case of perfectly competitive firms. So long as an additional unit of output adds more to the firm's revenues than it does to the firm's costs, profit on that unit will be positive and total profits will be increased (or losses decreased) by producing and selling the unit. Alternatively, when MC exceeds MR and $M\pi$ is negative, total profits can be increased (or losses decreased) by decreasing the rate of output. In Figure 10-10(a) short-run profits are maximum at an output of Q_2 units per period of time. This is the output rate at which the marginal cost curve intersects the marginal revenue curve. Moreover, it corresponds exactly to the value of Q_2 in Figure 10-10(b). At Q_2, the tangents to TR and TC have identical slopes. Since the slope of TC equals MC and the slope of TR equals MR, MR must equal MC at exactly the output where TR exceeds TC by the greatest amount.

The highest price which the firm can charge and still sell Q_2 units is P_2 dollars. The profit maximizing price thus corresponds to the point on the demand-AR curve associated with the output at which $MC = MR$. Average total cost at Q_2 units of output is ATC_{Q_2}. Total profit in the short run equals $(P - ATC_{Q_2})Q_2$, or the shaded area in Figure 10-10(a). At outputs smaller than Q_2 units, MR exceeds MC, and larger outputs up to Q_2 will add more to total revenue than to total costs; accordingly, total profit will rise as the output rate is raised. At an output rate beyond Q_2, MC exceeds MR, and additional sales cause total costs to rise faster than total revenue, thereby decreasing total profit. Note that the firm can realize at least a normal profit by selling at a price as high as P_1 or as low as P_3, but that a price of P_2 dollars will yield the greatest economic profit. Prices P_1 and P_3 may be thought of as the "breakeven" prices and outputs Q_1 and Q_3 may be thought of as the "breakeven" output rates.

Calculation of the Profit-Maximizing Output. The mathematical procedure for determining the profit-maximizing price and output for a firm with a downsloping demand function is analogous to the calculations for a firm in perfect competition. Suppose the firm's demand function is given by the equation $P = 11,100 - 30Q$ and the firm's total cost function is given by the equation $TC = 400,000 + 300Q - 30Q^2 + Q^3$. From the preceding discussion we know that profit is maximized at the output where $MR = MC$. Both MR and MC can be obtained from the information given. If the demand function is $P = 11,100 - 20Q$, then

$$TR = P \cdot Q = (11,100 - 30Q)Q = 11,100Q - 30Q^2,$$

and

$$MR = \frac{dTR}{dQ} = 11,100 - 60Q.$$

The MC function, being the first derivative of the TC function, is

$$MC = \frac{dTC}{dQ} = 300 - 60Q + 3Q^2.$$

Equating MR with MC gives

$$11,100 - 60Q = 300 - 60Q + 3Q^2,$$

which reduces to

$$3Q^2 = 10,800.$$

Solving for Q yields the two roots $Q = -60$ and $Q = 60$. Obviously, output can never be negative; hence, the profit-maximizing rate of output is 60 units. As indicated earlier, it can be proved that the larger of the two roots is always the profit-maximizing (or loss-minimizing) output rate. It is a simple matter, however, to calculate total profit at each positive value of Q for which $MR = MC$ and see which root is associated with the greatest profit.

The profit-maximizing price is found by substituting the profit-maximizing output rate into the demand function and solving for P. In terms of our example, the profit-maximizing price is

$$
\begin{aligned}
P &= 11,100 - 30Q \\
&= 11,100 - 30(60) \\
&= 11,100 - 1,800 \\
&= \$9,300.
\end{aligned}
$$

Total profit at this price and output can be calculated by subtracting TC at 60 units of output from TR at 60 units of output. The reader should verify that total profit at 60 units of output will be $32,000 per period of time.

Total Profit or Loss. If demand is weak, then the monopolistically competitive firm may be unable to make an economic profit or even a normal profit. In such cases the firm must decide whether to shut down its operations in the short run and wait for demand conditions to become more favorable or whether to continue operating at a loss. The firm's short-run price and output decision hinges upon whether or not demand is strong enough to allow the firm to cover variable costs at some output rate.

Consider Figure 10-11(a). Between outputs of Q_1 and Q_3 units per period, the firm's demand-AR curve lies above its AVC curve; hence, unit contribution profit $(P - AVC)$ is positive at all outputs greater than Q_1 and less than Q_3. As a consequence, between these outputs the revenues obtained by the firm are more than sufficient to cover total variable costs, and some total contribution profit can be earned to pay at least a portion of the firm's total fixed costs [see Figure 10-11(b)]. The firm should definitely continue to operate in the short run, since losses will be less than the amount of TFC —the amount it will lose if production and sales are temporarily discontinued. The question now is where between Q_1 and Q_3 to operate. Clearly, the firm

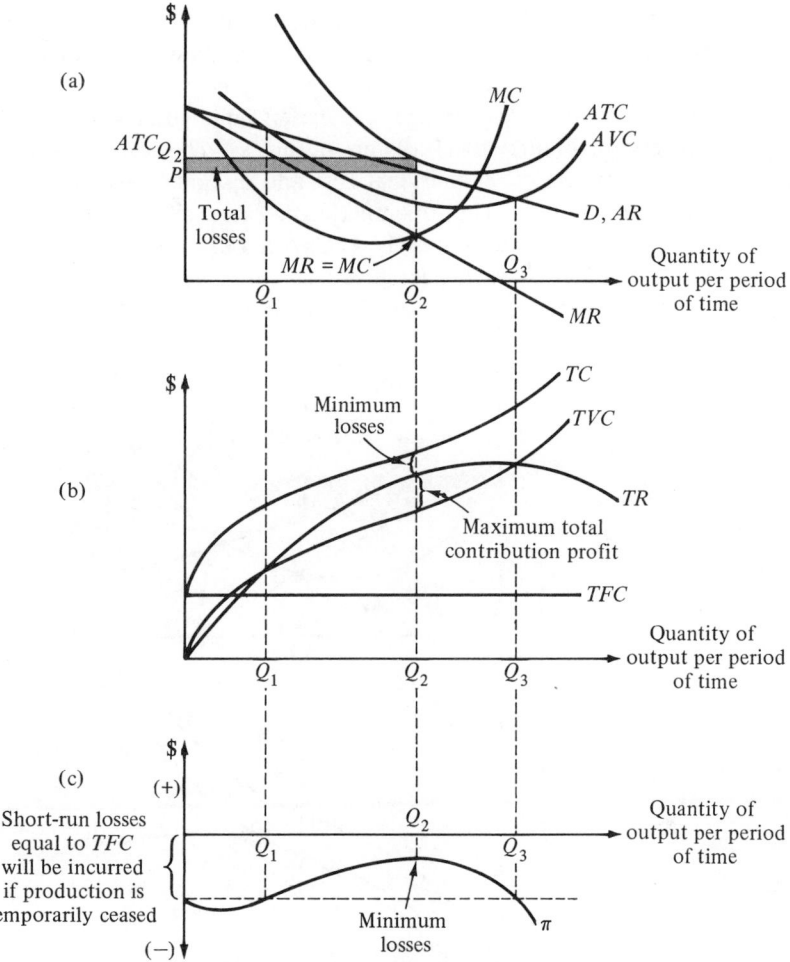

Fig. 10-11   The Short-Run Loss-Minimizing Price and Output for a Monopolistically Competitive Firm

is motivated to obtain as much total contribution profit as possible and thereby cover as large a portion of its total fixed costs as conditions will permit. Total contribution profit is maximum at the output where TR exceeds TVC by the greatest vertical distance. In Figure 10-11(b) this occurs at an output rate of Q_2 units, where a tangent to the TR curve has the same slope as a tangent to the TVC curve. By inspection, the vertical distance by which TC exceeds TR is a minimum at Q_2, meaning that at Q_2 the firm's short-run losses are minimized. Therefore, from the standpoint of TC-TR analysis, short-run losses are minimized at the output rate where total contribution profit is the greatest. This output coincides exactly with the output where the vertical spread between TC and TR is smallest. The corresponding total profit function reaches its highest level at Q_2, although it still lies entirely in the negative (loss) range. Insofar as unit costs and unit revenues are concerned [Figure 10-11(a)], an output of Q_2 units corresponds exactly to the intersection of marginal cost and marginal revenue, where marginal profit equals zero. The loss-minimizing price is P dollars. At an output of Q_2 units, average total cost is ATC_{Q2}; the firm's short-run losses will equal $(P - ATC_{Q2})Q_2$—which is shown as the shaded area in Figure 10-11(a). Thus, provided at least a portion of the demand-AR curve lies above the

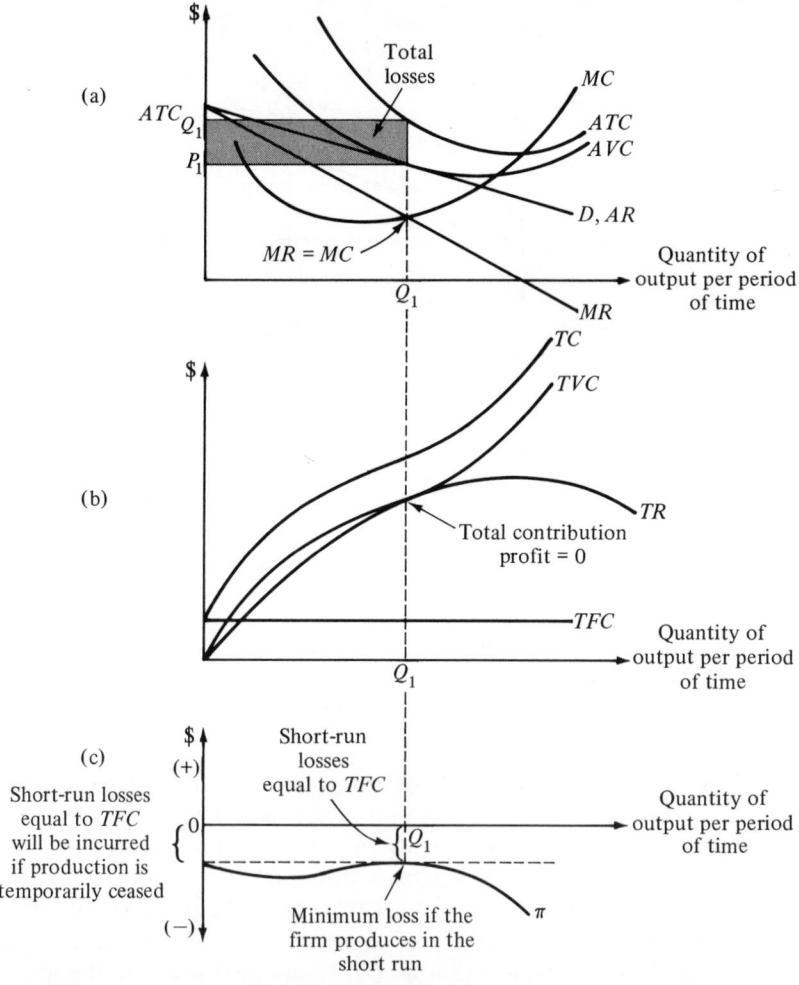

Fig. 10-12 The Short-Run Loss-Minimizing Price and Output for a Monopolistically Competitive Firm when the Demand Curve Is Just Tangent to the AVC Curve

AVC curve (so that $P > AVC$), we see that the $MR = MC$ rule, along with
its corollary, $M\pi = 0$, identifies not only the short-run profit-maximizing
output but also the short-run loss-minimizing output.

Figure 10-12 illustrates a situation where the firm's demand-AR curve
again lies below the ATC curve, foreclosing the opportunity for earning
a normal profit in the short run. Note that the demand-AR curve is tangent
to the AVC curve at a single output—Q_1 units. At Q_1, demand is just strong
enough to permit the firm to sell at a price that will cover AVC. Unit contribution profit equals zero at Q_1; likewise, total contribution profit is zero,
since $TR = TVC$ [see Figure 10-12(b)]. From a profit-loss standpoint the
firm will be indifferent as to producing and selling Q_1 units or closing down
production in the short run. In either event, short-run losses will equal TFC,
and this is the best the firm can do [see Figures 10-12(b) and (c)]. At any
other price and output combination TR will be insufficient to cover even
TVC, both total and unit contribution profit will be negative, and short-run
losses will exceed TFC by the amount of TVC not covered by TR. Given
that selling Q_1 units at a price of P_1 dollars will have no adverse effects on
its profit-loss position (as compared to temporarily closing down operations),
the firm will undoubtedly elect to continue production. In doing so, the firm
will protect its market share and, by continuing to place its product before
the public, stand a better chance of realizing a favorable shift in demand
conditions in the future.

Now consider Figure 10-13, where the firm's demand-AR curve lies
entirely below the AVC curve. At no output rate can sufficient revenues be
accumulated to cover the variable costs of production. The vertical spread
between TR and TC is always greater at output rates above zero than at zero.
Both unit and total contribution profits are negative at all positive outputs.
The total profit function is even more negative at positive output rates than
at zero output. Therefore, in this instance the firm will minimize short-run
losses by temporarily ceasing production and waiting for a favorable shift
of the demand-AR curve; short-run losses will equal total fixed costs.

Of course, if the weak demand conditions are perceived as permanent
and if over time the firm's costs cannot be lowered sufficiently to allow a normal profit to be earned, then the firm should begin to divert its energies
and resources into the production of other more profitable commodities or
else dissolve entirely. Short-run losses can be sustained only temporarily.
As the time perspective lengthens, some sort of readjustment must be made.

The curious reader may be wondering why we have not discussed
graphical treatment of industry supply and demand curves. The reason is
that under conditions of monopolistic competition the representation of
industry supply and demand *conditions* by means of industry supply and
demand *curves* is less than satisfactory. Product differentiation makes the
product units sold by one firm somewhat different than the product units
sold by another. Bottles of hair oil differ from tubes of hair cream. Aerosol

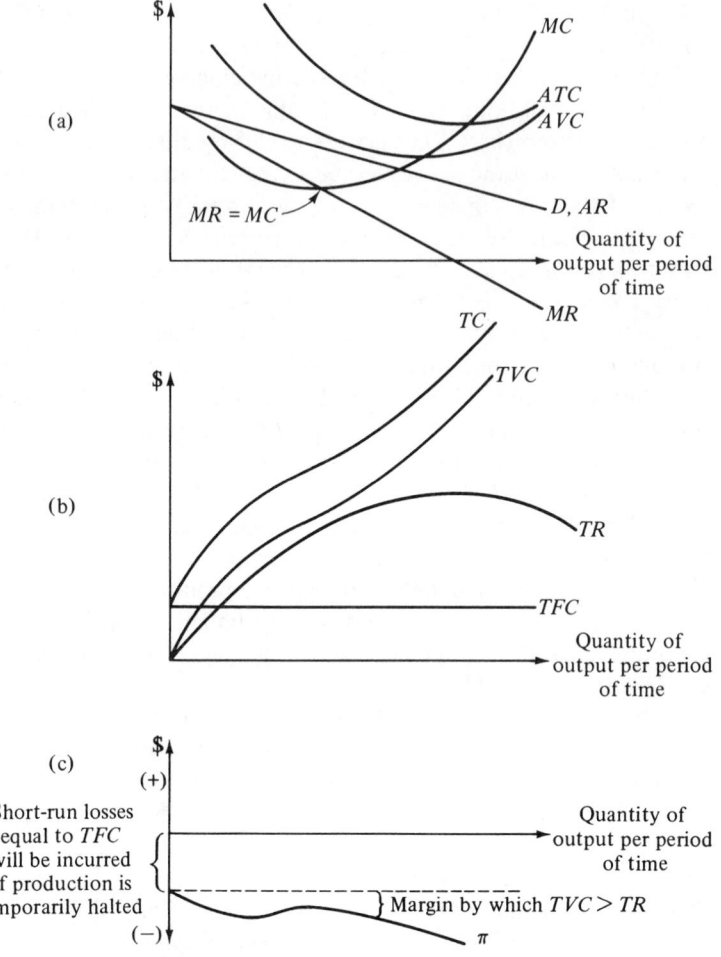

Fig. 10-13   The Short-Run Close-Down Position for a Monopolistically Competitive Firm

cans of hair spray are still different. Thus, there is some difficulty in constructing the quantity axis for industry curves. Furthermore, no single price prevails for the products of firms in the industry. Each firm may charge a slightly different price, according to the costs of producing its particular product and the strength of consumer demand for it. As a result of the price and product variations among firms, it is difficult to speak of a specific amount of output being supplied or demanded at a specific price. Moreover, what a firm is willing to produce at a given point in time hinges upon both MR and MC—the former varies with the demand for the product and the latter is a function of input prices and the firm's technology. There is no unique price for each alternative output; it all depends upon the shape and position of the demand-AR curve as to what the profit-maximization price is for any given output at which $MR = MC$. Thus the price-output decisions of firms cannot be meaningfully translated into an industry supply curve. The market as a whole is there, but it is described better in linquistic than in graphic terms.

Long-Run Adjustments of Monopolistically Competitive Firms. We saw earlier that with free entry and exit firms in a perfectly competitive industry are unable to earn more than a normal profit. Under monopolistic competition similar forces are present, though they are not quite so powerful as to eliminate completely the earning of economic profit or to guarantee each firm as much as a normal profit. The most which can be said is that *a tendency exists* for profits to move toward normal rates of return.

In the long run the firms in a monopolistically competitive industry can alter the scale of their operations or leave the industry. New firms can enter the industry without undue difficulties. When short-run economic profits exist generally throughout the industry, established firms can be expected to pursue additional economies of scale, new technologies, and other profit-enhancing, cost-reducing options. New firms, attracted by the above-normal rates of return, will be motivated to enter the industry.[9] The entry of new rivals, assuming constant market demand for the products of the industry, will cause the demand curve of each firm to shift to the left. Why? Because each firm will necessarily have a smaller market share, since more firms will be dividing the relatively constant total market among themselves. Moreover, the demand curve will become somewhat more elastic, owing to the presence of a larger number of close-substitute products. These shifts in demand will tend to narrow profit margins and cause economic profits gradually to dissipate. Provided the attraction of economic profits is sufficiently strong to induce the entry of enough new firms and provided established firms are unable to discover innovative means of earning economic profits, there will exist a tendency for all economic profits to be eliminated in the long run. Figure 10-14 illustrates the long-run equilibrium position of the representative firm. In panel (a) the demand-AR curve is shown tangent to the $SRAC$ curve and the $LRAC$ curve at the profit-maximizing output. Output Q_1 is the long-run equilibrium output and price P_1 is the long-run equilibrium price. Since price equals $SRAC$ at Q_1 units of output, the firm is just covering *all* of its costs, including implicit and opportunity costs. The accounting profit reported by the firm will be equal to a normal profit or a normal rate of return in the economic sense. In panel (b) the TC curve is tangent to the TR curve at an output of Q_1 units. The total profit function in Figure 10-14(c) climbs just to the zero-economic-profit level at

---

[9] For simplicity, we shall assume that the entry and exit of firms has no effect on input prices and, consequently, upon the $SRAC$ and $LRAC$ curves of the firms. In other words, the long-run adjustment process is presumed to take place in a constant-cost environment. Shifts in the $SRAC$ and $LRAC$ curves as firms enter or leave the industry would unduly complicate the discussion without altering the conclusions.

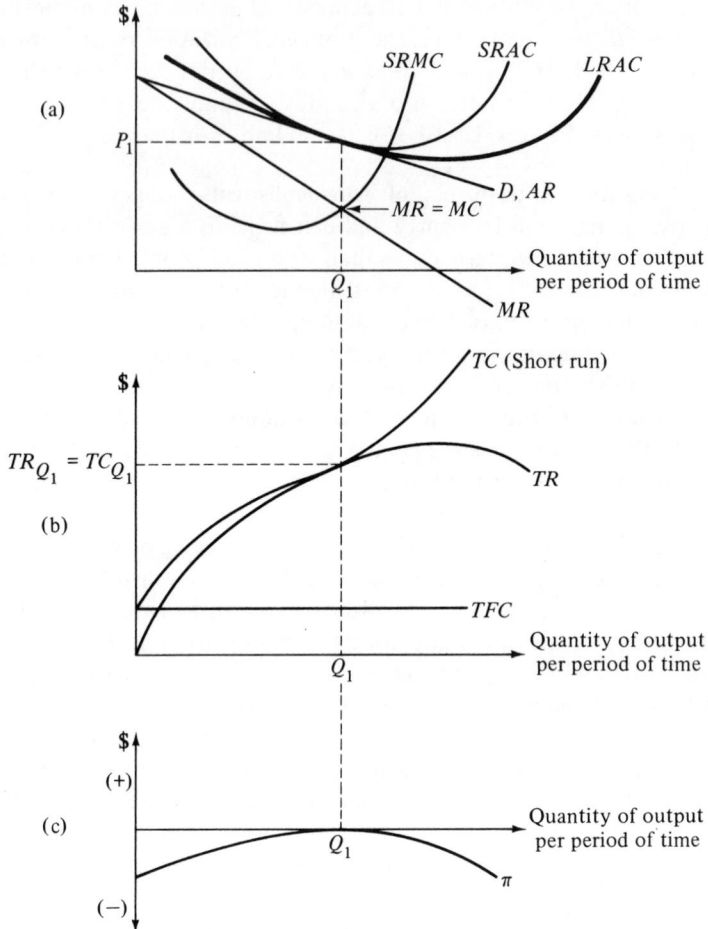

Fig. 10-14 Long-Run Equilibrium for a Monopolistically Competitive Firm

Q_1 units. Plainly, any deviation from an output of Q_1 and a price of P_1 will yield revenues which are insufficient to cover *all* production costs including a normal profit. And since economic profits have dwindled to zero, no incentive exists for additional firms to enter the industry.

Should weak demand conditions preclude established firms from earning a normal profit (as illustrated in Figures 10-11, 10-12, and 10-13), the least-efficient, highest-cost firms which are sustaining the largest losses are the most probable candidates for leaving the industry. The remaining firms can be counted upon to seek out ways to increase efficiency, reduce costs, stimulate demand, and thereby trim their losses. The exodus of firms from the industry will tend to shift the demand-AR curves of the remaining firms to the right, since the now fewer firms can divide the total market into larger pieces. Also, the reduction in the number of good substitutes will make the demand-*AR* curve a little less price elastic. The net result will tend to be an improvement in the profit-loss position of the representative firm to the point where at least a normal profit can be earned.

Observe that at the long-run equilibrium position, the representative firm is operating short of the minimum point on the *LRAC* curve. Each company is too small to achieve the lowest possible unit cost. In one sense there are too many firms in the industry. The same total output could be produced by a smaller number of firms, each operating at capacity. Thus, *excess production capacity* may be said to exist in the industry. Also, the long-run equilibrium price is higher than the minimum value of *LRAC*. Economists have made much of these two results; however, it is debatable how significant a criticism they constitute. The apparently excessive number of firms derives from consumer preferences for one brand over another, as reflected in the downsloping demand-*AR* curve. Consumers evidently believe they *gain* by being able to exercise their preferences for a brand or a store; otherwise, brand and store loyalty would vanish and the demand-*AR* curves of firms would tend to be horizontal (perfectly elastic).

An interpretative comment is in order here. Few economists seriously believe that long-run equilibrium conditions will be approximated in monopolistic competition as closely as in perfect competition. The sequence of events leading to long-run equilibrium in monopolistic competition is too easily interrupted. In the first place, some firms may be able to develop unique features in their product which are patentable and which give them a significant marketing edge over competitors even over the long term. Second, some firms may obtain an especially favorable location for their business which allows them to earn sustained economic profits; this arises often in the case of motels, service stations, restaurants, and shopping centers. Third, through product research and the implementing of new technologies, firms may be able to gain an advantage over their rivals which is sustainable for long periods. Finally, entry is not totally unrestricted; the added financial investment associated with product differentiation and sales promotion activities may pose some barrier to the entry of new firms, thereby allowing modest economic profits to persist in the long run. At the other end of the ladder, below-normal profits may also persist in the long run. The suburban florist may accept a return less than he could earn elsewhere because he likes living near a metropolitan area and because he likes designing floral arrangements. The proprietor of the corner grocery store may be content with a meager existence because his business is a way of life to him. Consequently, market forces will seldom be powerful enough in monopolistic competition to drive price all the way to equality with short-run and long-run average cost. Nevertheless, a *tendency* will exist for market forces to *limit* the profits and to *restrict* the losses of monopolistically competitive firms.

PRODUCT VARIATION DECISIONS

In monopolistic competition firms have the option of changing the characteristics of their product as well as changing their price and output. Indeed, varying the nature of the firm's product is a potent sales-increasing strategy. And from a broader social viewpoint, product competition is an important stimulant to technological innovation and product betterment over a period of time.

Suppose we consider the ramifications of product variation decisions. However, it should be kept in mind that the tendency to move toward the long-run equilibrium conditions depicted in Figure 10-14 is not obviated by the introduction of product changes. The entry and exit of firms operates to contain economic profits and to reduce economic losses no matter which variation of the product the firm selects, although the adjustment process may indeed be rendered somewhat slower and less powerful.

Let us approach the product variation decision of the representative firm by assuming for the moment that the price and product quality of rival firms are fixed. Given a goal of profit maximization, the representative firm can be expected to search among the various possible product variations for the one it perceives to be the most profitable. The problem is to select it under conditions of less than perfect knowledge. One approach is to use the best information available to estimate the most profitable price for each known variant of the product, given the prices and product characteristics of rival firms. Then the maximum profits that can be made with each variant can be estimated and the variation with the highest expected profit identified. By selecting this variant of the product, along with the corresponding profit-maximizing price and output rate, the firm can maximize expected profits.

Naturally, over time rival firms can be counted upon to change both the character of their products and the prices they charge. As this occurs, the representative firm will likely find further adaptions in its product and price to be profitable. A never-ending sequence of product variations is set in motion. Over time technological discoveries and product research will undoubtedly generate a steady stream of alternative changes which can be made in the firm's products. As new variations persistently emerge, some of them will be perceived as profitable enough to warrant their being selected—at least until more profitable variations appear.

Some firms will perceive it more profitable to adopt product variations which appeal to price-conscious consumers, with the result that their products are slightly less expensive and of lower quality. Other firms may view it most profitable to cater to the portion of the market desirous of superior quality goods, with the result that their products carry above-average prices and meet above-average performance standards. Still other firms may pursue a product variation strategy based upon "gimmicks," style, and image-related features. Such different product variation strategies reflect the fact that the market is comprised in part by consumers who are strongly quality-conscious but not especially price-conscious, in part by consumers who are willing to sacrifice quality to get a lower price, and in part by consumers who are susceptible to gimmickry and clever sales promotion schemes. This facet of consumer tastes and preferences makes it feasible and profitable for firms to pursue product-variation strategies that are diverse rather than uniform. At the same time it provides consumers with a wide range of product qualities, performance features, and prices, thereby permitting each consumer to choose the product which appears best-suited to his preferences.[10]

Product alterations will cause the firm's $SRAC$ and $LRAC$ curve to shift either up or down, according to the amounts and prices of the resource inputs needed to implement the new variations. They will also cause the demand-AR curves of each firm to shift both in position and slope as consumers respond to the product variations. It is easy to see that differences in the products and differences in the cost curves of the firms can make the long-run equilibrium positions differ from firm to firm. High-quality firms can exist alongside low-quality firms. Higher-priced firms can exist alongside lower-priced firms. This condition is readily observed in the sale of drugs and cosmetics, where retailers display on the same shelf the high-priced, better-known brands and the lesser-know, cut-price varieties. Moreover, at a given moment, some monopolistically competitive firms may be earning sizable economic profits, others may be earning only a normal profit, and others may be sustaining losses.

PROMOTIONAL EXPENSE DECISIONS

The third type of strategy which monopolistically competitive firms may employ to strengthen their market position concerns sales promotion. Imaginative sales promotion schemes are a strong complement to the firm's pricing and product-variation strategies. True, sales promotion adds to the firm's costs. But cleverly conceived promotional expenditures can be expected to shift the firm's demand-AR curve to the right and make it slightly *less* elastic as well. This is accomplished by successfully tempting people away from other brands which they previously purchased and by strengthening the

---

10 Product differentiation is not, however, without its drawbacks. Critics warn that the proliferation of product varieties may so confuse the consumer that the exercise of rational choice becomes virtually impossible. Some consumers, confronted with a myriad of similar products, may fall into the "trap" of judging quality by price alone. Critics also point out that many product alterations consist of frivolous and superficial changes which are of dubious value in improving durability, efficiency, or usefulness. In the case of durable and semidurable consumer goods, the process of product development seems to follow a pattern of "planned obsolescence;" firms make gradual but regular changes in their products aimed at increasing the frequency with which consumers become dissatisfied with their present model and trade it in on the new model. As partial remedies for product proliferation, a number of economists propose that information about products be provided to consumers in greater amounts and that laws and penalties regarding infringement on brands and trademarks be relaxed. Increased information and a weakening of trademark protection are held to increase "competition" by promoting a greater degree of product standardization and thereby lessening the powers of producers to vend differentiated products. The end result should be a movement in the direction of perfect competition. For a more thorough argument of this point, see Edward Chamberlin, *The Theory of Monopolistic Competition* (Cambridge, Mass.: Harvard University Press, 1933), pp. 271–274, and George J. Stigler, "The Economics of Information," *Journal of Political Economy*, Vol. 69, No. 3 (June 1961), pp. 213–225.

382

brand or store loyalty of existing customers. As long as revenues increase by more than enough to compensate both for the promotional expenses and for the extra production costs associated with greater outputs, the firm will have improved its profit position, thereby staving off the forces of adjustment toward long-run equilibrium.

Suppose we look first at the possible effects of promotional expenses upon the firm's long-run average costs. Initially, for the sake of argument, suppose promotional outlays substantially increase the demand for the firm's product and, consequently, the firm's most profitable long-run output rate. What, then, is the effect on the firm's long-run average costs? As depicted in Figure 10-15, sales promotion outlays obviously will shift the LRAC

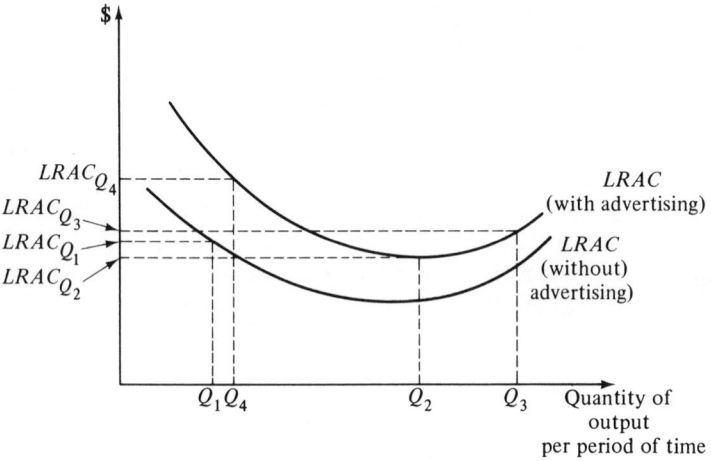

Fig. 10-15   The Effect of Sales Promotion Expenditures Upon Unit Costs and Output Rates

upward. However, if the demand-AR curve shifts so that production is more profitable at Q_2 than at Q_1, unit costs will decline from $LRAC_{Q_1}$ to $LRAC_{Q_2}$ because of economies of scale available to the firm. Greater production efficiency more than offsets the increase in unit costs associated with promotional expenses. On the other hand, output expansion realized from sales promotion may force diseconomies of scale upon the firm, as indicated by the movement from Q_1 to Q_3; in this case, unit costs would rise from $LRAC_{Q_1}$ to $LRAC_{Q_2}$. Some observers contend that a great portion of sales promotion efforts by firms are self-canceling, resulting in only slight increases in output—as suggested by the movement from Q_1 to Q_4.[11] In this instance, unit costs may be

[11] The cigarette, soap, beer, and toiletries industries are good cases in point. Like the Red Queen in *Alice Through the Looking Glass*, each firm has to run as fast as it can in its promotional activities just to keep up with where it is. This correctly recognizes that some promotional activity is defensive in nature and is undertaken to protect a firm's position as well as to enhance it.

driven up substantially by the decision to adopt an aggressive sales promotion strategy. Plainly, each of these three results is entirely plausible; which one will actually occur in a particular case varies with the shape of the $LRAC$ curve and the effect of sales promotion upon the profit-maximizing output.

A somewhat more interesting question relates to the effect of sales promotion activity upon the firm's price and profits. Consider Figure 10-16. In panel (a) is illustrated a situation where sales promotion outlays have the effect of *lowering* the firm's price and *raising* profits. In the absence of promotion, the profit-maximizing price and output are P_1 and Q_1, respectively, and total profit equals $(P_1 - SRAC_{Q_1})Q_1$. Initiating promotional activity shifts the demand-AR curve rightward from (D_1, AR_1) to (D_2, AR_2) and the $LRAC$ curve upward from $LRAC_1$ to $LRAC_2$. The firm will find it advantageous to expand output to Q_2 and to lower price to P_2; total profit will be

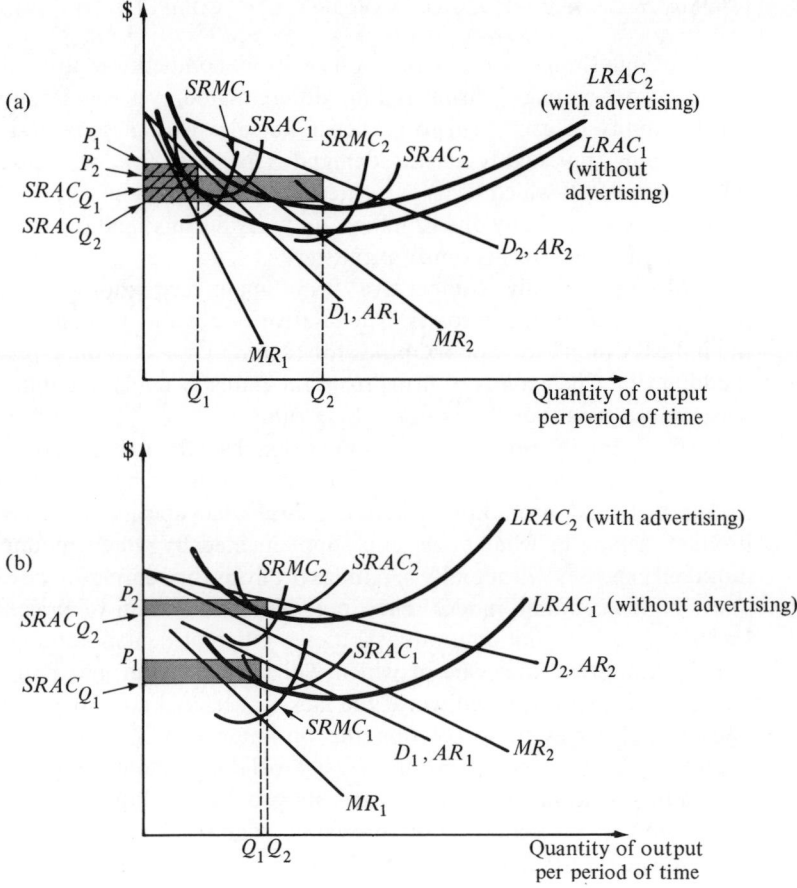

Fig. 10-16 Possible Effects of Sales Promotion Activity Upon Prices and Profits

$(P_2 - SRAC_{Q_2})Q_2$ dollars—an amount which dwarfs the profits earned when no promotional activity is undertaken. Panel (b) shows a situation where promotional activity causes price to rise and profits to fall. Before a promotional strategy is initiated, profit maximization occurs at P_1 and Q_1 with a resulting total profit of $(P_1 - SRAC_{Q_1})Q_1$ dollars. With promotional activity, the profit-maximizing price and output are P_2 and Q_2 and total profit is only $(P_2 - SRAC_{Q_2})Q_2$ dollars. Other possibilities exist: promotional activity can cause price to rise and profits to rise, price to fall and profits to fall, and so on. No general answer can be given as to the effect of promotional strategies upon a firm's costs, price, output, or profits. It all depends upon the effect which promotional expenditures have upon the position and shape of the firm's demand-AR curve and its $LRAC$ curve.

SUMMARY OF THE MODEL OF MONOPOLISTIC COMPETITION

The distinguishing features of monopolistic competition are: (1) many small, owner-managed firms selling differentiated, yet similar, products; (2) the ability of each firm to influence its sales by changing its price; (3) downsloping, but highly elastic, demand-AR curves for the firms; (4) the relative ease with which firms can enter and leave the industry; (5) the small effect the actions of any one firm have upon rival firms; and (6) firms' behaving as if they seek to maximize profits.

Monopolistically competitive firms may earn short-run economic profits or incur short-run losses. The relative ease with which firms can enter the industry limits the opportunities for earning large economic profits over the long run. The exodus of firms from the industry tends to eliminate or at least reduce economic losses in the long run.

The firm in monopolistic competition has three basic strategies for pursuing its principal goal of maximum profits—price changes, variations in its product, and promotional activity. Just what specific variation of the product, selling at what price, and supplemented by what amount of promotional expenses will actually maximize profits is too complex to be expressed in a simple economic model. Each possible combination of price, product variation, and promotional outlay poses a different demand and cost situation for the firm, some one of which will yield the firm maximum profits. Needless to say, in the real world the lack of perfect knowledge will present awesome obstacles to forecasting the optimum combination of the three strategies. Practical considerations will compel the firm to use a trial-and-error procedure in deciding upon its price, its product qualities, and its promotional outlays. Nevertheless, the preceding analysis should serve as a useful guide to decision-making in monopolistically competitive enterprises and as a framework for understanding the behavior of such firms in the marketplace.

The Market Behavior of Periphery Firms

Our purpose in presenting a detailed description of the models of perfect competition and monopolistic competition has been to gain understanding into the functioning of a modern industrial economy—in particular, the capitalistically-oriented economy of the United States. In Chapter 1 we saw that the United States economy embraces two distinct sectors—the periphery economy and the center economy. It turns out that the theoretical models of perfect competition and monopolistic competition provide an accurate portrayal of firm and market behavior in the periphery firm sector of the economy.[12] When large numbers of periphery firms sell a homogeneous product, price and output patterns correspond quite closely to those described in the perfectly competitive model. Where large numbers of periphery firms sell differentiated products, firm behavior regarding prices, outputs, product variation, and promotion parallels the model of monopolistic competition.

COMPETITION AMONG THE MANY IN THE REAL WORLD

Numerous bits of evidence are available to confirm these observations. Real-world examples of industries where almost perfectly competitive conditions prevail include such agricultural markets as corn, wheat, cotton, wool, barley, oats, and livestock, the bituminous coal industry, the manufacture of cotton cloth, and some financial markets involving stocks, bonds, and loans to business. Conditions approaching monopolistic competition are found in such industries as machine tools, pharmaceutical preparations, valves and pipe fittings, concrete blocks, brick, wood and upholstered furniture, sawmills, screw machine products, paperboard boxes, shoes, paints and varnishes, millinery, costume jewelry, lighting fixtures, men and boy's suits and coats, and women's dresses, suits, coats, and skirts; monopolistic competition is also prevalent in wholesaling and retailing, especially in the more populated urban centers. The characteristics of perfect and monopolistic competition are exemplified in industries comprised predominantly of small, owner-managed, single-product enterprises. In addition, *segments* of other industries exhibit the characteristics of these two models. As we shall describe presently, in industries where numerous periphery firms operate alongside a few center firms, the power relationships between the two types of firms often result in the periphery firms' exhibiting behavior patterns closely akin to that of perfect or monopolistic competition—conditions in the steel, tire, dairy, retail grocery, soap, petroleum refining,

---

[12] The student is urged to review at this point the specific traits of periphery firms as outlined in the section on "The Economics of Periphery Firms" in Chapter 1 (p. 23).

plumbing fixtures, machinery, and electrical appliance industries serve as examples.

The behavior of prices, outputs, and profits in the above mentioned industries (or segments thereof) compares favorably with the conclusions drawn from the two theoretical models of perfect and monopolistic competition. Rates of return on investment hover about the 6 to 10 percent range, so the tendency to earn little or no economic profit is well observed. However, as might be anticipated, earnings tend to be somewhat higher in the faster-growing industries and somewhat lower in the slow-growth industries. Output is generally responsive to changes in consumer demand, rising most dramatically where market demand curves are shifting rapidly to the right. Outputs and prices also respond to cost changes. Industries where technological change has tended to reduce unit costs show a relative decline in prices and a relatively large expansion of output.[13] Consumer demand, output, and cost movements are correlated. Where consumer demand and output are vigorously expanding, technical progress is stimulated and firms take advantage rather quickly of existing scale economies. The number of firms producing the product increases. Cost reductions coupled with expanding production capabilities give rise to price cuts which, in turn, reinforce the expansion process by triggering higher sales and output; this is a familiar cycle during the early and intermediate stages of the life cycle of a product or product group.

It is clear, then, that the models of perfect and monopolistic competition have empirical validity; both are able to predict and explain market behavior in certain circumstances.

THE BENEFITS OF COMPETITION AMONG THE MANY

Among economists, and especially among economic theorists, the conventional wisdom is that market conditions of perfect competition and monopolistic competition offer consumers the best of all possible worlds. If consumers are willing to accept a homogeneous product, a perfectly competitive market structure will supply it at the lowest possible price consistent with the costs of production. Under conditions of long-run equilibrium each firm operates at the minimum points of its short-run and long-run average cost curves and thus achieves maximum production efficiency. Price is driven to the level of minimum average cost, and investors receive a rate of return just sufficient to induce them to maintain their investment at levels adequate for producing the industry's equilibrium output most efficiently. Firms which fail to attain the lowest possible unit cost incur losses and eventually are driven from the industry. Consequently, resources tend to be employed at maximum production efficiency in a perfectly competitive industry.

---

[13] Evidence of this during the 1950's is reported in Harold Solozin, "Inflation and the Price Mechanism," *Journal of Political Economy*, Vol. 67, No. 5 (October 1959), pp. 463–475.

If consumers exhibit a preference for differentiated products, as usually they do because of the diversity of tastes among individuals, then monopolistically competitive conditions are held to produce optimum consumer benefits. Consumers tend to pay a price not much higher than that barely required to keep firms in business in the long run. However, in long-run equilibrium monopolistically competitive firms tend to build less-than-optimum-scale facilities because the demand-AR curve is tangent to the $LRAC$ curve just short of the minimum cost point; thus maximum production efficiency is not quite obtained. Nevertheless, the overall result is as good as can be achieved with differentiated products. In both perfect and monopolistic competition, the organization of firms and of productive capacity is highly responsive to consumer tastes and preferences. For these very important reasons the industry structures of perfect and monopolistic competition are commonly thought to yield industry prices, outputs, and profits that are most advantageous to consumers.

SOME DISADVANTAGES OF COMPETITION AMONG THE MANY

Yet, it is crucial to our understanding of business behavior to go beyond industrywide prices, outputs, and profits and look critically at the specific traits which an environment of perfect and monopolistic competition imposes upon individual firms. We have seen that every example of perfect competition and monopolistic competition involves industries where periphery firms predominate. There is, in other words, a very close correspondence between (a) the existence of near perfect competition and of monopolistic competition and (b) the presence of periphery firms. This is more than mere circumstance. The representative firm operating under conditions of perfect or monopolistic competition is small, both relatively and absolutely. It *must* be small relatively, because both models are predicated on the presence of large numbers of firms, no one of which has a sizable share of the market. In practice, it is small absolutely. Firm size is severely limited by the relatively quick appearance of diseconomies of scale. Were significant economies of scale present, firms would tend to be large—not small—relative to the total market. Then, too, firm size and growth is constrained by the lack of economic profits with which to help finance expansion and by the fact that, once scale economies are taken full advantage of, increased industry output is achieved by the entry of new firms rather than by the expansion of existing firms. The limitations upon firm size and upon firm growth that are imposed by perfect and monopolistic competition tend to guarantee that the firms in such industries be small and therefore take on the character of periphery firms.

This is not to say that wherever periphery firms exist, conditions of perfect or monopolistic competition prevail, but it does say that perfect and monopolistic competition are found only in markets comprised of periphery firms. Center firms are conspicuously absent from those industries previously cited as examples of perfect and monopolistic competition. Indeed, there are no examples of perfect competition or monopolistic competition where the business population is made up of center firms. This point, though often overlooked, is especially noteworthy because of its significance for the understanding of the structure of markets, the behavioral patterns of firms comprising these markets, and the criteria for judging the effectiveness with which markets function.

Consider some of the specific traits of firms which operate in an environment of atomistic (perfect or monopolistic) competition. To begin with, the representative firm in atomistically competitive industries is preoccupied with short-run problems. Decisions and actions are short-run oriented and circumscribed by market forces well beyond the firm's control. Since the firm's market power is nonexistent in perfectly competitive markets and only slight in monopolistically competitive markets, the firm is placed in the position of *reacting* and *responding* to changing market conditions. It exercises little control over its destiny. Like a small boat caught in the midst of a hurricane, the firm in atomistic competition faces a tower of uncertainty and insecurity. Its future survival is at the mercy of the market and its fortunes can be crushed at the drop of a hat—witness the relative distress of the typical small businessman over the past half century in times of economic downturns. There is no realistic alternative but for the periphery firm to attempt to maximize short-run profits. The profit margin is usually too slim to do otherwise. Product prices change frequently in response to changing demand and supply conditions. Falling demand may produce severe financial retrenchment, bankruptcy, or exit from the industry. Rising demand, on the other hand, offers dim prospects for steady, dependable expansion because of the ease of entry of new firms and because access to financial capital is limited.

For the periphery firm in perfect competition, market forces are especially harsh and unrelenting. The firm is always walking the tightrope of economic survival, with the winds of economic change just as likely to blow in the direction of losses as of profits. In monopolistic competition, the same forces are present, but they operate somewhat less powerfully; thus, the firm's predicament is not quite so insecure. Profit margins are not quite as volatile. However, in both instances the firms and their industries are subject to periods of considerable instability and disequilibrium, giving rise to an especially uncertain environment for decision-making. Profit incentives and financial capacities for risk-taking, for research, and for innovation are definitely impaired by the firm's small size and susceptibility to stringent treatment by market forces.

Not surprisingly, therefore, the pace of technological advance is slower, not faster, in environments of atomistic competition as compared to competition among the few. In many cases, periphery firms use technologically inferior equipment. The periphery economy contains none of the showcases of American technological achievement and superiority. In periphery firms industrial research and product development is normally undertaken on a small scale, if at all, owing to the firm's limited research needs and financial resources. A little bit of bigness—up to sales levels of $100 million to $250 million in most industries—is good for invention and innovation. Firms of this size and larger find a well-rounded research and development program and the new ideas it generates to be an asset in maintaining their viability and growth. Moreover, they can afford the talent needed to staff such an effort. Naturally, exceptions exist; some periphery firms are known for their technological prowess, being extraordinarily prolific in generating new ideas and in developing relatively uncomplicated processes and products.[14] But, *generally*, small periphery firms are not especially innovation-minded or technologically dynamic. This is partially because market forces and competition combine to keep profits so small that periphery firms are deprived of the venture capital requisite for financing technological research and for instituting innovative production processes. And it is partially because periphery firms operate on too small a scale to justify a significant research effort; research and development activities are seldom justifiable expenditures from a short-run profit-and-loss viewpoint—the criterion employed by periphery firms in atomistically competitive market environments.

Consequently, the social benefits to consumers of prices just sufficient to give firms a normal profit may be temporary. This is borne out by the fact that the conditions of perfect and monopolistic competition are typically associated with low-wage, low-skill industries having low productivity and below-average rates of productivity increase. Moreover, such industries are characterized by relatively low capital investment requirements, and they evidence a distinct propensity to lag behind other industries in pushing back technological frontiers—witness many of the firms in the agriculture, food products, textiles, apparel, sawmill, fabricated metal products, and electrical equipment industries. Experience has indicated that progress is more rapid where the rigors of short-run competitive forces are not so relentless as to make firms unwilling and unable to bear the risks and costs of research and innovation.

Furthermore, it is questionable whether the instability and insecurity of firms in such circumstances is conducive to high incomes and noninflationary full employment. Such industries are forever trouble spots in the overall economic picture—the prolonged death throes of the New England textile industry, of many of the Appalachian coal fields, and of the small farmer serve as cases in point. In the long run it is the rate of economic growth and technical progress, not low consumer prices, which determines whether per capita real incomes will be high or low and whether the quality of life will rise or fall.

---

[14] Control Data Corporation was a tiny firm when it led the way to very high-speed digital computers for scientific applications.

Thus, upon closer examination the market structures of perfect competition and monopolistic competition are not without their flaws and drawbacks. In fact, the case for competition among the many is not as strong as it first appears. Whether the advantages of perfect and monopolistic competition outweigh the disadvantages is a highly significant issue. We defer its consideration to Chapter 13, until such time as we have examined the models of oligopoly and monopoly along with the price and output behavior of center firms.

SUGGESTED READINGS

ARCHIBALD, G. C., "Chamberlin *versus* Chicago," *Review of Economic Studies*, Vol. 29 (1961), pp. 2–28.

BISHOP, ROBERT L., "The Theory of Monopolistic Competition After Thirty Years: The Impact on General Theory," *American Economic Review*, Vol. 54, No. 3 (May 1964), pp. 33–43.

CHAMBERLIN, E. H., *The Theory of Monopolistic Competition* (Cambridge, Mass.: Harvard University Press, 1933).

COHEN, K. J., and R. M. CYERT, *Theory of the Firm* (Englewood Cliffs, N.J.: Prentice-Hall, Inc., 1965), Chap. 11.

DOYLE, P., "Economic Aspects of Advertising: A Survey," *Economic Journal*, Vol. 78, No. 311 (September 1968), pp. 570–602.

KALDOR, NICHOLAS, "The Economic Aspects of Advertising," *Review of Economic Studies*, Vol. 18 (1949–1950), pp. 17–21.

ROBINSON, JOAN, *The Economics of Imperfect Competition* (London: The Macmillan Company, 1933).

SCHERER, F. M., *Industrial Market Structure and Economic Performance* (Skokie, Ill.: Rand McNally & Company, 1970), Chap. 14.

————, "Research and Development Resource Allocation under Rivalry," *Quarterly Journal of Economics*, Vol. 81, No. 3 (August 1967), pp. 359–394.

STIGLER, GEORGE J., "Monopolistic Competition in Retrospect," *The Organization of Industry* (Homewood, Ill.: Richard D. Irwin, Inc., 1968), pp. 71–94.

————, "Price and Non-Price Competition," *Journal of Political Economy*, Vol. 76, No. 1 (January-February 1968), pp. 149–154.

TELSER, RICHARD G., "Advertising and Competition," *Journal of Political Economy*, Vol. 72, No. 6 (December 1964), pp. 537–562.

Problems and Questions for Discussion

1. (a) A firm's total revenue can be determined by adding the values of MR for each unit sold. True or false? Explain.
   (b) A firm's total cost can be determined by adding the values of MC for each unit produced. True or false? Explain.
   (c) A firm's total profit can be determined by adding the values of $M\pi$ for each unit produced and sold. True or false? Explain.

2. Total profit is maximum at the same output at which total contribution profit is maximum. True or false? Explain.

3. Unit contribution profit $(P - AVC)$ is greatest at the same output that total contribution profit $(TR - TVC)$ is greatest. True or false? Explain.

4. Why is competition said to be "perfect" in a perfectly competitive market? Just what is so perfect about perfect competition?

5. How do perfectly competitive firms compete? In what form is "competition" present in a perfectly competitive market?

6. Graphically illustrate the short-run supply curve for a perfectly competitive firm which has a short-run production function characterized by decreasing returns to variable input over the entire range of its output capability.

7. Suppose in a perfectly competitive industry that market supply and demand forces combine to produce a short-run equilibrium price of $70. Suppose further that a firm in this industry has a weekly total cost function expressed by the equation

$$TC = 200 + 25Q - 6Q^2 + 1/3Q^3.$$

Determine the perfectly competitive firm's profit-maximizing output rate and the amount of its short-run profits or losses.

8. The Morgan Chair Company manufactures rocking chairs and sells them under conditions of monopolistic competition. The owner of the company has estimated its demand function as $P = 1625 - 6Q$, where P is in dollars and Q is in dozens of chairs sold per month. The company believes its monthly expenses vary with output according to the equation

$$TC = 25,000 + 25Q - 6Q^2 + 1/3Q^3.$$

(a) Determine the firm's short-run profit-maximizing price and output rate.
(b) How much profit will the firm earn at this price and output rate?
(c) Suppose the Morgan Chair Company's total fixed costs rise by 10 percent. Calculate the impact upon the firm's price, output, and profits. How do you account for these results?

9. Using the unit cost and unit revenue curves, graphically illustrate the short-run profit-maximizing price and output for a perfectly competitive firm which has a production function that exhibits decreasing returns to variable input over its entire range of output capability. [*Hint:* Determine the shape of the ATC and MC curves that correspond to a production function characterized by decreasing returns to variable input and then locate the price and output at which $MR = MC$.] Indicate on your graph the area which represents the firm's total profits.

10. Using the unit cost and unit revenue curves, graphically illustrate the short-run profit-maximizing price and output for a monopolistically competitive firm which has a production function that exhibits constant returns to variable input over its entire range of output capability. [*Hint:* First determine the shape of the ATC and MC curves which correspond to a production function characterized by constant returns to variable input; then find the price and output at which $MR = MC$.] Indicate on your graph the area which represents the firm's total profits.

11. Using *TR-TC* analysis, graphically illustrate the short-run profit-maximizing output for a monopolistically competitive firm which is faced with a linear, downsloping demand curve and which has a production function displaying decreasing returns to variable input over its entire range of output capability. Then derive the corresponding total profit function for the firm.

12. Suppose a firm operating under conditions of monopolistic competition is faced with a linear, downward-sloping demand curve and that its production function is of cubic form ($a + bX + cX^2 - dX^3$). Using the unit cost and revenue curves (*AR, MR, ATC, AVC,* and *MC*), graphically illustrate the price and output at which short-run profit will be maximized. Indicate on your graph the area which represents the firm's total profits.

13. In Chapter 5 it was shown that a linear, downsloping demand curve is half elastic and half inelastic; that is to say, the coefficient of price elasticity is greater than one along the top half of the demand curve and less than one along the bottom half. Is it possible for a monopolistically competitive firm which is confronted with a linear, downsloping demand curve to maximize short-run profits at a price and output corresponding to the inelastic portion of the demand curve? Why or why not?

14. Graphically illustrate a situation where the use of sales promotion activity by a monopolistically competitive firm results in a higher price and higher profits.

15. The purpose of sales promotion expenditures is to shift the firm's demand-*AR* function to the right and, at the same time, to make it more steeply sloped (less elastic over the relevant price range). Assuming that a firm achieves this purpose, graphically illustrate the effect this has upon the shape and position of the firm's total revenue function.

11

The Price
and Output Decisions
of Profit-Maximizing
Center Firms

The previous chapter emphasized "competition among the many." Here the spotlight is on "competition among the few." Far and away the most prominent and most important examples of competition among the few are found in the center economy—the domain of large corporate enterprises. The list of markets where a *few* very large corporate enterprises supply most of the industry output is a veritable *Who's Who* of American manufacturing. It includes the markets for such commodities as aircraft, aluminum, automobiles, alcoholic beverages, appliances, cigarettes, computers, copying machines, copper, electrical equipment, flat glass, certain food products, gasoline, gypsum products, locomotives and railroad cars, metal cans, phonograph records, sewing machines, steam engines and turbines, steel, synthetic fibers, telephone equipment, tires and typewriters. Several markets in the mining, construction, finance, retailing, and service industries are also served by firms which supply the lion's share of the total output. Taken together, these markets define "the center economy"—the heart of a modern industrial system. A distinctive feature of the center economy is that competition takes on the character of a contest among giants. Large enterprises compete primarily with other large enterprises. The number of firms in the market for any one commodity is small. These features make the models of oligopoly and monopoly especially applicable to describing center firm behavior.[1]

We shall, therefore, orient the presentation of oligopoly and monopoly theory to capture the specific facets of center firm behavior; periphery firm markets exhibiting the characteristics of oligopoly and monopoly will be given scant attention, even though many of the conclusions we draw will have some application to such markets.[2] We begin our examination of the price and output decisions of center firms with a survey of the more relevant models of oligopoly behavior. The final section of this chapter concerns the special case of pure monopoly. The assumption that the firm's overriding goal is to maximize profits will be continued; however, we shall relax this assumption in Chapter 12 and examine there the effect of alternative goals upon business behavior.

Models of Oligopoly Behavior

THE DISTINGUISHING CHARACTERISTICS OF OLIGOPOLY

Oligopoly epitomizes competition among the few. Oligopolistic markets arise whenever a small number of firms supply the dominant share of an industry's total output. Firms are necessarily large relative to the size of the total market they serve; and in the case of center firms they are large not just relatively but absolutely as well. The principal effect of fewness of firms is to give each firm such a prominent market position that its decisions and actions have significant repercussions on the other firms. Firms are acutely conscious of their interdependence, and competition among them is a highly personalized matter. Every firm recognizes that its best course of action in a decision situation depends upon the courses of action its rivals elect. This is true whether the decision concerns a design innovation, new promotional strate-

---

[1] It must be readily acknowledged that the models of oligopoly and monopoly behavior are not limited in their application to just the behavior of center firms. They may also accurately portray the behavior of periphery firms operating in markets so small that there is room only for a few firms. The small town with its two or three banks, auto mechanics, dry cleaners, building contractors, and so on, illustrates this possibility. In manufacturing, a number of highly specialized parts, components, gadgets, tools, and speciality products have a total market demand (even nationwide) so limited that a few small firms can easily supply the entire output. Hence, the conditions of competition among the few can arise where periphery firms are involved as well as where center firms are involved. The zone of demarcation between competition among the many and competition among the few, therefore, does not correspond exactly with the zone between periphery firms and center firms. Some periphery firms, because they cater to a limited market, operate under conditions of competition among the few.

[2] Recasting the traditional theory of oligopoly and monopoly into the mold of explaining the behavior of center firms to the virtual exclusion of explaining periphery firm behavior has much to recommend it. Generalizing oligopoly and monopoly theory to the point where it applies to both periphery and center firm environments forces one to exclude the rich institutional detail which supplies powerful understanding of the behavior of large corporations in a modern industrial economy. Such an exclusion is a serious disadvantage when one is trying to explain the functioning of an economic system dominated by the presence of large corporations. It is very difficult to construct satisfactory models of business behavior which describe equally well the behavior of entrepreneurial firms and the behavior of large managerial firms. After all, the behavior of a hardware store functioning as an oligopolistic firm in a small community differs in several important respects from IBM's behavior in the oligopolistic computer market. Thus, while orienting the presentation of oligopoly and monopoly theory to capture specific facets of center firm behavior may suffer slightly from a lack of generality, this weakness is more than offset by the gains in explaining real-world corporate behavior. This approach is also strong pedagogically because it provides students with highly visible illustrations of the relevance of oligopoly and monopoly theory.

gies, price changes, customer service policies, acquisitions and mergers, or whatever. Since rival firms may have numerous alternative courses of action, forecasting their actions and reactions introduces a new and exceedingly complex dimension to the decision process. But guessing the response of rival firms is an exercise no oligopolist can afford to neglect, for the probability is high that a change in the firm's tactics will elicit prompt and pointed reactions from rival firms. The great uncertainty is *how* one's rivals will react; this is the feature which distinguishes oligopoly from other market structures.

The other characteristics of an oligopolistic market structure may be accorded lesser notice. To begin with, rivalry among the few may involve either standardized or differentiated products. If the firms in an industry produce a standardized product, the industry is called a *pure oligopoly*. The most common examples of virtually uniform products marketed under conditions of oligopoly include steel, aluminum, lead, copper, cement, rayon, fuel oil, sheetrock, tin cans, roofing, explosives, and industrial alcohol. If a few firms dominate the market for a differentiated product, the industry is called a *differentiated oligopoly*. The most visible differentiated oligopolies involve the production of automobiles, aircraft, cereal, cigarettes, television sets, electric razors, computers, farm implements, refrigerators, air conditioners, soft drinks, soap, and gasoline.

Entry into an oligopolistic industry is typically formidable, though by no means impossible. The most pervasive barrier to entry is the presence of substantial economies of scale. In industries where technology is complex, large machine units are used, and sales promotion requirements are substantial, the optimum scale of operation is large. Minimum average costs occur at output rates so large that a few firms can supply the entire market. Firms of lesser size are forced to operate at costs so much higher that the entry of small-scale firms is generally not profitable. Moreover, the fact that existing firms produce well-known, highly advertised products and sell them through long-established marketing outlets works against the successful entrance of new firms. It is a hazardous undertaking for a relatively unknown firm to introduce a new product to compete directly against the brands of firms whose names are known to everyone. Certainly, such an entry will require a commitment of venture capital which *new* organizations will seldom be able to muster. The most likely candidates for entry into established oligopolies are other giant enterprises which do have the financial and organizational resources that it takes. This is not, however, an especially common occurrence, because the added production of another large-scale firm tends to increase supply to the point of driving price below average cost for all firms. Therefore, the profit prospects for new entrants, large or small, are dim, and entry is effectively discouraged.

Like firms in monopolistic competition, oligopolistic firms, and especially those producing differentiated products, rely upon differences in price, quality, reliability, service, design, rapid product development, promotional outlays, and product images to promote their sales and increase their profits. They attempt to create a very strong awareness among consumers of brands and product images. Everything that was said in Chapter 10 about the role of product variations and promotional outlays applies on an even grander scale among center firm oligopolists. The dimensions of competition under oligopoly are limited only by the imagination of the firms themselves.

A comment is in order about the analytical implications of the foregoing characteristics of oligopoly markets. Since many reasonable assumptions may be entertained about what rival firms will decide to do and how they will react in a given situation, no clear-cut solution to the oligopolistic firm's price and output decision problem exists. Unlike the models of perfect and monopolistic competition, in oligopoly no one pattern of behavior stands apart from the rest. Experience indicates almost anything can happen. As a consequence, economists have developed literally dozens of models of oligopoly behavior, each of which explains certain specific facets of oligpolistic conduct and performance, but none of which tells the whole story. It is not likely that oligopolistic behavior can ever be generalized to the point of a single model which will yield explanations and predictions of tolerable precision—the range of oligopoly behavior is simply too diverse and complex. Rather, we must be content with a number of models, each restricted to a manageable set of behavior patterns and institutional characteristics. Even then, the best that can be expected is models possessing a modest degree of explanatory and predictive power, but subject to substantial error on occasion. Accordingly, the discussion which follows consists of a series of models of center firm behavior. Taken together, these models give a reasonably accurate portrayal of those center firms whose behavior closely resembles profit maximization. In the next chapter we complete the picture of the center economy by presenting models of center firm behavior when the goals of enterprise extend beyond the realm of maximum profits.

THE KINKED DEMAND CURVE AND PRICE RIGIDITY

In oligopolistic markets there is a strong tendency for firms to avoid frequent price changes. One explanation for the relative stability of oligopoly prices, despite shifts in both demand and costs, is contained in the kinked demand curve model.[3]

In this model the oligopolistic firm is held to believe that if it cuts price below the prevailing level, rival firms will quickly follow with price cuts of their own. For rivals to do otherwise would allow the price-cutting firm to make significant inroads into their market shares and thereby increase its sales and profits at their expense. Consequently, rival oligopolists can be re-

---

[3] The kinked demand curve model was first advanced by Paul Sweezy in 1939. For a more intensive discussion of this model see his article "Demand Under Conditions of Oligopoly," *Journal of Political Economy*, Vol. 47 (August 1939), pp. 568–573. For an evaluation of the model see George J. Stigler, "The Kinky Oligopoly Demand Curve and Rigid Prices," *Journal of Political Economy*, Vol. 55 (October 1947), pp. 432–449.

liably counted upon to lower their prices in response to a price cut; such a retaliatory move will have the effect of limiting the gain in sales of any firm to its share of the overall gain in industry sales. More importantly, perhaps, a price cut by one firm may be construed by rivals as an aggressive attack which is deserving of a vigorous counterattack; a vicious price war may ensue in which all firms end up as losers.[4] On the other hand, if one firm independently raises its price above that currently being charged by its rivals, it can expect the rival firms to ignore the increase. Why? Because the rivals of the price-increasing firm stand to gain customers from the price booster. Some, though not all, of the customers of the now-higher priced firm will switch their purchases to rival firms, thereby enhancing the sales, market shares, and profits of the firms which hold the price line.

The matching of price cuts and the ignoring of price increases by rival firms has the effect of making an oligopolist's demand-AR curve highly elastic above the ruling price but much less elastic or even inelastic below the going price. Figure 11-1 illustrates this type of demand-AR curve and its

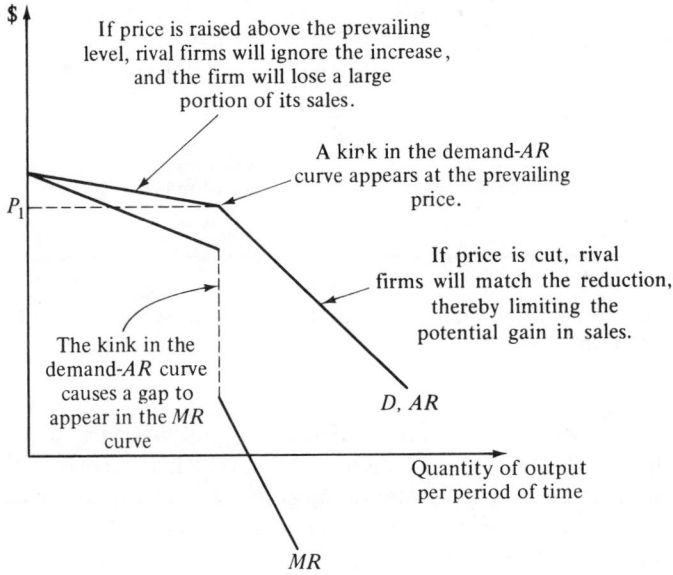

Fig. 11-1   The Kinked Demand Curve

corresponding marginal revenue curve. Observe that a kink in the demand-AR curve occurs at the prevailing price of P_1 dollars. Because of the kink in the demand curve, the marginal revenue curve consists of two disjointed segments. The upper segment corresponds to the more elastic portion of the

---

[4] The likelihood of a price war and the extent of damage it may do to the firms concerned tend to be greater (1) the more standardized are their products, (2) the more inelastic is the market demand for their output, and (3) the lower are the marginal costs of production. Industries such as petroleum, tires, and steel have a "high-risk" rating on all three counts.

demand-AR curve, whereas the lower segment corresponds to the less elastic portion of the demand-AR curve. The kink in the demand-AR curve causes the associated MR curve to have a vertical discontinuity at the prevailing price.

From the discussion in Chapter 10 we know that profits are maximized at the output rate where $MR = MC$. Suppose, then, an oligopolist faced with a kinked demand-AR curve also has a marginal cost curve of MC_1, as shown in Figure 11-2. The short-run profit-maximizing output rate is Q_1 units, since

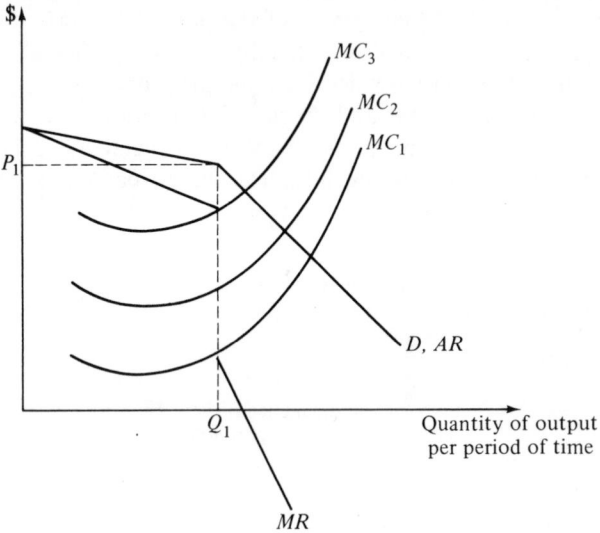

Fig. 11-2   The Profit-Maximizing Price and Output for an Oligopolistic Firm Faced with a Kinked Demand Curve

at outputs less than Q_1 units $MR > MC$ and at outputs more than Q_1 units $MC > MR$. In the event that rising input prices (such as wage increases or increases in raw material prices) should push the firm's marginal cost function up to MC_2, a selling price of P_1 dollars and an output of Q_1 units is still the most profitable price-output combination. In fact, the marginal cost function must rise above MC_3 before the firm would benefit from either a price change or an output change. So long as the MC function intersects the discontinuous portion of the MR function, the firm has no profit incentive to change either price or output.

The same rigidity of prices but not of outputs may occur even though the demand for an oligopolist's product intensifies. In Figure 11-3, for instance, the firm's demand-AR curve shifts rightward from D_1, AR_1 to D_2, AR_2, generating a new MR function (MR_2). However, it is possible that the MC function will still intersect the new MR function in the discontinuous segment. In such a case there is no incentive to change price from P_1 dollars, although

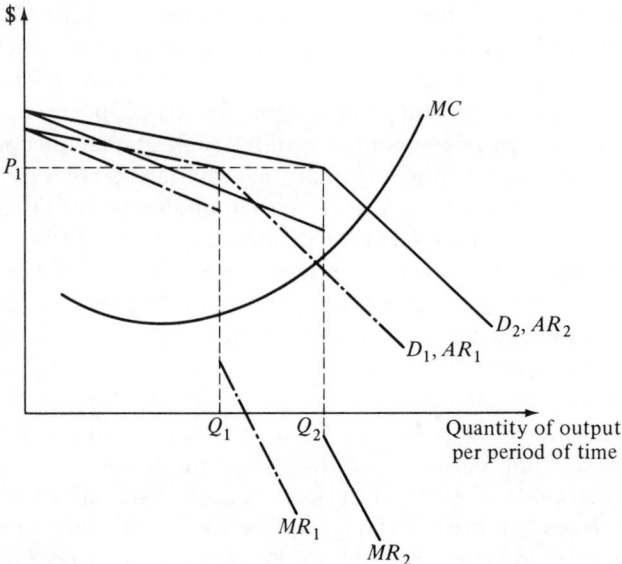

Fig. 11-3   The Effect of Demand Shifts upon an Oligopolist's Price and Output Rate

the profit-maximizing output rate does rise from Q_1 to Q_2 units. As long as the shift in demand is not so large as to result in MC's intersecting the new MR curve outside the discontinuous segment, then no change in the firm's selling price is called for.

The kinked demand curve model therefore yields five main predictions about the market behavior of oligopolistic firms:

1. An oligopolistic firm will refrain from *independently* raising its price for fear that the newly created price differential will cause a substantial drop in its sales, profits, and market share.
2. An oligopolistic firm will refrain from *independent* price cutting, since rivals will follow promptly and nullify the chance for sizable sales and profit gains.
3. Oligopolists will charge the same or nearly the same price for their products, since the ease with which their products are substitutable causes patronage to flock to the low-priced sellers. (Oligopolists cannot coexist by charging significantly different prices for essentially the same commodity.)
4. The price and output rate of an oligopolistic firm has a tendency to be rigid in the face of moderate cost changes.
5. An oligopolist's price will tend to be sticky but its output rate will tend to be responsive in the face of moderate changes in demand conditions.

All five predictions are consistent with observed behavior in both pure and differentiated oligopolies. Prices in oligopolistic industries do indeed appear to be generally more stable as compared to prices in perfectly and monopolistically competitive industries. Experience further indicates the prices charged by firms in an oligopolistic industry tend to be *identical* where the products are standardized or else weakly differentiated. Where their products are strongly differentiated, oligopolists tend to charge prices which are *comparable*. A common price policy is readily visible among oligopolists in a wide range of industries. Moreover, antitrust cases and studies of business pricing practices reveal a widespread conviction on the part of businessmen that price cuts *will* be matched.[5] During periods of economic decline and falling product demand, oligopolistic industries have typically been characterized by relatively small price declines and relatively large output declines.[6] Thus the kinked demand curve model does have demonstrated ability to predict and explain some significant facets of pricing behavior.

Nevertheless, the model is not without its faults. In the first place alternative explanations for price rigidity can be found. For instance, frequent price changes disrupt customer relations by introducing an important element of uncertainty as to future prices; regular buyers of a commodity prefer some degree of price stability. Firms which sell their product at "nationally advertised prices" not only encounter strong customer resistance to recurrent price changes but they face practical limitations upon the frequency with which their prices can be altered. Then, too, repeated changes in price enhance the risks of price warfare. Oligopolists may rationally elect not to rock the boat unduly by postponing price changes until cost or demand conditions have shifted so plainly as to leave no doubts among rivals as to the nonaggressive aspect of the action.

A second, and very important, limitation of the kinked demand curve model is its inability to explain how oligopolists initially arrive at the prevailing price. In other words, the model is much better at explaining why price persists at a particular level than how it reached that level or under what circumstances it might change. It is an *ex post* rationalization of price stability rather than an explanation of price determination. This is a most serious shortcoming which we shall attempt to remedy in subsequent models of oligopoly behavior.

Finally, the assumptions underlying the kinked demand curve itself do not always hold. When all firms in an oligopolistic industry experience similar shifts in cost or demand conditions, there may arise an incentive to change price that is mutually advantageous to all concerned and that is also generally recognized by all concerned. For example, industrywide price

---

[5] Actual examples may be found in Harold M. Fleming, *Gasoline Prices and Competition* (New York: Appleton-Century-Crofts, 1966), Chap. 5; R. B. Tennant, "The Cigarette Industry," in Walter Adams, ed., *The Structure of American Industry*, 3rd ed., (New York: The Macmillan Company, 1961), pp. 370–372; the records of the Salk vaccine case (*U.S.* v. *Eli Lilly et al.*) and the tetracycline case (*F.T.C.* v. *American Cyanamid et al.*); and A. D. H. Kaplan, J. B. Dirlam, and R. F. Lanzilotti, *Pricing in Big Business* (Washington: The Brookings Institution, 1958), p. 174.

[6] Gardiner C. Means, *Industrial Prices and Their Flexibility* (Washington, D.C.: Government Printing Office, 1935), p. 8; also, Gardiner C. Means, "The Administered Price Thesis Confirmed," *American Economic Review*, Vol. 62, No. 3 (June, 1972), pp. 292–306. In contrast, in industries where firms were more numerous and the characteristics of competition among the many prevailed, price declines were relatively large and production fell by relatively small amounts.

adjustments frequently follow wage increases imposed uniformly upon the firms by collective bargaining. Knowing its rivals are confronted with comparable cost increases, a firm can boost price in confidence that rivals will follow suit.[7] It is more than coincidental when U. S. Steel announces a price hike following a new settlement with the steelworkers union that other steel firms follow promptly. Therefore, when the incentives for a price change appear generally throughout the industry, a price increase may be followed rather than ignored, and the crucial assumption of the kinked demand curve model is contradicted. As a result, the model fails to account for how oligopolistic prices move to new levels when demands or costs change, although it can explain why they may remain stable once new levels have been reached.

MODELS OF OLIGOPOLY PRICE-OUTPUT DETERMINATION

Now that we have seen why, in an oligopolistic market, firms have reasons for changing prices only infrequently and why, when they do alter price, they do so more or less simultaneously, the time has come to delve more deeply into how oligopolists decide upon a particular price. Unfortunately, no one general procedure recommends itself in oligopoly pricing. The whole issue of oligopoly pricing has proven to be a most troublesome one for businessmen (and, more especially, for economic theorists) and it is, as yet, quite unresolved. Nonetheless, a number of aspects lend themselves to analysis. Let us begin with a fairly simple model and then gradually introduce greater realism.

Equal Market Shares and Equal Costs. Consider an industry containing only two firms—firm A and firm B. Suppose both firms sell identical products, have exactly the same production costs, and divide the market on a 50-50 basis. Since each firm serves one-half the industry demand, their demand-AR curves lie on top of one another and are located halfway between the vertical axis and the industrywide demand curve at each price, as shown in Figure 11-4. With identical demand-AR curves, the marginal revenue curves of A and B necessarily are the same. And having the same cost structure means their MC and ATC curves coincide as well. Maximizing profits at the price and output rate where $MR = MC$ results in both firms charging the same price ($P_{A,B}$) and producing at the same output rate ($Q_{A,B}$). Each firm will earn a short-run economic profit equal to the shaded area in Figure 11-4. The significant point here is that no pricing conflict exists between the two firms. Each firm maximizes profits at the same price. No formal or informal collusion is either called for or beneficial. Each firm can act independently in full confidence that its own best price-output strategy will be found "satisfactory" to its rival.

---

[7] Linking price increases to wage or tax hikes has the added benefit of making it appear that the blame rests with greedy unions or a revenue-hungry government; such maneuvers help the firm to escape public criticism and charges of profiteering.

402

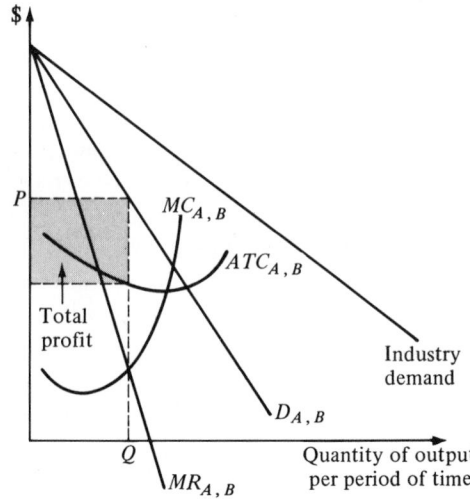

Fig. 11-4 The Price and Output Decisions of Two Firms with Equal Market Shares and Equal Costs

Equal Market Shares and Different Costs. Suppose, however, we introduce a cost differential between the two firms, other factors remaining unchanged. Specifically, suppose firm B has a higher MC curve, as indicated in Figure 11-5. Firm B's higher costs might reflect older, technologically inefficient production facilities or higher labor costs due to an unfavorable geographic location with respect to its resource markets. Examination of Figure 11-5 indicates that firm A's profit-maximizing price and output are P_A and Q_A, while firm B's are P_B and Q_B.

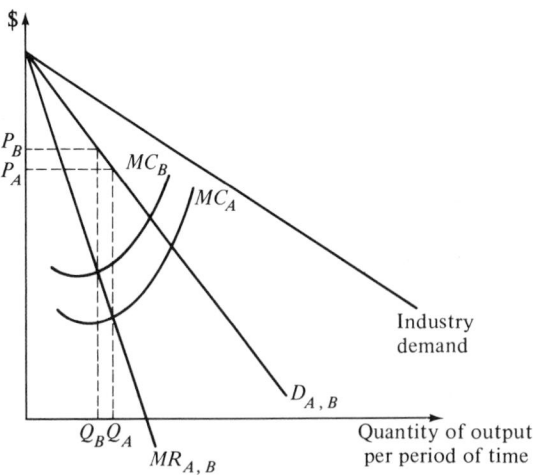

Fig. 11-5 The Price and Output Decisions of Two Firms with Equal Market Shares and Different Costs

A pricing conflict is immediately apparent. Each firm is worse off, profitwise, at its rival's favored price than at its own, and therefore each will prefer to see its own profit-maximizing price established on an industry-wide basis. If, as is likely, product standardization forecloses the possibility of a lasting price differential, some method of conflict resolution must be devised. One obvious, but sometimes fragile, way is for the two firms to reach a compromise via a gentlemen's agreement or formal collusion.[8] Alternatively, firm A, which prefers the lowest price, may choose to force its will upon firm B. Because of its cost advantage and because buyers flock to the low-priced seller, the firm with the lowest price preference is in a strong position to impose its preferences. However, if the profits of the high-cost firm are unacceptable at the low-cost firm's preferred price, it may slash prices below the preferred price of the low-cost firm in the hopes of coercing the latter into a more cooperative stance. A full-fledged price war may break out in which both firms suffer. Should warfare fail to yield a price that is "acceptable" to all concerned, then the high-cost firm can (1) innovate and bring its costs into line with (or even lower than) the low-cost firm, (2) shift into the production of other commodities where expected profits are higher, or (3) do the best it can at the prevailing price.[9] These three alternatives are not mutually exclusive, and the high-cost firm can pursue them all if need be. But one outcome is clear: *With standardized products "price equilibrium" in an oligopolistic industry requires that firms charge the same price for their products.* If a firm attempts to sell at a higher price, then it will suffer erosion of its sales, its market share, and its profits; conceivably, it will be driven from the market entirely over the long term.

Analogous pricing conflicts arise when the firms produce differentiated products that give rise to cost differentials among firms in the industry. However, the conflict may not be quite as intense if the products are sufficiently differentiated to permit a lasting price differential. Oligopolists are not as strongly compelled to sell at a uniform price when their products are differentiated as when they are identical. Buyers can be persuaded to tolerate modest price differences. But when product differentiation results in significant cost differentials among firms, and thereby drives a large wedge between their profit-maximizing prices, the pricing conflict among the firms in the industry intensifies.

[8] Collusive arrangements of any variety are fragile because each firm tends to have a large incentive to cheat on the other firms. The collusive price is necessarily a compromise price that is higher than would prevail in the absence of collusion. The chances are good, therefore, that by negotiating secret price concessions with individual customers, a firm can pick up a lot of profitable new business provided it is discreet and successfully avoids provoking rival firms. But what underscores the fragility of collusion is that the incentive to cheat is widespread. If and when one or two firms yield to the temptation, collusion quickly disintegrates. Mutual trust and faithful adherence to the bargain are essential for collusion to be maintained—neither is easy to come by or long preserved in a competitive atmosphere where millions of dollars are at stake and where cheating is lucrative. Consequently, collusive arrangements seldom offer a viable and long-lasting solution toward resolving pricing conflicts.

[9] Going out of business and dissolving the firm is not mentioned here as an alternative because the demise and death of a center firm is a rare event—much more so than in the case of periphery firms. Center firms normally respond to extreme market adversity by (a) gradually withdrawing from an unprofitable industry and shifting their organizational resources into more profitable endeavors or (b) mobilizing organizational resources to combat adversity in a long-term struggle which it is believed can be won.

404

Different Market Shares and Equal Costs. Next consider the case where firms have identical costs but different market shares, the latter arising, perhaps, from product differentiation. All three panels of Figure 11-6 illustrate demand situations where firm A has 60 percent of the total market at each price and firm B has the remaining 40 percent. The nature of the pricing conflict varies with the shape of the marginal cost function confronting the two firms. In Figure 11-6(a) the products of the firms are produced under conditions of identically rising marginal costs. Firm A maximizes its profits by producing where $MC_{A,B} = MR_A$; accordingly, A's preferred price is P_A and its preferred output rate is Q_A units. Firm B's profit-maximizing price and output are P_B and Q_B, respectively. A clash of pricing preferences arises again. The firm with the *larger* market share prefers the higher price.

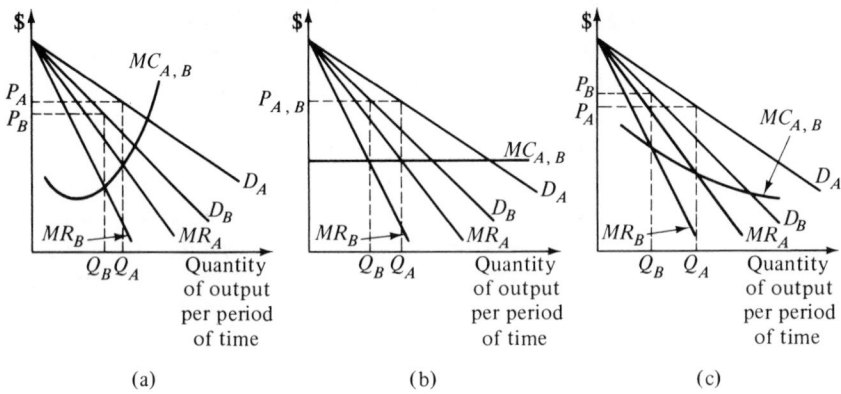

(a)   (b)   (c)

Fig. 11-6 The Price and Output Decisions of Two Firms with Different Market Shares and Equal Costs

Other things being equal, this result holds not just for a 60–40 market split but also for any other uneven division of the market. Moreover, the more divergent the market shares of the two firms, the greater is the disparity in their respective profit-maximizing prices. In this situation, whether the large-share firm will accede to the price preference of the small-share firm, whether the reverse will be true, or whether some compromise price will evolve is impossible to say. It all depends. The firm with the larger market share may try to intimidate the firm with the smaller share and coerce it into accepting a price close to the higher of the profit-maximizing prices. On the other hand, if the small-share firm is in a position to withstand pressure from the large-share firm, then it holds the upper hand, and price equilibrium is likely to be attained near the lower of the two profit-maximizing prices. Still another possibility is for the two firms to compromise and split the difference on price.

In Figure 11-6(b) both firms produce under conditions of identical and constant marginal cost over the relevant output range. (We saw in Chapter 8 that constant MC is not an uncommon occurence in the range of plant sizes employed by large-scale manufacturing enterprises.) In this instance firm A will maximize profits by producing Q_A units and firm B will maximize profits by producing Q_B units. However, the profit-maximizing prices of the firms coincide at $P_{A,B}$. Such a result is not circumstantial, but rather is an inherent geometrical trait of linear demand curves with a common vertical intercept. And it holds for any market-share division, whether it be 60–40, 75–25, or whatever. Therefore, when oligopolists have identical and constant marginal costs, no conflict over price arises, irrespective of the firms' market shares. This is a particularly important conclusion, given that many modern industrial enterprises have constant marginal costs up to 90 percent of capacity [refer back to Figure 8-5(b)] and also encounter constant returns to scale as they expand output over the long-run [see Figure 8-8(c)].

Figure 11-6(c) shows declining marginal cost prevailing for both firms over the relevant output range. Here, firm A prefers a lower price (P_A dollars) than firm B prefers (P_B dollars). The firm with the larger market share prefers the lower price because of the lower marginal costs associated with higher outputs. The production economies stemming from larger outputs will likely make firm A less willing to compromise its lower price preference with firm B's preference for a higher price. In fact, firm A has an incentive to expand its market share in order to take advantage of still lower costs; this may lead firm A to adopt an aggressive pricing strategy calculated to capture a portion of firm B's market. However, in the U.S. the antitrust laws will undoubtedly serve to restrain firm A from pursuing so large a share of the market that it provokes antitrust action. Nevertheless, the stage is set here, subject only to the constraint of antitrust legislation, for one firm to grow larger at the expense of its rivals by putting persistent downward pressure on price.

Different Market Shares and Different Costs.   Usually, both market shares and production costs vary from firm to firm. Product differentiation together with plant facilities and production technologies of differing vintage and efficiency virtually guarantee the presence of differences in market shares and production costs among oligopolistic firms. When the market shares and production costs of the firms vary simultaneously, almost anything can happen. The small-share firms may prefer a lower price or the large-share firms may prefer a lower price. Conceivably, no pricing conflict will arise, because differences in market share and costs cancel out. Yet, if price preferences do differ, a uniform price or at most a narrow band of prices will still tend to be established.[10] The ease with which the product of one firm

---

[10] An experiment conducted by J. W. Friedman revealed a tendency for price equilibrium to be reached more than 75 percent of the time. Despite the opportunity to cheat once equilibrium agreements were reached, the agreed-to price was honored in nine out of ten cases. However, Friedman found that a price equilibrium was reached somewhat less often under conditions of different market shares and production costs as opposed to equal market shares and costs. For further details see "An Experimental Study of Cooperative Duopoly," *Econometrica*, Vol. 35, No. 3–4 (July-October 1967), pp. 379–397.

can be substituted for the product of another firm guarantees that this will be so.

Therefore, pricing conflicts between firms are likely to be more latent than overt, though differences in preferred prices may occasionally become visible in the form of short-term price wars, discovery of price-fixing arrangements, and competitive behavior of a cutthroat or predatory intensity. More usually, pricing conflicts are gradually resolved via long-term adjustments on the part of the firms, including cost reduction schemes, technological innovation, new product research and development, product diversification, aggressive advertising and sales promotion tactics, and other forms of nonprice competition. Experience has shown that such adjustments are more reliable forms of conflict resolution than mutually unprofitable price wars and collusive arrangements. In the meantime, the firms against whom the conflict is resolved will suffer lower profits and maybe even short-run losses.

The major conclusion to be drawn at this juncture is that, despite the difficulties involved, some attempt at reaching a mutually acceptable price structure *must* and *will* be made by oligopolistic firms. In either the short or the long run, oligopolists have no realistic alternative to selecting identical or comparable prices for their products, irrespective of market share and cost differences. Hence, the fact that they reach this result is not evidence of collusion, either formal or informal; instead, it reflects a fundamental principle of oligopoly pricing. To conclude, as some observers have done, that identical prices are *prima facie* proof of "price-fixing" is utter nonsense. Collusion is, of course, one way of resolving pricing conflicts, but it is a far cry from being the only way or even the typical way. Several avenues of decision-making and conflict resolution can be rationally and independently pursued to arrive at mutually acceptable prices.[11] Collusion is neither inevitable nor expected.[12] On the contrary, when firms are so strongly interdependent, as oligopolistic center firms are, they can scarcely fail to recognize the imperatives of uniform pricing. Even the most foolish of firms will quickly learn this fact of life.

The attempt at reaching mutually acceptable prices may take the form of

[11] For one fascinating version of how uniform prices can be attained without collusion or communication between the firms, see Thomas C. Schelling, *The Strategy of Conflict* (Cambridge, Mass.: Harvard University Press, 1960), Chaps. 2 and 3. Schelling develops a theory of focal points in which it is contended that a tendency exists for choices among alternatives to converge on some prominent value intuitively perceived by those concerned. The focal point owes its prominence to precedent, analogy, an obvious split-the-difference situation, habit, institutional idiosyncracies, educated guess, or the like.

[12] In the United States, of course, formal collusion to fix prices is illegal; so is informal collusion (spontaneous meetings in smoke-filled backrooms, secret agreements, publicized pricing formulas, predetermined splitting of the market, prearranged output quotas, cooperation through an exclusive selling agency, and so on). In Japan and in many European countries, however, collusion is a legitimate practice.

The most spectacular contemporary example of outright price-fixing among American firms is found in the electrical equipment industry, where General Electric, Westinghouse, and a number of other firms were convicted in 1960 of fixing prices and dividing up the market for circuit breakers, switchgears, and related products. See *U.S.* v. *Westinghouse Electric Corp., et al.*

More recently, a federal grand jury in 1966 charged eight plumbing fixture manufacturers, eight corporate officials, and a trade association with conspiring to fix the prices of enameled cast iron and vitreous china fixtures. Ten corporate and individual defendants, plus the trade association, pleaded no contest and were fined. But American Standard, Borg-Warner, and Kohler and three officials chose to stand trial. Each of the six defendants was found guilty in federal district court; the three corporations were fined, and the three officials were both fined and given jail sentences.

joint profit maximization, wherein member firms of the industry arrive at a price which they perceive yields the largest possible collective profit. Or it may take the form of *independent profit maximization*, where one firm is sufficiently dominant to impose its wishes upon the others and thereby can choose the price that will maximize its own profits. Or it might assume some form of *hybrid profit maximization*, in which a compromise is reached between pricing together for maximum joint profits and pricing independently for maximum individual profits. Or, finally, it might involve adding a "fair" profit margin to "normal" average total costs ("formula pricing") to reach a mutually acceptable price. All of these price-coordinating procedures are observable in actual situations, but none stands out as the predominant form of reconciling price differences among the firms. Each pricing conflict tends to be resolved in its own unique fashion.

But the really significant issue in oligopoly pricing is not *how* pricing conflicts are resolved; the overriding concern is whether the price equilibrium finally chosen is at the *high* or *low* end of the conflict range. We shall dodge this issue temporarily and postpone a final judgment until Chapter 13, when more evidence has been accummulated. Some preliminary generalizations are possible now, however. If collusive actions on the part of the firms are feasible and maintainable, price is surely to be higher than otherwise. In the absence of collusion and coercion, the price equilibrium is just as surely to be at the low end of the conflict range, owing to the upper hand which the firms preferring a lower price have over those preferring a higher price.

THE CONTRIBUTIONS OF GAME THEORY TO OLIGOPOLY BEHAVIOR

The rudiments of game theory discussed in Chapter 2 have special application in decision-making under conditions of conflict. By organizing the consequences of alternative strategies into the form of a payoff matrix, the firm can obtain a powerful methodological device for determining its own "best" course of action, the "best" course of action of rival firms, and thereby the optimal solution to the conflict existing between the firms concerned.

To the extent that oligopolists set market share as their prime competitive objective (in the belief that profits vary directly with sales and market share), the oligopoly problem may be posed in the form of zero-sum games, since one firm's market-share gain is necessarily equivalent to the market-share loss of rival firms. However, zero-sum game models do little justice to the realities of oligopoly.

A more revealing portrayal of oligopoly decisions is found in nonconstant-sum games where the payoffs of the firms do not add to zero. Suppose two firms, A and B, are faced with a pricing conflict of the nature posed in the previous section. Let firm A's profit-maximizing price be $100 and firm B's profit-maximizing price be $90. For the moment, assume these are the only two alternative prices under consideration by the two firms. The payoff matrixes below summarize the annual expected profit payoffs (in millions of dollars) for each firm:

Firm A's Payoff Matrix			
		Firm B's Price Strategies	
		$90	$100
Firm A's **Price** **Strategies**	$ 90	$25 m.	$45 m.
	$100	$10 m.	$70 m.

Firm B's Payoff Matrix			
		Firm B's Price Strategies	
		$90	$100
Firm A's **Price** **Strategies**	$ 90	$50 m.	$10 m.
	$100	$75 m.	$20 m.

Looking first at firm B's payoff matrix, we see that its expected profits are always higher at its preferred price of $90; in the language of game theory, the $90 price dominates the $100 price. If firm B picks the $90 price, firm A is forced to do likewise or else face the penalty of even lower profits. It is not at all inconceivable that firm A will find this arrangement unacceptable, since its profits are far below what it could earn were firm B to choose the $100 price. Confronted with this predicament, suppose firm A considers two additional prices: a "compromise price" of $95 and a "war price" of $70. The two payoff matrixes then become:

Firm A's Payoff Matrix

Firm B's Price Strategies

		$70	$90	$95	$100
	$ 70	−$ 7 m.	−$ 4 m.	$ 0	$ 2 m.
	$ 90	−$10 m.	$25 m.	$40 m.	$45 m.
Firm A's **Price** **Strategies**	$ 95	−$25 m.	$20 m.	$50 m.	$65 m.
	$100	−$40 m.	$10 m.	$45 m.	$70 m.

Firm B's Payoff Matrix

Firm B's Price Strategies

		$70	$90	$95	$100
	$ 70	−$5 m.	−$15 m.	−$25 m.	−$50 m.
	$ 90	−$1 m.	$50 m.	$30 m.	$10 m.
Firm A's **Price** **Strategies**	$ 95	$0	$65 m.	$35 m.	$15 m.
	$100	$2 m.	$75 m.	$40 m.	$20 m.

Inspection of the expanded payoff matrixes reveals that by selecting a $70 price, firm A can "punish" firm B for choosing a $90 price, though not without inflicting losses upon itself as well. Yet, if firm A becomes desperate or if it believes it is better able financially to sustain temporary losses than is firm B, then provoking a price war is firm A's best response to B's choice of a $90 price. Faced with the prospect of a price war if it pursues its own self-interest at the expense of firm A, firm B may be persuaded to adopt the compromise price of $95.[13] Although both firms earn less-than-maximum profits at $95, the compromise price in this instance yields profits which both firms are likely to find acceptable in view of the alternatives.

Consider another situation where two firms, A and B, are forced to choose between prices of $10 and $15. The annual expected profits (in millions of dollars) for each firm appear in matrix form as follows:

Firm A's Payoff Matrix				Firm B's Payoff Matrix		
		Firm B's Price Strategies				Firm B's Price Strategies
		$10	$15			$10	$15
Firm A's Price Strategies	$10	$100 m.	$180 m.	Firm A's Price Strategies	$10	$ 80 m.	$ 30 m.
	$15	$ 50 m.	$150 m.		$15	$170 m.	$120 m.

Examination of firm A's payoff matrix indicates that the $10 price strategy dominates the $15 price strategy. And if firm A selects the $10 price, firm B's best act is to choose the $10 price also. However, the apparent rationality of such a mental process is misleading; both firms will end up with lower profits by selling at a price of $10 than they could earn by selling at a price of $15. This paradoxical result is an illustration of the prisoner's dilemma described in Chapter 2.

The solution to such a dilemma rests with information and experience. Provided conditions are reasonably stable, the dynamics of continuous rivalry among oligopolists afford ample opportunity for learning to make decisions which are mutually advantageous. Pricing strategies undergo periodic reassessment and evaluation. It cannot be too long before one or both of the firms recognize the value of information-sharing and communication.[14] When this happens, a cooperative pricing strategy can readily be devised and competition speedily channeled into the nonprice areas.

A further prediction about oligopoly behavior is now possible: oligopolists selling similar or identical products under stable demand conditions are more likely to establish a mutually acceptable price equilibrium than

---

[13] J. L. Murphy reported a finding of higher prices and higher profits when rivals faced a threat of flagrant price-cutting than when they did not. See his article "Effects of the Threat of Losses on Duopoly Bargaining," *Quarterly Journal of Economics*, Vol. 80, No. 2 (May 1966), pp. 296–313.

[14] Several controlled experiments have been conducted which tend to confirm the ability of players to "solve" the prisoner's dilemma type of game as they acquire experience and information. See Lester B. Lave, "An Empirical Approach to the Prisoner's Dilemma Game," *Quarterly Journal of Economics*, Vol. 76, No. 3 (August 1962), pp. 424–436; L. E. Fouraker and Sidney Siegel, *Bargaining Behavior* (New York: McGraw-Hill, Inc., 1963), pp. 50–51, 165–166, and 199.

oligopolists selling differentiated or rapidly changing products under conditions of variable demand. This prediction has empirical validity. Despite a long record of price uniformity among standard brands of cigarettes, the introduction of new filter-tip and king-size cigarettes by the major firms during the 1950's was accompanied by several years of frequent price adjusting before the firms again settled upon a uniform price structure.[15] The tire industry, where eight firms account for almost 90 percent of total output, is noted for its unstable price structure. The maze of conflicting grades and qualities of tires, coupled with the 100-plus firms which purchase from the major manufacturers but sell under "private labels," has made a tangle of the tire price structure in complete defiance of any notion of equilibrium.[16] Retail tire outlets feature a procession of sales, special discounts, allowances, and guarantees—some factory-authorized, some not. In addition, product research has produced a steady stream of innovations in tire technology that renders the market for tires even more volatile. Pricing in the steel industry, though generally stable, typically breaks down when vigorous competition from foreign imports or depressed business conditions appear.[17] Other examples pertaining to electrical equipment, railroading, rayon, copper, glass, and petroleum could be cited.[18]

At this point in our survey of oligopoly pricing it is useful to indicate the range of factors which impede price equilibrium among oligopolists: (1) unstable industry demand conditions, (2) the frequency with which producers' cost functions are modified by technological change and the extent to which these changes are diffused unevenly among firms in the industry, (3) different market shares among the firms, (4) extreme product differentiation, and (5) frequent product variations. Given that one or more of these price-destabilizing factors are to be found in almost every oligopolistic market, the fact that oligopolists still price uniformly is powerful testimony to the imperatives of pricing to meet the competition. The enormous degrees of interdependence and personal awareness among oligopolistic firms guarantee near uniformity of price.

PRICE LEADERSHIP

One obvious way of arriving at a common price policy in an oligopolistic industry is for one firm (or maybe two or three firms) to take the initiative and serve as price leader for the industry. In such instances, it is customary

---

[15] Tenant, "The Cigarette Industry," pp. 376–377.
[16] Kaplan, Dirlam, and Lanzilotti, *Pricing in Big Business*, p. 203.
[17] *Ibid.*, pp. 19–24.
[18] The curious reader may wish to consult Harold C. Passer, *The Electrical Manufacturers: 1875–1900* (Cambridge, Mass.: Harvard University Press, 1953), pp. 62, 161–162, 263–264, and 352–353; Jesse W. Markham, *Competition in the Rayon Industry* (Cambridge, Mass.: Harvard University Press, 1952), pp. 103, 130, 127–136, and 150–153; J. L. McCarthy, "The American Copper Industry: 1947–1955," *Yale Economic Essays* (Spring 1964), pp. 64–130; G. W. Stocking and M. W. Watkins, *Monopoly and Free Enterprise* (New York: Twentieth Century Fund, 1951), pp. 121–126; and E. P. Learned and Catherine C. Elsworth, *Gasoline Pricing in Ohio* (Boston: Harvard Business School, 1959), pp. 108, 131–135, 147–149, and 237–252.

for list price changes to be announced first by the price leader, with the remaining firms accepting the leader's judgment on price and following suit. The two major forms of price leadership are exemplified by the *dominant-firm* model and the *barometric-firm* model.

Dominant-Firm Price Leadership. Dominant-firm price leadership arises when one firm accounts for a much larger market share than any of the other firms. Typically, the dominant firm is a large corporate enterprise whose only rivals consist of numerous "competitive-fringe" firms, none of which is able to exert a material influence on the market through its price-output decisions. On rarer occasions, the industry is composed of one dominant center firm, several lesser center firms, and a host of competitive-fringe periphery firms.

The assumption underlying the dominant-firm model is that the dominant firm chooses the price and allows the competitive-fringe firms to sell all they wish at that price; the dominant firm then produces an amount sufficient to meet the remaining demand at the chosen price. In essence, the competitive-fringe firms behave just like perfectly competitive firms. They can sell all they want at the price set by the dominant firm and therefore face a horizontal demand curve at the established price. Each of the firms pegs its output at the rate where $MC = MR$; MR is equal to the price set by the dominant firm, since the latter lets the fringe firms sell all they please.

The determination of the dominant firm's optimum price is illustrated in Figure 11-7. Suppose the dominant firm believes the total market demand curve to be D_m. Suppose further that it estimates the amount of output which will be supplied by the competitive fringe firms at various alternative prices to be S_{cf}—found by summing together the portions of the marginal cost curves lying above average variable cost for each fringe producer. Once the dominant firm estimates how much of the total market demand will be served by the

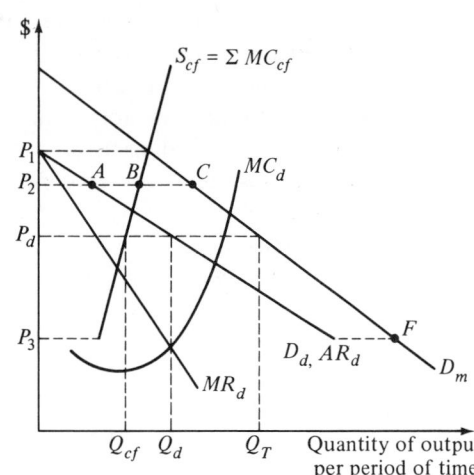

Fig. 11-7   Price and Output Decisions for
a Situation of Dominant-Firm
Price Leadership

competitive fringe, it can calculate how much will be left over for itself. For example, at prices of P_1 and higher, the competitive fringe is willing to supply all the output the market will absorb, leaving no sales potential for the dominant firm. At price P_2 total market demand is P_2C units; of this, the fringe producers would produce P_2B units, leaving BC units for the dominant firm. To locate the dominant firm's demand curve at price P_2 we set point A such that BC units equals P_2A units of output. This procedure can be repeated for other assumed prices. In each case the dominant firm's demand is found by subtracting the fringe firms' output at a given price from the total industry demand at that price. The result is a series of points which, when connected, gives the curve D_d, AR_d. Observe that at prices below P_3 the dominant firm has the entire market to itself; no output will be supplied by the fringe firms when price is less than the minimum average variable cost of every fringe firm. Thus, the dominant firm's demand curve below price P_3 coincides with the segment of the industry demand curve labeled FD_m. The dominant firm's entire demand curve is D_d, AR_d plus the segment FD_m.

The dominant firm determines its profit-maximizing price and output in the customary fashion of equating marginal revenue and marginal cost. The marginal revenue curve corresponding to D_d, AR_d is MR_d, and the dominant firm's marginal cost curve is shown as MC_d. Its profit-maximizing output rate is therefore Q_d units and its profit-maximizing price is P_d dollars. Total market demand at price P_d is Q_T units. Of this, the dominant firm supplies Q_d units, and the competitive fringe firms supply the remainder $(Q_T - Q_d)$, which equals Q_{cf} units in Figure 11-7.

One of the better current examples of dominant-firm price leadership arises in retailing where a nationally known seller (such as K-Mart, A&P, or Sears) dominates a local market for the commodities it carries. The numerous small, locally-owned retail firms carrying comparable products constitute the competitive fringe. The local firms must sell at prices approximating the dominant marketer or risk loss of a major portion of their customers. Thus, they are more or less forced to follow the leader. Moreover, they must be wary of undercutting the leader very much. If they get far out of line, the center firm is more than able to punish them by slashing prices even further, thereby dealing them severe losses. It is a simple matter for a large retailer to sustain losses temporarily in one local market and make them up in the other localities it serves.[19] The one-store or one-locality retailer has no such option.

In markets where one firm clearly dominates sales, parallel pricing among firms stems from either of two reasons. If economies of large-scale production give the dominant firm a distinct cost advantage over competitive-

---

[19] This is not to say, however, that large firms will readily resort to local price warfare. The dominant firm's profit sacrifices are likely to be quite large relative to the harm it inflicts upon small rivals. Price wars to discipline minor firms and to teach them the value of cooperation are worthwhile only if the aftermath produces an environment much more conducive to the earning of profits. Otherwise, it may take an inordinately long time to recoup the sacrifices of profit which a price war entails.

fringe firms, the dominant firm will probably select a price below that preferred by the competitive fringe but which, nevertheless, they must match or else face erosion of sales. If the dominant firm has a cost disadvantage and, consequently, elects a price higher than might otherwise prevail, the followership of the fringe firms stems from implicit coercion and potential punishment by the dominant firm and not from genuine popularity of the leader's chosen price. In either event if would not be far wrong to conclude that dominant-firm price leadership is an inevitable consequence of an industry composed of one dominant firm and a host of competitive fringe firms.

In times past, dominant-firm price leaders have included U.S. Steel in steel, Firestone in tires, Birdseye in frozen foods, Standard Oil in petroleum, R.J. Reynolds in cigarettes, International Harvester in farm implements, Alcoa in aluminum, IBM in computers, and American Can in tin cans. With the exception of IBM, however, the dominant firm is no longer as dominant in these industries. Rivals of important size and influence have emerged and gradually eroded the once overwhelming market power of the dominant firm.

The rather general trait of dominant firms to lose their dominance correctly suggests that the dominant-firm market structure may be a short-run situation which will eventually disintegrate into highly competitive oligopoly. The reasons are clear-cut. When the dominant firm's price allows fringe firms to realize positive economic profits, then, over time, they are encouraged to take advantage of scale economies and expand their outputs.[20] Since the dominant firm is a "quantity follower" and in effect makes room for fringe-firm expansion by curbing its own output, the most aggressive smaller firms, via steady expansion, will begin to increase their market shares at the expense of the dominant firm. Sooner or later, the dominant firm will find itself confronted with several emerging rivals of growing influence and power, and its dominant position will be effectively undermined.

The major point here is that the dominant firm, if it wishes to retain its position of advantage in the market, must deviate from the pattern of letting the small firms produce as much as they please. It is "suicide" for it to buy price leadership at the cost of quantity followership. Instead, to preserve its position the dominant firm must abandon the short-run profit-maximizing behavior portrayed in the dominant-firm model in favor of long-run profit maximization. Among other things, the latter entails adjusting its short-run profit-maximizing price downward so as to deter small-firm expansion and the entry of new rivals. The dominant firm must be wary of creating short-run market conditions conducive to the growth of the competitive fringe. Of course, it may be that it has no choice in this regard. The antitrust laws and the shape of the long-run average cost curve may preclude the

---

[20] The steel industry provides a classic example. In 1901 U.S. Steel controlled 65 percent of the industry's ingot capacity. As the dominant firm and price leader, it established a high price policy which stimulated the entry and expansion of smaller steel firms. By 1915 U.S. Steel's share of ingot capacity was down to 52 percent; its share has fallen steadily to 28 percent in 1960 and 21 percent in 1968.

establishment of a price that will perpetuate the dominant firm's position.[21] But even if long-term dominance is not sustainable, all is not lost for the dominant firm; temporary high profits may suffice to create a fortune for the stockholders. And there is no compelling reason why acceptable profits cannot be earned after even formidable rivals appear on the scene.

Barometric Price Leadership. Barometric price leadership exists when there are *several* principal firms, surrounded or not, as the case may be, by a competitive fringe of small firms. No one of the large firms is powerful enough to impose its will upon the others consistently. As a result, the identity of the barometric price leader changes. Sometimes one, sometimes another of the principal firms will take the lead in initiating price changes. For instance, in rayon yarn, American Viscose (the largest seller) and DuPont (the second largest seller) have in recent years shared the role of leader. In copper, price leadership has been exercised by all of the Big Three—Anaconda, Kennecott, and Phelps Dodge. In automobiles, General Motors is the recognized price leader. R. J. Reynolds and American Tobacco share the lead in cigarettes. U. S. Steel, Bethlehem, and occasionally a lesser firm bear the burden of price leadership in steel.

By and large, the barometric price leader appears to do little more than become the first firm to announce new prices consistent with current market conditions. Seldom does the barometric firm possess power to coerce the rest of the industry into accepting its lead, even though it may aspire to wield such control. In the usual case, the barometric firm acquires its status as leader because of its experience and respect throughout the industry, because other firms may be unable or unwilling to accept the responsibility of continuously appraising industry demand and supply conditions, or because other firms are hesitant to stick their necks out and formally recognize what is already being acknowledged in private. Thus, the barometric firm commands adherence of rivals to its price announcements only to the extent that it has accurately perceived the winds of change in industry demand and supply conditions. Even then, industrywide assent to the price change may not be forthcoming immediately; rival firms often temporize with a wait-and-see strategy for a period of several days or weeks.

Conclusions Concerning Price Leadership. Successful price leadership has the important effect in oligopoly of eliminating the kink in the demand curves of the firms. The price leader whose leadership role is widely and consistently accepted can count upon rivals to follow price increases as well as price cuts. However, the kink remains for firms whose price increases are frequently rejected. And for barometric firms whose lead is sometimes undermined by failure to follow, the existence of a kink lies in the realm of uncertainty.

---

[21] A penetrating and definitive analysis of dominant-firm pricing is found in Dean A. Worcester, "Why 'Dominant Firms' Decline," *Journal of Political Economy*, Vol. 65, No. 4 (August 1957), pp. 338–347.

The evidence is not clear whether price leadership sets a price structure higher than it would otherwise be. On some occasions, price leadership undoubtedly facilitates the raising of prices. Yet, when the price leader is the lowest-cost producer, it may hold price below levels preferred by rival firms. Then, too, price leaders can sometimes assume a statesmanlike position of not raising price during prosperous times in order to cooperate with federal anti-inflation requests and also to avoid claims of profiteering and greed that might tarnish their image and jeopardize long-run profit objectives.

Special Features of Center Firm Price and Output Decisions

The preceding models of oligopoly have focused upon the knotty problem of price-conflict resolution and the mechanics of reaching a mutually acceptable price. We turn now to matters of internal operations within the center firm and their effect upon price and output decisions. On numerous occasions we have indicated that center firms operate many plants, sell in many different markets, and produce many products. In addition, center firms have some unique strategies for dealing with market uncertainty and changing demand conditions. The time has come to bring these facets into our analysis of center firm behavior.

MULTIPLANT OPERATIONS

The total demand for such commodities as tin cans, storage batteries, biscuits and crackers, cement, building materials, dairy products, tires, apparel, computers, floor coverings, and steel, among others, is far larger than the existing firms can accommodate by operating one plant.[22] As a result, firms operate several plants to manufacture the same product. Decisions must then be made regarding how to allocate the firm's optimum total output among its several plants in order to minimize total production costs and maximize total profits.

The chances are that the various plants of a particular firm not only are located in different regions but also incorporate different technologies, obtain raw materials and labor inputs at varying prices, and therefore have different cost structures. An illustrative case is presented in Table 11-1. The firm operates two plants with marginal costs as shown in columns 2 and 3. Inspection of the marginal cost functions shows that if the firm wishes to produce three or less units of output it should use plant 1 exclusively, since it has the lowest marginal cost ($3, $5, and $7 compared to $8 for plant 2). However, the fourth through ninth units should definitely be produced in plant 2. Continuing in this fashion, we can derive the combined marginal cost

---

[22] In contrast, in producing typewriters, soup, sewing machines, photographic equipment, steam turbines, transformers, and locomotives, plants are quite large relative to the size of the total market, and multiplant operations are much less in evidence.

Table 11-1 The Allocation of Output Among Plants

(1) Total Output of the Firm	(2) Marginal Cost, Plant 1	(3) Marginal Cost, Plant 2	(4) Marginal Cost for the Firm	(5) Price	(6) Total Revenue	(7) Marginal Revenue
0				$30	$ 0	
1	$ 3	$8	$ 3	29	29	$29
2	5	8	5	28	56	27
3	7	8	7	27	81	25
4	9	8	8	26	104	23
5	10	8	8	25	125	21
6	11	8	8	24	144	19
7	12	9	8	23	161	17
8	capacity	capacity	8	22	176	15
9			8	21	189	13
10			9	20	200	11
11			9	19	209	9
12			10	18	216	7
13			11	17	221	5
14			12	16	224	3

curve for the firm (column 4). As usual, profit maximization requires that the firm select the output rate at which the marginal revenue from the last unit sold equals the marginal cost of the last unit produced. This occurs at an output of 11 units and a price of $19; here, the marginal cost of the eleventh unit is $9 and the marginal revenue from selling the eleventh unit is $9.

Given that the optimum total output of the firm is 11 units, how should production of the 11 units be divided between the two plants? The answer is: produce 4 units at plant 1 and 7 units at plant 2. *Production must be allocated among the various plants such that the marginal costs of the last units produced at each plant are equal both to each other and to the value at which the firm's overall marginal cost equals the marginal revenue of the last unit sold.* Unless the marginal costs of the last units produced at each plant are equal, the firm can lower its total production costs for a given output by shifting production from the plant where marginal cost is higher to the plant where marginal cost is lower.

In general, then, whenever a firm operates a number of plants to produce a given commodity, proper application of the profit-maximizing rule involves three sequential steps. Step one is to determine the firm's overall marginal cost curve from the marginal cost curves of the various plants. Step two is to pinpoint the firm's most profitable output by finding the output rate where overall marginal cost equals marginal revenue. Step three is to allocate the profit-maximizing output among the various plants so that the marginal costs of the last units produced at each plant are equal. In mathematical terms, the firm should arrange its production activities so that

$$MR = MC = MC_{P_1} = MC_{P_2} = \cdots = MC_{P_n},$$

where MR is marginal revenue from all sales of the commodity, MC is the combined marginal cost, and MC_{P_1}, MC_{P_2}, $\cdots$, MC_{P_n} are the marginal costs of the respective plants which the firm has for producing the commodity.

The effect of this rule in actual practice is to concentrate production activity in the most efficient plants and to use older, technologically inferior production facilities as sparingly as conditions will permit. Modern plants employing the latest technologies are nearly always operated at or near capacity rates in order to realize lowest unit costs. Less efficient plants are relied upon primarily to fill out the balance of the firm's total output and to help fill the firm's need for production capacity in periods of peak demand. In fact, it is partially because a firm's less efficient production facilities are used more and more intensively that marginal and average costs turn up rather sharply at outputs beyond 90 percent of rated capacity.

MULTIMARKET OPERATIONS

Up till now we have implicitly assumed that a firm sells a given product at a uniform price to all buyers. This is a tolerable first approximation, but many exceptions exist. Center firms, especially, sell their products in a variety of geographically separated or distinct markets (local, regional, national, and international) and they sell to diverse classes of customers (industrial users, commercial users, household users, large-quantity buyers, small-quantity buyers, regular customers, occasional customers, one-time customers, and so on). Firms sometimes find it more profitable to sell identical product units to different customers at different prices, depending upon the market they are in, and to sell identical product units to a single customer at different prices, depending upon the quantity he purchases. They may also sell products with different costs at the same price (i.e., airlines serve full-course dinners on some flights but only snacks on others, yet ticket prices are the same; manufacturers charge all customers the same delivered price even though the freight costs are less for nearby customers than for distant customers).[23] Pricing practices of this type are labeled by economists as *price discrimination*.

For a firm to employ price discrimination tactics in a profitable fashion, three conditions must be satisfied. First, the firm must face a downsloping demand curve and thus have some discretion in the price or prices it charges buyers of the product. With a horizontal demand curve, the firm has no motive for selling at different prices; in fact, selling at less than the full market price involves a sacrifice of profits. Second, the firm must have easily identifiable groups of customers with different types of demand for the product in question. Put another way, the shape of the demand curve for one class of customers must differ from the shape of the demand curve for another class of

---

[23] Such practices are not restricted to business enterprises. Universities, for example, charge the same tuition for a large freshman class taught by a graduate teaching assistant as they do for a small senior seminar taught by a premier professor.

customers. Third, the firm must be able to segregate its sales to each group of customers in such a way that customers paying the lower price cannot resell the item to customers paying a higher price; the different groups of customers must, in other words, be sealed off from one another so that transferring the product from one group to another is severely constrained, if not impossible.

Two distinct types of price discrimination serve to highlight the attractiveness of charging different prices for the same product. Consider first the case where the price the customer pays depends upon the quantity he purchases (most prominently illustrated by the sales of gas and electricity). Suppose the individual customer has a demand curve DD', shown in Figure 11-8. The firm

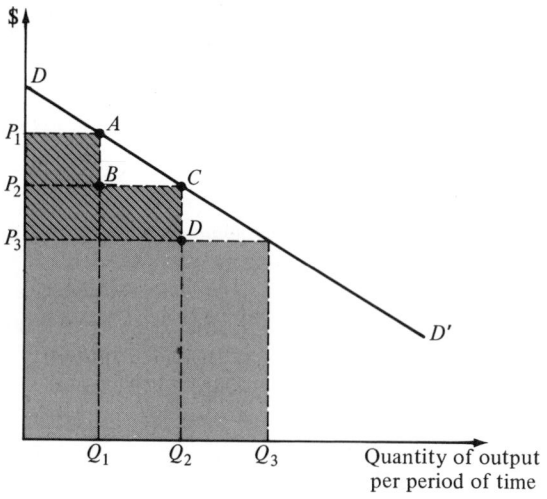

Fig. 11-8   The Revenue Effect of Pricing According to Volume Purchased

charges a price of P_1 dollars per unit if the customer buys Q_1 or fewer units per period. The firm reduces its price to P_2 dollars per unit on those units purchased in excess of Q_1 but no greater than Q_2 units. For all units purchased in excess of Q_2, the firm charges a price of P_3 dollars. If a customer elects to purchase a total of Q_3 units in a given time period, the firm's total revenue (the customer's bill) is calculated as follows:

$$TR = P_1(Q_1) + P_2(Q_2 - Q_1) + P_3(Q_3 - Q_2).$$

This amount is equivalent to the shaded area in Figure 11-8. The benefits to the firm of systematically reducing price as purchases increase should now be apparent. Under a single-price policy, sales of Q_3 units would call for charging a maximum of P_3 dollars per unit. Total revenue would amount to only $(P_3 \cdot Q_3)$ dollars, a figure P_1ABCDP_3 dollars less then obtained with a multiple-price policy.

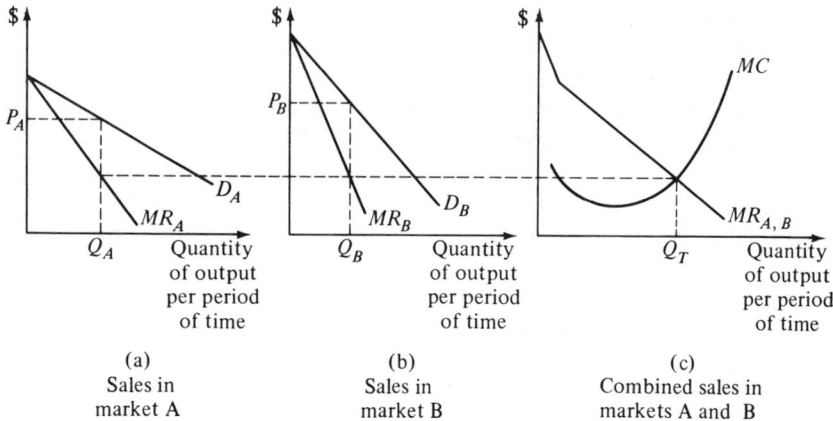

Fig. 11-9   Two-Market Price Discrimination

Figure 11-9 illustrates a situation where a firm charges different prices to customers in two different markets, A and B. The respective demand and marginal revenue curves of the two classes of buyers are given in panels (a) and (b).[24] The firm must decide upon its most profitable combined sales volume, how much should be sold to buyers in each of the two markets, and the price to charge in each market As usual, the most profitable output rate is where MR equals MC—however, the appropriate marginal revenue concept in this instance is not MR in *each* market *separately*, but rather MR in both markets *combined*. The marginal revenue curves in markets A and B are summed *horizontally* to obtain combined MR, shown as $MR_{A,B}$ in Figure 11-9(c). The intersection of $MR_{A,B}$ with MC in panel (c) defines the most profitable output rate (Q_T) for the firm. Next, a decision must be made as to how much of the total output of Q_T units to sell in market A and how much to sell in market B. The rule for profit maximization in such situations calls for allocating total sales between the markets in such a way that marginal cost at the optimal output equals marginal revenue *in each market*. In terms of our example, the rule requires that

$$MC = MR_{A,B} = MR_A = MR_B.$$

To equalize marginal revenue in the two markets at the profit-maximizing output, a horizontal line is projected from the point in panel (c) where $MC = MR_{A,B}$ to panels (a) and (b) to find where $MC = MR_{A,B} = MR_A = MR_B$. This gives an optimal sales level of Q_A units in market A and Q_B units in market B ($Q_A + Q_B = Q_T$). The profit-maximizing prices, P_A and P_B, are found from the respective demand curves in each market. The firm will

[24] Two-market price discrimination is quite common. Many center firms sell their products at one price in international markets and at another price (sometimes higher, sometimes lower) in domestic markets. In the case of products sold nationwide, prices are often higher west than east of the Rocky Mountains.

420

necessarily earn higher total profits by engaging in price discrimination than it could earn by following a single-price policy of charging the same price to all buyers. Furthermore, it can be proven mathematically (see mathematical capsule 9) that the firm's selling price is always higher in the market where demand is less elastic.

MATHEMATICAL CAPSULE 9

The Mathematics of Price Discrimination

When a firm sells its product in markets that are economically isolated and when the respective market demand curves confronting the firm are different, the firm maximizes total profit by charging different prices in each market. The conditions for maximizing profits may be derived very simply. For illustrative convenience we shall restrict the analysis to a two-market situation.

Suppose the firm's total revenue from sales of output in market A is represented as

$$TR_A = f(Q_A),$$

the firm's total revenue from sales of output in market B is represented as

$$TR_B = g(Q_B),$$

and the firm's total costs from combined sales in both markets is represented by

$$TC = h(Q_A + Q_B) = h(Q),$$

where Q is total output no matter in which market specific units are sold. In other words, TC depends upon the output rate and not upon where the output is sold.

As usual, total profit (π) is equal to total revenue minus total cost:

$$\pi = TR - TC.$$

Substituting into this expression gives

$$\pi = TR_A + TR_B - TC,$$

which can be rewritten as

$$\pi = f(Q_A) + g(Q_B) - h(Q).$$

The profit-maximizing conditions are

$$\frac{\partial \pi}{\partial Q_A} = \frac{\partial f}{\partial Q_A} - \frac{\partial h}{\partial Q} = \frac{df}{dQ_A} - \frac{dh}{dQ} = 0,$$

$$\frac{\partial \pi}{\partial Q_B} = \frac{\partial g}{\partial Q_B} - \frac{\partial h}{\partial Q} = \frac{dg}{dQ_B} - \frac{dh}{dQ} = 0.$$

But, by definition, $df/dQ_A = MR_A$, $dg/dQ_B = MR_B$, and $dh/dQ = MC$. Thus, profit maximization requires that

$$MR_A - MC = 0 \quad \text{and} \quad MR_B - MC = 0,$$

which in turn is equivalent to

$$MR_A = MR_B = MC.$$

Now let us prove that the higher of the two profit-maximizing prices is found in the market with the less elastic demand. Let $P = f(Q)$ represent any demand curve, where P is price and Q is the quantity demanded. Then total revenue is

$$TR = PQ,$$

and marginal revenue, according to the rule of differential calculus for the derivative of a product of two variables, is

$$MR = \frac{dTR}{dQ} = P + Q\frac{dP}{dQ}.$$

Multiplying the last term of the expression by P/P gives

$$MR = P\left(1 + \frac{Q}{P}\cdot\frac{dP}{dQ}\right).$$

Recalling from our definition of point elasticity that $\epsilon_p = (dQ/dP)\cdot(P/Q)$ and substituting this into the expression, we get

$$MR = P\left(1 + \frac{1}{\epsilon_p}\right).$$

This latter expression can now be used to demonstrate our proof that price is higher in the market where demand is less elastic. From the above expression, it follows that

$$MR_A = P_A\left(1 + \frac{1}{\epsilon_A}\right),$$

$$MR_B = P_B\left(1 + \frac{1}{\epsilon_B}\right).$$

Since at the optimal output $MR_A = MR_B$, then

$$P_A\left(1 + \frac{1}{\epsilon_A}\right) = P_B\left(1 + \frac{1}{\epsilon_B}\right),$$

which can be rewritten as

$$\frac{P_A}{P_B} = \frac{1 + \frac{1}{\epsilon_B}}{1 + \frac{1}{\epsilon_A}}.$$

Suppose $\epsilon_A = -4$ and $\epsilon_B = -2$ at the respective profit-maximizing prices of P_A and P_B; then demand is more elastic in market A than in market B. By substituting these values into the last expression, it is clear that $P_A/P_B < 1$ and that $P_B > P_A$. This result is obtained for any values of ϵ_A and ϵ_B such that $|\epsilon_A| > |\epsilon_B|$. Accordingly, two-market price discrimination always leads to a higher price in the market where demand is less elastic with regard to price.

The case of two-market price discrimination is easily expanded to allow for any number of markets. Whenever the firm sells a commodity in a variety of markets for which demand is different, four steps are required for determining the profit-maximizing prices and outputs in each market. Step one is to ascertain the firm's combined marginal revenue curve by horizontally adding together the separate marginal revenue curves in each market. Step two is to pinpoint the firm's most profitable combined output rate for all markets by locating the output rate where marginal cost equals combined marginal revenue. Step three is to allocate the profit-maximizing output among the various markets in such a way that marginal cost at the optimal output rate is equal to the marginal revenues from the last units sold in each market. In mathematical terms, this means the firm must divide its output such that

$$MC = MR = MR_1 = MR_2 = \cdots = MR_n,$$

where MC is marginal cost, MR is the combined marginal revenue, and MR_1, $MR_2, \ldots, MR_n$ are the marginal revenues of the respective markets in which the commodity is sold. Step four is to determine the prices in each market from the respective market demand curves.

A tremendous variety of price discrimination practices can be found in the real world. Table 11-2 summarizes the principal types, along with examples of each. The information contained in this table provides a useful portrayal of pricing policies commonly used by business firms.

Table 11-2   Types of Price Discrimination

INDIVIDUAL CUSTOMER DISCRIMINATION

1. *Bargain-every-time.* Each sale is an individually negotiated deal. The classic case is the purchase of new and used cars; other examples include made-to-order sales and objects of art.

2. *Size-up-his-income.* Wealthier customers are charged more than less affluent customers; price is partially a function of income. Standard examples are the pricing of medical, legal, accounting, and management consulting services.

3. *Cut-price-if-you-must.* Departures from list price are made when buyers shop diligently for the best price; sellers grant secret concessions as a last resort. Examples include the transactions between steel firms and auto makers for hot and cold rolled sheet steel and virtually any industrial product sold to skilled purchasing agents who are always on the look-out for a lower price.

Count-the-use. Price is based upon the level of use, even though unit costs do not vary appreciably with volume. For example, the rental fees on Xerox copying machines are based upon the number of copies made.

GROUP DISCRIMINATION

1. *Promote-new-customers.* New customers are offered "special introductory prices" lower than those paid by established customers in the hopes of enlarging the firm's regular clientele. Record and book clubs and magazine publishers are avid practitioners of this pricing policy.

2. *Forget-the-freight.* All customers are charged the same delivered price, even though transportation costs vary from customer to customer according to the distance located from the production site. Nearby customers are discriminated against in favor of far-away customers. Examples include cement and steel pricing and, additionally, any commodity which is sold at "nationally advertised prices" irrespective of transportation cost differentials.

3. *Get-the-most-from-each-market.* Prices are persistently held higher in markets where competition is weak than where it is strong. Import quotas and tariff barriers allow some firms to charge higher prices in domestic markets than in international markets (sugar, oil, and domestic wool).

4. *Favor-the-big-buyer.* Large purchasers of a commodity are given price cuts perhaps exceeding the cost savings derived from large-scale transactions. The large chain discount retailers buy many of their goods at prices below those of the small retailer; firms which purchase in "carload lots" obtain discounts not allowed to purchasers of just a few units.

5. *Skim-the-market.* A product is introduced at a high price within reach mainly of only high-income buyers. Periodically, price is then reduced step by step (and in conjunction with the availability of new production capacity) to allow steady, but gradual, penetration of broader markets. The pricing of television sets and Polaroid cameras has followed this pattern.

PRODUCT DISCRIMINATION

1. *Make-them-pay-for-the-label.* Manufacturers sell a relatively homogeneous commodity under different brand names, charging higher prices for the better-known, more prestigious brand names. Automobile tires, paints, articles of clothing, and food products are examples.

2. *Appeal-to-quality.* Products are offered in packages ranging from the budget variety to the super deluxe. Differences in price are *more* than proportional to the differences in cost. Household appliances are an obvious example. Traveling first class as compared to tourist class is another example.

3. *Get-rid-of-the-dogs.* Price concessions in the form of "special" sales are made periodically, or continuously in the bargain department of the retail store, in order to reduce stocks of poorly selling items and to make room for new merchandise. The seemingly perpetual end-of-the-model sales, close-out specials, anniversary sales, and inventory reduction sales serve as good examples.

4. *Switch-them-off-peak-periods.* Lower prices are charged for services identical except for time of consumption in order to encourage fuller and more balanced use of capacity. Off-season rates at resorts and the lower rates for long-distance calls made at night and on Sundays are examples.

SOURCE: This table is a composite of the observations of several writers, including Fritz Machlup, "Characteristics and Types of Price Discrimination," contained in the National Bureau of Economic Research conference report, *Business Concentration and Price Policy* (Princeton, N. J.: Princeton University Press, 1955), pp. 397–435; Joel Dean, *Managerial Economics* (Englewood Cliffs, N. J.: Prentice-Hall, Inc., 1951), pp. 419–424 and 503–548; and Ralph Cassady, Jr.,·Techniques and Purposes of Price Discrimination, *Journal of Marketing*, Vol. 11, No. 2 (October 1946), pp. 135–150.

Whether price discrimination is good or bad hinges upon subjective evaluations over which reasonable men may disagree. Value judgments inevitably creep into the picture. Most academic economists are suspicious of

424

price discrimination because, if systematically practiced, it facilitates ad-herence to a collusive price structure. In addition, since firms choose freely whether to use a single- or a multiple-price policy, the implication is clear that profits are higher with discrimination than without, thereby causing a redistribution of income from customers to the firm. On the positive side, charging different prices in different markets affects the total output of the product little if at all.[25] And since customers with more elastic demands (and for whom price is lower) are likely to have incomes lower than the customers comprising the less elastic markets, price discrimination may work to the advantage of the economically weak and therefore produce "socially beneficial" effects. Moreover, situations may exist in which the costs of pro-duction cannot be covered unless revenues are enhanced by multiple pricing. Hence, where profits can be increased with multiple pricing, the added profits may be the margin between supplying a good or service and not doing so.[26] Finally, price discrimination can enhance competition by en-couraging more price experimentation. Whereas producers are reluctant to engage in across-the-board price changes, they may be much more willing to test the consequences of a price change in one market or for one class of cus-tomers. On balance, the complex crosscurrents at work make it prudent to judge each particular instance of price discrimination on its merits.

MULTIPRODUCT OPERATIONS

Almost all firms of any size and consequence produce a variety of products. These products may be sold in markets of widely varying competitive intensity. The center firm is sure to enjoy stronger positions of market advantage for some of its products than for others. Consequently, profit margins on some of its products will be wider than those on others. Since in the short run there are restraints upon how much the firm can produce, the question arises as to how the firm should best use its limited production capacity to maximize the combined profits from all of its products. There may not always be sufficient resources available to permit pushing the output of all commodities to their respective profit-maximizing rates. Consider first the simplified case of a two-product firm.

For a two-product firm to maximize total profits from both products, it must divide its limited resource inputs between them in such a way that it receives an equivalent amount of extra profit from the last unit of input allocated to the production of each one. If this condition is violated, the firm can increase total profits by shifting units of input out of the production of the commodity where profit is less and into the production of the com-modity where profit is greater. As a numerical illustration, consider a firm

[25] For a treatment of the output effects of price discrimination see E. O. Edwards, "The Analysis of Output Under Discrimination," *Econometrica*, Vol. 18, No. 2 (April 1950), pp. 163–172, and Joan Robinson, *The Economics of Imperfect Competition* (London: The Macmillan Company, 1933), pp. 188–195.
[26] George J. Stigler, *The Theory of Price*, 3rd ed. (New York: The Macmillan Company, 1966), pp. 213–214.

which has a total of 300 hours of skilled labor available for producing products A and B. The estimated profits from alternative uses of this labor are as indicated below:

Product A

Hours of Skilled Labor	Total Profit from A	Added Profit
0	0	
		$500
100	$ 500	
		$600
200	$1100	
		$400
300	$1500	

Product B

Hours of Skilled Labor	Total Profit from B	Added Profit
0	0	
		$600
100	$600	
		$500
200	$1100	
		$400
300	$1500	

Suppose the firm is now using 100 hours of labor to produce A and 200 hours of labor to produce B, with resulting joint profits of $1,600 ($500 from A and $1,100 from B). Is the firm obtaining maximum total profit from both products? The answer is no. Combined profits can be increased by shifting 100 hours of skilled labor time out of producing B and into producing A. In doing so, the firm gives up $500 of profit from the production and sale of B but gains $600 profit from A—for a net gain of $100 and a joint profit total of $1,700. By using 200 of the 300 hours of skilled labor to produce A and only 100 hours to produce B, the firm receives $600 profit from the last hundred units of skilled labor used to produce A and also $600 profit from the last hundred units of skilled labor used to produce B. It has equalized the added profit yields of the last batch of input allocated to each product.

The two-commodity situation is easily expanded to n number of commodities and restated as follows: Limited resource inputs should be allocated among the production of commodities $C_1, C_2, C_3, \ldots, C_n$ in such a way as to yield an equivalent amount of profit from the last unit of input allocated to the production of each commodity. The significance of the profit-maximizing rule for multiproduct enterprises is that the limited availability of resource inputs often makes it more profitable to diversify into new products and to move into new markets *before* attempting to squeeze the last dollar's worth of profit from existing products and product markets. The most efficient and most profitable use of the firm's limited productive capabilities requires that the available resources be channeled into the production of commodities with high incremental profit prospects and out of commodities where incremental profits are low. Thus, short-run profit maximization for a multiproduct enterprise does not require that marginal revenue be equated to marginal cost for each and every product the firm produces. This latter holds only if the firm has adequate resources and sufficient production capacity in the short run to carry the production of every current and potential product to the rate where $MR = MC$. From a total organization viewpoint, price and output decisions require a careful balancing of adjustments among specific product markets to yield the optimal divisional and companywide profits.[27]

OTHER DIMENSIONS OF CENTER FIRM STRATEGY

Given that price differences and price changes are somewhat traumatic for center firm oligopolists, they divert the main thrust of their competitive efforts to the nonprice areas of product innovation, customer service, terms of credit, technological superiority, product performance features, and extensive promotional efforts. The intensity with which center firms compete on these points is unparalleled. The reasons are simple. Since the prices of the firms must be comparable, the major basis for gaining new sales necessarily proceeds along the many avenues of nonprice competition. No responsible management can afford to leave any stone unturned in its struggle for competitive success and acceptable organizational performance. Product innovation quickly becomes absolutely essential; so does investment in modern production technology. Certainly, few center firms will pass up the opportunity to increase the effective differentiation of their products in the minds of their customers. Indeed, they spend billions of dollars each year in efforts to maintain and strengthen their market positions. To do otherwise is to jeopardize and perhaps permanently impair the firm's long-term profitability.

Center firms may attempt to insulate themselves from aggressive competition from rivals and from adverse cost changes by means of vertical integration. Backward vertical integration spares center firms the uncertainty of being dependent upon other firms for crucial inputs, as well as the uncertainty of what prices must be paid for the inputs. By bringing the production of raw materials and critical component goods under its ownership and control, the center firm obtains *reliable* sources of supply at *reliable* prices. Such a move may be eminently desirable for defensive reasons if there is a good chance that rival firms will do the same or if favorable input prices are essential to preserving the firm's profit margins. Moreover, backward integration *internalizes* such problems as labor disputes, rising production costs, production breakdowns, and delays in scheduled deliveries. A center firm is better able to control daily operating problems when they fall within the purview of its own management than when they are the problems of other managements. Integrating backward has the further advantage of allowing the firm to better coordinate and systematize the many facets of its overall

---

[27] The pricing of steel products for a large multiproduct corporation like U.S. Steel provides a good illustration. In the production of steel rails and steel cables, where demand is less elastic and also where competition is less intense, U.S. Steel charges proportionately higher prices and maintains wider profit margins. In the markets for stainless steel, galvanized sheets, and tin plate, where U.S. Steel is in strenuous direct and potential competition with aluminum and lumber as well as other steel producers, prices are more than proportionately lower and profit margins are much narrower. Thus, product market elasticities and profit margin differences are indeed major decision variables in U.S. Steel's divisional price and output strategies. For greater detail see Kaplan, Dirlam, and Lanzilotti, *Pricing in Big Business*, pp. 172–173.

production process, thus deriving efficiency and cost benefits. Holiday Inns, for example, is rapidly diversifying into activities such as carpeting, candies, furniture items, foodstuffs, and a school of motel management—all of which complement its main product and serve to supply its 1,000-plus inns with basic support services. In general, the reductions of market uncertainty accompanying backward integration are valuable contributors to coordinating and routinizing the center firm's production cycle, thereby allowing the organization (a) to escape the disruptive influence of unreliable suppliers and supply prices, (b) to realize the mass production efficiencies of which it is capable, and (c) to insulate itself from the repercussions of tactical maneuvers by rival firms. Integrating backward thus makes the center firm more a master of its own destiny and less a slave to fortuitous circumstances beyond its control.

Also, to increase security and reduce uncertainty, center firms may be motivated to integrate forward into ownership and control of distribution outlets. Access to product markets must be dependable. Where ownership of distribution channels is impractical, center firms may employ such strategic devices as franchise systems, leasing provisions, and exclusive dealing arrangements to give them a stronger foothold in dealing with wholesale and retail outlets. For instance, while most gasoline service stations are locally operated, the facilities are leased to the operator by the brand-name refiner under terms which permit the refiner to maintain a watchful eye over operating procedures and merchandising policies. In a similar vein, a large manufacturer often grants a wholesaler or a retailer an exclusive franchise to handle its product in a specified geographic area; in return, the franchisee agrees to conform to certain prices, terms of credit, customer service policies, and product guarantees and warranties. Exclusive dealerships are commonly found in tires, automobiles, appliances, farm implements, road machinery, and building materials.

Finally, center firms may diversify their product offerings in order to round out their product line or to keep from tying the fortunes of the firm to a single product. To mount a strong marketing effort frequently requires each producer to have a full line of products and thereby offer the customer a "total package." Specializing in the production of only one or two items can entail serious market disadvantages, as well as less than full utilization of organizational resources and expertise. Several major oil companies, for example, are diversifying into coal and other fuels in an effort to become total energy firms. Soft-drink firms are moving into the production of complementary types of food products. The major cigarette producers are attempting to ward off decline by diversification into totally different product lines.

The deployment of the foregoing strategies tends to enhance or at least to help maintain a center firm's market position vis-à-vis rival firms. Such devices particularly tend to confer a tactical advantage upon the large, diversified firm in competing against periphery firms. Although a periphery firm can sometimes equal the production efficiency of center firms (where technology is not especially complex or large-scale, and where the marginal costs of production are constant over a wide output range), the periphery firm is hard-pressed to match the center firm in terms of overall organization capability, especially with regard to total marketing effort, long-range technological accomplishments, and managerial technology. Yet, these devices frequently become a virtual necessity in competing with center firms. When large corporate enterprises meet each other head-on in the marketplace, they can scarcely afford to be unprepared for the test. They can be expected to arm themselves with whatever tactical weapons can be mustered and to employ them in whatever degree of intensity may be required to accomplish organizational objectives. As a consequence, the dimensions of nonprice competition among center firms know only the bounds of managerial inventiveness. This aspect of center-firm competitive behavior is of no small significance in evaluating their conduct and performance, a matter which we shall explore more thoroughly in Chapter 13.

THE ROLE OF INVENTORIES AND ORDER BACKLOGS

The economic environment in which oligopolists operate is typically characterized by ongoing changes in consumer tastes, incomes, technology, and resource prices. Such changes tend to preclude oligopolists from maintaining precise equality in MR and MC—in other words, a strict enforcement of the profit-maximizing rule is impossible. At the same time, large corporate enterprises are likely to find current sales and current production at least slightly out of balance. In perfectly and monopolistically competitive markets, imbalances in sales and production can be corrected without undue difficulty; output rates are readily adjusted, and prices rise and fall promptly in response to changing market conditions. Consequently, other things being equal, periphery firms are fairly well able in the short run to keep marginal revenue in approximate equality with marginal costs. This is *not* true of oligopolistic markets or of center firms.[28] Not only are frequent price changes out of the question in oligopoly, but it is also impractical for large corporate enterprises to continually fine-tune production rates to meet transitory demand fluctuations. Center firm technology is typically complex, the various stages of the production process being systematically connected and carefully harmonized. It takes time to reschedule production and realign workloads. More im-

[28] In perfect competition, where the demand curve is horizontal, a firm can be confident of selling its entire output. To a lesser degree, monopolistically competitive firms can also anticipate selling their outputs, though perhaps after some price adjustment. Periphery firms with little or no market power generally carry relatively small inventories. In contrast, center firms with their downsloping demand-AR curves are somewhat uncertain how much they can sell at a given price. The higher a firm's selling price relative to marginal cost, the more profitable it becomes for firms to carry sizable inventories to minimize the risk of losing sales in periods of peak demand. This is especially true for firms with high fixed costs and low variable costs; they clearly prefer building up inventories to shutting plants down. See Edwin S. Mills, *Price, Output and Inventory Policy* (New York: John Wiley & Sons, Inc., 1962), pp. 72–83, 96, and 116–117, and Merton J. Peck, *Competition in the Aluminum Industry* (Cambridge, Mass.: Harvard University Press, 1961), pp. 88 and 92.

portantly, frequent production-rate changes impair mass–production efficiencies and cause unit costs to creep upward. As a result, large corporate enterprises wait for well-defined demand changes before altering production. They find it less disruptive, as well as cheaper, to respond to minor demand fluctuations by adjusting inventory levels and/or unfilled order backlogs (promised delivery dates) as opposed to interfering with optimum production rates.

This modus operandi is of special significance in oligopoly, for it provides firms with a realistic and readily invoked alternative to price and output changes as the means of balancing sales with production in any given period.[29] Although firms may base their output decisions for the next period upon an attempt to bring projected MR into equality with expected MC, mistakes will inevitably be made. If too much is produced relative to current sales at the prevailing price, inventory levels can be increased or unfilled order backlogs reduced. If production falls short of sales, inventories can be drawn down or delivery times extended. By keeping close tabs upon changes in new order flows, order backlogs, finished-goods inventory levels, and outgoing shipments, the firm can estimate the current position of its demand curve, the direction in which it is shifting, and expected future demand levels. The role of inventories and unfilled order backlogs is therefore twofold. They serve as *buffers* to compensate for minor production-sales imbalances, thereby avoiding firm or industry price adjustments. And they serve as *feedback signals* to facilitate the coordination of future production with future demand. Only when the signals of changed demand conditions come through loud and clear is a decision to modify production rates or to alter pricing policy seriously entertained.

We find, then, that inventory and order backlog adjustments are another factor accounting for price rigidity in oligopoly. Minor demand changes are accommodated via changes in inventories and backlogs, rather than by changing price or output in order to reequate MR and MC. Short-run profit maximization is abandoned in favor of long-run profit maximization or some other goal. Price and output revisions are undertaken only in response to clear-cut changes in long-run demand and cost conditions.

Although evidence is limited, it does tend to confirm that oligopolistic center firms rely more heavily upon inventory and order backlog variations in adjusting to demand fluctuations than upon price variations. Professor Markham's study of the rayon industry revealed that only when sales declines persisted for several months was production trimmed back; price changes were resisted even longer.[30] The three major copper producers, Anaconda, Kennecott, and Phelps Dodge, have repeatedly maintained copper prices by building up their inventories in periods of slack demand.[31]

---

[29] The material that follows draws heavily from the analysis of F. M. Scherer, *Industrial Market Structure and Economic Performance* (Skokie, Ill.: Rand McNally & Company, 1970), pp. 149–157.

[30] Markham, *Competition in the Rayon Industry*, Chap. 7.

[31] Kaplan, Dirlam, and Lanzilotti, *Pricing in Big Business*, pp. 176–181.

In the durable consumer goods and capital goods industries where center firms predominate, unfilled order backlogs may run in the hundreds of millions or even billions of dollars and inventory/sales ratios fluctuate over a relatively wide range. In contrast, in nondurable goods industries, where periphery firms are more numerous, order backlogs are virtually nonexistent; inventory levels are kept to a minimum to reduce the risk of spoilage and style obsolescence. Additionally, price cuts in response to short-run demand conditions are discernibly more numerous, and inventory/sales ratios are lower and less variable.[32]

The Special Case of Pure Monopoly

On rare occasions one firm accounts for the total supply of a commodity in a given market or markets. Such a market situation is called *pure monopoly*. Strictly speaking, pure monopoly can exist only when there are no close substitutes for the product of the single seller. Not only can there be no rival firms producing the same product, but there can be no firms producing products varying in only minor ways. The pure monopolist's product must be clearly and substantially different. Thus, the monopolistic firm faces no direct competition from rival firms and, as a consequence, acquires significant market power.

Real-world examples of pure monopoly are few and far between. Firms in the business of providing electricity, natural gas, telephone communications, and certain transportation services approach the position of pure monopoly. In years past, conditions approximating pure monopoly have prevailed in the production of aluminum, nickel, magnesium, molybdenum, shoe machinery, and Pullman cars.

The chief reason for the occurence of pure monopoly is the presence of pronounced economies of scale. Low unit costs and therefore low consumer prices are achievable only when one firm supplies the entire market demand for the commodity. High unit costs at small- or medium-scale outputs effectively bar the entry of new firms; indeed, consumers are likely to be better off with just one producer from which to buy the commodity. Thus, while it may be *technologically feasible* to have two, three, or more firms, it nevertheless is *economically inefficient* to have more than one. Industries where this occurs are called *natural monopolies*. In the normal case, natural monopolies are granted exclusive rights by government to serve a particular market or geographical area; in return the firm agrees to submit to government regulation to prevent abuse of its monopoly power. Public utility firms typify the natural monopoly type of enterprise.

Although pure monopoly is a rare market phenomenon, an examination of the price and output decisions of a pure monopolist will provide additional explanation of certain patterns of business behavior.

[32] Scherer, *Industrial Market Structure*, p. 155.

THE PRICE AND OUTPUT DECISIONS OF A MONOPOLISTIC FIRM

We shall assume for the time being that the pure monopolist's market price and output decisions are unconstrained by government regulation. We shall also continue to assume that the principal objective of the firm is to maximize profits.

The key difference between the market situation confronting a pure monopolist and that confronting other enterprises is that the firm's demand-AR curve coincides with the industry demand curve. The firm is the industry. Figure 11-10 illustrates the revenue and cost functions for a firm operating under conditions of pure monopoly. For all the usual reasons, the firm's profit-maximizing price and output correspond to the output where the

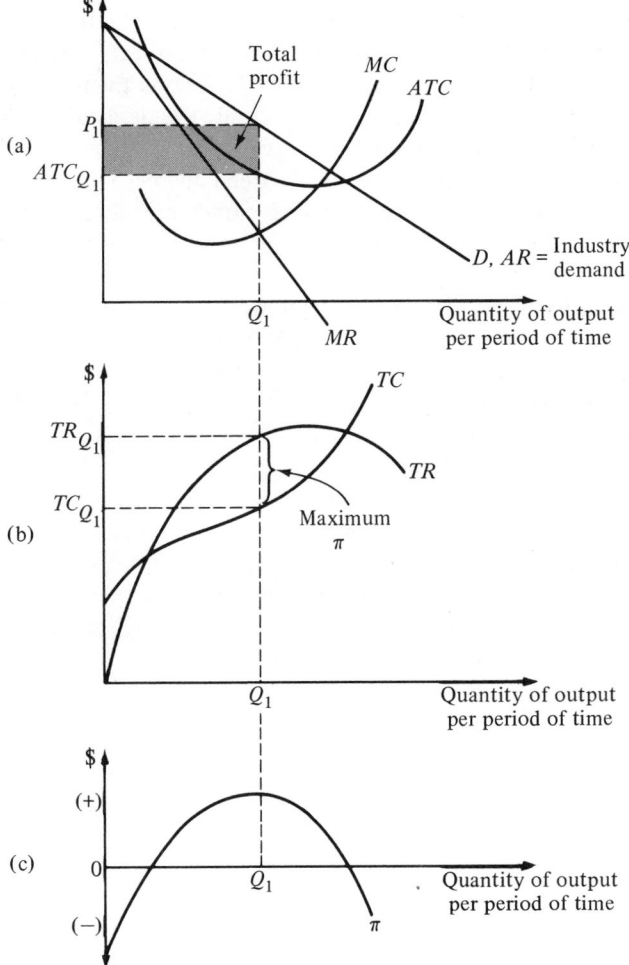

Fig. 11-10   The Profit-Maximizing Price and Output of a Pure Monopolist

firm's marginal revenue equals its marginal cost—shown as price P_1 and output Q_1 in panel (a) of Figure 11-10. In panel (b) it is apparent that total profit (π) is greatest at Q_1 units, where total revenue exceeds total cost by the greatest amount. And in panel (c) the peak of the total profit function also corresponds to an output of Q_1 units.

In the long run the monopolistic firm will adjust its scale of operations to accommodate changing demand conditions. Increases in demand for the firm's product may prompt an increase in plant and firm size, whereas declining demand calls for reductions in production capacity and firm size. The relation between the monopolist's market demand curve and its long-run average cost curve determines whether the firm should build optimum-scale, less-than-optimum scale, or greater-than-optimum-scale production facilities.

Thoughtful scrutiny of Figure 11-10 explodes a number of popular fallacies concerning the price and output decisions of monopolistic firms. A monopolist *does not* "charge the highest price it can get." There are many prices above P_1 in Figure 11-10(a), but the firm rejects them because of the lower profits which those prices entail. Second, the demand curve for the monopolistic firm's product is not "inelastic." As we discussed in Chapter 5, most demand curves are elastic at the upper end of the price range and inelastic at the lower end; linear demand curves are half elastic and half inelastic. The output that maximizes a monopolistic firm's profits will *always* fall within the elastic range of the demand curve—not the inelastic range. This proposition is quickly demonstrated. Since marginal cost is positive at all outputs, the output at which $MC = MR$ must necessarily correspond to outputs where MR is also positive. And as was shown in Chapter 5, marginal revenue is positive only at output rates where the price elasticity of demand is greater than one.[33]

Another common misconception about monopolistic firms is that they reap exorbitant profits. Weak demand and high costs are no less injurious to the profitability of a monopolist than they are to firms which face the rigors of direct competition. True, a monopolistic firm because of its market power has a superior opportunity to earn economic profits, but there is no guarantee that it will do so. It is quite possible for the demand-AR curve to lie everywhere below the firm's ATC curve (as illustrated previously in Figure 10-12); similarly, industry demand may be so weak that only normal profits can be earned (as illustrated in Figure 10-14).

THE CONSTRAINTS UPON THE BEHAVIOR OF A MONOPOLISTIC FIRM

Although being the sole producer of a commodity for which there is no close substitute does indeed confer a great deal of monopoly power, certain market restraints are nevertheless imposed upon the unregulated monopolist's behavior. Three such restraints deserve comment.

---

[33] The relationship between price elasticity, total revenue, and marginal revenue is described in the section "Elasticity and Total Revenue" in Chapter 5 (p. 166).

The first and foremost restraint upon the exercise of monopoly power is the fear of government intervention and regulation. The monopolistic firm producing what consumers view as a "necessity" risks drawing bitter outcries from consumers if it fully exploits its short-run profit opportunities. Widespread and persistent public criticism can be counted upon to produce, rightly or wrongly, some form of government action—whether it be antitrust action, government support of new competitors, or rate regulation (as in the case of natural monopolies). Thus, the monopolist may temper its price and curtail its pursuit of profits in order to escape consumer resentment and the likelihood of government regulation.

Second, a monopolist may deliberately limit its profits so as not to encourage direct competition. When a monopolist exploits its market power fully and earns large economic profits in the short run, it risks attracting the attention of center firms which may have the financial and technological resources to crack the monopolist's entry barriers. The monopolist may also trigger efforts on the part of its customers or on the part of other firms to develop acceptable substitutes. In other words, high monopoly profits activate the forces of *potential competition* from both new firms and new products. This threat is very real. The business landscape is littered with ex-monopolists which have been the victims of emerging competition—Alcoa, American Can, Standard Oil, DuPont, United Shoe Machinery, Ford, International Nickel, Dow Chemical, and Gillette, not to mention all the railroads whose monopoly profits have been permanently slashed by competition from truck carriers and the airlines. Therefore, rather than set price at the level which maximizes short-run profits but invites competition (or regulation), the monopolistic firm may decide to lower price to a level which deters potential competition and wards off government regulation and antitrust action. Such a pricing practice is called *limit pricing*. The exact level of the limit price depends upon how effectively entry is blocked, the probability of government regulation, and the degree of technological difficulty in developing substitute products. The obvious purpose of limit pricing is to forego short-run profit maximization in favor of profits over the long term.

The third restraint upon the exericse of monopoly power is the systematic propensity for *countervailing power* to develop on the buying side of the market.[34] Center firms waste little time in attempting to negate the monopoly power of sellers with whom they must deal. Major food packers, for example, have repeatedly threatened to enter into tin can manufacturing; to avoid the loss of these customers the two major tin can manufacturers have been forced to exercise price restraint. Electric utility firms have threatened to build nuclear-powered generating facilities if the railroad firms did not reduce freight rates on coal shipments to their coal-fired steam generating facilities. In certain circumstances, therefore, "across-the market" competition may be

---

[34] The theory of countervailing power and its application to center firm behavior was originated and developed by John Kenneth Galbraith in his book *American Capitalism: The Theory of Countervailing Power* (Boston: Houghton Mifflin Company, 1952); see especially Chap. 9.

successful in checking the power of a monopolistic firm and in reducing its price to levels more consistent with competition. Once price is lowered, the monopolistic firm has an incentive to increase output and make its product available to a broader segment of the market.

Taken together, these three restraints undoubtedly reduce the effective market power of monopolists to levels lower than commonly imagined. True, at a given moment a monopolist may possess substantial power to raise price above competitive levels; it may also earn sizable economic profits. But the situation tends to be short-lived. Monopolists which produce "necessities" and other essential goods—public utility firms, for example—quickly find their prices regulated and their profits reduced to socially acceptable levels. Over time, technological change regularly undermines the market power of the unregulated monopolists. And center firms forced to do business with monopolists attempt to neutralize their market power via bargaining and threats of vertical integration.

Summary and Conclusions

Suppose we try now to tie together the chief lessons emerging from our survey of center firm price and output decisions. The hallmark of the markets in which center firms operate is a high degree of mutual interdependence; each firm must try to anticipate the actions and reactions of rival firms in reaching its own decisions. The pricing decisions of center firms provide an outstanding example of oligopolistic interdependence. Where center firm oligopolists produce standardized products, a uniform price is imperative, since firms which attempt to charge higher prices will gradually be squeezed out of the market. Where center firm oligopolists produce either weakly or strongly differentiated products, prices must be comparable, though not necessarily identical, since customers will tolerate price differentials they believe are justified.

Yet, differences among rival firms regarding market shares and production costs give rise to divergent price preferences which somehow must be resolved. Whether the firms with high price preferences win out over the firms with low price preferences all depends. Collusion to maximize joint profits certainly is one possibility; however, collusive arrangements are fragile and are under increasing antitrust fire. Price leadership is another possibility if follower firms are prone to cooperate with the leader's price judgment. Nevertheless, agreements on a "cooperative" price are susceptible to secret price-cutting, conflicts over the best price, and stubbornness on the part of maverick firms. Cooperation to hold prices above the preferences of the low-price firms is less likely to be successful the more firms there are in the industry, the larger the output of the competitive fringe firms, the more strongly differentiated and rapidly changing are the firms' products, the more opportunities there are for secret price concessions, the more unstable are industrywide demand conditions, the more rapid the rate of technical progress, and the greater the degree of suspicion and mistrust among company executives. More importantly, the firms that perceive their profits to be greater at lower than at higher prices are frequently in a much stronger position to impose their preferences than are the firms which prefer higher prices. Long-run product substitution and the threat of entry by new firms also places a ceiling—sometimes a low one—upon the ability of oligopolistic producers to peg price at a collusive level.

The extremely strong pricing interdependence among center firm oligopolists is further demonstrated by the infrequency with which they change price and by the fact that when they do alter price they do so more or less simultaneously. The belief that competitors will ignore price increases and match price cuts, and the practice of using inventory and order backlog changes to buffer minor demand fluctuations, combine to produce relatively stable prices in center firm markets.

Because of the imperative to charge comparable prices for their products, center firm oligopolists are seldom able to use price as a strategic device for enhancing their market position in the short run. Rather, the competitive emphasis among center firms is shifted to product quality and performance, product innovation, design and styling, customer service, advertising, and the like. In several important respects, competition is focused around new product development and marketing strategies. In addition, center firms may be induced to integrate vertically as a means for avoiding uncertainty and circumventing the unreliability of both independent suppliers and distributors. And to the extent that vertical integration moderates the intense degree of interdependence among the firms, the autonomy of center firm management is modestly enhanced.

The market structure of pure monopoly is a special case where one firm completely controls the output of a product so unique that there are no close substitutes. In such cases the firm obviously has a great deal of monopoly power which it may be able to use to its own advantage. However, the market power of monopolists tends to be tempered by weak demand conditions, actual or threatened government intervention and regulation, potential competition from new firms and new products, and the exercise of countervailing power on the part of buyers.

SUGGESTED READINGS

BAIN, JOE S., "Price Leaders, Barometers, and Kinks," *The Journal of Business*, Vol. 33, No. 3 (July 1960), pp. 193–203.

BISHOP, R. L., "Duopoly: Collusion or Warfare?" *American Economic Review*, Vol. 40, No. 5 (December 1960), pp. 933–961.

BOULDING, KENNETH E. *Economic Analysis*, 4th ed. (New York: Harper & Row, Publishers, 1966), Vol. I, Chap. 22.

DEWEY, DONALD, *The Theory of Imperfect Competition: A Radical Reconstruction* (New York: Columbia University Press, 1969).

GALBRAITH, JOHN KENNETH, *American Capitalism: The Theory of Countervailing Power* (Boston: Houghton Mifflin Company, 1952), Chap. 9.

KAPLAN, A. D. H., J. B. DIRLAM, and R. F. LANZILOTTI, *Pricing in Big Business* (Washington: The Brookings Institution, 1958), Chaps. 1 and 4.

SCHERER, F. M., *Industrial Market Structure and Economic Performance* (Skokie, Ill.: Rand McNally & Company, 1970), Chaps. 5, 6, 7, and 8.

STIGLER, GEORGE J., "The Economics of Information," *Journal of Political Economy*, Vol. 69, No. 3 (June 1961), pp. 213–225.

————, "A Theory of Oligopoly," *Journal of Political Economy*, Vol. 72, No. 1 (February 1964), pp. 44–61.

WESTON, J. FRED, "Pricing Behavior of Large Firms," *Western Economic Journal*, Vol. 10, No. 1 (March 1972), pp. 1–18.

WORCESTER, DEAN A., "Why 'Dominant Firms' Decline," *Journal of Political Economy*, Vol. 65, No. 4 (August 1957), pp. 338–347.

Problems and Questions for Discussion

1. (a) Graphically illustrate the profit-maximizing price and output for an oligopolistic firm confronted with a kinked demand curve and whose production function reflects constant returns to variable .input throughout the firm's range of output capability. Indicate on your graph the area which represents total profit.

   (b) Illustrate the effect upon the firm's optimum price and output of a decrease in the demand for its product.

2. Is it possible for an oligopolistic firm confronted with a kinked demand curve situation to increase its short-run profits by increasing its short-run expenditures on sales promotion? Justify your answer by means of a graph.

3. Is it possible for a pure monopolist to benefit from sales promotion expenditures, given that there are no close substitutes for the monopolist's product? Explain and justify your answer graphically.

4. Titanic Corporation and Mammoth Enterprises are the only two firms selling robots to perform selected domestic services. The Titanic Corporation believes that the annual demand for its particular style of robot is given by the equation

$$P_T = 2400 - .1Q_T.$$

Mammoth Enterprises estimates that the annual demand for its robots is given by

$$P_M = 2400 - .1Q_M.$$

Because their robots have different performance features, the cost of producing Titanic's robot differs from the cost of producing Mammoth's. The estimated total cost function for Titanic's robots is

$$TC_T = 400,000 + 600Q_T + .1Q_T{}^2,$$

where TC is in dollars per year and Q_T is Titantic's annual output of robots. The estimated total cost function for Mammoth's robots is

$$TC_M = 600,000 + 300Q_M + .2Q_M{}^2,$$

where TC is in dollars per year and Q_M is Mammoth's annual output of robots.

(a) Determine the profit-maximizing price and output for both Titanic Corporation and Mammoth Enterprises.
(b) Does a pricing conflict exist between the two firms?
(c) If you were the president of Titanic Corporation, what price would you pick? Why?
(d) If you were the president of Mammoth Enterprises, what price would you pick? Why?
(e) Would a collusive arrangement between the firms be advantageous? Why or why not?

5. Reston Enterprises and Super-Technical Corporation are the only two firms producing pollution-free turbine engines for use in automobiles. Reston engines account for one-third of the total turbine engine sales, while Super-Technical engines account for two-thirds. Except for several minor features, both engines compare favorably in terms of quality, performance, and economy of operation.

(a) Suppose both firms produce their engines under conditions of identically rising marginal costs. Will there arise a conflict of price preferences between the two firms, assuming a goal of profit maximization? Illustrate graphically. Venture a judgment as to how the pricing conflict might be resolved in this particular situation. Is some form of collusion a distinct possibility here? Why or why not? Justify your reasoning.
(b) Suppose both firms produce their engines under conditions of identical and constant marginal costs. Will there then be a divergence of pricing preferences? Is it unreasonable to expect marginal costs to be constant?
(c) Suppose both firms produce their engines under conditions of identically declining marginal costs. Describe and graphically illustrate the nature of the pricing conflict, if any. If you were the president of Super-Technical Corporation, would you be willing to compromise your firm's preferred price with that of Reston Enterprises? Explain. Is some form of collusive arrangement likely to be reached under these circumstances? Why or why not?

6. The American Cracker Corporation has three plants for producing soda crackers. The marginal cost functions of the three plants and the firm's estimated demand-AR schedule are as follows:

Daily Output in Cartons	Marginal Cost of Plant 1	Marginal Cost of Plant 2	Marginal Cost of Plant 3	Price of Cartons of Soda Crackers
0				$.50
1	$0.14	$0.13	$.10	.48
2	0.16	0.14	.13	.46
3	0.18	0.15	.16	.44
4	0.20	0.16	.16	.42
5	capacity	capacity	capacity	.40
6				.38
7				.36
8				.34
9				.32
10				.30
11				.28
12				.26

Determine the most profitable price and output for the American Cracker Corporation. Then determine the optimal allocation of output among the firm's three plants.

7. Waxy Products, Inc. has discovered a new way to produce a "plastic wax" which, when once applied to hardwood floors, creates a permanent, waterproof, scuffproof, shiny surface absolutely guaranteed under any conditions to last for 12 months. Waxy Products, realizing the vast market potential for its plastic wax, has employed a market research team to estimate the demand function for plastic wax in both national and international markets. The market research team reports that its estimate of plastic wax demand in the domestic market is

$$P_D = 100 - 5Q_D,$$

and that its estimate of demand in the international market is

$$P_F = 60 - 5Q_F,$$

where P is in dollars and Q is daily sales in cases.

Waxy Products estimates that the short-run production function for plastic wax is $Q = 10X$, where $X =$ units of variable input; units of variable input cost $200 each.

The president of Waxy Products, not knowing very much about price policy, asks you to assist him in *maximizing* his firm's profits. Calculate for him the *specific* price and output levels that will maximize profits from the sale of plastic wax.

8. (a) Do you think competition among oligopolists is more strenuous, less strenuous, or about equally strenuous as compared to compeition among perfectly competitive firms? Explain your reasoning. Which type of market structure do you think is the more "socially beneficial"?

(b) Do you think competition among oligopolists is more or less strenuous than competition among monopolistically compeititive firms? Explain your reasoning. Which type of market structure do you think is the more "socially beneficial"?

9. Do you think firms which are pure monopolists (or nearly so) should have their prices regulated by government? Do you think regulated firms and industries are more progressive in terms of product innovation, customer service, and so on than are nonregulated firms and industries? Why or why not?

12

The Price
and Output Decisions
of Center Firms
with Multiple Goals

The managers of large corporate enterprises, although very profit conscious, are not necessarily inclined to base their decisions *solely* upon profit considerations. As we saw in Chapter 9, other goals tend to creep into the decision-making process of large corporations, especially when profits reach a sustainable level of acceptability. The time has come to examine in some detail how nonprofit goals can affect the price and output decisions of center firms. In this chapter we explore some of the newest and most prominent models of contemporary corporate behavior; in all of these models, corporate decisions and corporate strategies are predicated upon a hierachy of goals. Particular attention will be accorded the roles of sales and growth goals. At the same time we will focus less upon short-run price and output decisions and more upon long-run price and output decisions as the latter are conditioned by multiple goals, new product development, technological change, and competitive pressures. By lengthening the time frame over which the market behavior of center firms is analyzed we put ourselves in a much stronger position to judge their overall market conduct and market performance.

Models of Contemporary Corporate Behavior

PRICING TO EARN A TARGET RATE OF RETURN

Although profit is unquestionably a major concern of large corporations, the evidence is not strong that managerial estimates of the relationship between marginal revenue and marginal cost actually form the basis for price selection.[1] Rather, studies of corporate pricing policy indicate a widespread reliance upon *target return pricing methods*.

A *target return price* is designed to yield the firm a predetermined profit from the sale of specific products or product groups. The desired profit is typically based upon dollar sales (total revenue) or upon some measure of invested capital and may be expressed either as a percentage rate or as a dollar amount. For example, the desired profit target may be stated as a profit on sales of 5 percent, a profit return equal to 10 percent of total assets, a profit return equal to 15 percent of net worth (stockholder's equity), a profit return equal to 20 percent on net worth plus long-term debt, or simply a specific dollar figure. The size of the profit target tends to hinge upon such considerations as (1) industry custom, (2) competitive pressures, (3) what managers believe to be a "fair" or "reasonable" return, (4) a desire to equal or better the firm's recent profit performance, (5) a desire to stabilize industry prices, (6) whether the firm's product is new or a unique specialty item, and (7) the firm's related goals of sales, market share, and growth. Specific profit targets tend to differ among industries and firms, reflecting differing degrees of competition and differing priorities among alternative goals. Normally, however, *after-tax* profit targets tend to fall within the range of 5 to 10 percent of sales and 10 to 20 percent of invested capital.

The mechanics of target return pricing may be set forth briefly in terms of two examples—the first illustrating *pricing to achieve a target return on investment* and the second illustrating what is commonly referred to as *cost-plus pricing*.

1. Assume a firm has $100 million invested in the production of a particular commodity and desires to earn a long-run average annual return of 20 percent before taxes on its investment. This, of course, translates into an annual profit target of $20 million. The initial step is to determine average total cost at some "normal" output rate (often referred to as the standard volume). Usually, the normal output rate is arbitrarily pegged somewhere between two-thirds and four-fifths of the capacity rate, instead of being

[1] The literature on the subject is immense. Among the more definitive studies are R. L. Hall and Charles J. Hitch, "Price Theory and Business Behavior," *Oxford Economic Papers*, Vol. 2 (May 1939), pp. 12–45; A. D. H. Kaplan, J. B. Dirlam, and R. F. Lanzilotti, *Pricing in Big Business* (Washington, D.C.: The Brookings Institution, 1958), Chap. 2; Burnard H. Sord and Glenn A. Welsch, *Business Budgeting*, (New York: Controllership Foundation, 1958), pp. 88–89 and 148; James H. Miller, "A Glimpse at Practice in Calculating and Using Return on Investment," *N. A. A. Bulletin* (June 1969), p. 73; W. W. Haynes, "Pricing Practices in Small Firms," *Southern Economic Journal*, Vol. 30, No. 4 (April 1964), pp. 315–324.

related to the firm's actual operating rate. Many firms base their normal output rate upon what they believe to be their long-run rate of plant utilization. Suppose ATC is estimated to be $50 at the normal output rate of 2 million units. Since the firm wishes a total profit of $20 million on sales of 2 million units, profit per unit must average $10. The target price is then calculated by adding the necessary profit margin of $10 to the projected average total cost of $50 at the normal output rate, giving a price of $60. The target price serves as the initial basis for the firm's price decision; it may be adjusted upward or downward according to prevailing business conditions, actual or potential competition, long-run strategic objectives, and other relevant factors of the moment. Once the target price is chosen, the firm sells whatever amount is then demanded at the target price.

2. *Cost-plus pricing* is a widely used procedure whereby price is calculated by adding a predetermined percentage markup to the estimated unit cost of the product. To determine unit cost, the firm first computes the costs of labor, raw materials, and other variable inputs to get an estimate of AVC; to this is added the projected AFC at the "normal" operating rate (or standard volume). To illustrate, suppose the firm is producing a commodity under conditions of constant returns to variable input such that $MC = AVC = \$30$. Further suppose that 75 percent of capacity is viewed as the normal operating rate, and at this output rate AFC is estimated to be $15. Average total cost is therefore $45 at the normal output rate. To this figure is added a markup of 5, 10, 20, 50, or whatever percent is required to achieve the firm's target profit. (The size of the markup frequently reflects what managers believe is an "equitable" relation to cost.) If the firm desires a 10 percent return on sales, it should add a margin of $5 to its unit cost estimate of $45 to give a selling price of $50, which in percentage terms is equivalent to a markup slightly in excess of 11 percent over cost. If the firm desires a 25 percent return on sales, it should add a margin of $15 to its $45 unit cost to give a price of $60—a percentage markup of $33\frac{1}{3}$ percent over cost. As with pricing to achieve a target return on investment, cost-plus prices are subject to modification by competitive conditions and other pertinent considerations.

There are numerous variations of these two approaches to pricing. Cost estimates may be based on "normal" operating rates, forecasted costs, or costs for the most recent accounting period. The amount of the "plus" or the target profit may be based on either short-run or long-run considerations; it may be fixed for all products of the firm or variable among products; it may be computed as a percentage of costs, invested capital, or sales. In other words, the specific "formula" used depends upon each firm's peculiar circumstances and goals. Multiproduct firms generally have different profit targets for different products, depending upon such factors as the competitive situation, the intricacy and originality of the product and its design, and the estimate of the product's economic worth and utility to the customer.

Another common use of target return pricing is found in center firm strategies for new product development and product innovation.[2] In con-

---

[2] An excellently documented example of International Harvester's use of this strategy is found in Kaplan, Dirlam, and Lanzilotti, *Pricing in Big Business*, pp. 69–79.

templating the introduction of a new product or the revamping of an existing product, the typical procedure is for the firm first to identify a target selling price using such criteria as the prices of similar products, competitors' prices, and the estimated performance value to the customer. Product design and planning then proceeds toward producing at a cost that fits within the target market price and at the same time allows a margin of profit sufficient to yield the firm's target rate of return. Engineering and production personnel are assigned the task of designing a product which will conform as closely as possible to the targeted unit cost, price, and profit margin. Hence, the firm, in developing and pricing new products, starts from established or preconceived prices and works backward to see whether it can profitably offer the product at or below competitive prices. Failing this, the firm may pursue the question of whether higher costs can be justified by a product that on comparative performance can command a somewhat higher price than the ruling price average and still yield the desired target returns. The attempt to design a product within the target cost-price-profit figures is sometimes successful, sometimes unsuccessful. In the unsuccessful instances, whether the go-ahead is given depends' upon management's estimate of the nature of the product in its overall product line. If the product is one which strongly complements or creates substantial demands for other of the firm's products, the firm may well decide to produce the item regardless of the estimated profits. Therefore, determining the prices of all the firm's products entails a careful balancing of adjustments to individual product markets so as to obtain an overall profit performance compatible with company wide targets.

Attributes of Target Return Pricing. In practice, both pricing to achieve a target return on investment and cost-plus pricing offer relatively simple and expedient methods of price determination which have a demonstrated ability to yield "adequate," "fair," or "reasonable" profits. The profitability of the two methods is evidenced by the avowed use of some sort of target return pricing by such "blue-chip" firms as Alcoa, DuPont, General Electric, General Foods, General Motors, International Harvester, Johns-Manville, Standard Oil (N.J.), Union Carbide, and U.S. Steel.[3]

Once the target price is chosen, the usual procedure is for the firm to stick by its price and sell whatever amounts of output that short-run demand conditions will permit. The target return price is therefore a stable price— an attribute which highly recommends itself to oligopoly situations where infrequent price changes are a standard feature. This may partly explain the popularity of target return pricing among center firm oligopolists. However, target return pricing does have the effect of making profits quite variable; on a year-to-year basis, actual profits may turn out to be either higher or

[3] R. F. Lanzilotti, "Pricing Objectives in Large Companies," *American Economic Review*, Vol. 48, No. 5 (December 1958), pp. 921–940.

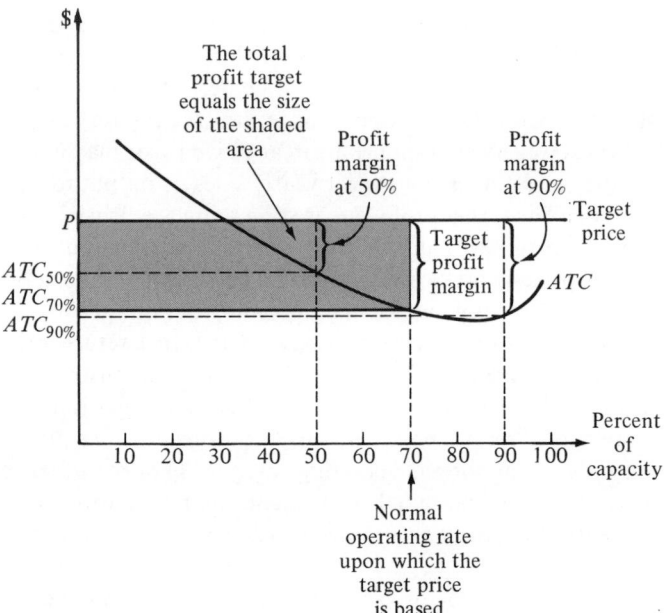

Fig. 12-1   The Effects of Demand Fluctuations upon Achieving the Target Rate of Return

lower than the target profit rate. Suppose, for example, a firm has a short-run average total cost curve as illustrated in Figure 12-1; the target price is P dollars, the "normal" operating rate is 70 percent of capacity, the target profit margin is $(P - ATC_{70\%})$, and the target amount of total profit is equal to the shaded area. If in a particular year demand is especially strong and actual output corresponds to 90 percent of capacity, then total profits will be pushed up well above the targeted level. Two reasons can account for this. First, the firm's actual sales of output will exceed the rate required to achieve the profit target. Second, unit costs at 90 percent of capacity may be lower than at 70 percent of capacity because of the lower average fixed costs associated with higher production rates. The realized profit margin on each unit sold of $(P - ATC_{90\%})$ may therefore be larger than the margin of $(P - ATC_{70\%})$ needed to reach the target. The combined effect of wider profit margins and above-normal sales is a realized profit which may be considerably in excess of the target rate of return, as shown in Figure 12-1. On the other hand, if demand for the firm's product is weak and actual sales of output amount to only 50 percent of capacity instead of the "normal" 70 percent, then the profit target will in all probability not be achieved. At production rates below the normal 70 percent figure, average fixed costs are sure to be higher, and average variable costs may be higher if the production process cannot be operated efficiently at less than normal rates.

With average total cost at 50 percent of capacity exceeding that at 70 percent, the realized profit margin of $(P - ATC_{50\%})$ will be narrower than the targeted margin of $(P - ATC_{70\%})$. This, together with lower sales, produces total profits well below the target rate of return (see Figure 12-1).

The firm is well aware that profits in any given year may not correspond to the profit target; it does not expect yearly sales of output to exactly equal the normal rate. The target profit rate is something the firm hopes to achieve over the long run rather than the short run. This is apparent from the fact that the target price is predicated upon a normal rate of production instead of the forecasted sales volume for the upcoming period.

It follows from the discussion above that target return pricing is *not* a strategy for maximizing profits.[4] This is easily demonstrated. Since the target return price is keyed to the firm's normal operating rate (or standard volume), the target return price and the profit-maximizing price will coincide if and only if the normal operating rate just happens to correspond to the output rate where marginal cost equals marginal revenue. Certainly, there is no reason to expect this to occur—except by mere circumstance and coincidence.

Actually, the concept of target return pricing exemplifies a behavior pattern closely approximating satisficing. The target rate of return, according to the evidence available, tends to be based upon managerial concepts of what is an "equitable" or "reasonable" or "satisfactory" rate of return, given the degrees of risk and uncertainty involved. Few managers believe— or, more accurately perhaps, admit—that their profit targets are indicative of the "maximum" obtainable rate of return. Managers exhibit a propensity to use target return pricing techniques because information is often too sketchy or too expensive to allow a full-fledged analysis of the relevant factors. In essence, target return pricing is an imperfect expedient designed to facilitate, in a rough but ready manner, the handling of a thorny decision problem under conditions of uncertainty. Parenthetically, it should be added that executives use similar "rules of thumb" in other decision situations. Advertising expenditures are frequently determined by setting aside some fixed percentage of total revenue; inventory levels may be pegged to some preset turnover norm. By translating complicated problems into simple routines, rule-of-thumb procedures economize on executive time and may

---

[4] Some economists have argued that if the firm's target rate of return is based upon some concept of the *largest* rate of return the firm perceives it can get, then the firm's behavior reflects a goal of profit maximization. This is misleading if not erroneous. To illustrate why, suppose a firm believes the maximum rate of return market conditions will allow is 20 percent. The critical question now becomes whether the perceived maximum rate of 20 percent can be obtained just as well via target return pricing as by marginal cost-marginal revenue pricing. The answer is only by rare circumstance. If 20 percent is truly the maximum profit rate, then the only way it can be attained is for the firm to elect the price and output corresponding to the intersection of MC and MR. Since the target return price is based upon the "normal" operating rate (or standard volume), the target return price and the profit-maximizing price will coincide only if the normal operating rate just happens to be the output rate where $MR = MC$. This is a little too much to expect. Thus while a firm's managers may believe the target return price will yield the maximum rate of profit, the facts of the matter are to the contrary. In a sense, the fallacy in their thinking is akin to the fallacy that maximum profit is achieved at the output where profit per unit $(P - ATC)$ is greatest. As was demonstrated in Chapter 10, the output rate at which price exceeds ATC by the greatest amount *does not* correspond to the output rate where $MR = MC$.

even contribute to overall operating efficiency. In any event, they serve as classic examples of precisely what is meant by satisficing—the seeking of satisfactory workable solutions to complex decision problems.

REVENUE MAXIMIZATION WITH A PROFIT CONSTRAINT

The best known of the contemporary models of corporate behavior is the model of sales-revenue maximization with a profit constraint. This model, first proposed by Professor William Baumol, is founded upon the premise that once profits reach acceptable levels, the firm's profit goal becomes subordinate to its goal of increasing sales revenue (the rationale underlying this goal hierarchy was presented in Chapter 9).[5] According to Baumol, the sales goal assumes such strong proportions that the firm's managers are willing to forego higher profits to obtain greater sales revenues.

Figure 12-2 illustrates the revenue-maximization model. The firm's TR, TC, and π curves are shown in their conventional shapes. Total profit

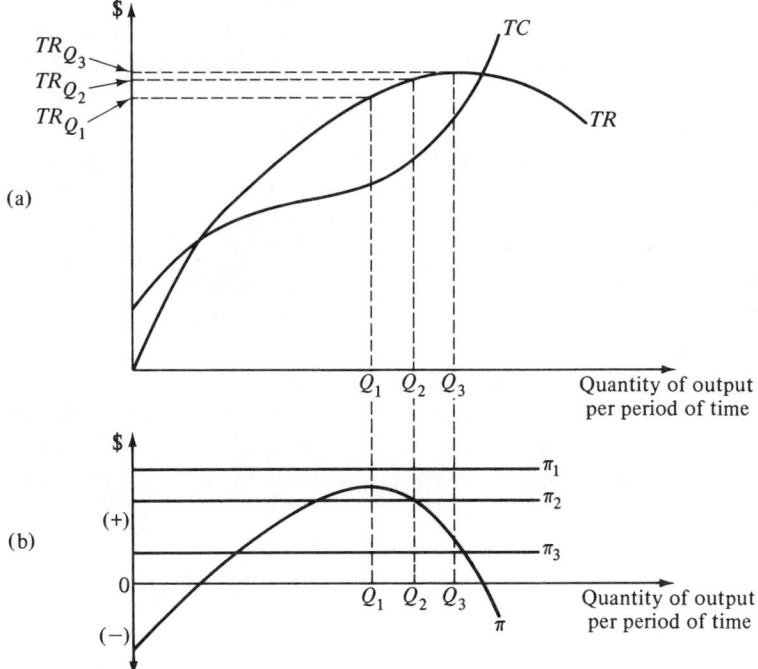

Fig. 12-2   The Revenue-Maximization Model

[5] Professor Baumol's model with all of its price-output and policy ramifications is presented in his book *Business Behavior, Value and Growth*, rev. ed. (New York: Harcourt Brace Jovanovich, Inc., 1967), Chaps. 6, 7, and 8.

is maximum at an output rate of Q_1 units and TR is maximum at an output rate of Q_3 units. Thus, it is evident that the firm cannot simultaneously maximize short-run profits *and* sales revenue. Profit is always maximum where $MR = MC$, whereas TR (or sales revenue) is maximum where $MR = 0$. The price and the output rate which maximize profits definitely do not correspond to the price and the output rate which maximize sales revenue. Suppose the firm has a profit target of π_1 dollars [Figure 12-2(b)]. If profits of π_1 dollars are required before other objectives such as sales revenue maximization are pursued, then the firm is in no position to increase the sales of output beyond Q_1 units, since even at the profit-maximizing output the profit target is still out of reach. The firm must produce at Q_1 units just to come as close as possible to satisfying its profit constraint. However, if profits of π_2 dollars will fulfill its profit requirements, the firm is in a position to pursue a sales revenue goal as well as a profit goal. By a lowering of its price, the output rate can be expanded to Q_2 units and sales revenues pushed up to TR_{Q_2} dollars. Profits will still be the desired amount of π_2 dollars, though they will be below the potential maximum of π_1 dollars. Nonetheless, the firm is able to meet its profit objective and it enjoys a higher level of sales revenues than it would at the profit-maximizing output of Q_1 units. This is what is meant by sales revenue maximization with a profit constraint. Finally, suppose the profit constraint is only π_3 dollars. Then price can be lowered yet further, the sales of output pushed to Q_3 units, and revenue pushed to the maximum value of TR_{Q_3} dollars. The firm has no motive to expand its output rate past Q_3, even though its profit goal of π_3 dollars is overfulfilled. The reason? Additional output can be absorbed in the market only at prices reduced so much that total revenue will fall. Hence, revenues are smaller at output rates greater than Q_3 than they are at Q_3, effectively undermining the firm's revenue incentive to push sales past Q_3 units.

Observe that at outputs below Q_1, a strategy of lowering price and increasing output enhances both profits and sales revenues. Up to an output of Q_1 units, the two goals are complementary in the sense that success in achieving higher sales is concomitant with success in achieving higher profits. On the other hand, between outputs of Q_1 and Q_3 units, lower prices and greater outputs cause profits to fall but sales revenues to rise. Therefore, between Q_1 and Q_3, greater sales revenues are achieved at the expense of profits—the two goals compete with one another. Beyond an output of Q_3 units, a lower price and consequently larger sales of output result in lower profits and in lower sales revenues.

A chief conclusion to be derived from the sales revenue maximization model is this: *if a firm has a goal of maximizing its sales revenue subject to a profit constraint and if the firm's profit constraint (or profit target) is below the maximum attainable profit, then the firm will charge lower prices for its products and will produce greater outputs than it would with a goal of profit maximization.*

Advertising Expenditures and the Goals of the Firm. The decision as to how much to spend on advertising and sales promotion is also influenced by the firm's choice of goals. A revenue-maximizer tends to spend more money promoting its products than does a profit-maximizer. This proposition is illustrated in Figure 12-3. The horizontal axis in panels (a) and (b) represents

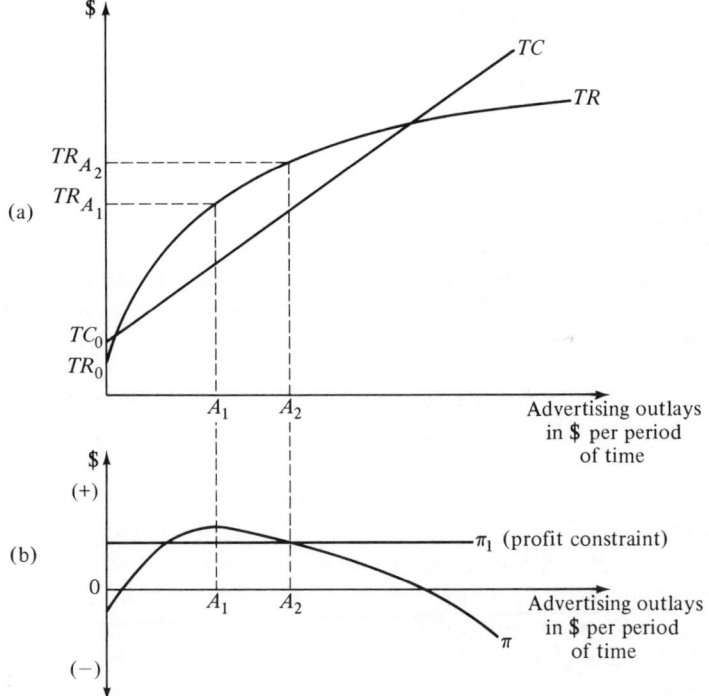

Fig. 12-3   Advertising Expenditures and the Goals of the Firm

the dollar magnitude of advertising outlays; the vertical axis measures dollar costs, revenues, and profits. For simplicity, total cost is shown to increase linearly with advertising expenditures, starting from a value of TC_1 dollars where advertising is zero. The TC curve includes all production and selling costs, including advertising outlays. The total revenue curve is drawn on the reasonable assumption that increased advertising tends to increase sales of output and revenue, but by progressively lesser amounts. In other words, diminishing returns to promotion exist, and additional advertising expenditures result in ever more slowly increasing revenues. The total profit (π) curve in panel (b) is found by subtracting total costs from total revenues at each level of advertising outlay; it indicates the profitability of various-sized advertising outlays.

Figure 12-3 indicates that the profit-maximizing amount of advertising outlay is A_1 dollars. In contrast, a revenue-maximizing firm with a profit constraint of π_1 dollars has an optimal advertising outlay of A_1 dollars. The additional advertising pushes sales revenues from TR_{A1} dollars to TR_{A2} dollars without causing total profits to fall below the targeted level of π_1 dollars. So long as the revenue-maximizer's profit target is *less* than the maximum profit level, the revenue-maximizer will find it advantageous to spend more heavily on advertising than will a profit-maximizer. The revenue-maximizer's output rate will, accordingly, be greater than the profit maximizer's output rate. However, the revenue-maximizing firm's selling price may be higher, lower, or equal to the profit-maximizing firm's, depending upon the effect advertising has upon unit costs and upon customer demand for the firm's products (see Figure 10-16). On occasions, the extra advertising undertaken by the sales maximizer may shift the firm's demand-AR curve so as to make it advantageous to charge a price slightly above that of rival firms. On other occasions, the additional advertising may simply result in selling more units at the prevailing price level. And on rare occasions, the extra advertising may entail a lower price as well as expanded sales.

The Effect of Fixed Cost Changes. One of the most surprising and interesting aspects of the economics of the firm is the effect of fixed cost changes upon price and output decisions. Consider Figure 12-4, where the firm's initial cost-revenue-profit functions are given by TFC_1, TC_1, TR_1, and π_1. Note that if the firm's primary goal is profit maximization, then its optimum output rate is Q_1 units; but if its primary goal is sales revenue maximization with a profit constraint of π dollars, then its optimum output is Q_2 units. Now suppose the firm experiences a rise in the prices of its fixed inputs such that total fixed costs rise to a level indicated by TFC_2. This will cause the firm's total cost function to shift upward by the amount of the rise in fixed costs to TC_2. The rise in fixed costs will further cause the firm's profit function to shift downward from π_1 to π_2, with the amount of the downward shift being equal to the increase in fixed costs.

What effect does this sort of cost increase have upon the firm's optimum price and output rate if the firm's principal goal is profit maximization? The answer, surprisingly enough, is *none*. The rise in fixed costs *lowers* the peak of the total profit curve, but it moves the peak neither to the right nor to the left. Moreover, changes in fixed costs have no effect whatsoever upon MC or upon MR, thus leaving the point at which $MC = MR$ completely undisturbed. Hence, total profit is maximized at precisely the same price and output as before the rise in total fixed costs. And we have the inescapable conclusion that changes in fixed costs do not influence the short-run price and output decisions of profit-maximizing firms so long as it is possible to earn positive contribution profits.

But what of the effect upon a revenue-maximizing firm? From Figure 12-4 it is apparent that given the downward shift in the total profit curve an

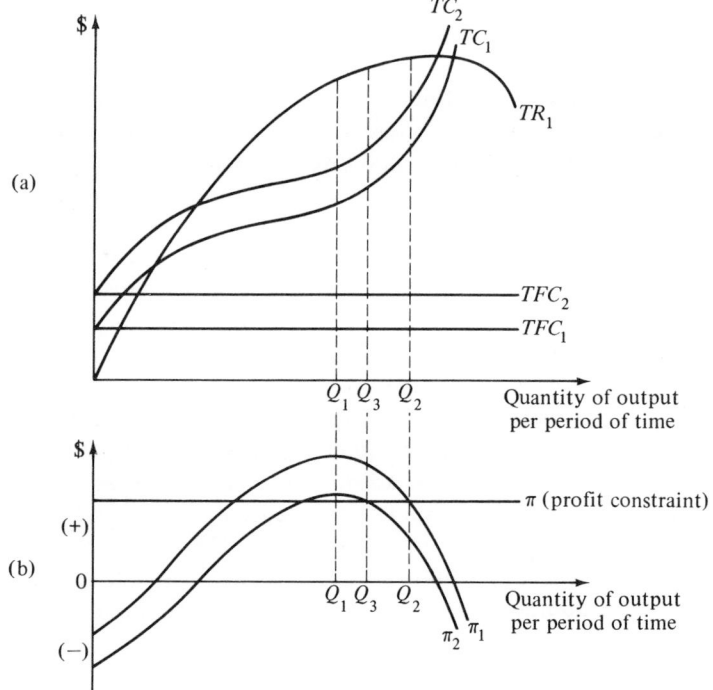

Fig. 12-4   The Effect of Fixed Cost Changes upon the Firm's Optimum Price and Output

output of Q_2 units will result in profits below the minimum acceptable level. The revenue-maximizing firm will therefore be compelled to reduce output to Q_3 units to meet its profit constraint; concomitantly, it will raise price as the vehicle for effecting the reduction in unit sales. Thus, the goal of the firm is the pivotal factor in analyzing its response to a rise in fixed costs. Firms which seek to maximize profits will leave their price and output rates unchanged when fixed costs change, whereas firms which seek to maximize sales revenue subject to a profit constraint will tend to reduce their outputs and raise their selling prices in response to an increase in fixed costs.

Insofar as actual business practice is concerned, there is little question which of the two responses to fixed cost increases is the more commonly observed. An increase in fixed costs is usually an occasion for serious consideration of a price increase, especially in center firm markets. This sort of behavior implies that center firms do have a sales revenue goal and are not singularly motivated by the desire to earn higher profits.

The Effect of Tax Changes.   Whether a firm is a profit-maximizer or a revenue-maximizer has significant public policy implications. An outstanding

450

illustration concerns the use of federal taxation policies to control inflationary tendencies. Increases in corporate tax rates have in recent years
become a standard weapon for helping contain inflationary forces and
achieve price stability and full employment. The logic seems plain enough:
with steeper corporate profits taxes, the business sector has fewer after-
tax dollars to spend for new capital investment and less of a profit incentive
to invest these dollars, so that investment spending is curtailed and the
investment component of aggregate demand is reduced. In turn, the pressure of aggregate demand upon production capacity is relieved somewhat and
the motive of business enterprises to raise product prices is dampened.

    However, the successful use of increases in corporate profits taxes as
a weapon for fighting inflation depends implicitly upon the principal goal
of business enterprises. This can be seen from the cost-revenue-profit curves
shown in Figure 12-5. Given a total revenue curve of TR_1, a total cost curve
of TC_1, a net-profit-after-taxes curve of π_1, and a profit target of OA dollars,
the profit-maximizing and revenue-maximizing outputs are Q_1 units and
Q_2 units, respectively. Now suppose an additional tax of 10 percent of all
profits is imposed upon the firm. The effect of the tax is to shift the firm's
after-tax profit curve downward at each level of *profitable output* by the
amount of the additional tax, as shown by π_2. Observe that the peak of π_2

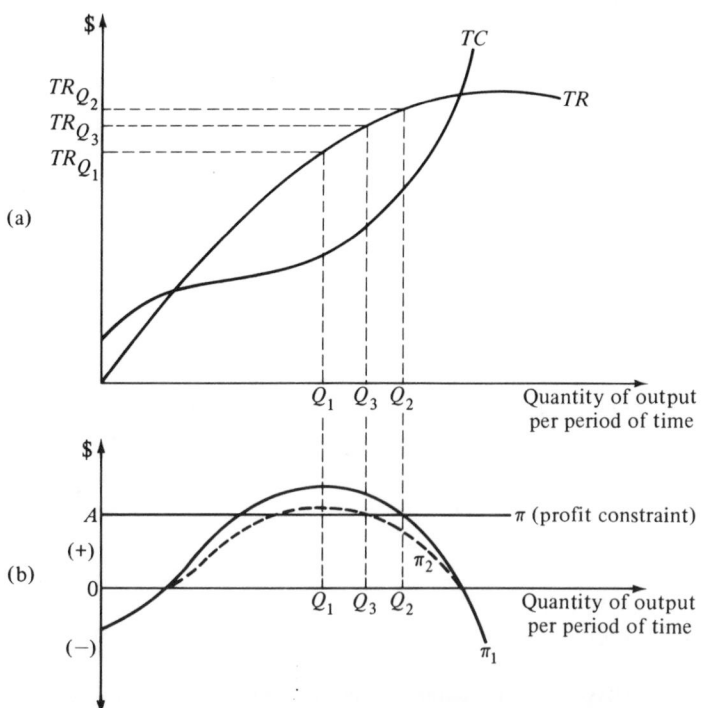

Fig. 12-5   The Effect of Tax Changes upon the Firm's Optimum Price and Output

corresponds to the same output as does the peak of π_1. Hence, we may correctly conclude that the profit-maximizing output rate is the same after the additional tax is paid as it was before. The profit-maximizing firm therefore has no incentive to change either its output rate or its price. But the same cannot be said if the firm's goal is to maximize sales revenue subject to a profit constraint! Imposing additional corporate profits taxes upon a revenue-maximizing firm induces the firm to restrict its sales of output to Q_3 units and to raise its price as the means of reducing sales of output from Q_2 to Q_3 units. Raising price and restricting output is the only strategy available to the firm in the short run which will allow it to meet its profit constraint.

To the extent, then, that business firms are revenue-maximizers and not profit-maximizers, higher corporate profits taxes help to intensify upward price pressures rather than dampen them. This may partially explain why the 10 percent tax surcharge imposed upon business firms in the 1968–70 period had little perceptible effect in easing inflationary pressures and may in reality have helped *increase* the rate at which prices rose.[6]

The preceding analysis highlights the effects of different goals upon the optimal price and output decisions of the firm. It indicates how seriously wrong predictions of business price and output behavior can be unless care is exercised first in determining the actual goals of business enterprises.

The Extent of Revenue-Maximizing Behavior. The evidence is inconclusive whether or not a significant number of business firms actually base their price and output decisions upon a goal of maximizing sales revenue subject to a profit constraint. The major obstacle is that the decision process of large corporations is exceedingly complex. Many factors influence and constrain corporate pricing decisions; it is quite difficult to know just what set of motivations and priorities are reflected in managerial decisions. In addition, the behavioral differences between profit maximization and revenue maximization are difficult to detect with the available empirical data because so many economic forces must be untangled. The few available studies of business behavior, the public pronouncements of business executives, and the consulting experiences which several academicians have had with major firms do, however, combine to give credence to the revenue-maximization model.[7] The numerous examples of target return pricing are also quite consistent with a revenue-maximizing goal. Nevertheless, the final verdict is still out on the extent of revenue-maximizing behavior among business enterprises.

---

[6] A more complete discussion of some of the microeconomic responses to changes in federal fiscal policy is contained in Arthur A. Thompson and Walter J. Klages, "An Evaluation of Alternative Approaches to the Application of Stabilization Policy," *Business Perspectives*, Vol. 7, No. 1 (Fall 1970), pp. 25–34.

[7] See, for example, the instances cited by Baumol, *Business Behavior, Value and Growth*, Chap. 6; Marshall Hall, "Sales Revenue Maximization: An Empirical Examination," *Journal of Industrial Economics*, Vol. 15 (April 1967), pp. 143–154; J. W. McGuire, J. S. Y. Chiu, and A. D. Elbins, "Executive Income, Sales, and Profits," *American Economic Review*, Vol. 52, No. 4 (September 1962), pp. 753–761; and B. D. Mabry and D. L. Siders, "An Empirical Test of the Sales Maximization Hypothesis," *Southern Economic Journal*, Vol. 33, No. 3 (January 1967), pp. 267–277.

THE RELATED GOALS OF SALES, PROFIT, AND GROWTH:
AN INTEGRATIVE MODEL

All of the preceding models of center firm behavior have been largely *static* in their approach. They have concentrated upon pinpointing the firm's optimal price and output decisions at a particular moment, given some specified set of cost and revenue conditions. The result has been an illuminating snapshot description of firms and markets in motion. But a complete picture of business behavior and market performance requires that the time frame of our analysis be lengthened to include the long-run goals of business enterprise and the dynamic influences of such powerful forces as technological progress, shifts in consumer buying patterns, and long-run competitive pressures. Progress in raising the quality of economic life is best gauged by *trends* in prices, in product quality, in rates of growth in output, and in the pace of innovation, rather by their respective values at some moment of time.

As was emphasized in Chapter 9, large corporate enterprises may exhibit interest in such goals as profits, sales revenues, market share, long-run survival, security, managerial autonomy, technological virtuosity, and rising dividend rates, as well as fulfillment of the personal objectives of top management. The surest strategy for achievement of these goals over the long term is maintaining the growth and expansion of the firm itself. Searching for some optimum short-run equilibrium condition and then seeking ways to maintain it is a strategy totally abhorrent and foreign to managers. Instead, the energies and resources of firms are focused upon escaping the throes of a static state and the stagnation and decline which it soon entails. Every management is acutely aware that the activities upon which the firm presently relies will over time lose their sustaining power through changes in consumer tastes, the appearance of superior commodities, increased competition from foreign and domestic rivals, and growth in the market power of suppliers and customers. Change is certain. Thus progressive business firms, and especially progressive center firms, are strongly growth-conscious and expansion-minded. Expanding sales revenues and expanding profits—the two most focused-upon measures of business growth—are sure to be foremost in the typical center firm's goal hierachy.

The concern with growth has very important implications for price and output decisions. In all probability, a growth-conscious management will avoid employing any sort of short-run strategy which interferes with the attainment of long-run goals. For example, firms commonly elect to deviate from their short-run profit-maximizing prices and output rates in order to better achieve long-run profit maximization. This was indicated in Chapter 11, where dominant firms and near monopolists were seen to have strong incentives for choosing actual selling prices below those at which $MC = MR$ and for increasing short-run output rates past the $MC = MR$ intersection. Via this short-run price-output strategy, these firms (a) discourage the entry and expansion of rival firms, (b) reduce the chances of government intervention, and (c) contain the motives for countervailing power. The intent of such a strategy is, of course, to forsake short-run for long-run profit maximization. In the same vein, firms may price new products below short-run profit-maximizing levels in order to open up more uses for the product, attract more new customers, and thereby enhance their long-term profits, sales, and market shares. Some firms may invest heavily in technologies which they know have little or no short-run payoff but which offer substantial long-run benefits in terms of costs and efficiency, given expected changes in input prices. Target return pricing, which makes use of long-run "normal" operating rates as the basis for price determination, is another situation where long-run considerations dominate those of the short run.

Growth Equilibrium. Given that growth and expansion comprise the major strategy for long-run goal achievement, it is imperative that growth considerations be incorporated into our analysis of business behavior. Specifically, we shall concentrate upon the criteria for determining how rapidly the firm should expand its production activities in pursuit of its goals. The analysis follows closely the lines proposed by Professor Baumol in his "growth-equilibrium" model.[8]

Consider first the effects of growth and expansion upon a firm's total costs. Two types of cost arising from the growth process are of particular interest: (1) *output costs*—ordinary fixed and variable costs stemming from the operation of production processes with greater output potential and (2) *expansion costs*—costs associated exclusively with the expansion process. Output costs can reasonably be expected to increase linearly as a firm's annual rate of growth in output rises—in other words, constant returns to scale may be said to characterize the expansion of production capacity. Once the optimum scale of plant for a productive activity is identified, a firm can build as many such plants as may be required to satisfy output needs. Technical progress also helps to ward off more-than-proportional increases in output costs as production rates are expanded or as the scope of a firm's activity is widened.

In contrast, the faster a firm seeks to grow, the faster *expansion costs* can be counted upon to rise. The reasons for this deserve brief mention. First, to shorten the time required to build a new plant facility or to build more plants of the same sort at a given time is likely to strain the abilities of construction firms and add substantially to the prices at which they will agree to build such facilities Second, ever more rapid expansion requires ever more money to finance it. Beyond some point, firms generally find that the more money they must raise for investment, the higher is the cost of obtaining it. The amount of growth which can be funded by retained earnings is limited. Issuing large amounts of new stock or selling bonds drives

8 Baumol, *Business Behavior, Value and Growth*, Chap. 10.

their prices down and so raises the cost of obtaining capital. Negotiating loans also tends to become more expensive, since lenders may well insist upon higher interest rates for larger and more frequent loans. Third, growth of a firm entails the recruitment of more executives, middle- and lower-echelon managers, technical staff, and production workers. It takes time for them to be trained and to gain experience in their assignments. The more rapidly a firm tries to assimilate new personnel into the organization, the more opportunity there is for inefficiency and rising costs to accompany growth.

Consequently, as a firm seeks to accelerate the rate of expansion in its long-run production capabilities, it typically finds it difficult to accommodate faster growth without encountering severe "growing pains" and a concomitant rise in inefficiency. Construction costs, capital costs, and organizational staffing costs all increase disproportionately, causing the firm's total cost function to rise more and more sharply. Thus, while ordinary output costs tend to increase linearly in view of the prevalence of constant return to scale, expansion costs can be counted upon to transform an otherwise linear total cost curve into one which increases at an increasing rate as a firm's annual growth rate of output becomes progressively larger. This is illustrated in Figure 12-6.

Now, what about the effect of growth upon a firm's total revenues?

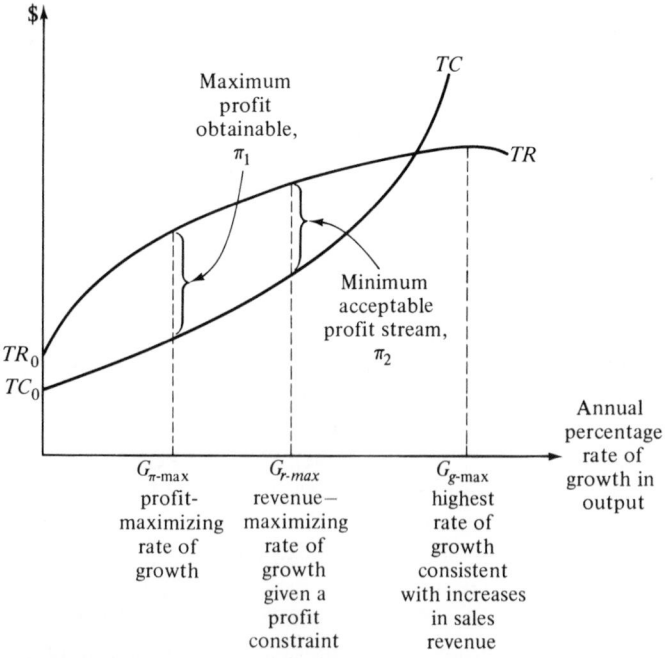

Fig. 12-6 Growth Equilibrium for the Firm

Barring totally unfavorable market conditions, a firm's total revenues can be expected to rise as the rate of growth in output rises above zero. However, market conditions will seldom permit a firm to expand without limit and still realize increases in total revenue. True, a firm is usually capable of fostering greater sales via some combination of lower prices, advertising, innovation, and diversification, but the ability to generate greater revenues over the near term is not boundless. Internally generated strategies to spur sales are likely to encounter diminishing success even in a favorable market environment. Hence, the firm's total revenue curve tends to increase at a decreasing rate, as shown in Figure 12-6.

It is obvious from Figure 12-6 that different rates of growth in output result in different degrees of profitability. The gap between TR and TC widens, then narrows, as the annual rate of growth in output increases. A firm will therefore find it unprofitable to expand either too slowly or too rapidly, and there is some rate of output expansion that will maximize long-run profits. The profit-maximizing growth rate, shown as $G_{\pi-\max}$, results in a maximum profit stream of π_1 dollars. It follows from this analysis that a firm grows partly because growth makes the firm more profitable.[9]

However, as we have emphasized on numerous occasions, center firms may have objectives other than profit. One very plausible alternative to long-run profit maximization is maximization of the *rate of growth* of sales revenue subject to a profit constraint. Given that corporations stress the *percentage* by which sales and profits have grown rather than the *amount* of sales and profits, *growth rates* may more accurately describe corporate goals than absolute dollar values.

From a long-run viewpoint, profit serves not so much as a constraint upon a firm's behavior as it does an instrument variable for attaining such goals as secure future profits, rising dividends, rising stock prices, strong market position, and target rates of return on investment. For instance, profits are the means for obtaining the funds to finance growth and expansion. Retained earnings are a major source of funds for investment; dividend payments help induce outside investors to provide risk capital; and evidence of profitability is essential to establish the firm's credit and borrowing power among lenders. Profits are essential if the firm is to be able to finance new product development and technical innovation—both major tactical weapons for achieving growth. Thus, a firm desirous of maximizing its rate of growth of sales revenue will of necessity have a corollary objective of earning sufficient profits to finance the growth it desires. This profit stream may be less than the maximum profit stream the firm is capable of earning.

---

[9] The conclusions that a firm pursues growth because it is profitable to do so is, of course, just as true of periphery firms as of center firms. The motives for profitable growth are not the exclusive province of center firms, despite the fact that absolute growth in the center economy tends to dwarf that in the periphery economy. Over the years more than a few periphery firms have chalked up respectable records of profitable growth. Some have been so successful in achieving higher profits via aggressive growth strategies that they now stand in the ranks of the center firms; examples include Control Data Corporations, Holiday Inns, Textron, TRW, and Xerox.

Referring again to Figure 12-6, suppose a profit stream of π_2 dollars will suffice to meet capital needs as well as to satisfy stockholders' expectations. Then the firm can push its rate of growth past $G_{\pi-\max}$ to $G_{r-\max}$—$G_{r-\max}$ may be delineated as the maximum rate of expansion consistent with maximizing sales revenues *and* attaining the desired profit. Hence, a firm with an objective of maximizing its rate of growth of sales revenue will tend to expand production faster than a profit-maximizing firm. It is apparent that past a growth rate of $G_{\pi-\max}$, profits and sales *compete*—higher revenues can be achieved only by sacrificing some profits. Yet, if growth is carried too far, the profit stream will be too small to generate the needed investment capital. This explains why the firm stops short of a growth rate corresponding to the peak of the *TR* curve (shown as $G_{g-\max}$ in Figure 12-6).

Three very important conclusions are implied by this analysis. First, the center firm's behavior over the long term (as well as over the short term) varies according to its goals. The price and output decisions of profit-maximizers differ from those of revenue-maximizers and those of growth-maximizers. The implication is strong that the pursuit of other goals will entail still different price-output decisions and growth-strategy sets. In other words, prices, outputs, and growth rates all vary according to the priorities which center firms assign to their respective goals.

Second, the center firm has a very powerful motive to expand its rate of output over time. Irrespective of whether the center firm's ultimate goal is to maximize long-run profits or future sales revenues or something else, growth of its long-run output rate is a virtual certainty. This is not to say that the output rate for each and every product will be increased—obviously, shifts in consumer demand may dictate otherwise—but it does say that the combined physical output rates of the firm's products will tend to rise over time. A positive rate of output growth—and maybe a substantial rate—is a virtual prerequisite to achievement of the center firm's goals.

Third, and most important of all, because of their strong motivation to expand production, center firms are the engine of economic growth for the entire economy. They initiate, nurture, and implement the expansion of output. The imperatives for satisfactory sales-profit-market share performance and the large corporation's immense capacity to undertake research, new product development, technological innovation, and capital investment all combine to thrust center firms into the vanguard of generating and promoting long-run economic expansion. On reflection, this conclusion reduces to pure common sense. It cannot be seriously contended that the small-business sector exerts significant influence over the pattern and process of national economic growth. The role of government, though definitely influential, is ordinarily that of a watchdog and a permissive partner rather than an active agent. Thus, the driving force of economic growth necessarily emanates from center firm activities. Certainly, center firms are the dominant organizational and institutional vehicle through which economic growth is achieved. It would not be far wrong to maintain that the actual rate of growth of the economy is partially a reflection of the degree to which center firms as a group have achieved their growth goal.

Aspects of Center Firm Growth. In the center economy the motives for vigorous output expansion are highly contagious. One firm hell-bent on growth can so jeopardize the market position of other firms in the industry that they must follow suit or face an unpleasant squeeze into relative obscurity. Few firms opt the latter; hence, the growth of one or a few firms catalyzes the growth of other firms and causes a strong growth psychology to pervade the entire industry. In addition, once growth competition appears, the posture of the center firm towards growth tends to become active rather than passive. Managers understand thoroughly the tactical advantage a firm gains from staying in the ranks of the growth leaders. It is much more satisfactory to seize the initiative in pursuing growth, because this permits the firm to pick the specific strategy and timing that seem most propitious.

However, from the center firm's standpoint, expansion should be steady and prudent; bursts of innovation and expansion are undesirable. Erratic growth is a destabilizing influence as regards staffing, financial planning, and capital investment. In addition, extraordinary but unrepeatable sales and profit performances are embarrassing to management. A record of vigorous, uninterrupted progress is the most enviable. This has led to an attempt to fund research and development programs in ways calculated to generate a dependable flow of new but pretested ideas. These ideas are then implemented at a tempo sufficient to yield the firm's target growth rate, provided adequate financing is available and provided the economic environment is not hostile to expansion. At the same time, wide fluctuations in the firm's investment spending have been reduced and its investment expenditures put on a more regular, programmed basis.

On balance, the effect of center firm growth strategy upon the economy as a whole is quite favorable. Not only is national economic growth stimulated by expansion-minded center firms, but business investment is made less volatile and full employment is made somewhat easier to achieve.

Growth Equilibrium for the Firm and for the Economy. Although the drive for growth permeates the center economy, a critical issue yet remains. How can the firm, year after year, find customers for its ever-growing flow of output? One answer is that if there is simultaneous growth in the production activity of a large segment of the center economy, many new job opportunities will be created, and wage and salary incomes will expand. At the same time, investment spending for new production capacity and purchases of more inputs will cause the incomes of suppliers to rise. In due course the ripples of center economy expansion will permeate the periphery economy. The rise in incomes triggered by center and periphery expansion has the effect of generating increases in the total demand for goods and services throughout the economy and thereby expanding the markets in which the increased production can be sold. The process of growth thus begets the increases in demand needed to ratify and sustain the firm's expansion. Provided growth occurs neither too slowly nor too rapidly among firms and among industries, the entire economy can be kept on a path of reasonably balanced growth and full employment equilibrium. Such is the skeleton of the economic links between growth equilibrium for the firm and growth equilibrium for the economy. More will be said about this in Chapter 15.

Summary and Conclusions

We have seen that the firm's goals have a definite effect upon its price and output decisons. A profit goal in terms of target rates of return will not lead to the same price and output decisions as will one based on marginal revenue and marginal cost concepts. A firm whose primary goal is revenue maximization subject to a profit constraint tends to produce at a greater output rate and to sell at a lower price than does a firm whose goal is profit maximization—other things being equal. Whereas a profit-maximizing firm has no incentive to alter its price and output in the face of increases in either fixed costs or taxes, a revenue-maximizing firm tends to respond by curtailing output and raising selling prices. A revenue maximizer also tends to spend greater amounts on advertising and sales promotion, which, if effective, will tend to push its output rate beyond that of a comparable profit-maximizing firm.

Unless confronted with an unfavorable economic environment, center firms will exhibit a strong propensity to grow. This holds whether their principal goal is long-run profit maximization or some combination of higher profit, greater sales revenues, and stronger market position. A powerful growth psychology tends to develop among center firms. Over the long term, growth competition tends to emerge as a major dimension of competition among center firms. The effect is to thrust center firms into the role of providing the driving force behind overall expansion of the economy. In a very real sense, center firms are the engine of economic growth and economic progress. They are at once both the impetus and the organizational vehicle for improving the quality of economic life.

SUGGESTED READINGS

BAUMOL, WILLIAM J., *Business Behavior, Value and Growth*, rev. ed. (New York: Harcourt Brace Jovanovich, Inc., 1967), Chaps. 6–10.
KAPLAN, A. D. H., J. B. DIRLAM, and R. F. LANZILOTTI, *Pricing in Big Business* (Washington, D.C.: The Brookings Institution, 1958), Chap. 2.

MARRIS, ROBIN, "A Model of the 'Managerial' Enterprise," *Quarterly Journal of Economics*, Vol. 77, No. 2 (May 1963), pp. 185–209.

————, *The Economic Theory of 'Managerial' Capitalism* (New York: The Free Press, 1964).

PENROSE, EDITH, *The Theory of the Growth of the Firm* (New York: John Wiley & Sons, Inc., 1959).

SHEPHERD, W. G., "On Sales-Maximizing and Oligopoly Behavior," *Economica*, Vol. 29, No. 116 (November 1962), pp. 420–424.

WESTON, J. FRED, "Pricing Behavior of Large Firms", *Western Economic Journal*, Vol. 10, No. 1 (March 1972), pp. 1–18.

WILLIAMSON, JOHN, "Profit, Growth and Sales Maximization," *Economica*, Vol. 33, No. 129 (February 1966), pp. 1–16.

WILLIAMSON, OLIVER E., "A Model of Rational Managerial Behavior," which appears as Chapter 9 of Richard M. Cyert and James G. March, *A Behavioral Theory of the Firm* (Englewood Cliffs, N.J.: Prentice-Hall, Inc., 1963), pp. 237–252.

————, *The Economics of Discretionary Behavior: Managerial Objectives in a Theory of the Firm* (Englewood Cliffs, N.J.: Prentice-Hall, Inc., 1964).

————, *Corporate Control and Business Behavior* (Englewood Cliffs, N.J.: Prentice-Hall, Inc., 1970).

Problems and Questions for Discussion

1. If a firm selects its selling price via some sort of "cost-plus" technique, is it possible for the firm to ever lose money? Why or why not?

2. Minnick Corporation has invested $50 million in facilities and equipment to produce miniature portable color TV sets with a 4-inch screen. Minnick's annual production capacity is 2 million sets. Over the last five years, Minnick's sales of these miniature TV sets have averaged 1.6 million per year. The company's fixed costs have remained relatively stable at $10 million per year. The firm estimates its annual total variable cost function to be

$$TVC = 120Q + 10Q^2,$$

where Q is *millions* of units of TV sets sold per year.
   (a) If Minnick desires to earn a target rate of return on its investment of 30 percent (before taxes), what target return price should Minnick select?
   (b) If Minnick's pricing policy is to add 15 percent to its normal production costs to determine selling price, what price should it charge, based upon the above information?

3. In the college textbook business, it is standard practice for the author's royalty to be some percentage of the total revenue which the publisher receives from sales of the book. The publisher, of course, incurs all costs of manufacturing, promoting, and distributing the book. Would the price and the sales volume (the number of books sold) which maximize the publisher's profits on the book also maximize the author's royalty payments? Why or why not? Demonstrate your answer graphically.

4. Suppose in the short run a firm produces under conditions of constant returns

to variable input over the entire output range for which it has production capability. Suppose further that the firm selects its selling price in order to earn a target rate of return on its investment and follows the practice of selling at the target return price no matter what short-run demand conditions happen to be.

(a) Graphically illustrate the firm's short-run AVC, MC, and ATC curves.

(b) On the same graph illustrate a target return price.

(c) Under these circumstances what is the value of MR?

(d) At what output rate would the firm maximize short-run profits?

(e) At what output rate would the firm maximize sales revenues?

5. Suppose a firm's short-run production function is characterized by constant returns to variable input. Suppose further that the firm faces a linear, downsloping demand curve for its product.

(a) Graphically illustrate the firm's TR, TC, and π functions.

(b) Indicate on your graph the profit-maximizing output.

(c) Indicate on your graph a profit constraint which is smaller than the maximum amount of profit.

(d) Indicate the revenue-maximizing output, given the profit constraint.

6. The Harco Beverage Corporation has estimated its weekly demand function to be

$$P = 416 - 7Q,$$

and its weekly total cost function to be

$$TC = 1{,}700 + 16Q + Q^2.$$

(a) If Harco's goal is to maximize sales revenue subject to the constraint that profits equal no less than $2,500 per week, what is Harco's optimum price and output rate? [*Hint:* Recalling that $\pi = TR - TC$, substitute the appropriate expressions into this equation and solve for Q.]

(b) If Harco's goal is to maximize profits, then what is its optimum price and output rate? How does the profit-maximizing price and output compare with the revenue-maximizing price and output?

(c) Suppose Harco's total fixed costs rise from $1,700 to $1,875. Determine the impact upon Harco's profit-maximizing price and output rate.

(d) Determine the impact of the increase in total fixed costs from $1,700 to $1,875 upon Harco's revenue-maximizing price and output rate, given the profit constraint of $2,500.

13

Business Behavior and Economic Welfare

Now that we are armed with an understanding of business behavior as portrayed in the various market models, it is time to stand back and appraise the social consequences of the price and output decisions of center firms and periphery firms. Which, if any, of the four types of market structures is the "best" one from society's standpoint? Does a perfectly competitive periphery-firm type of market structure typically result in a lower price and a greater output than an oligopolistic center-firm type? How much and what kinds of competition are socially and economically desirable? In the long run is the style of competition found in the center economy more socially beneficial than the style of competition found in the periphery economy? Are consumers at the mercy of big business? Are some of the goals of center firms more socially responsible than others? What is the economic impact upon society of collusion, monopolistic practices, the exercise of market power, and weak competitive pressures?

These are very tough questions. They involve thorny issues which bear directly upon the overall economic welfare of society. Unfortunately, we will not be able to find definitive answers. An objective evaluation of business conduct and market performance is replete with analytical difficulty. In the first place, actual business behavior and market conditions do not neatly correspond to the theoretical models of perfect competition, monopolistic

461

competition, oligopoly, or pure monopoly. There are numerous inter-mediate and borderline situations; many industries embody characteristics of two or more of the conventional models and therefore cannot be categorized as behaving in a manner analogous to any of them. More importantly, the currently existing theories of business behavior are overwhelmingly *static* in their analytical approach; that is, they are primarily concerned with deter-mining what sort of business behavior will result from a particular set of market circumstances. The models are presented as operating towards an equilibrium, the essence of which hinges upon the original set of market conditions. And the nature of this equilibrium commands the center of attention, with only incidental concern for the time and the path for reaching equilibrium. This sort of analytical procedure is called *comparative statics*, since it ultimately involves comparing results at some equilibrium point with those obtained at another equilibrium point.

The fact is, however, that the static equilibrium results of particular business decisions are part of a process which takes considerable time to re-veal its true features and ultimate effects. Hence, it may be misleading to de-termine a firm's equilibrium price and output decisions at some moment of time and attempt to draw conclusions about whether these decisions work in the best interests of society. Rather, if a true and objective judgment is to be rendered, then the time frame of the evaluation period must be widened and business performance examined as it unfolds over a period of years. Price *trends* and output *trends*, taken in conjunction with quality improvements, new product innovation, technological change, and the *patterns* of economic change, give a more meaningful and valid evaluation of business behavior and its social implications. Competition is a *dynamic* process, not a mecha-nism of equilibrium, and its effectiveness is not readily determined from statically-oriented models of business behavior.

For these reasons, the many static models of business behavior stop short of allowing economists to describe in accurate and rigorous analytic fashion just how business behavior affects society's economic welfare over the long term. While these models do yield valuable insights into business be-havior (and for that alone they are worthwhile), they are far from being the ultimate in microeconomic theory. These is much more to learn about the mechanics and processes of disequilibrium adjustment, the almost infinite variety of market situations, the implications and the impact of decision making under conditions of uncertainty, the long-term effects of corporate behavior patterns, and the long-run competitive effects of technological change, innovation, and economic growth.

All this amounts to saying that the state of microeconomic theory is too underdeveloped and too untested to permit *unequivocal* answers to the questions posed above. Besides, as we shall see shortly, numerous subtle value judgments quickly creep into any discussion of what is and what is not in the best interest of society. However, we shall not use these circumstances as an excuse to dodge the issues. Having come this far, the reader has a right not to expect a "cop out"; there is, indeed, an obligation to try to tie things together—if only provisionally—and to seek answers to some of these questions—even if they are tentative and weighted by value judgments. The reader therefore is dutifully forewarned that what follows is neither totally accepted nor thoroughly tested economic doctrine. Moreover, the discussion below is not rigorous, systematic analysis; it is instead laced with generalizations about "the way things really are." No economist pretends that this is a satisfactory state of affairs, but it is about the best that can be done, given the existing body of economic knowledge and economic theory.

THE CRITERIA FOR EVALUATING BUSINESS BEHAVIOR

The first step in launching an evaluation of business behavior is to decide upon the standards for judging market conduct and market performance. This, in itself, is a controversial task, because it necessarily entails subjective judgments as to what is important and what is not. Reasonable men can disagree over both the criteria and the priorities. Nonetheless, some common ground does exist.

We begin with the fundamental assertion that the business sector of the economy performs well when it provides consumers with whatever goods and services they want to buy at prices no higher than required to make production feasible and sustainable. From this statement follow several explicit criteria or standards for judging business behavior, not necessarily listed in order of their priority or social importance:

1. The production decisions of business firms regarding output rates and the range of quality must be responsive to consumer demand.
2. Production activity should be undertaken according to the most efficient technological and organizational means.
3. The operations of business firms should be progressive in the sense that new technological achievements both for increasing output per unit of input and for producing new and superior products are encouraged and exploited.
4. The constraints upon discretionary business decisions should be severe enough to preclude firms from securing rewards (profits) far in excess of those needed to call forth the desired amount of productive activity.
5. The operations of business firms should facilitate (or at least not hinder excessively) the achievement of such national economic goals as full employment, price stability, economic growth, a rising standard of living, an increasing quality of life, economic freedom, an equitable distribution of income, and so on.

Unfortunately, these criteria are not always completely consistent. Conflicts may arise which cannot be resolved without invoking basic value judgments as to which should take precedence. Different individuals and groups may place different priorities on these criteria. Still, good industrial performance implies that all five goals be satisfied to the greatest extent feasible.

THE MANY DIMENSIONS OF COMPETITION

In a capitalistically-oriented economy, the built-in mechanism for achieving good industrial performance is *competition*. The essence of competition is an *independent striving for patronage* by firms selling competing products. Except for the unique circumstances of natural monopoly, there can really be no argument as to the desirability of competition among business enterprises, large or small. Indeed, the necessity of having "vigorous competition" in a free-enterprise economy is widely accepted and its benefits generally acknowledged. Competition is what protects consumers from excessive prices and what disciplines producers to synchronize their production activities with those wants highest on the priority lists of consumers. Competition, in conjunction with the profit motive, forces producers to employ the most efficient production techniques that are available. By giving customers a choice of firms from which to purchase a product, competition acts to contain the power of firms that have maneuvered themselves into positions of advantage in the markets they serve. Hence, with adequate amounts of competition, discretionary business behavior is limited and business decisions are monitored in ways designed to protect society from business exploitation.

By and large, the extent to which competitive forces are actually strong enough to perform the above functions determines just how good business performance will be. However, competition assumes many forms and many shades of intensity. There is price competition, technological and innovational competition, quality competition, growth competition, and potential competition. In addition, business firms strive for greater patronage and increased market shares via advertising and sales strategy campaigns, thereby giving rise to what might be termed promotional competition. Still other dimensions of the competitive process relate to such matters as location, convenience, terms of credit, delivery, design and styling, customer repair service, guarantees, performance and durability, and status.

As might be suspected, society derives considerably more benefit from some of these forms of competition than from others. We can illustrate this proposition dramatically by comparing the style of competition in the periphery economy with that in the center economy.

Contrasts in the Competitive Behavior of Periphery Firms and Center Firms

Although numerous fundamental differences in the economics of periphery firms and the economics of center firms were presented in Chapter 1, there is more to the story. In particular, there are some significant differences in the style and vigor with which periphery and center firms compete. These contrasts in competitive styles and intensities are important, because they provide the touchstones for weighing the relative merits of periphery firm and center firm behavior.

PRICE COMPETITION IN PERIPHERY AND CENTER FIRM MARKETS

In the periphery economy, the individual firm has little discretion over the price it charges. This is because periphery firms often operate in market environments approximating the conditions of either perfect or monopolistic competition. In such cases the number of firms is relatively large, and the forces of market demand and market supply play a dominant role in price determination. No one firm is able to exert a significant price-determining influence unless its product is strongly differentiated. We are not far wrong, therefore, to think of most periphery firms as price-takers—they must take as given whatever price is established by demand and supply conditions.

Price competition in periphery firm-dominated markets thus means that firms struggle to produce profitably at the price established by supply and demand. This is particularly true where the products of the firms are for all practical purposes homogeneous and each firm's demand-AR curve is horizontal at the prevailing market price. In periphery firm markets where demand conditions approximate the model of perfect competition, price competition does *not* mean that firms compete for a greater market share by cutting price below the prevailing level. With perfectly elastic demand, there is no profit to be made from charging prices below the going rate. Instead, price competition in perfectly competitive markets means being forced to compete at a particular price irrespective of whether that price exceeds average total cost.

In contrast, where periphery firm markets embody the essential characteristics of monopolistic competition, price competition tends to assume its normal connotation. Product differentiation, when made effective in the minds of buyers, can result in price differences and therefore price competition among the firms involved. Firms may employ lower prices as a major tactic for increasing patronage for their products. However, different selling prices among periphery firms may be more a reflection of real (or imagined) quality differences than a measure of producers' attempts to attract more patronage by selling at a price lower than rival firms.

On the other hand, in center firm markets price competition takes on yet another dimension. Center firms use their prominent market position to frame their own price policy. Although by no stretch of the imagination can they charge whatever they please for their products, center firms do have price-making capabilities which in general exceed those of periphery firms. This is illustrated by the propensity of center firms to use target return pricing and price leadership as a means of price determination. Nonetheless, competing center firms, like competing periphery firms, still tend to sell their products at comparable prices, though for slightly different reasons.

Oligopoly conditions ordinarily characterize center firm markets. The close personal rivalry among center firms, the rapid shift of patronage to a lower-priced seller, and the strong mutual interdependence among center firms regarding price all combine to give center firm oligopolists overwhelming motives to establish a common price. This is invariably true if their respective products are homogeneous or weakly differentiated. The sales and market shares of competing center firms are much too sensitive to price differences to allow for much, if any, price deviation. Hence, whereas competing periphery firms are constrained by market demand and supply conditions to sell at similar prices, competing center firms sell at comparable prices because of the intense personal competition among them. Price competition among oligopolists thus often results in firms' selling at identical or comparable prices, rather than at different prices, irrespective of cost differences or profit margins. Firms which find the common price too low to earn a profit are forced to accept short-term losses until they can reorganize their production techniques and institute a cost-reduction program or until demand conditions warrant a common price increase; if these fail to materialize, they can be expected to cease production of the item altogether.

What can we conclude about the vigor of price competition in the periphery and center economies and its ultimate benefit to society? Insofar as *theory* is concerned, we can be rather definite in our answer. Theoretically, the style of price competition characterizing periphery firm markets should tend to result in a short-run price closer to average total cost than the style of price competition characterizing center firm markets. Since periphery firm markets usually resemble rather closely the models of perfect competition and monopolistic competition, we know that periphery firms are subjected to competitive forces that *tend* to push price in a given market to a level where it equals average total cost. We found no such automatic tendency to occur in our survey of center firm price decisions. Hence, other things being equal, the implication is strong that price competition among periphery firms will lead to lower prices and narrower profit margins than will price competition among center firm oligopolists.

From this theoretical conclusion we obtain the fundamental social benefit of periphery firm markets. Over the long run, competition among large numbers of periphery firms producing identical products acts to drive market price to the level of minimum average total cost—the results parallel those of the model of perfect competition. The profits of firms move toward levels just sufficient to induce them to produce a quantity of output consistent with the industrywide equilibrium output. And since, under conditions of long-run equilibrium, each firm operates at the minimum point of both its short-run and long-run average cost curves, maximum production efficiency for the firm and the industry tends to be attained. Some firms may be unable to compete at the equilibrium price established by the market. Such firms will incur losses, and eventually will be driven from the industry, unless they discover means of bringing their production costs down to a level which allows them to earn at least a normal profit. Thus, price competition tends to drive inefficient periphery firms from the industry or else forces them to become efficient enough to survive at the prevailing market price.

If consumers exhibit a preference for differentiated products, as is likely given the diversity of consumer tastes, then a market structure closely akin to monopolistic competition can be counted upon to produce a price not far above average total cost. The economic profits of periphery firms operating under conditions of monopolistic competition will tend to be dissipated by price competition among existing firms and/or among new firms attracted into the industry by the prospect of above-normal profits. Although in monopolistic competition periphery firms may operate at output rates which are short of the least-cost point on their cost curves, the resulting price and operating efficiency is as good as can be achieved with differentiated products.

Thus, in theory, the style of price competition which characteristically inhabits markets comprised of large numbers of relatively small firms tends to be sufficiently potent to yield product prices just equal to or barely above production costs. The social benefits are evident. With low prices (and consequently low profits), consumer demand is stimulated and consumers can enjoy the benefit of the greater volumes of output accompanying the low prices. In the short run consumers can really expect no better performance from the business sector.

In reality, however, the profit margins of periphery firms may not *always* be smaller that the profit margins of center firms. Only when long-run equilibrium conditions are approached do we find that periphery firm industries earn no more than the minimum return required to attract capital and stay in business. In practice, needless to say, the conditions of long-run equilibrium seldom are present, owing to the dynamics of technological progress, economic growth, new product innovations, and changing consumer tastes. Real-world economic conditions simply are not static enough to allow long-run equilibrium to be reached. Thus, the forces of dynamic economic change pave the way for periphery firms to earn substantial *short-run* economic profits, in which case the profit margins and rates of return of periphery firms and center firms may not always diverge as much as the theory suggests.

The Empirical Evidence.   There is confirming evidence that *on the whole* the prices of commodities produced by periphery firms are closer to average total costs than are prices of center firm produced commodities. Table 13-1 presents the relevant statistics for all U.S. firms engaged in manufacturing. Both for simplicity and for convenience in collecting the data, suppose we define center firms as being the 500 largest manufacturing corporations in terms of sales, and periphery firms as being all the remaining manufacturing corporations. This is in accord with our concept of center and periphery

Table 13-1 Estimated Profit Margins and Rates of Return for Periphery Firms and Center Firms in Manufacturing, 1958–1971

Year	After-Tax Profits as a Percentage of Sales Revenue		Rates of Return on Stockholder's Equity	
	Periphery Firms[a]	Center Firms[b]	Periphery Firms[a]	Center Firms[b]
1958	2.41	5.41	6.63	9.51
1959	3.05	6.07	8.92	11.00
1960	2.55	5.67	7.17	10.08
1961	2.51	5.55	7.18	9.59
1962	2.61	5.88	7.76	10.59
1963	2.80	6.05	8.39	11.10
1964	3.39	6.46	10.45	12.10
1965	3.86	6.71	12.99	12.99
1966	4.01	6.63	14.01	13.23
1967	3.51	5.96	11.58	11.75
1968	3.48	5.96	11.70	12.19
1969	3.42	5.54	11.35	11.49
1970	2.77	4.67	8.64	9.55
1971	3.63	4.65	10.73	9.77

Sources: The Economic Report of the President, 1972, p. 281, and *The Fortune Directory of the 500 Largest Corporations*, 1958–1971.

[a] Periphery firms are defined here to include all manufacturing firms in the U.S. except the 500 largest corporations in terms of sales.

[b] Center firms are defined here as the 500 manufacturing corporations in the U.S. having the largest sales revenues, coinciding exactly with "Fortune's 500" in any given year.

firms, though drawing the dividing line at 500 is obviously arbitrary. The relationship between prices and average total costs is indirectly reflected in the figures for after-tax profits as a percentage of sales revenue; the larger the percentage of profits to sales, the greater is the relative margin between price and average total cost. In essence, after-tax profits as a percentage of sales revenue gives the average amount of profit (in cents) per dollar of sales revenue for all commodities produced by the firm—a statistic which is indicative of average profit margins.

Examination of Table 13-1 reveals that during the 1958–1971 period the after-tax profits per dollar of sales realized by center firms have consistently averaged 5.0 to 6.5 cents as compared to 2.5 to 4.0 cents per dollar of sales for periphery firms. This correctly suggests that the relative margin between price and average cost is greater for center firm produced commodities than for periphery firm produced commodities. Periphery firm profit margins widened from about 2.5 cents per dollar to 3.5 and 4.0 cents per dollar during the strong business upswing of the 1965–69 period; this, along with the rising rates of return on invested capital (stockholders' equity) realized by periphery firms, is indicative of the higher (above-normal) profits which they may earn in the short run as a result of fortuitious changes in business conditions. Insofar as the rate of return on invested capital (stockholders' equity) is concerned, we find that the difference in the profitability of center and periphery firms is much less. This stems from the fact that periphery firms have a smaller amount of invested capital per dollar of sales than do center firms. As we have noted, center firm production activities typically entail a much heavier capital investment than do those of the periphery firm. For instance, during the 1958–1971 period the total invested capital of the 500 largest manufacturing corporations was an average of three times the size of the total invested capital of the remaining 400,000-plus manufacturing firms. Moreover, over this period the 500 largest firms had about $1 in invested capital for each $2 worth of goods sold, whereas all the remaining manufacturing firms had an average investment of only $1 for each $3 worth of goods sold.[1]

We may draw several conclusions from the data in Table 13-1.[2] First, the prediction of economic theory that market forces will exert strong pressure to push the prices of commodities produced by periphery firms close to average total cost is largely confirmed by the available evidence. Periphery firms do realize profits per dollar of sales revenue which on the average are smaller than those of center firms. Second, the historical long-run average rate of return among periphery firms is only *slightly* below that among center firms. However, we must be cautious on one very important point. We have no way of knowing for sure whether these two results are due to more vigorous price competition among periphery firms than among center firms, to differences in the intensity of other forms of competition, or to some other economic factors. Nor can we say that consumers and society as a whole derive more benefit from periphery firm competition (whatever its makeup) than from center firm competition just because periphery firm profit margins are smaller. Other crucial aspects must still be examined—to which we now turn.

TECHNOLOGICAL AND INNOVATIONAL COMPETITION IN PERIPHERY AND CENTER FIRM MARKETS

One of the most powerful and socially beneficial forms of competition is that associated with the emergence of the new product, the new technology,

---

[1] Derived from *The Economic Report of the President*, 1972, and *The Fortune Directory of the 500 Largest Corporations*, 1958–1971.

[2] Corroborating evidence has been gathered by numerous economists using the *concentration ratio* approach of measuring market power. Simply stated, a concentration ratio is the proportion of sales revenue (or assets or output) accounted for by the largest firms ranked in order of size as compared to all firms in the same industry. If, for example, the combined passenger car sales of General Motors, Ford, and Chrysler amounted to $20 billion and the total sales of all passenger cars in the U.S. came to $25 billion, then the three-firm sales concentration ratio would be .80. By implication, the higher the concentration ratio the greater is market power concentrated in the hands of a few firms and the "less competitive" the industry is held to be. This implication appears to be substantiated; profits do tend to increase with the degree to which a few firms dominate the sales of a commodity. However, valid doubts remain, considering the methodology used to test this hypothesis. More research with better data is needed. Among the best and most recent studies relating profits to the number and size of firms are Joe S. Bain, *Barriers to New Competition* (Cambridge, Mass.: Harvard University Press, 1956), pp. 192–200; H. Michael Mann, "Seller Concentration, Barriers to Entry, and Rates of Return in Thirty Industries," *Review of Economics and Statistics*, Vol. 48, No. 3 (August 1966), pp. 296–307; Norman R. Collins and Lee E. Preston, "Price-Cost Margins and Industry Structure," *Review of Economics and Statistics*, Vol. 51, No. 3 (August 1969), pp. 271–286; and William S. Comanor and Thomas A. Wilson, "Advertising, Market Structure, and Performance," *Review of Economics and Statistics*, Vol. 49, No. 3 (November 1967), pp. 423–440. For a discussion of the conceptual and data problems of testing the hypothesis that profits increase with market power, see F. M. Scherer, *Industrial Market Structure and Economic Performance* (Skokie, Ill.: Rand McNally & Company, 1970), pp. 50–57.

the new source of supply, and the new type of business enterprise.[3] The competitive response which follows the emergence of a successful innovation can scarcely fail to improve the quantity or quality of output, through both the innovation itself and the pressure it exerts on rival firms. The impact of new things has, as a matter of historical fact, regularly undermined the established positions of market advantage possessed by monopolistic or oligopolistic firms. Victims of technological and innovational competition include the steel firms, which now face strong competition from plastics, aluminum, and other metal alloys; the railroad firms, whose share of freight traffic has been substantially eroded by the emergence and growth of the truck carriers and the airlines; the motion picture industry, which has been plagued by the advent of television; and the domestic automobile firms, which are confronted with the popularity of small foreign cars. Gillette's monopoly position in the safety razor market has been weakened by the emergence of electric razors and the development of long-lasting blades by other firms.

Still another example is provided by the innovations in retailing which have occurred over the past several decades. Not so many years ago, competition among retailers consisted primarily of the rivalry among the firms concentrated in and about the main downtown shopping district. Yet, as almost any downtown retailer will quickly point out, the new competition that has really mattered has arisen not from additional downtown retail outlets of the same type, but from innovative retailing organizations—the chain store, the mail-order house, the shopping mall, the discount store, the supermarket, the self-service department store, and the convenience store.

Thus, in a technologically dynamic environment, new products are constantly replacing old products; some firms are faced with rapidly expanding markets, others with shrinking markets; some types of business enterprise are experiencing vigorous expansion and relative prosperity while others are on the decline or dying out. The procession of new innovations gives birth to new firms and new industries whose very success serves to erode the market position of established firms and industries. The faster the pace of technological change, the shorter becomes the life cycle of more and more commodities. A "perennial gale of creative destruction" literally rises forth from technological and innovational competition. It is largely this perennial gale that stimulates increases in the standard of living and feeds the engine of economic progress.

Society, therefore, has a major stake in the extent to which competition acts to spur the pace of technological change and innovation. The truly efficient business enterprise must do more than just achieve the lowest production costs at some point in time; it must also make adequate provision for

---

[3] Joseph A. Schumpeter, *Capitalism, Socialism and Democracy*, 3rd ed. (New York: Harper & Row, Publishers, 1950), p. 84; John K. Galbraith, *American Capitalism: The Concept of Countervailing Power* (Boston: Houghton Mifflin Company, 1952), Chap. 7.

the research and technological development which brings into being new and higher-quality goods, new and more efficient production processes and methods of transportation, new markets, new sources of supply of raw materials or partially manufactured goods, and new forms of enterprise. In other words, it is not enough that a firm operate at the minimum point of its short-run and long-run average total cost curve; it must, in addition, be aggressive in seeking new technologies (a) for lowering costs even further, (b) for increasing output per unit of input, and (c) for producing new and superior products.

Over the long run, whether a firm is technologically progressive is much more crucial to society than whether it achieves the lowest possible unit costs. Dynamic performance is ultimately what counts, because it is principally from technological change and innovation that society realizes gains in productivity (output per unit of input), gains in the quantity and quality of output, and gains in the level of per capita income. This leads to the crucial question of this section. Is a market environment which tends to squeeze profit margins and force price close to minimum average total cost in the short run compatible with the achievement of a high rate of technological progress and innovation?

Based upon real-world industrial performance, the answer to this question is apparently no. We noted earlier that prices tend to be closer to average costs in the periphery economy than in the center economy. And it is in the periphery economy that competitive forces are most powerful in pushing individual firm output rates toward the least-cost point. Nonetheless, technological and innovational competition reaches its most dramatic heights in the center economy. The center firm—not the periphery firm—is the economy's major organizational vehicle for innovation and technological achievement.

Center-Firm Participation in Technological and Innovational Competition. A number of interrelated reasons account for the greater emphasis on technological and innovational competition in the center economy than in the periphery economy. Center firm oligopolists, for reasons explored in Chapter 11, find price competition an ineffective and unrewarding strategy for enhancing their sales-profit-market share positions. Competing on the basis of new product variations, innovation, and production superiority is far more fruitful—especially over the long run. Experience shows that innovation is the single most effective tactic for earning substantial economic profits—as IBM, Xerox, Polaroid, Eastman Kodak, DuPont, and other high-technology firms have demonstrated so vividly. But, at the same time, an innovator can scarce afford to rest on past laurels. A decided advantage currently will gradually be dissipated as rivals successfully imitate or even better the original innovation. It thus behooves each firm persistently to press forward to develop still better products and production processes. Indeed, the list of firms earning

472

sizable long-term economic profits on the basis of some strategy other than innovative leadership is quite short.

Second, the presence of strong and aggressive rival center firms puts each under severe pressure to remain efficient and technologically progressive. Failure to do so will soon allow rivals to cut severely into the laggard firm's market share. The terrific pressure which technological competition brings to bear upon the highly personalized competitive environment of center-firm markets is illustrated by events in the computer industry. On June 30, 1970, IBM announced it was bringing out a new family of superscale computers. Within eight months all of the remaining major computer makers announced they would soon market new and more powerful computers with capabilities comparable to those made by IBM. The speed with which IBM's rivals responded testifies to the power and effectiveness of technological and innovational competition in the center economy.

Third, center firms are in general more able than periphery firms to undertake innovations and to compete on the basis of technology. Technological progress may be viewed as occurring in four steps: invention, development, implementation, and diffusion. Invention is the act of conceiving a new product or process and working out the details in its essential but rudimentary form. Development is the lengthy sequence of trial-and-error testing through which the invention is modified, perfected, and worked out in finest detail to make it technically ready for practical application. Innovation involves implementing the finalized version of the invention and putting it into practice for the first time. Diffusion relates to the rate and speed at which the innovation comes into widespread use as other enterprises follow the lead of the innovator. The available evidence indicates that steps one and two (invention and development) are often relatively inexpensive and can be undertaken on a small scale.[4] They are thus within the reach of both periphery and center firms. The third step, however, can be a costly, time-consuming process, especially if the innovation has broad appeal. To transform a new and proven idea into a common everyday commodity requires large-scale production facilities and a national and international distribution system. This kind of commitment is frequently beyond the reach of periphery firms; in all but a few instances they lack the scientific and engineering expertise, the managerial know-how, and the substantial amounts of money required to carry it off profitably—even on a gradual basis. Several years may be required before the anticipated profit payoff is realized. The product may have to be test-marketed, the unforeseen technical bugs eliminated, new productive facilities built or expanded, marketing channels organized, promotional campaigns designed and instituted, and the competition from other products surmounted. Such a process is not cheap, and experience indicates it is not likely to be undertaken on a regular and sustained basis by periphery firms locked in a struggle for short-run survival.

[4] For an excellent discussion of this and related points see Scherer, *Industrial Market Structure and Economic Performance*, Chap. 15, especially pp. 350–352.

These organizational shortcomings on the part of periphery firms explain why many inventions which originated among periphery firms have ended up as major products of center firms. Well-known examples include air conditioning, the jet engine, cellophane, the cotton picker, the helicopter, power steering, and the cracking of petroleum.[5] For the same reasons, center firms end up shouldering the burden of developing and implementing numerous inventions of academicians, independent inventors, and specialized R&D firms. Examples include titanium metals, Eastman Kodak's Kodachrome color film, DuPont's Dacron fibers, and Xerox's development of copying equipment. A number of other innovations have required large-scale funding. The development and implementation cost of civilian jet airliners has soared past the $100 million mark on several occasions. DuPont reportedly spent $27 million and several years developing nylon for commercial use (and it lost $100 million over an eight-year period in a futile attempt to make Corfam, a man-made leather product, a profitable innovation). RCA reputedly sank $65 million into R&D on color television before achieving a product with mass market potential. Many millions have also been spent by IBM in developing computers, by Alcoa in aircraft metals fabrication, by General Electric in refining X-ray equipment, by Westinghouse in designing nuclear-powered generating equipment, by steel firms in developing continuous casting of steel, and by General Motors in its development of the diesel locomotive, the automatic transmission for automobiles, and the liquid-cooled aircraft engine. One surmises that the Big Three of the automobile industry will spend billions of research dollars in making the automobiles of the future safer and more pollution free. And it is a fairly safe bet that center firms will play the major role in conquering the problems of general environmental pollution. Periphery firms simply do not have the organizational capacity for initiating the necessary technological break-throughs.

Periphery Firm Participation in Technology and Innovational Competition. Even so, there are numerous instances of innovation in the periphery economy. By no means do all or even most innovations require such heavy investments of time, money, and risk that they can be undertaken only by center firms. A census of the innovations in any one year would unquestionably reveal that the number of less costly, minor innovations is far greater than the number of very expensive, more spectacular ones. Many technical challenges can successfully be met by periphery firms willing to bear the risks. That periphery firms suffer no real handicap in implementing uncomplicated innovations is confirmed by the frequency with which they introduce new products, product variations, and improved production methods without fanfare and at comparatively little expense. Examples include specialized applications of computer technology, the development of semiconductors and electronic circuitry technology, containerized shipping, nonreturnable

---

[5] John Jewkes, David Sawers, and Richard Stillerman, *The Sources of Invention* (New York: St. Martin's Press, Inc., 1958), pp. 71–85.

soft-drink bottles, the instituting of self-service shopping, the application of numeric process control equipment, the use of bank credit cards, and the emergence of the convenience food store. In addition, periphery firm participation in the innovational process arises when the managers of large corporate enterprises are skeptical of the possibilities of proposed new products or new processes; in such instances it is left to imaginative and determined entrepreneurs to pioneer a new industry, provided financial barriers can be overcome.[6] Then, too, genius is not always easily accommodated in large corporate research laboratories, which emphasize highly-structured, result-oriented programs.[7] For these reasons, periphery firms must be accorded a significant role in advancing the cause of technological progress. Experience shows that no single size and type of firm is uniquely conducive to technical progress.

Nevertheless, it is indisputable that the greatest technological achievements are to be found in the center economy—with regard to both production process innovation and new product development. Center firms comprise the vanguard of the process of creative destruction. And it is center firms which compete most vigorously in the arena of technology and innovation.

Research and Development Efforts.   To be able to pioneer innovations or to respond speedily when rivals assume the lead in introducing novel discoveries, enterprises must invest in research and development activities to whatever extent is necessary to maintain their market position and to fulfill their growth objectives. In essence, each firm must create its own source of supply of innovations and it must see to it that this source of supply is reliable. That center firms have moved decisively in this direction is amply supported by the evidence. During the past fifteen years, center firms in the United States have emerged as leaders in establishing their own research and development laboratories to create new products and new processes and to make innovation less of random, haphazard occurrence. They have employed much of the nation's best scientific and engineering talent and they have purchased the specialized equipment which makes experimentation easier and more precise. Many center firms have deliberately sought to bring together into one unified organizational effort the critical combination of a fertile mind, a challenging problem, and the motivation to solve it.

[6] The *Wall Street Journal* in its March 15, 1971, issue reported just such a reaction by General Motors and other auto manufacturers regarding the possibilities of a "windup" car. The idea for the windup car, which apparently originated in a physics research lab at Johns Hopkins University, is based upon "flywheel energy storage." The car's engine is wound up by a small electric motor which spins a heavy flywheel up to very high speeds. To drive the car, a switch is turned that allows the spinning motion of the flywheel to be converted back into electricity for powering the drive shaft. The flywheel would lose its energy (or unwind) after 100 or so miles and would require a 20 minute rewind cycle. Detroit engineers have scoffed at the idea and believe "it just won't work." In their view serious danger to passengers is posed by spinning a 225-pound flywheel at 2,000 miles per hour (three times the speed of sound). Nevertheless, the originators of the idea are proceeding on their own, assisted by a $190,000 federal grant, to develop a prototype engine and windup car.

[7] Within the last twenty-five years, hundreds of research enterprises have been founded by entrepreneur-minded scientists and researchers who became disenchanted with the environs of the research labs of high-technology center firms. See E. B. Roberts, "Entrepreneurship and Technology," *Research Management*, Vol. 11, No. 4 (July 1968), pp. 249–266, and A. H. Rubinstein, "Problems of Financing New Research-Based Enterprises in New England," *New England Business Review* (July and August, 1958).

The R&D efforts of center firms relative to periphery firms is readily documented. Statistics compiled by the National Science Foundation show that as of 1969 firms having 5,000 or more employees accounted for 90 percent of the total R&D expenditures; firms with 1,000 to 4,999 employees accounted for 6 percent; and firms with fewer than 1,000 employees, the remaining 4 percent.[8] (The category of firms having 5,000 or more employees coincides almost exactly with the population of center firms as we have defined them; the class of firms with fewer than 1,000 employees matches up quite well with the concept of periphery firms; and firms with 1,000 to 4,999 employees have the characteristics of both center and periphery firms and may be thought as comprising the "in-between" group.) About 98 percent of all industrial R&D is performed in 1,200 companies, nearly all of which are large firms. Of the 515 companies with 5,000 or more employees, 480 had R&D programs of $200,000 or more and 417 spent more than $1 million.[9] Moreover, more than 86 percent of the scientists and engineers engaged in R&D were employed in firms with 5,000 or more employees.

It is very likely that large-scale research and development programs are more productive than small-scale ones in terms of results and perhaps even in the vital idea-generating stage of the innovation process. The division of labor has not progressed far enough in periphery firms to make formal, intensive R&D programs economically feasible, as is evidenced by the fact that fewer than 4 percent of the R&D scientists and engineers are engaged in R&D programs with expenditures of less than $200,000 per year.[10] Periphery firm efforts to compete on the basis of technological superiority and innovation tend therefore to be somewhat more casual and haphazard than center firm efforts.

Some Tentative Conclusions. What then may we conclude about the social benefits of technological and innovational competition as it appears in the center economy and in the periphery economy? In general, it appears that technological progress is enhanced more by center firms than by periphery firms. Center firms are uniquely well suited to engage in technological and innovational competition of the highest order of magnitude; periphery firms are not. The center firm's larger and more stable profits, its ability to absorb the losses from research which proves unfruitful, its superior access to capital for financing innovation, and its greater organizational capacity in terms of scientific, engineering, and managerial know-how place it ahead of the periphery firm as the *potential* pacesetter for pushing back the barriers to technological progress. When the center firm's *capacity for innovation* is combined with its motives for competing on the basis of technological superiority, the result is an organizational vehicle of significant social importance

---

[8] National Science Foundation, *Research and Development in Industry, 1969* (Washington, D.C.: U.S. Government Printing Office, 1971), p. 33.
    [9] *Ibid.*, p. 46.
    [10] *Ibid.*, p. 41.

476

for advancing the cause of technological progress. The rise of the large corporate enterprise and its attendant scientific and managerial establishment goes far toward explaining the perceptible increase in the rate of technological advance and the strong increases in per capita income which characterize modern industrial economies.

This brings into sharp focus a major consideration for evaluating industrial performance. *An industry composed of firms which all tend to produce at an output rate corresponding to minimum average cost but whose rate of technological progress results in a slower growth of output will in the long run prove to be less efficient and will make less of a contribution to society's economic welfare than will an industry composed of firms which produce at output rates other than minimum average cost but which have a high rate of technological achievement.* Consider, as an example, the following situation.

Assume an industry is composed of 100 periphery firms, each producing 10 units of output and operating at the minimum point of its respective average cost curve. Total industry output is therefore 1,000 units, which, let us say, can currently be sold at a price of $6 apiece. Suppose further that new uses of technology allow the periphery firms to expand output by 3 percent each year and still maintain full production efficiency by operating at minimum *ATC*, and that competition causes any resulting cost savings to be passed on to consumers via price reductions of 1 percent annually. At the end of 5 years industry output will have risen to 1,160 units and the market price will have fallen to $5.71. Now let us assume that this same industry had been composed of three center firms each producing 300 units of output, but operating at output rates other than that of minimum *ATC*. Total industry output initially would total 900 units, or 10 percent less than the output under a periphery firm market structure. The lesser initial output of the center firm, assuming identical market demand conditions, will allow the three center firms to obtain a higher price, say $6.30. But because center firms invest more heavily in R&D and compete more vigorously on technological grounds, suppose they are able to expand output by 5 percent per year using the same inputs (but still producing at other than the minimum point of their new *ATC* curves). And suppose that they also pass along part of the cost savings to consumers by reducing selling price by 2 percent per year.[11] At the end of 5 years the total output of the three center firms will be 1,160 units and their selling price will have fallen to $5.70—results that are equivalent to the periphery firm market performance even though the center firms started out with a lower total output and higher prices. Moreover, every year thereafter the center firm market structure will *outperform* the periphery firm market structure on both *price* and *output* by an *increasing* margin. Center firm prices

[11] Some critics might argue that none of the savings will be passed on to consumers. They would contend that the market power of center firms and the lack of price competition allows them to keep prices up and thereby earn greater economic profits. However, evidence will be presented later (in Tables 13-2 and 13-3) to the effect that such has not historically been the case in a significant number of instances involving major center firm product groups.

will fall by 2 percent compared to only 1 percent in the periphery firm market structure; center firm output will expand by 5 percent compared to only 3 percent for the periphery firm market structure. These results occur (a) despite the fact that the center firms do not produce at the minimum points of their *ATC* curves, (b) despite the fact that center firm profits may be much greater per unit of output, and (c) despite the fact the center firms were not assumed to possess any economies-of-scale advantage over the periphery firms.

This example, although oversimplified, illustrates most vividly why it is long-run dynamic performance that really matters in evaluating market structures and business behavior. Indeed, it is the rate of technical progress, not the efficiency with which a firm operates at any particular moment of time, that ultimately determines the quality and quantity of output. For this reason alone, it follows that the socially optimum type of market structure is the one most conducive to achieving technological advance and innovation, yet competitive enough to protect consumers against abuses of market power. Center firm oligopoly seems to be closer to this optimum than are either perfectly or monopolistically competitive periphery firm markets. Ideally, a market structure of center firms operating under conditions close to monopolistic competition might prove best if market demand for the product were sizable enough to support a large number of relatively large firms. Unfortunately, national and international markets for specific products are usually too limited to allow such structures to exist.

QUALITY COMPETITON IN PERIPHERY AND CENTER FIRM MARKETS

By *quality competition* is meant an independent striving among firms for increased patronage based upon differences in durability, performance, functional design, reliability, efficiency, esthetic value, and the degree of completeness with which the commodity in question fulfills a consumer need. Thus, quality competition emphasizes the competitive aspect of something *better*, whereas technological and innovational competition emphasizes the aspect of something *new*.

Competition among firms on matters of quality appears both in the periphery economy and in the center economy, and of necessity reaches its most intense proportions in markets where the products of the firms are differentiated. When the firms produce homogeneous products, quality competition is a short-lived phenomenon; firms may strive to improve their products, but the improvements are quickly adopted by rival firms, thereby wiping out quality differentials. Obviously, were this not to happen, the firms would soon be producing differentiated products.

Quality competition interacts with the processes of technological change and innovation on a broad front. Product improvements are a result of research and development efforts aimed specifically at developing superior

478

products. On the other hand, using a marketing strategy predicated upon offering consumers a high-quality product acts as a spur to product research and product innovation over a period of time.

Consumers derive major benefits from vigorous quality competition. They tend over time to get a higher-quality product at often no higher prices than before. Quality competition gives consumers a wider range of choice, balanced between economy and luxury models, and it gives firms an incentive to promote durability where the consumer's interest calls for it. It leads firms to cater to the interests of small groups of consumers with specialized tastes as well as to the preferences of the great mass of consumers. And consumers are the beneficiaries of the new products and of the technological advance which is a by-product of quality competition.

There is not much doubt but that the center economy is characterized by a healthy degree of quality competition. The reasons are plain. Not only is quality competition an alternative to price competition, but obtaining a decisive quality advantage over rival firms' products is also a surefire technique for strengthening one's own market position, particularly when the higher-quality product can be sold at a price equal to or not much above the prices of lesser-quality products. Having a reputation for quality can give a firm a significant and perhaps long-lasting marketing edge that extends not only to the markets in which it currently competes but the markets that it may seek to enter as well. Thus, rival firms are very conscious of the quality differentials in their products, and they tend to be quite aggressive in seeking to develop quality features which will give them a competitive advantage. They are fully aware that sustained success in the marketplace depends upon consumers' remaining satisfied with the quality of the item; it is repeat business and not one-time business that generates long-term economic profits.[12] At the same time, intense quality competition among center firms has developed because market pressures make it essential to charge the same price as do competitors offering identical or closely substitutable products.

Center firms have made creditable strides in improving the quality of their products. For instance, the development of FM stereo radio equipment has given listeners greater fidelity of sound and more enjoyment. Refrigerators are now "frost-free" and come equipped with automatic ice makers. Electric ovens are self-cleaning. Whereas in 1955 there was an average of three service calls a year on an automatic washer, today the average is one call every four years. Since 1958, the number of service calls required for a new household appliance during the first year of ownership has decreased almost 50 percent among the leading brands. Even casual observation is enough to detect that such products as color TV's, dishwashers, air conditioners, transistor radios,

[12] Although quality competition impels firms to protect their reputations and those of their products by testing new and improved products for the performance features on which customer satisfaction will depend, there still is no guarantee that all the "bugs" will be eliminated. There are many dangers to health and safety against which public safeguards are needed, and many products no doubt contain dangers that no one yet knows about—despite governmental regulations and rigorous testing by the producer.

and automobiles have been continually upgraded each new model year. The effectiveness of quality competition in the center economy is thus readily apparent, even to an untrained observer. Additionally, it is clear that center firms deliberately try to build up an image of quality and reliability; this is reflected in the two well-known mottos "You Can Be Sure If It's Westinghouse" and General Electric's "Progress Is Our Most Important Product."

Periphery firms with their characteristically smaller activity in new product research and development are, generally speaking, not heavily represented in the vanguard of business enterprises waging spirited battles on quality. The technological pioneering type of periphery firm is, of course, an exception, but such firms are not relatively numerous. Quality competition in the periphery economy often takes the form of specializing in the production of hand-crafted or custom-made commodities for a very limited group of customers who want and can afford "the very best." Examples include furniture, articles of apparel, decorative items, and jewelry. Since economies of scale are negligible in producing these types of commodities and since the markets for them are limited, periphery firms tend to dominate their production. This type of quality competition is important to only a small elite group of consumers; it cannot be said to rank in overall social importance with the style of quality competition found in the center economy. Quality competition among center firms has the benefit of increasing consumer satisfaction and living standards on a broad front, since the products of center firms are commonly found in all but the very poorest of households. The vast majority of consumers benefit from more reliable performance of major household appliances and the numerous new features which center firms steadily incorporate into them.

Quality competition also has another dimension. Consumers do not share the same tastes. Whereas some are very quality-conscious and are willing to pay a little more to get what they believe is a better product, others would rather pay a little less and accept in return a product which has fewer performance features, is not quite as durable, is a little less stylish, and so forth. Hence, quality competition also involves producing a range of quality gradations of any given product. This has the advantage of widening the consumer's choice and allowing him to select the specific variation which best suits his tastes and needs. Significantly, each center firm tends to provide consumers with a wide range of choice for a given product. For example, General Motors has numerous styles and models of automobiles with an almost infinite array of accessory options. Each of the several producers of kitchen appliances, TV's, stereos, radios, sewing machines, or typewriters offers the consumer a choice of the regular model, the deluxe model, or the super deluxe model, each in a variety of colors and designs. In contrast, periphery firms commonly produce a more limited range of commodities; each tends to specialize in one or a few such styles, sizes, and quality gradations. Consumers of periphery firm-produced commodities may nonetheless end up with a wide range of choice by choosing from among many different firms, each of which caters to a specific segment of the market. This is most apparent in the case of apparel firms, where some concentrate upon producing the finest in wearing apparel, others are middle-line firms, and others aim their product at the price-conscious and the budget-conscious consumer.

On balance, it seems fair to conclude that the type and intensity of quality competition which permeates the center economy is typically more socially advantageous than that in the periphery economy. Over time, the improvement in the quality of consumer goods produced by center firms has been substantial and has benefited many consumers. This is not to say, however, that center firm performance could not have been better. There is, undoubtedly, truth to the charge that center firms resort to "planned obsolescence" as a means of getting consumers to replace certain commodities more frequently. Sometimes they deliberately engineer products to have a short life. Some of their so-called new or improved products can scarcely be said to meet a popular, pressing demand; rather they create an artificial "need" of doubtful social value or significance. Firms may fail to incorporate some known improvements because the resulting increase in the durability of the item may have the effect of greatly reducing total sales and hence total profits over time (the longer-lasting light bulb serves as a good example). Firms focus strongly on the aspects of quality that are most visible and profitable and neglect others. Such practices are naturally wasteful of the economy's resources and can in no way be condoned. And as many disgruntled consumers can testify, there is ample room to improve yet further the quality of many consumer products—the prevalence of such consumer attitudes at least partially explains the recent rise of "consumerism." Nonetheless, the overall performance of the large corporate enterprise has been good as regards quality improvements and the range of products offered to consumers.

GROWTH COMPETITION IN PERIPHERY AND CENTER FIRM MARKETS

The character of competition in periphery and center firm markets is further dichotomized by differences in goals and objectives. The harsh whip of market forces and the style of "competition among the many" to which periphery firms are generally subjected makes them defense-minded; they have little choice but to focus their energies upon the immediate and pressing problem of dodging losses and avoiding being thrust into a cost-price-profit squeeze. Hence, entrepreneurial decisions are made with an eye toward short-run profits, and the behavior of periphery firms is closely akin to short-run profit maximization. The preoccupation with short-run problems, coupled with their less distant planning horizon, tends to give periphery firms less of a growth orientation than center firms. This attitude also derives from their limited product line, their limited resources for expansion, and, most importantly, from the ease of entry into periphery firm markets. Once scale economies are taken advantage of (and these are usually small in periphery firm markets), increased industry output is achieved not so much by expansion of existing firms as by the entry of new enterprises into the industry. Thus, in the periphery economy circumstances often combine to inhibit the growth of individual periphery firms; output is expanded by increasing the number of periphery firms in the industry or, if profit opportunities are especially attractive, by the entry of one or more center firms into the market. Only in the exceptional case is a periphery firm able to surmount the barriers to long-term growth and cross into the zone of prospective center firms.

The goals of center firms are typically more diverse and longer-range than those of periphery firms. Center firm managers are most anxious to post persistent and steady gains in profits and sales revenues; they evidence a strong interest in strategies that will strengthen their firm's market position; and they pursue numerous other subsidiary goals compatible with the achievement of their firm's primary goals. Relative to periphery firms, center firms tend to emphasize long-run performance over short-run performance. Their behavior is more nearly approximated by long-run profit maximization, or revenue maximization, or satisficing, than by short-run profit maximization.[13] An especially distinctive feature of center firm behavior is their influential role in determining the speed of economic expansion and the directions of economic growth. Center firms are growth leaders and growth initiators, whereas periphery firms tend to be growth followers. The growth consciousness of center firms is so pervasive and so strong that *growth competition* tends to spring up among rival center firms.

Center firm oligopolists may for a time keep out of one another's way, may respect one another's markets, and refrain from direct price competition.[14] But such a relaxed competitive environment is short-lived, particularly when cost differentials exist among rival firms, as indeed is usually the case. The most profitable of the center firms will be better able to finance investments in improved products and production methods, and in time it will begin to slice into the market shares of the laggard, higher-cost, less progressive firms. Given their drives to grow and expand, center firms will scarcely fail to seize opportunities to increase their market shares at the expense of complacent rivals, unless inhibited by antitrust laws. Aggressive expansion by one firm stiffens competitive forces in center firm markets by impressive proportions, precipitates a battle for market position, and catalyzes the process of growth and growth competition among the firms involved. Thus, managements which fail to keep their organizations on their toes and under pressure toward goals ahead of their performance are jolted out of their complacency by the use of fresh strategies on the part of rival firms.

---

[13] Actual evidence to this effect was reported by Bjarke Fog in a study of international price-fixing agreements. Fog found that, in the industries he studied, small firms preferred a price which was most advantageous in the short term, while large enterprises favored a longer-range pricing policy. For further details see Bjarke Fog, "How Are Cartel Prices Determined?" *Journal of Industrial Economics*, Vol. 4 (November 1956), pp. 16–23.

[14] G. C. Allen, "Economic Fact and Fantasy," Occasional Paper 14, The Institute of Economic Affairs, London, 1967, p. 20.

Once center firm oligopolists have reached the limits of expansion in one market, either because of market saturation for the commodity or because of rumblings in the Antitrust Division of the Justice Department, they will begin to cast about for new outlets for their investment capital. Diversification into new product lines, both related and unrelated to existing products, will be contemplated. So, also, will expansion into international markets. Even the product markets long dominated by one firm are liable to attack from center firms previously engaged in other industries, unless, of course, entry is blocked or profit opportunities are especially dim. Expansion-minded center firms are likely to be attracted particularly toward the invasion of fast-growing periphery firm markets where local or regional monopolies exist.

The power of center firms to move into new industries, new markets, and new product lines is quite strong, and their growth strategies generate a formidable set of competitive forces. Seldom can even well-entrenched center firms block invasion from another center firm when the latter is seriously bent on entering.[15] This is not the case when firms of lesser size and capability attempt entry. It is at this juncture that the path of expansion pursued by one center firm begins to intrude upon the territories of center firms in other industries. In this way established positions are constantly being challenged or else becoming ripe to be challenged. As a general rule, growth competition is most prevalent in markets where product demand expands vigorously over a short period and where, consequently, there is ample room for new firms to maneuver. In markets where demand is growing more slowly and can easily be absorbed by those companies already in operation, entry is less attractive and growth competition is much less active.

The competitive pressures created when large corporate enterprises enlarge their scope of operations and enter markets hitherto the province of others comprise a major feature of competition in the center economy. Examples include the invasion of the U.S. steel market by Japanese steel firms; the invasion of U.S. firms into Western Europe and the Common Market; the rise of the small foreign-made car in the U.S.; the decision of IBM to invade the field for copying equipment dominated by Xerox and the decision by Xerox to initiate the production of computing equipment; the thousands of acquisitions of enterprising periphery firms by center firms seeking immediate footholds in emerging markets and industries; and the

---

[15] A good example of how a center firm invades the markets of other center firms and thereby touches off a major competitive struggle is provided by Procter & Gamble's invasion of the market for household paper products. For years Scott Paper Co. was the undisputed leader in the household paper products field (toilet tissue, paper towels, and disposable diapers). But in 1957 P&G elected to enter the paper products market. Using its potent marketing muscle, which included heavy advertising (P&G is the nation's biggest advertiser), head-on invasions of new territories, the introducing of colors, scents, and designs, and a dazzling array of discounts, coupons, and special promotion deals, P&G steadily upped its share of the roughly $1.2 billion market for toilet tissue, paper towels, and disposable diapers from 0 to 25 percent. Scott Paper's overall market share now has fallen below 40 percent. According to Nielsen figures reported in *The Wall Street Journal*, P&G as of 1971 held 16.2 percent of the single-ply toilet tissue market, which gave it a slim edge over Scott; it held 13.6 percent of the paper towel market, compared to Scott's 27.7 percent; and its Pamper diapers had grabbed off almost 100 percent of the disposable diaper market, forcing Scott to discontinue its disposable diaper line at a loss of $12.8 million. (The remainder of the household paper-products market is divided up primarily among American Can, Kimberly-Clark, Georgia-Pacific, and Crown Zellerbach.) A blow-by-blow account of how P&G pulled off its invasion and put the squeeze on Scott is given in the October 20, 1971, issue of *The Wall Street Journal*, pp. 1 and 22.

formation of the giant conglomerate enterprises with their special emphasis upon diversified growth by merger.

The emergence of the giant corporation, with its wide variety of expertise, its contact with several branches of the economy, and its ambitions for growth and expansion, has by no means relaxed competitive pressures so much as it has altered their form. The notion that the economic history of modern times shows a steady progression from highly competitive markets to monopolistic markets is remote from the truth—the number of firms is not nearly as accurate an index of the strength of competitive pressures as some observers are prone to think. Corporate managements, in the course of pursuing their growth objective, create a generally dynamic economic environment containing effective long-term competitive pressures that are based upon technical progress and new and better products.

PROMOTIONAL COMPETITION IN PERIPHERY FIRM AND CENTER FIRM MARKETS

Business enterprises seek to gain a strategic advantage over rival firms by the many means of product promotion at their disposal. This process may be thought of as *promotional competition.*

Depending upon the circumstances, product promotion may enhance competitive forces in ways that are socially beneficial or it may serve to diminish competition and, consequently, diminish overall economic welfare. Promotional activity which is aimed at identifying sellers, giving instructions for use, describing performance features, and giving terms of sale facilitates competition by informing consumers more fully about the products that are available. Advertising is the medium through which new firms, new products, and improvements in existing products are made known. Advertising enables innovative firms to reach larger numbers of potential buyers rapidly and efficiently, enhancing the profits from innovation, and strengthening the incentive for investing in innovative endeavors.[16] It also permits the realization of production economies which might otherwise be unattainable. Additionally, advertising *may* signal a certain level of quality; commodities which are advertised and have been produced by well-known manufacturers are more likely to prove satisfactory than are nonadvertised products about which consumers know little or nothing. Brands and trademarks help consumers select products of high quality and reliability, and they help consumers reward through repeat purchases those firms whose products they find especially appealing. Hence, the practice of using brands and trademarks as an aspect of product differentiation motivates firms to maintain adequate quality standards. Multiproduct firms are particularly aware that one poor product, through the adverse reputation it creates, can impair the sales of others of its products.

---

[16] Jules Backman, *Advertising and Competition* (New York: New York University Press, 1967), pp. 23–27.

484

On the other hand, it is doubtful whether consumers benefit from the more persuasive aspects of advertising and the exaggerated claims that "ours is better than theirs." The notorious soap, beer, toiletries, gasoline, soft-drink, and (now-departed) cigarette commercials are of dubious social benefit, except insofar as they serve to finance the entertainment supplied by the radio and television programs which they sponsor. The reason is that such advertising tends to be "self-canceling." The million-dollar advertising campaign of one brewery is quickly countered by the other breweries to protect their market position. Few additional people will drink beer because of the beer ads; about all that happens is that the firms fight over whose brands will be favored by those who will drink beer anyway. The extra advertising thus drives up the costs of the brewers and results in higher prices than might otherwise prevail. It unnecessarily raises the financial barriers to the entry of new firms by increasing the costs which they must incur to penetrate the market. And it wastes economic resources which undoubtedly might be put to better social use in other endeavors.

There is a sound theoretical reason to expect promotional competition to be stiffer in center firm than in periphery firm markets. Where consumer's regard one firm's product as a close substitute for that of another and the individual firms are small relative to the market, then the commodity will tend to be less intensively advertised.[17] This is because one firm's advertising expenditures will promote the commodity almost as much as it promotes the particular *brand* of the commodity of the advertiser. The advantage of advertising is thereby greatly diluted. However, if individual firms are large relative to the market, advertising is more likely to pay off even if buyers view rival brands as close substitutes. In the latter case, the market share of the advertising firm is large enough relative to the total market so that its sales gains justify the advertising expense, even though its advertising may spill over and benefit rival firms by persuading consumers to buy more of the commodity as well as more of its own brand. Moreover, because the competition among center firms is so personal and because they are so sensitive to each other's marketing strategy, they are often forced to advertise heavily not merely as a strategy for expanding their market share but as a means of *defending* their existing position from the promotional tactics of rival firms.

It is difficult to generalize, on the basis of the empirical evidence, whether promotional competition in the periphery economy is more or less socially beneficial than that in the center economy.[18] It is plain that *infor-*

[17] Lester G. Telser, "Advertising and Competition," *Journal of Political Economy*, Vol. 72, No. 6 (December 1964), pp. 540–541.
[18] Among the more recent and the more definitive studies of the competitive effects of advertising are Telser, "Advertising and Competition," pp. 537–562; Comanor and Wilson, "Advertising, Market Structure, and Performance," pp. 423–440; H. Michael Mann, J. A. Henning, and J. W. Meehan, Jr., "Advertising and Concentration: An Empirical Investigation," *Journal of Industrial Economics*, Vol. 15 (November 1967), pp. 34–45; Richard A. Miller, "Market Structure and Industrial Performance: Relation of Profit Rates to Concentration, Advertising Intensity, and Diversity," *Journal of Industrial Economics*, Vol. 17 (April 1969), pp. 104–118; W. S. Comanor and T. A. Wilson, "Advertising and the Advantages of Size," *American Economic Review*, Vol. 59, No. 2 (May 1969), pp. 87–98; and Leonard W. Weiss, "Advertising, Profits, and Corporate Taxes," *Review of Economics and Statistics*, Vol. 51, No. 4 (November 1969), pp. 421–430.

mative advertising undertaken by either periphery or center firms can contribute to rational consumer choice. But the zone between informational advertising and persuasive advertising is fuzzy, and most promotional efforts contain elements of both.

It is readily observable that advertised brands are generally more expensive than nonadvertised brands. Whether this reflects the powers of persuasive advertising or the existence of quality differences among the two classes of products is unclear, but it is clear that large numbers of consumers generally consider highly advertised brands as being superior to less advertised brands. We have only to observe the sometimes striking price differentials among competing brands of aspirin, toiletries and cosmetics, soap, alcoholic beverages, and canned goods to recognize the extent to which consumers (rightly or wrongly) associate quality with price. One study of advertising and competition found that in some of the heaviest advertised groups (particularly cigarettes, and health and beauty aids) the introduction of new and improved products is more frequent.[19] This implies a high degree of new product entry and new product competition within these commodity groups, since advertising is the major means of introducing new and improved commodities to the consumer. Particular brands within these product categories were also found to be unable to maintain consumer acceptance for as long a time as branded products in other categories. Therefore, heavy advertising may be indicative of the relative ease with which new products can squeeze out old products; in such cases competitive pressures would appear to be strong even though the number of firms remains the same.[20]

Nevertheless, advertising and sales promotion can be carried well past the point where it is informative, serving merely to barrage consumers with half-truths, misleading claims, exaggerations, and mutually canceling persuasion. The most visible offenders seem to be center firms—in particular those engaged in producing soaps and detergents, beer, soft drinks, headache pills, toothpaste, mouthwash, cereal, tires, gasoline, and automobiles. The major consequences are higher prices and the wasteful use of economic resources which could better have been used to produce much needed goods and services—of either a public or a private nature.

THE CONTRIBUTIONS OF PERIPHERY AND CENTER FIRMS TO NATIONAL ECONOMIC GOALS

Earlier, we noted that one of the criteria for judging business behavior and market performance is the extent to which the operations of business firms facilitate, or at least do not hinder, the pursuit of national economic goals. The issue upon which we will focus attention in this section is the relative

[19] Telser, "Advertising and Competition," pp. 549–551, 556–557.
[20] These days, much of the most formidable competition comes from the branching out of existing firms into new product areas or new markets rather than from the creation of altogether new firms.

486

contribution of periphery and center firms towards achieving national economic objectives. Although empirical evidence on the issue is less than definitive, there are a number of points on which some judgment can be rendered.

The Goal of Price Stability. On an economywide basis, the term price stability refers to a general economic condition in which prices *on the average* are neither rapidly rising (inflation) nor rapidly falling (deflation). In other words, price stability requires that the average price level change by no more than 1 to 2 percent per year.

There is good reason for arguing that center firms contribute more to price stability than do periphery firms. We have seen that the prices of commodities produced by center firms change less frequently than do the prices of periphery firm-produced commodities. This is partly because center firms rely upon changes in inventory levels and order backlogs to smooth out temporary demand fluctuations and because the tactics of price leadership and target return pricing are predicated upon fundamental long-run market conditions rather than very short-run conditions. Center firms are also hesitant to alter prices frequently because of a perceived kink in the demand curves for their products. Periphery firms, however, are less able to withstand the pressures of short-term changes in market demand and supply conditions. Having little or no position of advantage in the market and having relatively slim profit margins, the periphery firm often has little choice but to alter its price-output decisions when demand and supply conditions change. Thus, prices in periphery firm markets respond not only to fundamental market changes but also to short-lived imbalances in demand and supply.

More importantly, center firms seem to have greater organizational capacity for dealing with inflationary forces than do periphery firms. This applies both to demand-pull and cost-push types of inflation.[21] Insofar as demand-pull inflation is concerned, center firm ambitions for growth plus their greater attention to long-range planning and to anticipation of long-run shifts in demand reduce the probability that center firms will be caught short of production capacity to meet consumer demand for their products. Consequently, it is a relatively rare event for center firms to be confronted with the necessity of raising prices as a means of rationing short supplies of their products. This implies that under normal circumstances demand-pull inflationary conditions are less prone to inhabit center firm markets than periphery firm markets. Whereas the output of center firm-produced commodities is increased largely by increases in the production capacity of existing center firms, expanding the output of periphery firm-produced commodities requires the entry of new firms (as represented by the transition from short-run to long-run

[21] *Demand-pull inflation* refers to situations where consumers are anxious to buy a larger volume of goods and services than producers are presently capable of supplying. Hence, a current demand level in excess of productive capacity tends to *pull* prices upward as sellers find they can sell all that they can currently produce at prices higher than the prevailing level. Prices are then raised as a means of rationing the available supplies among those buyers who are most willing and able to pay for them. *Cost-push inflation* is said to represent situations where rising raw material prices and rising wage rates push prices upward; firms are "forced" to raise prices in reponse to rising production costs in order to preserve a margin between prices and average total costs that is consistent with target rates of return and "fair" profits.

equilibrium in the perfectly and monopolistically competitive market models). The entry of new periphery firms is almost certain to take longer than the expansion of a growth-minded center firm, especially when the latter devotes much top management attention to planning for and anticipating expansion in the first place.

Center firms also seem better equipped to cope with rising production costs and the forces of cost-push inflation than do periphery firms. This conclusion follows from our previous observations that center firms are masters at using managerial technology, automation, vertical integration, and technological innovation to suppress rising costs. The superior managerial talents of center firms, their ample financial resources for attacking the problems creating rising production costs, and their propensity to invest in research and development combine to give center firms an advantage over periphery firms in holding the line on selling prices during periods of rising input prices.

Some crude evidence of the relative contributions of center firms and periphery firms to the goal of price stability is given by the data in Tables 13-2 and 13-3. Table 13-2 compares changes in the consumer price indexes for products produced primarily by center firms with the price indexes for products produced primarily by periphery firms for the period 1947 through 1971. Table 13-3 shows relative price changes for periphery and center firm commodities at the wholesale level for the same time period. Although the index values in both tables are imperfect measures of center and periphery prices, since separate price indexes for center firm products and periphery firm products are nonexistent and since shifts in consumer demand undoubtedly account for some portion of the relative price differences, the indexes are still sensitive enough to indicate the relative extent to which prices in the periphery economy have risen faster than prices in the center economy.

As indicated in Table 13-2, the average prices of several products produced principally by giant corporations have risen at a much slower pace over the past 25 years than have the average prices of many periphery firm-produced items. The consumer price indexes for the eleven center firm-dominated product groups shown in Table 13-2 rose by an average of just 10.0 index points between 1947 and 1971; this compares most favorably with an average increase of 54.4 index points for all consumer goods and with an average increase of 66.0 index points for the eleven periphery firm-dominated product groups. In the case of two widely-used center firm products—household appliances and radios—prices have fallen by almost one-third since 1947. At the same time, the prices of electricity, telephone service, automobiles, gasoline, and tires—all of which are largely produced by center firms—have risen at rates far below the prices of such products as apparel, footwear, fruits and vegetables, newspapers, and services of all kinds where small firms are the primary producers. Significantly, it is in the periphery-firm dominated service sector of the economy that the steepest price rises of all have been recorded. While it must be acknowledged that a vigorous

Table 13-2 A Comparison of Consumer Price Indexes for Selected Center Firm-Dominated and Periphery Firm-Dominated Product Groups, 1947 through 1971 (1967 = 100)

Product Group	Year																		
	1947	1949	1951	1953	1955	1957	1959	1960	1961	1962	1963	1964	1965	1966	1967	1968	1969	1970	1971
LARGE-FIRM DOMINATED PRODUCT GROUPS																			
Canned Baby Food	—	—	—	90.9	89.9	93.5	94.3	95.0	98.9	100.2	101.9	101.8	100.2	98.6	100.0	101.5	104.6	106.7	110.9
Building Materials	—	—	—	—	—	—	—	—	—	—	—	95.1	95.8	97.7	100.0	103.8	110.8	113.7	119.0
Electricity	88.9	90.6	91.5	93.6	95.2	95.9	98.5	99.8	100.1	100.1	100.1	99.6	99.1	99.1	100.0	100.9	102.8	106.2	113.2
Residential Telephone Services	73.3	80.4	88.4	94.8	92.3	95.2	100.2	101.8	102.1	102.3	102.3	102.3	100.8	98.7	100.0	100.0	101.3	102.6	108.0
Household Appliances	140.8	140.9	146.4	138.8	126.4	120.6	118.7	117.9	115.2	111.6	109.2	107.4	103.9	100.7	100.0	101.2	102.4	104.1	105.5
Laundry Soaps and Detergents	95.5	82.4	88.7	82.2	87.6	93.9	97.5	97.0	96.0	95.8	96.6	96.6	96.6	98.0	100.0	101.1	102.3	106.0	109.8
New Automobiles	69.2	82.8	87.4	95.8	90.9	98.4	105.9	104.5	104.5	104.1	103.5	103.2	100.9	99.1	100.0	102.8	104.4	107.6	112.0
Gasoline, Regular and Premium	62.2	72.3	73.9	80.3	83.6	90.0	89.9	92.5	91.4	91.9	91.8	91.4	94.9	97.0	100.0	101.4	104.7	105.6	106.3
New Tubeless Tires	71.1	72.0	93.7	93.2	89.8	92.9	94.1	87.4	83.2	87.4	91.5	92.0	94.2	96.4	100.0	105.6	109.7	113.1	116.3
TV Sets, Portable and Console	—	—	156.3	132.6	116.8	122.4	126.2	127.1	123.8	117.7	114.7	112.1	107.3	102.1	100.0	99.8	99.6	99.8	100.1
Radios, Portable and Table Models	—	—	145.0	144.9	133.8	132.0	127.3	125.1	122.9	119.0	117.2	114.6	108.5	101.8	100.0	99.6	99.0	98.8	98.5
All Items	66.9	71.4	77.8	80.1	80.2	84.3	87.3	88.7	89.6	90.6	91.7	92.9	94.5	97.2	100.0	104.2	109.8	116.3	121.3

SMALL-FIRM DOMINATED PRODUCT GROUPS

Product Group																			
Fresh Fruits and Vegetables	60.3	65.4	66.9	73.3	73.2	78.0	79.7	84.6	83.3	85.5	90.6	95.9	97.9	99.7	100.0	109.4	111.1	116.3	121.0
Construction, Repair and Maintenance Services	—	—	—	—	—	—	—	—	—	—	—	87.0	89.4	94.2	100.0	107.1	116.9	128.4	140.0
Residential Water and Sewerage Services	—	—	57.2	65.9	73.5	80.9	83.5	85.6	87.8	91.1	92.0	94.4	97.7	100.0	104.7	111.8	120.4	133.4	
Housefurnishings	92.7	94.9	106.0	102.9	99.2	99.7	99.0	99.3	98.7	98.1	97.7	97.6	97.1	98.0	100.0	103.9	108.1	111.4	114.3
Apparel Commodities	80.4	82.0	88.7	86.7	85.8	88.2	89.0	90.3	90.8	91.2	92.0	92.8	93.6	96.0	100.0	105.6	111.9	116.5	119.8
Footwear	57.5	62.3	71.6	70.0	71.6	77.8	82.2	85.1	85.9	87.1	88.0	88.4	90.0	95.3	100.0	105.3	111.8	117.7	121.5
Auto Repairs and Maintenance	56.4	61.1	67.0	72.3	76.5	82.4	85.5	87.2	89.3	90.4	91.6	92.8	94.5	96.2	100.0	105.5	112.2	120.6	129.2
Medical Care	48.1	52.7	56.3	61.4	64.8	69.9	76.4	79.1	81.4	83.5	85.6	87.3	89.5	93.4	100.0	106.1	113.4	120.6	128.4
Daily Hospital Service Charges	22.0	27.8	32.0	37.4	41.5	47.2	52.7	56.3	60.6	64.9	69.0	72.4	76.6	84.0	100.0	113.2	127.9	143.9	160.8
Recreational Services	—	—	—	—	—	—	—	—	—	—	—	89.0	92.0	95.7	100.0	107.1	112.8	119.0	125.2
Newspapers, Street Sale and Delivery	46.6	54.1	55.6	61.2	62.4	68.8	73.9	75.4	77.2	78.8	83.8	90.4	93.2	96.3	100.0	106.3	111.4	119.4	129.6

SOURCE: U.S. Department of Labor, Bureau of Labor Statistics, *Handbook of Labor Statistics 1972*, Tables 116 and 117.

Table 13-3 A Comparison of Wholesale Price Indexes for Selected Center Firm-Dominated and Periphery Firm-Dominated Product Groups, 1947 through 1971 (1967 = 100)

Product Group	Year																		
	1947	1949	1951	1953	1955	1957	1959	1960	1961	1962	1963	1964	1965	1966	1967	1968	1969	1970	1971
LARGE-FIRM DOMINATED PRODUCT GROUPS																			
Manmade Textile Fiber Products	137.7	135.7	138.3	124.2	123.5	116.9	115.6	112.7	108.0	108.6	108.6	110.8	109.8	103.5	100.0	105.0	106.6	102.1	100.8
Refined Petroleum Products	74.2	81.4	91.8	92.6	92.0	104.1	94.4	95.5	97.2	96.1	95.1	90.7	93.8	97.4	100.0	98.1	99.6	101.1	106.8
Industrial Chemicals	82.1	79.9	100.2	97.6	98.2	102.6	102.9	103.2	101.0	98.9	97.3	96.7	97.5	98.3	100.0	101.0	100.3	100.9	102.0
Plywood	109.4	108.6	131.4	124.8	120.4	110.0	115.5	109.6	107.3	103.6	104.8	103.5	103.5	104.0	100.0	115.7	122.5	108.5	114.7
Drugs and Pharmaceuticals	119.8	106.5	108.8	105.7	105.6	106.2	106.1	106.6	104.6	102.1	101.2	101.1	100.4	100.5	100.0	99.3	99.8	101.1	102.4
Steel Mill Products	45.5	56.4	64.0	70.5	77.2	91.8	96.5	96.4	96.0	95.8	96.3	97.1	97.5	98.9	100.0	102.5	107.4	114.3	123.0
Agricultural Machinery and Equipment	53.3	63.8	70.8	72.1	72.6	78.7	84.5	86.1	87.7	89.5	90.8	92.2	94.0	96.8	100.0	103.9	108.5	113.0	117.0
Home Electronic Equipment	124.2	133.7	119.9	—	120.0	121.8	119.7	117.8	115.4	110.3	107.3	105.6	103.1	101.2	100.0	98.1	94.7	93.6	93.8
All Commodities	76.5	78.7	91.1	87.4	87.8	93.3	94.8	94.9	94.5	94.8	94.5	94.7	96.6	99.8	100.0	102.5	106.5	110.4	113.9
SMALL-FIRM DOMINATED PRODUCT GROUPS																			
Dairy Products	69.8	70.2	78.3	80.3	77.1	81.1	83.1	86.1	88.2	87.7	88.2	88.4	89.0	97.2	100.0	104.8	108.2	111.2	115.4
Beverages and Beverage Materials	68.3	72.6	83.6	86.8	93.1	95.4	93.0	92.8	92.6	93.0	94.7	99.7	99.2	99.3	100.0	102.8	106.0	112.9	115.8
Apparel	95.1	89.9	97.6	93.4	92.6	93.6	94.0	94.9	94.6	95.0	95.4	96.3	97.1	98.3	100.0	103.6	107.2	111.0	112.9
Lumber and Wood Products	73.4	77.7	97.2	94.3	97.1	93.5	98.8	95.3	91.0	91.6	93.5	95.4	95.9	100.2	100.0	113.3	125.2	113.7	127.0
Hardware	48.2	54.9	65.2	68.7	75.9	85.4	89.6	90.3	91.2	91.4	91.5	92.1	93.1	96.3	100.0	102.7	105.9	111.4	116.5
Structural Clay Products (excluding refractories)	62.3	69.0	78.0	79.2	83.8	89.4	92.2	93.7	94.2	95.0	95.5	95.8	96.6	98.2	100.0	102.6	106.0	109.8	114.2
Toys, Sporting Goods, Small Arms, etc.	77.7	81.3	93.1	91.0	90.9	94.2	94.0	94.7	95.4	95.3	95.5	95.5	97.1	98.4	100.0	102.4	105.2	109.4	112.6

SOURCE: U.S. Department of Labor, Bureau of Labor Statistics, *Handbook of Labor Statistics 1972*, Table 120.

expansion of consumer demand for services accounts for a portion of the strongly rising prices of services, there nevertheless is a strong implication that periphery firms in the service sector have been slow in expanding their output capabilities and generally unable to solve the problems of rising costs.

The figures in Table 13-3 provide further confirmation of center firm ability to overcome inflationary forces relative to periphery firms. The average wholesale prices of such center firm commodities as home electronic equipment (TV's, tape recorders, stereos, radios, and so on), drugs and pharmaceuticals, and manmade textile fibers have been trending downward since 1947. The wholesale prices of industrial chemicals and plywood rose but modestly over the period. One of the chief exceptions to price stability in the center economy has been in the area of steel mill products; the steep climb in steel prices is probably due to the general lack of efficiency, technological achievements, and managerial astuteness widely believed to characterize the industry. Overall, the wholesale prices of the eight center firm-dominated product groups increased an average of only 10.7 index points during the 1947–1971 period. In stark contrast, the wholesale price index of all commodities spurted up from 76.5 in 1947 to 113.9 in 1971—an increase of 37.4 index points in 25 years. The mean increase for the seven periphery firm commodity groups was even larger—45.8 index points.

The statistics contained in Tables 13-2 and 13-3 testify to the organizational capacity of center firms to help contain inflationary forces. And the price behavior in periphery firm-dominated markets makes it equally clear that price performance where there is "competition among the many" is not necessarily as socially beneficial as is implied by the models of perfect and monopolistic competition. At the same time, the data in the two tables emphasize why it is dynamic performance, not static performance, that really counts in evaluating industrial performance. Although center firms seem to have wider profit margins and to earn slightly greater rates of return on investment than do periphery firms, the *long-run trend of prices* of many center firm products has clearly been superior to that for periphery firm products. Given the widespread increase in resource input prices (especially labor), the ability of center firms to hold the line on prices and still preserve profit margins is indeed impressive. Such performance strongly suggests that center firms have been quite successful in using new managerial technologies and new production techniques to keep productivity and efficiency rising at rates sufficient to offset a large portion of the rising cost pressures to which their operations have been subjected. In markets where this occurs, center firm performance must be ranked ahead of periphery firm performance, irrespective of the fact that center firm profit margins and rates of return may entail substantial economic profits.

The Goal of National Economic Growth.   There can be little doubt but that the chief impetus for national economic growth emanates from the activities of large-scale enterprises. Large corporations display strong propensities to expand; they are committed to the cause of technological advance, as evidenced by their heavy expenditures on research and development. Even though they are not the source of many major inventions, they are nonetheless society's main organizational vehicle for *implementing* new discoveries. They are part and parcel of nearly all of the showcases of technological achievement. As a consequence, it is in the center economy that most technological breakthroughs are transformed into "better things for better living," that increases in productivity (output per unit of input) are most persistent and usually above average, and that wage rates and salaries are highest. Such are the foundations of increases in per capita incomes, living standards, and the quality of economic life. For these reasons, large corporations are the dominant influence in determining the speed and pattern of economic growth.

Increasingly, of course, government is becoming a significant factor in the process of economic expansion. Governmental expenditures for new national defense technologies and capabilities, for space explorations, and for pure scientific research frequently yield technologies and products which have profitable application in the private sector of the economy. In addition, government policymakers deliberately apply monetary and fiscal policies in ways which actively encourage and support economic growth.

Periphery firms are therefore relegated to a position no higher than third in order of relative contribution to the process of national economic growth. Theirs is largely a supportive, following role in economic expansion. In one sense, though, some periphery firms and industries are major beneficiaries of center economy expansion and the concomitant productivity increases which are realized. The above-average gains in productivity which center firms have typically achieved have in turn slowed their needs for scarce labor inputs, as evidenced by the very modest employment growth in center firms engaged in manufacturing. This has the effect of increasing the supply of labor available to other enterprises, particularly periphery firms outside the manufacturing sector, and thereby accelerating the potential expansion of the types of goods and services they produce.

Contributions Toward Solving Social and Economic Ills. Patently, the U.S. public is dissatisfied with social and economic performance in the fields of housing, urban development, and urban transportation. Sources of dissatisfaction range from the existence of slums and the scarcity of low-cost housing to the more general issue of how to revitalize the cities and overcome the knotty problems of urban decay and urban congestion. Then, too, scattered throughout the economy are pockets of economic depression (the so-called depressed areas) which have emerged primarily from the decline in economic significance of small-scale farming, the New England textile industry, and coal mining in Appalachia. One wonders whether it is a coincidence that the industries most closely related to these problems (the construction industry and the real estate business, in addition to agriculture, textiles, and coal mining) all are dominated by the periphery firm type of enterprise. Large managerial corporations are conspicuously absent in these economic sectors. One of the most commonly proposed solutions to these social and economic ills has been to persuade large corporate enterprises to come to the rescue. Firms such as IBM, Xerox, and Eastman Kodak have located new plants in slum areas to provide jobs expressly for the urban poor. Westinghouse, U.S. Steel, and virtually all of the building material firms have undertaken to design innovative forms of low- and moderate-cost housing which can be mass produced.[22] Numerous other corporate enterprises have attacked social problems boldly, though obviously only a small dent has been made so far. But the organizational talents and resources of large corporations are potentially a principal vehicle through which many social and economic problems can be eliminated. One suspects that if federal monies were provided for massive urban projects on a scale comparable with the military and space programs, the organizational and productive genius of center firms would quickly be focused upon the urban-housing, depressed-area problem complex and an even more substantive commitment obtained from large enterprises to attack these problems.

In addition, it is worth noting that the social problems of poverty and low living standards, to the extent that they are industry-related, are associated almost exclusively with periphery firm-dominated industries. This is entirely predictable. The style of competition in many periphery firm markets provides little margin for wages that are much, if at all, above minimum levels; the pressure to keep costs down is too great. Handicapped or relatively inefficient firms may be forced to make up for their disadvantages via substandard wages and working conditions. Furthermore, the low capital investment and the lesser emphasis upon research and technology restrict the productivity gains of periphery firms and reinforce their tendency to pay below-average wages and salaries. In contrast, center firms are wage and salary leaders. Their wider profit margins, their greater capital investment per production worker, and their propensity to adopt new technologies gives them the ability to pay top wages and salaries. As a consequence, the employees of center firms tend to enjoy a standard of living which on the average exceeds that of the representative periphery firm employee. Center firms are less likely to rely upon substandard wages and working conditions as a means of competing. This is borne out by actual experience, since it is in agriculture, food products, apparel, textiles, lumber, furniture, leather products, fabricated metals, and the service industries, where periphery firms predominate, that wages are lowest and that the living conditions of employees are closest to subsistence levels. Hence, it is not really surprising that federal minimum wage laws have their greatest impact upon periphery firms; center firms almost never have to raise wage levels to meet the requirements of minimum wage laws.

22 "The War That Business Must Win," *Business Week*, November 1, 1969, pp. 63–74. For a broad survey of the efforts of major corporations to solve social problems, see Jules Cohn, *The Conscience of the Corporations* (Baltimore: The Johns Hopkins Press, 1971).

ANTICOMPETITIVE PRACTICES IN PERIPHERY
AND CENTER FIRM MARKETS

It has often been observed that businessmen think competition is a good thing—so long as it affects *other* businessmen. But to the managers of firms subjected to competitive rigors, competition is most irksome. Competition limits discretionary action; it impedes efforts to obtain a secure position of advantage in the market; and it reduces the level of economic profits.

Both periphery and center firms have been ingenious in devising ways to escape the discipline and regulation which competition imposes. Scores of anticompetitive practices, some outlawed and some still legal, have been instituted to keep prices at higher levels and to restrict output so as to keep prices and profits from tumbling. Although nearly every form of collusive agreement, formal or informal, to fix prices or to restrict output is illegal in the United States under the antitrust laws, several violations are uncovered each year and unknown numbers of schemes go undetected.

Some anticompetitive practices are spontaneous, casual, and short-lived; others have proved more enduring. Collusive arrangements may pertain to base prices, shipping allowances, charges for extra features, guarantees, warranties, service policies, output quotas, market shares, or the specific geographic areas or product lines that are to be regarded as each firm's exclusive sphere of interest. In addition, firms may reach understandings regarding product standards, specifications, and the frequency with which products will be restyled and redesigned. Industry trade associations may be formed to promote information-sharing and communication flows among the member firms (these are popular in the lumber and wood products, electrical products, textile, aerospace, alcoholic beverage, utility, transportation, and insurance industries). Among steel, copper, oil, and chemical firms, joint ventures are a popular means of instituting interfirm cooperation, and conceivably they serve to enhance anticompetitive practices. Some firms have knowingly and willingly, though not necessarily collusively, acceded to price leadership in order to avoid price competition. Other firms have persuaded state legislatures to enact so-called "fair trade" laws, whereby manufacturers are given the right to refuse to sell to retailers who do not agree to sell branded products at the manufacturer's "suggested" retail price. Still other firms have used the tactics of merger and acquisition to sidestep strong rivalries, although this practice runs afoul of the antitrust laws when the effect is to *substantially* lessen competition.

Another restrictive and rather popular practice relates to the patent system. Some firms have abused the patent laws by aggressively buying up patents, licenses, and copyrights so as to preclude the emergence of competition from rival products.[23] For instance, when DuPont scientists invented nylon, they did not just patent the basic superpolymer composition and the

---

[23] Scherer, *Industrial Market Structure and Economic Performance*, pp. 390–392.

processes for producing it, but they systematically investigated the whole array of molecular variations with properties similar to nylon and then blanketed their findings with hundreds of patent applications to prevent other firms from developing an effective substitute. Similar tactics have been pursued by firms in such fields as plastics, cellophane, shoe machinery, photo supplies, electric lights, copying equipment, computers, telephone equipment, television, and synthetic rubber. Thus, firms have attempted to insulate themselves from competition by systematically building up an impregnable portfolio of patents. Inevitably these portfolios include many inventions which the firms have no real intention of using directly but which they patent simply to prevent others from using. Thus, inventions are suppressed that might have been commercialized to the advantage of consumers.

A restrictive approach that is often used because of its effectiveness and compatibility with antitrust and patent laws is for firms holding a monopolistic patent position to insert competition-reducing provisions into the patent licenses which it may grant (willingly or unwillingly) to potential rival firms.[24] These provisions take several forms. First, firms to which licenses are granted may be constricted to sell only in a specified geographic area. Second, the price of the licensed product may be stipulated as one of the terms of the license. And third, direct or indirect output limitations may be incorporated into the licensing agreements. For example, the royalty rate that the grantor of the license receives may increase if the sales of the grantee exceed some specified number of units or some predetermined market share. As a case in point, General Electric in the 1930's granted a license to Westinghouse to produce improved light bulbs that called for a royalty rate of 1 to 2 percent on the sales made by Westinghouse up to 25.4421 percent of the two firm's combined sales but a royalty rate of 30 percent for sales exceeding this quota.[25] Also, Westinghouse had to sell the bulbs at prices and terms set by General Electric.

To the extent that anticompetitive practices exist, they are somewhat more prevalent in center firm than in periphery firm markets. The oligopolistic character of most center firm markets makes them inherently well suited to some sort of collusive agreement, since fewness of firms is a necessary prerequisite for reaching viable arrangements. And the prospect of economic profits running into the millions of dollars provides a potent motive for center firms to attempt to suspend some of the stringent pressures of competition. It is more than circumstantial that the most prominent examples of price-fixing and other forms of collusion involve oligopolistic center firms. In contrast, restrictive practices are virtually impossible to institute where markets are comprised of large numbers of relatively small firms, although small businessmen may be equally desirous of escaping the control of market forces. For a large number of firms to reach an acceptable and enforceable

---

[24] *Ibid.*, p. 162.
[25] George W. Stocking and Myron W. Watkins, *Cartels in Action* (New York: The Twentieth Century Fund, 1947), p. 309.

agreement is exceeding difficult; so difficult, in fact, that collusion of any form is almost totally absent in markets which approximate the conditions of monopolistic competition and perfect competition. Such is one of the built-in social benefits of competition among the many. This is not to say, however, that periphery firms do not engage in monopolistic practices. At the local and regional level periphery firms may compete in small enough numbers and may possess enough market power to "rig the market" to their own advantage. Oligopoly, it must be recalled, is not unique to center firm markets; it may well characterize certain local and regional markets dominated by periphery firms.

Nevertheless, anticompetitive agreements in periphery firm markets have neither the frequency nor the overall social impact and social significance of those in center firm markets. Unlike center firm activities, which typically transcend national and international markets, periphery firm operations are much narrower and influence far fewer consumers. While a limited impact in no way excuses restrictive practices among periphery firms, it is in center firm markets where such practices assume their greatest severity. This explains why the Antitrust Division of the Justice Department consistently appears more suspicious of the competitive behavior of large corporations and directs most of its energies toward detecting and prosecuting center firm violations of the antitrust laws. Certainly, on theoretical grounds, there is ample reason why oligopolistic and monopolistic markets should be scrutinized more closely and more frequently than markets structured along the lines of monopolistic and perfect competition.

But even so, restrictive practices should be regarded as the exception rather than the rule—even in oligopolistic center firm markets. The frailty of collusive agreements, the ambitions for growth and expansion, the general existence of spirited nonprice competition, the more rapid pace of technological change and innovation, the fear of potential competition, and the antitrust laws all combine to make collusive arrangements in center firm markets more illustrative of deviant than of normal behavior. The antitrust laws contribute especially to maintaining and encouraging competition. The inclination of the Antitrust Division of the Justice Department towards prosecuting the parties to restrictive agreements, punishing abuses of monopoly power, opposing acquisitions and mergers which tend to consolidate market power and lessen competition, and blocking avenues for creating new kinds of monopolistic arrangements has unquestionably improved the functioning of oligopolistic center firm markets.

THE WELFARE LOSS FROM ANTICOMPETITIVE PRACTICES AND ABUSES OF MARKET POWER

Several estimates have been made of the short-run economic impact of monopolistic practices, business inefficiency, and resource misallocation arising from competitive deficiencies and market imperfections.[26] These estimates indicate that the reduction in total output ranges from less than 1 to as much as 12 percent of the gross national product, with most estimates placing the loss in the neighborhood of 5 to 6 percent of GNP. Professor Scherer has compiled the most comprehensive and explicit estimates of the loss in output associated with imperfect competition. His estimates are summarized in Table 13-4. Although Scherer admits that each of his individual category estimates is subject to a wide margin of error, he concludes that if the "true" output loss could be ascertained, it would probably fall within the 3 to 12 percent range. The estimates of the other experts in the field place the static annual loss at less than 6 percent.

The wide disparity in the estimates of the welfare loss arising from monopoly power suggests that they all be taken with the proverbial grain of

Table 13-4   Best-Guess Estimates of the Output Losses Attributable to Collusion, the Exercise of Market Power, and Related Breakdowns in the Competitive Process, Expressed as a Percentage of 1966 GNP

Causes of Output Losses	Estimated Percentage Reduction in 1966 GNP
Output losses due to monopolistic resource allocation in the unregulated sectors of the U.S. economy	.9
Output losses due to pricing distortions in the regulated sector of the U.S. economy	.6
Inefficiencies in production and higher costs associated with enterprises insulated from competition and therefore not compelled to use the lowest-cost production technology	2.0
Inefficiencies due to deficient cost control by defense and space contractors	.6
Wasteful advertising and sales promotion efforts	1.0
Producing at less than optimal scale for reasons other than product differentiation	.3
Extra transportation costs stemming from inefficient plant locations	.2
Idle and inefficient production capacity due to monopolistic practices and collusion	.6
TOTAL LOSSES	6.2

SOURCE: F. M. Scherer, *Industrial Market Structure and Economic Performance* (Skokie, Ill.: Rand McNally & Company, 1970), p. 408.

[26] Arnold C. Harberger, "Monopoly and Resource Allocation," *American Economic Review*, Vol. 44, No. 2 (May 1954), pp. 77–87; David Schwartzman, "The Burden of Monopoly," *Journal of Political Economy*, Vol. 68, No. 6 (December 1960), pp. 627–630; David R. Kamerschen, "An Estimation of the 'Welfare Losses' from Monopoly in the American Economy," *Western Economic Journal*, Vol. 4, No. 3 (Summer 1966), pp. 221–237; Harvey Leibenstein, "Allocative Efficiency vs. 'X-Efficiency,'" *American Economic Review*, Vol. 56, No. 3 (June 1966), pp. 392–415; Scherer, *Industrial Market Structure and Economic Performance*, pp. 400–409; and William G. Shepherd, *Market Power and Economic Welfare* (New York: Random House, Inc., 1970), pp. 195–198.

salt. Their main significance is to indicate that the *static* effects of slack competitive pressures probably do not place an undue burden on the economy, especially considering that dynamic performance is the truly significant determinant of society's overall economic welfare. If, as has been argued, the style of competition in the center economy is indeed a spur to economic growth, then the static burden of market power and inefficiency is more than offset by the superior dynamic performance that seemingly characterizes numerous center firm markets—many of which coincide with the very markets where the static burden is estimated to be greatest. But at the same time, society's economic interests will still be best served by keeping the static welfare loss from the exercise of market power to the lowest level consistent with good dynamic industrial performance.

Summary and Conclusions

Despite the danger of sweeping generalizations, it is worthwhile to attempt a summary appraisal of the relative performance of periphery and center firm markets and to indicate the character of a socially optimum market structure. However, the reader is forewarned that this is inherently a subjective task, because it requires judgments as to which of the conflicting trends of business behavior are the more important and the more dominant. The following conclusions are tentatively offered.

1. On the whole, industrial performance in both the periphery economy and the center economy is quite good. In fact, considering periphery firms' deficient organizational capacity for improvement and growth, their preoccupation with short-run problems, the positions of advantage which center firms often possess in the markets for their products, and the prevalence of oligopolistic market structures in nearly all of the key industries, overall market performance is almost remarkable. Still, there is room for improvement.

2. Competition among the many tends to produce relatively lower prices and relatively narrower profit margins *in the short run* than does competition among the few. Herein lies the fundamental social benefit of markets structured along the lines of perfect and monopolistic competition. Since, in practice, center firm markets are overwhelmingly oligopolistic, and since the characteristics of perfect and monopolistic competition are to be found only in periphery firm markets, the implication is strong that the prices of periphery firm products are typically closer to average total cost than are the prices of center firm products. This implication has some empirical support (Table 13-1). Accordingly, it follows that the static short-run results of competition among large numbers of periphery firms will tend to be superior to those among oligopolistic center firms.

3. In the long run the dynamic performance of center firms appears distinctly superior to that of periphery firms. Despite an initial handicap imposed by the exercise of market power, collusive and other monopolistic practices, and various breakdowns in competition, center firm performance is stimulated over the long run by the desire for growth and expansion and by market mandates for technological virtuosity. The center firm's large and stable profits, its greater access to financial capital, its ability to withstand short-term setbacks, and its scientific, engineering, and managerial know-how render it better suited to engage in quality competition and technological and innovational competition than is the representative periphery firm. For much the same reasons, center firms also evidence greater organizational ability to suppress rising cost pressures. Finally, center firm contributions to the process of national economic growth far outweigh those of periphery firms. Consequently, the long-term price and output performance of center firm markets tends to rank well above that of periphery firm markets. From the late 1940's to the early 1970's many center firm prices have risen more slowly than many periphery firm prices; center firms have been pacesetters in implementing new product innovations and in pushing back the barriers to technological progress; center firms have realized above-average gains in output per unit of input; and center firms have been in the forefront of enterprises which have raised wages faster than prices. It is precisely on such performance features that the principal foundations of economic progress and rising standards of living rest. Hence, the dynamic pattern of center firm behavior appears to have socially beneficial results which overwhelm the perhaps superior short-run performance of periphery firms. However, some qualification is needed. It must be recognized that while the long-run competitive forces in the center economy do have a restraining effect upon center firm decisions and market independence, the effect nonetheless operates unevenly among the various center firm industries. The long-run dynamic performance of center firm industries consequently varies from "not so good" to "very good" and even "excellent."

4. Ideally, products should be marketed under conditions which would combine the short-term results of competition among large numbers of periphery firms with the long-term performance of competition among oligopolistic center firms. It seems best to have enough firms producing similar products so that short-run competitive forces are strong enough (a) to prevent collusion, (b) to keep profit margins narrow, and (c) to force firms to operate at or very near the minimum points of their short-run and long-run average cost curves. Yet, firms should be large and diverse enough to acquire the organizational traits of center firms that are responsible for their superior long-run market performance. The economic welfare of consumers ultimately depends upon markets being structured so as to achieve the optimum dynamic performance, and it cannot be denied that the large corporate

enterprise has several inherently strong features which are crucial to good industrial performance over the long run.

Several prescriptions for improving the functioning of periphery and center firm markets follow from these conclusions. In some periphery firm markets, notably agriculture, textiles, food products, mining, and certain service industries, representative firm sizes are too small and profits too slim to allow ambitious research and development efforts to thrive and bold innovations to be undertaken; thus, greater concentration may be warranted in order to enable periphery firms to participate more fully in the activities that produce optimum dynamic performance. The forces of short-run competition in oligopolistic center firm markets need to be strengthened in order to (1) eliminate excess production capacity, (2) curtail wasteful promotional efforts which raise costs and prices, (3) minimize the effect of restrictive practices, and (4) inject a short-run competitive element that trims center firm profits margins in markets where profits appear unduly "excessive" or "monopolistic." The thrust of public policy should be geared toward enforcing as much competition as is consistent with achieving economies of scale, product differentiation, technological progress, innovation, and economic growth. Whenever conflicts appear between policies which stiffen short-run competitive pressures and policies which stiffen long-run competitive forces, the long-run oriented policies should take precedence, since sacrifices in short-run performance are sooner or later overwhelmed by improvements in long-run performance.

In general, it would appear that the philosophy of the antitrust laws should be to foster competition and punish restraints of trade. Any sort of collusive arrangements to fix prices, restrict production, divide markets, forestall innovation, or bar entry of new firms should definitely be prohibited. However, it is doubtful whether the national interest is served by specifying any particular limits to size, market share, or market power. Mergers of a horizontal, vertical, or conglomerate variety may be consistent with the public interest, unless they reveal a manifest attempt to restrain competition. The optimum market structure is different in different industries, depending upon technological considerations, organizational capacities for research and innovation, the size of the relevant market, the strength of competition from foreign firms, and other factors. A fiercely competitive struggle where firms are locked in a perpetual battle for survival and walk the tightrope of zero economic profits seldom is preferable to a competitive style that allows firms to provide steady jobs at good pay, earn acceptable profits, produce ever-higher quality products, foster technological progress, and stimulate economic growth.

SUGGESTED READINGS

CLARK, J. M., *Competition as a Dynamic Process* (Washington: The Brookings Institution, 1961), Chaps. 4, 8, 10 and 19.

FERGUSON, C. E., *A Macroeconomic Theory of Workable Competition* (Durham: Duke University Press, 1964), especially pp. 26–31 and 48–82.

MARRIS, ROBIN, "Is the Corporate Economy a Corporate State", *American Economic Review*, Vol. 62, No. 2 (May 1972), pp. 103–115.

SCHERER, F. M., *Industrial Market Structure and Economic Performance* (Skokie, Ill.: Rand McNally & Company, 1970), Chaps. 2 and 17.

SCHUMPETER, JOSEPH A., *Capitalism, Socialism and Democracy*, 3rd ed. (New York: Harper & Row, Publishers, 1950), Chaps. 7 and 8.

SILBERSTON, AUBREY, "Price Behavior of Firms," *Economic Journal*, Vol. 80, No. 319 (September 1970), pp. 511–575.

SOSNICK, STEPHEN, "A Critique of Concepts of Workable Competition," *Quarterly Journal of Economics*, Vol. 72, No. 3 (August 1958), pp. 380–423.

STIGLER, G. J., and J. K. KINDAHL, *The Behavior of Industrial Prices* (New York: National Bureau of Economic Research, 1970).

TELSER, LESTER G., "Advertising and Competition," *Journal of Political Economy*, Vol. 72, No. 6 (December 1964), pp. 537–562.

Questions for Discussion

1. Would it be fair to say that while center firm oligopolists do not compete on the basis of price in the short run (since they all charge identical or comparable prices), they nevertheless compete strenuously on the basis of price over the long run via new product variations, quality differences, and innovation? Explain and evaluate.

2. Do you think that large corporate enterprises are in a position to exploit consumers in terms of the prices they charge for their products? In terms of the quality of the products they offer consumers?

3. Explain why the *incentive* for undertaking technological advance may be weak in the periphery firm sector of the economy.

4. Is the number of firms an important determinant of the degree of competition which will tend to exist in the market for a commodity? Is the size of the firms comprising an industry an important determinant of the degree of competition?

5. Should business enterprises undertake to solve social and economic problems? Is it socially desirable for business firms to direct a portion of their energies toward solving such problems as urban congestion, poverty, slum housing, and racial discrimination? What impact would you expect such behavior to have upon these firms' prices and output rates?

6. Do you think it is possible for competition to be "too strong"? What are the social and economic consequences of an "overly" competitive environment—if there is such a thing? Do you think these consequences are better or worse than those which arise when compeition is "too weak"? Explain.

V

RESOURCE INPUT
DECISIONS
AND
GROWTH EQUILIBRIUM

14

The Resource
Input Decisions
of Business Enterprises

In this chapter we shift attention from product markets to resource markets. The involvement of business enterprises in the functioning of the markets for resource inputs is evident. Engaging in productive activity of any sort requires that firms purchase resource inputs. Moreover, any change in output dictates a change in resource usage. Business behavior in product markets thus quickly reverberates into resource markets, affecting both resource prices and resource employment.

The analysis of this chapter is aimed first at the firm's input decision, with the specific goal of identifying what determines the amount of a resource input a firm is willing to purchase at various input prices. The input decisions of business enterprises are then used as the takeoff point for examining on a broader front the employment rates of resources, the prices of resource inputs, and ultimately the incomes that accrue to resource owners.

In order to bring out the principles governing the operation of resource markets, it will be necessary to examine the resource input decisions of business firms in three contexts: (1) when the firm sells its output in a perfectly competitive product market and buys its input in a perfectly competitive resource market, (2) when the firm sells its output in an imperfectly competitive market and buys its input in a perfectly competitive resource market, and (3) when the firm is confronted by imperfectly competitive conditions in both the product and the resource markets. These are the three situations most frequently approximated in practice.

SOME PRELIMINARY CONSIDERATIONS

Before we embark on the analysis of resource markets, three points warrant mention. First, the concepts of demand, supply, revenue, production, and costs apply to input decisions as well as to price and output decisions. The prices of resource inputs, for example, are in large measure determined by the interaction of demand and supply. However, as regards input markets, the roles of the firm and the consumer are reversed. Resource inputs are demanded by firms, not consumers; and some important inputs, such as labor and managerial talents, are supplied by consumers, not firms.

Second, while a firm's inputs may be broadly classified as consisting of land, labor, capital, and managerial ability, the fact remains that each of these classifications contains an enormous variety of particular inputs. The range of labor inputs for a firm extends from the unskilled to the highly skilled, with each job class having its own wage rate. Thus, even within the same plant the types of labor services employed by the firm may include such diverse sorts as those provided by an aerospace engineer, a secretary, a machinist, a maintenance man, a computer programmer, a drill press operator, and a shipping clerk. Since each type of labor service is characterized by its own unique wage rate and demand and supply conditions, it is not really very meaningful to speak of *the* demand for labor or *the* price of labor. The models of input markets will therefore be presented in terms of an unspecified input. Because the principles underlying input decisions and the operation of input markets are essentially the same, the models presented will have general applicability to almost every resource market—irrespective of whether the input is some type of land, labor, capital, or managerial talent.

Third, although firms may have a variety of goals, the principles of resource pricing and employment are indicated most easily by assuming that the only goal of the firm is to maximize profits. Accordingly, throughout this chapter, we shall assume a goal of profit maximization. This assumption in no way disturbs the thrust of the analysis and the resulting conclusions.[1]

---

[1] For an illustration of the effect which a goal of sales revenue maximization has upon the firm's input decision, see William J. Baumol, *Economic Theory and Operations Analysis*, 3rd ed. (Englewood Cliffs, N.J.: Prentice-Hall, Inc., 1972), pp. 328–330. Baumol demonstrates that a minor adjustment in the profit-maximizing input rules will give the revenue-maximizing input conditions.

The Resource Input Decisions of a Firm
Operating under Conditions of Perfect Competition
in Its Product and Resource Markets

The simplest case of resource pricing and employment arises in an environment where firms sell their products in a perfectly competitive market and buy their inputs under perfectly competitive conditions. For our purposes the most important aspect of a perfectly competitive *product* market is that the firm can sell additional units of output at the going price; consequently, the firm's demand-AR curve is horizontal and product price equals marginal revenue. In perfectly competitive *resource* markets the essential feature is that the firm can purchase as many units of an input as it may wish without affecting its price. In other words, the supply curve for an input which confronts the firm is horizontal at the prevailing input supply price.

THE PERFECTLY COMPETITIVE FIRM'S INPUT DECISION:
THE ONE-VARIABLE INPUT CASE

To identify the key factors underlying the perfectly competitive firm's input decision, suppose we consider first the situation where the firm has only one variable input, all the other resource inputs being fixed. The profit-conscious firm in a perfectly competitive environment will evaluate the outcomes of employing different quantities of its single variable resource— suppose we call it resource X—by their comparative effect upon total revenue and total cost. If using more units of resource X per period of time will add more to the firm's revenues than to its costs, then the extra input unit will increase the firm's total profits (or decrease its losses). On the other hand, if employing more units of resource X per period of time causes costs to rise by more than revenues, then using these input units will result in lower total profits (or larger losses). Hence, *to maximize profits a firm should purchase additional units of a resource input until the added costs associated with employing one more unit are equal to the added revenues it contributes.* This is the basic principle underlying the optimum input decision of a profit-maximizing firm.

The Revenue Gain from a Unit of Variable Input. When a firm employs another unit of variable input per period of time, its output rate rises by an amount equal to the marginal product of the variable input (MP_x). But the prime motivation of the firm for employing more of an input is not the output gain so much as the subsequent revenue gain. If the firm sells under conditions of a horizontal demand-AR curve, then each additional unit of output—suppose we call it product A—can be sold at the prevailing market price (P_A), which in turn equals marginal revenue (MR_A). The perfectly competitive firm's revenue gain from using one more unit of variable input may thus be calculated by multiplying the marginal product of the additional unit of input (MP_X) by the amount of revenue which the firm receives from selling another unit of the product (MR_A). For instance, if adding one more machine operator to the firm's production line causes the output rate to increase by 10 units per day and if each of these units can be sold for $5 each, then the firm's revenue gain is $50.

The change in total revenue associated with using one more unit of variable input (X) is called the *marginal revenue product* of the input (MRP_X), and it may be calculated according to the expression

$$MRP_X = MP_X \cdot MR_A.$$

Alternatively, marginal revenue product may be conceived as the change in total revenue resulting from a change in the use of variable input X, which in discrete mathematical terms is equivalent to the expression

$$MRP_X = \frac{\Delta TR}{\Delta X}.$$

As usual, MRP_X may be more rigorously defined as the rate of change in total revenue as the rate of usage of variable input X changes, or

$$MRP_X = \frac{dTR}{dX}.$$

Note carefully that the concept of MRP differs from that of MR. Whereas MRP refers to revenue changes which result from changes in the usage of *variable input*, MR refers to revenue changes associated with changes in the rate of *output*.

A second and more restricted concept of the revenue change from using more or less of variable input X may be referred to as the *sales value of the marginal product* of the input $(SVMP_X)$. The $SVMP$ is just what its name implies. It is the dollar value of the increased output associated with using another unit of variable input. Put in another way, the $SVMP_X$ is the amount of extra output (MP_X) multiplied by the average price per unit at which it can be sold (P_A), or

$$SVMP_X = MP_X \cdot P_A.$$

Inasmuch as the perfectly competitive firm's selling price equals its marginal revenue $(P_A = MR_A)$, it follows that $SVMP_X = MRP_X$. However, the equality between $SVMP$ and MRP holds true only for a perfectly competitive firm. If the firm must reduce product price to sell the extra output (as is the case in all market situations other than perfect competition where firms face downsloping demand-AR curves), then product price is always greater than marginal revenue, and the values of $SVMP_X$ will exceed the values for MRP_X at a given input rate. Thus, in reality, the concept of $SVMP$ is only a special case of MRP: the case where price equals MR—a situation unique to a perfectly competitive product market.

Although in a perfectly competitive market structure $SVMP$ equals MRP, we shall nevertheless use the concept of MRP to refer to the change in total revenue resulting from a change in input usage. The concept of $SVMP$ will be reserved to apply only to the gross market value (in dollars) of the marginal product of a unit of input.

The Profit-Maximizing Rate of Input Usage.   To illustrate how a firm can ascertain the profit-maximizing rate of usage of variable input X, consider the hypothetical production, cost, and revenue data in Table 14-1. The first three columns of the table show how the output of product A (Q_A) and the marginal product of variable input X (MP_X) change as successively larger doses of variable input X are combined with the available fixed inputs.[2] The price of product A (P_A) is constant at $20 (column 4) because of the perfectly competitive product market, and the corresponding total revenue from the sale of product A (TR_A) is shown in column 5. The values for marginal revenue product (MRP_X) are shown in column 6 and are found by either (a) multiplying the gain in output from using another unit of X (MP_X) by the revenue which the firm receives from the sale of a unit of output (MR_A) or (b) subtracting the successive values of TR_A in column 5 to find the change in total revenue per unit change in variable input. Column 7 indicates the price at which units of variable input can be purchased; the constant price of $180 correctly implies that the firm can buy as many units of variable input as it wants at the given price without inducing a change in the input price. Hence the marginal cost of an additional unit of variable input is the same as its price. We shall find it convenient to refer to the amount which each additional unit of variable input adds to the firm's costs as the *marginal resource cost* (MRC).[3] Since the supply price of X is fixed, $P_X = MRC_X$, and the supply function for X coincides precisely with the MRC function for X. Column 8 lists total variable costs (units of variable input X multiplied by the price per unit P_X). The last column in the table shows the amounts of total contribution profit ($TR - TVC$) at each input rate; total contribution profit reflects total profit inasmuch as the former differs from the latter only by the amount of total fixed costs.

---

[2] Hypothetical amounts of fixed inputs, the prices of the fixed inputs, and the resulting amount of total fixed costs are not included in the table, since they do not really enter into the determination of the profit-maximizing rate of variable input.

[3] As with all other marginal concepts, marginal resource cost may be defined mathematically as the rate of change in the firm's costs as the rate of usage of variable input changes; in symbols this becomes

$$MRC = \frac{dTC}{dX} = \frac{dTVC}{dX},$$

where X refers to the units of variable input. Marginal resource cost differs from margnal cost in that the former refers to the changes in costs associated with a change in *input* whereas the latter refers to a change in costs stemming from a change in *output*.

Table 14-1 The Profit-Maximizing Rate of Resource Input Usage for a Firm Operating in Perfectly Competitive Product and Resource Markets

(1) Units of Variable Input (X)	(2) Units of Output (Q_A)	(3) Marginal Product (MP_X)	(4) Price of Product A ($P_A = MR_A$)	(5) Total Revenue from the Sales of Product A ($TR_A = P_A \cdot Q_A$)	(6) Marginal Revenue Product ($MRP_X = MP_X \cdot MR_A = \Delta TR_A / \Delta X$)	(7) Supply Price of the Variable Input ($P_X = ARC_X = MRC_X$)	(8) Total Variable Cost ($TVC = P_X \cdot X$)	(9) Total Contribution Profit ($TCP = TR - TVC$)
0	0		$20	$ 0	$	$180	$ 0	$ 0
1	14	14	20	280	$280	180	180	100
2	40	26	20	800	520	180	360	440
3	60	20	20	1,200	400	180	540	660
4	78	18	20	1,560	360	180	720	840
5	94	16	20	1,880	320	180	900	980
6	108	14	20	2,160	280	180	1,080	1,080
7	120	12	20	2,400	240	180	1,260	1,140
8	130	10	20	2,600	200	180	1,440	1,160
9	138	8	20	2,760	160	180	1,620	1,140
10	144	6	20	2,880	120	180	1,800	1,080

Observe that total contribution profit is maximized at an input of 8 units of resource X, which means that total profit is maximum (or losses minimum, depending on the amount of total fixed costs) at this input rate. By interpolation, it is seen that $MRP_X = MRC_X$ at 8 units of variable input.

As stated above, profit maximization requires that the firm purchase additional units of input until the added cost of one more unit just equals the added revenue it contributes. Given that the price of variable input remains unchanged irrespective of how many units the firm purchases, the cost of an additional unit of variable input is a constant equal to $180 (column 7). The revenue contribution of a unit of variable input is given by the *MRP* figures (column 6). A comparison of columns 6 and 7 in Table 14-1 indicates that it will pay the firm to employ 8 units of variable input. Increasing the usage of variable input from 7 to 8 units adds $200 to the firm's revenues but only $180 to costs. Should the firm employ the ninth unit of variable input, revenues will rise by $160 but costs will rise by $180; thus, to employ 9 units of variable input is clearly a less profitable act. By interpolation, it is evident that at 8 units $MRP_x = MRC_x$, which satisfies the profit-maximizing condition and, in fact, is the rule by which the firm identifies its profit-maximizing rate of input usage. Inspection of the total contribution profit figures in column 9 confirms that 8 units is the optimum amount of variable input. Total contribution profit is greatest when 8 units of variable input are used. Since total profit is maximum where total contribution profit is maximum, the profit-maximizing rate of variable input usage is 8 units per period of time.

The determination of the profit-maximizing rate of variable input can be illustrated graphically. We have just seen that a firm's input decision is based upon a comparison of how much an input is worth relative to what it costs. How much an input is worth in essence determines the firm's demand for the input, whereas what an input costs is a function of the available supplies of the input and the demand for it in the total market. The firm's input decision can therefore be approached by an analysis of the firm's demand and supply curves for the input.

The demand and supply approach to the firm's input decision is shown in Figure 14-1(a), using the same data as in Table 14-1. The firm's demand curve for a variable input is obtained by plotting the *MRP* figures in column 6 of the table. The *MRP* curve is synonomous with the demand curve for resource X if X is the only variable resource employed. The reason? A firm's demand for a resource input is necessarily predicated on what the resource is worth to the firm in terms of the revenue contribution it can make; this is precisely what is meant by *MRP*. The *MRP* curve rises briefly and then falls because the marginal product of the variable input first increases (due to increasing returns to variable input) and then decreases (due to the inevitable occurrence of diminishing marginal returns to variable input). The relevant portion of the *MRP* curve is the downsloping segment where MP_x is declining but positive.[4] The firm's supply curve for the input

[4] For reasons explored in Chapter 7 (pp. 223–226), the firms will find it profitable to use enough variable input to get beyond the point of diminishing marginal returns unless product demand is very weak or the cost of variable input so high as to make production unprofitable. Hence the truly relevant portion of the *MRP* curve is the downsloping segment.

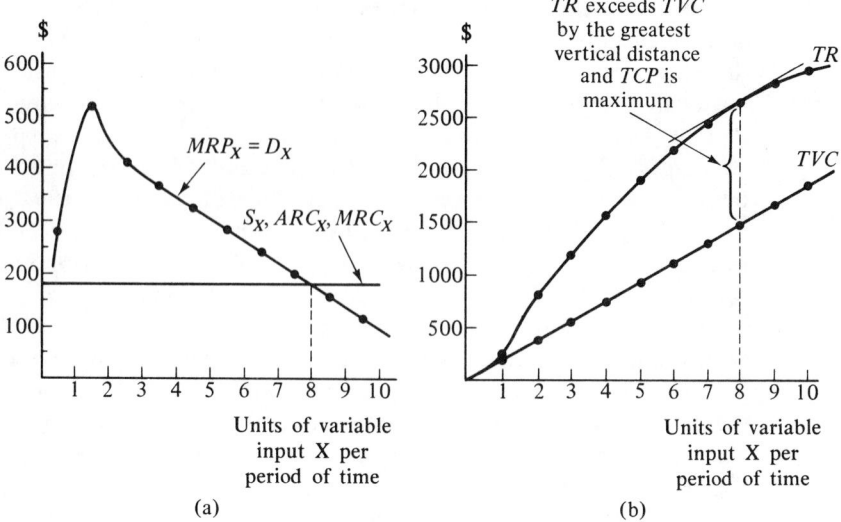

Fig. 14-1 The Profit-Maximizing Rate of Input Usage for a Firm Operating in Perfectly Competitive Product and Resource Markets

is determined by the entries in column 7 of Table 14-1. It is a horizontal line at the level of \$180—the prevailing market price of the input. Since the input supply price is a constant, the input's price is exactly equal to both the *average resource cost* (*ARC*) and the marginal resource cost (*MRC*) of adding more variable input. Or, to put it another way, when perfectly competitive conditions prevail for input X, it follows that $P_X = ARC_X = MRC_X$ and that the supply curve for X coincides with the ARC curve for X and the MRC curve for X. These relationships are so indicated in Figure 14-1(a).

The firm's demand and supply curves [Figure 14-1(a)] intersect at a point corresponding to eight units of variable input. This intersection identifies the profit-maximizing amount of variable input. At inputs of fewer than 8 units per period of time an additional unit of variable input adds more to total revenue than it adds to total cost, thereby giving the firm a clear incentive to increase its variable input usage. This is the same as saying *MRP* exceeds *MRC* at inputs below 8 units. However, to go beyond 8 units per period of time will result in total costs rising faster than total revenues, and the additional variable input will fail to "pay its own way." Hence, the firm will reduce its total profits (or increase losses) by purchasing more than 8 units of variable input. Therefore, it can be concluded from the demand and supply analysis that *a perfectly competitive firm will maximize profits by employing additional units of variable input until the point is reached where the input's marginal revenue product equals its marginal resource cost.* The rationale underlying the $MRP = MRC$ rule is analogous to the $MR = MC$ rule. The only real difference is that the former refers to the profit-maximizing rate of input usage, the latter to the profit-maximizing rate of output. The two rules give the same operating results in terms of price, output, and profit, but they approach the determination of the profit-maximizing conditions via a different route.

Plotting the total revenue and total variable cost data in columns 8 and 9 of the table verifies the $MRP = MRC$ rule from another vantage point [see Figure 14-1(b)]. Note that in Figure 14-1(b) the horizontal axis has been drawn to represent units of variable input rather than units of output, thereby relating TR and TVC to the usage of variable input rather than to output. The maximum vertical distance between TR and TVC occurs when their slopes are equal. The slope of the TR curve when variable input (X) is plotted on the horizontal axis is dTR/dX, which, by definition, is MRP_X. Similarly, the slope of the TVC curve in these circumstances is $dTVC/dX$, which corresponds precisely to the meaning of MRC_X. Hence, the profit-maximizing rate of variable input usage is reached when the revenue gain from using more variable input (MRP_X) equals the added cost of purchasing the variable input (MRC_X). Can you explain the economics of the shapes of the TR and TVC curves in Figure 14-1(b)? Why is the TVC curve linear? Why does TR increase at a decreasing rate? [*Hint:* Your answers should concern the fact that the graph shows TR and TVC to be a function of the usage of variable input rather than the quantity of output.]

MATHEMATICAL CAPSULE 10

The Profit-Maximizing Input Rate under Conditions of Perfect Competition in the Product and Resource Markets

The proposition that a perfectly competitive firm will maximize profits by purchasing units of a variable input until the point is reached where MRP equals MRC is easily demonstrated in mathematical terms.

Let the firm's production function for producing product A be

$$Q_A = f(X),$$

where Q_A = units of output of product A and X = units of any variable resource input. Then the marginal product function for input X may be written as

$$MP_X = \frac{dQ_A}{dX} = f'(X).$$

The firm's profit function may be expressed as

$$\pi = TR - TC.$$

But by definition

$$TR = P_A Q_A$$

and

$$TC = TFC + TVC.$$

Since $TVC = P_X X$, we can rewrite the expression for TC as

$$TC = TFC + P_X X.$$

Substituting into the profit function gives

$$\pi = P_A Q_A - (TFC + P_X X).$$

However, since $Q_A = f(X)$, the expression for TR_A becomes $P_A \cdot f(X)$, which when substituted into the profit function gives

$$\pi = P_A \cdot f(X) - TFC - P_X X.$$

In mathematical terms, profit maximization requires that

$$\frac{d\pi}{dX} = 0,$$

which, translated into words, means variable input must be added to the point where profits cease to increase.

Taking the derivative of the profit function with respect to X gives

$$\frac{d\pi}{dX} = P_A \cdot f'(X) - P_X.$$

Setting this expression equal to zero to satisfy the profit-maximizing condition gives

$$P_A \cdot f'(X) - P_X = 0.$$

For this condition to be met, it is apparent that the first term of the above expression must equal the second term or that

$$P_A \cdot f'(X) = P_X.$$

But $f'(X)$ is, by definition, the same as MP_x, which gives

$$P_A \cdot MP_X = P_X.$$

The term $P_A \cdot MP_X$ is precisely equal to MRP_X, because in perfect competition $P_A = MR_A$. And $P_X = MRC_X$, because the input supply price in a perfectly competitive resource market is a constant value. So the condition for obtaining the profit-maximizing input rate becomes

$$MRP_X = MRC_X,$$

which is what we set out to establish.

THE PERFECTLY COMPETITIVE FIRM'S INPUT DECISION:
THE TWO-VARIABLE INPUT CASE

When the firm's production process utilizes two or more variable inputs, its input decisions become considerably more complex. The reason rests with the interdependence which exists among the variable inputs. A change in the price of one variable input not only affects the amount it will pay the firm to use of that input but also alters the optimum amounts of the other variable inputs. Moreover, these alterations in the usage of the other variable inputs will trigger changes in the marginal product of the variable input whose price changed, thereby resulting in still further input adjustments.

To illustrate the nature of the firm's input decision when several resource inputs can be varied, consider the simplest case where the firm has only two variable inputs—X and Y. To keep things manageable, we shall restrict the discussion to determining just the firm's optimum input rate for X. Suppose the price of input X is initially fixed at P_{X1} and the amount of input X which will maximize the firm's profits is X_1, as shown in Figure 14-2. When the amount of resource Y is held constant, the marginal revenue product curve for X is MRP_1. Now suppose a shift in the supply conditions for input X causes the price of X to fall from P_{X1} to P_{X2}. The change in the supply price of X has three effects which are pertinent to determining the new profit-maximizing input rate of X: the *substitution effect*, the *output effect*, and the *marginal cost effect*.

The substitution and output effects were explored briefly in Chapter 7 and may be indicated by means of isoquant-isocost analysis.[5] As explained in Chapter 7, when the price of one input falls, the firm will be induced to use more of it and less of other variable inputs. Let the initial prices of

---

[5] For a review of this material see the section in Chapter 7 on "The Impact of Changes in Resource Prices," pp. 243–247.

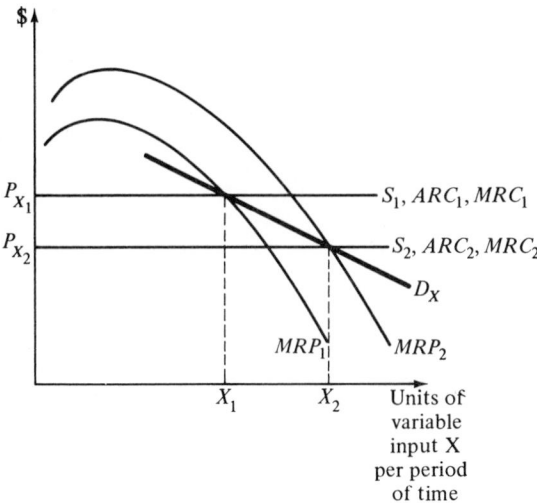

Fig. 14-2 The Perfectly Competitive Firm's Input Decision for Two or More Variable Inputs

inputs X and Y be P_{X_1} and P_{Y_1}, the initial output be on isoquant Q_1, and the equilibrium input rates be X_1 and Y_1 at point A, as shown in Figure 14-3. If the price of X falls from P_{X_1} to P_{X_2}, the isocost line rotates to the right, allowing the firm to produce Q_2 units of output with the same total cost outlay, using X_2 units of variable input X and Y_2 units of variable input Y (point B).

The movement from A to B can be broken down into the substitution effect and the output effect. The substitution effect shows the change in the optimum input combination that would result if the firm decided to continue to produce Q_1 units of output; it is indicated graphically by the movement from point A to point C on isoquant Q_1 in Figure 14-3. Point C is found by drawing a third isocost line tangent to isoquant Q_1 but parallel to the isocost line with extreme points TC_1/P_{Y_1} and TC_1/P_{X_2}. The isocost line tangent to Q_1 at point C has a slope equal to the new price ratio of inputs X and Y (P_{X_2}/P_{Y_1}) and is indicative of the optimum input combination for producing Q_1 units of output, given input prices of P_{X_2} for X and P_{Y_1} for Y. The difference in the input combinations at A and C indicates the extent to which the firm is induced to use *more* of input X and *less* of input Y when the price of X falls from P_{X_1} to P_{X_2}, the price of Y remains fixed, and the firm decides to produce the *same* amount of output after the reduction in the price of X as before the price change. The relevance of the substitution effect to the firm's input decision is that the substitution of input X for input Y will cause the marginal product curve for input X to shift downward, thereby making the values of

MP_x smaller at each input rate of X than before. The lower marginal productivity of X arises from the fact that having fewer units of input Y to work with makes input X less productive.[6]

The output effect is represented by the movement from point C to point B in Figure 14-3. It reflects the change in optimum input combination which is associated solely with a change in the firm's output rate, the ratio of input prices being held constant. The output effect can be counted upon to result in an increase in the usage of both inputs X and Y.[7] Taken by itself, the output effect will shift the marginal product curve for input X upward because the presence of more of input Y will make X more productive. In other words, having more of input Y to work with will cause the values of MP_x to be higher at each input of X than they otherwise would be. (Note that the impact of the output effect upon MP_x is in the opposite direction as the impact of the substitution effect.)

The marginal cost effect stems from the lower price of input X. When the supply price of resource X falls from P_{x_1} to P_{x_2}, the marginal cost of

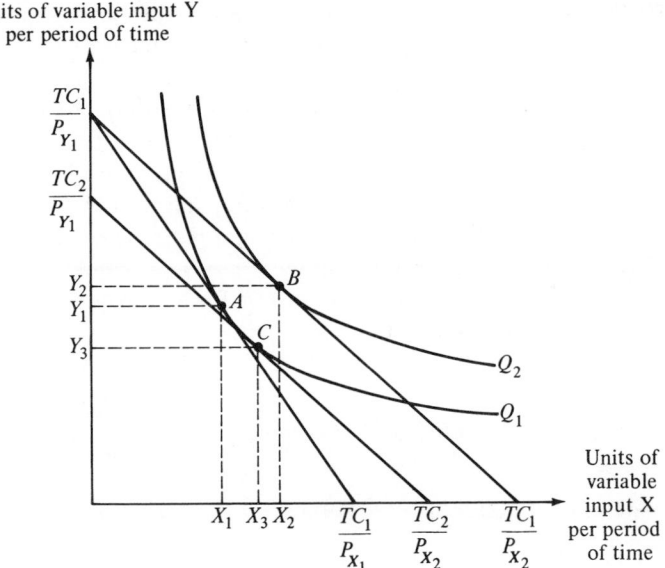

Fig. 14-3   The Substitution and Output Effects Resulting from a Change in an Input's Supply Price

[6] The logical basis for this statement may be more apparent if one recalls that in situations where one input is variable and the remaining inputs are fixed, a reduction in the amount of fixed inputs causes the production function to shift downward, reflecting lower marginal productivity for the variable input. Consequently, it follows that reductions in the use of input Y will make input X less efficient because the units of X have fewer units of complementary input with which to produce the product.

[7] Only in rare and relatively unimportant cases will the output effect fail to affect both variable inputs in the same manner. Increases in the output rate normally require increased usage of all variable inputs. Similarly, decreases in output usually are accompanied by reductions in the use of each variable input.

producing each unit of output is reduced, because it costs less than before to obtain the variable input needed to produce more output. Thus, the marginal cost curve shifts downward, with the result that the firm's marginal cost curve will intersect the firm's marginal revenue curve at a *larger* output than before (the reader should verify this statement for himself by drawing a graph). Accordingly, the profit-maximizing rate of input for the firm is increased. The marginal cost effect thus leads to an expansion of output; in turn, more of both inputs X and Y will be required, and the marginal product curve for input X will shift upward.

To recapitulate, when the price of variable input X falls (the prices of all other variables inputs remaining constant), the substitution effect (by itself) tends to shift the marginal product curve for input X *downward*. In contrast, the output and marginal cost effects precipitate an *upward* shift of the MP_X curve. The net result will be a shift of MP_X upward (and quite possibly a change in its slope at each point as well).[8]

The consequently larger values of MP_X at each level of input, when multiplied by the firm's marginal revenue from additional sales, will cause the firm's MRP curve for input X to shift upward and to the right. Now, turning back to Figure 14-2, suppose the input adjustment and the subsequent changes in MP_X combine to shift the firm's marginal revenue product curve from MRP_1 to MRP_2. The new MRP curve, coupled with the new supply price of P_{X_2}, will generate a new profit-maximizing equilibrium input rate at X_2 units. By changing the price of X again, tracing through the substitution, output, and marginal cost effects upon MP_X, and then finding the new MRP curve for input X, other profit-maximizing input rates for X can be generated. The resulting equilibrium supply prices and input rates, when connected, form the firm's input demand curve for X, shown as line D_X in Figure 14-2. The points along D_X show the quantities of input X which will maximize the firm's profits when the prices of other variable inputs are held constant and the usages of all other variable inputs are appropriately adjusted for changes in the supply price of X.

THE FACTORS INFLUENCING A FIRM'S INPUT DEMAND

We are now in a position to indicate explicitly the factors which ultimately determine a firm's demand for a resource input.[9] These factors may be grouped into two classes: (1) those which influence the *location* of the firm's

[8] Unfortunately, a proof of this statement involves an onerous mathematical exercise. The reader is thus asked to accept the statement on faith. Those who desire to pursue the point should consult Charles E. Ferguson, "Production, Price, and the Theory of Jointly Derived Input Demand Functions," *Economica*, Vol. 33, No. 132 (November 1966), pp. 454–461; and Charles E. Ferguson, "'Inferior Factors' and the Theories of Production and Input Demand," *Economica*, Vol. 35 No. 138 (May 1968), pp. 140–150. An additional treatment may be found in Charles E. Ferguson, *The Neoclassical Theory of Production and Distribution* (London and New York: Cambridge University Press, 1969), Chaps. 6 and 9.

[9] This discussion is equally applicable to firms operating in either perfectly or imperfectly competitive product markets.

input demand curve and which cause it to *shift* and (2) those which determine the sensitivity or elasticity of the firm's input demand to input price changes.

Changes in the Firm's Input Demand. As the previous discussion suggests, the determinants of a firm's input demand relate to the input's productivity and to the revenue contribution it makes to the firm's activities. However, we can be much more specific than this.

First, it is obvious that a firm's input demand is derived from the demand of consumers for the firm's products. The more intense is consumer demand for its products, the greater will be the firm's need for resource inputs to produce them. If improvements in a product or reductions in its price stimulate consumer demand, then the firm's input demand will also increase. A resource input that is very proficient in helping to produce a commodity in strong demand by consumers will itself have a strong demand. On the other hand, a firm's demand for an input will be slight if its product demand is small, irrespective of the input's own productivity. There will be no demand for an input which is enormously capable of producing something no one wants to buy.

Second, a firm's input demand is dependent upon known technology and the directions of technological change. The technological character of a firm's production process is a fundamental factor in determining the marginal product function for each and every input. And, clearly enough, technological change alters the marginal productivity of a firm's resource inputs. Thus, technological progress that makes an input more productive also increases the demand for that input. Technological progress which makes an input less productive relative to other inputs ultimately reduces the demand for the input and may even eliminate demand for it entirely.

Third, the price of an input relative to other inputs influences input demand. As isoquant-isocost analysis demonstrates, the relative prices among substitutable inputs determine a firm's choice of production technologies from the array of known production recipes. If an input becomes cheaper relative to other inputs, the demand for it will gradually increase as producers alter their production techniques so as to substitute the lower-priced resource inputs for the relatively higher-priced ones.

Fourth, the demand for an input will be greater the higher is the marginal revenue which the firm receives from additional sales of output. Whatever the marginal product of an input is, the higher the value of MR the larger will be the input's marginal revenue product. Since an input's MR values are of paramount importance in determining the profit-maximizing input rate, it necessarily must be true that anything which increases MRP will also increase the firm's input demand—other things being equal.

And last, the greater the quantity of other inputs employed, the greater the demand for a given input. This proposition follows from the fact that giving an input more of other inputs with which to work and produce allows the input in question to be more productive and thereby have a higher marginal product at each input rate than otherwise. For example, providing automobile workers with more high-speed metal-stamping machines and automated assembly equipment will result in their being more productive and more capable of achieving a greater output per man-hour worked—which clearly means a higher marginal product of labor and, in turn, a higher marginal revenue product for labor.

The Firm's Elasticity of Demand for a Resource Input. Four important factors influence the degree to which a firm's input demand will respond to changes in the price of an input. As is customary in economics, we shall refer to this responsiveness or sensitivity as the firm's elasticity of demand for a resource input.[10]

First, the rate at which the marginal product of an input changes as the firm increases or decreases its usage has a bearing upon the degree to which a firm will alter its input rate as a consequence of a change in the input's supply price. This follows from the fact that the marginal revenue product of an input is equal to $MP \cdot MR$. Whatever the value of MR, the faster the value of MP declines, the more rapid will be the decline in MRP and the less elastic will be the firm's demand for the input. If, for example, the technological character of a firm's production function is such that the marginal product of variable input X declines slowly as larger doses of X are combined with the fixed inputs, then the effect will be to cause the MRP values for X to decline more slowly than otherwise. This will enhance the elasticity of the firm's demand for the input. On the other hand, if the marginal product of X falls off sharply as more of X is used, then the effect is to cause the MRP curve for X to decline more swiftly, thereby reducing the elasticity of the firm's input demand.

Second, the derived nature of resource demand necessarily makes the elasticity of a firm's input demand dependent upon the elasticity of demand for the firm's product. A decline in the price of a product having an elastic demand will give rise to a sharper increase in output and therefore a stronger increase in the amounts of the variable inputs used to produce it than will a comparable decline in the price of a product having an inelastic demand.

Third, the degree to which resources can be substituted for one another determines an input's demand elasticity. The larger the number of substitutes for an input and the greater the ease with which substitution can be initiated and accomplished, the greater will be the elasticity of demand for that input. If a book publisher finds that some six or seven grades of

[10] It will be recalled from earlier discussion (Chapter 5) that the concept of elasticity is nothing more than a ratio of percentage changes. The elasticity of demand for a resource input X (ϵ_X) may be thought of as

$$\epsilon_X = \frac{\text{percent change in the input rate of X}}{\text{percent change in the supply price of input X.}}$$

paper are equally satisfactory in manufacturing college textbooks, then a rise in the price of any one grade of paper can be counted upon to cause a very sharp drop in its demand as other grades of paper are readily substituted. At the other extreme, where an input has few if any good substitutes, the demand for it tends to be highly inelastic. For instance, the lack of good substitutes for sheet steel in manufacturing automobile bodies, for electricians in performing electric wiring functions for new construction projects, or for crude oil in the refining of motor fuels explains why their demands are relatively unresponsive in the short run to increases in their supply prices.

Finally, the elasticity of demand for a resource input is determined in part by the fraction of total production costs accounted for by the input. The construction industry offers a good illustration of this proposition. In construction, labor costs are approximately 50 percent of total costs. If the wage rates of all the many types of construction labor rise by 10 percent, then total construction costs will rise by 5 percent. Rising construction costs will push the prices of new construction upward and reduce new construction activity. In turn, the demand of construction firms for construction labor will be weakened. However, suppose only the wage rates of bricklayers rise by 10 percent, the wage rates of other types of construction labor remaining fixed. Further suppose that the total wages paid to bricklayers amount to only 2 percent of total costs. Then a 10 percent rise in bricklayers' wages will cause total costs to rise by only .2 percent—an amount not likely to affect the demand for new construction to any important degree nor therefore the demand for bricklayers and other construction labor. Hence as a general rule, the smaller the fraction of total costs accounted for by an input, the more inelastic will be a firm's demand for the input.[11]

THE INDUSTRY DEMAND FOR A RESOURCE INPUT

The total industry demand for a resource input is found by combining the amounts of input that all firms in the industry will employ at a given price. This is slightly different from horizontally summing the individual firm demand curves for the input, because in perfect competition, when all firms change their output rates simultaneously, the market price of the product will also change. The resulting change in marginal revenue will trigger a shift in each firm's *MRP* curve for the input. Despite these complexities the industry demand curve for the input can be determined; the procedure is illustrated in Figure 14-4.

The profit-maximizing input rates for a representative firm in a perfectly

---

[11] It is, incidentally, the small portion of total costs coupled with a lack of good substitutes which explains why craft unions having more or less monopoly control over the supply of a specific type of labor have been consistently able to negotiate substantial wage rate increases for their members. The 6 to 10 percent annual wage increases which the various craft unions in the construction industry achieved during the 1968–1971 period are a case in point.

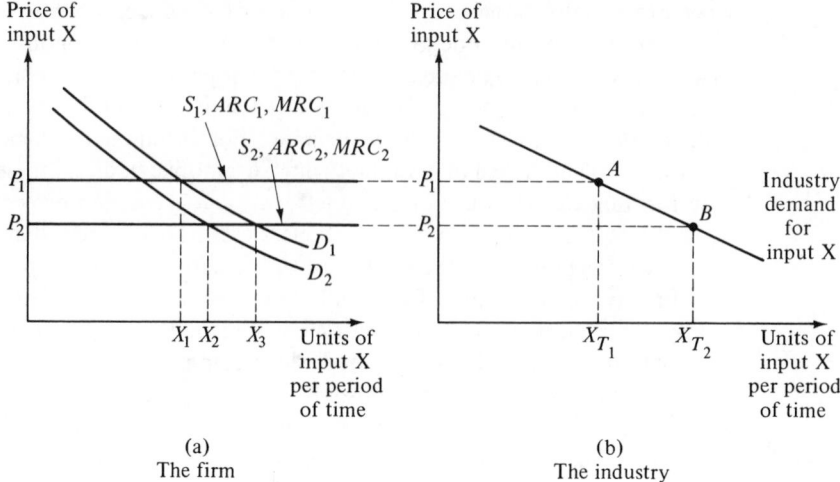

Fig. 14-4 Deriving the Industry Demand for a Resource Input in a Perfectly Competitive Environment

competitive industry are shown in panel (a). Given some market price for the firm's product, the firm's demand for input X is represented by the curve labeled D_1, derived according to the method described in Figure 14-2. If the supply price of the input is P_1 dollars, the firm's equilibrium input is X_1 units. Adding together the optimum input usages of all the firms in the industry gives a total demand of X_{T_1} units at input price P_1, shown as point A in Figure 14-4(b).

Now suppose the price of input X falls to P_2, perhaps because of greater available supplies of the input. This shifts the firm's marginal cost curve downward at each output rate and causes MC to intersect MR at a greater output rate. Assuming nothing else changes, the representative firm will expand its output rate by moving along D_1 in panel (a) and increasing its usage of X to X_3 units per period. However, we cannot assume that nothing else changes; what the representative firm does, the other firms will find it advantageous to do as well. The lower price of X affects the MC curves of all the firms. Hence, when the price of input X falls, *all* firms will be induced to expand their output rates and thereby use more of input X. The industry-wide expansion of output will shift the industry supply curve for the product to the right, causing the market price of the product to fall. In turn, the lower product price means a lower marginal revenue and thus a lower marginal revenue product for X at each input rate. The effect is to shift the firm's input demand curve for X down and to the left, say from D_1 to D_2. The new profit-maximizing input rate for the representative firm at input price P_2 therefore is X_2 units and not X_3 units. Aggregating for all firms in the industry gives a total industry demand of X_{T_2} units at input price P_2, shown as point B in Figure 14-4(b). Points in addition to A and B can be determined by considering still other input prices. Connecting these points by a line gives the industry demand curve for input X.

THE INDUSTRY SUPPLY OF A RESOURCE INPUT

The supply of a resource input to an industry refers to the various input quantities which owners of the input are willing and able to make available to firms in the industry at various prices. Since in a free economy resource owners have a choice of supplying their resources to one line of production or another, it is reasonable to presume that they will direct them to the use and to the industry which offers the greatest prospect of reward—and not necessarily just the greatest monetary reward, because the reward package often includes nonmonetary as well as monetary elements.

Insofar as capital and land inputs of various types are concerned, the expected monetary reward is generally the predominant consideration. However, the case of labor inputs is more complicated. Wage rates and salaries are certainly important, but so are such features as the time and expense in learning a job or entering a profession, the opportunity for obtaining personal satisfactions from the job, the prospects for promotion and advancement, the regularity of employment, the environmental conditions under which the work is performed, the specific community and geographical area in which the job is located, and the social status of the occupation. Each job type offers a package of monetary and nonmonetary considerations that each potential worker may evaluate differently in the light of his own preferences. Given a choice of occupation and jobs, each member of the labor force can reasonably be expected to choose the one which he perceives as offering the best total package relative to his interests, skills, and capabilities. Nonetheless, the supply of labor inputs may be expressed as a function of monetary rewards in the short run. Experience indicates that the nonmonetary elements affecting resource allocation change rather slowly and can therefore be treated as a constant for purposes of short-run analysis.

Logic dictates that a positive relation between input prices and input supplies will exist for most all types of land, natural resource, manpower, and capital goods inputs. As the amount of monetary reward accruing to an input rises, resource owners will ordinarily be induced to supply the input in larger quantities per period of time. For instance, higher prices for minerals and natural resources intensify efforts to discover and tap more sources of supply. As wage rates in one occupation rise relative to wage rates in other occupations, the number of people seeking employment in that occupation will tend to rise. The greater the wage differential between firms, the more will workers gravitate from low-paying to high-paying firms; similarly, the greater the wage differentials between industries and between geographical regions, the more mobile will workers become.[12] Accordingly, input supply curves are upward sloping, owing to the tendency of inputs to be drawn to employments where the rewards are highest.

How responsive input supplies will be to changes in input prices depends on several factors:

1. The size of the economic unit under consideration—the total economy, a locality, an industry, or a single firm. The supply of an input to the economy as a whole may be fixed in the short run, while at the same time the supply to a particular locality, industry, or firm may be highly elastic or even perfectly elastic. Although at any given time there is just so much land, labor, or capital input in the entire economy (or in a more restricted geographical area), firms and industries may be able to obtain as much of the available supply of an input as they may need without changing their offer prices because they may require only a negligible fraction of the available supply of an input.

2. The period of time considered. The response of input supplies to input price changes is greater over the long run than over the short run, primarily because the degree of resource mobility increases with time. It takes time to discover and develop new mineral deposits, to shift capital investment out of less profitable endeavors into more profitable endeavors, to convert land from one use to another, to retrain workers or induce them to move into areas where job opportunities are expanding, and to inform people preparing to enter the labor force of the changing prospects of economic reward in the various professions. Hence, the elasticity of supply of an input becomes greater with the expansion of the time frame under consideration.

3. Whether the input is unique to a particular industry or whether it is widely used. The supply of an input used only by a single industry tends to be less elastic than inputs which are used by a number of different industries, though in both cases the input supply curve is upward sloping to the right. The more versatile and mobile an input is, the more elastic will be its supply to a particular industry.

The value of the elasticity of supply, however, is not of paramount importance for our purposes. The basic analysis will be the same whatever the shape and degree of elasticity of the industry supply curve—even if it is vertical or backward rising.[13]

---

[12] Sometimes substantial wage differentials exist and are maintained for long periods, but beyond some point a wage differential can become too great for a firm, or an industry, or a locality, or a region to maintain without affecting labor supply conditions. The wages workers expect from one firm bear some relationship to the wages similar workers elsewhere receive, and if workers' expectations are grossly unrealized, the supply of labor is bound to be affected. The supply of job applicants may not totally dry up, but their quality may deteriorate. Moreover, labor turnover is likely to be above average as workers' dissatisfaction with their wages pushes them to look for alternative employment.

[13] The backward-bending supply curve for an input arises from that fact that above certain input price levels, resource owners prefer to withdraw some units of input from the market to meet leisure-time or other

THE PRICING AND EMPLOYMENT OF A RESOURCE INPUT

The industry demand and supply curves for an input determine the equilibrium price which firms in the industry pay for the input and the equilibrium amount of the input employed in the industry. Figure 14-5 shows the industry demand and supply curves for input X. Their intersection determines the industrywide equilibrium input price of P_1 dollars and employment rate of X_{T_1} units per period of time. If the prevailing price exceeds P_1 dollars, the available supply of the input will exceed the quantity which firms are willing to employ. Some units of the input will be either idle altogether or else used only part of the time. The excess supply of the input will generate a downward pressure on its price. On the other hand, if the actual price of X falls below P_1, the quantity demanded by firms in the industry will exceed the quantity supplied to the industry and upward price pressures are automatically activated.

Thus, market forces push resource prices and employment rates toward levels that will clear the market. Multiplying the equilibrium input price by the equilibrium employment rate of X gives the amount of money income which the owners of input X will receive from the firms in the industry. Aggregating the income of input X over all industries which use input X gives the total money income received by the owners of X and the share of

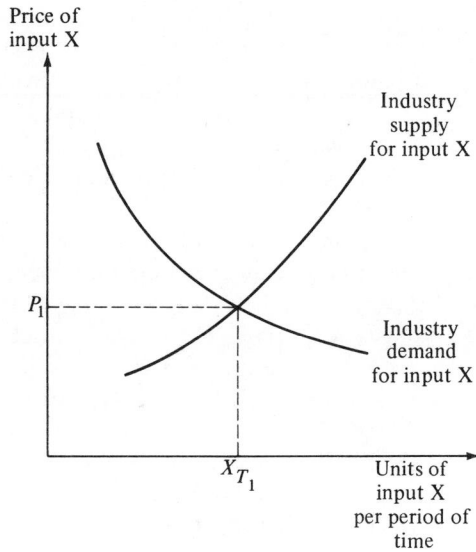

Fig. 14-5 The Pricing and Employment
of a Resource Input

---

personal preferences, since those units still being supplied will provide an income which is regarded as adequate. Hence, above some input price level, the higher the price the smaller the quantity of the input supplied by resource owners. The effect is to cause the supply curve for the input to bend backward and upward—or to be backward rising.

the economy's output they will earn from having supplied X. This explanation of how the income accruing to resource owners is determined is called the *marginal productivity theory of income distribution*. It derives this name from the fact that particular input prices and employment rates are a function of the input's marginal productivity.

However, it must be recognized that if the input is widely used in many industries and if its supply to a particular industry is very sensitive to input price changes, it is misleading, if not wholly inaccurate, to examine input equilibrium in terms of one industry alone. The reason is that what firms in one industry pay for an input and the amounts they use of this input necessarily are related to the prices that firms in other industries pay and the amounts of that input they employ. In fact, input prices and employment rates among the various industries using that input are interconnected; price or employment adjustments in one industry transmit pressures and influences to other industries, though with "impulses" of varying degrees of intensity. The linkages between industries are usually sufficiently strong to cause input prices to *tend* toward the same level in all industries which use that particular input. Different input prices for the same quality input can prevail without stimulating the movement of input supplies among firms and industries, but at some point the tolerance of resource onwers for differentials becomes stretched so thin that firms and industries, in order to keep the inputs they need, will be forced to lessen the gap. Consequently, where an input is employed in several industries, the appropriate focal point for analyzing input prices is at the level of the total market for the input rather than at the level of the firm or industry.

The total market demand for an input on an economywide basis may be thought of as the sum of all the various industry demand curves, where the industries may be structured along any sort of lines and may contain any number of firms of various types and sizes. Similarly, the total market supply of an input is the result of combining the industry supply curves. Again, the intersection of the market demand and market supply curve determine the input's economywide equilibrium price and rate of usage per period of time. The resulting price and employment rate form the basis for ascertaining the total amount of income which owners of the input in question will receive per period of time.

While it is generally agreed among economists that resource prices and employment rates are outcomes of supply and demand forces, in particular situations the operation of supply and demand forces may be suspended or modified. The presence of labor unions, the imposing of minimum wage requirements, the employment practices of large corporations, a wage-price freeze, plus a host of other institutional considerations, combine to cause input prices and employment rates to deviate from the free market results. We shall discuss some of the ramifications of these market aberrations in the concluding section of this chapter.

It goes almost without saying that the model of the firm's input decision under conditions of perfect competition in both the product and resource markets is most applicable to a few periphery firm markets where the products of the firms are homogeneous and where the number of firms comprising the product market is quite large. Only under these conditions is perfect competition in the product market even approximated. Thus, strictly speaking, the preceding model of resource pricing and resource employment provides a theoretical description of but a small segment of the economy. Nevertheless, many of the principles governing business behavior in perfectly competitive product and resource markets are much the same as in other types of market structures. In this sense, the perfectly competitive input model is valuable for its introduction to more realistic models of resource pricing and employment.

The Resource Input Decisions of a Firm Operating under Conditions of Imperfect Competition in Its Product Market and Perfect Competition in Its Resource Market

A somewhat more prevalent model of the functioning and behavior of resource input markets concerns the situation where the firm sells its product under conditions of imperfect competition (i.e., monopolistic competition, oligopoly, or monopoly), yet buys its inputs in a perfectly competitive resource market. This model characterizes much of the periphery economy and portions of the center economy, at least insofar as some inputs are concerned.

THE IMPERFECTLY COMPETITIVE FIRM'S INPUT DECISION:
THE ONE-VARIABLE INPUT CASE

When the firm sells its product in an imperfectly competitive market structure, its input decision is determined in a manner analogous to the perfectly competitive case, but with a slightly modified calculation procedure. In monopolistic competition, oligopoly, or pure monopoly the firm's product demand curve is downsloping, and the firm must lower price in order to increase its sales volume. This has a very important consequence. Whereas the *MRP* curve of an input used by a perfectly competitive firm falls solely because the marginal product of the input declines, the *MRP* curve of an input used by an imperfectly competitive firm declines for two reasons: a declining marginal product and a lower marginal revenue from the sale of additional output. The perfectly competitive enterprise can sell additional output at a constant price and obtain a constant MR, so that its MRP curve falls at the same rate as does the MP curve of the variable input. But when an imperfectly competitive firm adds one more unit of variable input and output rises by the amount of its marginal product, it is forced to lower selling price to sell the increased output. Barring the opportunity for price discrimination, the price decrease applies not just to the marginal product of the last unit of variable input but also to the units of output previously produced.[14] Hence, the marginal revenue received from additional sales is a decreasing function, and the firm's MRP curve for variable input falls faster than the rate of decline in MP. In other words, the MRP curve for a firm selling under conditions of imperfect competition is necessarily more steeply sloped than it otherwise would be if the firm sold its output under conditions of perfect competition. However, in either case, MRP still equals the net addition to total revenue associated with a change in the variable input rate.

The Profit-Maximizing Rate of Input Usage. To illustrate how a firm confronted with a downsloping demand-AR curve can ascertain the profit-maximizing rate of usage of a single variable input (X), consider the hypothetical production, cost, and revenue data in Table 14-2. Column 4 shows the extent to which the firm must lower price in order to sell the extra output of each successive unit of X, while columns 5 and 6 concern the corresponding TR and MR values. Column 7 contains the $SVMP_X$ figures, obtained by multiplying MP_X by the price at which the added output can be sold. Observe carefully that unlike the perfectly competitive case, the figures for $SVMP_X$ in column 7 do *not* coincide with MRP_X values in column 8. The figures for the sales value of the marginal product represent the gross addition to total revenue attributable to an additional unit of X. However, the firm's total revenue does not rise by the amount of $SVMP$, because to sell the added output the firm must reduce its price on the preceding units of output, thereby causing the *net* addition to TR to be less than the gross addition. To illustrate: The eighth unit of X has a marginal product of 10 units of output; these can be sold for \$17 apiece for a total of \$170—the figure for $SVMP$. But this is not the MRP value for the eighth unit of X because, to sell these 10 units of output, the firm must accept a \$1 price reduction on the 120 units of output produced by the preceding seven units of X. Hence, the MRP of the eighth unit of X is [\$170 − 120(\$1)] or \$50, as shown in column 8. The other values in column 8 can be determined in like fashion. The figures in columns 9, 10, and 11 of the table are obtained in the usual way.

The principle upon which the imperfectly competitive firm's input decision is based is precisely the same as that of the perfectly competitive firm: the firm should purchase additional units of a variable input up to the point where the added cost of more input equals the added revenue it con-

---

[14] We shall assume throughout the following discussion that the firm employs a single price policy and does not therefore engage in any of the several forms of price discrimination.

Table 14-2 The Profit-Maximizing Rate of Resource Input Usage for a Firm Operating in an Imperfectly Competitive Product Market and a Perfectly Competitive Resource Market

(1) Units of Variable Input (X)	(2) Units of Output (Q_A)	(3) Marginal Product (MP_X)	(4) Price of Product A (P_A)	(5) Total Revenue from Sales of Product A $(TR_A = P_A \cdot Q_A)$	(6) Marginal Revenue (MR_A)	(7) Sales Value of Marginal Product $(SVMP_X = MP_X \cdot P_A)$	(8) Marginal Revenue Product $(MRP_X = MP_X \cdot MR_A = \Delta TR_A / \Delta X)$	(9) Supply Price of Variable Input $(P_X = ARC_X = MRC_X)$	(10) Total Variable Cost (TVC)	(11) Total Contribution Profit $(TCP = TR - TVC)$
0	0			$ 0					$ 0	$ 0
1	14	14	$25	336	$24.00	$336	$336	$140	140	196
2	40	26	24	920	22.46	598	584	140	280	640
3	60	20	23	1,320	20.00	440	400	140	420	900
4	78	18	22	1,638	17.67	378	318	140	560	1,078
5	94	16	21	1,880	15.12	320	242	140	700	1,180
6	108	14	20	2,052	12.29	266	172	140	840	1,212
7	120	12	19	2,160	9.00	216	108	140	980	1,180
8	130	10	18	2,210	5.00	170	50	140	1,120	1,090
9	138	8	17	2,208	-.25	128	- 2	140	1,260	948
10	144	6	16	2,160	-8.00	90	-48	140	1,400	760
			15							

530

tributes. In short, the usage of variable input must be carried to the rate where $MRP = MRC$. A comparison of columns 8 and 9 in Table 14-2 indicates that the profit-maximizing input rate is 6 units of X. For the firm to go beyond this point and employ the seventh unit of X will result in revenues increasing by $108 but costs rising by $140—plainly an unprofitable act. For the firm to stop short of using 6 units of X will result in smaller total contribution profits (see column 11) and hence smaller total profits (or greater losses).

The profit-maximizing input decision can be approached graphically in a somewhat more general fashion. Figure 14-6 shows an imperfectly competitive firm's MRP curve for a variable input. Suppose the input supply curve is S_1, with a resulting input price of P_1 dollars. The profit-maximizing input rate is X_1 units, where $MRP_X = MRC_X$. Should the input supply price fall to P_2 dollars, giving a new input supply curve at S_2, the firm's profit-maximizing input rate would expand to X_2 units per period of time. And should the input supply curve shift downward to S_3, the new equilibrium input rate would become X_3 units. Consequently, the profit-maximizing input rate of X is found along the input's MRP curve, which makes the MRP_X curve the firm's demand curve for input X, provided only one variable input is used in the firm's production process.

THE IMPERFECTLY COMPETITIVE FIRM'S INPUT DECISION: THE TWO-VARIABLE INPUT CASE

When the firm's production technology incorporates the use of two or more variable inputs, the interdependence among the several variable inputs renders the determination of the firm's input demand more complex. The

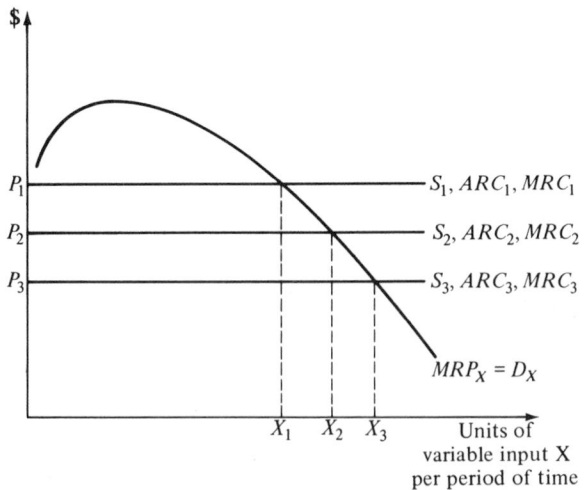

Fig. 14-6 An Imperfectly Competitive Firm's Demand for a Resource Input

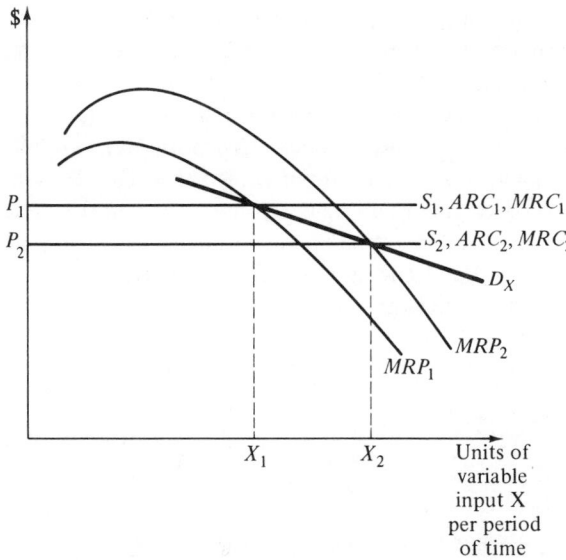

Fig. 14-7 The Imperfectly Competitive Firm's Input Decision When Two or More Inputs are Variable

MRP curve is no longer the firm's input demand curve but rather is the starting point for deriving its input demand curve. The analysis for an imperfectly competitive firm using two or more variable input parallels that for the perfectly competitive firm.

As portrayed in Figure 14-7, suppose that the supply price of input X is temporarily fixed at P_1 and that the input's marginal revenue product curve is MRP_1. The profit-maximizing rate of input is therefore X_1 units per period of time.

Now let the supply price of X fall to P_2. This change triggers four effects at the level of the firm: the substitution effect, the output effect, the marginal cost effect, and the marginal revenue effect. The substitution, output, and marginal cost effects operate in exactly the same way for firms in monopolistic competition, oligopoly, or pure monopoly as they do for firms in perfect competition.

However, the *marginal revenue effect* is unique to imperfectly competitive product markets and arises from the fact that the firm's marginal revenue will change as a consequence of the output changes induced by the shift in the price of input X. The decline in the price of X lowers the firm's marginal cost curve, causing a new intersection of *MC* and *MR* at a *larger* output, a *lower* price, and a *lower MR* value. (The reader should verify this statement for himself by drawing a graph.) Since $MRP_X = MP_X \cdot MR$, then a decline in *MR* necessarily acts to reduce MRP_X.

On balance, the output and marginal cost effects will override the substitution and marginal revenue effects, with the result that a decline in the supply price of X will shift the MRP curve for X upward and to the right, say from MRP_1 to MRP_2.[15] The profit-maximizing input rate for the imperfectly competitive firm thus becomes X_2 units at a supply price of P_2 dollars. Other profit-maximizing input rates for X can be generated by changing the price of X again and again, tracing through the substitution, output, marginal cost, and marginal revenue effects, and finding the new position of the firm's MRP curve. Connecting the points formed by the equilibrium input supply prices and input rates gives the firm's input demand curve for X, labeled as D_X in Figure 14-7. The points along D_X show the various quantities of input X that maximize the firm's profits when the prices of other variable inputs remain constant and the usages of all other variable inputs are appropriately adjusted for changes in the supply price of input X.

THE INPUT DEMAND OF AN IMPERFECTLY COMPETITIVE INDUSTRY

To derive the industrywide demand for an input when the firms compete under conditions of imperfect competition requires that the demand curves of the individual firms somehow be combined into a single input demand curve for the industry. In an imperfectly competitive market of two or more firms, whatever shade of oligopoly or monopolistic competition may exist, the demand curves of the firms cannot simply be summed horizontally to give the industry demand curve.[16] This is invalid for the same reason it does not work for perfect competition. To begin with, a change in the input's supply price affects the optimum output rate of each firm in the industry. A change in the firm's output rate leads then to a price change. The price and output adjustments made by the firm will combine to shift the MRP curve of the input via the substitution, output, marginal cost, and marginal revenue effects. In turn, the shift in MRP alters the firm's optimum input demand at the new input supply price. In such situations, the industrywide input demand curve is derived by first finding the profit-maximizing input rate for each firm at each possible input price after allowing for shifts in the MRP curve and then by summing these optimum input amounts over all firms in the industry. The rationale and the graphical analysis are identical to that described in Figure 14-4 and need not be reiterated here.

Once the industry demand for the input is determined, the industrywide equilibrium price and input rates are found at the intersection of the industry demand and supply curves for the input. The nature of the input's industry

---

[15] For a formal proof of this claim the reader may consult the references in footnote 8.

[16] Obviously, if the industry is one of pure monopoly, no combining is necessary, because the firm's input demand and the industry input demand are one and the same.

supply curve, discussed in an earlier section of this chapter, is unaffected by the existence of imperfect competition in the product market. Again, however, the equilibrium price of an input on an industrywide basis is bound to be affected by the price of the input in other industries. When resource inputs are versatile enough to be used by several industries and when they are relatively mobile between industries, the equilibrium price and employment rates of an input are best analyzed on a marketwide or economywide basis rather than on an industrywide basis. Barring the existence of resource immobility or other powerful institutional determinants of an input price, the tie between a resource input's price in one industry and its price in other industries is usually strong enough to cause the overall price of the input to *tend* toward the same level in all industries using that input. A valid explanation of how input prices are determined must therefore hinge upon overall market demand and supply conditions rather than upon demand and supply in any one industry.

The Resource Input Decisions of a Firm
Operating under Conditions of Imperfect Competition
in Its Product and Resource Markets

Up to this point perfectly competitive conditions have been assumed to characterize the supply side of the firm's input decision; the firm has been viewed as such a small purchaser of any one input that its input decision has no perceptible effect on the supply prices of inputs. The time has come to relax this assumption and to consider the situation where the price a firm must pay for an input is affected by how much of the input the firm elects to utilize.

In numerous geographical areas the supply of an input *in the short run* is relatively limited. Enterprises with large plants in the area may utilize such a sizable fraction of the local input supply that their decisions to employ more or less of the input have a discernible impact on the input's short-run local supply price. The effect is to make the firm's input supply curve upward-sloping. The more of an input the firm wishes to obtain, the higher the price it must offer to bid supplies of the input away from alternative users.[17] The less of an input the firm needs, the smaller the price it can get by with paying, since it does not have to bid as high to attract the desired supply away from other firms.

Several types of input supply situations other than perfect competition may be delineated. A resource input market in which only *one* firm uses the

---

[17] As regards labor inputs, it should be recognized that a large firm may be able to expand the size of its labor force without raising the going wage rate by increasing recruiting efforts and/or by lowering its standards for hiring new employees. Either of these strategies, however, really means that the effective price of a given quantity and quality of labor is rising, even though the nominal wage scale remains the same.

input is referred to as *monopsony*.[18] If only a *few* firms are the predominant purchasers of the input, the resource market is designated as *oligopsony*. Where *many* firms are using an input but their numbers are still small enough to allow each firm a small influence over the input's supply price, the resource market may be characterized as *monopsonistic competition*. A particular firm can sell its output under conditions of oligopoly yet buy its inputs under conditions of monopsonistic competition. Likewise, it is possible for a firm to sell its product under conditions of monopolistic competition and to obtain its inputs under conditions of monopsony; this could occur if the numerous small producers were geographically dispersed but still large enough to dominate the market for labor in a local area. Plainly, a variety of product and resource market combinations can result: monopoly-monopsony, oligopoly-monopsony, oligopoly-monopsonistic competition, perfect competition-oligopsony, and so forth. However, in any sort of imperfectly competitive input market, whether it be one of monopsony, oligopsony, or monopsonistic competition, the analytical considerations governing the supply aspects of the firm's input decision are the same. Thus, it is sufficient merely to examine imperfect competition in the input market to learn about the firm's input decision in other than a perfectly competitive resource market.

THE MARGINAL RESOURCE COST CURVE
AND A RISING INPUT SUPPLY CURVE

The key feature of an imperfectly competitive input market is an upward-rising input supply curve. With a rising supply curve the firm is forced to pay a higher price if it wishes to secure more of the input, and the firm can get by with paying a lower price for the input should it choose to use less of the input. Since the supply curve for an input represents the firm's average cost for obtaining the input, the firm's *ARC* curve is also upward-sloping and coincides with the supply curve. This has a most important consequence insofar as the firm's marginal resource cost is concerned.

Under imperfectly competitive input supply conditions, the *MRC* curve does not correspond to the input supply and average resource cost curve. Consider the hypothetical data in Table 14-3. Columns 1 and 2 show how much the firm must increase its offer price in order to obtain additional units of X; these two columns represent the firm's input supply and *ARC* schedules. Column 3 presents the total cost of input X associated with each

---

[18] The term monopsony is on occasions also used to refer to product market situations where there is only a single buyer of a commodity. Hence, strictly speaking, monopsony refers to a single buyer—it matters not whether the buyer purchases an input or a final good or service. Likewise, pure monopoly refers to a single seller —whether the seller is selling a product or an input again really makes no difference. For example, the craft union which is able to unionize all persons having a particular skill is just as much a monopolist in "selling" the skill it controls as is the local telephone company in rendering telephone service. Analogous meanings and interpretations can be attached to the terms oligopoly, oligopsony, and so on.

of the various input rates of X. Column 4 shows the marginal resource cost of each additional unit of X and can be calculated by successive subtraction of the TC_X figures; that is, $MRC_X = \Delta TC_X / \Delta X$.

Table 14-3 Marginal Resource Cost for a Firm Operating Under Conditions of Imperfect Competition in the Resource Input Market

Units of Variable Input (X)	Supply Price of Variable Input $(P_X = ARC_X)$	Total Cost of Variable Input (TC_X)	Marginal Resource Cost (MRC_X)
1	$5.00	$ 5.00	
			$ 6.00
2	5.50	11.00	
			7.00
3	6.00	18.00	
			8.00
4	6.50	26.00	
			9.00
5	7.00	35.00	
			10.00
6	7.50	45.00	
			11.00
7	8.00	56.00	
			12.00
8	8.50	68.00	
			13.00
9	9.00	81.00	
			14.00
10	9.50	95.00	

When the firm must pay a higher price to obtain larger amounts of input X, the marginal resource cost of each extra unit will be higher than the input's supply price and average resource cost. As shown in Table 14-3, suppose the firm increases its usage rate of X from 7 to 8 units per period. The price of the eighth unit is $8.50. But this value is not the marginal resource cost of the eighth unit. To obtain the use of 8 units of X, the firm must pay $8.50 for *each* one.[19] Hence the firm's cost of obtaining each of the previous seven units of X rises from $8.00 to $8.50 for an added cost of $3.50 (7 × $.50). Adding this to the $8.50 cost of the eighth unit gives a total increase of $12.00 in the firm's cost of upping the input rate of X from 7 to 8 units. Thus, the marginal resource cost of the eighth unit is $12.00. The MRC of the other units can be derived in the same fashion.

A graphical portrayal of the relationships among the firm's input supply curve (S_X), the average resource cost curve (ARC_X), and the marginal resource cost curve (MRC_X) is depicted in Figure 14-8. The MRC_X curve lies above the input supply and average resource cost curve at each and every input rate. The rationale is the same as for the relationship between ATC

---

[19] This is not only required by the supply conditions, but it is also equitable. Since we assume each unit of X is just alike, there is no cause for the firm to reward one unit of X any differently from the others. If, for example, the firm has 8 identical units of input X, then the second unit (assuming it can be picked out from the rest) is no more "valuable" than the fifth or the eighth unit. The *order* in which the units of X are hired has no real bearing on their worth to the firm. Nor is it usually feasible for the firm to pay different units of the same input a different price. Consequently, the price which it takes to get the *total* amount of X that is desired is what determines the price *each unit* must be paid.

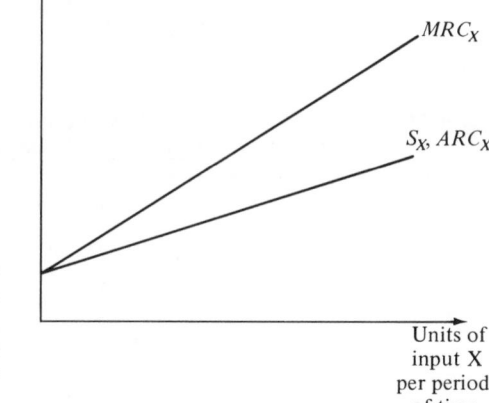

Fig. 14-8 The Relationships Among the Input Supply Curve, the Average Resource Cost Curve, and the Marginal Resource Cost Curve in an Imperfectly Competitive Input Market

and MC; in fact, the ARC_x-MRC_x relation parallels that of ATC and MC. As is the usual case with marginal and average concepts, if the average cost (or supply price) of input X is rising, then the marginal cost of input X (MRC_x) must be greater than average cost and the MRC curve for X must lie above the input supply and average resource cost curve.

The mathematics of the relationship between S_x and MRC_x is easily indicated. Assume, for convenience of illustration, that the input supply curve for X is linear and upward-sloping. Then the general equation for the supply curve is

$$P_x = ARC_x = a + bX.$$

The total cost of the input at any input rate is

$$TC_x = P_x \cdot X = ARC_x \cdot X = (a + bX)X = aX + bX^2.$$

Marginal resource cost is, by definition, the rate of change in the total cost of the input as the input rate changes, which in terms of calculus is the first derivative of the input's total cost function. The equation for MRC_x thus becomes

$$MRC_x = \frac{dTC_x}{dX} = a + 2bX.$$

A comparison of the equation for the input supply-average resource cost curve and the equation for the MRC curve indicates that the MRC_x curve will rise twice as fast as S_x-ARC_x when S_x-ARC_x is linear and upward-sloping. The marginal resource cost curve can be determined in like fashion for other types of input supply-average resource cost functions.

THE IMPERFECTLY COMPETITIVE FIRM'S INPUT DECISION
IN AN IMPERFECTLY COMPETITIVE RESOURCE MARKET:
THE ONE-VARIABLE INPUT CASE

Determining the firm's profit-maximizing input rate with respect to resource X follows the same principle when imperfect competition exists in the input market as it does when there is perfect competition. As we have just seen, the distinctive feature of an imperfectly competitive resource market is an upward-rising input supply curve and an even more rapidly rising marginal resource cost curve. Nonetheless, the firm will still find it advantageous to increase the usage rate of X so long as additional units of X add more to revenues than to total costs. As before, the firm's net revenue gains from using additional units of an input are given by the input's *MRP* function, whereas the extra costs incurred are indicated by the input's *MRC* function as derived from the input's supply and *ARC* functions.

The relevant curves are shown in Figure 14-9. The firm's profits will be maximum at an input rate of X_1 units, where $MRP_X = MRC_X$. To use more than X_1 units per period of time would add more to the firm's total costs than to its total revenues. To stop short of using X_1 units would mean a sacrifice of some profits, because the marginal revenue product of all units below X_1 exceeds their respective marginal resource costs. Clearly, then, X_1 is the profit-maximizing input rate. But now the question becomes: what price must the firm pay to obtain X_1 units per period of time? Although the marginal revenue product at X_1 is MRP_{X_1}, this is not the price which the

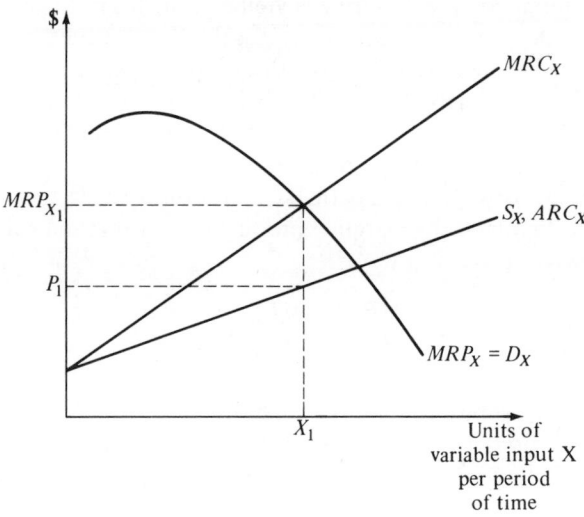

Fig. 14-9   The Profit-Maximizing Input Rate for a Firm Operating in Imperfectly Competitive Product and Resource Markets

firm need pay to get X_1 units. The input supply curve (S_x) shows the price which the firm must pay for various quantities of the input. From S_x it is apparent that to obtain X_1 units of resource X, the firm will find it necessary to pay a price of P_1 dollars—this, then, is the firm's equilibrium input price.

THE IMPERFECTLY COMPETITIVE FIRM'S INPUT DECISION
IN AN IMPERFECTLY COMPETITIVE RESOURCE MARKET
WHEN SEVERAL VARIABLE INPUTS ARE USED

Ordinarily, a firm's production technology will call for the use of several inputs—some fixed in the short run, others variable, but all subject to change in the long run. Consequently, it is important to consider how the firm's profit-maximizing input combination is determined when several inputs are variable.

In Chapter 7 it was shown that to minimize its total costs for a given output the firm must adjust its input mix so as to obtain an equivalent amount of output per dollar spent on the last unit of each input used. In more formal terms this requires the firm to combine its various inputs (X_a, X_b, X_c, ..., X_n) such that

$$\frac{MP_{X_a}}{P_{X_a}} = \frac{MP_{X_b}}{P_{X_b}} = \frac{MP_{X_c}}{P_{X_c}} = \cdots = \frac{MP_{X_n}}{P_{X_n}}.$$

If the least-cost input combination rule is violated, the firm can either obtain more output for the same total cost or else get the same output for less total cost. Suppose, for instance, a dollar's worth of input X_a contributes more to output than a dollar's worth of input X_b. Then the firm would find it advantageous to shift its expenditures on inputs; more dollars should be allocated to the purchase of X_a and fewer to the purchase of X_b—the firm should substitute input X_a for input X_b. As the substitution is made, the marginal product of X_a declines and the marginal product of X_a rises; the substitution process ceases when

$$\frac{MP_{X_a}}{P_{X_a}} = \frac{MP_{X_b}}{P_{X_b}}.$$

However, this proposition holds if and only if the inputs are purchased in perfectly competitive resource markets. If the firm's input supply curves are all upward sloping such that input prices vary with the quantity used, then a substitution of one input for another entails input price changes as well as marginal product changes. The firm must therefore consider an input's marginal resource cost (MRC) rather than its supply price when making its input decision. The rule for minimizing the cost of a given output under imperfectly competitive input conditions thus becomes

$$\frac{MP_{X_a}}{MRC_{X_a}} = \frac{MP_{X_b}}{MRC_{X_b}} = \frac{MP_{X_c}}{MRC_{X_c}} = \cdots = \frac{MP_{X_n}}{MRC_{X_n}}.$$

To see the rationale underlying this proposition consider the two-input case where inputs X_a and X_b are being used in such proportions that

$$\frac{MP_{X_a}}{MRC_{X_a}} > \frac{MP_{X_b}}{MRC_{X_b}}.$$

This inequality says that at the existing input combination the firm can realize a greater increase in output per additional dollar outlay on input X_a than on input X_b. Consequently, by substituting X_a for X_b the firm can realize more output for the same cost or else it can get the same output for less cost. As substitution is initiated, the marginal product of X_a declines and the MRC_{X_a} increases, whereas the marginal product of X_b increases and the MRC_{X_b} declines. Sooner or later the substitution of X_a for X_b will result in equality in the ratios of MP and MRC. At the point of equality, no further change in the firm's input mix will prove beneficial from the standpoint of costs or output.

The preceding discussion shows, albeit in a nonrigorous fashion, that if a firm *buying its inputs* under conditions of imperfect competition is to achieve the lowest possible total cost for a given output, then it should adjust its input combination to the point where the ratio of marginal product to marginal resource cost is the same for all inputs used. An interesting question now arises: what adjustments in the rule, if any, are necessary to identify *the profit-maximizing resource input combination*? Is the rule for attaining the least-cost resource combination for a given output also adequate for ascertaining the profit-maximizing input mix? The answer to the latter question is *no*, though the reason may not be apparent at first glance.

The rule for determining the least-cost resource combination for a *given output* reveals only the correct *proportions* in which to employ variable inputs. It says nothing about which output rate maximizes profits, and therefore it leaves unanswered the question as to the correct *absolute amounts* of each variable input. To illustrate the significance of this point, consider the following numerical example. Suppose a firm is using 10 units of input X_a and 15 units of input X_b to produce 3,500 units of a particular product per week. Suppose further that at this input combination the specific values of marginal product and marginal resource cost for X_a and X_b are $MP_{X_a} = 40$ units of output, $MRC_{X_a} = \$10$, $MP_{X_b} = 60$ units of output, and $MRC_{X_b} = \$15$. The least-cost rule that

$$\frac{MP_{X_a}}{MRC_{X_a}} = \frac{MP_{X_b}}{MRC_{X_b}}$$

is satisfied, as we can see by substituting the *MP* and *MRC* values into the above expression:

$$\frac{MP_{X_a}}{MRC_{X_a}} = \frac{40 \text{ units of output}}{\$10} = 4 \text{ units of output/\$,}$$

$$\frac{MP_{X_b}}{MRC_{X_b}} = \frac{60 \text{ units of output}}{\$15} = 4 \text{ units of output/\$.}$$

At the current input combination, the firm obtains 4 units of output per dollar spent on each input, which says that there is no advantage to be gained from shifting the input mix insofar as cost or output is concerned. However, how do we know whether or not it would be more *profitable* to use more (or less) of both inputs X_a and X_b? There is no way to tell from the information given. Thus, while it is clear that the firm is using its inputs to the best advantage to produce the current output of 3,500 units, we do not know from the information given whether 3,500 units is the profit-maximizing output rate and therefore whether 10 units of X_a and 15 units of X_b constitute the profit-maximizing input combination.

This shortcoming in the least-cost rule is easily disposed of by bringing the marginal revenue products of the two inputs into consideration. Suppose the marginal product of the tenth unit of input X_a (40 units of output) adds \$20 to the firm's total revenue and the marginal product of the fifteenth unit of X_b (60 units of output) adds \$30. Then, clearly, the *MRP* of both inputs exceeds their respective marginal resource costs of \$10 and \$15, and the firm will find it profitable to increase its usage of both X_a and X_b. As demonstrated previously, the firm should increase an input's usage to the point where $MRP = MRC$. This rationale applies to any and all resources. Thus, *in general it can be said that a firm attains the profit-maximizing input rate when each and every variable input is employed to the point where its marginal revenue product equals its marginal resource cost.* In algebraic terms this becomes

$$\frac{MRP_{X_a}}{MRC_{X_a}} = \frac{MRP_{X_b}}{MRC_{X_b}} = \frac{MRP_{X_c}}{MRC_{X_c}} = \cdots = \frac{MRP_{X_n}}{MRC_{X_n}}.$$

Hence, converting the numerator of each term of the least-cost rule from a measure of marginal product to a measure of marginal revenue product gives the expression for the profit-maximizing input combination. This latter expression satisfies the need for determining both the absolute quantities and the proportions of the various inputs that will maximize total profits, since it incorporates measures of each input's productivity (marginal product), revenue contribution, and cost—all of which are essential for input optimization. However, since each input must be used at a rate such that its

$MRP = MRC$, then it follows that the input ratios must not only be equal to each other but they must also be equal to 1. In other words, to use each variable input in the profit-maximizing *proportions* and in the profit-maximizing *absolute amounts*, the firm must adjust its input mix to the point where

$$\frac{MRP_{X_a}}{MRC_{X_a}} = \frac{MRP_{X_b}}{MRC_{X_b}} = \frac{MRP_{X_c}}{MRC_{X_c}} = \cdots = \frac{MRP_{X_n}}{MRC_{X_n}} = 1.$$

It should be recognized that (1) changes in an input's marginal productivity, (2) changes in the marginal revenue received from the sale of output, or (3) changes in an input's marginal resource cost will tend to change both the proportions and the absolute amounts of the inputs which a firm will find it most profitable to use.

The profit-maximizing rule derived above is applicable to firms operating under any and every type of product and resource market combination. This is necessarily so because, as we have seen, every firm—no matter what sort of market circumstances it faces—finds it advantageous to adjust its input rate of a variable resource to the point at which the input's marginal revenue product equals its marginal resource cost.

An Evaluation of the Marginal Productivity Approach to Input Pricing and Employment

The discussion in this chapter has so far been chiefly theoretical with little emphasis on actual practice. The principal reason is that something of an abnormal gap exists between theoretical models of input decisions and of the functioning of input markets on the one hand and what goes on in the real world on the other hand. This gap has left the economic theories of input pricing, input employment, and income distribution in a very unsettled state, with a host of honest differences prevailing among various authorities.

The problem lies partly with the almost countless number of institutional interferences, market imperfections, and artificially imposed restraints that have gradually become an integral feature of input markets. A representative sample of some of the most important of these interferences and imperfections includes (1) the enactment of minimum wage laws, (2) the exercise of whatever monopoly power unions have to obtain wage increases in excess of productivity gains, (3) the imposing of wage-price freezes, (4) restrictive union work rules and featherbedding practices, (5) the long-standing traditions regarding the size of wage differentials between certain types of occupations, (6) job discrimination and wage discrimination based upon race or sex, (7) the educational, apprenticeship, and license-to-practice requirements for entering an occupation, (8) the regulation of rates of return to monopolistic enterprise, (9) the effects of monetary policy upon interest rates, (10) zoning regulations which preclude the use of land for certain types of activities, and (11) the relative immobility of resource inputs among firms, industries, and geographical areas—at least in the short run.

The effects which such factors have upon input prices and employment are well worth illustrating. Two examples will be given, both taken from the labor input sector because of their widespread applicability to real-world events.

THE IMPACT OF MINIMUM WAGE LAWS UPON LABOR MARKETS

Minimum wage legislation is generally aimed at accomplishing three things: (1) reducing the poverty associated with wage payments which do not afford workers a "decent" standard of living; (2) curtailing the practice whereby marginal firms pay substandard wages to a relatively immobile work force, thus keeping production costs low enough to enable them to compete with other enterprises (this practice is sometimes labeled as "unfair competition"), and (3) increasing the purchasing power of low-income families. By and large, the firms affected by minimum wage laws are small companies operating on slim profit margins and stressing short-run profits, their work force is non-union, and they have a relatively low capital investment per worker. Almost without exception such firms are periphery firms operating in perfectly or monopolistically competitive product markets.

The higher wages and higher labor costs which minimum wage laws impose upon the affected firms puts them under severe pressure to correct their already precarious cost-price-profit position. When higher minimum wages are legislated, there is likely to arise a sort of "shock effect" which forces the affected firms to upgrade management practices, implement new production technologies, and increase labor performance and efficiency if they are to survive. Several specific responses present themselves, and each has, in fact, been observed to occur in practice. Management can improve plant layout and the quality of supervision; labor saving equipment can be installed; inefficient employees can be weeded out; new employee selection standards can be raised; working conditions can be improved so as to reduce labor turnover and to increase the general efficiency and morale of the firm's labor force; the amount of overtime work offered employees can be cut back; and jobs which no longer pay their way can be eliminated entirely.

But whatever response set each affected firm elects, one important outcome is almost certain to emerge: the opportunities for employment in the affected occupations will be less than otherwise. The minimum wage law will peg the supply price for such labor above the level which would be determined by the forces of market demand and supply for such labor—

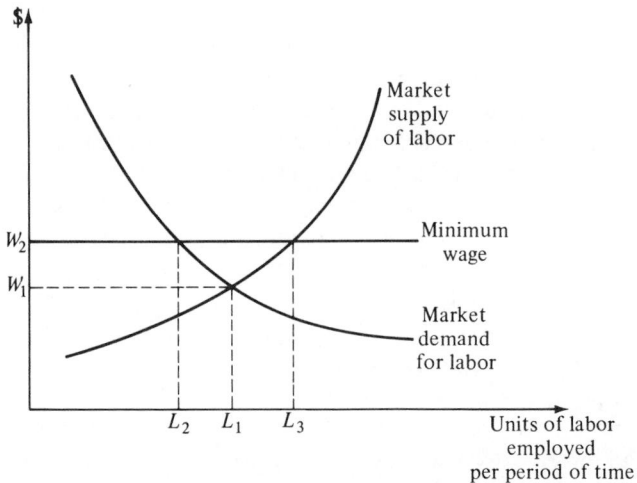

Fig. 14-10   The Employment Effect of a Minimum Wage Law

otherwise the minimum wage has no *raison d'etre*. The outcome of a higher-than-equilibrium input supply price is a reduced optimum employment rate, as depicted in Figure 14-10.[20] If the minimum wage is set at W_2 dollars, given the market demand and supply curves for labor of a particular type, then firms will adjust their employment rate downward from L_1 to L_2 units per period of time, and $L_2 L_3$ units of labor will be involuntarily unemployed. The reduction in employment takes the form of dismissal of the least efficient employees, the closing down of marginal firms, cutbacks in the average number of hours worked per employee, or reductions in the number of new job opportunities in the affected occupations. Studies indicate that the groups hit hardest by the lower employment rates tend to be teenagers, blacks, and persons lacking in skills and training.

Hence the economic effect of minimum wage laws upon resource pricing and employment is (1) to push wage rates for the lowest-paid occupations up above the equilibrium rates that would prevail in their absence and (2) to suppress employment rates in the affected occupations. On the whole, however, more persons are probably benefited by the minimum wage laws than are hurt by them, owing to the progress made in achieving the three

[20] Empirical studies of this phenomenon are numerous. See, for instance, *Studies of the Economic Effects of the $1 Minimum Wage, Effects in Selected Low Wage Industries and Localities*, Wage and Hour and Public Contracts Divisions, United States Department of Labor, January 1959; H. M. Douty, "Some Effects of the $1.00 Minimum Wage in the United States," *Economica*, Vol. 27, No. 106 (May 1960), pp. 137–47; N. Arnold Tolles, "American Minimum Wage Laws: Their Purposes and Results," *Proceedings of the Twelfth Annual Meeting of the Industrial Relations Research Association* (Madison, Wis.: Industrial Relations Research Asssociation, 1960), pp. 116–133; Neil W. Chamberlain, *The Labor Sector* (New York: McGraw-Hill, Inc., 1965), pp. 529–533; and Finis Welch and Marvin Kosters, "The Effects of Minimum Wages on the Distribution of Changes in Aggregate Employment," *American Economic Review*, Vol. 62, No. 3 (June 1972), pp. 323–332.

aforementioned objectives of such legislation.[21] Inefficient firms are also forced to bring their operations up to par or else face the penalty of low profits or losses. For our purposes, the major point to be noted about minimum wage legislation is that it *artificially* causes the supply prices of low-skill, low-productivity types of labor to be higher than they would be if the forces of market demand and market supply were allowed to function freely. In this sense, governmental policy toward minimum wage rates, not labor's marginal productivity, is a major factor in determining wages, employment, and income in the affected occupational categories.

It is also worth noting that minimum wage laws can affect wage rates in occupations which carry higher than the minimum wage. A higher minimum wage allows unions to press for further wage increases through collective bargaining. The unions' philosophy is that while they will use their bargaining power to become wage leaders, upward adjustments in the federal minimum rates provide them with a new platform from which they can launch demands for still higher union wages on the grounds of maintaining historical wage differentials.

SOME ECONOMIC EFFECTS OF UNIONS

In modern industrial economies trade unions are an integral and accepted part of the functioning of labor markets, especially in the manufacturing sector. In the United States, nearly 85 percent of the workers in plants employing 100 workers or more are unionized; union membership totals approximately 18 million persons; and the pattern-setting wage settlements reached in certain key industries are quickly transmitted to other sectors of the economy. Thus unions have a major impact upon national labor markets; their presence does make a difference. The added power workers gain by union organization creates a very strong presumption that the resulting wage and employment rates will be different from what they would have been had workers remained unorganized. Consequently, any analysis of wage rates and employment which ignores the impact of collective bargaining is suspect in its ability to explain and to predict the behavior of real-world labor markets.

Incorporating union behavior into the analysis of labor markets first requires some notion of the economic goals of unions. Casual observation suggests that unions pursue some satisfactory, and perhaps quite complex, balance of increased wages and incomes, increased leisure, and an adequate number of job opportunities for current and potential union members. However, depending on their own unique circumstances, different unions may

---

[21] When the demand for labor is *inelastic*, a rise in the minimum wage may lessen employment opportunities, but the total income of those who remain employed will definitely be greater than before. However, when the demand for labor is *elastic*, increases in the minimum wage will reduce both employment and the total income accruing to those who remain employed. Hence, only when labor demand is relatively inelastic do increases in the minimum wage have their most beneficial impact.

place differing emphases and priorities on these goals; collective bargaining is by no means a uniform process whereby each union consistently pursues the same objectives with the same intensity.

The Wage-Employment Preference Path.

A union's preferred tradeoff between wages and employment can be viewed graphically. Suppose collective negotiations between a firm and a union result in the establishment of an average wage of W_1 dollars and an equilibrium employment rate of L_1 units of labor per period of time, as shown in Figure 14-11(a). Now consider the combination of wage and employment rates which the union would prefer and which it will attempt to attain in its negotiations with the firm. If the firm's product demand should shift in such a manner that its demand for labor input shifts from D_{L_1} to D_{L_2}, the union's preference is generally for substantial wage increases, say from W_1 to W_2 (which may, incidentally, be in the form of overtime wages), and modest increases in the number of persons employed, say from L_1 to L_2. This reflects the usual union attitude that its first responsibility is to the existing membership and that it is obliged to win them higher wages whenever the opportunity presents. Hence, the union's preference path is a steeply rising curve above the initial wage-employment combination.[22] However, the stronger the rise in the firm's demand for labor, the more the union is ordinarily willing to temper its wage demands in return for increases in employment (and gains in union membership). For this reason the portion of the union's preferred wage-

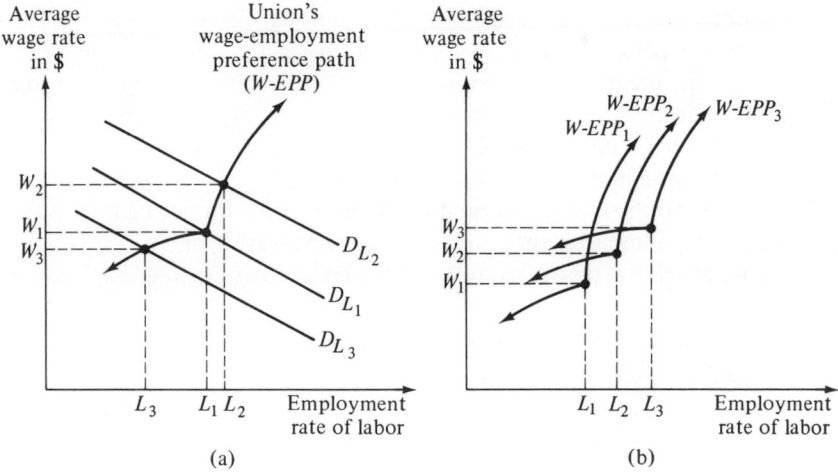

Fig. 14-11   The Wage-Employment Preference Path of a Typical Union

---

[22] An exception to this general case arises in instances where large numbers of union members are unemployed at the prevailing wage-employment combination. Here the union will undoubtedly pursue a policy of getting the unemployed members back to work before seeking major wage advances.

employment path above the prevailing wage-employment combination is shown as rising at a decreasing rate.

If economic conditions should shift the firm's demand for labor input downward, say from D_{L_1} to D_{L_3}, the union usually exhibits a strong preference for larger cutbacks in employment (say from L_1 to L_3) relative to wages (which might be reduced from W_1 to W_3). The reasoning behind such a preference is that wage reductions weaken the ability of the union to win wage gains in future bargaining sessions, whereas employment cutbacks are self-correcting as soon as business conditions pick up again.[23] Hence the lower section of the wage-employment preference path falls slowly and at a rate commensurate with employment reductions that are more than proportional to the wage reductions.[24] The union's wage-employment preferences therefore tend to produce a curvilinear pattern, kinked at the current wage-employment position. As new wage negotiations are consummated, the curve shifts to a new position and a kink appears at the newly instituted wage-employment combination, as depicted in Figure 14-11(b).

In viewing the union's wage-employment preferences, care must be taken not to view employment as referring solely to the number of workers employed. A firm's employment *rate (L)* is composed of n number of workers working h number of hours per period of time. Thus a reduction in the union's preferred employment rate may reflect preferences for cutbacks in the number of workers *or* in the number of hours worked by each worker *or* both. Similarly, increases in the union's preferred employment rate may mean more workers *or* more hours worked by each worker *or* both. By observing the composition of the employment rate the union bargains for over a period of time, it is possible to infer what the union's preference is toward greater membership versus more leisure time for the rank and file. Therefore, the union's wage-employment preference curve is indicative not only of the union's wage (and income) goal and its employment (and membership) goal but also of its leisure time goal.[25]

To the extent that unions are successful in imposing their wage-employment preferences upon firms, we have at least a partial explanation of why wages rise at above-average rates in periods of strong business expansion,

[23] An excellent discussion of the tactical advantages which the union receives from following such a policy is found in Allan M. Cartter and F. Ray Marshall, *Labor Economics: Wages, Employment, and Trade Unionism*, Rev. Ed. (Homewood, Ill.: Richard D. Irwin, Inc., 1972), pp. 245–246.

[24] Again, the preferred wage-employment path may assume a different shape if significant employment cutbacks have been recently imposed and many union members are already laid off. In such instances the union may be more amenable to cutting wages and maintaining employment, in which case the lower section of the curve may reflect a preference for relatively larger wage cuts and relatively smaller employment cuts.

[25] Unions historically have shown a keen interest in shortening the standard workday and workweek. During periods of depressed business conditions, shorter working hours are a means of sharing the available work among greater numbers of people. During periods of prosperity, the shorter workweek is a means of raising wage rates by instituting time-and-a-half overtime rates after fewer hours worked. On occasions, unions may find it easier to persuade firms to pay workers the same total income but allow them to work fewer hours to earn it (which is equivalent to raising the average wage rate) than to persuade them to pay workers a higher wage rate for working the same number of hours as before. The former does not raise the firm's total labor costs provided the same amount of work can be accomplished in the fewer working hours, whereas the latter is sure to increase the firm's total wage bill.

yet employment gains are modest, and why wages fail to fall and labor employment cutbacks are comparatively severe in times when business conditions are slack. Such wage-employment behavior is particularly prevelant in the center economy, where most firms have unionized labor forces.

The Effects of Unions on the Firm's Labor Input Decision. From a supply standpoint the effect of union-negotiated wage rates is to make the firm's supply curve for union labor horizontal (or perfectly elastic) at the agreed-to wage scale, at least until the supply of labor runs out at these wage rates. This is illustrated in Figure 14-12, where the firm's supply curve for labor in a nonunion (though still imperfectly competitive) labor market is S_L, the corresponding marginal resource cost curve for labor is MRC_L, and the firm's demand for labor is D_L, the latter reflecting the firm's marginal revenue product of labor in an imperfectly competitive product market. The intersection of MRC_L and MRP_L determines the equilibrium wage and employment rates for the firm—W_1 and L_1, respectively.

But if a union organizes the firm's employees and uses its bargaining power to push the effective average wage rate to W_2, the firm's supply curve for labor becomes the kinked line W_2CAS_L, which is horizontal over the range W_2CA. Observe the effect this has upon the unionized firm's optimum employment rate. Since the unionized firm's labor supply curve is the line W_2CAS_L, the firm's marginal resource cost curve for labor becomes $W_2CABMRC_L$. A new intersection of MRC_L and MRP_L occurs at point C, giving an equilibrium employment rate of L_2 units. Thus, not only can the union benefit its members by increasing wages, but it can also increase em-

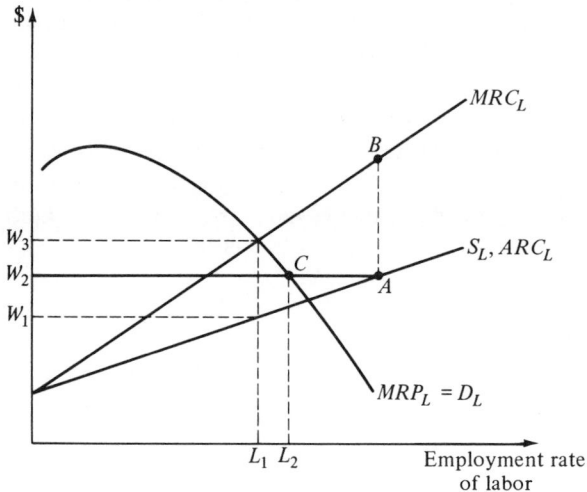

Fig. 14-12   The Effect of Union-Negotiated Wage Rates Upon the Firm's Labor Input Decision

ployment rates because of the effect which contract wage rates have upon the shape of the firm's labor supply curve. Actually, the union can push the average wage rate all the way up to W_3 before the firm will find it advantageous to reduce its labor employment rate below the preunionization rate of L_1 units. Thus, we have the rather surprising conclusion that a union *may* initially have the effect of increasing both a firm's average wage rate and its employment rate, provided it does not insist upon pushing the wage rate up too far. This indeed constitutes a powerful argument in favor of unions—at least from the standpoint of union members.

Referring again to Figure 14-12, suppose the union bargains for and gets wage increases that push the average wage above W_3, thereby making it advantageous for the firm to cut its employment rate below L_1. Further suppose that the union views this cutback as undesirable. The union can then use its bargaining power to preclude the firm from so reducing labor employment. A major aspect of collective negotiations between unions and managements concerns working conditions and, in particular, such matters as the content of jobs, how certain operations are to be performed, the size of work crews, the quantity of work which can be expected, safety rules, the length of paid vacations, the number of paid holidays, seniority provisions, guaranteed annual wages, and supplemental unemployment benefits. In other words, there is a *work and effort bargain* in the contract, just as there is a wage bargain. A principal effect of the provisions relating to the work and effort bargain is to give unions a measure of influence over the firm's employment rate, either directly or indirectly—at least in the short run.

Experience clearly indicates that unions use these provisions to "make work" and to keep the number of persons employed in specific jobs, firms, and industries higher than managements might otherwise maintain. The notorious instances of featherbedding in the railroad industry and the output quotas in the construction industry are classic cases in point. Consequently, in a unionized firm the mere fact that labor's *MRC* exceeds its *MRP* is no guarantee that the firm will adjust its input of labor downward. The discretionary action of the firm's managers in regard to the labor input decision is heavily constrained by the provisions of its collective bargaining contract. Because of this, managers of unionized firms find strict adherence to the $MRC = MRP$ rule a practical impossibility; work schedules, job assignments, and work loads can be altered only within limits. To some extent, therefore, the marginal productivity approach to input pricing and input employment is impeded, if not replaced, by the institutional mechanism of collective bargaining insofar as unionized firms are concerned. However, since most managements retain almost complete authority over the capital-labor input mix in building new production facilities, the power of unions to influence employment rates in the long run is somewhat less; managers are undoubtedly guided in their selection of the capital-labor input mix for new facilities by their perceptions of the expected relative contributions and costs of capital and labor.

The Effects of Unions on Economywide Wage Rates and Employment Rates.   Few economists would deny that unions in certain firms and industries have won highly favorable wage increases for their members. But whether unions have pushed wages up faster than they would have risen anyway is a much trickier (and hotly contested) issue.[26] And, significantly, the issue defies precise resolution, since it involves a comparison of what has actually happened with what might have happened under another set of circumstances. There simply is no way of knowing for sure what the relative wages of various industries would be if all industries were nonunion; any estimates to this effect are little better than educated conjectures.[27] Even so, it seems fair to say that unions are in a good position to win "above-average" wage gains on a consistent basis when (1) the percentage of unionized firms in the industry is high and it is difficult for nonunion firms to enter; (2) bargaining is on an industrywide basis so that all firms in the industry are equally affected; (3) industry and firm profits are high enough that the firms can "afford" substantial wage increases without endangering their competitive position; (4) the industry is a strategic one such that work stoppages have serious economywide implications; and (5) the union controls entry to the trade via apprenticeship and other regulations. On the whole, it is significant to note that in most occupational categories, wage rates in unionized firms exceed those in nonunion enterprises—even after allowing for differences in regional location, size of firm, size of community, and type of pay system (incentive wages or hourly wages).[28] Nor is it mere circumstance that above-average wage rates pervade the center economy where unions are strongest and where the wage agreements between large unions and large corporations set the pattern of wage changes throughout the economy. In manufacturing, center firms have proven easier to organize than periphery firms, mainly because the above conditions are found more frequently in the center economy than in the periphery economy. Particularly, the greater ability of center firms to pay higher wages offers unions an attractive target.

---

[26] The literature on this issue is large and contains a number of studies with conflicting findings. The interrested reader should consult, *inter alia*, Arthur Ross and William Goldner, "Forces Affecting the Interindustry Wage Structure," *Quarterly Journal of Economics*, Vol. 64, No. 2 (May 1950), pp. 254–281; Harry Douty, "Union and Nonunion Wages," in W. S. Woytinsky and Associates, *Employment and Wages in the United States* (New York: The Twentieth Century Fund, 1953), pp. 493–501; Frank C. Pierson, "The Economic Influence of Big Unions," in *Labor Relations in an Expanding Economy*, Annals of the American Academy of Political and Social Science (January 1961), pp. 96–107; Martin Segal, "Unionism and Wage Movements," *Southern Economic Journal*, Vol. 28, No. 2 (October 1961), pp. 174–81; Albert Rees, *The Economics of Trade Unions* (Chicago: The University of Chicago Press, 1962), Chap. 4; Gregg Lewis, *Unionism and Relative Wages in the United States* (Chicago: The University of Chicago Press, 1963); and Vernon T. Clover, "Compensation in Union and Nonunion Plants 1960–1965," *Industrial and Labor Relations Review*, Vol. 21, No. 2 (January 1968), pp. 226–233.

[27] Comparisons of wage movements between union and nonunion firms and industries are not really very satisfactory because of the differences which exist in geographical location, sizes and types of firms, competitive pressures, technological processes, the proportion of labor costs to total costs, productivity changes, and so forth. These factors, as well as the presence or absence of a union, affect wage movements and parceling out their separate effects presents almost insurmountable statistical difficulties.

[28] Douty, "Union and Nonunion Wages," pp. 496–497.

The wage-raising effects of collective bargaining, to whatever extent they exist, therefore fall first and most heavily upon center firms. As a consequence, the supply price of blue-collar labor services to center firms tends to be higher than for periphery firms—a fact which partially accounts for the greater tendency of center firms to substitute capital for production labor.

A much more apparent effect of union activity relates to the overall supply of labor. Unions have sought to limit immigration to the United States. They have set the pace in reducing the standard number of hours worked per day and per week. They have won longer paid vacations and more paid holidays for their members. They have worked actively to reduce the age at which persons may retire and begin to draw pension checks. They have supported strong child labor laws and minimum age requirements for entering certain hazardous occupations. All this adds up to a considerable reduction in the number of man-hours of work time which are available for hire at each wage rate. The outcome is an economywide supply curve for labor that is certain to be to the left of where it might otherwise have been. One can conclude with a high degree of confidence that the restriction of labor supply by unions has contributed to a higher level of wages in the United States.[29]

Summary and Conclusions

The marginal productivity approach to input pricing and input employment is a systematic attempt to analyze the principles governing a firm's input decision and to explain the functioning of the markets for resource inputs. Three basic models of input pricing and employment stand out: (1) the model of perfect competition in both product and resource markets; (2) the model of imperfect competition in the product market and perfect competition in the resource market; and (3) the model of imperfect competition in both product and resource markets. In all three models, one theme underlies the firm's input decision: to maximize profits the firm should adjust the usage of each input to the point where the added revenue the firm receives from using the last unit of the input equals the added costs associated with employing the input. A firm's usage of an input depends upon what the input is worth to the firm relative to the costs of using it. This principle holds irrespective of the type of market circumstance in which the firm's product is sold or in which the input is purchased. It is from the $MRP = MRC$ rule that input prices and input employment rates are ultimately determined and the incomes accruing to resource owners are ultimately derived.

As a first approximation to the functioning of input markets, the

[29] This point is made by Lloyd Reynolds, *Economics*, 3rd ed. (Homewood Ill.: Richard D. Irwin, Inc., 1969), p. 493.

demand and supply analyses of the three marginal productivity models is relatively sound. However, there exist numerous imperfections in and barriers to the free interplay of market forces. Collective bargaining, minimum wage laws, wage-price controls, and resource immobility, to mention only the more important, impede the attainment of free market equilibrium and cause outcomes which may deviate far and long from the equilibrium position suggested by marginal productivity analysis.

SUGGESTED READINGS

BAUMOL, W. J., *Economic Theory and Operations Analysis*, 3rd ed. (Englewood Cliffs, N.J.: Prentice-Hall, Inc., 1972), Chaps. 16 and 17.

BISHOP, ROBERT L., "A Firm's Short-Run and Long-Run Demands for a Factor," *Western Economic Journal*, Vol. 5, No. 1 (March 1967), pp. 122–140.

CARTTER, ALLAN M., and F. RAY MARSHALL, *Labor Economics: Wages, Employment and Trade Unionism*, Rev. Ed. (Homewood, Ill.: Richard D. Irwin, Inc., 1972), Chapters 8–11 and 13.

CHAMBERLAIN, NEIL W., *The Labor Sector* (New York: McGraw-Hill, Inc., 1965), Chaps. 17, 18, and 19.

DYE, HOWARD S., "A Bargaining Theory of Residual Income Distribution," *Industrial and Labor Relations Review*, Vol. 21, No. 1 (October 1967), pp. 40–54.

FERGUSON, CHARLES E., *The Neoclassical Theory of Production and Distribution* (London and New York: Cambridge University Press, 1969), Chaps. 6, 7, 11, and 12.

PERLMAN, RICHARD, *Labor Theory* (New York: John Wiley & Sons, Inc., 1969), Chaps. 1, 2, 5, and 10.

PIERSON, FRANK C., "An Evaluation of Wage Theory," *New Concepts in Wage Determination*, eds. George W. Taylor and Frank C. Pierson (New York: McGraw-Hill, Inc., 1957), pp. 3–31.

REDER, MELVIN, "The Theory of Union Wage Policy," *Review of Economics and Statistics*, Vol. 34, No. 1 (February 1952), pp. 34–55.

REES, ALBERT, "The Effects of Unions on Resource Allocation," *Journal of Law and Economics*, Vol. 6 (October 1963), pp. 69–78.

RUSSELL, R. ROBERT, "A Graphical Proof of the Impossibility of a Positively Inclined Demand Durve for a Factor of Production," *American Economic Review*, Vol. 54, No. 5 (September 1964), pp. 726–732; and the critique of this proof by David M. Winch, "The Demand Curve for a Factor of Production: Comment," *American Economic Review*, Vol. 55, No. 4 (September 1965), pp. 856–861.

Problems and Questions for Discussion

1. (a) Explain the difference between marginal revenue and marginal revenue product.
   (b) Explain the difference between marginal cost and marginal resource cost.

(c) What is the relationship between an input's *SVMP* and its *MRP* when the output is sold under conditions of perfect competition? Under conditions of imperfect competition?

2. Complete the following table for a firm.

Units of Input X	Quantity of Output	MP_X	Product Price	TR	MRP_X	Supply Price of X	MRC_X
0	0	——	$5	——	——	$50	——
1	20	——	5	——	——	50	——
2	44	——	5	——	——	50	——
3	64	——	5	——	——	50	——
4	80	——	5	——	——	50	——
5	92	——	5	——	——	50	——
6	100	——	5	——	——	50	——
7	104	——	5	——	——	50	——

(a) Do the figures in the table suggest a perfectly or imperfectly competitive product market? Why? Do the figures indicate a perfectly or imperfectly competitive input market? Why?

(b) What is the profit-maximizing input of X?

3. Suppose a firm employs only one variable input (X) and that the equation expressing the firm's marginal revenue product function for X is

$$MRP_X = 60 + 4X - X^2.$$

Suppose the firm's supply price for input X is fixed at $28 per unit. What is the firm's profit-maximizing input rate of X?

4. Complete the following table showing production, cost and revenue data for a firm having only one variable input.

Units of Variable Input X	Quantity of Output	MP_X	Product Price	TR	"Average" MR	MRP_X	Supply Price of X	TVC	MRC_X
0	0	——	$25	——	——	——	$400	——	——
1	50	——	24	——	——	——	420	——	——
2	110	——	23	——	——	——	440	——	——
3	160	——	22	——	——	——	460	——	——
4	200	——	21	——	——	——	480	——	——
5	230	——	20	——	——	——	500	——	——
6	250	——	19	——	——	——	520	——	——
7	260	——	18	——	——	——	540	——	——

(a) What type of product and resource markets are indicated by the figures in the table?

(b) What is the profit-maximizing input rate of X?

5. The Alpha-Omega Corporation uses only one variable input in its production process—input X. Studies of the firm's revenue data indicate the following relationship between *TR* and the input rate of X:

$$TR = 144 + 70X - X^2.$$

Studies also indicate that the input supply curve for X which confronts Alpha-Omega may be expressed by the equation:

$$P_X = 13 + .5X.$$

Determine the profit-maximizing input rate for X.

6. Given the following data for labor input; product prices; and wage rates:

Number of Workers of a Given Skill and Training	"Average" MP_L	Product Price	Daily Wage $(P_L=ARC_L)$
0	—	$2	—
10	18	2	$12
20	17	2	14
30	16	2	16
40	15	2	18
50	14	2	20
60	13	2	22
70	12	2	24
80	11	2	26

(a) Determine the profit-maximizing employment rate of labor and the equilibrium daily wage for a firm faced with the above schedules.

(b) Suppose a minimum daily wage of $24 is imposed upon the firm. Determine the profit-maximizing employment rate of labor.

(c) How do you reconcile the differences, if any, in your answers to (a) and (b)? Explain fully.

7. Consider the following two statements:
   "An increase in the demand for an input raises its price."
   "An increase in an input's price reduces demand for the input."

How can this pair of statements be reconciled? Does it make any difference in your answer whether perfect or imperfect competition characterizes the input market? The product market?

8. It has sometimes been advocated that firms should reward inputs according to their respective marginal product. That is to say, if the last unit of an input has a marginal product of 10 units and if these 10 units have a market value of $50, then the input is entitled to a monetary reward of $50. Any payment less than $50 entails "exploitation" of the input. What validity, if any, do you see in this position?

9. Suppose input X is the only variable input which a firm uses to produce product A. The firm sells product A under conditions of imperfect competition and buys input X under conditions of imperfect competition. What effect would you expect each of the following to have upon the firm's usage of input X? Be sure to distinguish between a movement along the firm's demand curve for X and a shift in the location of the demand curve. If any uncertainty exists as to the impact upon the usage of X, then specify the causes of the uncertainty.

(a) An increase in the demand for product A.

(b) The appearance of a new and very good substitute for product A.

(c) A technological improvement in the capital equipment which input X works with in producing product A.

(d) An increase in the supply of input X.

10. It is well known that average wage rates in the United States are higher than in foreign countries. Business firms often lament that this puts them at a severe cost disadvantage in competing with foreign firms. Unions reply that U.S. workers are generally healthier and better trained than workers in foreign nations and, further, that U.S. workers generally have more and better capital equipment with which to work. These factors, the unions claim, offset the wage rate differential.

  (a) Explain the rationale of the union argument in terms of marginal productivity analysis.

  (b) In recent years, Japan and several Western European nations have greatly closed the gap in worker productivity by raising the living standards of their population and by adopting the very latest production technologies. What implications does this have for the ability of U.S. firms to continue to pay higher wages and still compete in world markets?

15

Growth Equilibrium
for The Firm
and for The Economy

Preceding chapters have emphasized the decisions of consumers, firms, and resource owners and the functioning of both product and resource markets. The decisions of individual economic units and the workings of individual markets have been viewed separately and in isolation from one another— mainly because one cannot undertake a detailed analysis of everything at once and not because it actually works this way in the real world. In fact, of course, the decisions and behavior of consumers interact with and affect the decisions and behavior of firms; the decisions and behavior of firms interact with and affect the functioning of product and resource markets; and the operations of product and resource markets interact with and affect economic activity as a whole. Indeed, whatever goes on in one part of the economy is related either directly or indirectly to what goes on in another part, though sometimes the relationship is negligible or imperceptible. The point is that individual economic units and markets, taken together, make up an economy. Microeconomics is ultimately very concerned about how these units and markets fit together and how well the resulting *economic system* functions.

This chapter will provide an introduction to the branch of micro-economics that deals with the interactions and interrelationships among the various decision-making units and the various markets. Attention is first directed toward the conditions requisite for establishing static general equilibrium throughout the economy. Next, the analysis shifts to the problem of maintaining general equilibrium over time, with emphasis on dynamic growth equilibrium at the levels of the firm and the economy.

Static Equilibrium on an Economywide Basis

In broad terms, general equilibrium for an entire economy exists when all economic units simultaneously achieve equilibrium positions, when the quantity demanded equals the quantity supplied in each and every product and resource market, and when the major economic sectors are in balance. Suppose we examine these conditions in a bit more detail.

THE CONDITIONS OF GENERAL EQUILIBRIUM

Given the limitations of his income and the prices he must pay for the available goods and services, a consumer is in equilibrium when his expenditure-saving mix yields maximum satisfaction. This requires not only that he make full utilization of his income but that he arrange his purchases so the marginal utility per dollar spent on the last unit of each commodity is equal for all commodities actually purchased. For general equilibrium to prevail, all consumers must be at their perceived utility-maximizing equilibrium positions. However, this is not to say that the consumer is guaranteed satisfaction or happiness in this mechanism. All that is implied is that they realize the most advantageous combination of satisfactions, given the prevailing set of circumstances.

A business firm is in equilibrium when its product prices, output rates, and input rates have been adjusted to the point where the firm attains its set of goals (profit, sales, market share, and so on) to the fullest extent that demand and cost conditions will permit. As a point of clarification, it is long-run, not short-run, equilibrium that is the pertinent equilibrium state for the firm; this is because short-run equilibrium positions are temporary and market forces are working to move the firm to the long-run equilibrium position. Firms cannot really be said to be in a state of rest with no incentive or opportunity to make adjustments unless the markets in which they operate are in long-run equilibrium.

A resource owner is in equilibrium when the resource inputs he owns or controls are employed to their maximum advantage, balancing the consideration of monetary reward with his nonmonetary preferences. More specifically, workers are supplying labor at equilibrium rates when they have attained the most advantageous combination of work, leisure, and income, subject to the constraints imposed by their skills and abilities and the realizable opportunities for employment. The owners of property resources, being less affected by nonmonetary elements in deploying such resources, may be viewed as supplying property resources at equilibrium rates when the latter are allocated to the uses yielding the highest long-run monetary income and taking into consideration the attitudes of resource owners towards risk.

For the equilibrium conditions of consumers, business firms, and resource owners to be met simultaneously, a number of other less apparent conditions must be present. First, general equilibrium requires the price and output rate for each separate commodity to be pegged at levels consistent with demand and supply. Neither surplus nor shortage conditions for a commodity can exist, since the presence of either will elicit price and/or output rate adjustments by the firms concerned.

Second, the equilibrium which emerges in each commodity market must be based not only on the particular demand and supply conditions for that commodity in isolation but also upon demand and supply conditions for complementary and substitute products. That is to say, the various prices and output rates for all commodities must be mutually consistent. The flows of commodities through the economy must not result in the accumulation of surpluses in one sector and the appearance of shortages in another. This requirement is in recognition of the interdependencies among commodities and sectors. (We shall elaborate upon the specifics of this requirement later in the chapter.)

Third, the same equilibrium characteristics of commodity markets must be present in resource input markets. Input prices and employment rates must be at positions which allow for a mutually consistent equilibrium *among* input markets as well as for equilibrium in a particular input market. The average price of each input must call forth an overall supply of that input which, when allocated among the alternative uses of the input, results both in equilibrium employment rates in each of the alternative firms and industries and in an equilibrium demand-supply combination for the input on an economywide basis. Given the prevailing patterns of input prices, firms must have no motive for changing their input mix.

Although the market mechanisms of changing prices, output rates, and input rates are most prominent in the process of reaching equilibrium, other factors are present. Underneath the surface are the guiding forces of consumer tastes and preferences, production and managerial technologies, limitations of resource supplies, business goals, and national priorities. In a static analysis, these forces are generally assumed to be constant. Provided that they remain fixed long enough, it is conceivable that the entire pattern of economic activity could adjust to them. Then each product and resource market would reach its own unique equilibrium, the equilibrium results in all markets would be consistent, and no forces would be acting to cause further adjustments. The economic system would settle into a fixed pattern whereby the same amount of the same commodities would be produced via the same technology-input mix by the same firms and would be bought by the same consumers with the same-sized incomes. The overall rate of economic activity would neither rise nor fall. This state of affairs is what is meant by *static general equilibrium*.[1]

THE INTERRELATIONSHIPS OF INDUSTRIES AND MARKETS

The complexities of static general equilibrium are worth further exploration, especially as concerns the interrelatedness of product and resource markets. Suppose initially that a state of static general equilibrium exists and there then occurs an increase in the demand of consumers for mobile homes. Let us trace through some of the chief effects of this "disturbance" upon the system of markets.

The first response to the demand increase will be a shift in the optimum price of mobile homes. Most likely, the retail prices of mobile homes will stiffen (the discounts from list prices will be smaller) as retailers discover the greater willingness of consumers to pay a higher net price. The brisk sales stemming from the rise in demand will prompt the sellers of mobile homes to increase the orders they place with manufacturers. The mobile home manufacturers can be counted upon to react to the influx of new orders by stepping up production rates and perhaps by raising wholesale prices, depending upon how hard pressed they are to fill the additional orders from retailers and depending upon their relative preferences for more profits, faster growth, a larger market share, and so on. The rise in the output of mobile homes will affect the demand of those firms manufacturing the resource inputs used in the production of mobile homes—sheet aluminum, window glass, axles, tires, sinks, shower stalls, carpeting, electric wiring supplies, and light fixtures, as well as the labor services of the various semiskilled and skilled construction workers needed for the mobile home assembling process. Since these resource

[1] Economic theorists have spent a great deal of time and energy formulating mathematical models and deriving sets of equations in an effort to determine whether general equilibrium is possible. Most of the modern work has concerned general equilibrium in a *perfectly competitive environment*, primarily because of the mathematical simplicity and neatness of the perfectly competitive model. The results of these efforts do indicate that in a perfectly competitive economy it is possible to achieve general equilibrium without imposing unacceptable constraints upon the values of the relevant economic variables. However, no set of reasonably realistic, sufficient conditions for a stable equilibrium has yet been presented. For a simplified mathematical treatment of the theory of general equilibrium in a perfectly competitive economy, the reader is referred to K. J. Cohen and R. M. Cyert, *Theory of the Firm: Resource Allocation in a Market Economy* (Englewood Cliffs, N.J.: Prentice-Hall, Inc., 1965), Chap. 9. For more advanced discussions, see J. Quirk and R. Saposnik, *Introduction to General Equilibrium Theory and Welfare Economics* (New York: McGraw-Hill, Inc., 1968); R. E. Kuenne, *The Theory of General Economic Equilibrium* (Princeton, N.J.: Princeton University Press, 1963); Kenneth J. Arrow and Gerard Debreu, "Existence of an Equilibrium for a Competitive Economy," *Econometrica*, Vol. 22, No. 3 (July 1954), pp. 265–289; and Lionel McKenzie, "On the Existence of General Equilibrium for a Competitive Market," *Econometrica*, Vol. 27, No. 1 (January 1959), pp. 54–71.

But while it is valuable to be able to demonstrate that general equilibrium can exist in a perfectly competitive economy, the fact remains that real-world economies are far removed from being perfectly competitive and are becoming even further removed as the trend toward a corporate economy proceeds to run its course. Thus, the more relevant theoretical question revolves around the possibilities of an internally consistent general equilibrium in an *imperfectly competitive environment*. This problem so far has not been satisfactorily resolved by economic theorists, although in recent years it has received increasing attention. See Wassily Leontief, *The Structure of the American Economy* (New York: Oxford University Press, 1951), and the articles by Kenneth Arrow, John Lintner, and Robert Solow in *The Corporate Economy: Growth, Competition, and Innovative Potential*, edited by Robin Marris and Adrian Wood (Cambridge, Mass.: Harvard University Press, 1971).

Since the mathematics of general equilibrium in an imperfectly competitive environment entails a degree of sophistication well beyond the scope of this book, we shall confine our discussion to presenting a conceptual framework for economywide equilibrium in a corporate economy, sidestepping the issue of whether the conditions required are in fact wholly compatible with each other.

inputs will have to be bid away from other uses, their prices will tend to be pulled upward. The mobile home manufacturers, by intensifying the competition for the needed resource inputs, will be forced to increase their offer prices for inputs. As this occurs, the firms losing the inputs may find it necessary to increase their offer prices in order to counteract the shift of needed inputs to the mobile home industry. The higher input prices imply rising costs and narrowing profit margins in the affected firms and industries.

Furthermore, should the induced shift of labor to the mobile home industry entail either a geographic relocation of workers and their families or the construction of new mobile home production facilities in areas where the needed supply of labor is available, the construction firms and the suppliers of building matrials will experience an increase in the demand for their products (either from the demand for new housing or from the demand for new production facilities). This will further enlarge the affected product and resource markets, requiring additional price, output, and input adjustments.

However, the effects of the increase in the demand for mobile homes do not just reverberate back through the shifts in the input demands of the mobile home manufacturers. The higher demand for mobile homes will increase the demand for mobile home spaces in trailer parks, for compactly styled furniture, for equipment and accessories to transport mobile homes, and for portable power equipment. In addition, increases in mobile home ownership will elicit changes in the demand for other types of living accommodations—apartments, rental dwellings, and family-owned residences—thereby causing further adjustments in the residential construction and building materials industry. All of the businesses catering to consumer loans, home mortgages, and real estate financing (banks, savings and loan associations, and finance companies) will feel the effects of the resulting rise in the demand for credit to finance the purchase of mobile homes and the diminished demand for credit to finance other living accommodations. Insurance companies will need to respond to the shift in the demand for various types of homeowner's policies regarding fire, theft, property liability, and damage from acts of nature, perhaps, by instituting an entirely new form of policy designed to cover the special risks of mobile home ownership. The higher demand for mobile homes also implies a far-reaching shift in life styles and consumption habits which will eventually have ramifications in such markets as those for household appliances, lawn and garden accessories, recreation goods, automobiles, camping equipment, tourism, and local convenience services. The resulting product demand changes not only will entail additional price and output rate adjustments by the affected firms but also will be transmitted back into the resource input markets relevant to all these products.

This is still not all: an increase in the number of mobile home owners has important consequences for the supplies of labor and land. Greater use of mobile homes should make workers more mobile, thus rendering the supplies of some labor services more elastic over time. More land will be needed for mobile home parks, mobile home communities, mobile home campsites, and overnight parking facilities; less land will be needed for permanently located single- and multiple-family residences. In the public sector, the changing makeup of housing and living patterns will alter the nature of the demand for local government services and the structure of property taxation, the latter having implications for shifting the relative profitabilities of various types of housing investments and causing a realignment in real estate investment patterns. Finally, the whole array of price-output-input adjustments will affect wages, salaries, profits, rents, and interest rates in the affected firms and industries, causing some redistribution of personal income. These income changes will prompt yet another series of price-output-input reactions as the affected consumers revise their expenditure patterns and saving rates to conform to the new income constraints.

If one had the tenacity and the inclination, the entire sequence of equilibrium adjustments and market linkages could be pursued to its ultimate conclusion and the entire set of market interrelationships pinned down. But the major point is already apparent. Product and resource markets are linked together directly and indirectly to form a market *network*. Given a state of static general equilibrium, any initial disturbance, whether it be a change in product demand, a change in resource supply conditions, an increase in population, a breakthrough in production technology, or a new product innovation, will trigger a complex chain reaction through the network of product and resource markets. The initial disturbance creates effects which spill over into adjacent markets and cause them to move toward new equilibrium positions. These secondary effects in turn generate new waves and ripples, which are carried by the various market linkages into a third set of product and resource markets. The third-order changes may extend back into the primary market where the initial disturbance occurred or back into the secondary markets and may also generate still higher-order effects transcending yet more distant markets. Barring further disturbances, the effects of the initial disturbance will eventually dissipate, new equilibrium positions will be reached, and a state of general equilibrium will be restored.

THE INTERRELATIONSHIPS OF ECONOMIC SECTORS

The foregoing paragraphs explain how markets are linked together. We now turn to the linkages between economic sectors. The term *economic sector* refers simply to a grouping of closely related markets.

Figure 15-1 provides a convenient graphical summary and synthesis of the flow of dollars and commodities through the economy, showing how the major economic sectors are related. Starting at the box on the left, we see that the process of producing goods and services gives rise to an aggregate amount of income equal to the market value of what has been produced. This simple,

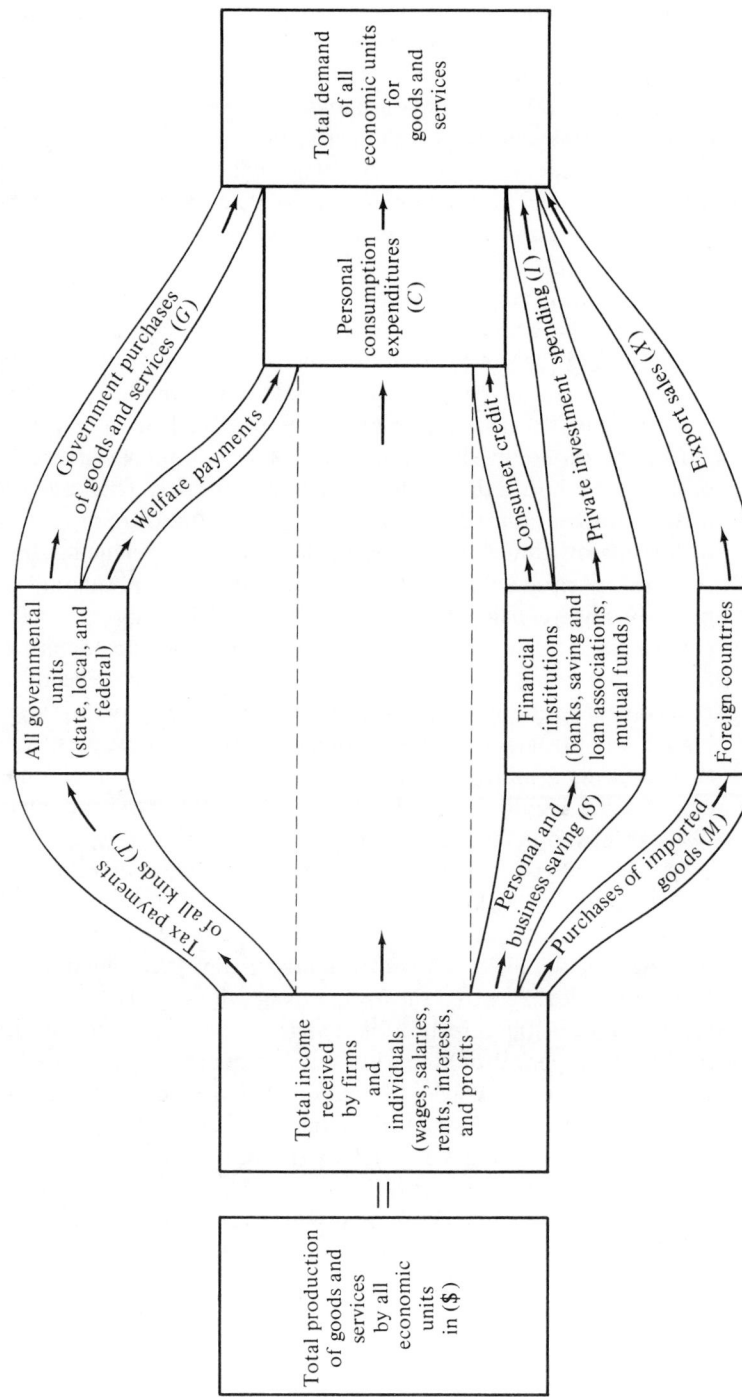

Fig. 15-1 A Simplified Model of the Operation of a Market Economy

but crucial, proposition follows from the fact that the monetary value of a commodity is determined by the market value of the economic resources required to produce it.[2] Four basic things can be done with the income which economic units (firms and households) receive from the production process: (1) a portion is paid to government in the form of taxes (T), (2) a portion is saved (S) and, temporarily at least, deposited in various financial institutions, (3) a portion may be used to pay for goods imported from foreign countries (M), and (4) far and away the major portion goes to purchase consumer goods and services (C).

Obviously enough, governmental units use the tax revenues they receive to pay for the goods and services required for carrying out governmental functions and for various income redistribution programs. Foreign countries use the dollars they receive from the sale of commodities to U.S. citizens to purchase goods which they desire to buy from us; hence the leakage of income out of the economy via imports tends to be counterbalanced by an inflow of money back into the economy from export sales. The flow of savings into financial institutions comes out in the form of funds for consumer credit and for private investment spending; the latter includes financing the replacement of worn-out production facilities, the expansion of production capacity, and new housing (considered as investment spending by national income accountants). The demand side of the economic picture therefore consists of four major components: (1) personal consumption expenditures (C), (2) government spending for goods and services (G), (3) private investment spending (I), and (4) sales of goods to foreign countries or exports (X). Figure 15-1 thus presents a model of the linkages between the major economic sectors, emphasizing the flows of dollars and commodities and the relationships between total supply and total demand.[3]

For analytical convenience suppose we refer to the tax, savings, and import flows as "leakages" and the government spending, investment, and export flows as "injections." The rectangular boxes across the diagram may be viewed as the main income-spending stream. It is evident that the balance between the leakages and the injections provides the key to overall economic stability and to the direction of change in the rate of economic activity. If during some period of time (a month, a quarter, a year, or whatever) the dollar sum of the leakages ($T + S + M$) is just equal to the dollar sum of the injections ($G + I + X$), then the total dollar value of the goods and services produced will be equal to the dollar value of total spending on goods and services. To put it differently, when the leakages equal the injections, then the income generated from the current rate of production is,

---

[2] This is a fundamental proposition of macroeconomics, usually explained in detail in principles of economics texts. See, among others, Campbell R. McConnell, *Economics*, 5th ed. (New York: McGraw-Hill, Inc., 1972), Chap. 10; and G. L. Bach, *Economics*, 7th ed. (Englewood Cliffs, N.J.: Prentice-Hall, Inc., 1971), Chaps. 5, 6, 7, and 8.

[3] This model can easily be expanded to portray in more detail the ties between various subsectors of the economy. However, for our purposes the simplified model of Figure 15-1 will suffice.

after being allocated to the various spending components, converted into a volume of expenditures just sufficient to provide a matching total demand; the total demand for goods and services is exactly equal to the total supply of goods and services. Assuming, not unrealistically, that the composition of these goods and services is in accord with buyer preferences, all markets will be cleared of their output and the economy may be said to be in equilibrium— no forces will operate to cause the overall rate of economy activity to either increase or decrease. Such is the nature of general equilibrium at the level of the whole economy.

On the other hand, whenever the leakages and the injections do not balance, a state of disequilibrium exists, and forces immediately and automatically spring into action to rectify the situation. Suppose, for instance, that a portion of the dollars flowing into government, or foreign countries, or financial institutions somehow get trapped and are not spent. Then the size of the leakage flow will exceed the size of the injection flow. This has the effect of causing the prevailing production rates to exceed the rates at which goods are being purchased. Total supply will exceed total demand. As business firms see sales slipping and inventories of unsold goods piling up, they will respond by cutting prices and/or curtailing production rates. Typically, the prices of perishable, seasonal, and faddish commodities, as well as those which are expensive to store, will be reduced in an effort to stimulate buying and eliminate unwanted surpluses. But, in the cases of durable and easily stockpiled items, firms may find it more profitable to maintain prices and cut back on production rates until demand conditions become more favorable. The combination of falling prices and lower production rates will reduce incomes—wages and salary incomes will be lower because of the lessened need for labor inputs, and profits will be lower because of lower sales volumes and slimmer profit margins. The decline in incomes and profits will cause tax revenues to fall and will also cause business firms to review the profitability of new investment spending, probably revising investment spending plans downward unless the downturn in economic activity is viewed as clearly a short-term disturbance. In general, then, when the leakages exceed the injections, the rate of economic activity will fall. The economic decline will continue until production rates and spending rates are brought into line and supply-demand equilibrium is restored in the various product markets.

At the other extreme, it is quite conceivable that the sum of the injections $(G + I + X)$ will exceed the sum of the leakages $(S + T + M)$. There are several ways in which this can occur. Governments, of course, can spend more than they collect in tax revenues by borrowing the difference; this practice, known as deficit spending, is commonly engaged in at all levels of government. Scarcely any unit of government has not at one time or another issued bonds to finance some project and then paid off the bonds over time with new tax revenues. Financial institutions can also provide new funds for investment and consumer credit in amounts which exceed current saving rates; banks, in fact, create new money whenever they exchange IOU's for demand deposits.[4] Thus both the government sector and the investment spending sector are fully capable of causing the injections flow to exceed the leakage flow at some moment of time. When and if such circumstances occur, current output rates will be inadequate to meet the total demand for goods and services; total demand will, in other words, exceed total supply. Producers who find the demand for their products outstripping current production rates have three alternative responses, which they can employ singly or in combination: (1) they can draw down inventories to help meet the excess demand; (2) they can increase production rates, provided they have unused production capacity and provided they can obtain the necessary labor and raw material inputs; and (3) they can raise prices to ration the available supplies among those buyers most anxious to obtain their products. Whatever response set producers elect—and most likely it will be some combination of all three—incomes will tend to rise, thereby stimulating further spending and expansion of economic activity. The general rise in incomes and in the overall pace of economic activity will cause tax revenues to rise, saving rates to increase, and investment in new production capacity to increase. Whether government spending will rise, fall, or remain unchanged is, of course, more a political than an economic question. The major point is that when the injections exceed the leakages, economic activity in the various economic sectors tends to be stimulated. The rise in economic activity will lose its steam when production catches up with demand and producers are just able to meet the demands for their products.

This thumbnail sketch of the interrelationships of the major economic sectors is sufficient to indicate why static general equilibrium requires not just equilibrium in each market and each related market but also balance between and among the major economic sectors. Spending patterns must be consistent with income patterns; production flows must in the aggregate match the rates at which commodities are purchased; the siphoning off of dollars in leakages must somehow be offset by the pumping of an equivalent amount of dollars back into the income-expenditure stream.

GENERAL EQUILIBRIUM AND THE OVERALL RATE OF ECONOMIC ACTIVITY

From the standpoint of society's overall economic welfare, the level of economic activity at which general equilibrium occurs makes a great deal of difference. For instance, national goals and priorities call for the achievement of full employment. Full employment requires two things: (1) that an adequate number of jobs be available for those persons who are willing and

---

[4] The money-creating activity of commercial banks is explained in all basic economic books. See, for example, McConnell, *Economics*, Chap. 17; Bach, *Economics*, Chap. 12.

able to work and (2) that the available human and property resources be deployed among alternative uses in an efficient manner. The question becomes: if general equilibrium is attained, then must it occur at a level of activity consistent with full employment?

The answer to this question is "not necessarily." Certainly there is neither an economic "law" nor a compelling force operating to peg the level of economic activity at the full employment position. As we have seen earlier, static general equilibrium requires that the total supply of goods and services be equal to the total demand for goods and services; or, putting it another way, the leakages must equal the injections. This condition guarantees that the flow of commodities through the major economic sectors will be mutually consistent; no forces will be operating to cause the overall rate of economic activity to rise or fall. Moreover, the composition of total output must be such that the demand and supply conditions for each separate commodity are consistent with equilibrium. This condition has several dimensions. Business firms must have no motives for altering prices or output rates, given the existing demand conditions. Consumers must be allocating their incomes in the optimum fashion, given the existing price and income constraints. Resource owners must be deploying their resources in the optimum pattern, given the existing demand for resource inputs and prevailing resource prices.

However, the static equilibrium position reached under these conditions may or may not represent a full employment equilibrium. Too low a level of total spending will call forth an equilibrium production rate requiring less than a full employment rate of input usage; unemployment rates for labor will rise above the tolerable and expected 3 or 4 percent target rate, and the related static equilibrium will be below the full employment level of economic activity. Too high a level of total spending will strain resource supplies and production rates to the point where higher product prices and input prices will be necessary to curb total demand and artificially bring it into line with total supply.

Nevertheless, the insatiability of consumer wants tends to generate a consistently "high" rate of economic activity; this tendency is further reinforced by the drive of center firms for growth and expansion and by the want-creating effects of new product innovation and sales promotion. But whether total spending will automatically be high enough to generate full employment is another matter. For this reason it is deemed desirable for the federal government to take an active role in using monetary and fiscal policy to promote full employment.

STATICS VERSUS DYNAMICS

The concept of static general equilibrium has practical importance because it is a useful tool of economic analysis. It would be a mistake, however, to conceive of static general equilibrium as either achievable or desirable. It is impossible in a modern industrial economy, especially a trillion-dollar economy like that of the United States, for the underlying economic conditions ever to remain fixed long enough for the forces of change to adjust to a point where they are in balance. Indeed, change is a product of the normal operation of a modern economy, and this change in turn affects the operation of the economy. The milieu of change transcends population size, consumer tastes and preferences, incomes, costs, product prices, output rates, business strategies, national economic priorities, the pattern of international competition, and so on. New technological processes and product innovations are constantly injecting new disturbances into the economic picture. Population growth, education, and training programs produce persistent rises in the quantity and quality of labor services available to producers. The net effect of these wide-ranging and perpetually emerging tendencies for economic change is to prevent a static general equilibrium from ever being achieved. Instead, new economic developments and new patterns of economic activity are constantly appearing in response to changing demand and supply conditions; in turn, product and resource markets are forever pursuing newly-created general equilibrium positions.

As indicated previously, the direction and the pace of economic change determine the gains in society's economic welfare. In a static stationary economy, the standard of living is fixed, and society as a whole is doomed to exist at the prevailing output, income, and employment rates. Progress is nonexistent. But in modern industrial economies things are quite different. Change is commonplace and all-pervasive. More important, the growth goals and growth strategies of large corporate enterprises tilt the forces of change toward economic growth—rising outputs, rising incomes, rising living standards, and a higher quality of life. Insofar, then, as economywide equilibrium in a progressive environment is concerned, the focus is not upon static general equilibrium but upon *dynamic growth equilibrium*.

Dynamic Growth Equilibrium

The study of dynamic equilibrium growth paths for an economy and the associated equilibrium growth patterns for firms constitutes one of the newest and least explored areas of economics. Moreover, because of the vast array of variables that must be taken into account, the theoretical models dealing with these topics are especially complex. For this reason, the body of theory which does exist is highly mathematical, involving a degree of sophistication well beyond the scope of this book.[5] We shall therefore restrict our considera-

[5] A representative sample of the literature of microeconomic and macroeconomic growth models includes W. J. Baumol, *Economic Dynamics*, 3rd ed. (New York: The Macmillan Company, 1970); Bent Hansen, *A Survey of General Equilibrium Systems* (New York: McGraw-Hill, Inc., 1970); Robert Dorfman, Paul A. Samuelson, and Robert Solow, *Linear Programming and Economic Analysis* (New York: McGraw-Hill, Inc., 1958), Chap. 11; Edith Penrose, *The Theory of the Growth of the Firm* (New York: John Wiley & Sons, Inc., 1959); Joan Robinson, *Essays in the Theory of Economic Growth* (New York: St. Martin's Press, 1964); and

tion of dynamic growth models and of the links between growth equilibrium for the firm and for the economy to a presentation of basic concepts, indicating in nonrigorous terms some of the basic relationships and some of the tentative conclusions which have been reached. Again, the reader is forewarned that what follows is in the formulative stages; by no means has it survived sufficient empirical testing to warrant great confidence.

GROWTH EQUILIBRIUM FOR THE ECONOMY

In an industrialized economy the quality of economic performance is judged by how well the economy adheres to a path of stable growth and noninflationary full employment. The less frequent the deviations from a path of orderly economic expansion and the smaller such deviations from the full-employment level of economic activity, the better an economy's performance is judged to be. So long as the pace of economic activity is proceeding at a rate commensurate with a stable growth path, the economy may be said to be in *growth equilibrium*.

The character of growth equilibrium on an economywide basis has a number of fundamental features. Ideally, the total output of goods and services must expand fast enough to provide employment opportunitites for all persons seeking jobs, but not so fast as to strain resource supplies to the point of unleashing wage-price-cost spirals and the knotty inflationary problems which such conditions present. Given the economy's resource capabilities, the optimum growth rate of total output is one that is consistent with the limits of technological progress and with the simultaneous achievement of price stability and full employment. Professor Joan Robinson has called such a smooth, steady expansion "a golden age" of growth.[6]

For the optimum growth rate to be realized, the leakages $(S + T + M)$ and injections $(G + I + X)$ must be kept in balance, growing in step with each other as expansion occurs. The total demand for goods and services must grow at the same pace as does the overall output rate of producers; otherwise, the size of the market for the new output will be deficient. Ordinarily, the process of growth is capable of generating the increases in income and spending needed to sustain the growth of output over time; this is because economic expansion generates new investment spending and creates new

---

Edwin Burmeister and Rodney Dobell, *Mathematical Theories of Economic Growth* (New York: The Macmillan Company, 1970). More specific studies and also more advanced mathematical discussions of economic growth paths include J. A. Mirrlees, "Optimum Growth When Technology Is Changing," *Review of Economic Studies*, Vol. 34, No. 97 (January 1967), pp. 95–124; T. C. Koopmans, "Objectives, Constraints, and Outcomes in Optimal Growth Models," *Econometrica*, Vol. 35, No. 1 (January 1967), pp. 1–15; T. C. Koopmans, "On the Concept of Optimal Economic Growth," in *The Econometric Approach to Development Planning* (Skokie, Ill.: Rand McNally and North-Holland Publishing Co., 1966); Robert Solow and Paul A. Samuelson, "Balanced Growth Under Constant Returns to Scale," *Econometrica*, Vol. 21, No. 3 (July 1953), pp. 412–424; and the Symposium on the Theory of Economic Growth, *Journal of Political Economy*, Vol. 77, No. 4, Part II (July/August, 1969).

[6] Mrs. Robinson has attached corresponding nicknames to other possible phases of growth: a limping golden age, a leaden age, a restrained golden age, a galloping platinum age, a creeping platinum age, a bastard golden age, and a bastard platinum age. See her *Essays in the Theory of Economic Growth*, pp. 51–59.

employment opportunities in amounts sufficient to provide the income requisite for purchasing the additional goods and services produced. A steady state of expansion then rolls smoothly along, with technological progress and productivity gains paving the way for increases in real incomes. New production technologies are implemented as firms build new production capacity. Profits are sufficiently high to continue to attract and provide the money capital requisite for expansion. Firms may be said to be in growth equilibrium because their realized expansion rates are, on the average, compatible with what is possible.

One may further characterize an economy in growth equilibrium by supposing that technological advances, combined with gains in the quantity and quality of resource inputs, allow for a 5 percent annual increase in the total output of goods and services when production rates are maintained at the full employment rate of input usage. Investment spending for the new production capacity needed to increase output rates and an increased demand for raw material inputs will serve to push the incomes of suppliers upward. Similarly, the new production activity will give rise to new job opportunities for blue- and white-collar workers and for managers, thus increasing wage and salary incomes. Suppose the 5 percent increase in production yields a 5 percent gain in total income. If the leakages are in balance with the injections, then the 5 percent rise in total income will in turn produce a 5 percent increase in total spending, thereby providing ample market potential for selling the additional production. Repeating this process year after year would put the economy on a steady growth path of 5 percent, which, if attained, would constitute a stable "golden age" growth equilibrium for the economy.

GROWTH EQUILIBRIUM FOR THE FIRM

Although growth equilibrium entails even and steady expansion of total output for the economy as a whole, it would be erroneous to view the output rates of each and every commodity as expanding at the economywide equilibrium growth rate. The very process of economic growth will give birth to changes in consumer tastes and preferences and to variations in the intensity of competitive pressures. Some products will die out and others will rise to prominence via the perennial gale of creative destruction. The discovery and implementation of new production techniques will alter optimum input mixes and economies of scale. These changes will provoke a variety of responses in the business sector, and all of them will play a role in determining the growth equilibrium for particular firms.

Growth equilibrium for a firm may be thought of as the path along which the firm must continually adjust its prices, output rates, and input rates so as to optimize the attainment of its complement of goals (profits, sales revenue, market share, growth, technological virtuosity, security, and so on), given the constraints imposed by the economic environment. Whatever the particular goal set of the firm, management's function in attaining growth equilibrium is to search out the particular activity mix which yields the best perceived outcome insofar as the firm's goal set is concerned. Decision makers must juggle price-output-input combinations so as to obtain the best performance, given the existing uncertainties. This is not to say that once the optimum price-output-input combination has been identified, it should be maintained into the indefinite future. Realistically, new developments arising from further economic growth of the economy will cause the optimum combination to change; thus, managers will continually be forced to modify the firm's strategy set, revising prices and output rates, adding new products and dropping old ones, implementing new technologies, shifting the organization's resources into new activities, and revamping the organization's structure and orientation to meet new priorities.

Where the demand for a commodity is increasing faster than average, firms will be motivated to respond with above-average increases in production rates. Where the demand for a commodity is increasing at below-average rates, production rates can be expected to rise more slowly than the average. Where demand is shrinking or on the verge of disappearing entirely, firms will be forced to cut back production and perhaps to go out of business or shift into the production of items with more attractive profit and sales opportunities. The variability in the growth rates of the demand for various commodities will change the composition of the economy's total output. In turn, firms will have to realign the usage of the various resource inputs in accord with demand changes and technological developments. The chief requirement which economywide growth equilibrium imposes upon producers is that the required output and input adjustments for specific products be orderly. When slack appears in one firm or industry or economic sector, it must be absorbed by expansion elsewhere in the economy; otherwise the achievement of full employment is jeopardized. Individual product prices and input prices can be raised or lowered, but on the average product prices cannot rise or fall by more than 1 or 2 percent and input prices must be kept in line with productivity changes, lest inflationary or deflationary pressures interfere with attainment of price stability.

The growth equilibrium position of particular firms will vary according to two factors: (1) the quantity and quality of the opportunities for expansion offered by the overall economic environment and (2) the respective organizational capabilities of firms regarding the quality of management, the financial resources they can marshal, and their propensities for undertaking new activities. These relationships warrant further attention, because they comprise the link between growth equilibrium for the firm and growth equilibrium for the economy.[7]

Insofar as any one product is concerned, the firm's optimum growth

---

[7] However, to the extent that the operations of firms take on an international character, rather than being constrained by the boundaries of a single national economy, the link between growth equilibrium for the firm and growth equilibrium for the economy is supplemented by a link between growth equilibrium for the firm and growth equilibrium of the international economy in which the firm operates.

rate is clearly a function of the market potential of that product—the rate at which demand is rising (or falling), the profit opportunities, the strength of competitive pressures in that product market, and the like. But firms are not restricted to producing a single product; they may widen the range of their activities to include any number of related or unrelated products and they may extend their activities to include producing and selling in international markets rather than just national markets. This is why the growth equilibrium of a particular firm is a function of the *entire* set of economywide expansion opportunities which are open to it and not just growth in the demand for the commodities it currently produces. It is clear that the size of the set of opportunities for expansion is very much dependent upon the growth equilibrium path of the economy as a whole. An economywide growth of 5 percent per year will necessarily offer firms greater expansion potential than a growth rate of only 2 percent. One may think of the economy's equilibrium growth path as opening up a certain amount of new expansion potential for firms each period which, if taken advantage of, will result in achievement of the equilibrium growth rate.

Given the full range of opportunities for expansion offered by growth equilibrium on an economywide basis, firms may be viewed as competing for the available new market potential, with each firm's own growth equilibrium being a function of (a) its perceived role in the economic setting, (b) the strategic position it has for meeting the new commodity demands generated by growth, and (c) its aggressiveness in committing resources to the available expansion opportunities. Some firms are content to continue to operate within the bounds of their current activities; thus, their growth rates are pegged directly to the expansion of the product markets in which they operate—the steel and railroad firms serve as examples. Other firms take a broader view of their capacities and branch out into new products and new markets as they approach the limits of expansion in their present products—the popularity of this strategy is reflected by the pronounced trend toward diversification by merger and acquisition evidenced by U.S. firms during the late 1960's. Firms confronted by shrinking markets and declining profit opportunities are faced with the choice of accepting a negative growth equilibrium path or else breaking out of their traditional molds and launching into new activities and new markets. In some cases, firms are in position to initiate and shape the course of economic expansion by means of new product innovations and new managerial technologies; other firms will be growth followers. Some firms are able to achieve high growth rates not so much because of careful planning and foresight but because they just happen, fortuitously, to be engaged in activities for which demand vigorously increases. Some firms may lack the financial resources to exploit fully the new opportunities which present themselves, while others will expand cautiously, engaging only in those activities which are viewed as low-risk. A variety of growth equilibrium patterns for firms present themselves. These patterns are especially distinct as between center firms and periphery firms.

CENTER FIRMS, PERIPHERY FIRMS, AND GROWTH EQUILIBRIUM

In Chapter 12 it was argued that the major impetus for growth and expansion emanates from the center economy. Indeed, the growth goals and growth strategies of center firms provide a reliable force for keeping the fires of economic expansion burning, subject only to the qualification that the economic environment remains conducive to growth. At this point it should be apparent that the major reason why center firms can, year after year, find buyers for their ever-growing flow of output and thus satisfy at least partially their drives for growth is the permissive environment generated by a growing economy.[8] Without economic growth, there are only limited opportunities for center firms to expand output rates and thereby climb to higher plateaus of goal achievement. With economic growth, the growth targets of center firms become more realizable. Thus, the growth of center firms and the growth of the economy are interwoven—the drives of center firms for expansion are the impetus for growth of the economy, but at the same time the ambitions of center firms for expansion over the long term can be translated into reality only in a growth economy. And once the growth process is initiated, the ripples of center firm expansion spill over into the periphery economy, where new demands for periphery-firm produced commodities serve to reinforce and widen the spheres of new economic activity.

There is one rather noteworthy difference between the mechanisms of economic adjustment in the periphery economy and in the center economy. In periphery firm dominated markets, shifts in equilibrium output rates are accommodated largely by the entry or exit of firms. For example, where the demand for periphery firm commodities increases, new firms are often organized to supply the increased demand, and the necessary resource supplies are bid away from alternative uses. Where the demand for periphery firm products decreases, some firms are pushed out of the industry, often dissolving entirely and leaving resources free to be used elsewhere. Adjustment to change in periphery firm markets therefore typically involves an *external* reallocation of resources in the sense that resources are forced to move *between* firms and *between* industries in the course of reaching a new equilibrium. The adjustment process relies heavily on *interfirm* resource mobility. In the center economy, however, the appearance of new firms and disappearance of old firms is a rarer phenomenon. More frequently, adjustment to changes in demand takes the form of an *internal* reallocation of resources within the corporation; that is to say, the center firm responds to change by shifting its organizational resources out of activities that are on the decline and into activities that are on the upswing. Thus, there is a relatively greater emphasis upon *intrafirm* resource mobility.

---

[8] In the 1965–1970 period, for example, the market value of total annual output in actual dollars (money GNP) in the United States rose by an average of $60 billion each year, and the market value of total annual output in constant dollars (real GNP: 1964 = 100) rose by almost $40 billion each year. This reflects substantial opportunities for business expansion in terms of both sales revenues and output.

The intrafirm aspect of resource reallocation in the center economy became quite distinct in the 1960's as an important by-product of the center firm's attention to long-range planning and forecasting as well as a necessary strategy for achieving the firm's growth target. In effect, the giant corporation with its financial capacity for undertaking new projects, its contacts with many areas and regions, its growing array of products, and its pool of managerial and technical expertise has evolved into sort of a subeconomy of its own with rather considerable powers to rechannel its energies as circumstances may require. Seldom does a center firm find itself so inflexible and locked into a stagnant or declining industry that liquidation is the most viable alternative; rather, opportunities for diversification are nearly always present, thereby allowing the firm to accommodate change by internally redeploying its resources.

A major consequence of the differential response of center and periphery firms to changing conditions is that there tends to be less *involuntary* movement of resources between firms and between industries in the center economy than in the periphery economy in order to accommodate demand-induced variations in the size and composition of total output. In an atomistically competitive environment, where the livelihood of firms rests largely on a single commodity, the adjustment to changing demands is certain to entail a heavy reliance upon interfirm resource mobility. In accordance with the models of perfect and monopolistic competition, firms must come and go in order to keep each firm operating at or near the low point of its long-run average cost curve. Such an instability in the number of firms producing a commodity causes considerable worker dislocation and compels a high degree of resource mobility if firms are to adjust rapidly to changing market conditions. Quite conceivably, the degree of mobility required for optimal adjustments may exceed societal and worker preferences. Intrafirm resource reallocation poses no such problems. Ordinarily, it is easier and faster to shift labor and other inputs from one activity to another *within a firm* than it is for marginal firms to be forced out of business, pushing the released resources out into a search for new employment in new or expanding firms. Moreover, intrafirm resource mobility circumvents the institutional barriers to interfirm resource mobility arising from family and community ties, educational and apprenticeship requirements, severance pay provisions, company retirement plans, and the like.

Two common occurrences may be cited to support the relative ease with which intrafirm resource reallocation is accomplished. First, experience has shown the seriousness of the problems in getting unemployed workers either to move to locations in other communities and regions where jobs are available or to undergo whatever retraining may be necessary to make them employable.[9] In contrast, initiating transfers of workers from one plant location to

---

[9] The long time-lags and the expense of getting the average hard-core unemployed worker retrained and relocated are well documented. So also are the problems of labor mobility between firms. See J. John Palen and Frank J. Fahey, "Unemployment and Reemployment Success: An Analysis of the Studebaker Shutdown,"

another within a corporation's sphere of activity and offering them whatever on-the-job retraining may be necessary is an everyday occurrence which, in comparison, is less painful to the workers, less time-consuming, and less expensive. Second, where unions enter the picture, we find that union leaders are not likely to oppose attempts to eliminate jobs in one of the firm's activities when the firm is willing to shift the dislocated workers to new jobs in other of its activities. But when output changes will displace workers and force them to look for employment in other firms and industries, union leaders assume a decidedly less cooperative posture towards facilitating resource reallocation in the direction of new equilibrium positions.

Thus, it seems fair to conclude, all things considered, that the internally oriented resource reallocation mechanism of the large corporation is probably more streamlined and more efficient than the externally oriented mechanisms of periphery firm markets, both because of the smaller incidence of involuntary unemployment associated with interfirm resource reallocation and because of the smaller attendant loss of production effort.

NATIONAL ECONOMIC POLICY AND GROWTH EQUILIBRIUM

It goes without saying that the achievement of a stable growth equilibrium on an economywide basis is an enormously complex task. Not only must the process of economic change be kept orderly and tidy and the proper degree of flexibility in the production mechanism be maintained, but the economic environment must also be kept conducive to just the right rate of business expansion. None of these is likely to be accomplished without design and carefully executed strategy, despite the tendency for the economy to move toward growth equilibrium. The only institution capable of promoting and coordinating growth equilibrium on an economywide front is the federal government.

In general terms, the aim of national economic policy is to see to it that the target rate of national economic growth and the associated growth equilibrium become a reality. When stimulation of investment or consumption spending is needed to provide a boost to the economy, it is the responsibility of the monetary and fiscal authorities to design an appropriate strategy and to implement it at the proper time. Such a strategy may include tax cuts, increases in government spending, increases in the money supply, and lower interest rates in whatever combination is deemed most appropriate for the particular situation. On the other hand, when growth proceeds so fast that inflation is a by-product, then the economic pulse must be slowed by means of some combination of tax increases, restraints upon government spending, a tightening up of the money supply, higher interest rates, and

Industrial and Labor Relations Review, Vol. 21, No. 2 (January 1968), pp. 234–250; Richard J. Solie, "Employment Effects of Retraining the Unemployed," *Industrial and Labor Relations Review*, Vol. 21, No. 2 (January 1968), pp. 210–225; Kenneth O. Alexander, "Employment Shifts in Areas of Persistent Unemployment," *Industrial and Labor Relations Review*, Vol. 22, No. 1 (October 1968), pp. 73–84; and Paul S. Goddman, "Hiring, Training, and Retraining the Hard-Core," *Industrial Relations*, Vol. 9, No. 3 (October 1969), pp. 54–66.

wage-price controls. In other words, the federal government has the responsibility of orchestrating national economic policy such that the economic throttle is kept turned to the right speed; otherwise, the possibility of attaining a stable growth equilibrium is remote.

Actually, of course, keeping a trillion-dollar economy directly on the path of a stable growth equilibrium over the long term is really too much to expect of policymakers, given the uncertainities of economic change, the lack of well-defined and coordinated policies for maintaining economic stability, and the political constraints which are inevitably present. Steering a course of noninflationary full employment and at the same time keeping the rate of increase in economic activity steady is much like trying to guide a raft through swirling rapids on an unknown river—the course ahead is uncharted, the going is tricky, and the margin for error to either side is razor thin. Thus, a more realistic interpretation of the role and function of public policy is for it to attempt to minimize the size and the frequency of deviations from the target growth path. But even this objective is likely to prove elusive— as is amply testified to by the recurrent ups and downs in the pace of economic activity, and by the frequently unrealized predictions of governmental policymakers.[10] Nevertheless, attempting to keep the economy as close to the target equilibrium growth path as is possible is a very reasonable way of conceiving the goal of national economic policy.

At the same time that policymakers are engaged in promoting a golden age of economic growth and noninflationary full employment, consideration must also be given to the *directions* of growth and expansion. In recent years, a few economists and a number of young people from the middle- and upper-income classes have questioned the wisdom of a strong growth orientation.[11] They have argued that the consequences of industrial expansion entail greater environmental pollution, urban congestion, and faster depletion and spoilage of natural resources. They suggest that a more desirable objective is to raise the "quality of life." Their point about "the growth of what for whom" is well-taken (and is in the process of being heeded), but it is erroneous to conclude that economic growth *per se* is in conflict with improving the quality of life. Rather, economic growth, if properly channeled, is the key to achieving a better environment, just as it always has been. After all, it is economic growth which has freed societies in industrialized nations from their struggle against hunger, disease, poverty, ignorance, long work days, and short lives, thereby allowing them to attain their present quality of life.

Without further economic growth, it is unclear how the problems of urban decay, housing shortages, slum living conditions, inadequate public facilities, a lack of comprehensive medical care, crowded highways, and better living standards for low-income families are to be solved. Moreover, it is a virtual certainty that the majority of people interpret a higher

[10] The reasons for the failure of economic policy and the complexities of designing a policy mix for growth equilibrium are discussed by Robert Eisner, "What Went Wrong," *Journal of Political Economy*, Vol. 79, No. 3 (May-June 1971), pp. 629–641.

[11] For one critique of the current forms of economic growth, see E. J. Mishan, *Technology and Growth: The Price We Pay* (New York: Frederick A. Praeger, Inc., 1970).

quality of life to mean having more and better goods and services with which to enjoy living. Therefore, economic growth is quite compatible with what most people consider as a higher quality of life. Once satisfactory technological solutions are found to industrial pollution and resource depletion problems—as is inevitable—then increased production will cease to pose a threat to the environment and the quantity and quality of goods and services can be increased in whatever ways and whatever directions society elects.

Indeed, there can be no question in a free society that the growth equilibrium path must be consistent with consumer preferences, social goals, and human values, national priorities, and preservation of the environment. In the United States, at least, living standards are approaching the point where economic growth just for the sake of growth is an untenable policy. It is becoming increasingly possible to stress the quality of goods and services as well as the quantity, and it is certainly imperative that society's technological apparatus be pointed in the direction of solving the problems of environmental pollution that are a by-product of industrialization and economic growth. Moreover, the problems of poverty, discrimination, and urban decay are crying for attention.

However, while there is general accord on the nature of a socially desirable type of growth equilibrium, there exists a wide diversity of opinion as to the specific policies which ought to be deployed to support its achievement. Furthermore, differences exist as to priorities. Plainly enough, there is room for reasonable men to disagree as to whether clamping down very hard on industrial pollution is more important than keeping plants open and avoiding widespread unemployment or whether protecting the domestic steel industry from foreign imports is more important then encouraging the growth of world trade or whether the federal government should finance research and development activities in the aerospace industry but not in the drug industry. For this reason, even if it could be assumed that policymakers are wise enough to know just what sort of policy mix is called for in specific situations, it would not be possible to prescribe an "optimal" growth equilibrium strategy. Thus, economic policy issues will necessarily remain in the realm of conflict, despite the powers of economic analysis to explain and to predict economic phenomena.

Summary and Conclusions

The part of economic theory that concerns the interdependencies and linkages among prices, output rates, and input rates in all of the various markets and economic sectors is called general equilibrium analysis. The purpose of such analysis is to determine what the equilibrium configuration of prices, output rates, and input rates will be for each firm and in each market, given the guiding forces of consumer tastes and preferences, production technologies, available resource supplies, business goals, and national priorities.

In a state of static general equilibrium there are no forces operating to cause the pace of economic activity to rise or fall. The leakages equal the injections, and the total supply of goods and services equals the total demand for goods and services. At a lower level, each product market is in equilibrium; so is each input market. Consumers, business firms, and resource owners have no motives for changing what they are doing, given the prevailing economic circumstances. In theory, general equilibrium can occur at, above, or below full employment, depending upon the level of total spending.

In practice, however, static general equilibrium is never attained because the underlying forces are never constant long enough for all product and resource markets to reach their respective equilibrium positions. The real world is very much dynamic, with changes occurring constantly in such basic economic forces as consumer tastes and preferences, the range of possible products and production technologies, the quantity and quality of available resource inputs, the distribution of income, the styles of managerial technologies, and so on. Over the long term in a progressive society, the most appropriate concept of general equilibrium is growth equilibrium—a state of stable growth and noninflationary full employment, the optimal growth rate being a function of technological progress, the availability of new resource supplies, and societal preferences.

Insofar as firms are concerned, the character of economywide growth equilibrium is important because it determines the extent of expansion opportunities open to enterprises and ultimately their own individual growth equilibrium positions. The individual firm's own growth equilibrium path depends upon the strategic position it has for meeting the new commodity demands generated by growth and the aggressiveness with which managers commit organizational resources to the available expansion opportunities. Growth equilibrium for the firm thus may be thought of as the path along which the firm must continually adjust its prices, output rates, and input rates so as to optimize the attainment of its complement of goals.

Even though there are strong tendencies for the economy to move in the direction of the growth equilibrium path, deviations and lags in adjustment are inevitable. Change is too frequent, resource mobility too imperfect, and the adjustment mechanism too slow in responding to change for the economy to remain fixed on a steady, even growth path. For this reason, it is appropriate for the federal government to play an active role in promoting economywide growth equilibrium and in facilitating the process of adjustment to economic change.

SUGGESTED READINGS

BAUMOL, W. J., *Economic Dynamics*, 3rd ed. (New York: The Macmillan Company, 1970), Chaps. 17 and 18.

HAHN, F. H., and R. C. O. MATTHEWS, "The Theory of Economic Growth: A

Survey," *Economic Journal*, Vol. 74, No. 296 (December 1964), pp. 779–902; reprinted in *Survey of Economic Theory*, Vol. II (New York: St. Martin's Press, 1965).

HANSEN, BENT, *A Survey of General Equilibrium Systems* (New York: McGraw-Hill, Inc., 1970).

COHEN, K. J., and R. M. CYERT, *Theory of the Firm: Resource Allocation in a Market Economy*, (Englewood Cliffs, N.J.: Prentice-Hall, Inc., 1965), Chap. 9.

PATINKIN, DON, *Money, Interest, and Prices*, 2nd ed. (New York: Harper & Row, Publishers, 1965).

SCHUMPETER, JOSEPH A., *The Theory of Economic Development* (New York: Oxford University Press, 1961), Chaps. 2, 4, and 6.

Questions for Discussion

1. Trace through the economic effects of:
(a) An innovation which allows waste paper to be recycled and made reusable.
(b) A permanent increase in the demand for sports entertainment.
(c) A sharp decline in the number of women seeking employment.
(d) A precipitous decline in natural gas reserves.

2. Distinguish between static general equilibrium and dynamic growth equilibrium for an economy.

3. (a) Do you think that some deviations from economywide growth equilibrium are inevitable? Why or why not?
(b) Would it be fair to state that the economywide pace of economic activity *tends* toward the growth equilibrium path?
(c) Is it likely that the nature of an economy's growth equilibrium path can be (and is) altered by basic changes in the economic environment? If so, what sorts of basic changes can cause the growth equilibrium path to shift?

4. Explain the relationships and the linkages between growth equilibrium for the economy and growth equilibrium for the firm.

5. Do you think managers of firms are able to keep their respective firms steered on a course of steady growth? Why or why not? Do they try to do so even though they may not succeed? Why or why not?

6. What, if any, guarantee does society have that growth of the economy and of firms will proceed in directions consistent with societal preferences and priorities?

7. It has been observed that business enterprises thrive on "problems," that these problems typically precipitate a search for technological solutions, that the resulting technological discoveries point the way to new investment opportunities, and that the resulting new investment spending is the cornerstone of economic growth. Critically evaluate this sequence of events as an "explanation" or "cause" of economic growth and expansion.

Index

579